972.08   Rutz
The Great Rebellion

MILLIS PUBLIC LIBRARY
MILLIS, MASSACHUSETTS

The Great Rebellion

Mexico, 1905–1924

BY THE SAME AUTHOR

Labor and the Ambivalent Revolutionaries: Mexico, 1911–1923
Cuba: The Making of a Revolution
Mexico: The Challenge of Poverty and Illiteracy

EDITED WORKS

The Mexican War: Was It Manifest Destiny?

An American in Maximilian's Mexico, 1865–1866: The Diaries of William Marshall Anderson

Liberation in the Americas: Comparative Aspects of the Independence Movements in Mexico and the United States (with Robert Detweiler)

Interpreting Latin American History: From Independence to Today

RAMÓN EDUARDO RUÍZ

The Great Rebellion

Mexico, 1905–1924

MILLIS PUBLIC LIBRARY
MILLIS, MASSACHUSETTS 35787
NOV. 1 0 1980

W· W· Norton & Company NEW YORK · LONDON

Copyright © 1980 by W. W. Norton & Company, Inc.
Published simultaneously in Canada by George J. McLeod Limited,
Toronto. Printed in the United States of America.
All Rights Reserved
FIRST EDITION

Library of Congress Cataloging in Publication Data
Ruíz, Ramón Eduardo.
    The great rebellion.

    Bibliography: p.
    Includes index.
    1. Mexico—History—1910–1946.   I. Title.
F1234.R9114 1980   972.08   79-27659
ISBN 0-393-01323-5
ISBN 0-393-95129-4 pbk.

1 2 3 4 5 6 7 8 9 0

*Con cariño a Natalia, a mis hijas,
Maura y Olivia, y con profundo
agradecimiento a mis padres,
Ramón Ruíz y Dolores Urueta.*

Contents

Preface

This book is about a momentous event in the history of Mexico, popularly called La Revolución, a civil war that erupted in 1910; before coming to a close, it claimed the lives of untold numbers of Mexicans and put to the torch millions of dollars of private property. The drama covers the years between 1905 and 1924. However, it is not a simple chronology but an interpretation of events. It is my view of what took place, that Mexico underwent a cataclysmic rebellion but not a social "Revolution."

Ostensibly, I began to write this book in 1970, when I went to Mexico for a year of archival research. Yet, in truth, its origins antedate 1970 by decades; they go back to my childhood, when I would listen to my father, often in company with friends from Mexico, discuss what had taken place in the country he had recently fled. A magnificent storyteller, my father eagerly shared his wealth of anecdotes and opinions with all of his children. There was never a dearth of listeners, for even my mother, who had left her home in Chihuahua for other reasons, became an avid fan. As I grew older, I promised myself that I would someday write, to borrow a phrase from Bernal Díaz del Castillo—one of the soldiers who accompanied Hernán Cortés on his conquest of Mexico and lived to write a chronicle of his experiences—a "true history" of La Revolución. I set out to write a scholar's book, one that would be both controversial and, as they say in the trade, solidly researched and perhaps even "objective," whatever that word means. In all candor, however, I cannot claim to have written an impartial book; on the contrary, it is an interpretive history. Its point of view is in part inspired by what my father, who grew to manhood in the Mexico of the Old Regime, told us, in part tempered by the wisdom of my mother, whose family often had a different version of those times and events. In addition, I have devoted a good part of a lifetime to learning about Mexico and have spent many years in the country of my parents. Yet, whatever the merits of my work, I suspect that I may have written a "Mexican" version, at times sympathetic to the strengths and weaknesses of the Mexican *ambiente* and character, but likewise, colored by a sense of *desconfianza*, an attitude of disbelief and distrust shared by Mexicans of all classes. To some readers, this may be a weakness; but, from my perspective, this attitude of "prove it" may keep the story from straying too far from that much vaunted but seldom uncovered historical "truth."

The book is divided into four sections with an Introduction. Part One, "The Whys and Whereofs of Rebellion," examines the causes of discontent and revolt. "On the Meaning of Revolution," the introductory chapter, takes up the question of "what is Revolution," a question which must be defined precisely lest it become meaningless. My central thesis is that Mexico did not have a "Revolution." Part Two, "The Cast of Chieftains," discusses the key figures of rebel leadership. In the "Chronicle of What Was Done," Part Three, I have written about their accomplishments and failures. The concluding section, Part Four, "The Ubiquitous Barriers," looks at special obstacles in the path of change and ends with my evaluation of why Mexico had a rebellion but not a social revolution.

I can blame no one but myself for the faults in the book. Its strengths, whatever they may be, I owe in large measure to the wisdom and help of friends and colleagues. Michael C. Meyer, a fellow Mexicanist, read the entire manuscript, and in the process, helped correct errors along the way, as did James Scobie, my colleague at the University of California at San Diego. I am grateful to both for their help. In addition, I learned much from discussions with scores of Mexican scholars and friends. I am particularly indebted to Luis Villoro, Enrique Florescano, and Moisés González Navarro, distinguished scholars of Mexican history. Without their insights, and that of other students of Mexican events, I could not have written my book.

Calendar of Events

Porfiriato, 1876–1911
Porfirio Díaz, President of Mexico, 1876–1880, 1884–1911
Financial crash, 1907
Francisco I. Madero, *La Sucesión Presidencial en 1910*
Creelman interview, 1908
Rise of anti Díaz protest, 1908–1910
Re-election of Díaz and Ramón Corral, 1910
Plan de San Luis Potosí, October, 1910, Madero's declaration of rebellion
Francisco Villa and Pascual Orozco join Madero's revolt, November, 1910
Emiliano Zapata revolts in Morelos, 1911
Fall of Ciudad Juárez, May, 1911
Francisco León de la Barra, Interim-President of Mexico, May-November, 1911
Madero, President of Mexico, November, 1911–February, 1913
Plan de Ayala, Zapata's land reform program, November, 1911
Tragic Ten Days, fall of Madero, February, 1913
Victoriano Huerta, President of Mexico, February, 1913–August, 1914
Plan de Guadalupe, Venustiano Carranza refuses to recognize Huerta's presidency
Constitutionalists topple Huerta, August, 1914
Villa and Zapata break with Constitutionalists, 1914
Adiciones al Plan de Guadalupe, December, 1914
Decree of January 6, 1915
Convention of Aguascalientes, 1914–1915
Battle of Celaya, defeat of Villa, April, 1915

Triumph of Constitutionalists, 1915
Carranza, Provisional President of Mexico, 1915–1917
General John J. Pershing invades Mexico, 1916–1917
Constitution of 1917
Carranza, President of Mexico, 1917–1920
Founding of Confederación Regional Obrera Mexicana (CROM), 1918
Death of Zapata, April, 1919
Fall of Carranza, 1920
Alvaro Obregón, President of Mexico, 1920–1924
Treaty of Bucareli, 1923
Adolfo de la Huerta rebellion, 1923
Plutarco Elías Calles, elected President of Mexico, 1924

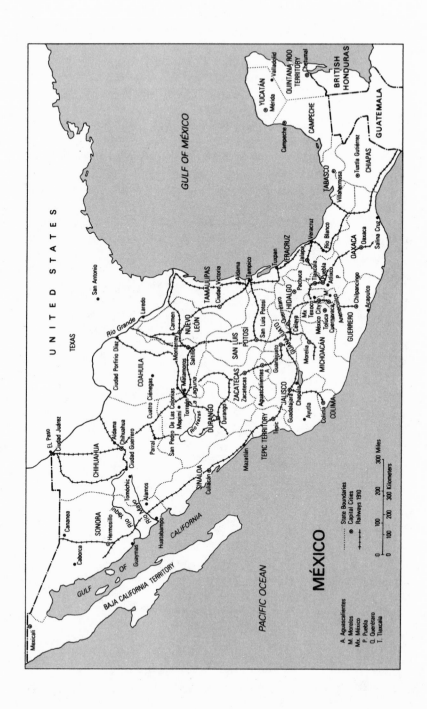

PART I THE WHYS AND WHEREOFS OF REBELLION

ONE *On the Meaning of Revolution*

"The Revolution is the Revolution"

Luis Cabrera

WHAT IS Revolution? Until recently, scholars of contemporary Mexico seldom questioned the assertion of the men who toppled the regime of Porfirio Díaz that they had spawned a "Revolution." To distinguish the upheaval ignited by Francisco I. Madero's call to arms, from the scores of *cuartelazos,* uprisings, which had harried the Republic in the first half of the nineteenth century, Mexicans, scholars and laymen alike, baptized it with a capital "R." Madero's uprising, set for November 1910 in the Plan de San Luis Potosí, became La Revolución. According to this interpretation, which took hold when both Madero and the defenders of the Old Regime labeled his rebellion a Revolution, earlier armed movements, which in their time had also been called Revolutions, were downgraded to simply coups or revolutions spelled with a small "r." To simplify terminology, the 1810 struggle against Spain, proclaimed by Father Miguel Hidalgo, became the War for Independence, or at best, the Revolution for Independence. The mid-nineteenth century clash between the Conservatives and the Liberals led by Benito Juárez, which also might legitimately claim revolutionary status, acquired the name of La Reforma.

Yet a "Revolution," if indeed more than a mere change of rulers, heralds the dawn of a new age, in an economic and social as well as a political sense. It is not just a change of rulers, not simply a matter of throwing the rascals out, but a transformation of the basic structure of a society. A Revolution, in its capital "R" meaning, is a social catharsis that, among its other accomplishments, dramatically alters the prevailing economic system, and transforms the class structure as well as the patterns of wealth and income distribution. Moreover, in the twentieth century, a Revolution must modify the nature of a nation's economic dependency on the outside world. By this definition, only a fraction of modern upheavals fit into the category of Revolution. In the eighteenth century, the classic model is the French Revolution, which upended the Ancient Regime and replaced it with a capitalist state run by the bourgeoisie. Not until the twentieth century did similar explosions occur. Doubtless, the Russian, Chinese, and Cuban Revolutions, substituting Marxist economies for capitalist ones, merit a place alongside the French example. By altering the fabric of society, turning the class structure upside down, and ending old colonial relationships, these upheavals meet the requirements of Revolution.

Still, if the criterion is depth of change any social transformation of major consequence can wrap itself in the mantel of Revolution. Two which come to mind immediately are the repercussions resulting from the advent of modern commerce and industrialization. Historians refer to the former as the Commercial Revolution, tracing its origins to late sixteenth-century England, and to the latter as the Industrial Revolution, which centers on the invention of the steam engine in 1750 and its impact on manufacturing. Without a doubt, the Industrial Revolution, encouraged by earlier commercial changes, had tremendous consequences for the Western world. England, and ultimately France, Germany, and the United States underwent a metamorphosis that fundamentally transformed their societies. Perhaps no upheaval in the history of mankind ranks with the alterations wrought by the steam engine and its later offshoots.

However, as previously indicated, the Industrial Revolution, as well as its commercial ancestor, occurred over decades if not centuries. The industrial age, now labeled the era of science, is still with us: it continues to revolutionize societies, both in the "capitalist" West and in the so-called Third World. The Second

World of the Marxists, a response to the evils of unbridled capitalism, is also one of its offspring. But, to repeat, the Industrial Revolution was neither sudden, nor in a literal sense violent, which the term Revolution, by its character in France, Russia, China, and Cuba, apparently demands. Paradoxically, therefore, the word that most fittingly describes the process of the Industrial Revolution is *evolution*. Its change developed in an evolutionary manner, not by way of Revolution.

Considering this definition of Revolution as a sudden, violent, social and economic catharsis, to what extent can the Mexican upheaval of 1910 be considered a Revolution? The answer, obviously, requires that rhetoric be separated from fact; it calls for distinguishing the ideals often spelled out in the new laws from what the leadership really intended, and from what it actually accomplished. Did Madero, Venustiano Carranza, or Alvaro Obregón, the *caudillos* of the rebellion, plan and carry out a Revolution? Did their supporters, regardless of their rhetoric, envisage a total metamorphosis of the social, economic, and political fabric of the Old Regime? Was their objective to rid the country of the capitalist system that, whatever its limitations and drawbacks in Mexico, emulated the economic and political models of Western Europe and the United States, and to substitute for it a fundamentally different socio-economic structure? Did the laws implemented by the rebel rulers of Mexico after 1911 break with the past and lay the foundations for a new order and for a new economic independence? To what extent were they carried out? Or, to put the question succinctly, were the *caudillos* and their disciples intent on reform only, not radical change?

If time is a critical ingredient, how deep a transformation had Mexico enjoyed when, in 1923, the rebel masters had consolidated their control? At that juncture, the shape of future policy, as well as the accomplishments of the past, was no longer in doubt. Any modifications that might occur in the future, including the radical measures of Lázaro Cárdenas from 1935 to 1938, more properly belong under the heading of reform. This interpretation, furthermore, has precedence in Mexican history. In the mid-nineteenth century, Juárez and his Liberals, whose struggle against the Conservatives contained radical features, unpretentiously and candidly called their movement La Reforma. As Luis Cabrera, one of the political luminaries of his day, observed, for three decades, while don Porfirio governed, "everyone, when speaking of his calls to arms, referred to them as the 'Revolution of the Noria' or the 'Revolution of Tuxtepec'; but history, fully aware of how sycophants can distort truth, now says 'the Plan of the Noria'. . . ." [1]

The United States, which from Woodrow Wilson's time had watched the unfolding drama in Mexico with jaundiced eye, had also set limits on the degree of reform the rebels might expect to fulfill without outside interference. The Bucareli Agreements of 1923, dealing specifically with the petroleum issue, substantially limited the nationalistic goals of Mexicans, as exemplified in the Constitution of 1917. Further, the accord between Obregón and the Harding administration complicated the enforcement of agrarian and labor legislation.

Nor were the goals challenged by Washington clearly revolutionary. To begin with, the architects of the uprising, nearly always young and not unprosperous, represented, with the exceptions of the Maderos and Carranzas, the middle class, the offspring of the progress of the Díaz era. Only a tiny minority embraced radical doctrines. Despite their rhetoric, which at times exalted socialist gospel, the majority of the rebel spokesmen pressed for reform and not for destruction of the existing system. The ambivalent progeny of the Old Regime wanted entrance into the inner circle of government and business. None of those who climbed the pinnacles of power as a result of the Revolution seriously considered the substitution of capitalism with Marxism. The Constitution of 1917, of course, prominently featured labor and agrarian legislation that, if faithfully carried out, might have dramatically transformed the social fabric of Mexico. Its enactment, however, did not result in the destruction of Mexico's capitalist framework. The legislation, while tempering the ideals of former rulers, upheld the principles of private property, of unfettered competition, and the sacred rights of the individual. Like their contemporaries, the Progressives in the United States or the Radical party in Argentina, the prophets of the post-Díaz period were as capitalist as their predecessors. They wanted to modernize the system, to profit personally from it, and certainly in the thinking of their left wing, to maximize its benefits for labor and the peasants. In Section VI of Article 27, the patrons of the Constitution conferred legal status on the *ejido*, an indigenous communal system of land ownership. Yet the *ejido*, and other cooperative ventures, stood on the periphery of the major goals. The Magna Carta of 1917 essentially revised its predecessor of 1857, adding a broader and more modern economic platform. In ascending to power, the middle classes, actually a new generation, failed to make a sharp break with the past. Even Positivism, the political philosophy castigated by the rebels, survived to become part of the intellectual baggage of "modern" Mexico.

The Great Rebellion, perhaps a more accurate description of what transpired between 1911 and 1923, was as much a phenomenon of the nineteenth century as it was a harbinger of the future. Its roots and its principles, reflect, of course with significant modifications, ideals enshrined in the French Revolution and in successful operation in England and the United States. Its *raison d'être* was still the capitalist formula, streamlined and updated to meet Mexican conditions of the early twentieth century. In the opinion of key insurgents, Díaz and his cohorts had subverted the formula. The tiny band in disagreement wanting more radical change suffered failure and even death, as is exemplified by the fate of Emiliano Zapata and Ricardo Flores Magón. Given its narrow goals, the rebellion was essentially a face-lifting of Mexican capitalism. If it was indeed a Revolution, it was the last of the Revolutions that hark back to the French model.

Revolution and violence, the destruction of property and the loss of life, go hand in glove. One must not confuse violence with Revolution; the two are not always the same. Yet in Mexican history, the violence of the period from 1913 to 1915 is often taken as proof of a Revolution. That the rebels had to fight vigorously to unseat General Victoriano Huerta, who had driven Madero from the National Palace, hardly needs documentation. Still, Mexicans, with a keen sense of truth, acknowledge that much of the violence, while characteristic of the era after Huerta, involved factional squabbles. While social and economic principles might have occasionally been at stake, the armed clashes were actually factions of the rebel family pitted one against another. Undoubtedly, Zapata, conferred with the title of "Attila of the South" by his rivals, stood for social change. Measured by the standards of Lenin and his disciples, his contemporaries in Russia, he falls woefully short of being a revolutionary. Zapata's coreligionists at the Convención de Aguascalientes, who on occasion spoke for social change, fit into a similar category. No scholar, however, has verified the revolutionary credentials of Francisco Villa, the ally of Zapata and the major enemy of the Constitutionalists, who were the ultimate victors. At best, the evidence contradicts the view of Villa as a revolutionary. Venustiano Carranza, the First Chief of the Constitutionalists, by his own admission, had no use for revolutionaries or radicals. Violence in Mexico, in summary, did not necessarily signify Revolution.

TWO *The Ambivalence of*

Progress

———

"Everything is doubtlessly true: our economic, industrial, commercial, and mining progress is undeniable."

Francisco I. Madero, 1908

"A revolution in Mexico is impossible."

El Imparcial, 1909

———

I

WHAT *El Imparcial* misinterpreted and what Madero, with his plaudits for the transformation of Mexico unconsciously expressed, is that Revolutions originate not in the souls of people crippled by hunger and want, but with those who have tasted the fruits of change. The dashed hopes of a beneficent future or their sudden loss are the seeds of rebellion. Such was the condition of Mexicans, as a new century replaced the age of Victoria. "In every corner of the Republic reigned prosperity and an enviable peace," reported the steel magnate Andrew Carnegie after a visit with Díaz, the master of Mexico for three decades.[1] From the perspective of Julio Sesto, a Spanish poet and tourist, "not a cloud darkened the horizon." Economic stability guaranteed peace; an eternal peace, he went on, "because Mexicans, yesterday's children, are now sophisticated adults." [2]

The opinions of the poet Sesto and the practical business-man Carnegie withstand the scrutiny of half a century. Under

Díaz, concedes Fernando Rosenzweig, a distinguished Mexican scholar, Mexico embarked upon an era of economic development.[3] Don Porfirio's peaceful *patria,* attracted an army of investors from the United States and Europe with an eye for profits. Mexico's natural resources and Díaz's benevolent tax and financial policies kept them there. Between 1893 and 1906, the gilded age of the Mexican economy, the value of mined metals, the country's leading industry, jumped from 40 million pesos to 170 million pesos, and nearly all of this increase was due to foreign investments, technology, and markets.[4] After a trip to Mexico, Winchester Kelso, an expert in mines, declared that mining enjoyed a prosperity unequalled in the history of the Republic.[5]

The mining bonanza built cities, laid the foundations for the railroads, and helped give birth to commercial agriculture. Mines of silver, gold, and copper, joined later by mines of lead, zinc, and a host of other industrial metals, dotted the landscape. Commercial agriculture for export altered the terrain of Yucatán, Morelos, Coahuila, and Sonora, while northern cattlemen with access to American markets carved out huge empires. On the Gulf of Mexico, Americans and Englishmen competed to exploit rich deposits of petroleum. Textile plants manufactured cotton cloth in the corridor from Córdoba to Mexico City with others in Guadalajara, Durango, Nuevo León, and Chihuahua, for a total annual production by 1904 valued at 45.5 million pesos. Iron smelters belched black smoke over the skies of Monterrey and Ciudad Chihuahua; those in Monterrey produced 60,000 tons of steel and iron.[6] In addition, there were paper mills; plants for beer and liquor; tobacco factories turning out enough cigars and cigarettes to meet national demand; a sugar industry subsidized by foreigners who bought land, planted cane, and mechanized its cultivation; jute mills; meat-packing plants; and manufacturers of glycerine, dynamite, fine crystals, glass, henequen twine, cement, and soap. From Guaymas, a port on the Gulf of Cortés, iron-makers shipped wagons to Central America.[7] Railroad growth had been spectacular, expanding from a meager 650 kilometers in 1876 to 24,000 kilometers by 1910. This progress resulted in the development of a Mexican middle class, small but important beyond its numbers. When Mexicans celebrated their centennial of independence, foreigners came to pay homage to don Porfirio who had made the miracle possible, a man, to cite the eulogy of one American admirer, not to be compared to William Howard Taft but to George Washington.[8]

Progress conferred multiple gifts. Budget deficits as old as the Republic were ended.[9] After 1895, declared José I. Limantour who, as minister of the treasury, managed the economy, financial problems no longer plagued the budget.[10] In the fiscal year ending in 1896, national income stood at 50,500,000 pesos; ten years later it had almost doubled.[11] States soon to shelter rebels enjoyed similar blessings. From 1878 to 1910, Chihuahua's budget jumped from 119,666 pesos to 1,243,481 pesos; Coahuila's increased from 77,532 to 436,666 pesos; the income of Nuevo León tripled, while that of Yucatán multiplied eight-fold. The national budget, in the interval, grew from 7,679,066 pesos to 23,883,920 pesos.[12] The larger budgets reflected growth in state and national revenue, as well as rising costs and added expenditures.

Growth and development, however, exacted a price. It was not without social change, even in rural Mexico.[13] With the building of railroads, the advent of industrialization, and the trappings of a modern economy, the traditional way of life clashed with new aspirations and needs. If industry were to prosper, a domestic market had to grow apace. But signs indicated that the buying power of the consumer had failed to stay abreast of the ability of the manufacturer to produce. Textiles, for example, one of the indicators of industrialization, lagged in development, not merely because of outdated machinery and antiquated methods, but because a limited market hampered its modernization. Since the industry manufactured cheap cotton cloth for the lower classes, its growth required higher wages for its consumers—urban workers and peasants in rural villages—a goal calling for drastic alterations in prevailing economic and political formulas.

Instead, however, the men who ran the regime began to contemplate the export of industrial products, especially to Latin America, a palliative that, if successful, would have postponed the need to cope with domestic inequalities.[14] As Andrés Molina Enríquez pointed out in his eloquent analysis of Mexico's social problems, *Los Grandes Problemas Nacionales,* only industries producing for export had experienced success. Two examples were the tobacco and henequen industries. Those relying on the domestic market, on the other hand, had faltered upon arriving at a certain stage of growth. To the manufacturer, the only way to get beyond this point was to export his products. Failure to do so meant stagnation because it was impossible to build industry on the buying power of the masses.[15] Given the nature of the domestic economy, therefore, exports held the key to prosperity.

Yet, ironically, the cyclical fluctuations of foreign markets, a product of economic currents outside the control of Mexico, made reliance on exports hazardous. During the bonanza years of henequen, to use a story told to Sesto, a clerk counting money in a store in Mérida accidentally dropped a quarter, and seeing a janitor standing nearby, asked him to pick it up. To which the janitor replied: "Bah! I don't stoop for a *pinche* quarter." [16] After the bottom fell out of the export market for henequen, that same janitor, if he were lucky to have a job, labored from dawn to dusk for a quarter or less.

The uneven nature of economic development, characteristic of the society of Díaz, was one of the contributing causes of the upheaval of 1910. Reliance on the vagaries of the export market, the failure to build a large consumer class, and the slowness of social change undermined the old structure. As Frank Tannenbaum wrote, the coming of "the revolution . . . bore a logical relationship to the cumulative difficulties growing out of the efforts to industrialize the country." [17] Eventually, given the emphasis on economic development, Mexico had no choice but to acknowledge the need for social change: such as labor reforms, higher wages, shorter working hours, and an end to the exploitation of women and children. The necessary reforms also included wider opportunities for the middle class. To stimulate agricultural output which had remained at low levels during the entire Díaz regime, agrarian measures included the break-up of the nonproductive estates, and the mechanization of the fields.[18] Failure to heed the call of modernization, an inevitable demand of development, cost Díaz and his companions dearly.

The modern technology, capital, and machines introduced

in the days of Díaz, as well as close ties with the industrial world, particularly with the United States, had made the traditional structure incompatible with Mexico's progress. One example was the railroads, a major achievement of the Porfiristas, which helped usher in the final social crisis. As the ironhorse came to dominate the Mexican countryside, it upset land prices, exacerbated an already inequitable pattern of land distribution, disrupted the old political and economic balance in many states, and increased the disparity between rural and urban Mexico. The railroad had a disruptive influence even in rural Mexico. The use of peasants to build railbeds encouraged their social mobility, and on occasion, brought their release from the *haciendas*. Additionally, the ironhorse facilitated the movement of people from the less prosperous central and southern states to the north, and across the border to the United States.[19]

Specifically, the introduction of the railroads brought the northern provinces into the vortex of change. In Sonora, the first railroads appeared in 1882 and by 1910 ran the length of the state, with trunk lines connecting the mining centers with Arizona. From the 1880's on, the railroads entered Chihuahua, bringing the Ferrocarril Noroeste de México; lines were built between Ciudad Chihuahua and Santa Eulalia, from Jiménez to Parral, and the Kansas-Mexico City line was completed.[20] Similar developments occurred in Coahuila and Nuevo León. The railroads encouraged the exploitation of the mining, commercial, and agricultural wealth of these provinces. As their economies prospered, so did a middle class of merchants, miners, artisans, professionals, and *rancheros*—small, landed proprietors. In Sonora, particularly, which had attracted a large colony of Americans, a clash inevitably arose between the foreigners and a new class of affluent Mexicans, who gave voice to local interests.[21]

The railroads spurred a mining boom, which was of special importance in the northern states. Because of its mining industry, Sonora became the richest and most prosperous state in the Republic.[22] Foreigners played a leading role in the drama. Americans controlled an investment of 45 million dollars, three-fourths of it in mining. Approximately 5,400 individuals owned mines and there were four major mining corporations. The axis of the mining empire was Cananea. In 1910, Sonora exported ores worth 26 million pesos, three-fifths of which was in cop-per.[23] During the boom, the population of the mining towns grew rapidly. Cananea led the way with barely 100 inhabitants in 1891, about 900 ten years later, and 25,000 in 1906. It was then the largest city in Sonora.[24]

As the railroads encouraged mining, so did they also open the way for agriculture, and the development of other regions of Sonora. In the rich agricultural district of Alamos, the popula-tion jumped from 43,346 in 1891 to nearly 60,000 by 1910; Navojoa, its center, had 1,334 people in 1884 and 10,882 after the arrival of the Southern Pacific Railroad.[25] On lands watered by the Mayo and Yaqui rivers *hacendados* planted corn, wheat, and garbanzos for export. The *hacendados* of the Mayo valley, recent conquerors of the Yaquis, traveled the path to wealth with the garbanzo bean, which was purchased by the Spanish merchants of Mazatlán, Hermosillo, and Alamos for export to Spain. A steady rise in the price of garbanzos, from 2 pesos a bushel to over 16 pesos by 1910, added to their prosperity. The rising fortunes of the garbanzo lords coincided with the economic crisis of 1907 and the decline of mining which, for agriculture, meant the coming of cheap labor into the Mayo valley from less pros-perous regions.[26] In 1909, while the mining towns languished, *El Imparcial* could still write of lands being cleared for plant-ing along the Río Yaqui and of people coming to work there in growing numbers.[27] Bacum, its hub, had over 5,000 inhabitants.

The American colony, a factor in Sonora's progress, began to grow rapidly in 1900. One of the newcomers was the Richardson Company, which, after surveying *tierras baldías*, so-called idle and unclaimed lands, in the Yaqui valley, acquired 76,000 hectares of land, subdividing and selling it in smaller plots to colonists from California. With the backing of the state's oli-garchy, the national government granted the Richardson Com-pany extensive water rights to the Yaqui River. The concession brought the company and the American farmers, who cultivated fruits, vegetables, and grains for export, into conflict with older Mexican interests. The authorities of the state, however, sided with the newcomers, thus contributing to the rebellion of 1910.[28]

The ebullience of individual enterprise spilled over into

the public domain. Ramón Corral and other leaders of Sonora built roads, constructed public buildings, developed the port of Guaymas, and poured money into public education.[29] The schools offered teaching jobs to scores of chieftains of the forth-coming rebellion, including Alvaro Obregón and Plutarco Elías Calles. Francisco C. Aguilar, the mayor of Ures, although chastized for holding office for two decades, nevertheless won public acclaim for his encouragement of public education. Corral and Aguilar, in their support for public schools, went beyond the call of duty; few of their colleagues in office in other parts of the Republic acted with equal concern for education. Governor Miguel Cárdenas of Coahuila, for example, used 500,000 *pesos* set aside for the schools in the municipality of Parras to subsidize the Coahuila y Pacífico railroad.[30] In Sonora, 35 percent of the population could read and write, as compared to a national average of less than 15 percent.[31] Coahuila, with identical statistics, and Chihuahua, only slightly less well read, still had literacy rates twice the national average. At the other extreme, Guerrero, Oaxaca, and Chiapas, latecomers to Madero's camp, had less than 10 percent literacy. Only the Federal District, the site of the Republic's capital city, had a higher percentage of literacy than the northern provinces.[32] The social élite of Guaymas, the commercial entrepôt of Sonora, patronized the Teatro Almada where Adolfo de la Huerta, a companion-in-arms of Obregón and Calles, was achieving fame as a singer. The prosperity of mining and agriculture made this level of education possible. The highest wages in the Republic were earned in these northern states: miners earned between 2 and 6 pesos a day; leather workers of Hermosillo received 2.50 pesos; the minimum wage was over a peso in Sonora. By comparison miners in central Mexico, previously the best paid workers, earned much less.[33]

Chihuahua, with the arrival of the railroads and the wealth of its mines, shared a similar prosperity. Its progress, Sesto recalled, had "astonished the natives of Mexico City who accompanied Díaz on his journey to El Paso . . . for his meeting with President Taft."[34] From 1895 to 1909, the economic development of Chihuahua had annually attracted nearly 10,000 newcomers, giving it the sixth largest rate of population growth in the country, and the highest of the northern provinces.[35] Chihuahua had more people than Sonora, Coahuila, or Nuevo León.[36] An intelligent and hard-working breed, who possessed all the virtues of the Protestant ethic as Andrew Carnegie might have observed, inhabited the small but thriving capital city of almost 40,000.[37] *El Imparcial* euphorically claimed for Chihuahua "one of the brightest futures in all of the Republic." [38]

Indeed, if official statistics merit study, Chihuahua had crossed the threshold of progress. The value of its mineral production had multiplied, from less than 7 million pesos in 1899, to over 23 million pesos ten years later. Its livestock industry annually sold 70,000 cattle to American buyers, and the affluent citizens of Chihuahua consumed 2.5 million pesos of beef a year. Between 1902 and 1908, the value of Chihuahua's local commerce rose from approximately 8.2 million to nearly 13 million pesos.[39] According to its tax rolls, which were notorious for their low assessments, private and public property in 1908 was worth almost 20 million pesos, compared to 7 million pesos in 1877. Untaxed properties were valued at 192 million pesos, of which 85 million were in mining. Mining production in 1898 had a value of 6.8 million pesos, and ten years later had increased to over 23 million pesos.[40] Besides mining—the backbone of the economy, and the livestock industry—the origin of vast fortunes, Chihuahua could boast of other industries. The Guggenheim Corporation had built an iron smelter on the outskirts of the capital. Smaller plants manufactured cube sugar, *piloncillo,* and leather goods, while a host of shops turned out handicrafts. The state produced its own salt, while Talamantes and Dolores had textile mills.[41] The Banco Minero had few peers among the provincial banks of the Republic.

Under Díaz, acknowledged Madero, Coahuila too, had received the benefits of progress due to technological change.[42] One of these was the ubiquitous railroad. The Central and the Internacional, which met at Torreón, the hub of the Laguna, had transformed that sleepy town into a commercial depot of 35,000 people. Torreón offered abundant opportunity for ambitious entrepreneurs. To capitalize on the cotton grown nearby, some of them built a textile mill and a plant to produce oil from its seed. Others erected iron foundries, breweries, and a softdrink business. A grid of electric trolleys, the first in Mexico, connected Torreón with Ciudad Lerdo and with Gómez Palacio, home of a bottle factory with national distribution.[43] On the banks of the Río Nazas, *hacendados* cultivated cotton for export and for sale to the Republic's textile mills. As in Sonora, clashes over water rights helped drive a wedge between the planters and Díaz. Industry, the railroads, and cotton brought to Torreón a population hungry for jobs. With the arrival of hard times after the crisis of 1907, hundreds of them took up arms against the Old Regime.[44]

But Coahuila was more than Torreón. At Río de Sabinas, foreigners operated the largest coal mines in Mexico. Farmers and *hacendados* became concerned that better paying jobs in the mines, on the railroads, and in the thriving construction industry, threatened to deprive agriculture of its field hands.[45] Coahuila, like Chihuahua, Zacatecas, and Durango, had discovered an added source of income in guayule, a bush that grew wild in the arid regions of the north. Its elastic rubber gum found a market in England, Germany, and especially in the United States.[46] Between 1904 and 1907, more than twenty guayule processing plants were built in the northern states—the majority in Coahuila—some costing as much as 500,000 pesos. With a total investment of over 15 million pesos, the industry annually exported guayule valued at 10 million pesos. Through its subsidiary, the Continental Rubber Company of New York, the United States Rubber Company virtually controlled the guayule industry, to the unhappiness of Mexican competitors, including the Maderos.[47] During the years of high exports, guayule lands, formerly selling for 20 to 30 centavos a hectare, sold for 100 pesos or more. The end of the guayule bonanza in the final years of the Díaz regime sorely hurt the economy of Coahuila. Around Parras, *hacendados* cultivated grapes and bottled wines. As in the cotton and guayule industries, the Maderos played salient roles in the grape and wine business; grapes from Coahuila sold in Mexico City while its wines were shipped to all corners of the Republic.[48] All told, the value of Coahuila's trade had more than doubled in the last fifteen years of the Díaz regime.

The railroad, which made its appearance in 1890, transformed Monterrey, the capital of Nuevo León, into the Manchester of Mexico. By 1910, the city had nearly 80,000 people—as against 35,000 in 1880. With 1800 telephones and an electric trolley, Monterrey, the *sultana* queen, of the north, possessed smelters and steel mills, the only ones in the Republic. There were breweries making the finest beers in the country, glass factories, textile mills (one owned by the Maderos), large commercial houses, and the shops of the railroads. A small band of enterprising Mexican families—Sada, Garza, Calderón, Muguerza, and Milmo—eventually interrelated by marriage, not only controlled the commerce and small industries of Monterrey, but also one of the steel mills. Skilled workers earned as much as 10 pesos a day. Bernardo Reyes, the *caudillo* of the *regiomontanos,* the natives of Monterrey, had given his blessings to labor legislation which, among other features, offered compensation for industrial accidents.[49] The city, meanwhile supported 57 public schools.

Yet, ironically, despite their economic progress, all of these northern states complained of labor shortages at one time or another. As *El Correo de Chihuahua* pontificated in 1906, the shortages endangered the industry of the state and in particular its agriculture.[50] In Sonora, the construction of the railroad from Guaymas to Guadalajara nearly stopped because of the lack of workers.[51] To attract workers to harvest their cotton crop, planters in the Laguna first offered double wages, and when that failed, added bonuses, but still met with defeat. According to *El Imparcial,* the problem resulted from the shiftless character of the Mexican worker who, accustomed to just getting along, lacked the incentive to improve himself. The proprosed remedy was to import foreign workers.[52]

In truth, however, the worker had been merely given an opportunity to nibble on the fruit of progress. Despite the opinion of newspaper editors, the benefits hardly satisfied the needs of the worker and his family. So lamentable was the worker's situation, as Madero recognized in *La Sucesión Presidencial,* that he often chose to emigrate to the United States where, in the face of almost certain humiliation, he fared better than in his homeland.[53] To Molina Enríquez, the complaint by employers of labor shortages had the ring of hypocrisy; with the harvest in, or the work of industry completed, the employers cut wages to the bone, leaving the worker to survive as best he could. The worker at least, had reason to be ambivalent about progress.

II

Still, partisans of the Old Regime had belatedly endeavored to update more than technology and machines. Wealth and the security it granted the holder widened horizons and the range of subjects of prime concern. A sense of social responsibility began to creep into government circles and even to infect the society of the rich. Despite the worship of Social Darwinism, which identified success with the white man of Europe and the United States, an awareness of the Indian and of the importance of his heritage was developing. Disturbed by the age-long neglect of the Indian, and apprehensive for the survival of his culture, influential figures in government and society sponsored a conference in 1908 to discuss the Indian's plight. At the invitation of Francisco Belmar, a noted jurist, President Díaz, with Enrique Creel—then minister of foreign relations—in attendance, opened the conference. After much discussion, the delegates, among them dignitaries of society, voted to organize a Sociedad Indigenista Mexicana to study the Indian question, to find remedies for it, and to back reforms.[54] The year before, the government had built a special school in Tepic for Indians, the first of others to follow. Newspapers in Mexico City welcomed the attempt to meet the special needs of the Indian student.[55] On the outskirts of the capital, archeologists began the restoration of the ancient metropolis of San Juan de Teotihuacán, site of the great pyramids. To indigent but promising artists, among them Francisco Goitia and Diego Rivera, the government offered scholarships for study in Europe. With pride, *El Imparcial* reported their triumphs abroad. Rivera achieved an international reputation in Paris as a Cubist painter with money furnished by the Old Regime.

Near the close of the nineteenth century, Díaz named Justo Sierra, intellectual, poet, and politician, to the position of head of the new Ministry of Public Instruction. Not since the early years of that century had the national government taken the responsibility for public education. Although limiting their activities to the Federal District and territories, this was a gigantic first step for authorities in Mexico City, who immediately undertook to expand the number of schools and to coordinate their programs. Undoubtedly, had this beginning been allowed to prosper, it would ultimately have led to a nationwide federal system of public education. Tragically, with the fall of Díaz, his successors eventually disbanded the Ministry of Public Education, thus putting an end to Sierra's famous experiment; it was not revived until 1921.

The Old Regime clearly favored higher education. It spent 121.38 pesos on each of its students, but only 7.06 pesos for the pupil in primary school.[56] Still, it had not entirely closed its eyes to public schooling in the lower grades. Between 1878 and 1908, the number of primary schools grew from 5,194 to 12,068, while school enrollments jumped from 141,780 to 658,843.[57] Slowly the regime had awakened to the need for rural education; in his last message to Congress, Díaz reported the building of seventeen new schools.[58] Some states also, had taken an interest in rural education. Zacatecas, for example, supported 251 rural schools in 1910, while San Luis Potosí had 70 of them. In Tabasco and Yucatán, *maestros ambulantes,* travelling teachers, went from village to village teaching the three R's. A number of states, Mexico for instance, compelled the *hacendados* to maintain rural schools for the children of their *peones,* while in Querétaro, in an effort to encourage *hacendados* to build schools, taxes were cut if they built them.[59] In the meantime, the Church, often accused of controlling education under Díaz, had only 586 schools with 43,720 students in 1910, a small fraction of the total student population.[60]

In public education, the northern provinces led the way. Both Enrique Creel and Ramón Corral, potentates of the Old Regime, helped improve schooling in Chihuahua and Sonora. As governor of Chihuahua, Creel appointed a blue-ribbon committee to watch over the quality of public education and personally chaired its meetings. He established a state board of education, named inspectors to supervise the schools, and labored to increase their number. At the end of his term in office, Chihuahua had 226 primary schools, an additional 110 schools receiving state funds, and one school for every 1,061 inhabitants.[61] Creel took the financial burden for education off the municipalities and made it a state responsibility. He established a normal school to train teachers, and to improve farm output, had the state help subsidize a private college of agriculture in Ciudad Juárez. Under Creel, the state legislature set up a retirement system for teachers and public employees, and passed laws to encourage the "incorporation and betterment" of the Tarahumara Indians.[62] Corral won plaudits for similar measures in Sonora. In the years from 1895 to 1910, the number of school-teachers in both Sonora and Chihuahua doubled and increased from 275 to 921 in Coahuila.[63] Whether because of schools or teachers, Chihuahua began to give birth to scores of newspapers; one, *El Correo*, published by Silvestre Terrazas, helped fan the fires of discontent.

By providing public jobs and diplomatic posts to its writers and intellectuals, the Old Regime helped make Mexico a bastion of the arts. True, as the architecture of the Palacio de Bellas Artes in the capital clearly showed, to the rulers of the Republic all that was European, whether in poor taste or not, glittered. Nonetheless, Mexico became a haven for *modernismo*, the first literary school with roots in Spanish America. Its luminaries, Amado Nervo, Manuel Gutiérrez Nájera, and Salvador Díaz Mirón won international acclaim for Mexico. Federico Gamboa, a diplomat and disciple of Emile Zola, wrote *Santa,* one of the first novels to emerge out of the Spanish New World. In the world of art, José Guadalupe Posada, a caricaturist, gained a public following for his biting satire of Mexico's gilded age and also won the admiration of aspiring young painters, among them José Clemente Orozco, who in a few years was to become a muralist of international reknown.

More significantly, Orozco and his companions stood on the brink of a renaissance of the arts, which during its heyday in the 1920s and 30s, would make Mexico a Mecca for artists from the entire Western world. In 1910 to celebrate a hundred years of Mexican independence, the government had arranged to sponsor a program of "public spectacles," including an Exposition of Contemporary Spanish Painting. But, pleaded Dr. Atl (Gerardo Murillo) a painter-politician and spokesman for the intrepid band of young Mexican artists, why not also include their work, especially since it was the independence of their country that was being celebrated? The Ministry of Public Instruction heard their pleas, and gave them 3,000 pesos to begin their exhibition. During that Centennial Celebration of 1910, "our showing," recalled Orozco, "was an immense, an unexpected success." The exposition by the Spanish painters "was more formal, more stylishly made up, but ours," he went on, "for all that it was improvised, was more dynamic, more varied, and more ambitious. . . ." Held at the Academia de San Carlos, Mexico's leading art school, the exhibit filled its patios, its corridors "and whatever halls were available" with crowds of admiring Mexicans who came to see what their compatriots could do.

Filled with enthusiasm over their triumph, Orozco, Atl, and their friends decided to organize a society of artists, calling it the Centro Artístico. Its goal was to secure from the government the walls of public buildings upon which to paint murals. Having voted on a plan of action, the ebullient artists went off to discuss their project with the Ministry of Public Instruction, asking that they be allowed to paint their first murals on the walls of the Preparatoria. A jubilant Orozco reported that "it was granted, and we portioned out the panels and set up scaffolding." It was early November, 1910. On the twentieth of that month, unfortunately for the dreams of Orozco, Madero revolted. Concluded Orozco: "There was a panic, and our projects were ruined or postponed." Had Díaz continued in office, Mexico would have enjoyed its now-famous mural renaissance a decade earlier—on the very same walls of the Preparatoria.[64]

III

"Don't," Díaz was wont to say, "stampede my horses." By "horses" Días meant the Mexican masses. The less said of liberty and social justice, in his judgment, the better off were he and Mexico. With this assumption as a yardstick, Díaz confined participation in politics to the few. Unfortunately for him, he failed to apply this formula to his economic policies. Had he barred all progress from Mexico, he might have died in office. The fire-brands of rebellion had little support from backward Mexico, as the histories of Chiapas and Oaxaca demonstrate. Most of the southern states, which had been bypassed by the tides of modernization, only belatedly jumped on the rebel bandwagon. Only Morelos, both victimized and blessed by the arrival of the railroad and the development of a modern sugar industry, voiced a protest early. Meanwhile the inhabitants of Oaxaca, more typical of southern Mexicans, watched the fall of Díaz and its aftermath from afar. Isolated from the core of the Republic by mountains and the absence of roads, the peasants of Oaxaca, often Indian in language and attitudes, remained passive. No agricultural monster such as the sugar industry of Morelos had driven them from their lands. Oaxaca had over half-a-million villages, nearly all surviving on a marginal existence, but not for want of political autonomy.[65] As in Oaxaca, immunization against the epidemic of progress kept peace in the majority of southern states. In the border provinces, to the north, the ambivalence of progress, a concoction of the past and the trappings of the twentieth century, upset the balance.

THREE *Age and the Politics of Rigidity*

"*He [Díaz] has governed the Mexican Republic for over thirty years and wedded his life to its singular events, but now nearly eighty years of age he is more a part of history than a contemporary.*"

Francisco I. Madero

I

Accord to a political axiom, governments wield power as long as their leaders believe in their ability to rule, and at the same time, are able to keep the loyalty of those classes with a stake in the status quo. On both counts, the potentates of the Old Regime had lost their right to govern by 1910. Regardless of whatever else went askew, it was the internal decay of the Old Regime that ultimately undermined its stability. After thirty years in office, the rulers of the Republic had failed to keep abreast of the transformations wrought by their success. Time and changing conditions demanded fresh accommodations if the masters were to cling to power. Unable to adjust, Díaz and his allies lost their popularity and their legitimacy. To Antonio Manero, who watched the unfolding drama closely, the aging actors had outlived their roles. "The normal evolution of ideas and events themselves," he concluded, "led to the collapse of the Old Regime and planted the seeds of revolution." [1]

Díaz had governed effectively for three decades because his

policies, sanctioned by eminent political sages and philosophers, responded to practical necessities. But by 1910, even in the opinion of Jorge Vera Estañol, a conservative with fond memories of yesteryear, only social and political inertia kept Díaz and his administration in the National Palace.[2] Francisco Bulnes, the caustic critic of politicians, for his part, judged as an exageration the boasts of rebels that they had toppled a dictatorship; in his opinion, the extent of the power of the Old Regime was a figment of their imagination. Had Díaz and his cohorts still wielded absolute control, their enemies could not have destroyed them. By the same token, the rebel's success eloquently verified the government's loss of legitimacy and authority.[3]

As Madero, the voice of the rebels, acknowledged, Díaz had not always governed with the tools of the dictator. His motto, commented Madero, of "a minimum of terror and a maximum of benevolence"—or to quote a slogan of the time—"General Díaz tightens the noose but does not hang"—suggests an administration with a considerable measure of concern for public opinion.[4] During much of his administration, Díaz controlled politics with the consent of the classes and people who counted in society. Obviously, as Bulnes conceded, Díaz did not rule democratically, a form of government alien to Mexico's history. The fathers of Mexican independence in 1821 had understood neither the meaning of a republic, nor of liberty, nor of democracy. On the other hand, it was absurd to assert that the nature of politics depended solely on the whims of one man. On the contrary, the character of a society, itself the product of historical circumstance, determined the nature of the government. For better or worse, Bulnes concluded pessimistically, "people had the type of government they deserved."[5] To cite Manuel Calero, a favorite of both the old ruler and of Madero, Díaz could not be held accountable for the death of democracy in Mexico, but merely for his failure to inculcate respect in the popular conscience for democratic institutions, and hence his failure to make them an integral part of the Mexican political tradition.[6] Given the character of the national reality, Díaz could be blamed only for not attempting to reshape it. Public dissatisfaction, and not the capture of Ciudad Juárez by the rebels, an insignificant border town, had brought his administration to a close.[7]

II

By 1910, key segments of society stood to gain from a change in government. These were not "unprosperous" people; they were upwardly mobile groups more annoyed or restrained than oppressed. The "outs," essentially the middle class, which were offshoots of the years of progress, demanded a new political and economic accommodation. They looked with increasing disfavor upon a system that showered benefits upon a few aging men who had achieved prominence with the triumph of Díaz. The majority of the rebels condemned the "cliquish" control of Mexico's economy and politics. They wanted full access to current opportunities and not just token acceptance.

The monopoly denounced by the "outs," the older generation's pre-eminence in national life, dated from the decision of Díaz to rule by conciliating the powerful elements of society. A keen student of history, Díaz ascribed the instability which had plagued ·the Republic since its birth to factional strife. To rid Mexico of political turbulence, he adopted the politics of conciliation. In return for backing, he granted key segments of society access to the national pork barrel. Unlike Benito Juárez and his Liberals, whose implacable distrust of clergy and Conservatives invited retaliation, Díaz made his peace with both groups, in the meantime placating the military. To gain use of their talent and capital he opened Mexico's resources to the exploitation of foreign businessmen. In the beginning, Díaz placed wealth, power, and entrance into the social élite at the beck and call of everyone willing to work with him. He turned his back only on the poor, particularly the peasantry. In the interval, he not merely made peace with the ancient foes of the Liberals, but invited them to share the banquet table with him. The supporters of Díaz won a monopoly of the seats in Congress and the state legislatures, as well as of appointments to the judiciary and the governorships. These were the old and the newly rich, an élite of physicians, lawyers, and engineers, plus leaders in commerce, banking, and agriculture, and increasingly, luminaries in science, literature, and the arts.[8] The stalwarts of the Old Regime, recalled Luis Cabrera, eventually a distinguished rebel spokesman, were businessmen, financiers, the clergy, and the *hacendados*.[9]

But despite the opportunities offered by the early Díaz regime, for three decades a select few shared the spoils of politics and business. Fresh blood was seldom infused into the inner circles. Díaz ran the affairs of the Republic from Mexico City. In his cabinet, Ignacio Mariscal ruled Foreign Relations for twenty-six years; Manuel González Cosío managed the War Department for nineteen years; for nearly two decades Leandro Fernández presided over Communications; and José I. Limantour for seventeen years had no rival in the Treasury. Some of the governors established records of longevity: both governors Francisco Cosío in Querétaro and Próspero Cahuantzi of Tlaxcala enjoyed office for twenty-six years; Alejandro Vásquez del Mercado in Aguascalientes and Aristeo Mercado of Michoacán for twenty-four years; for eighteen years Mucio P. Martínez and Teodoro Dehesa governed Puebla and Veracruz. Two clans, the Terrazas in Chihuahua and the Corral clique in Sonora monopolized politics in their respective states for decades. Mexico was ruled by old men in 1910. Of the twenty-four governors only one was under fifty years of age, and sixteen had celebrated their sixtieth birthday. The Chief Justice of the Supreme Court was eighty-three years old, while 60 percent of the country's judges were over seventy years of age. Men eighty and ninety years old sat in the Chamber of Deputies, while the Senate, to cite Bulnes, "housed a collection of senile mummies in a state of lingering stupor." [10]

Still, the evil did not necessarily lie in the age of the incumbents. Quite a few of the governors and cabinet officers, although well along in years, dispatched their obligations efficiently. By most accounts, age had not impaired Governor Dehesa's abilities in Veracruz or tarnished the reputation of General Bernardo Reyes in Nuevo León. Nor had Díaz limited his choice of governors to the social élite, those usually white of skin and Spanish by ancestry. Próspero Cahuantzi, the *cacique*, or undisputed chieftain, of Tlaxcala, could pass for an Indian, but to cite Julio Sesto, was "an Indian with a European soul who could plow his lands with the best, lead with deft hand troops in battle, draw up legislation, and hold a *soirée* in the governor's mansion." [11] It was the rotation of the same men in office, the denial of opportunities to others, and not age, that the opposition resented. To make matters worse, on the morning of the rebellion, Díaz, despite his promise to open up the system, imposed his candidates on Morelos, Sinaloa, and Yucatán. The independent bloc in Morelos favoring Patricio Leyva for governor included Otilio Montaño, a school-teacher, who shortly became one of the drafters of the Plan de Ayala, the Zapatista banner.

Cliquish control of politics extended down to the lowest levels. Governors named the *jefes políticos,* the political bosses, of the municipalities, often without consulting the local citizenry.[12] Many of the *jefes políticos,* miniature autocrats, spent a lifetime in office. However, until late in the nineteenth century, the municipalities had exercised a strong voice in the selection of their officials. Resentment against the *jefes políticos* helped ignite the flame of rebellion in the northern provinces. Local management of communal lands had given villagers a stake in the politics of the municipalities of the central states. Díaz and his provincial bosses took advantage of the rape of village lands, and the subsequent loss of interest by villagers in running their affairs, to impose *jefes políticos* at odds with local sentiment. Governors went so far as to choose as *jefe político* an *hacendado* or one of his friends.[13] To quiet the swelling resentment, Díaz, in his final presidential message, vowed to put an end to the monopolistic system, but, until he sailed for Europe on the *Ypiranga,* he made no effort to keep his word.[14]

To stifle opposition, Díaz forbid political parties. The ban, perhaps initially justified to end factional squabbles and petty rivalries, actually confined political careers to a chosen few, and eventually curtailed liberty of thought. While Díaz lavished rewards on this admirers and the opportunistic, he punished dissidents. After years of successful rule, Díaz' outlook hardened; he abandoned his former policy of conciliation, in effect, confining the fruits of his administration to those men who had long ago climbed aboard the official bandwagon. Díaz did not tolerate deviation. When General Reyes timidly challenged his authority, Díaz sent him off on a mission to Europe. Reyes' abject surrender left his followers, among them Venustiano Carranza in Coahuila, at the mercy of Díaz. When Madero and his supporters, rebuffed in their attempts to name one of their own to the vice-presidency, stood up to Díaz, Madero was jailed, and with the help of a cooperative judiciary, fraudulent legal procedings were begun against the Madero properties.[15]

To insure control of political office by the inner clique, which his increasing age jeopardized, Díaz and his congressional allies passed an amendment creating the office of the vice-president. In addition, the president and his subordinate were given six-year terms. Given Díaz' advanced age, the plan made sense; it guaranteed a smooth transition of presidential authority should he die unexpectedly. However, unless Díaz permitted outsiders a voice in the selection of his running mate, the measure strengthened the control of the vested clique. Ironically, the amendment to the Constitution unleashed the pent-up ambitions not solely of outsiders but within the official family. Reyes became the first victim of the hoax because Díaz never intended the vice-presidency for potential rivals. Wanting a man he could trust to keep his place, Díaz picked Ramón Corral, a candidate backed strongly by Limantour and the barons of business, finance, and industry.[16] Intimately identified with the traditional interests of Sonora, Corral proved an unpopular choice; his selection exacerbated political conflicts in Sonora between old and new economic groups. Apparently oblivious to Corral's unpopularity—or because a vice-president without a following posed no danger to him— Díaz again chose him as his running mate in the 1910 elections. The imposition of Corral was a cardinal miscalculation.

Keeping government in the proper hands required a deferential, trustworthy judiciary. Whether intentionally or not, Díaz' government put justice at the service of the élite. From the perspective of the disenfranchized, the structure of the judiciary system caused a thousand evils. Only scions of the leading families and their friends could aspire to successful legal careers. From the Supreme Court to the provincial benches, the executive branch or the state governors were responsible for all judicial appointments. To enter the system, a young lawyer, if he was by chance given the opportunity of a legal career, had to abandon textbook principles and loyalties to ideals.[17] More detrimental, because it touched all of society, a compliant judiciary compromised justice and ultimately eroded public confidence in the law.

By 1910, the corruption of justice, an old problem in Mexico, and the loss of public confidence in the legal system had reached epidemic proportions. Lawyers, remembered Aquiles Elorduy, a graduate of the national law school in the waning days of Díaz, believed that in making decisions the lower and higher courts, as well as the Supreme Court itself, merely obeyed dictates from above—of a *jefe político,* a governor, a cabinet minister, or the president of the Republic.[18] Magistrates in rural Mexico did the bidding of the *hacendados* or sold justice as though it were a cash commodity. Without money for a bribe, lamented Rafael de Zayas Enríquez, there was no justice for the aggrieved, because "even the janitor of a courthouse will not perform his duties without a tip." [19] Tardily, Díaz pledged to put his house in order; but, when the curtain came down on the drama, neither the cast of characters nor the script had been changed.

III

The monopolistic sins of politics had their counterparts in the spheres of business and finance: laissez faire commerce, free competition, rugged individualism, and the rest of the trappings of nineteenth-century capitalism. But, as the small entrepreneur understood well, a huge gap separated doctrine from practice. From the perspective of those at the bottom of the social system, reality was the "special privileges granted the friends of officials." [20] Government drew its strength, affirmed Luis Cabrera, from the privileges of a small coterie in business, banking, industry, commerce, mining, and petroleum.[21] These special advantages ruled out free competition, supposedly the cornerstone of the prevailing economic philosophy. Given this situation, the small entrepreneur hardly had an opportunity for success.

Cabrera, Manero, and critics of similar bent placed the responsibilities for these evils on the doorsteps of the *científicos,* Díaz' kitchen cabinet of businessmen and politicians.[22] When President Venustiano Carranza attempted to eliminate the monopolies, he uncovered an elaborate web intricately tied to the banks of Mexico or to foreign corporations claiming international immunity.[23] Consumers and small businessmen paid taxes, but not the large companies or the inner circle of favorites—which were also exempt from paying import duties. A similar situation existed in the municipalities where, to the mounting anger of local natives, the political machine exempted the friends of the powerful from taxation. An act of political disloyalty, therefore, cost not only membership in the club but freedom from paying taxes. Supporters of Reyes' abortive attempt to become vice-president, including relatives of Carranza in Torreón, found themselves in this predicament in 1909.[24]

Not surprisingly, the chosen amassed vast fortunes. As Bulnes wrote in *El Verdaero Díaz y la Revolución,* many profited enormously.[25] One such beneficiary was Iñigo Noriega, a man of humble origins who acquired a fortune of 8 million *pesos,* an *hacienda,* and a third of the lands of his native Tamaulipas, by relying, charged Francisco Múgica, upon the Leyes de Tierras Baldías to rape the villages.[26] By these laws, so-called "idle and unclaimed" lands could be surveyed and acquired by private individuals. General Gerónimo Treviño, an intimate of the Madero clan, became a millionaire. Tomás Braniff multiplied a small fortune into 10 million pesos. Bulnes estimated the wealth of Manuel Calero, once a penniless lawyer and afterwards a supporter of Madero, at 600,000 pesos.[27] One of the public scandals of the day, of benefit to a small band of speculators, involved the former governor of Jalisco, Manuel Cuesta Gallardo. With the blessings of Díaz, the Banco Nacional had loaned Cuesta Gallardo a large sum of money for a real estate venture near Lake Chapala in Jalisco. The Compañía Eléctrica e Irrigadora de Chapala, the front for Cuesta Gallardó, abandoned the venture without ever repaying the loan. Meanwhile, by granting the concession to his friend, Díaz had antagonized the local *hacendados,* also with lands to sell, who threatened to make their anger public. To silence them, Díaz asked the Banco Central to finance the purchase of their lands at a price fixed by them. As a result, lands worth 16 million pesos sold for over 45 million pesos. So enormous was the amount of money involved that the Banco Nacional had to help the Banco Central float the transaction. Cuesta Gallardo and the *hacendados* made a tidy profit from the shady scheme.[28]

IV

Sonora could be considered a microcosm of the national ills. Cronyism, exaggerated tenures in public office, and regional rivalries had shaken the fabric of the state. Curiously, in the entire Republic, only Sonora had a law forbidding the re-election of its governors.[29] To circumvent the statute, a triumvirate managed the politics of the state. Between 1883 and 1911, Luis Emeterio Torres and his two proteges, Ramón Corral and Rafael Izábal, rotated the office of governor among themselves. Their rule occurred during an era of expansion that until 1900 showered benefits chiefly on the mining districts of the northwest and western Ures. Its axis was Hermosillo, the capital of the state. There Corral, in league with foreigners, amassed a large fortune. Corral earned his reputation and multiplied his wealth in business and mining. He was not an *hacendado,* but a speculator in the world of finance, a man who loved urban life and the society of the frock coat, as well as an efficient administrator and able politician. An occasional writer, he saw himself as something of an intellectual.[30]

Until 1900, both the old and the new economic groups looked to Corral for leadership. The coming of American investors and the Yaqui wars, which split businessmen and *hacendados* into opposing camps, the arrival of hordes of workers in the booming mining towns, and the growth of Guaymas and other commercial rivals of Hermosillo, upset the political balance. From this juncture, Corral could count on the support of only the older, traditional interests. Izábal was a land baron, the owner of four *haciendas* in the district of Hermosillo, where he and his neighbors, with modern farm implements, cultivated wheat, corn, and beans for sale on the domestic market. By 1910, Izábal and his band of *hacendados* were confronted with the formidable challenge of farmers in other regions of Sonora, particularly in the prosperous, labor-intensive, export-geared *haciendas* of the Mayo and Yaqui river valleys. In the end, Izábal and his clique of northwest *hacendados* lost their leadership of the state's agriculture. Concomitantly, the coming of the railroads, which linked Naco, Cananea, and the mining camps of the northeast with Arizona, cost the Hermosillo oligarchy its place at the top of commerce and business. Despite these fundamental changes calling for a new political accommodation, Governor Izábal, and Corral, then vice-president (Torres had died), attempted to keep the monopoly of power in their hands. Their wars against the Yaquis, the major source of workers for the southern farms, angered the *hacendados* of the Mayo and Yaqui region, while their mishandling of the strike at Cananea, which they had put down by importing gun-toting Americans to kill Mexicans, inflamed the passions of nationalists already upset by the heavy influx of foreigners.[31]

The careers of Corral and Izábal, which epitomize the clannish politics and business climate of Sonora, help explain the resentment that became rebellion. Both men, first under the tutelage of Torres and then on their own, had, at one time or another held every political office. Corral, who began his political career by joining the rebellion against Governor Ignacio J. Pesqueira, was elected to Congress in 1877, and eventually became president of the Chamber of Deputies. Shortly afterwards, he returned to Sonora as lieutenant governor, then became its governor, and from that office went on to be mayor of the Federal District, vice-president of the Republic, and minister of *gobernación,* the key cabinet post, in 1904 and 1910.[32] Before assuming the governorship, Izábal had been elected to five state legislatures and twice to the national Congress. From 1879 to 1911, just seventy-four men, most of whom were friends or relatives of Torres, Corral, or Izábal, occupied the 208 seats of the sixteen state legislatures, each a three-year term.[33]

The ruling clique managed the politics of Sonora with an iron hand. Chosen by Díaz, the governor carried out the wishes of the national and state oligarchies. After 1891, all nine districts in Sonora had prefects appointed by the governor, who also controlled the presidents of the municipalities. By fraud, or because the corrupt nature of politics discouraged opposition, these petty bosses elected themselves over and over again. The prefect of Ures, to give one example of longevity, stayed in office for twenty-one years.[34] Accountable only to the governor, the prefects became miniature tyrants who dispensed or withheld favors at whim. Meanwhile, the national government reduced the number of municipalities, from eighty-nine in 1900 to seventy, ten years later.[35] Local autonomy fell by the wayside. It was this *caciquismo pueblerino,* the abuse of authority by petty tyrants, writes a noted historian Antonio G. Rivera, that fanned the flames of rebellion in Sonora.[36]

The loss of municipal autonomy, moreover, blocked not merely political rights but opportunities for profit as is illustrated by the experience of Benjamín Hill, who later became a major rebel military figure. A budding entrepreneur of thirty-six, Hill expected to make his way in life by taking his share of benefits from the growth and development of the Mayo River valley. Although he had easily mastered the skills of the land speculator, he soon learned that it took more than talent to guarantee success. To escape the flooding of the Mayo which heavily damaged Navojoa each year, the town council, manipulated by a small clique with the concurrence of state authorities, had voted to transfer the seat of government up the valley. Immediately, the distribution and sale of land sites for homes in the new community attracted the attention of speculators. But, recalled Hill, no sooner had the lands been subdivided into lots than the town council sold them off cheaply to its friends, excluding Hill and his allies from the lucrative business deals. The episode alerted Hill to the importance of municipal politics. Not long after, Hill and his friends were meeting in the home of Flavio Bórquez, a dissident landlord, to discuss how to handle the *caciques* on the council.[37] At this point, Madero published his book, *La Sucesión Presidencial en 1910,* which included a strong indictment of the attack on municipal autonomy. Not illogically, in Sonora, Hill became the president of the first club opposing Díaz' re-election.[38]

Conversely, the decline of mining hurt Alamos and incited factional strife. One of the four towns in Sonora with over 5,000 inhabitants, Alamos suffered acutely after mining fell on evil days. By 1910, Alamos had actually lost population, to the unhappiness of its merchants. Many former residents had left for Navojoa, Echojoa, and Huatabampo, all thriving agricultural towns. Alamos was a colonial bastion, with a strong merchant class, *hacendados* with large land holdings, and old and distinguished families. Blaming Alamos' decline on Corral and his henchmen, its inhabitants eventually joined the ranks of the malcontents. To the southwest, the struggle to control the water of the Río Yaqui pitted *hacendado* against *hacendado,* especially after the expulsion of the Yaquis had opened more land for cultivation. Squabbles over water rights aggravated political rivalries.

On the coast, the growth of Guaymas endangered the preeminence of Hermosillo. By 1910, Guaymas had become the state's major port, where minerals from the interior were shipped abroad, where merchants imported and sold guns and ammunition for the wars against the Yaquis, and where the Yaquis in turn, purchased their weapons. The arrival of the railroad in Guaymas offered further avenues for profit: from the handling of materials for the construction of the railroad; from the supplies shipped through Guaymas to Americans working on the railroads; and from the traffic of agricultural goods hauled by railroad to Guaymas for shipment to California. As the economy of Guaymas flourished, its population expanded to 38,000 inhabitants, surpassing Hermosillo's 31,000. Yet Hermosillo still controlled politics. Thus, when Madero visited Sonora on his political campaign, the merchants of Guaymas gave him an enthusiastic reception. One wealthy *hacendado* of the port city, José María Maytorena, became president of the Club Maderista; its secretary was Adolfo de la Huerta, of the city's banking community. Not one of the old families of Hermosillo embraced Madero.[39]

The political portrait of neighboring Chihuahua bore a marked resemblance to Sonora's. In the process of acquiring ownership of half of this arid land, the Terrazas clan won sole control of its politics. Advocates of rebellion, writes Francisco R. Almada, the distinguished chronicler of Chihuahua's history, found fertile soil there because of local anger.[40] It was the bitter resentment of the economic and political monopoly of the Terrazas clan and not discontent with the national leadership that converted Chihuahua into a hotbed of rebellion.[41] "In my presence," Bulnes remembered, Abraham González, one of the dissidents in Chihuahua, claimed that he had "initiated the revolution not out of hatred for Díaz but because of his hatred of the Terrazas family as represented by the government of don Enrique Creel." [42]

After helping Benito Juárez put down an abortive military coup by Porfirio Díaz in 1872, Luis Terrazas, a native of Chihuahua, had set out to conquer his province. Ultimately, he built an empire in cattle, banking, textiles, and meatpacking, and along the way, established himself as a political monarch.[43] Because of his early opposition to Díaz, who eventually defeated Juárez' successor, Terrazas had to bide his time. Finding the doors to the statehouse closed to him, he stayed in the shadow of Colonel Miguel Ahumada, the *cacique* of Chihuahua. However, in 1893 Terrazas' nephew and son-in-law, Enrique C. Creel, used his influence with politicians in Mexico City to bring about peace between his uncle and don Porfirio.[44] From then on, the political destinies of Terrazas took a turn for the better as he and Díaz joined hands to rule Chihuahua. His rapprochement permitted Terrazas to expand his already sizeable empire and to become the pilot of the state's politics. By 1910, Almada wrote, the monopoly of the Terrazas' clan, which confined opportunities to a favored minority, had awakened deep animosities among those left out.[45]

The monopoly of the Terrazas' family limited roles on the political stage to one cast of characters. Between 1903 and 1911, with only brief interludes, either Terrazas or Creel sat in the statehouse. At one point, Creel, the son of an American consul and one of Terrazas' sisters, was both governor of Chihuahua and minister of foreign relations. Before that he had been Mexico's ambassador to Washington. Partly Yankee, Creel never fully won the trust of his nationalistic Mexican compatriots. As Bulnes put it, Creel was "half yankee by blood" and "by character and education a yankee-and-a-half." [46] A group of fifteen deputies returned year after year to the state legislature. One group of twenty-seven men monopolized the seats in four legislatures, each of two years duration.[47] From 1881 to 1911, only eighty-six men sat in the state legislature, fifty-five of them on two, three, ten, or more occasions. Just thirty-one were not re-elected. A handful represented their own districts or a neighboring one; many, in the course of their political careers came to represent each of the fifteen legislative districts of Chihuahua.[48]

The Terrazas' clique abolished even the pretense of local government. The state constitution of 1847 had divided Chihuahua into sixteen cantons or districts (later increased to twenty-one), each split into municipalities and submunicipalities. Elected by popular vote for a two-year term, the *jefe político* of the district presided over the town council of its principal center. Elected municipal presidents governed the less important towns and districts. In 1887, the ruling clique began to undermine the system, first giving the governor the right to appoint permanent *jefes políticos,* and then two years later abolishing the job of municipal president of the chief towns. Governor Creel carried the attack on local government one step further in 1904, giving himself the authority to name the president of even the smallest municipality.[49] To make matters worse, the *jefes políticos* chose the police. Silvestre Terrazas, a distant relative but no ideological kin to the clan and editor of *El Correo de Chihuahua,* accused the *jefes políticos* of even hiring natives of other states as police.[50] As the Terrazas tightened their control of politics, so did the complaints of outsiders multiply in number and volume, especially in Parral and Guerrero, which eventually became havens for rebels.

In the financial world, the Lujáns, Asúnsolos, and Falomirs shared the spoils with Terrazas and Creel. From the beginning, they were the landowners, businessmen, industrialists, bankers, and cattle barons. The favored Americans arrived later: the Guggenheims; Colonel William C. Greene, the lord of mining and lumbering; and William Randolph Hearst, who tended cattle on his giant estate. Ties of friendship, if not always of blood, bound the favored Mexicans, and barred the ambitious outsider from participating in the state's prosperity. The concessions conferred on insiders by the governor or the state legislature included an array of special privileges: the right to postpone the payment of state and local taxes; monopolies of certain industries; lucrative contracts to build highways, public buildings, and railroads; permits to sponsor lotteries; and the ownership of *tiendas de raya,* company stores.[51] Concomitantly, in his fiscal policies, Creel put the burden on the least able to pay. The tax system favored the rich and the corporation over the poor and the small merchant. On a business valued at 500 pesos, the owner paid up to a peso a month in taxes; on a business of 10,000 pesos or less, a tax up to ten pesos a month; but on a business worth over 20,000 pesos, a monthly tax of fifteen pesos or less.[52]

When, in 1867 the triumphant Liberals set out to dictate the course of Mexican history, the western lumbering and mining district of Guerrero dominated politics. Guerrero was hurt by the entrance of the railroad into the city of Chihuahua in 1884, which paved the way for a profitable cattle industry in the central flatlands. With access to markets in Texas, the economy of Ciudad Chihuahua prospered, helping the Terrazas to put together an empire. Creel, who profited along with the Terrazas, made his millions in corporate business. Like Corral in Sonora, Creel worked hand in glove with American investors who poured money into mining and lumbering, and as the history of the Palomas Land and Cattle Company demonstrates, into the purchase of land. The economic shift came at the expense of Ciudad Guerrero, which by 1892 had lost its political leadership. With its headquarters in Ciudad Chihuahua, the Terrazas clan sat in the driver's seat.[53]

Guerrero's decline left behind a rubble of broken dreams and ambitions. One such disappointed *politico* was Abraham González, who later, with the victory of Madero, would become governor of Chihuahua. His early life epitomizes the dashed hopes of those of the gentry in disfavor with the oligarchy. A native of Ciudad Guerrero, González belonged to a distinguished family; both his maternal grandfather and his uncle Celso González had governed the state. Educated in the Preparatoria of Mexico City and at Notre Dame University in the United States, González was a man of learning who spoke English fluently. Although not a millionaire, he was, by the standards of Chihuahua, very well off: he was the owner of farmlands on the outskirts of Ciudad Guerrero. As long as his uncle Celso's band ran state politics, González held promising jobs, one of which was head cashier of the Banco de Chihuahua. With Celso's downfall in 1892, the date which marks the Terrazas' rise to prominence, González' fortunes took a turn for the worse. When the Terrazas gained control of the Banco de Chihuahua, González lost his job. To compound his difficulty, the lands he owned yielded only modest profits, while foreign corporations blocked his attempts to invest in mining. By 1910, a once promising career had ended in a series of minor jobs: as a translator; editor of *El Padre Padilla,* a small weekly newspaper; and as a cattle buyer for an American company. In that role he met Pancho Villa, a cattle rustler and bandit.[54]

Stymied in his efforts to move upwards, González became an advocate of reform. Yet he never championed the destruction of the system, merely its modification. He wanted opportunities for men of his class and generation. He flirted briefly with the Partido Liberal Mexicano, but its intoxicating agenda of social change had little appeal for him. [55] As he admitted to Bulnes, his unhappiness with the Terrazas' dynasty eventually encouraged him to hoist the banner of rebellion. Not even the return to the governorship of the popular Miguel Ahumada, who promptly lowered taxes and began to sweep out the corrupt bosses in the municipalities, dissuaded González.[56] For the men of Guerrero, the belated reforms of Ahumada hardly compensated for damaged careers and thwarted expectations.

The ups and downs in the career of González probably best explain why Chihuahua became a hotbed of sedition. Undoubtedly, as students of Mexican history emphasize, other reasons must be taken into account. The proximity of Chihuahua and sister border provinces to Arizona, New Mexico, and Texas, which supplied northern Mexicans with a close view of American politics and economics, while facilitating the acquisition of war materials, may have encouraged the spirit of protest. The hostile, arid topography, as well as the isolation from Mexico City, lent itself to guerrilla warfare, as did the rugged individualism of the people of the north.[57] To some, the curtailment of individual liberties by the Terrazas and by Díaz helped ignite the conflagration.[58] Yet, as one from Chihuahua succinctly pointed out to Alvaro Obregón, the natives of the state, because of their isolation from authorities in Mexico City, had always enjoyed a healthy dose of personal liberty.[59]

Despite rebel claims to the contrary, Madero's clarion call did not signal an uprising against a regime based simply on terror or military might. Even a superficial glance at the history of the three decades reveals a picture at odds with the legend. To the astonishment of countless observers, both Mexicans and foreigners, the military proved no match for the insurgents, who were poorly equipped and ill-trained. Only the battles of Zacatecas and Torreón, where Villa's troops routed the federal army, and Obregón's triumphs at Guadalajara and Celaya rank as major military engagements. The others were *tiroteos,* skirmishes of varying magnitudes between rifle-toting bands. But, paradoxically, the myth still remains that a powerful military buttressed the Old Regime. Given that conviction, it is difficult to explain how that army, a loyal ally for years, failed to defend its benefactor.

The mystery, in truth, rests on a falacious assumption: the dependence of the Old Regime on military backing. Its survival and successes in actuality ultimately stemmed not from its military strength, but from its popularity. Don Porfirio stayed in the National Palace because he had the support of the majority, and particularly, the people who counted. His slogan of "Peace, Order, and Progress," his practice of showering gifts on the literate, had few disbelievers until the first decade of the 1900's. Only when the formula faltered, especially with the financial crisis of 1907, did enthusiasm wane. After the hectic turmoil of the Santa Anna years, Mexicans had no stomach for more internal strife. Peace and order offered benefits beyond what the sword promised. Once don Profirio had consolidated his authority, he had scant reason to rely on a powerful military. As José I. Limantour, the guiding genius in the Treasury, argued, the popularity of don Porfirio explains his long and successful rule.[60]

An avid student of the politics of longevity, Díaz wanted no challenge by the military to his regime. To keep the generals in their place, and to avoid a repetition of the ubiquitous *cuartelazo,* the military coup of the age of Santa Anna, Díaz deliberately kept the army impotent. It was a police force employed to maintain law and order. In rural Mexico, the "Mounties" of Mexico, the *rurales,* recruited from unruly residents who had a stake in disorder, helped protect the patrons of the status quo. Yet by 1910, the supposedly powerful and efficient *rurales,* existed mostly as a figment of the imagination.[61] Grown old and fat, some of their legendary captains could only mount their horses with herculean efforts. In 1909, as Díaz publicly acknowledged, Mexico had only 3,000 *rurales*—too few to impose on the countryside a peace by the sword.[62]

Only indirectly concerned with their combat readiness and to assure the loyalty of his troops, Díaz placated their officers, promoting them on schedule, permitting the generals to age gracefully in rank, and closing his eyes to their graft and incompetence. By allowing his officers access to the public trough, thus making the career of the warrior monetarily attractive, Díaz won their loyalty and subservience. A large slice of the money earmarked for the purchase of military hardware, as well as for the recruitment of soldiers, found its way into the pockets of generals and colonels. Phantom regiments existed in the army. By 1910, a frantic rush by Díaz' army to purchase rifles and cannon, proved in vain because soldiers to use them could not be found.[63]

When Limantour investigated the army, he discovered, much to his dismay, how well Díaz' benign neglect had worked. While the budget included funds for infantry battalions of 2,000 men, theft in the military had cut their numbers by a third. The situation was even worse in the cavalry. When Madero revolted, the bulk of the troops were stationed in the Federal District or in other urban centers where the uprisings were anticipated. The soldiers dispatched to combat the enemy lacked equipment and supplies, while their commanders, because of their inexperience, quickly revealed their incapacity for leadership. The attempts of the aged Díaz to direct operations in the field added to the confusion.[64]

Nonetheless, the ineptness of the army, which astonished Mexicans of that time and continues to baffle some scholars, did not come as a total surprise to officials of the Old Regime. In his *Apuntes,* Limantour describes how he had to guard against granting the military its requested funds because of its propensity for graft. He admitted that he had discouraged the growth of the army as well as the modernization of its equipment lest the money be misspent.[65] Francisco Bulnes, the caustic critic with entrance to the official corridors of government, recounted how General Bernardo Reyes, upon appointment as minister of war discovered an army staffed with incompetents and grafters.[66] Another Porfirista, Jorge Vera Estañol, thought the army ill-equipped, badly trained, and incompetently led by officers devoid of either theoretical knowledge or battlefield experience.[67] Peculation, said Antonio Manero, a politician who once admired don Porfirio, had left the army virtually useless.[68] Or, to cite Manuel Calero, a lawyer in the Mexico of Díaz, the army served merely for "military parades." This point was reiterated by Arturo Langle Ramírez, author of a book on Villa's army, who asserted that while Díaz's soldiers might know how to march in parades, "their command of battle tactics bordered on the ludicrous." [69]

What graft and kindred sins could not sabotage, age and senility did. As Bulnes bitterly remembered, old men ran the army, "giving to the public the image of a funeral carriage pulled by mummies reeking of the stench of camphor." [70] Colonels eighty years of age and older commanded troops; there were captains of seventy years of age, lieutenants of sixty years, and sublieutenants only slightly less ancient, on active service. Of the four *generales de división,* the youngest, Reyes, was sixty years of age, another seventy-nine, and the others eighty.[71] According to General J. Refugio Velásquez, one of the generals, a huge cultural gap divided the officers and their men, who were almost always conscripts from the worst elements of the lower classes, many of them even criminals from jail.[72] When that source dried up, the army filled its quotas by raiding villages of illiterate Indian peasants. A sarcastic Bulnes labeled the Mexican army "the worst in the world." [73] Little wonder, therefore, that the rebel soldiers, usually with only a rifle and scarce ammunition, defeated the paper tiger. But, then, Díaz had long ago discounted the need to rely on an efficient military.

One incident, the Creelman interview of 1908, lit the tinder box. The pledge of don Porfirio given in this interview, to step down at the end of his current term in office, set off a chain reaction which toppled his fossilized regime. Díaz, strange as it may seem, had not discussed the interview with his cabinet; Limantour recalled that he learned of it by reading a newspaper. But Madero and the *científicos* took Díaz' promise seriously. Rosendo Pinedo, one of the kitchen cabinet, went so far as to write a letter to the editor of *El Imparcial* applauding as "our rights" the awaited metamorphosis of Mexican politics.[74] Teodoro A. Dehesa, the governor of Veracruz, in a burst of naïveté brought his friend Madero to talk to Díaz.[75]

The aging president, nonetheless, never intended to step down; he rigged the elections of 1910 and proclaimed himself and Corral Mexico's leaders for another six years. But, although his admirers immediately accepted the decision, the decrepit Díaz proved incapable of ruling. His regime had not merely lost its ability to govern but its faith in its ability to do so. Not until February 1911 did it take steps to quell the rebellion which had broken out the previous year. During the interval, Díaz and his advisers committed untold blunders, publicly displaying their incapacity to govern. The shaky regime collapsed with the loss of Ciudad Juárez to a tiny band of poorly armed rebels whom Díaz, bed-ridden with a tooth-ache, had been unable to defeat. The Old Regime disintegrated, concluded Limantour, because Mexicans tired of being ruled by a government they thought strong, but which, in reality, could not maintain either order or fulfill public aspirations.[76]

FOUR *The Ungrateful Scion*

"But the shift in the center of gravity brought about by the growth, both in numbers and power of the middle class and the appearance of a large, organized lower middle class, was not understood by the Old Regime which, on the decline, merely had eyes for the past."

Jorge Vera Estañol

I

A SOCIETY THAT shunts aside its progeny carries within itself the seeds of its own destruction. And so it occurred in the age of Díaz, which had vigorously paved the way for the growth of a middle class, and then shut the doors of opportunity to it. Not permitted to share the distribution of power with the old guard, the more ambitious and frustrated of the middle class ultimately rebelled against the society which had fathered them.

Progress spurred the formation of the middle class, which had been tiny and nebulously defined at the time of the Reforma. "A legitimate child," to cite *El Imparcial,* the class "evolved from Díaz' successful transformation of Mexico." Without the economic formulas of Díaz, which he defended in the face of adversity, no such class would have developed. Its origins, explained *El Imparcial,* began with the initial manifestations of public wealth: the appearance of industry, the arrival of the railroads, and the availability of loans to small business.[1] Its appearance, which Díaz authenticated by granting it a stake in peace and order, sounded the death knell for the old Regime. Or as the poet and intellectual Guillermo Prieto commented, industrialization had given birth to a middle class with a life of its own, with its own resources, and with opportunities for success. By joining hands with the ruling élite, it had pledged not to question the prevailing formulas. Yet its arrival on the scene, as Prieto recognized, brought "a profound change." [2] Tragically for the rulers of Mexico, lamented Jorge Vera Estañol, they shut their eyes to it. Instead of welcoming it into the inner salons, the old guard barred the doors of upward mobility to all but a few of the new class.[3]

II

Had the Old Regime taken the time to examine its progeny, careful study would have revealed a middle class no less important because of its complexity. Although referred to as a middle class, in effect, it lacked the credentials of a true class: a strong awareness of itself or a consciousness of class. Defined by the terminology of Western Europe or the United States, the Mexican middle class had not jelled. Its homage to the Protestant ethic, characteristic of the middle class in the industrialized world, often had a hollow ring. While Díaz could speak of it as the cement of Mexico's democracy and eulogize it as the class most dedicated to hard work, reality only partly upheld his professed convictions.[4] As Vera Estañol observed, the Protestant ethic, whatever its merits, did not always find disciples among the middle class. Instead, the middle-class Mexican was more apt to seek to rub shoulders with the rich, to copy their dress, to live in the most luxurious home his income could provide, and to emulate the life of the country squire. He lived beyond his means: rather than save for a rainy day, he discounted the future; his quest for the good life kept him on the verge of bankruptcy; in order to enjoy a vacation in Acapulco or Veracruz, he went into debt and spent the rest of the year trying to make ends meet.[5] "Our middle classes," to quote *El Imparcial,* "live on a day-to-day basis . . . regardless of the size of their income." [6] Even the educated among them, declared Antonio Manero, were suspicious and distrustful of others.[7] Such a class fell an easy victim of the crisis of 1907, which was the origin of the middle-class leadership for the upheaval three years later.

That the middle class was ambitious, thirsty for gain, and suspicious of others, most observers agreed. But as to its actual composition, the critics had varying opinions. Most saw the middle class as a hodgepodge of sectors or groups situated between the rich and the poor. Julio Sesto, said its elements could rightfully claim to "embody the vigor of the Republic, and by their culture and abnegation, stand as models of dignity," and he spoke of "four or five groups" above the masses yet loosely identified with them.[8] From Vera Estañol's vantage point, the middle class stood between the poor and the rich and consisted of upper and lower sectors.[9] Antenor Sala in another classification included skilled laborers, *rancheros,* small businessmen, public and private employees, professionals, artists and artisans, independent mine operators, and the owners of workshops and small cargo and fishing boats. He calculated their number at approximately 4 million —over one-fourth of the Republic's total population in 1910.[10] As Sala's definition reveals, the middle class had rural as well as urban roots, particularly in the northern provinces where the expansion of the great estates was concurrent with a dramatic explosion in the number of small and medium-size *ranchos.*[11] To Andrés Molina Enríquez who, like Sala, grouped skilled workers with public employees and small businessmen, rural middle class meant *mestizos*—those of mixed Spanish and Indian ancestry— who, "of greater intelligence, a higher culture, and more energetic," would not toil on *ejidos,* communal farms, in the manner of Indian peasants.[12] Ambassador Henry Lane Wilson, an intimate of the old guard, thought of the middle class as "sturdy tradesmen, usually of Indian extraction . . . industrious, intelligent," with "acute interest in public affairs . . . impatient of existing conditions and constantly exerting a stronger and wider influence." Almost always critical of the regime and its leaders, Wilson went on to suggest that "the vast majority" of the members of this class "will rise to the support of ambitious men offering remedies for present evils."[13] Events on the horizon proved Wilson a prophet.

The middle class prospered in the fertile soil of the northern provinces. The railroads and the development of mining gave impetus to its growth and prosperity. During the last fifteen years of the Porfiriato, the population of Sonora, a mirror of the transformation of the border states, jumped from 191,281 to 265,383, an increase of 40 percent. Almost one-fourth of its population lived in communities of over 2,500 inhabitants—small urban centers. In comparison with other regions of the Republic, urban growth in the north had wider ramifications. Northern towns were truly urban environments, not the *pueblos* or villages of the south where peasants lived in traditional rural settings. Offsprings of a mining bonanza, and with an economy "increasingly geared to the market," the urban towns of the north sheltered a population of "agricultural entrepreneurs." [14] All of the border provinces, particularly Sonora, Chihuahua, and Coahuila, enjoyed a substantial growth of professional groups. The number of school teachers multiplied rapidly, as did, although on a smaller scale, physicians and lawyers.[15] Resentful of their exclusion from the inner circles of politics and business, *rancheros*, merchants, and professionals eagerly heeded the call to arms.[16]

As one Mexican scholar writes, the "outs" joined Madero —men who aspired to enter the charmed circle of politics—as well as "lawyers without clients and budding bureaucrats in search of public jobs." [17] Do not be misled, Rafael de Zayas Enríquez told Díaz, the middle classes "reflect" the discontent of industrial labor, "out of necessity and to satisfy aspirations." [18] Even sales clerks in the prestigious Palacio de Hierro in Mexico City, a group not noted for the espousal of egalitarian ideas, had taken up the cry for Sundays off—along with bartenders and salesmen who had organized a society in the capital entitled "Sundays Off" that, as its name implied, wanted the sabbath made a day of rest, and a shorter work week.[19] Its demands echoed in Chihuahua, San Luis Potosí, and sundry provincial cities and towns.[20]

Middle-class unrest, which gave shape and articulation to the rebellion of 1910, had limited objectives in the beginning. Conservative by conviction and upbringing, the majority of the middle class cared little about ideological matters. With the exception of Ricardo Flores Magón and his disciples, whose crusade for social justice drew a meager army, the middle class generally turned a deaf ear to radical messiahs. In time, however, the restrictions on upward mobility began to irritate the less docile. The political monopoly reserved for the élite, conferring social as well as economic benefits, eventually alienated the more ambitious.[21] From a middle-class perspective, the élite, vulgarly labeled the *cientéficos*, by blocking access to the top, had become the enemy. It was equally certain, that not one of the middle class, the *gente decente*, wanted to drop out of a class that had cost so much sweat and toil to join. Fear of the economic pinch, which had been exacerbated by the financial crisis of 1907, the daily struggle to keep up with the family next door and to provide wife and children with the proper home, food, and clothing—in short, the dilemma of the "unrich," observed Felix F. Palavicini a lawyer of moderate reform proclivities—led the middle class to the threshold of rebellion.[22] Or, as Bulnes said, the middle classes feared not tyranny and subservience, but the specter of poverty, the high cost of meat and bread, and fundamentally, the necessity of belt tightening.[23]

Only late in the Porfiriato, after the crisis of 1907 had turned the economy upside down and begun to empty pocketbooks, did the middle classes unfurl the flag of rebellion. Yet they wanted no truck with the Partido Liberal Mexicano, the vehicle of the Flores Magón. Instead, the timid disciples of change cautiously championed the candidacy of General Bernardo Reyes, the provincial *caudillo* from Nuevo León who had an ambivalent attitude toward labor. Francisco I. Madero undoubtedly molded his platform with the opinion of the middle classes in mind, among them the "poor intellectuals who had escaped the corrupting influence of wealth." The restless, he conceded, also included the "select group" of industrial workers "who aspire to a better way of life and who, by attempting to organize labor unions, had taken a big first step to win their rights and to fulfill their ideals." [24] At the same time, perhaps reflecting his class prejudice, Madero expressed scant hope for the poor who, "never compelled to attend school and always able to satiate their bestial craving for liquor . . . stoically accept their lot and give no thought to whether they can improve themselves." Still, "despite their ignorance," he acknowledged, "they understand that everything told to them is a lie." [25]

The anger of the middle class focused, ironically, not on the octogenarian Díaz but on his confederates. The targets were the *cientificos* and the provincial hierarchy of political cronies. With a few exceptions, the firebrands of the *gente decente* judged the president sacrosanct. Nobody in 1906, reported Zayas Enríquez, whom Díaz had asked to investigate the reasons for labor unrest, "dreamed of the presidency, aspired to it, or conspired against it." If censure there was, it merely held Díaz accountable for keeping in office a gang of useless sycophants.[26] Or, as Vera Estañol commented, rarely did middle-class censors urge radical measures; on the contrary, they counseled the gradual substitution of men in political office and cautious reform.[27] In 1909, confessed Francisco Vásquez Gómez, once personal physician to Díaz and afterwards a temporary ally of Madero, "nobody envisaged a thorough house cleaning, merely a transitional government." [28] The devil had political horns. When Madero and his faultfinders met to form the Centro Antirreeleccionista in 1909, they vehemently castigated the sins of politics, singling out for acrimonious censure the re-election of Díaz and the absence of honest elections, while urging a change in administration; but, recalled Vásquez Gómez, they "said not a word about social and economic evils." [29]

Belatedly, the clandestine, middle-class opposition press, which had tempered its criticism of the government's handling of the labor disputes at Cananea and Río Blanco, came out openly against Díaz. As Zayas Enríquez believed, apprehension for the consequences of their revolutionary propaganda may have kept its editors and journalists from taking the fatal plunge.[30] Given the antics of the reluctant rebels, Díaz supposed that they merely wanted a house-cleaning of personnel.[31] To stay in office, it would only be necessary to throw some of the rascals out. In his final message to Congress, Díaz described his recent cabinet shuffle as a response to his critics.[32] He pledged to revise the judiciary, to enact an effective electoral law, and to retire to private life at the end of his presidential term.[33] With ample justification, Díaz maintained that understanding until the spring of 1911.

Paradoxically, instead of keeping the wolves at bay, the concessions, to paraphrase Manero, emboldened them. Seen as a sign of weakness, the concessions radicalized the enemy. Yet, to continue with Manero's analysis, Madero's triumph left undisturbed the structure of the Old Regime. Manero interpreted as meaningless the promises of universal suffrage and no re-election of presidents in a country where the majority of the people, because of past neglect, were political neophytes. On the surface, the hated autocratic trappings would disappear; but, sooner or later, a party or a leader, either through fraud or force, would again monopolize political power. With Madero's victory, the outs—by implication the middle class—had replaced the ins.[34]

This middle-class version of Mexico's problems, which vented its ire on the coterie around don Porfirio, rested on one assumption. The evil was not so much in the *jefe* who dispensed public jobs, but in the choice of office holders. To the rebels who supported Madero, the ills lay not with the system but in its administration. A broom was needed to sweep out the present occupants of public office. Díaz had become aware of this need, but too late. This view of politics had deep roots in Mexico. Since colonial days, the government bureaucracy had served as the principal employer of the educated man. Mexico's commerce and industry, which had always been of limited size, offered only scattered opportunities. For the white-collar man, the federal and local bureaucracies were a haven. The hunt for public jobs, *empleomanía* Luis Villoro called it, colored the early history of the Republic. With some justification, some historians see the Reforma, the confrontation between the Liberals of Juárez and the Conservatives, as a battle for public office. Obviously, the Liberals espoused remedies beyond the simple substitution of personnel. Still, in the days of Juárez, to survive, the tiny middle class required admittance to public jobs.

The progress of Mexico's gilded age left the picture unaltered. True, economic development opened careers in industry, mining, and transportation, and by 1910, more Mexicans held jobs in private industry than ever before. The population, had almost doubled, from 8,743,000 in 1874 to 15,460,000 in 1910, and concomitantly, economic progress had resulted in a numerical growth of the middle class. With ample justification, Díaz could take credit for its existence. However, by the same token, there were additional political mouths to feed. In Justo Sierra's words, "although a beggar, the state was paradoxically, the richest man in Mexico." As in former years, to keep the ship of state afloat it was necessary to make bureaucrats of the *gente de medio pelo,* those who were "unrich" but not poor.[35] Or, as Bulnes jocularly reminded his audience, "when the Church waxed rich, the middle class lived off the altar of God"; after the victory of the Reforma, a mortal blow to clerical ascendancy, "the middle class feasted at the public trough." [36] To keep alive the middle class, Mexico, in the fashion of other Latin American republics, had to spoon-feed it by converting the bureaucracy into a refuge for it. So Díaz conceded it a virtual monopoly of the lower public jobs.[37] Of the middle class in 1876, a minuscule section of the total population, only 16 percent held public jobs; when General Díaz boarded the *Ypiranga* for exile in 1911, the middle classes made up 70 percent of the bloated bureaucracy.[38] Mexico spent 7.7 million pesos on the salaries of bureaucrats in 1868, but 70 million by 1910. "General Díaz," Bulnes recalled in retrospect, had "become the sublime redeemer of the middle classes." [39]

But, unfortunately for the old autocrat, the growth of the economy, especially after the crisis of 1907, failed to match the numerical expansion (as well as the explosion of aspirations) of the *"gente de medio pelo."* By 1900, the drain on the national Treasury occasioned by salaries of public employees had compelled José I. Limantour, who managed the budget, to place a ceiling on them and to limit their number. This austerity measure worsened the plight of the middle classes which was further aggravated by the collapse of the economy in 1907. To complicate matters, there was almost no turnover in government jobs because, in the absence of any retirement system, federal and local governments permitted the aged and the infirm to hang on until death.[40] Governor Enrique Creel's retirement legislation in Chihuahua was a singular initial step in dealing with this problem. Limantour's economy measure, however, failed to slow down public spending; budget increases in the last years of don Porfirio's reign included funds to keep salaries of public employees abreast of the rising cost of living.[41] Unhappily, this occurred as food prices doubled and the cost of housing, clothing, and bare essentials rose steadily. Yet even before the calamity of 1907, the supply of candidates had exceeded the available public jobs—because even a government clerk, with a yearly salary of 600 pesos, earned much more than the average worker.[42] It is no surprise, therefore, that innumerable intellectuals who cast their lot with the rebellion had earlier coveted public jobs, Among the disappointed job-seekers were Luis Cabrera and Jesús Urueta.[43] Both later accused Limantour of mishandling public funds.

The professional man with a university diploma, or a title of even uncertain origins conferring special status, made the quest for public employment into a ritualistic pilgrimage. The list of job hunters, almost always headed by the ubiquitous *licenciado,* a lawyer by university degree or special claim to learning, included engineers, architects, agronomists, writers, poets, teachers, and physicians all with pretentious titles and inflated ambitions. These were the intellectuals either because they claimed the distinction or because society, although not always deferentially, conferred it. Not everybody, if the word of Bulnes can be trusted, coveted high public office; most middle-class bureaucrats stoically accepted their posts and salary; but not the intellectual, in Bulnes' version the office holder with a professional title who wanted the glories of higher responsibility and a commensurate salary.[44] Lawyers were especially guilty in this regard. Bulnes, himself a *licenciado,* calculated that Mexico had one lawyer with an official diploma for every one thousand inhabitants, or 15,000 of them, nearly all on the government's payroll.[45] *Ingenieros,* engineers, were another problem, said Bulnes. Believing that the backwardness of Mexican agriculture stemmed from the paucity of *ingenieros agrónomos,* agronomists, the administration had built the Escuela Nacional de Agricultura. It was urgent, according to the pundits, to expand the number of agronomists, and in that manner, improve yields in rural Mexico. Had the program been fully carried out, so Bulnes argued, it would have meant 36,000 *ingenieros agrónomos,* each expecting a government salary of 3,000 pesos a year, at a cost of 108 million pesos to the Treasury. Since the value of agricultural production seldom went beyond 260 million pesos, 40 percent of it would have gone to pay the salaries of the agronomists—if all had found jobs with the government. Fortunately, perhaps, the Escuela Nacional de Agricultura graduated only a fraction of the projected army of *ingenieros agrónomos.* Even so, many of them, explained Bulnes, never found work in their chosen field, becoming a floating population of unemployed professionals demanding "decorous jobs" from the government, and upon not finding them, joining the ranks of the rebels.[46]

Deliberately or not, Bulnes may have exaggerated the number of hungry *licenciados, ingenieros,* and fellow professionals in 1910. His principal allegation, nonetheless, withstands scrutiny. Vast numbers of professionals and intellectuals made a career of public office, aspired to higher posts and better salaries and, when unsuccessful, listened eagerly to the prophets of doom. Lawyers, engineers, and physicians formed a majority of the Mesa Directiva, the central committee, of the Partido Antirreeleccionista, as well as that of the party in Chihuahua, where Madero ultimately confronted Díaz.[47]

School teachers, also on public salaries, formed a similar interest group. Between 1895 and 1910, their numbers multiplied from less than 13,000 to over 21,000, a rate of growth higher than that for the population as a whole. For every one thousand inhabitants, the increase was from ten to fourteen teachers. Sizeable growth in their ranks occurred in the border provinces during the second half of the Porfiriato, doubling in Chihuahua and Sonora and multiplying more than three times in Coahuila.[48] Many of them were graduates of the normal schools, initially established in Veracruz by Governor Joaquín Baranda. Manuel Chao, for example, general and governor of Chihuahua in the days of Pancho Villa, had made the trek north to establish schools after completing his studies at the normal school in Jalapa. A majority of the teachers were the offspring of lower middle-class families and, in the provinces, from small towns. On an income between 8 and 20 pesos a month, the life of the school master was a daily battle for survival. Even with a salary of 20 pesos, or 72 centavos a day, lamented *El Imparcial,* a primary-school teacher could not make ends meet. How could he, on that income, the newspaper asked, "think of a better future for his wife and children?" [49] When the time came the teacher joined the rebels in droves. With the possible exception of lawyers, no other group contributed a larger share of revolutionary chieftains and planners. Bulnes phrased it succinctly: "to educate is to govern." [50] When the Díaz regime put learning at the disposal of the lower middle class, but denied it commensurate salaries and opportunities for advancement, it signed its own death certificate.

Meanwhile, Limantour's efforts to balance the budget widened the split between the higher and the lower bureaucracy. The chances to move upward from clerical jobs declined in the decade before 1910 while, at the same time, the economic pinch reduced the number of openings in business, journalism, and law. Díaz' policy of keeping his cronies indefinitely in office, froze opportunities for advancement, and increased the split. As the "veterans . . . converted government jobs into sinecures," wrote Bulnes, "the hatred of the lower bureaucracies for the higher" exploded[51] To summarize what Zayas Enríquez told Díaz, the people had wearied of immobile public functionaries and employees, and unwilling to tolerate any longer the denial of what they considered their right to high government jobs, hardly concealed their "hatred for a political clique that does as it pleases with public offices while milking the profits of business." [52] Writing in *El Diario,* Luis Cabrera maintained that the *cientificos,* the inner clique, had cornered three out of four administrative posts—the jobs in the higher bureaucracy.[53] Those at the bottom of the bureaucratic totem pole, to cite Bulnes, listened avidly to politicians who promised to rid them "of the gang of fossilized oldsters" who kept them locked into their menial posts.[54]

III

In November, 1910, in the city of Puebla de los Angeles, Aquiles Serdán, a young newspaperman, one of the few foolish enough to heed Madero's call to arms, fired the opening salvo of the rebellion. Serdán had acknowledged no other ruler in his life but don Porfirio. Born in 1876, the year Díaz claimed the presidential throne for himself, Serdán had spent his childhood, adolescence, and maturity under one man. His futile attempt to bring down the house Díaz had built, which cost him his life, encapsulates one more element of the bureaucratic stalemate—middle class youth.

A new generation had reached maturity in the years of

Díaz' reign. Yet, just as the lower bureaucrat found the path to upward advancement barred to him, so did the young find the avenue of economic and political mobility closed. Even the fortunate, those willing to accept the tutelage of the old and to pay homage to the past, had to play second fiddle to the élite.[55] As Francisco R. Almada described life in Chihuahua, middle-class youth, who had reached maturity in the three decades of the Porfiriato, inherited a society in which an entrenched clique monopolized both politics, and in league with foreigners, lucrative jobs in business. Unable to crash the inner circle, the young were sympathetic to the oracles of change.[56] To them, the demise of Díaz signaled fresh career opportunities.[57] One such man was Abraham González, a frustrated bank clerk who, with the victory of Madero, became governor of Chihuahua. His career was not atypical; Alvaro Obregón, Plutarco Elías Calles, Luis Cabrera, and countless companions, generally in their late twenties or early thirties, rose to prominence with the departure of the old clique. Somehow Díaz, who himself had rebelled against Juárez because of his hunger for public office, had forgotten how dangerous it was to deny upward mobility to the young and gifted. The aging Díaz could not surmount the generation gap inadvertently widened by his own record of economic success. As Manuel Calero—one of the fortunate young men to pass through the sacred portals—explained, don Porfirio could not conquer his fears of the innovations likely to take place if doors were unlocked to another generation.[58]

Whether consciously or not, Madero's call for political change in La Sucesión Presidencial had been anxiously awaited by middle-class youth. Madero, lamented El Progreso Latino of Chihuahua, had committed the cardinal sin of undermining the confidence of youth in the future of their country.[59] Madero's propaganda touched deep roots of frustration in the provinces. Even before Madero had openly challenged the Old Regime, students in the professional schools of Guadalajara had taken to the streets to warn against the re-election of Díaz.[60] However, students and professors at the National University of Mexico, recalled Jorge Prieto Laurens, only occasionally heeded the propaganda; the large majority maintained its faith in Díaz.[61] Guadalajara, after all, was miles away from Mexico City, from where the nation's political chieftains picked the chosen for the rewards of public office.

The bitterness of youth, the hunger of the lower bureaucrats for promotions and recognition, and the malaise of the middle class merged to form a ground swell of resentment in the provinces. By 1910, the northern states particularly were a hotbed of thwarted ambitions and dreams. In the provinces, Díaz learned from Zayas Enríquez, unhappiness with the control of politics by the governors and their *compinches,* which dashed the "legitimate hopes of many," was rampant.[62] As Manuel González Calzada wrote about Tabasco, popular discontent with monopolistic politics planted the seeds of rebellion: sixteen years of control by Governor Abraham Bandala and his cronies; the exploitation of the economy for their own advantage; and the re-election of Díaz. Tabasco did not rebel because *hacendados* stole lands from peasants or because surveying companies carved out empires. Of the peasants exploited unmercifully by the lumber magnates, only a handful joined the rebellion. The uprising occurred because of the subjugation of the urban middle class—artisans, shopkeepers, *licenciados,* physicians, and public employees—to the whims of a small band of high government officials, powerful merchants, and a coterie of chosen *hacendados* in league with Bandala.[63] It was in the provinces where Filomeno Mata's *Diario del Hogar* circulated widely. As Ramón Prida observed, it had enthusiastic readers in San Pedro de las Colonias and Parras, both in Coahuila, as well as in Chihuahua, and along the Costa de Sotavento in Veracruz.[64]

At this juncture oblivious to these pent-up aspirations and thwarted careers, Díaz, either through senility or a mistake in political judgment, granted James Creelman the famous interview. After three decades of benevolent tutelage, stated Díaz, Mexico was ready for democracy. In 1910, he pledged, he would step aside and permit others to govern. The unexpected declaration—published in newspapers in the United States—hit Mexico like a bomb; not, however, because of the promise of democracy, of scant significance to most Mexicans, but because the vow to vacate the National Palace offered fresh horizons to countless Mexicans. Particularly, it meant opportunities for political, economic, and social advancement for a middle class denied the fruits of progress. In that lies the significance of the Creelman interview: the anxiously awaited access to prestigious public jobs, the hope of joining a favored group of Mexicans in industry and commerce, and perhaps, the displacement of foreigners who monopolized key sectors of the economy. Don Porfirio broke his vow, but he lived long enough to witness the results of his error. Had he permitted the middle classes a larger share of the results of Mexico's progress, he probably would have kept their loyalty.

FIVE

On the Ramparts

of Industry

"If nobody cares about the rights of the rural peon, and if that is not so with the industrial workers, it is because they constitute better material for those who want to change the status quo, because of their higher intellectual level, their combative nature, and because they can be organized."

Rafael de Zayas Enríquez

I

FROM ATTEMPTS to piece together the structure of a modern economy, to expand and develop mining, to build a railroad network and ports on the Gulf of Mexico and the Pacific Ocean, to lay the foundations for factories and mills, and to exploit rich petroleum deposits recently discovered, emerged an industrial labor sector, itself one of the goals of planners in Mexico City. By 1895, it is calculated, Mexico had 693,000 industrial workers, and by 1910 over 800,000. These were the workers, Zayas Enríquez warned Porfirio Díaz in his confidential report, who were courted by men unhappy with the status quo, and prophetically, who were destined to be the first to defy the Old Regime.

This neoteric class, affirmed Jorge Vera Estañol, could be found the length and breadth of the Republic: in the mines of Sonora, Chihuahua, Durango, Guanajuato, Mexico, and Michoacán, as well as in the coal fields of Coahuila and in the foundries of Mapimí, Velardeña, Chihuahua, Torreón, Monterrey, Matehuala, Aguascalientes San Luis Potosí, and Texiutlán; in the fertile Laguna, and around the cities of Hermosillo, Chihuahua, Monterrey, Guadalajara, Toluca, Cuernavaca, Mexico

Orizaba, and Jalapa; in the textile centers of Querétaro, Veracruz, Jalisco, Puebla, and Mexico; in the petroleum camps of the Huasteca, along the corridors of the railways, and in the large commercial entrepôts, particularly the ports. The industrial laborer, unlike the rural *peón,* read newspapers, joined mutual aid societies, and knew how to stand together against his employer. Along the northern border, proximity with the neighboring Republic helped convince the worker that only the avarice of his masters stood between him and the fruits of progress.[1]

Notwithstanding the tinsel and glitter of Mexico's gilded age, labor had to endure a multitude of hardships. For the worker, the hours of toil were long and the wages poor. Factories opened their doors before the break of day and closed them long after dark. Textile workers, for example, whose daily schedule was common to most industry, arrived at the mills at five or six in the morning and remained locked up until eight or later at night. On Saturday—the short day—the worker left his job at six in the evening. He had two forty-five minute rest periods, one for breakfast and another for lunch.[2] Management deducted money from his paycheck for the support of the Church, for religious services and festivals; levied arbitrary fines as punishment; hired and fired at will; and held him responsible for shopworn shuttles and spindles.[3]

Nor were employers known for their bountiful hearts. Workers earned the highest wages in mining, generally in the northern provinces, and less in the ballyhooed *industrias de transformación,* the factories and mills supposedly doing a facelift on the economy of Mexico. In addition, the invasion of village lands by the *hacienda* which drove a steady stream of the landless into the cities and created a surplus labor market, resulted in an abundance of cheap labor for the factories. Higher wages were paid in the extractive industries, which were isolated from the cities, many located in the far north, and offering risky jobs.[4]

AVERAGE DAILY WAGES IN INDUSTRY, OTHER THAN MINING [5]

Year	North	Gulf	Pacific North	Pacific South	Central Zone	Republic
1880	.21	.24	.30	.16	.28	.24 pesos
1910	.66	.51	.98	.27	.52	.59

At the mills in Orizaba, with the top wages in textiles, workers earned up to 1.25 pesos a day.[6] The copper barons of Cananea, who claimed the largest payroll in Mexico, paid miners three pesos for up to twelve hours of work in the pits, and a labor élite as much as eight pesos.[7] However, in the coal mines of Coahuila, as in Guanajuato, miners earned the more prevalent scale of two pesos a day.[8] Miners in Sonora, meanwhile, had to purchase at inflated prices corn and wheat imported from the central grain states; food in Guanajuato cost far less. Masons, carpenters, and mechanics in Mexico City earned between two and three pesos a day. Women fared much worse. In the textile mills of the Federal District, reported Julio Sesto, women earned as little as 25 centavos a day. Many of the women were no more than children, "forsaken girls of Mexico spending an embittered adolescence in the shops and factories." [9] Management, to the growing anger of the worker, often paid wages in *vales,* chits redeemable only at the company store, the *tienda de raya,* notorious for selling low-grade goods at bloated prices.

By all appearances, industrial workers—men, women and children—spent a good part of their lives in sweatshops, crowded into unventilated and unheated rooms that hot weather turned into furnaces and in winter's cold into iceboxes. Indifferent supervisors had scant regard for the safety of their workers. One mine in Pachuca had over 600 accidents, a fourth of which were fatal.[10] Between 1906 and 1910, according to calculations by *El Imparcial,* five hundred men died in coal mine disasters in Coahuila.[11] Nor did the mining moguls bestir themselves to compensate adequately the victims of accidents. More likely than not, they exhibited a "callous attitude . . . beyond belief." [12] Ernest Gruening, author of a noted book on Mexico, spoke of a man who had lost both legs in a mine accident; the company had covered his hospital costs and had given him five pesos. He spent the rest of his life begging for alms on the streets. Other companies, Gruening learned, paid ten to fifteen pesos for the loss of an arm or leg—plus hospital expenses. Yet the mining barons were no more callous than other employers.[13] On a political level only governors Vicente Villada and Bernardo Reyes of Mexico State and Nuevo León had taken steps to compel management to acknowledge its responsibility in the case of industrial accidents.[14]

The specter of unemployment continually haunted the worker. The jobless chart followed the ups and downs of Mexican industry. Until 1900, the industrial labor force had grown at a faster pace than the population as a whole. But mechanization and the cyclical fluctuations of the economy took their toll. The almighty machine, which multiplied production by 55 percent, helped diminish the employed labor force by 26 percent between 1895 and 1910. New machinery, in addition, cost 16,000 workers their jobs. Between 1900 and 1905, industrial labor had grown to represent from 14.6 to 15.6 percent of the entire national work force; all the same, by 1910, because of the larger number of machines in use, as well as the crash of 1907, the percentage had dropped to 15 percent.[15]

National ills had repercussions in the mining sector. As a result of the collapse of the market for copper and sister metals in 1907, miners lived with the nightmare of unemployment. In fact the miners at Cananea rebelled partly out of fear of losing their jobs.[16] By the fall of 1907, mines in Oaxaca, Hidalgo, Durango, Guanajuato, and Sonora had laid off countless men.[17] As the year ended in Sonora, a floating population of jobless men had invaded Guaymas; others stayed behind in Cananea, expecting the mines to resume operations. Unhappily, the copper slump persisted, and desperate men began to plot.[18] Unemployment plagued Cananea until the eve of Díaz' flight. In neighboring Chihuahua, the financial crisis shut down the copper mines at Río Tinto and left 500 men out of work; at Parral, the closing of the American Smelting and Refining Company and Guggenheim foundries in 1908 cost 1,300 men their jobs. Over 1,000 jobless miners walked the streets of Pachuca after the Real del Monte mines shut down. By 1907, Pachuca had over 12,000 unemployed miners and their numbers grew daily. The city of San Luis Potosí, the fifth largest in the Republic, had armies of men out of work in its streets.[19]

The situation in textiles was no less grim. The textile industry totally dependent upon the domestic market, had always either grown slowly or stagnated. Consumer demand continually lagged behind productive capacity. In the years before 1910 the industry, which manufactured cheap cotton cloth for the lower classes, suffered acutely. Mills went out of business because of the decline in consumer demand, an offspring of hard times. To safeguard profits, management cut wages and let workers go. Jobless mill hands encouraged the strike at Río Blanco in 1907.[20]

By the same token, squalid housing, was the lot of the worker and his family. Homes ranged from the caves described by the American consul at Monterrey to small houses of stone or adobe in the mining camps. At Nacozari, a Phelps Dodge complex in Sonora, miners lived in a company town of one-room shacks fifteen-feet square.[21] At Río Blanco, textile workers and their families shared large wooden pavilions with sheet metal roofs, divided into rectangular rooms—one per family—each with its door and window. For his "apartment," the worker paid one half of his wages in rent.[22] Sesto called the *casas de vecindad,* tenement houses, home to the workers of Mexico City, "diabolical mansions where hygienic conditions sparkle by their absence." [23] Scenes of towns in the petroleum region revealed rows of dirty, wooden shacks, open sewers, and women drawing water from stagnant pools.

Illness and disease found fertile soil in the homes, mines, and factories of the worker. Between 1895 and 1911, the death rate in Mexico was almost double that of the United States; the mortality rate in Mexico City topped that of Cairo and Madras.[24] Workers suffered from tuberculosis, syphilis, and pellagra, and from silicosis in the mines. Typhoid, small pox, and intestinal disorders plagued the life of adult and child alike. In Pachuca, an epidemic of hookworms first infested every mine in its vicinity and then spread to the people of the city.[25]

"He that giveth unto the poor shall not lack" runs a biblical proverb. Unfortunately, it had scant credibility in the world inhabited by the Mexican worker. To the contrary, he faced the hostility not merely of management but of government and the courts. Employers early began to join together to resist the petitions of labor: the Centro Industrial de México spoke for the textile lords, the mining barons had their club, as did businessmen elsewhere. Don Porfirio and his friends, Mexicans and foreigners alike, upheld the doctrine of laissez faire; government was simply a *gendarme,* intervening only when labor got out of hand. Both state and federal authorities backed management in the famous strikes of Cananea, Río Blanco, and of the railroads in 1908. Said a lawyer of the era: Díaz "set aside the civil code for the rich and the penal code for the poor." [26] To deal with the recalcitrant, the masters of Mexico relied on Article 925 of the penal code of the Federal District, which levied a fine or jail sentence on anyone convicted of exerting either moral or physical force to alter wages or to impede "the free exercise of industry or labor." [27] A law in Sonora punished workers who joined labor unions.[28] In the mining camps, employers used *rurales* to break up labor protests.[29] Article 4 of the textile codes, a general expression of management's attitude, permitted the worker to complain in writing to the head of his department, but left the final decision to others.[30] Yet, despite this harsh lot, industrial labor enjoyed marked advantages over rural workers and the peasantry. It was the industrial workers' fate to live in the ambiguous world of progress, where the future and the past met in a mixture of hope and despair. The miner who descended into the bowels of the earth in Sonora earned eight times the wages of the rural worker, but had to endure many of the identical hardships.

Until 1900, all workers had enjoyed a slight increase in real wages. But the rise in the cost of living, exacerbated by the drop in the price of silver which comprised half of Mexico's exports, and the international depression of 1907, eliminated the laborer's meager gains. Between 1891 and 1908, food prices rose dramatically: corn by 95.6 percent; wheat by 99.8 percent; and beans by .64 percent.[31] All were staples of the working-class diet. To cite an editorial in *El Correo de Chihuahua,* strikes occurred because income lagged behind prices.[32] The monetary reform, placing Mexico on the gold standard, did not restore the buying power of the peso.[33]

DAILY MINIMUM INDUSTRIAL WAGES [34]

Year	North	Gulf	Pacific North	Pacific South	Central Zone	Republic
1900	.40	.40	.58	.25	.43	.40 pesos
1905	.37	.36	.52	.14	.34	.33
1908	.37	.33	.64	.25	.34	.35

Worse still, foreign workers fared much better than their Mexican counterparts. Attitudes, however, had begun to change, although slowly. By 1906, according to *El Imparcial,* the nation had adopted a fresh slogan: "Mexico for the Mexicans." The worker, the editors confessed, could take credit for it.[35] *El Imparcial,* the voice of the government and a newspaper notoriously kind to foreign investors, had belatedly conferred its blessings on nationalism. Yet for years labor had demanded that Mexicans share the benefits savored by outsiders.

To Mexicans, these benefits appeared grossly unfair. Most foreigners, in their opinion, looked down on Mexicans judging them both inefficient and untrustworthy. For a long time, the Mexican had kept his rancor to himself, aware that his protest would fall on deaf ears. Not so after 1906, when he began increasingly to vent his bitterness. Anger over the higher wages paid Americans set off the strike at Cananea. Resentment against the prices at the *tienda de raya* owned by a Frenchman helped ignite the fuse at Río Blanco. The explosive strike of 1908 stood for the "Mexicanization" of the railroads. By 1910, Mexican labor judged the special status of foreigners as an insult and believed itself by intelligence and skills fully qualified to handle the tasks monopolized by aliens. Nationalism, perhaps the cardinal plank of the rebels of 1910, symbolized a concrete and practical goal to Mexican workers: to acquire for themselves the jobs held by foreigners.

II

Labor's ire slowly caught the attention of the Master of Mexico. In his speech to Congress in 1906, Díaz had bemoaned attempts by workers to organize themselves in order to impose their will on management.[36] *El Imparcial,* unquestionably voicing the fears of the administration, pointed an accusing finger at "Jacobins" who had captured and subverted the labor movement; by distortions to fit their own selfish needs, socialists, anarchists, and nihilists had brainwashed the gullible workingman.[37] For his part, Zayas Enríquez, whom Díaz had asked to look into labor discontent, conceded that the worker distrusted both government and business but was neither socialist nor the enemy of capitalists.[38]

Indeed, as Díaz and his backers feared, labor had taken steps to get management off its back and to fend for itself. In the nineteenth century, attempts to establish mutual aid societies had met with considerable success; however, the cooperative movement, a more ambitious design, never got off the ground. The Gran Círculo de Obreros, the first of the large labor organizations, appeared in the textile industry. To no one's surprise, it split into warring camps, with one group answering the siren call of Díaz. Two of its messiahs and editors of *El Socialista,* Juan de Mata Rivera and Prisciliano Díaz González, by permitting themselves to be "elected" to Congress, set an odious precedent for others.[39] In the meantime, other labor groups, to the shock of staid conservatives in power, adopted slogans and doctrines with a socialist tint.

Americans, the minority most envied and distrusted, ironically, helped plant the seeds of the labor union movement in Mexico. Through 1908, the railroad companies had employed large number of American workers affiliated with labor organizations across the border, specifically the Knights of Labor and the Industrial Workers of the World. To better their lot and to close the wage gap, Mexicans, learning from the experience of their rivals, began to organize brotherhoods and ultimately labor unions. Their initial effort, the Sociedad de Ferrocarrileros Mexicanos, took root in 1887 in Nuevo Laredo, a border town facing Texas. One year afterwards, Nicasio Idar, a Mexican who had worked on the railroads in the American Southwest, became the spearhead for the Orden Suprema de Empleados Mexicanos del Ferrocarril, and an early victim of Díaz' cupidity. Even so, discouraged but by no means beaten, others picked up the banner taken from Idar to form the Confederación de Sociedades Ferrocarrileras de la República Mexicana a decade later. Workers in Puebla founded the Unión de Mecánicos Mexicanos, which immediately began to branch out into the provinces. On its heels came the Unión de Calderos Mexicanos, the Unión de Forjadores Mexicanos, and the Unión de Carpinteros y Pintores del Ferrocarril.[40]

At this point, the rising nationalist tide, which was battering even the doors of the National Palace, inadvertently gave the railroad workers an unexpected but welcomed ally. Fearing a Wall Street monopoly of Mexican transportation, the minister of the treasury, José I. Limantour, on behalf of the government, had begun to buy stocks in the railroad companies. By 1909, the government had become the majority stockholder in the National Railways of Mexico.[41] More important, one year earlier, after a heated interview with a delegation of Mexican workers, Limantour, in compliance with their demands, had begun to substitute Mexican telegraph operators for Americans on the railroads. To protest the decision, all Americans on the railroads walked off their jobs, but Limantour, instead of bowing to their tactics, replaced them with Mexican workers. After this, Mexicans ran the trains.[42]

Even before, however, the ups and downs of the economy had intensified the struggle between natives and foreigners. Responding to the economic difficulties, which cut jobs and lowered wages, Mexicans unfurled the banner of the labor strike, first at San Luis Potosí in 1903 and then in Nuevo León. In 1906, in the railway shops of Aguascalientes, Mexicans abandoned their jobs to underscore their anger over the dismissal of one of their leaders and the inflated pay of Americans. That same year, 300 Mexicans went on strike in the shops of the Ferrocarril Central Mexicano in Chihuahua; their grievances included the issue of equal pay for Mexicans and the recognition of the Unión de Mecánicos y Maquinistas. The strike paralyzed San Luis Potosí, Torreón, Monterrey, and Aguascalientes.[43] The year before, in Cárdenas, a railway hub in San Luis Potosí, a pitched battle between American and Mexican railroad workers, after leaving eighteen dead, ignited another strike. Earlier, Mexicans on the railroads had banded together in the Gran Liga de Ferrocarrileros Mexicanos, with headquarters in Jalapa, which shortly claimed branches in various provinces. The Gran Liga, the first of the railroad groups with the trademark of a labor union, became the model for others. It accepted only Mexican citizens as members and asked that Mexicans run the railroads. By 1908, approximately 15,000 railroaders looked to the Gran Liga for guidance.[44] At nearly the same time, *El Ferrocarrilero*, the voice of the railroad men, appeared in the labor camps.

By the turn of the century, Mexicans in sundry jobs had emulated the precedent set by their companions on the railroads. In far-off Mérida, anarchists led by José Zaldíver, a Spaniard, had

formed a political cell, while José María Pino Suárez, in a few
months to be the running mate of Francisco I. Madero, headed a
less doctrinaire group. The printers of Guadalajara, who had organized themselves into a labor group, published *El Obrero
Socialista;* their goal was to encourage workers to form labor
unions. Of more importance, the Flores Magón brothers had
organized the Partido Liberal Mexicano, a friend of labor
unions and of the right to strike. To unite all the miners in the
Republic, Esteban Baca Calderón, one of the strike leaders at
Cananea, had devised the grandiose scheme of building a Liga
de Mineros de los Estados Unidos Mexicanos. The textile workers
of Puebla, Veracruz, and Tlaxcala, after establishing labor cells
in each of the states, joined together to form the Gran Círculo
de Obreros Libres, a name chosen because of its ties to the labor
group of the nineteenth century. It weathered only the first
storms, but its successor, of identical title, survived to play a major role in the strike at Río Blanco. It published *La Revolución
Social* and eventually established branches in Oaxaca, Querétaro,
Jalisco, Hidalgo, Mexico State, and the Federal District, as well
as in Veracruz, Tlaxcala, and Puebla. The Liga Obrera, open to
workers in all industries, was organized in Mexico City. The
miners of Coahuila established the Unión Minera Mexicana,
while the workers of Torreón formed a Confederación del Trabajo. Yucatán had an Unión Sindicalista. At its meeting in
Mexico City in 1906, the Liga de Fabricantes de Tabaco, a radical band, adopted a resolution urging all guilds to become labor
unions.[45] With a few exceptions, these groups upheld the ideal
of the strike and advocated social and economic reforms.

Not to be outdone, the Catholic Church, to the bewilderment of the Old Regime, shared with malcontents of the era an
active interest in the organization of the worker, specifically
after the publication of the Rerum Novarum of Pope Leo
XIII in 1891. Until then, the prelates of the Church had
merely urged the worker to accept his fate, while reminding the
rich to set a good example and to be charitable. Following the
encyclical, the Church underwent a metamorphosis, demanding
of employers better working conditions, an eight-hour day, and
the end of child labor. A Catholic layman, José Refugio Galindo,
founded the Obreros Guadalupanos, which published *La Demo-*

cracia Cristiana and *Restauración*. It set out to organize the workers in the textile mills, sponsored congresses in the provinces to discuss agricultural problems, and lobbied for the enactment of reform legislation. Father José María Troncoso, in 1908, united all Catholic workers in the Unión de Obreros Católicos.[46] By 1911, the Confederación Católica Obrera could boast of having 46 *círculos obreros* with 12,230 members, and 15,000 four years later. Like the Church, it lobbied for a minimum wage; the abolition of child labor; the barring of married women, for their own sake, from working in the factories; for decent housing, accident insurance, and old-age benefits, while advocating the compulsory arbitration of industrial disputes.[47] According to Church prelates and laymen alike, membership in the Catholic unions would shield the worker from the pitfalls of socialism, isolate him from the dangers of radical trade unions, and teach him the error of espousing class conflict. The triumph of the Constitutionalists put a stop to the Catholic crusade until 1919. Despite its cautious stance, the Díaz regime and most employers greeted the efforts of the holy Church coldly.

Management, meanwhile, refused to deal with any labor union, Catholic or not, or to bargain with spokesmen for the workingman. To retaliate, the workers fell back on the strike, approximately 250 times between 1881 and 1911. A wave of strikes erupted in 1905, fed by the hard times that were descending upon the country. In 1907 alone, the nation witnessed the outbreak of twenty-five major strikes, chiefly in textiles, tobacco, bakeries, and transportation, many within earshot of Díaz and his cabinet. Veracruz and Puebla both with big textile complexes, had the largest number of industrial disputes. The textile industry suffered the largest number of strikes (75), next the railroads (60), and then tobacco (35).[48] No state with any degree of industrial progress escaped the turmoil of the strike.

Of the sundry strikes, three set the stage for the rebellion of 1910. The north witnessed two: the uprising of the miners at Cananea in 1906 and the railroad walkout of 1908. The other occurred in the south, between the textile workers and their bosses at Río Blanco in 1907. Joined by common roots, the three industrial disputes reveal much about the nature of labor unrest. All three were the result of modernization, erupted in the progressive sectors of the economy and in key industries. At Cananea, the strike halted operations in the leading mining center of Mexico. With 25,000 inhabitants, Cananea was one of the biggest cities of Sonora, enjoyed one of the highest percentages of growth in the Republic, and basked in the sunlight of the copper bonanza.[49] Initially worth 260,000 pesos, by 1906 the annual value of copper exports had climbed to 32 million pesos.[50] At Río Blanco, the strike closed the doors on the largest textile center, Mexico's most highly developed industry.[51] Because of Río Blanco, an integral part of the Orizaba textile zone, the state of Veracruz had blossomed, become a leading manufacturing nucleus, and the commercial entrepôt of the Republic. The railroads, site of the third major strike, laid the foundations for both the growth of textiles and the prosperity of mining.

Declining export markets linked two of the strikes. Copper, sold mainly in the United States, and the railroads running between San Luis Potosí and Texas, needed foreign customers for their prosperity. The world financial debacle of 1907, felt earlier in Mexico, hurt both copper and the transportation industry. On the railroads, a lag in business kept wages low in the face of the spiraling cost of living, and increased competition for jobs between Mexicans and foreigners.

Fear and envy of foreigners played a leading role in the three strikes. Price gouging by the French proprietor of the *tienda de raya* lit the fuse at Río Blanco, an industry owned and managed by Frenchmen who paid foreign workers higher wages.[52] An acute stage of antiforeign sentiment applied the torch on the railways. Buffeted by the crisis of 1907, which shook the rickety wage structure and swelled the ranks of the unemployed, Mexican workers, with growing popular backing, demanded access to the jobs taken by foreigners. At Cananea, William C. Greene, the copper mogul, employed 5,360 Mexicans and 2,200 foreigners, mostly Americans.[53] He paid his compatriots from across the border five pesos in gold for a day's labor, but Mexicans only three silver pesos, less than half of what Americans earned. To Greene's annoyance, Mexicans asked for equal wages, access to the better jobs, an eight-hour day, and the dismissal of two arbitrary American foremen at the Oversight Mine.[54]

Greene's adamant refusal gave vent to the pent-up anger of

the Mexicans. Before the strike subsided, half a dozen Americans had died, while federal troops, with the aid of American rangers brought in from neighboring Arizona at the behest of Governor Rafael Izábal, killed thirty Mexican miners.[55] The invasion of Mexican soil by armed Americans raised a public outcry in the Republic. Newspapers called on Díaz, to cite an editorial by the noted author and soldier Heriberto Frías, in *El Correo de Chihuahua*, to punish Izábel for his crime.[56] In Mexico City, Zayas Enríquez cautioned Díaz not to take the public clamor lightly, advice the aging ruler brushed aside.[57]

Miners, textile workers, and railroad men had ample grounds for their grievances. Yet quixotically, compared to workers elsewhere in the Republic, peasants in particular, not a few workingmen belonged to the *clases altas* or *privilegiadas,* the labor élite discussed by Andrés Molina Enríquez, which included machinists, electricians, mechanics, boilermakers, shop foremen, mine technicians, skilled factory hands, and railway employees.[58] No one disputed that Greene paid the highest wages in Mexico. To cite Governor Izábal, the miners dressed in the clothes of the middle class, equipped their homes with modern appliances, and purchased the latest furniture.[59] None of the strike leaders actually toiled below the surface of the earth: Esteban Baca Calderón, Manuel M. Diéguez, and Francisco Ibarra, the outspoken champions of the rank and file, sat behind desks. Diéguez earned seven pesos a day, twice the wages paid miners.[60] Over 65 percent of the miners had savings on deposit, totalling approximately 40,000 pesos, in the Banco de Cananea.[61] Still, judged by the income of miners in Arizona, just a stone's throw away, Mexicans fared poorly. Nor did Mexicans enjoy job security which, as Francisco Bulnes noted, occurred only with high copper prices.[62] While low in comparison with Cananea, wages in the textile industry ranked above the national average. "Men who once plowed the land with oxen for 50 or 60 centavos a day," *El Imparcial* reminded its readers, "earned up to 2 pesos daily in the mills." [63] The lot of the railroad workers was no worse.

To relish both the sorrows and the joys of the "ambivalence of progress"—this was the destiny of the workers at Cananea, in the textile mills, and the railroads. Jobs in industry had given them the liberty to escape the plight of the rural poor. With a better job and higher pay went a certain degree of political sophistication. Through personal effort, the worker concluded, he could improve his situation. He had become a convert to the idea of progress. Meanwhile, the favored status of the foreigner, in the north proximity to the wealth of American labor, and the opulence of the rich at home served to remind the Mexican worker that he had merely taken a first step up the ladder. Aspirations to rise still further led him to confront his employer, not because he suffered more than others, but on the contrary, because he had experienced some progress. He wanted a larger slice of the pie.

Unfortunately for the worker, the official response to the troubles at Cananea, Río Blanco, and on the railroads, locked the door to additional benefits. In his message to Congress in 1907, Díaz gloated over his speedy victory at Río Blanco, hardly concealing his glee over the failure of the strike at Cananea. Cost what it might, he warned, he meant to make the worker respect the rights of private property.[64] At Cananea, Díaz had watched events from afar; however, at the request of the textile workers, who mistakenly looked to him for help, Díaz had arbitrated the dispute at Río Blanco. His dictum, which favored management and offered paltry concessions to labor, left no doubt where he stood in the conflict between employers and workers. His decision, which ironically conceded the justice of the workers' complaints, abandoned them to the whims of capitalists and political bosses. Díaz in effect told them that the worker might plead his case before the rulers of Mexico, but under no circumstance could he join with his companions to defend his interests. He could only beg for mercy. The rebel leaders of 1910 quickly learned to exploit the rancor of labor.

Political dissidents of the late-Díaz era therefore uncovered fertile soil in labor's ranks. General Bernardo Reyes, aspirant to the throne and a *caudillo* with a mild record of social reform, gained innumerable adherents in the factories and railroads. The Partido Antirreeleccionista, the sponsor of Francisco I. Madero, had startling success in industrial areas.[65] Marcos González, a labor dignitary, figured prominently in its ranks, while others helped to organize branches of the party in Río Blanco, Nogales, and Santa Rosa.[66] Madero bitterly indicted public officials for their attacks on his labor supporters in Cananea, Atlixco, Puebla, and Tlaxcala.[67] Had Díaz not interfered, the candidates of the Partido Antirreeleccionista would have won the political contest there.[68] Workers who made up the rank and file of the Partido Nacionalista Democrático put heavy pressure on its leaders to march in step with movement opposing re-election.[69] The middle classes had provided leadership and ideology to the drive to dump Díaz, said Juan Sánchez Azcona, a Madero partisan; but, he went on, it inherited its vigor and robustness from its labor following.[70] Ultimately, the key rebel uprisings occurred in the mining camps and other labor centers of Sonora, Chihuahua, Puebla, Veracruz, and in the Federal District. According to the memoirs of a woman who, as a young girl had lived through the events of the day, in Coahuila, the home of Madero, large numbers of miners, had abandoned the coal pits of Palau, Las Esperanzas, and La Conquista to take up arms on his behalf.[71]

SIX *The Responsibility of the Agrarian Sector*

_____

"The agrarian question, in recent years the cause of social disturbances with sundry consequences, had a very different character and was infinitely less acute in the time of . . . Díaz."

José I. Limantour

_____

I

MOST ATTEMPTS to explain why Mexicans rebelled in 1910 whether written by natives, foreign scholars, or by rebels who lived to tell of their adventures, point an accusing finger at the "agrarian question." The landless and their champions, the enemies of the octopuslike *haciendas*, kindled the armed protest. Yet, as the embittered but sagacious Limantour recalled from exile in Paris, the character of the famous "agrarian question" underwent a transformation in retrospect.

The old Porfiristas had ample reason to complain. To credit the discontent of landless for the rebellion is to simplify, if not to distort, the nature of the situation. As Limantour observed, to argue from hindsight that "popular agitation for land and water ignited the revolution . . . intentionally falsifies the facts on behalf of a cause that either did not exist or only vaguely had begun to take shape. . . ." [1] Francisco Bulnes put the matter succinctly. Long before Francisco I. Madero challenged don Porfirio, messiahs of agrarian reform had called the country to arms; yet, its proponents, the Magonistas, only managed to get themselves jailed in the United States. The landless of Coahuila and Chihuahua did not heed their call. A few months later, nonetheless, Madero, hardly the archenemy of the *hacendados,* uncovered fervent revolutionaries in the northern provinces. If the hunger for land had put the match to the fuse, asked Bulnes, why had not northerners rushed to enlist in the ranks of the Magonistas?[2] Moreover, the tragic course of the revolt records the deaths of distinguished apostles of land reform at the hands of their companions in arms. Both Emiliano Zapata, the inflexible champion of land reform, and General Lucio Blanco, the first to distribute the lands of an *hacienda* to its peons, won the laurels of history but paid with their lives for their convictions.

All the same, nothing can mask the deplorable backwardness of large segments of rural Mexico. Official policy, by deliberate design, abandoned the welfare of the countryside for the sake of industrial and urban progress. This decision, in the beginning, received the stamp of approval of Mexicans in diverse walks of life. Still, despite the growth of industry and commerce, agriculture, with its technical lag, remained one of the mainstays of the economy.[3] The contrast between modern and rural Mexico became a festering sore on the national body. Most important, the antiquated agrarian structure imposed the yoke of a subsistence economy that constrained the growth of industrial production, circumscribed the circulation of goods, made impossible a healthy labor class, and prevented the development of a vigorous internal market.

The picture is not all one-sided, however. A huge gap separated commercial agriculture from subsistence farming. Impressive steps had been taken to develop commercial crops for export. Yucatán's henequen industry not only grew by leaps and bounds but became a source of revenue for the national government. By the early 1900's, Mexico was a leading exporter of henequen fiber. During the same interval, the production of cotton and sugar doubled. Veracruz grew tobacco for domestic consumption and for export. American buyers purchased guayule from Coahuila, Durango, Zacatecas, and Chihuahua. Farmers in Sonora were exporting citrus fruits and vegetables to consumers in the American Southwest, while others cultivated garbanzos for sale to Spain. Stockmen in Chihuahua sold their cattle in the Texas market. No attempt to arrive at a balanced assessment of agriculture can ignore these accomplishments.

But the failures and omissions of policy, with all of their tragic consequences, cast a mighty pall over the rural scene. One stark and revealing statistic tells all: although three out of four Mexicans inhabited rural villages, just 2 percent of the total population tilled land of its own. While 3 million Mexicans cultivated the land, fewer than 1,000 *hacendados* controlled nearly all of it; the marginal lands belonged to 400,000 small farmers, almost always without the tools and equipment to cultivate them.[4] The *hacienda* and its owner, the *hacendado*, were synonymous with rural Mexico. On these baronies, the *peón*, who supplied the labor, scratched out a paltry existence. Whether living in a free village, or on *hacienda* lands, he was the forgotten man of Mexico. Exploitation of the peon was glaring, as was the nefarious *tienda de raya*, the company store, the theft of his lands, and the scandalous absence of justice for him in the courts. Not until late in the Porfiriato did officials in Mexico City take steps to teach him to read and write. The rural Mexican was illiterate, hungry, ill-housed, and marked for early death because of disease. Novelists, artists, and historians have vividly depicted his plight. To make matters worse, the exploitation of the peasant failed to make the traditional *hacienda* productive. Modern machinery only belatedly appeared in rural Mexico. Despite a 60 percent growth in population, Mexico harvested more corn and beans, the staple of the diet, in 1867 than in 1910.[5] To feed itself, predominantly rural Mexico had to import food.

Claims to the contrary, it is still risky to conclude that rural neglect and the exploitation of the poor spawned the rebellion of 1910. That these were elements encouraging discontent hardly requires additional comment. But, at what point and for what reason they become important is another matter. Clearly, the most persecuted, the peasantry of rural Mexico, neither plotted nor spearheaded the rebellion. Zapata, the valiant fighter for peasant rights, was neither its symbol nor its prophet. There is a curious dichotomy in peasant attitudes. The history of rural Mexico includes, as Moisés González Navarro says, a record of local rebellions in the days of Díaz, particularly in the central zone.[6] Before 1910, revolts had broken out in 1879, 1882, and 1905 in

San Luis Potosí.[7] Thefts of village lands had led to an uprising of peasants in Veracruz in 1906; *rurales* had to stamp it out.[8] The Yaquis of Sonora and the Maya of Yucatán gave their lives defending their lands. The novelist Heriberto Frías left for posterity the gallant story of Tomóchic in Chihuahua, a struggle in which villagers were pitted against the military. Important as these deeds were, they merely testify to the ancient record of peasant resistance.

Peasant attitudes, nevertheless, also included an apathy bordering on stoicism. With only a bleak life to look forward to, many peasants came to have "no initiative, no ambition, or desire to improve themselves," to quote Fernando González Roa, a proponent of agrarian reform.[9] High rates of alcoholism sapped their strength, as well as their resolve. As one penny-pinching *hacendado* in Morelos said, why pay the peasant more when he will "merely drink away the extra money."[10] Or, as Julio Sesto saw it, "ten million decadent Indians . . . [made] up the popular classes."[11] Yet, on occasion, even unsympathetic commentators had perceptive observations to make about the attitudes of the rural poor. As Bulnes pointed out, if peasants sometimes did not want land, and thus appeared to lack the desire to stand on their own, it was for a logical reason. For example, in regions of scarce or irregular rainfall, it was preferable to work as a sharecropper than as an independent farmer. With a poor harvest, the planter would look out for the peasant and his family. Conversely, in regions of bountiful rains, where nature blessed every harvest, peasants voiced strong demands for land.[12]

Neither were all the rural poor chained to *haciendas*. In regions of labor scarcity, especially on tropical *haciendas* producing a cash crop for export, the *hacendado* used the *tienda de raya* to keep a supply of cheap labor readily at hand. He lent credit freely to the peasant. On the other hand, in regions with an abundance of labor, the poor had less access to goods on credit at the company store. With perhaps the exception of Morelos, this was especially true of the central zone, heavily dotted with *haciendas*.[13] Where the *hacendado* could count on the labor to plant and harvest his crops, the worker was free to move about.

Nor did the intemperate mistreatment of peons light the flames of rebellion. Quite the contrary; the revolution fared poorly where the peon was most exploited, in Oaxaca, Tabasco, Campeche, and Chiapas. Yucatán was the only state where the *hacendados* ruthlessly exploited their workers and in which revolutionaries uncovered fertile soil. In Chiapas, which possessed one of the most abominable records of man's inhumanity to man, rebel propaganda stirred hardly a soul.[14] By the same token, central Mexico and peripheral areas, with large populations of peons, witnessed no early outburst of revolutionary activity—outside of Morelos, southern Puebla, the state of Mexico, and a slice of Hidalgo.[15] Interestingly, this region had the largest number of communal villages or *ejidos,* as well as the biggest share of the Republic's *haciendas.*[16] It appears that peasants, who tilled both their lands and those of the neighboring *hacienda,* had come to terms with the *modus vivendi.*[17] In some instances, peasants even took up arms to defend *haciendas* against rebel attacks.[18]

Nor, to complicate the problem, did regions with large populations of independent farmers or *rancheros* and free agricultural workers early hoist the banner of rebellion. Jalisco, Michoacán, and Guanajuato, on the sidelines during the initial skirmishes, not only had impressive numbers of *ranchos,* but their totals grew rapidly between 1877 and 1910: in Jalisco from 2,646 to 7,645; in Michoacán from 1,527 to 4,436; and in Guanajuato from 889 to 3,788.[19] Rebellion flared first in Sonora, Chihuahua, and Coahuila. Provinces with a high growth rate of *ranchos* suffered from a different mix of problems. The Bajío, for example, had large numbers of *peónes acasillados, hacienda* peons, and landless wage workers. In Chihuahua, meanwhile, the number of peons, both landless (wage workers), and bound to *haciendas,* doubled, but the number of small farmers, *agricultores* dropped by a third. Neither Coahuila nor Sonora had significant increases in the numbers of *hacienda* peons or wage workers.[20]

To many scholars, the growth in the number of *haciendas* from 1877 to 1910 verifies the relationship between agrarian unrest, implied by the proliferation of the great estates, and the coming of the rebellion. In that era, the number of *haciendas* went from 5,869 to 8,431. But, at the same time, their numerical importance, compared to the growth of other rural units, declined from 21 to 12 percent of the total.[21] Concurrently, the number of *ranchos* increased from 14,705 in 1877 to 48,633 in 1910.[22] While the *hacienda* and its growth undoubtedly figure among the causes of the rebellion, they do not alone explain its coming.

II

These rural maladies, which statistics easily document, were both endemic and complex. The thirty years of peace, order, and progress, the cardinal tenets of the positivists, exacerbated the ills but did not introduce them. What, then, brought the agrarian question to a head? To begin with, the evidence does not support the theory of a troubled Mexican social conscience. Not until late 1914 did the future masters of Mexico embrace, at least in theory, the doctrine of land reform. Before that, only José Wistano Orozco, who published in 1895 his monumental *Legislación y Jurisprudencia Sobre Terrenos Baldíos,* and his disciple, Andrés Molina Enríquez, author of the classic *Los Grandes Problemas Nacionales* that appeared nearly fifteen years later, had taken the trouble to examine the social implications of the rural problem. Both were lawyers and small-town magistrates, while Molina Enríquez was both a positivist and an admirer of Herbert Spencer. Orozco, for his part, had merely called attention to the inefficiency of the *haciendas,* to the fact that they were put together not by talent and hard work but by chicanery, and that they led to the exploitation of the poor. Yet, he had no social program to offer as a solution, although he spoke optimistically of small property, which he believed was more productive.[23] Until 1902, when Camilo Arriaga and José María Facha asked the Liberal Clubs of San Luis Potosí to open their hearts to the peons on the *haciendas,* the tiny group of dissidents met to discuss the political evils of the dictatorship. The initial Plan del Partido Liberal, made public in 1906, merely urged the recovery of the uncultivated lands, their distribution among Mexicans returning home from the United States, and an end to the alienation of the public lands.[24] However, scarcely anyone, as Bulnes says, listened to the Magonistas, the patrons of the Plan del Partido Liberal.

The growing awareness of rural problems was probably

caused by material considerations: a concern for the inefficiency and low productivity of Mexican agriculture. For twenty years Mexico had had to import corn and wheat from Argentina and the United States. Years of bountiful harvests cut the size of the imports but never eliminated the dependency. From the perspective of Bulnes and *científicos* of like opinion, this fact simply documented the inability of the land to feed its inhabitants; conversely, from the vantage point of their enemies, it symbolized the inefficacy of the system.[25] The reliance on imports, in the meantime, worsened during the last years of the Díaz regime. Between 1902 and 1906, the cost of imports of corn and wheat had never exceeded 439,000 pesos. Then, in 1907, their cost jumped to 2,198,000 pesos, to 4,756,000 pesos the next year, and to 15,487,000 pesos in 1909. When Madero called for armed rebellion, the imports of corn and wheat still required a public expenditure of 12,387,000 pesos.[26] Clearly, as both the Porfiristas and their critics recognized, something was wrong, either in the nature of the land or in the character of the *hacienda* system.

The debate began in 1907, well nigh by accident. Tlaloc, the fickle Mexican rain god, forgot to water the lands of his worshippers. Droughts, which had already damaged the crops of the two previous years, struck with devastating force, and continued to wreak havoc in the countryside until 1910.[27] One of the regions hardest hit was the Bajío, the Republic's bread basket; half of·the wheat harvest of Querétaro, for example, was lost in 1906.[28] By 1909, a series of droughts, exacerbated by cold weather, had driven authorities in the Bajío to purchase corn for sale to the starving poor.[29]

No major agricultural zone escaped the droughts. Harvests of corn, the national staple of the diet, and wheat, a key food in the towns and cities, dropped sharply. Mexicans who had looked to the harvest of 1907 to remedy the deficiencies of crop failures in 1905 and 1906, learned that, for all intents and purposes, it was a total loss.[30] From that point on, alarming reports of crop losses filled the country's newspapers. *Hacendados* in Morelos, called together by the governor to discuss food shortages, agreed to stop out-of-state corn sales, and if necessary, to import it.[31] Steps were taken in some states to divert the scarce water from wheat to irrigate the plantings of corn.[32] But, despite these measures, and the prayers of the holy fathers, the harvests of both corn and wheat were catastrophically poor. *El Imparcial,* which earlier had scoffed at the probability of such a failure, conceded it would have dire results.[33] Díaz, in his report for 1908, acknowledged the loss of nearly the entire wheat crop.[34] No sooner had the country digested this bit of bad news when authorities began to warn of yet another impending disaster for the coming year. From the pages of *El Imparcial,* Pedro Miguel Gorozpe, president of the prestigious Sociedad Agrícola Mexicana, cautioned Mexicans not to get their hopes up, for even if the rains fell the harvests would not feed Mexico.[35] His predictions quickly bore fruit, as Díaz again conceded in his message to Congress in 1909.[36] The losses included not merely corn and wheat, but beans as well.

To deal with the emergency, and the resultant sharp rises in the prices of foodstuffs, Ramón Corral, the vice-president and minister of *gobernación,* appointed a blue-ribbon committee to look into the complex problem. In his opinion it was so acute that he chaired the committee himself and asked Limantour, the minister of finance, to serve on it.[37] The committee, which voted to import corn and wheat for domestic distribution and to watch over prices, continued at work until December 21, 1910, when Díaz announced that recent harvests had made its activities unnecessary. Díaz acted prematurely; while the harvests of corn turned out well, the wheat yield was only half of what had been predicted.[38] Corral's committee, furthermore, had left unresolved a principal reason for the recent debacle. After three decades of railroad building, Mexico still lacked an adequate transportation system. During the crop disaster, it had proved impossible to ship corn and wheat from regions of some abundance to those of scarcity, and thus to alleviate the hunger of tens of thousands.

The disastrous droughts did not spare the northern provinces. In Chihuahua, the last plentiful rains had fallen in 1906. By May of the following year, *El Imparcial* began to report news of an "alarming drought with terrible consequences for agriculture in nearly all of the state." [39] The drought continued through 1908 and into 1909, severely damaging the wheat crop, and "leaving the countryside parched and dry, without a blade of grass for the cattle to feed on." By April, the livestock industry, labeled a leading source of Chihuahua's wealth by *El Imparcial,* confronted a "crisis of major proportions." [40] The drought hung on, compelling the purchase of corn from Corral's committee for sale in Chihuahua. One apocryphal story sums up the severity of the situation. In Miñaca, a village in the district of Guerrero, Chihuahua, soon to be a hotbed of rebellion, saloons, faced with a grave shortage of water, put up the following sign: "whiskey *solo,* twenty *centavos; con agua,* fifty *centavos.*" [41] Sinaloa reported severe droughts and grain scarcities, while droughts that crippled its food and water supply cost the city of San Luis Potosí one million pesos.[42] Nuevo León experienced severe shortages of corn. Farmers in arid Sonora, while suffering no unusual water problems, complained of frosts, cold snaps, and of insect hordes that reduced the harvests of wheat and garbanzos in 1907 and 1908.[43] Nature, it appeared, had decided to bless the cause of rebellion.

But its fickle hand fell unevenly across the Mexican landscape. The droughts crippled principally small farmers and *medieros,* tenant farmers or sharecroppers, who depended on Tlaloc to water their fields. Few of them cultivated irrigated lands. To cite Jorge Vera Estañol, the *medieros,* the proletariat of rural Mexico, "suffered extraordinarily during the final years of the Díaz administration because of three consecutive years of droughts." [44] Numerically large, the *medieros* blamed their plight on the *hacendados* who had denied them ownership of irrigated lands that would have helped them to survive the droughts. They had no sympathy for the arguments of academic oracles who put the responsibility for the agricultural debacle on such things as the 1907 international crisis that had curtailed bank credits to farmers.[45] The idea that Mexico could not feed itself never crossed their minds.

National shortages of corn and wheat reflected the plight of *medieros* and small farmers dependent on Mexico's rains to water their lands. As Molina Enríquez explained, small farmers harvested the bulk of the grains for sale to local markets; it was not the *haciendas,* even though they occupied nine-tenths of the cultivable land. It was the small farmer, he wrote, who supplied the corn and wheat consumed by the people of Mexico. Grain shortages, therefore, occurred at the expense of small farmers and *medieros* who, without irrigated lands, gambled on the weather.

The drought years penalized them and not the *hacendados,* who, to cite Molina Enríquez, seldom lost the harvests on their irrigated lands. To the contrary, the large landowners profited during years of scarcity because they were able to sell their corn and wheat at inflated prices.[46]

Harvests in short supply encouraged price increases. Expecting an early end to the era of droughts and grain scarcities, and unwilling to impose any kind of government regulation, authorities waited until 1909, when Corral organized his Junta de Provisión del Grano, to control supply and demand. In the interval, speculators with an eye for profit began to buy up the scanty supplies of corn and wheat for resale at exorbitant prices.[47] By 1909 *tiendas de raya* on *haciendas* on the outskirts of Pachuca, the capital of Hidalgo, were selling a bushel of corn for four pesos, a price labeled a "huge abuse" by *El Imparcial*.[48] No central or northern state escaped this curse.

The sharp rise in the price of foodstuffs, admittedly a long-standing problem in republican Mexico, but one greatly exacerbated by the droughts, coincided with the financial collapse of 1907. By closing down markets in the United States and Europe for Mexican minerals, the crises cut national revenues and damaged the buying power of the peso. As a result, prices of all articles went up. This disparity between income and the cost of living which the agricultural crisis aggravated, helped trigger the revolt against Díaz. Mexicans with fixed incomes, the so-called middle classes and industrial labor, especially suffered the consequences of the widening gap between income and the prices of food and key commodities. Wages and salaries never caught up with the spiraling cost of living.[49]

However, as earlier indicated, the droughts, although a major catalyst, had not given birth to this phenomenon. From the nineteenth century on, wages and salaries had stayed at about the same level, while their purchasing power, or real value, had declined steadily. Furthermore, the price of food and clothing rose rapidly after 1907. For residents of Mexico City, the influx of visitors arriving to celebrate the centennial of 1910 accentuated the price spiral with their lavish spending. As *El Imparcial* editorialized, all Mexicans suffered, "as each day the struggle to make ends meet becomes more acute."[50] To give examples of what the price spiral meant, between 1891 and 1908 the cost of flour, beans, wheat, corn, and chile nearly doubled. Rice had a smaller increase.[51] Even apologists for the Old Regime admitted that the price of corn had gotten out of hand.[52] The price of sugar, on the contrary, remained fairly steady, after years of sizable rises.[53] Ironically, the stability of sugar may have encouraged the *hacendados* of Morelos to expand their holdings at the expense of neighboring villages in order to plant larger amounts of sugar cane. The price spiral, moreover, accelerated during the final years of the Old Regime.

Inhabitants of cities and towns felt the gap between income and prices acutely. Complaints originated from virtually the entire map of the Republic, from Hermosillo and Guaymas in the northwest, across the expanse of the border communities, and south to Mexico City. The competition for scarce goods among relatively well-paid workers led to a frightening gulf between wages and prices in the ports of Tampico and Veracruz. Even distant Yucatán felt its effects. According to González Roa, while the cost-of-living index for the over-all population of Mexico City rose from 100 to 144.6 in the years from 1890 to 1910, for its working class it went from 100 to 163.47.[54] All classes suffered, but some more than others. As Vera Estañol remarked, the workers and the middle classes carried the brunt of the burden.[55] Although price increases had outstripped wage hikes, most members of the middle class, *El Imparcial* reminded its readers, had not received a raise in twenty years.[56] Caught between fixed incomes and skyrocketing prices, the middle classes could survive only by lowering their standard of living. In Mexico City, the demands of landlords for higher rents compelled many middle-class families to take flight to the less costly, and less prestigious, suburbs.[57]

III

Meanwhile, in the countryside, *hacendados* began to grumble about the lack of workers. The complaint arose from both the traditional *haciendas*, of marginal importance to the marketplace, and *haciendas* producing cash crops for export. So frantic were the planters of Coahuila by 1906 that they asked the army for soldiers to help pick the cotton of the Laguna; the soldiers, they swore, would be paid handsomely. Unable to find enough soldiers or other Mexicans to work for them, they began to import Chinese and Japanese coolies. The same lack of workers hampered the *haciendas* of Tehuantepec. Even in isolated and backward Chiapas the planters could not find enough workers to harvest the coffee beans. Faced with identical shortages, the henequen lords of Yucatán welcomed the Yaquis, then being forcibly driven from Sonora. Yet the influx of Yaquis, reported *El Imparcial,* hardly satisfied a tenth of the labor needs of the henequen industry.[58] An *hacendado* from Jalisco in 1907 testified that "in forty years he had never witnessed a comparable labor shortage." He told of *haciendas* that had normally harvested their corn by the end of February, unable to do so by mid-March. This occurred, he insisted, even though *hacendados* were paying seventy-five centavos a day, twice and three times the usual wage.[59] Further up the Pacific coast, the *hacendados* of Sinaloa, one of the powerful and productive groups in the Republic, underwent a "veritable crisis" because workers, despite offers of high wages, could not be found to harvest the crops. Taking a cue from their brethren in Coahuila, they too, began to urge the importation of Chinese coolies, and in addition, laborers from Jamaica. As late as 1910, similar shortages of labor hampered agriculture in Sonora, Chihuahua, and Coahuila, as well as in the Gulf states of Veracruz and Tabasco. Strangely, the economic doldrums touched off by the financial debacle of 1907 failed to end the problem of the absent worker.

    This curious paradox of labor shortages in times of economic difficulties had its roots in the character of Mexican agriculture. By the first decade of the twentieth century, many workers were simply unwilling to toil in the fields under the conditions endured by their fathers. Industry, the railroads, the mining boom, the growth of the port cities, the discovery of petroleum, and urban expansion had produced jobs with higher wages for Mexicans who might formerly have worked in the fields. As one student of the Laguna put it, the cotton planters of Coahuila could not compete for workers with better-paying industries.[60] The city of Torreón, the hub of the Laguna, and nearby Durango, for instance, provided jobs in textiles, soap factories, soft-drink plants, the cotton-seed oil industry, and on the railroads. In varying degrees all of Mexico's developing urban centers provided comparable opportunities.

But, principally, it was the prosperity of the northern states, mining in particular, that drew workers away from the fields of central and even southern Mexico. Between 1895 and 1910, approximately 150,000 of them settled in Chihuahua, and another 75,000 in Sonora. When the northern boom collapsed, the bold and the daring among the unemployed cast their eyes across the border. These were years of growth in the American Southwest. Men were needed to build railroads, to labor in the mines of Arizona, to harvest vegetables and fruits in California and Texas, and to pour tons of concrete for streets, public buildings, and hotels in burgeoning towns and cities. By comparison with Mexican *hacendados*, the Americans offered higher rewards. All regions of Mexico sent their offspring to the United States, but the largest blocs came from Guanajuato, Michoacán, Querétaro, and Jalisco. Both Zacatecas, a mining province hard hit by the crisis of 1907 and the decline of silver prices, and Aguascalientes, an impoverished arid land, also sent job seekers in droves across the border.[61]

No one knows exactly how many Mexicans, "usually the most energetic," left their homeland to test their luck in the land of the Yankees. Statistics are unreliable. According to the available figures, few Mexicans traveled to the Southwest before 1906. An article in *El Imparcial* taken from a report of the United States Office of Immigration, indicates that for 1902 just 715 emigrants left home, a figure undoubtedly low. With the collapse of the economy, their numbers grew, from nearly 6,000 in 1908 to 15,591 in the first six months of the following year.[62] Yet in 1908 alone, according to figures furnished by the local Mexican consul, 8,186 Mexicans had crossed through Laredo on their way to work in the United States, while in 1906, *El Correo de Chihuahua* reported with alarm that 22,000 Mexicans had entered Texas through Ciudad Juárez.[63] When asked by American authorities why they left, the immigrants listed the poverty of the countryside as the prime reason. Next in order was the monopoly of land by a few, followed by the absence of jobs in industry. At the bottom of the list of reasons, significantlly, were the want of law and justice, and acts of political persecution. Whatever the reliability of statistics, it is clear that Mexicans migrated across the border, almost always from rural villages, generally in search of jobs, and in growing numbers after the bubble burst in 1907 in Mexico.[64]

Yet, despite the significance of the crisis of 1907, the peculiar labor structure of rural Mexico determined the character of the exodus northward into mining, railroads, industry, and eventually into the American Southwest. Approximately 3.1 million Mexicans made their living from the land. The *peones acasillados* spent their entire lives under the tutelage of the *hacendado* who, in one way or another, took care of them. The degree of benevolence or exploitation varied among *hacendados,* as the books by John Kenneth Turner and Charles Flandrau document. Another group tilled small plots of their own, or those of the village. Both, not infrequently, carved out a meager existence; to feed their families they needed jobs on the neighboring *haciendas* for at least a part of each year. At the same time, the *hacienda's* monopoly of the land, plus the growth of the rural population, had created a landless proletariat seasonally employed by the *hacendados.* But to survive, this increasingly larger group required additional work. Unfortunately, the *haciendas* could not provide either jobs for the entire year or decent wages. As an article on the Bajío entitled "Why our Workers Emigrate," explained, the *hacendado,* on the average, paid twenty-five centavos for a day's work, but only for approximately half of the year. At best, he needed workers for two months to plant the corn, for another two to thin and weed it, and perhaps for an additional two months during the harvest.[65]

To keep at hand a reliable supply of cheap labor for the three key periods, *hacendados* relied on a system of debt peonage which, through the *tienda de raya,* kept the peons mortgaged to them. Both the indebted peon and the *hacendado,* Molina Enríquez pointed out, knew what was expected of each other. The peon knowingly borrowed more than he could repay, while the *hacendado* lent fully aware that the peon would not pay him back.[66] There was a limit, however, to the number of *peones acasillados* an *hacendado* could keep or entice to his *hacienda.* Most of them, after all, housed their flocks in *jacales,* punished them arbitrarily, and paid them the lowest wages in the Republic. No free worker, or anyone with an ounce of initiative, willingly put himself in the situation of the *peones acasillados,* the lowest class in Mexican society.[67] Nor, conversely, could the *hacendados* have employed all of the job hunters—even had they been willing to work under such conditions.

The jobless worker in rural Mexico, therefore, had limited alternatives. He could, if sufficiently desperate, put himself in the hands of an *hacendado* (if the *hacendado* would take him). If he happened to be an *ejidatario,* a resident of a village owning lands in common, or the owner of a small parcel of land, he could work for himself as well as for the nearby *hacienda;* or, if landless, he could attempt to survive on the six months of work an *hacendado* might provide. To complicate the problem for the landless worker, all rural jobs paid poorly, from a high of 1.25 pesos in Chihuahua to less than a fifth of that in Oaxaca. The average rural wage for the Republic in 1908, according to Frank Tannenbaum, was 31.6 centavos a day, just 2.6 centavos above what it had been in 1891. In Jalisco and Michoacán, just as in Puebla and Oaxaca, rural wages had actually declined between 1891 and 1908.[68] Only in Chihuahua had rural wages improved markedly. In reality, the publicized higher wages, so much in the news of *El Imparcial,* at best were a seasonal phenomenon. Once the harvest was over, either the job or the extra money disappeared.

A significant inference, or perhaps even a conclusion, about the nature of the rebels of 1910 can be drawn from this situation with agricultural labor. To cite Molina Enríquez, because only the lowliest of the rural population accepted the role of *peón acasillado,* the focus of protest in the countryside, logically, did not arise from the peasants on the *haciendas,* the most exploited. On the contrary, it came from the landless workers, by implication the most dissatisfied, but at the same time, the more able and aggressive of the rural sector, the tens of thousands unwilling to spend their lives under the tutelage of *hacendados.* This group increased dramatically in the years just before 1910. In truth, these were rural wage workers, often jobless and increasingly without decent alternatives after 1907. From this sector came the men who either emigrated northward, more and more to the

American Southwest, or, after the call to arms, enlisted in the rebel armies.[69] Paradoxically, the most exploited, the *peones acasillados*, the true peasants, generally watched the rebellion unfold from afar.

IV

The north had its version of Mexico's agricultural ills. With the exception of the Yaquis, of key significance to Sonora, the northern provinces lacked powerful or substantial Indian populations. Communal landholding systems and other pre-Columbian or colonial vestiges were of secondary importance, again outside the confines of the Yaqui question. Debt peonage was not an important part of the economy of the north; farmers, *hacendados*, and cattle ranchers relied primarily on free labor.[70] The *rancho*, that Mexican combination of small farm and livestock ranch, vastly outnumbered the *pueblos* or villages.[71]

By the same token, no other region matched in size the *latifundios* of the north. It was there that the infamous surveying companies, given legal sanction by the Leyes de Terrenos Baldíos of the 1880's, enjoyed unlimited opportunities. The size of the typical Mexican *hacienda* seldom exceeded 3,000 hectares—outside of Chihuahua, Coahuila, Nuevo León, and Durango, where it had 5,000 hectares. The *haciendas* of Sonora, on the other hand, with usually 2 to 3,000 hectares of land, ranked below the national average. As one Mexican writes, Sonora was not noted for large *haciendas*.[72] Still, with a few exceptions, nowhere in the Republic was the imbalance in the ownership of land so skewed as in the north, where a small élite monopolized it.[73] The spectacular growth of the large estates, so often associated with the Díaz era, took place primarily in the northern provinces. The empire of Luis Terrazas in Chihuahua epitomized this phenomenon. There and in Sonora, the *hacienda* was an entrenched feature of the rural scene. The railroads, which unlocked the door to the profitable cultivation of cash crops and the feeding of cattle for beef and hides for the export market, promoted the burbeoning land empires. With buyers waiting across the border, the planters, particularly in Sonora, began to purchase the latest farm machinery and to fertilize their fields with chemicals. In the interval, the price of lands for wheat, garbanzos, citrus fruits, and vegetables multiplied tenfold.[74]

To judge objectively the expansion of these huge baronies requires historical perspective. To start with, when Díaz toppled the former rulers of Mexico, none of the northern states had large populations. All were sparsely populated, while their cities were hardly more than small towns. As Juan Bautista Alberdi said for distant Argentina, "to govern was to populate." Luis Terrazas, accused by the rebels of hoarding lands, began his empire in a land empty of people. Originally, he robbed no one; quite the opposite. It was his genius for building a cattle and agricultural kingdom that laid the foundations for many villages and towns.[75] Díaz and his advisers, in accordance with the dictum of the Argentinian Juan Alberdi, believed that progress meant putting the public lands in the hands of private individuals. Eventually, of course, the alienation of the national real estate thwarted the property goals of recent arrivals and threatened the lands of villagers and small farmers who had lived in Chihuahua prior to the arrival of Terrazas and his companions. Although few in numbers, their anguished cries echoed loudly across the north by 1910.

Nowhere in Mexico was the alienation of the land so obvious. By the turn of the century, the activities of the surveying companies had become a national scandal. Four of them gobbled up two-thirds of Sonora, while others acquired large chunks of Sonora, Sinaloa, Tamaulipas, and Durango. Outside of the north, only in Tepic, Guerrero, and parts of Veracruz did the companies taste comparable success.[76] Of the seven states most exploited by the surveying companies, five were in the north: Coahuila, Chihuahua, Durango, Sinaloa, and Sonora. More than 3 million hectares were given away or sold for a pittance in Chihuahua and Sonora by national authorities; Sinaloa lost almost 2 million hectares; while small cliques acquired over 1.3 million hectares in Coahuila and Durango.[77]

The story of Chihuahua graphically portrays the scope of the land grab. Four companies had put their stamp of ownership on a territory equal in size to England and Wales.[78] Their conquests, and those of prominent citizens, left only marginal lands in key districts to villages, small farmers, and *rancheros*. In the districts of Guerrero, Rayón, Camargo, Meoqui, Aldama, Victoria, and Abasolo, Jesús E. Valenzuela and his partners claimed 2,795,191 hectares. A company headed by Ignacio López, with Creel as one of its associates, received 1,008,703 hectares in Galeana. An additional 395,372 hectares in Guerrero and Degollado went to a group headed by Mariano and Telésforo García, and another 661,748 hectares in Galeana and adjoining districts to Eugenio Schentz. Luis García Teruel acquired 712,300 hectares in Galeana and Bravos. The Gómez del Campo family received 1.5 million hectares. Meanwhile, to build the Ferrocarril Noroeste, the government gave away 1,047,769 hectares.[79]

On their own, or with the aid of the surveying companies, a small group of men carved out mammoth empires. Chihuahua, in the process, became known as the haven of the landed barons. There were nineteen *latifundios* which encompassed over 100,000 hectares, while twelve ranged in size from 40,000 to 100,000 hectares. The twelve largest *hacendados* owned 8,588,940 hectares; seventeen *hacendados* ruled over 130,145 kilometers of land, or two-fifths of Chihuahua, including nearly all of the land useful for agriculture or cattle. Terrazas, the biggest of the land barons, sat atop the pyramid; two of his sons, Juan and Alberto, controlled *haciendas* of over 200,000 hectares. The *latifundio* of Pablo Martínez del Río, the only one dating from colonial days, consisted of 1,382,426 hectares. Creel was master of 433,320 hectares, while William Randolph Hearst, a friend of Creel and Terrazas, escaped from the pressures of the publishing world on an estate of 349,699 hectares. Among the other Chihuahuan moguls were Carlos Zuloaga, Enrique Müller, Luis Faudoa, Ponciano Falomir, José María Luján, and Antonio Asúnsolo. In the meantime, the 201 *ejidos* of the state occupied a mere 1.5 percent of its land.[80] Equally significant, just 138,774 hectares in the entire state had water for irrigation, nearly all of which was the property of *hacendados*.[81]

A host of sins beset the alienation of the land in Chihuahua, which are typical of the history in the north. The frauds, cheating, and manipulations which accompanied it added fuel to the fires of rebellion. The epic uprising of Tomóchic vividly described by Frías, broke out in 1888 when the Limantour family arrogantly helped itself to 170,000 hectares of land in Guerrero and Abasolo. Soldiers brutally crushed the rebellion and the Limantours kept the land, selling it to the Cargil Lumber Company in 1906.[82] In the judgment of some historians, the uprising of Tomóchic signaled the opening shot of the upheaval of 1910. Despite the defeat at Tomóchic, angry denunciations of surveying companies and landed lords multiplied rapidly.[83]

Neighboring Coahuila had its own land problems, somewhat similar to Chihuahua's. While serious and complex, the situation was not the most acute in the north.[84] For one thing, the *ejidos* had not felt, at least to the same extent as in Chihuahua, the heavy hand of the land speculator and *hacendado*. On the other hand, depressed markets in the United States for cotton and guayule, two of the principal sources of revenue, further shook the local economy in the waning days of Díaz' regime. Until the end, guayule remained a surplus on the market. The cotton planters confronted an additional obstacle. In 1906, they had bemoaned unsold cotton bales in their warehouses; however, droughts from 1906 to 1909 turned the Nazas River, which watered the cotton, into a dry gulch, cutting the size of the harvest sharply. The harvest of 1907 was the lowest in a decade, and that of the following year no better.[85] In 1909, hordes of grasshoppers invaded the Laguna to feast on a cotton crop already damaged by drought.[86] When the crops failed, the jobless abandoned the Laguna, hurting the commerce of its towns. Accounts of local bankruptcies and bank failures traveled the length of the Republic. Then, in a sudden reversal the rainfall of 1909 converted the Nazas into a raging torrent of water that overflowed its banks, causing heavy damage to neighboring plantations.[87]

By 1908, according to Governor Miguel Cárdenas, a severe crisis faced Coahuila. A combination of droughts and of falling prices for cotton and guayule had sapped the vigor of the economy. From information given by Cárdenas, who had traveled to Mexico City to seek assistance, only the coal industry kept the economy afloat.[88] Meanwhile, as early as 1906, the planters had begun to discuss with Díaz the problem of declining markets for cotton, urging, as one of their solutions, controls on its production and sale.[89] Concurrently, a conflict had erupted between certain planters and the Compañía Industrial Jabonera de la Laguna which, according to complaints against it, had taken unfair advantage of a contract drawn up in 1889 to buy cotton seed at ruinously low prices. The Compañía Jabonera, the owner of the soap factories in Torreón, Gómez Palacio, and San Pedro de las Colonias, in reality, enjoyed a monopoly and used it to fix prices. Beyond that, the soap company had employed the courts and the local mortgage banks to compel planters to cultivate only cotton, and to deliver its seeds to the Jabonera. When planters attempted to sell their seed to independent buyers, the Jabonera, with the help of the courts, had an embargo placed on their crop. But, as the angry planters pointed out, not all of their companions were dealt with in identical fashion. The soap company played favorites; friends of the politically powerful were free to cultivate what they wished and to sell to whom they pleased. To aggravate matters, the Jabonera enjoyed the support of Limantour and Creel, kingpins of the administration, and employed as its lawyer, Jorge Vera Estañol, a favorite of the old rulers.[90]

In Sonora, the Yaqui question, intimately tied to the land problem, added one more twist to the tangled web of events which eventually toppled Díaz from his throne. Through the 1870s, the Yaqui Indians, a hard-working tribe, had cultivated the lands of their ancestors in the Mayo and Yaqui valleys, and made up 15 percent of the state's population.[91] As late as 1900, they had provided almost all of the workers in agriculture, as well as for mining and for the construction of the railroads.[92] In the 1880s, their fertile lands had begun to attract the attention of speculators. By opening up the valleys of the Mayo and Yaqui to farmers, the railroads had added impetus to the acquisition of lands there. Mexicans and Americans, individually or in association with surveying companies, rushed to stake their claims. Even by 1881, observed General Bernardo Reyes, then the military commander of Sonora, the claims, if honored, would "deprive the unfortunate Yaquis of even the means to feed themselves."[93] To the despair of the Yaquis, the rulers of Sonora, with the connivance of Mexico City, eventually honored these claims. As a result, a long and bloody clash broke out between the Yaquis and their voracious enemies.

Paradoxically some Yaquis, the *mansos* or domesticated ones, continued to provide most of the labor for a large group of *hacendados*. Without it, their lands would have lain fallow. All the same, other Yaquis, the *broncos* or unconquered ones, harassed the *haciendas* without respite, attacking towns and destroying property. Often the same Yaquis who tilled the fields belonged to marauding guerrillas, or lent them moral support and gave guns and food. Because of the tenacity of the Yaquis, it proved impossible to eliminate the guerrillas. Only the return of the lands to their rightful owners, a plea rejected by the masters of Sonora, would have restored peace.

To settle the matter once and for all, Governor Rafael Izábal, in the years between 1903 and 1907, launched a full-scale campaign against the Yaquis. With the backing of Díaz and Corral, he brought federal troops into battle, and in an effort to end hostilities forever, began to deport the Yaquis to the henequen plantations of Yucatán. To his chagrin, his formula, apparently beginning to succeed, backfired; rather than bring peace, it exacerbated political rivalries in Sonora. Threatened with the loss of their workers, *hacendados,* miners, and even Americans who had complained of Yaqui depradations joined together to oppose Izábal's policy, charging that authorities were deporting both the peaceful *mansos* and the warlike *broncos* Yaquis. But old vested interest groups with whom Izábal had close ties, particularly those around Hermosillo, urged him to push ahead. Where before Yaquis fought whites, now the campaign to exterminate them split the rulers of Sonora into warring camps.

Because Corral and Díaz sided with Izábal, his scheme brought a clash between leading business and agricultural groups in Sonora and politicians in Mexico City. The Yaqui issue shattered the fragile unity of Sonora.[94] One of the *hacendados* hurt by Izábal's tactics was Ramón Maytorena, sentenced to sixteen months in jail for harboring Yaquis. Not surprisingly, a member of the Maytorena family eventually played a key role in the downfall of the Díaz regime in Sonora. The *hacendados* there had no stomach for a policy that, at their expense, provided the planters of Yucatán with cheap labor.[95]

Yet the departure of Izábal did not cancel efforts to deport

the Yaquis.[96] In 1908, plans were unveiled to rid Sonora of all
Yaquis, the peaceful and warlike together. The local officials
claimed that until then, just the rebellious Indians had been
captured and shipped to Yucatán. Only by deporting every Yaqui,
El Imparcial blandly assured its readers, would the wars end.[97]
The threat failed to end Yaqui attacks on property and lives;
both survived the fall of Díaz. By 1908, according to an American miner, the Yaquis were no longer merely bandits, but
"rebels." [98]

The Yaqui wars, wrote Bulnes, cost the regime dearly.[99] As
Madero recognized, the attempt to exterminate the Yaquis
alarmed powerful agricultural interests in Sonora.[100] But, blind
to all protest, government authorities pushed ahead with their
plans, bleeding the state, damaging its economy, dividing its
inhabitants into antagonistic camps, and driving the Yaquis and
their employers into the vortex of rebellion. Fructuoso Méndez,
a Yaqui chieftain, helped swing the support of his tribe to
Madero. A guerrilla, he had been conscripted into the army by
his captors. While stationed in Cananea, he met Lázaro Gutiérrez de Lara, an advocate of social change, who secured his
release from the military. Méndez figured prominently in the
strike at Cananea in 1906 and later became a key officer in
the army of Alvaro Obregón.[101] Also, the Yaqui wars offered a
splendid opportunity for a flourishing contraband trade in arms
with Arizona, leading Governor Cubillas and Ramón Corral to
wonder if the guns were to be used against Yaquis or against
the government.[102]

V

Far to the south, the appearance of a modern, cash-crop agriculture upset the tranquility of tiny Morelos, which had been
home of the sugar *haciendas* since colonial times. Isolated from
central Mexico by a towering range of mountains, the sugar industry had scarcely changed in centuries. With only a small
market to supply, the *hacendados* had worked out a fragile peace
with the neighboring villages. Although not forgotten or forgiven,

the theft of village lands was a matter of historical record. Scores of villages still farmed their own lands.

The arrival of the railroad in Cuautla and Yautepec, lowering freight rates between Morelos and central Mexico, upset the delicate balance between *hacendados* and villagers. For the first time, planters could dream of a national market for their sugar—and perhaps export it to foreign consumers. When the Spanish-American War disrupted the Cuban sugar industry, which formerly supplied the national market, the planters of Morelos rushed to acquire its customers. To meet the expanding market, the planters began to build huge sugar mills and to equip them with the latest machinery. Hungry mills and expanding markets called for additional lands on which to plant cane, for irrigation water, and for fresh supplies of cheap labor. The "race was on to grab land, water, and labor." [103]

An early victim of these changes was the policy of coexistence with the landed villages. Before, the planters had occasionally taken village lands; with the quest for more and cheaper sugar, land theft became a major business. As villages fell to the control of *hacendados,* they became, for all intents and purposes, company towns. As in the mining camps of Sonora, their owners ruled the lives of their inhabitants, gave the *tienda de raya* a monopoly and meted out justice as they saw fit. The haphazard exploitation and cruelty of former years turned into the systematic oppression of the gilded age factory.[104] Judged by per capita retails sales, Morelos became one of the most commercialized states in the republic. The poor suffered in the process. With the help of authorities in Mexico City, and with the complicity of local courts, the *hacendados* made themselves masters of the land and water of Morelos. Emiliano Zapata and hundreds of other small farmers lost their lands, as did scores of villages, which converted their inhabitants into wage workers on plantations. Wages kept low by the demands for cheap sugar and the proclivities of *hacendados* for greater profits, worsened the predicament of the workers. It mattered little that big agriculture had brought labor-saving machinery, a profitable trade, and even a cultural renaissance to Morelos.[105]

In 1909, the planters elected Pablo Escandón, one of their

own, as governor of Morelos. Patricio Leyva, the defeated candidate, according to *El Imparcial*, had promised to return the stolen lands to their rightful owners.[106] When Escandón as governor was both ineffectual and a tyrant, the cauldron of rebellion boiled over. Not until 1919, when false leaders posing as revolutionaries murdered Zapata, did the rebellious, the poor of Morelos, lay down their arms. Nowhere else in Mexico, however, did masses of peasants with leaders of their own rise against the national government. The situation in Morelos was unique.

VI

Practical considerations, in summary, awakened concern for national agrarian problems. The future rebels enjoyed no monopoly over the concern. On the contrary, spokesmen for the Old Regime were among the first to voice dissatisfaction with the condition of rural Mexico. The financial crisis of 1907, which grievously wounded the mining industry, the country's principal source of revenue, vividly exposed the stagnation of agriculture. It was glaringly obvious that Mexico, in dire need of additional income, could not count on its *hacendados* for aid. With a few exceptions, agriculture was a burden on the national economy.

El Imparcial, a news organ subsidized by the administration, early began to alert the public to agricultural ills, particularly after knowledge of the mining debacle spread. Scores of editorials and articles appeared underlining the inability of agriculture to make up the loss in mining revenue. One commentary pointed out that the value of agricultural exports in the previous six months had grown by only 2.3 million pesos, sales of henequen representing half of the increase. Of the other agricultural exports, only garbanzos and tobacco had made slight gains.[107] Agriculture, as it had for years, "promised much but offered little." [108] Mining, another article stressed, "has been the principal —if not the sole—basis of our commercial expansion." Despite the drop in the price of silver, sales of copper and gold had enabled Mexico partly to meet the payments on its foreign debt. But, a commentary of May 23, 1908 went on, "our balance of trade will rest on a stronger base if we can accelerate the development of agriculture." The national welfare required a sharp increase in the exports of farm goods. It was time to face up to the problem and to modernize the agricultural sector.[109] It would be a tragic mistake, El Imparcial told its readers, "not to expand the foundations of Mexico's economy, or to rely again solely on the fickle fortunes of a mineral export." The economic troubles had demonstrated that Mexico must exploit wisely its agricultural potential.[110] Land was clearly the neglected resource. Low yields per hectare, giving Mexico half the wheat harvests of Argentina and the United States, and less than a sixth of what Germany and Denmark produced, were unacceptable.[111]

The commentaries in El Imparcial, moreover, went beyond a lament over the drop in exports; they included a growing concern over the inability of Mexico to feed itself. By cutting the value of the peso, the mining crisis had multiplied the cost of importing corn and wheat that the droughts had made necessary. Also, it appears likely that official awareness had taken into account the censure of rural ills voiced by political critics. By 1909, Molina Enríquez had published his perceptive study, while the Partido Liberal Mexicano had incorporated land reform into its platform. Still, it is more likely that the political critics as well as El Imparcial reflected a common preoccupation with rural maladies. As the newspaper put it, "the plethora of metals will not mitigate the hunger of our people." [112] As early as 1906, it had called attention to the shortage of foodstuffs that each year increasingly failed to meet national demands. Failures in production, "a chronic problem in the last ten years," had "brought in its wake a retinue of scarcities and high prices in the cities, as well as poverty and anguish in the countryside." [113] Not only must Mexico import wheat in ever greater quantities annually, but statistics for the production of corn revealed a steady decline from 1897 to 1904.[114]

The debate involved hacendados as well. At the first Congreso Agrícola Regional, held in Villahermosa in 1901, again at Tulancingo in 1906, and at Zamora a year later, hacendados met to discuss the problem. At these meetings, they listened to experts explain the advantages of chemical fertilizers, of scientific methods of farming, and of using modern machinery. At one session at Tulancingo, the *hacendados* even discussed whether to pay higher wages in order to encourage their workers to be more productive, an idea which most of them labeled irrelevant. A discussion at Zamora on the living conditions of the *hacienda* peon fared no better.[115] Still, despite their reluctance to improve life for their workers, the *hacendados,* by meeting, had conceded that not all was well. The enlightened among them, meanwhile, began to urge the improvement of farming methods, as the testimony of one *hacendado* reveals who, after a visit to the American Midwest, returned convinced of the need to replace antiquated machinery.[116] Only in this manner, he argued, could Mexico feed itself and produce a surplus for export. To encourage this effort, *hacendados,* with the backing of officials in government, established the Cámara Agrícola Central in 1908 that, with the assistance of the Sociedad Agrícola Mexicana, began to build a national organization of cattlemen and farmers. The Sociedad Agrícola pledged to do whatever was necessary to convey the "urgency" to improve agriculture.[117]

Nor did the negative attitude of the *hacendados* at Tulancingo and Zamora close the debate on labor. In 1909, one of their own bodies, the Cámara Agrícola y Ganadera de Tamaulipas voted to end the practice of lending money to peons on the *haciendas.* That resolution sounded the death knell of debt peonage in Tamaulipas. In the opinion of the Cámara, *hacendados* had nothing to lose, because the practice tied up scarce funds required to improve farming, undermined the initiative of their workers, and kept them from putting aside their own savings.[118] In the fall of that same year, *El Imparcial,* in a critical review of John Kenneth Turner's recent article, *Barbarous Mexico,* openly condemned debt peonage and promised forthcoming government action to end it. "Peonage," it declared, "will rapidly fall by the wayside" because of its incompatibility with modern agriculture.[119]

During the interval, the administration, with much fanfare, had announced a program to improve agriculture. In 1908, it began to build dams and irrigation canals. In his message to Congress in the fall of the next year, Díaz promised other reforms. One dealt with banks to provide long-term credit at low interest rates to farmers.[120] Of equal significance, Olegario Molina, the minister of *fomento,* in 1908, shelved for further study the notorious Leyes de Terrenos Baldíos; two years later Díaz suspended them indefinitely calling them "incomplete, disorganized, and unresponsive to geographical and economic realities." [121] A few months later, he dispatched special committees to Sonora and Chihuahua to rectify errors committed in the surveys of public lands, and in Sonora, to review the subdivisions and sales of lots in the towns along the banks of the Yaqui and Mayo rivers.[122] Lamenting that "previous efforts to subdivide the *haciendas* had failed," Díaz promised to make "the ideal a reality." [123] In March, 1910, he embraced a program of land reform, which included for subdivision into plots of eight to twenty hectares, the lands of the *haciendas* in the border provinces, and which could be purchased in ten annual installments.[124] With that measure, Díaz had gone beyond what Madero promised in his Plan de San Luis Potosí. Foreseeing no opposition to the project, *El Impracial* predicted that it would develop "our public wealth as well as guarantee peace in the future." Mexico, it insisted, more than other nation, had to turn its vision back to the land.[125]

SEVEN *Foreigners: The Blessings and the Bane*

"He plotted his Nation's path
And with vigor made it great;
But the Great Man died
Because of his love for the foreigner."

Mexican Popular Rhyme

I

NATIONALISM, an important factor in the rebellion of 1910, contains a logical yet striking paradox. Under the firm hand of Porfirio Díaz, Mexico had climbed from centuries of colonial neglect to modernity and respectability. Foreigners were one of the leading instigators of that progress. Mexico won entry into the twentieth century and acclaim in the Western world, as Francisco Bulnes had warned, through foreign investment and technology.[1] From this alien invasion, Mexico both profited and lost. Eventually, those Mexicans denied a place at the banquet table came to blame their plight on the foreign presence. Their bitterness sparked a wave of nationalism bordering on xenophobia which characterized the twilight years of the Old Regime and set the stage for rebellion.

By all accounts, Mexico had traveled a long road. When Díaz made himself master of the National Palace in 1876, Mexico had undergone half a century of economic chaos and civil strife. Benito Juárez, who had spent a lifetime combating the Conservatives and the imperial machinations of Napoleon III, had only recently begun to put the house in order. A scattering of commercial enclaves survived here and there. Around Mexico City, and on the corridor to Veracruz, infant textile mills represented the extent of industrialization. The Republic boasted of one railroad, from the capital to the Gulf of Mexico. What limited international trade and intercourse Mexicans carried on was primarily with Western Europe. Englishmen alone had invested money in Mexican mining, banking, and commerce. In the Federal District there was a tiny American colony of 350 persons, (130 adults, the rest children) by far the largest in Mexico, of whom a few dabbled in commerce, others taught in private or public schools, edited an English language newspaper, labored for the Mexico City-Veracruz railroad, or worked as civil engineers, administrators of *haciendas,* mechanics, or foremen.[2] A wide gap separated Mexico from the world of Queen Victoria, the harbinger of the industrial era.

Upon taking office, Díaz confronted a formidable challenge. Juárez and his successor, Sebastián Lerdo de Tejada, left behind merely the beginnings of economic development: a small railroad and timid attempts to revive mining, agriculture, and commerce. In their search for a formula for growth, the two Liberal administrations had embraced the positivist doctrine of peace, order, and progress. For Díaz, who followed, the question was how to alter the colonial structure of Mexico. All solutions, Díaz and his advisers concluded, required funds and know-how, of which Mexicans had little. What there was of domestic capital was tied up in land. At the same time, because of Mexico's inability to meet payments on its foreign debt, primarily to European creditors, the Old World had closed its resources to Mexico. Nor, must it be forgotten, this was the age of belief in the virtues of free trade, a doctrine embraced, albeit with some misgivings, by José I. Limantour, the guiding spirit of Mexican finance. A system of protective tariffs, he asserted, could not be "implemented overnight"; one had to keep in mind Mexico's particular circumstance, especially its geographical location adjacent to the United States.[3]

To break the impasse, the absence of foreign capital which barred economic development, Porfirian Mexico had just one alternative: to turn to its rich Yankee neighbor. Material progress could not wait for the growth of Mexican capital and hence would have to rely on investors from across the border. To make Mexico modern and to assure the national well-being, Díaz subordinated other interests and in effect sold to aliens the country's resources. As Limantour acknowledged, this decision, which ultimately converted Mexico into a dependent of the foreigner, brought with it obvious dangers. But, he attempted to convince his countrymen that the benefits, in the form of new industries or of help to older ones, contributed to the prosperity of all Mexicans. Limantour mistakenly predicted—as the history of modern nations that had relied on outsiders to finance their development shows—that the people of Mexico, better educated and prosperous, would someday redeem what had been sold to the foreigner and keep at home the remaining fruits of progress.[4] On this assumption of future redemption, Díaz invited the stranger into his home.

Railroad builders from the north were the first to arrive. A few months before the close of his initial term in office, and against the nationalistic sentiments of Congress, Díaz granted concessions for the construction of railroads to Ciudad Juárez and Nuevo Laredo. By 1910, foreigners, in particular Americans, controlled an enormous portion of the economy and land. "No other country in the world," solemnly announced the railroad magnate Edward Harriman, "offered greater advantages to American capital than did Mexico." [5] As if to thank his northern neighbors for the favors conferred on Mexico, Díaz went so far as to personally meet and welcome American tourists to the National Palace.[6] Foreign governments, in return, bestowed upon him their highest national honors. Meanwhile, Americans discovered a second home in Mexico, so much so that Julio Sesto, the peripatetic Spanish traveler, learned that English ranked in importance with the language of Cervantes. Mexicans, he commented in wonderment, enjoyed baseball, played tennis, drove American automobiles, and brazenly flaunted their American clothing and shoes.[7]

II

No one disputes that foreign entrepreneurs plowed fertile soil in Mexico. In 1902, American investments totaled $511,465.38 dollars; nearly all of them were made after 1877 and half of them since 1896. All told, there were 1,115 individual investors and firms. By 1911, American investments had grown to over $1 billion dollars, with railroad stocks and bonds accounting for $644,300,000 dollars.[8] American capital in Mexico exceeded the amount of all other foreign investments as well as those of the Mexicans themselves.[9] The value of the American investment was three times that of other foreigners, twice that of Mexicans, and greater than the value of property held by Mexicans and Europeans together. Of the total American investment abroad, over a quarter of it was in Mexico; only Canada had a larger share of American money.[10] Americans controlled 75 percent of the Mexican mines, 72 percent of the metallurgical industry, 68 percent of the rubber business, and 58 percent of the petroleum production.[11] Foreigners controlled 80 percent of Mexican industry, but Americans had invested a mere $10 million dollars in industry, just 1.49 percent of their total direct investment.[12] Obviously, Mexicans could not count on Americans to build their factories. Of equally ominous implications, over 75 percent of Mexico's foreign trade was with its powerful northern neighbor.[13] As Antonio Manero lamented, the Republic's export and import industries relied principally on American markets and business.[14]

To balance the American role, Díaz belatedly attempted to attract European capital, especially the British. Lured by visions of easy profits, English businessmen and speculators invested 52,967,260 pounds, the French 960,791,600 francs, Germans 109,817,500 marks, and the Dutch 51,000,000 dollars.[15] Mining and railroads drew the bulk of European capital. However, unlike Americans, Europeans, Spaniards included, invested in Mexican industries, many of them producing for the domestic market. A majority of the textile mills, for instance, were French, while the breweries of Toluca, Monterrey, Guadalajara, and Orizaba were owned by German capitalists; and Spanish, French, and English funds had found their way into the paper industry.[16] The percentage of direct English and French investment surpassed that of the United States.

Fortunately for Mexico, as Fernando González Roa said, foreigners infrequently purchased agricultural lands or became cattlemen. This picture, nonetheless, began to change in the last days of the Porfiriato, especially in the northern provinces, where American ownership of large tracts of land became a major irritant.[17] The jump in the value of American holdings was sizeable, from $30 million dollars in 1902 to $80 million by 1912, and to $125 million dollars by 1921.[18] Of the nearly 5,000 inhabitants of agricultural colonies—new farming units usually in the northern border states—half were foreigners. To exploit the recently discovered oil fields and, at the same time keep peace among the competing foreigners, Díaz turned over the lands lying between Tampico and Veracruz to the Huasteca Petroleum Company, an American conglomerate; and in the area south of Veracruz to El Aguila, a British monopoly. These two groups controlled 89 percent of Mexican petroleum production, while 92 percent of the yield from mining was in Anglo-American hands.[19]

With this picture vividly in mind, the nationalistic firebrands of 1910 held Díaz responsible for having betrayed Mexico to the foreigners. Worse, the developmental policies of the Old Regime, as critics saw it, had failed to transform the rickety economic foundations of the Republic, at the same time as delivering it into foreign arms. To the misfortune of Díaz, the economy took a downhill turn in the last decade of his rule. Until 1907, on paper at least, the annual value of exports had exceeded the cost of imports by 30 million pesos. Still, that surplus hardly gave a true picture. To start with, it overlooked an outward flow of 48 million pesos to cover payments on the public debt (24 million pesos), the railroads (20 million pesos), and on obligations of the Banco Nacional and the Banco de Londres y México.[20] Beyond that, the so-called surplus ignored the large amounts of capital siphoned out of Mexico in the form of profits by foreign investors. As *El Imparcial* publicly acknowledged in 1907, the surplus in the balance of trade failed to cover the flight of American profits from Mexico.[21]

This unhealthy picture, furthermore, did not go unnoticed by Limantour and his aides. They were fully aware of the cost of imports, the drain on Mexican savings brought about by payments on the foreign debt, and the flow of profits out of the country.[22] In response, Limantour took steps any nationalist would surely have advocated. To reduce imports, he imposed a higher tariff, providing domestic industries with greater protection from outside competition. He sought means to encourage the exports of raw materials and mining products. The goal, as Manero pointed out, was to make Mexico less dependent on foreigners.[23] In 1906, with the aid of a European loan, Limantour took another step to give Mexico a larger say in the management of its own destinies, that of buying the majority stock in the railroads.[24] To the anger of its Mexican workers, however, he left its operation in foreign hands.

To Limantour's sorrow, his attempts to restore ownership to Mexicans and re-establish control had only a minimal effect and came too late. Past mistakes could not be easily undone. The railway grid, for example, which cost Mexico dearly, only marginally met its transportation needs. To aggravate matters, while the Díaz regime had granted foreign enterpreneurs exorbitant subsidies to build the railroads, Mexico had borne 67 percent of the cost by 1896.[25] In return, the foreigners had built a network that joined Mexico City and the mining towns of the north to American markets and business. Only minimally did the railroads tie the capital to the provinces, open communication with the port cities, or destroy the barriers separating the Gulf Coast from the Pacific slope. Despite the millions of pesos spent, a national railway grid still remained an aspiration and not a reality. The regime's efforts to gain a larger measure of control over the mining industry fared even less well. In 1908, the administration announced forthcoming legislation to limit future foreign activity in mining, which included a law to prohibit the purchase by foreigners of additional mining properties or the acquisition of new mining rights.[26] *El Economista,* a conservative, influential organ that reflected the growing nationalism of the day, called the restrictions just and necessary.[27] All the same, confronted with the opposition of the Cámara Minera de México, manipulated by the foreign mining barons, the administration favored caution and recalled its controversial legislation.[28] To cite *El Imparcial,* which was always ready to dance to the tune of the government, the mining measure merely poured oil on the fires of xenophobia.[29]

Yet the administration had not abandoned its attempts to shake loose from its American captors. During the interval, Limantour had boarded a ship for Europe in search of funds to consolidate Mexico's foreign debt, and with the financial maneuver, lessen dependence on Wall Street. It was Limantour's hope that the involvement of European bankers would act as a brake on voracious American capitalists. Clearly, at this juncture, Limantour and Díaz no longer believed in the miracles wrought by outsiders, especially Yankees. This was not, moreover, a sudden change in the thinking of the regime. From the start, as Daniel Cosío Villegas maintains, Díaz and his allies, despite their public behavior, never fully trusted the United States. Ironically, the decision to open Mexico to American investors, commented Cosío Villegas, had originated in Díaz' fears of what he suspected were American designs on Mexican territory by the Rutherford B. Hayes administration. By giving American businessmen a stake in Mexico, Díaz pitted them against Hayes and his schemes.[30] Still, even granting that Díaz underwent a change of heart, his policies had to overcome the distrust of the United States of Liberals. Without question, Díaz lived to regret whatever faith he had placed in American capitalists and their government. Stung by the charges of treason hurled at him by his nationalistic foes, the old warrior labored until his death to vindicate himself. "I was never," he told an Argentine reporter who interviewed him in exile in Spain, "a darling of the Yankees." To the contrary, he claimed, his policies had cut short attempts by Americans to dominate Mexico. "That desire," he told the reporter, "is more than enough to justify fear for the future of my country." [31]

III

From the cherished dream to rid the country of alien potentates surfaced a strident cry of the upheaval of 1910: "México para los mexicanos." The apostles of rebellion hoisted the banner of nationalism, proclaiming their cause Mexico for Mexicans.[32] Although a twentieth-century crusade, it was an old gospel, with roots in the Spanish colonial era, the Joel R. Poinsett episode, the War of 1846, and even, as the commentary of Díaz and Limantour demonstrates, the age of don Porfirio. "In its origins," wrote Bulnes, "the Mexican Revolution had a markedly Boxer character . . . directed principally against the influence, prestige, and interests of the United States." [33] The rebels viewed the United States as the natural enemy of Mexico, All political attacks on the Old Regime, by the same token, implied censure of its investment policies for foreigners. The rejection of Díaz, to paraphrase Luis Cabrera, embodied an angry denunciation of the system of privileges, the largest and most preferential having been for foreigners. From the beginning, the battle against the Old Regime and foreign domination were one and the same.[34]

The outcry against Yankees and other aliens had deep, popular roots. The man on the street, who gave an enthusiastic hearing to condemnations of Uncle Sam and company, had seldom shared the élite adulation of the foreigner. For too long, in his opinion, official favors had fallen on intimates of Díaz and outsiders.[35] As one observer remarked, in commenting upon the nature of Yankees; "At the start, the newcomers were few and useful; but later, when they arrived in droves, with every one hundred honest men a thousand rascals appeared, boasting of talent and money, and claiming to speak for large industries, but who in the long run, turn out to be scoundrels in frock coats of no help to anyone." [36] By 1910, as *El Tiempo* suggested, the middle class was not just staunchly Catholic but "solidly anti-American." [37]

When the last of the Old Regime had taken flight, every rebel leader of any stature had pledged undying loyalty to the *patria*, publicly castigated worship of the foreigner, and vigorously censured the role of the *gringo* in Mexico. Public disenchantment with Americans, as distinct from the ancient distrust of the United States, dates from about the turn of the century. By then, not only had wealthy Yankees carved for themselves deep enclaves in the Mexican economy, but popular delight with Díaz had begun to wane. In San Luis Potosí, the Liberal

Clubs of 1901, precursors of the rebel hordes, had declared Mexican nationalism to be a cornerstone of their gospel. "We are at peace with the foreigner," lamented Antonio Díaz Soto y Gama, "even though he exploits us." [38] Ricardo Flores Magón and his Partido Liberal Mexicano so exalted their nationalist creed that they drew the ire of federal and state authorities. In the summer of 1906, rumors of a coming uprising, apparently headed by adherents of the Partido Liberal, reached Mexico City. *El Imparcial,* not one to take the possibility of rebellion seriously, nevertheless discussed the rumor, reporting that it was to occur in the border states, with the sole objective of driving out foreigners, especially Americans, Germans, and Englishmen. [39] "Our foreign policy," wrote Francisco I. Madero in *La Sucesión Presidencial,* "always exhibits an exaggerated compliance with the desires of the United States." Foreigners, in his opinion, enjoyed privileges at the expense of Mexicans, calling attention to the railroads where the foreign bosses set aside the best jobs for Americans and discriminated against Mexicans. [40] Before a large audience in Pachuca, he deplored the exploitation of Mexican miners by giant American corporations. [41]

Madero's views, because he headed the rebellion of 1910, should not be overlooked. His successors, moreover, gave equal voice to the antiforeign sentiment. Cabrera called *extranjerismo,* the worship of the foreigner, a major cause of the rebellion. He charged that *extranjerismo* had unfairly given outsiders advantages over Mexicans. [42] "Among us," said Andrés Molina Enríquez, "the foreigner is the guest we implore to come and receive with outstretched arms but who, for his part, treats us shabbily." [43] Americans sat at the head table of the dinner set aside for the élite. Mexico, to the anguish of Molina Enríquez, confronted the danger of becoming another Cuba or Panama. From his perspective, the interests of foreigners threatened the sovereignty of the Republic "because once their stake is endangered, if Europeans, they will in the name of civilization call upon the United States for protection, and if Americans, they will act on their own; which means, in summary, that the United States will speak for and defend them all." [44] Or to cite Felipe Angeles, a Porfirista general, "All Mexicans feel a repugnance for Americans, a sentiment that springs from the sense of danger we intuitively harbor in our hearts." He "admired the United States, which I equate with ancient Rome," he explained, "but I do not want it, as Rome did, to conquer the world." [45] Rogelio Fernández Güell, a friend of Madero, director of the National Library and an author, feared Mexico "had been transformed into an enormous market to which people of all nationalities flocked to make their fortunes, converting it into a land of adventurers, without country, religion, or family, whose god was gold." [46] To José N. Macías, a moderate politician and lawyer, the prosperity of Mexico was undeniable, "but it was an elusive gift, that of foreign capitalists who oppressed the country in order to multiply their resources with almost biblical prodigality." [47] Roberto V. Pesqueira of Sonora called attention to the exploitation of Mexico "by conscienceless traders who by means of money prostituted the government to their own vile ends, obtaining concessions and sinecures displeasing and irritating to the popular mind and feelings." Worse still, "the moneyed and conservative classes, preferring the security and growth of their millions to the progress and honor of the country and the name of the race," had become "ready collaborators of these foreign pirates." [48] Even Victoriano Huerta, who was at least partly indebted to Henry Lane Wilson, the American ambassador, for his accession to the presidency, upbraided the exalted powers of the embassy, which, in his opinion, converted its occupant into the guardian of the conduct of Mexican officials.[49] Huerta, who pictures himself as a nationalistic knight, swore to safeguard "México para los mexicanos." [50]

Mexican nationalism, however, embraced more than just a censure of political and economic roles set aside for aliens. It was also an effort to cast off the baggage of centuries-old colonial attitudes. To Mexican intellectuals, the countrys' longed-for rebirth required a spiritual rupture with the past. They rejected the servile imitation of foreigners and castigated the Mexican unwillingness to develop its own intrinsic culture. *Modernismo,* a cultural stew concocted out of foreign "isms"—Parnassim, symbolism, and impressionism—merited special rebuke by the rebel intellectuals.[51] It was equated with the mentality of the old aristocracy, as represented by such institutions as the Jockey Club. The literary nationalists turned their backs on the *modernista* disciples of the *Revista Azul* and the *Revista Moderna,* abjuring the preoccupation of Amado Nervo, a poet laureate of the Old Regime, with the "unknown," while ridiculing the lament of his contemporary, Manuel Gutiérrez Nájera, who "mourned the solitude and sadness of the soul in pursuit of Alfred de Musset." José Juan Tablada labeled the concerns of Nervo and the *modernistas* a façade without substance. But it was Enrique González Martínez who best expressed the disgust with *modernismo* when he urged men of letters to "wring the neck of the swan," the swan being the trademark of the poetry of Ruben Darío, father of *modernismo.* For intellectuals of such views, *modernismo* symbolized the betrayal of political and social concerns and an accommodation with the status quo.[52]

Nationalism, therefore, included within its folds the support of the principal sectors among the rebels: fledgling brokers of political power; reformers of all stripes; middle-class office seekers and ambitious entrepreneurs; industrial workers who demanded equal pay for equal work; intellectuals who contemplated the ephemeral revolutionary soul as well as mural artists waiting to draw peasants in vivid colors on the walls of public buildings. Only the peasants, perhaps, had no direct involvement in the new nationalism; and as events document, with the exception of Emiliano Zapata and his followers in Morelos, they were latecomers to the revolutionary game.

IV

As Bulnes perceptively noted, attacks on the Old Regime implied censure of its investment policies that, in the opinion of the dissidents, had opened wide the doors to an unabated flood of foreign speculators. In accordance with this axiom of Mexican politics, a close correlation should exist between regions of heavy American investments, on the one hand, and foci of rebellion, on the other. And it did. The highly nationalistic north, the border provinces of Sonora, Chihuahua, and Coahuila, along with the Federal District, accounted for 90.0 percent of all foreign capital invested in Mexico.

FOREIGN INVESTMENTS, 1910 [53]

Place	Percent of Total
Federal District	62.8
Coahuila	9.5
Sonora	7.3
Chihuahua	6.3
Nuevo León	2.2
Sinaloa	1.4
Durango	1.4
Total	92.9

Sonora, a hotbed of discontent amply meets the conditions of Bulnes' axiom. By 1910, its economy had closer links with the United States than with Mexico. This relationship influenced even political decisions in Sonora which, in theory, were to have been made in Mexico City. Foreigners, primarily Americans, owned and controlled mining—the key to the state's economy—along with a growing number of agricultural, commercial, and ranching enterprises. The railroads, provided an outlet for its products, joining Sonora to the American Southwest. As early as 1902, Sonora had received the second largest amount of foreign investment in the Republic; about 70 percent of it was in mining. Along the Yaqui and Mayo rivers, farmers from California, taking advantage of the expulsion of the Yaquis, had purchased 100,000 acres of land and fifty miles of irrigation canals from the Richardson Company. They and farmers around Hermosillo shipped vegetables, garbanzos, and fruits to California markets. Americans owned nearly 2.5 million acres of land in Sonora by 1902—and even more in neighboring Sinaloa.[54] The names of the huge American agro-businesses were bywords in the state: The Sonora Land and Cattle Company, the Sinaloa and Sonora Irrigation Company, M. M. Sherman, and the Richardson Company, among others. *El Imparcial,* meanwhile, continued to report sales of land to American buyers. One in the spring of 1909 was for 15 million pesos for the purchase of lands in the Río Yaqui valley for the cultivation of grains, fruits, and vegetables for export to markets across the border.[55]

The alien invasion which accompanied the influx of capital

and was almost always American increasingly troubled the natives of Sonora. From their vantage point, strangers grew fat off
the resources of the state while Mexicans struggled to survive
on the leftovers. The historian Antonio G. Rivera writes that an
American arriving in Sonora "literally came home because his
compatriots were its owners, men of identical race with similar
prejudices, particularly feelings of racial superiority." He looked
upon Sonora as his bailiwick, demanding and obtaining the
privileges accorded the conqueror. He expected to hobnob with
the local élite, and if he so desired, to receive entrance to its
social circle, along with special protection from the authorities
of the state.[56] After all, were not Colonel William C. Greene,
the master of Cananea, and Ramón Corral, Sonora's political
boss, friends?

In addition, all of the foreign corporations had established
company towns. The largest were those of the Cananea Consolidated Copper Company, the Moctezuma Mining Company, El
Tigre Mining Company, and the Creston Mining Company.
The owners controlled everything in these towns: food, housing,
schools (when available), the police, and city hall. Competition
from local independent merchants was discouraged because it
endangered the profits of company stores.[57] A backlash to this
alien invasion was inevitable, not solely from the old vested interests, ultimately distrustful of the newcomers, but from the
new social classes. These classes, ironically, thrived with the development of the economy of Sonora which had been undertaken
largely with American dollars and markets. The booms spurred
by mining and railroad construction helped open additional
lands to farmers, but also cut into the *hacendados'* supply of cheap
labor, and so helped kindle the fires of nationalism. These labor
problems, plus the curtailment of credit due to the financial
crisis of 1907, shook loose Díaz' ties to the landed classes of
Sonora.[58] Between 1895 and 1910, the foreign colony of Sonora
grew from 1,370 to 9,328, and elsewhere in the northern provinces
more than doubled.[59]

The nationalist pot reached the boiling point with the attempt to drive the Yaquis from their lands and the uproar over
the strike at Cananea. The attack on the Yaquis, which endangered the pool of cheap agricultural labor, iinfuriated the south-

ern *hacendados,* especially since American farmers were often the beneficiaries. Not surprisingly, both the ire of the *hacendados* and the Yaquis focused on Americans. By 1906, according to *El Imparcial,* armed bands of marauding Yaquis threatened to make the Yaqui River valley as well as the mining zones unsafe for Americans.[60] At this juncture, labor troubles flared at Cananea. To put the strikers down and to safeguard American property, Governor Rafael Izábal shamefully brought in armed Americans from Arizona. News of Izábal's actions spread like wildfire across the Republic, raising loud cries of protest from nationalists. Even the puppet press, admitted Bulnes, took up the hue and cry, calling Izábal a "traitor to his country." [61] A letter to Enrique Creel subtly reveals the nature of anti-American prejudice in Sonora. Commenting on the strike, its author, a friend from Sonora of the pro-American Creel, merely remarked in passing that the strikers had killed "two *gringos.*" [62] Madero, who had expressed only marginal sympathy for the wage demands of the textile workers in Orizaba, publicly condemned the use of American mercenaries to squash the strike at Cananea. Díaz, he said, should have compelled the owners to pay higher wages.[63]

The story of Chihuahua follows closely that of Sonora. People in Chihuahua rebelled, writes the historian Francisco R. Almada, partly because of the preference given foreigners over Mexicans and the "inviolability of their privileges." [64] To quote another historian of the state, "the protection granted foreign capital and its enthusiastic reception by the local élite could not pass unnoticed." [65] As in Sonora, the lure of mining drew the bulk of foreign investment, either Anglo-American or American. Until approximately 1870, Mexicans had owned and controlled mining; after that date the picture changed, as more and more of both the old mining centers, and those recently opened fell under foreign domination. After 1884 when the government abolished the colonial mining codes banning monopolies and prohibiting the acquisition of subsoil rights, the invasion of Chihuahua took on the character of a gold rush. By 1910, recalls Almada, the foreign mining barons had staked out empires in Chihuahua. To protect their extraterritorial rights from Mexican intruders, he continued, they put up miles of barbwire fences, giving their properties "the appearance of foreign legations." The companies hired rifle-toting guards to patrol their properties, while their stores purchased and sold goods with their own currency.[66] With few exceptions, the foreign monopolies in mining kept the door shut to Mexicans.

The mining bonanza attracted other foreign entrepreneurs, again almost always from north of the border. With the arrival of Colonel Greene, of Cananea fame, the exploitation of the forests of the Sierra Madre Occidental began. Pine trees unfit for the sawmills were cut to fuel locomotives or burned as firewood in the company towns. More foreigners entered Chihuahua when Governor Creel exempted their investments from taxes and granted new concessions. Foreigners owned and ran the metallurgical plants of Aquiles Serdán, Parral, Villa Escobedo, San Martín, Jiménez, Lluvia de Oro, Calera Cusihuiriachi, and San Julián; the cement factory of Ciudad Juárez; the railroads between San Isidro and Calera and from Camargo to La Boquilla; the hydraulic plant on the Río Conchos; the natural gas plants in Ciudad Chihuahua and Parral; and the race track in Ciudad Juárez. The concession given the American Smelting and Refining Company to build a foundry on the outskirts of Ciudad Chihuahua included a thirty-year exemption from paying taxes. It also granted to Juan Terrazas, cousin and brother-in-law of the governor, the lucrative contract to operate the company store.[67] As the number of foreigners grew, so did the exemptions from taxes and other privileges multiply. Of the nearly 300 concessions given out between 1879 and 1910, almost all of which were granted to foreigners, over two-thirds came during the final six years.[68] The list included concessions for every conceivable enterprise from ice-making plants, telephone installation, trolley operation, the manufacture of horse-drawn wagons, to a special permit for a company to hire out domestics to clean private homes.[69]

The surveying companies, offsprings of the notorious Leyes de Tierras Baldías, meanwhile, had a field day in Chihuahua, not infrequently to the profit of foreigners. Only in Veracruz, Tabasco, Yucatán, and Chiapas did the companies taste similar success. One Mexican nationalist commented that the surveying companies were a plague worse than the conquering armies of Hernán Cortés because they stole from Mexicans in order to enrich foreigners.[70] Four American groups acquired huge empires in Chihuahua: William Randolph Hearst, 3.1 million acres; the Corralitos Cattle Company and the Palomas Land Company, 5 million acres; and the T. O. Ranch, 2.47 million acres.[71] To the anger of nationalists and Mexicans eager to acquire lands of their own, the foreigners joined with the Terrazas clan to convert Chihuahua into their personal preserve.

Chihuahua's economic dependency, its proximity to Texas and reliance on American markets, was another irritant. The construction of the railroad, which joined the state to El Paso, had opened the gates to a flood of American goods and to a pattern of economic growth often at odds with local interests. Mexican merchants and manufacturers suffered in the process. Further, Chihuahua sold its cattle and minerals, its chief exports, to American buyers, which placed local economic well-being at the mercy of foreigners. Americans, in short, helped control the destinies of the people of Chihuahua. When the Congress of the United States, for example, proposed to pass the Payne Bill in 1909, designed to protect American zinc miners, *El Imparcial* warned that it would ruin the zinc interests of Chihuahua.[72] To shield Mexican manufacturers and merchants from outside competition, the Mexican Congress in 1905 abolished the duty-free zone of Ciudad Juárez; however, this merely encouraged the contraband trade from Texas to grow by leaps and bounds.[73]

An incident which occurred on the eve of Madero's call to arms graphically depicts the depth of anti-American resentment in Chihuahua and in the Republic. Early in November, 1910, an angry mob in Rock Springs, Texas, killed Antonio Rodríguez, a young twenty-year-old Mexican accused of having killed an American woman. His body was then burned although some alleged that he had been burned alive. The police of Rock Springs did nothing to prevent the murder of Rodríguez. The Mexican response, which was not long in coming, shook Chihuahua. Protests flared nearly everywhere. In Ciudad Chihuahua, teachers and students staged a public rally to condemn the death of Rodríguez and to charge Texas authorities with complicity in the affair. To the wrath of Mexicans, the police of the city, at the behest of the American consul, arrested a teacher and six students for their roles in the demonstration.[74] A huge protest with strong anti-American overtones in Mexico City, again led by students, included attempts to burn the offices of *El Imparcial,* which had been accused by popular opinion of condoning the crime. Irate students and workers attacked American property in Guadalajara, stoned the American consulate in Ciudad Porfirio Díaz, a border town in Coahuila, and organized noisy marches in Veracruz, Monterrey, and Aguascalientes.[75]

The picture in Coahuila, though on a smaller scale, was similar. Of the manufactured products sold locally, 90 percent came from across the border.[76] Guayule exports, the second largest industry, depended on American markets and capital. The Carbonífera del Norte, an American corporation, and according to Governor Miguel Cárdenas, "one of the most powerful in the country," owned and ran the major coal mines.[77] Americans controlled large tracts of land: one company, Piedra Blanca, had over 1.2 million hectares; another, San José de las Piedras, 460,000 hectares.[78] As in Sonora, water rights became an additional source of conflict. It ultimately involved prominent Mexican families—including the Maderos—in a confrontation with foreign bankers, and clouded the politics of Coahuila and the Republic until the very end.

In 1887, Díaz had granted the Compañía Tlahualilo, which began as a Mexican syndicate, a permit to develop and colonize lands recently purchased from an *hacendado* in the Bolsón de Mapimí. To complicate matters the syndicate, originally subsidized by the sale of bonds on the English market by London bankers, defaulted on its payments.[79] The concession of 1887 included the right to dig an irrigation canal joining the Nazas River to the lands of the Tlahualilo group nearly thirty miles away. Despite modifications in 1891 and 1895, the concession survived virtually intact until 1908. The company dug the canal at the upper end of the Nazas, not far from the triangle of Torreón, Gómez Palacio, and Villa Lerdo. Since the Nazas originated in the western Sierra Madre of Durango, the canal, which was located at the upper end of the rich delta called La Laguna, provided direct access to the river water. Priority of access was a life-and-death matter to the planters of the Laguna because for most of the year the Nazas was a dry riverbed. Yet, despite the unreliable nature of the Nazas, the Laguna had blossomed into the foremost cotton region of the Republic.

The initial success of the Tlahualilo venture had attracted other up-river planters, and in time, scores of planters at the lower end of the delta. Díaz' decision, which is perhaps understandable in light of the sparse population of the area in 1887, severely penalized cotton planters along the lower banks of the Nazas who were all Mexicans. Among them was Francisco Madero, the father of the Apostle of 1910. Lively quarrels soon broke out between the rival bands of planters, leading to sabotage of irrigation canals and dams, and even to murder. As early as 1896, Francisco and his brother Evaristo had joined with their neighbors to complain to Díaz, who turned a deaf ear to their pleas.[80] Eventually, a series of droughts that exacerbated the plight of the lower *ribereños*, produced renewed demands that the government curtail the privileges of the foreign-controlled Compañía Tlahualilo and of other up-stream planters.

In December, 1907, a group of planters met with Díaz in Mexico City to air their grievances against the Compañía Tlahualilo, and the up-river *hacendados*.[81] In response, the following year, Olegario Molina, minister of *fomento*, sharply modified the terms of the original concession, giving the planters along the lower banks exclusive rights to the waters of the Nazas between the twentieth days of August and September of each year.[82] When the Compañía Tlahualilo objected and Mexican courts ruled against it, its directors, then appealed to Washington.[83] However, Díaz ignored the protest, and upheld the revised concession.

Unfortunately for the aged ruler, his courage satisfied no one. The Maderos and their neighbors, who saw themselves as the victims of two decades of exploitation by the Tlahualilo company and up-river *hacendados*, hardly felt like celebrating a victory that kept their lands parched until late August. At the same time, the ruling damaged not merely the Tlahualilo interests but the large up-river *haciendas* which, while numerically few, had large numbers of tenant farmers and sharecroppers who, unable to irrigate their lands, abandoned them to swell the ranks of the penniless and unemployed.[84] The propaganda of rebellion fell upon their sympathetic ears. Antonio Manero called the clash in the Laguna one of the causes of the crisis of 1907. For nationalists, the conflict in the Laguna ended with an ironic twist. Luis Cabrera, who became a patriotic firebrand and prophet of rebellion, was one of the lawyers for the Compañía Tlahualilo, a foreign concern, while Jorge Vera Estañol, soon to be in the cabinet of Victoriano Huerta, and Manuel Calero, a cabinet officer under Madero but considered an enemy by the rebels, handled the government's case in court, which in essence was a defense of nationalist groups.[85]

Only in Monterrey, the capital of neighboring Nuevo León, did a core of ambitious and intelligent Mexican entrepreneurs survive the invasion of American capital. United by ties of blood and marriage, the Monterrey oligarchy not only managed to keep control of its fledgling industries but to expand its activities and to coexist with the large American corporations which eventually established themselves in the city. Still, the Guggenheims, a powerful American family, owned the largest iron and steel mill. And even in Monterrey, the native owners of manufacturing plants and stores learned to ask the federal goverment to protect them from outside competition.

Nationalists groups in San Luis Potosí, however, fared less well. During the depression of the 1890s which damaged the economy of the state, many of its leading citizens had applauded the arrival of American investors as an opportunity to recuperate lost fortunes.[86] Between 1897 and 1911, American investments multiplied fifteenfold. Americans gained control of the two principal elements of the state's economy: mining and the railway grid. The Guggenheims alone owned railroads and smelters for gold, lead, silver, zinc, cobalt, antimony, bismuth, and sulfur.[87] It was a case of too much American investment. Some of the families, who had earlier welcomed the foreigners, lived to regret their decision. Camilo Arriaga, a scion of such a family, whose father once owned one of the largest silver mines in San Luis Potosí, became a fervent nationalist, a founder of Liberal Clubs, and an enemy of Díaz. Another wealthy Mexican, Pedro Barrenechea, the state's leading native industrialist, helped Madero escape from San Luis Potosí after his arrest. Barrenechea, who had built his fortune by cooperating with foreigners, apparently saw an opportunity to add to it by eliminating his competitors.[88]

With the debacle of 1907, a similar outcry against Americans arose in Yucatán. Faced with financial disaster because of the drop in the price of henequen, growers, in Yucatán blamed the International Harvester Corporation, their chief customer. Beleaguered planters accused the monopolistic company of fixing prices at their expense.[89] In former years, the planters claimed, they had controlled the banks, the railroads of Yucatán, and the henequen industry; but now, after Americans had purchased large blocs of stock in the henequen industry, the foreigners, in conjunction with the Díaz clique, made key economic and political decisions.[90] Even *El Imparcial,* never very nationalistic, took up the hue and cry, urging a search for new markets for henequen in Europe and South America in order to free Yucatán from dependence on Yankee customers, upon whom it placed the responsibility for the henequen fiasco.[91] It was in Yucatán that José María Pino Suárez, a young lawyer and later vice-president under Madero, first won acclaim through his efforts to organize a Comisión Reguladora del Henequén to shield small growers from the "price-fixing tactics" of International Harvester.[92]

Obviously, nationalism, no matter how broadly defined, cannot alone be held accountable for the explosion of 1910. Yet, without taking into account the nationalism which had swept the country, which often bordered on xenophobia, no combination of events or ideas adequately explains why untold numbers of middleclass and wealthy Mexicans gambled their lives and fortunes on armed rebellion. Unquestionably, envy and distrust of Americans and other aliens occupied center stage in the unfolding drama.

EIGHT

Watershed of Rebellion

"*In the same year it surfaced in the United States, the economic crisis broke out in Mexico and, because it contaminated even Europe, hit us with double intensity.*"

Antonio Manero

I

AT A CRUCIAL juncture in the unfolding of rebellion, frequently one event ignites the fuse. The German defeat of Czarist Russia in 1915 toppled the aristocratic rulers and ultimately opened the doors to Lenin and his Communist allies. Historians write that the Intolerable Acts led the Thirteen Colonies to rebel against their English king. In Cuba Fulgencio Batista's cynical usurpation of power in 1952 undermined a regime which dated from the Spanish-American War. In Mexico, the financial crisis of 1907, an event which marked the swan song of fourteen years of prosperity, revealed gaping flaws in the national economic and social structure, and became the watershed of the rebellion.[1] Until the debacle paralyzed mining, commerce, and industry, the people paid homage to the Mexican miracle; with its onset, even former disciples of the Old Regime began to listen to the oracles of change.[2]

No class escaped the repercussions of 1907. For the beneficiaries of the years of progress, the unexpected financial crisis dashed hopes of greater things to come, lowering expectations, and shutting the gates to upward social mobility. The middle class was the hardest hit. Lawyers, physicians, engineers, bureaucrats, teachers, and small merchants saw their dreams evaporate in the wake of the economic disaster. Unemployment, poor wages, and a sharp rise in the cost of living, particularly in food prices, aggravated the already difficult plight of the army of workers in mines, railroads, and industry. Worse still, to stay afloat and to protect profit margins, foreign owned and controlled corporations cut wages and jobs; the small Mexican merchant often had to go out of business.[3] *El Imparcial,* which had previously been known for its running commentary on the Mexican miracle, carried more and more stories on the bankruptcies of commercial houses.[4] Before 1907, recalled Julio Sesto, the pages of *El Imparcial* advertised jobs in Mexico City for carpenters, masons, and painters"; but "the crisis and universal poverty tempered . . . the enthusiasm of those advertisements that were a hymn to Mexican progress." The depression, continued Sesto, had deeply hurt the housing industry, which had employed the largest number of workers in the capital.[5] Even distant Oaxaca, isolated from contact with the modern world, felt the reverberations of the crisis. Faced with huge losses in sales, merchants in its capital city dismissed employees and reduced salaries.[6] Despite talk of recovery by 1909 due to the encouraging rise in exports, the national economy, *El Imparcial* conceded a year later, still limped along. The last year of prosperity had been 1906.[7] Ironically, the tide of rebellion swept Díaz out of office as the depression began to recede; Mexico had a healthier balance of trade in 1911 than a year earlier.[8]

The financial disaster had no single cause. As Antonio Manero, banker, economist, and ambitious politician, remarked, multiple ills sapped the vigor of the economy.[9] The international financial panic of 1907, set in motion by events in the United States, headed the list. For all intents and purposes, the welfare of the Mexican economy was determined by decisions made by outsiders. The proximity of its northern neighbor, commercial ties nurtured by the railroad network joining the two countries together, and above all, heavy investments of American capital, explained Manero, made Mexico a tributary of the United States.[10] Only Cuba exported more to the United States, while Mexico ranked first among America's customers.[11] The crisis, Díaz informed Congress in 1908, by reducing the value of Mexico's exports, had rocked the foundations of its prosperity.[12]

Díaz' message had relevance nowhere more than in the

northern provinces. All of their economies depended on their neighbors across the border for the markets that kept them alive. The railroads carried northward nearly everything grown or dug out of the soil, mining ores as well as vegetables and fruits from Sonora for California markets, cattle from Chihuahua for the Kansas City stockyards, and cotton and guayule from Coahuila. Falling prices hurt large sectors of the population of the northern states. The drop in the price of cotton, for example, cut into the income of influential planters in Coahuila, among them the Maderos. Only the timely intervention of Ernesto Madero saved the family from bankruptcy.[13]

The hostile winds struck Chihuahua especially hard. According to *El Correo*, the state suffered keenly because its welfare was largely dependent on foreign capital.[14] Inhabitants of western Chihuahua, a mining and lumbering center, bore the brunt of the depression. Much of their fate was tied up with that of William C. Greene, a mining baron with a concession to exploit the forests of the districts of Galeana and Guerrero. Greene built lumber mills, a paper manufacturing plant, and a furniture factory. He became active in commerce and banking, and brought the Ferrocarril Noroeste de México to Madera, the heart of his empire. To develop his mining stake, the Greene Gold Silver Company, he cut a road through mountains thought impenetrable to link Temocáchic with the mining camps of Concheño and Ocampo. A marvel of engineering skill, the road was the first in Chihuahua. Both in Sonora and Chihuahua, the crisis of 1907 struck Greene's empire with devastating force. In a futile attempt to rescue his investments in Cananea, Greene shut down or curtailed operations in Galeana and Guerrero. It was to no avail. He lost control of his mining corporation, valued at $25 million dollars, and fared equally poorly with the Sierra Madre Land and Lumber Company.[15] Greene's debacle shattered the economy of the region. Merchants and small businessmen lost everything while over 2,000 workers and their families, reported *El Correo*, faced starvation.[16] To quell the anguished protest of the jobless, authorities brought in *rurales*.[17]

In the course of time, all of Mexico felt the explosion that rocked the districts of Galeana and Guerrero. The rebellion of Chihuahua grew out of its aftermath. A socialist member of the

Partido Liberal Mexicano, Praxedis G. Guerrero, fired the opening salvo in the summer of 1908 in the district of Galeana. His protest failed but Pascual Orozco, who ran wagon trains between the mining camps, continued the revolt. On December 4, 1910, Orozco captured Ciudad Guerrero, one of the initial victories of the dissidents in Chihuahua. There Orozco issued his strident *Manifiesto*, which formally called for the fall of Díaz and for reform. One of those who listened was Abraham González, a native of Guerrero with his future behind him. Early in 1911, Francisco I. Madero set up his revolutionary junta in Ciudad Guerrero, and with Orozco, moved northward along the tracks of the Ferrocarril Noroeste to attack Ciudad Juárez.[18]

In world trade, which decided whether Mexicans enjoyed the fruits of plenty or languished in hard times, mining ranked first in importance, exercising a tyrannical control. No one questioned the link between its prosperity and foreign markets; it was obvious even to the man on the street. The world economic debacle, as indicated earlier, wrought havoc to the mining industry, which had been the key to the golden years. A growing imbalance in trade resulted during 1905–06, the value of Mexican exports suffered a loss of 14 million pesos, while the value of imports rose by over 21 million pesos. An editorial in *El Imparcial* explained that the imbalance stemmed principally from a fall in the volume and value of mineral exports, in gold and silver as well as in copper and lead. At the same time the rate of decline increased precipitously after 1907.[19]

The misfortunes of silver, Mexico's venerable export, damaged many sectors of the economy.[20] Its problems, however, antedated the depression of 1907. The spectre of falling silver prices had haunted the entire history of the Díaz regime. In the 1850s, a brief decline in gold production had set off a frantic race by miners to sell silver. To share in the supposed bonanza, Díaz modified the mining codes in 1881 to encourage foreign investors to develop the silver mines. With the new legislation, Mexico's production of silver expanded rapidly. To Mexico's sorrow however, while investors sank fortunes into silver mining, and Mexican silver entered the market in larger amounts, more and more countries abandoned bimetalism for the gold standard. Even China and India, traditional customers stopped buying silver, while the United States, France, and Japan began to mint their own silver coin in place of the peso.[21] In 1892, the bottom fell out of the silver market, the price of silver plunged downward and by 1905 "the Mexican peso had largely lost its ancient and honorable place in the daily commerce of hundreds of millions of human beings." [22]

The stagnant but "kept" silver industry hurt business, labor, the railroads, agriculture, and the government itself. The value of the peso was pegged, until late in the Díaz era, to the price of silver. By fixing its currency to silver, Mexico built a tariff wall around itself. When the price of silver on the world market fell, everything purchased abroad or made with imported materials cost dearly, far beyond the buying power of labor and even the middle classes. The tariff wall placed workers and families on limited incomes at the mercy of inefficient Mexican businessmen and manufacturers hungry for profits. The noncompetitive textile industry, for instance, survived on its monopoly of the manufacture and sale of coarse cotton cloth to workers and peasants. For a brief period, too, the low value of the peso had benefited the exporters of tropical goods, particularly henequen; by paying the cost of its production in pesos, and then selling the product abroad for dollars, the planters had multiplied their profits. The lucrative exchange ended with the growing popularity of manila hemp and the substitution of baling wire for henequen fiber by farmers in the American Midwest.

Until the departure of Díaz, Mexicans watched the ups and downs of silver with apprehension. Its decline, added to the drop in sales of other metals, which by 1906 had begun to undercut the wages of over 100,000 miners and their families, and indirectly, threaten the wages and salaries of tens of thousands of Mexicans engaged in commerce and industry. Mexican newspapers faithfully reported the price of silver, periodically predicting an upturn on such fallacious assumptions as the eventual need for more silver coin because of the population growth of the United States.[23] Yet, until the bitter end, Díaz' messages to Congress laconically lamented the absence of any improvement in the price of silver. On the eve of the rebellion, the silver depression had paralyzed one mining sector and all of its subsidiary industries; and, warned *El Imparcial,* "nobody can predict how

long the crisis will last." [24] The drop in the price of silver ultimately compelled Mexico to adopt the gold standard, a decision
that temporarily, at least, victimized a large segment of the
population. One of the states to suffer was Sonora where, from
1906 on, silver mines began to close. Abandoned mining camps
came to dot the landscape of the district of Alamos, heart of
the old bonanza.

When the bottom fell out of the market for copper in 1906,
the mining industry, especially in Sonora, received another
blow. Since the birth of the electrical industry in the United
States, Americans had rushed to Sonora to exploit its rich deposits of copper. Colonel William C. Greene, who had established a copper kingdom in Cananea, was one of them. By 1905,
Cananea, the biggest copper camp in the world, had become one
of the largest cities in Sonora. In 1880, Mexico had exported copper worth 260,000 pesos; by 1906 the value of the copper shipped
abroad had jumped to 32 million pesos, nearly all of which
came from Sonora. Mexico was the world's third leading pro-
ducer of copper.[25] Then, in 1907 Greene was forced to shut
down his mines. Although he partly reopened some the next year,
Greene himself admitted that the jobless filled the streets of
Cananea. Many of them fled to Arizona and California. By 1911,
Cananea had lost two-fifths of its inhabitants, and not until that
year did its mines again pay dividends to their shareholders.
The copper doldrums spread like a cancer throughout Sonora,
shutting mines in the districts of Alamos and in Altar, already
damaged by the fall in the price of silver. Storekeepers in
Guaymas, the commercial capital of the state, felt the effects of
the mining slump. By 1908, conceded *El Imparcial,* Guaymas no
longer participated in prosperity.[26] On May 9, 1911, Cananea
fell to Juan Cabral and his men, the first city in Sonora to be
captured by rebels.[27]

Ultimately, the economic troubles engulfed every mining
state. The misfortunes of silver, to cite Governor Esteban
Fernández, dealt heavy blows to the economy of Durango, a
state which joined the rebellion early on.[28] Sesto visited
Guanajuato in the midst of a "depression" in 1909.[29] All twenty-
two mines in Taviche, a district in Oaxaca, were closed down;
shortly after, the Oaxaca Smelting Company went bankrupt.[30]

According to *El Imparcial,* with the end of operations at Real del Monte, "a crisis of alarming proportions" befell Pachuca, the capital of Hidalgo; approximately 1,000 jobless miners roamed the streets in search of work.[31] Mines in Coahuila and Nuevo León shut down. The closing of the Compañía de Peñoles left 3,000 workers without jobs and greatly diminished the sales of storekeepers in nearby Mapimí.[32] To aggravate the problem, the prosperity of textile mills in Coahuila, as well as in Chihuahua and Nuevo León, began to decline. Between 1901 and 1910, the labor force had dropped by 75 percent in the mills of Coahuila, and by 40 percent in Nuevo León. As Madero debated whether to rebel or not, industry in Coahuila employed 10,000 fewer workers than ten years earlier. Victimized by its mining problems, its cotton and guayule exports in trouble, and forced to accept a governor not of its choice, Coahuila became a haven for political malcontents.

II

Shortcomings of a different sort, meanwhile, exacerbated the difficulties created by the vagaries of the international markets. The years of prosperity had encouraged a wave of speculation in land, mines, and industry. Intoxicating prices for raw material and minerals, prompted marginal buying on the stock exchange, and fostered unstable growth in mining and agriculture. With easy profits at hand, mining speculators, planters of cotton, henequen, and guayule, and merchants expanded their operations, and then, with only limited capital, began the process all over again.[33] Eager to share in the prosperity, friends and relatives gambled their savings on the venture. When the bottom fell out of the boom, and banks proved unable to cover the losses, speculators and planters alike were faced with bankruptcy. With sizeable new investments, the northern provinces suffered particularly.

To complicate the picture, the depression triggered a banking panic that shook the entire financial structure of Mexico. No region escaped its effects. It was so severe that the government had to take drastic measures to uphold the value of the peso on the international market. At home, merchants, business-men, shopkeepers, farmers, and *hacendados* alike were con-fronted with shortages of money which, to quote Díaz' message to Congress in 1907, could be described without "hyperbole." [34] Again the next year he acknowledged the inability of the Treasury to come to the aid of commerce and business caught in the grips of the tight money situation.[35] When funds to rescue falter-ing enterprises could not be found, the economy ground to a halt, ending, *El Imparcial* complained, "the prosperity of Mexico." [36]

From the regime's perspective, factors it could not control had created the monetary disaster. Prior to 1907, between 50 and 60 million pesos of foreign investment had entered Mexico an-nually, explained Toribio Esquivel Obregón. When the finan-cial panic hit the United States—Mexico's principal source of outside funds—Mexico was cut off from the capital needed to develop its resources. Meanwhile, Mexican banks, unable to count on government aid and with their capital tied up in long-term loans, could not come to the rescue of ailing enterprises. Particularly acute was the shortage of funds for long-term loans. Esquivel Obregón placed the responsibility for the bank's pre-dicament on creditors who, having borrowed large sums, refused to pay off their obligations.[37] Whatever the merits of this de-batable assumption, the shortage of long-term loans chiefly punished the small entrepreneur. The wealthy, as Esquivel Obregón recognized, nearly always had access to short-term credit.[38] However, in the opinion of the small businessman or farmer, confronted with the loss of his life's savings, the banks could not loan money because they refused to foreclose on loans and mortgages held by the pampered rich, especially the landed barons. There was some truth in this view: *hacendados,* many of them relatives or friends of the bankers, held from 70 to 80 percent of all bank loans.[39]

Without reserves to meet the monetary crisis, the banks turned to the government for help. But the regime, unwilling to dip into its limited savings, refused to shore up the banks. Mexican officials believed that spending any part of the 32 mil-

lion pesos in the Treasury would have jeopardized the stability
of the national government.[40] Still, in an effort to head off a
wave of banking failures in Yucatán, the hardest hit province,
the national banks ultimately had to provide loans. Determined
to put an end to the banking scandals that had all but destroyed
public confidence in the financial world, Mexican officials in
1908 at an emergency meeting convoked to discuss the critical
situation, urged bankers to alter drastically their loan and credit
policies.[41] In addition, to end the flagrant speculation of bankers—the practice of lending large sums with insufficient capital in
reserve—the government enacted legislation requiring adequate
guarantees for loans.[42] Although obviously a necessary measure,
the legislation left unmet the urgent need for emergency financial aid, and in the case of the *hacendados* of Yucatán, already
heavily mortgaged but begging for further loans to save their
beleaguered empires, it set off a loud outcry against the *cientificos* in government. But in the opinion of Francisco Bulnes,
one of the *cientificos*, the legislation brought to a close the
hacendados' scandalous practice of "robbing . . . the banks." [43]
Contrary to this logic, the banking reform in Yucatán helped
bring about one of the first uprisings against the regime. Its
leaders had the enthusiastic backing of many unhappy *hacendados*. Delio Cantón, one of the rebel lords, was a bankrupt
merchant.[44]

The plight of the state banks revealed by the crisis of 1907
had old roots. A law in 1896 had authorized their establishment
under the nominal control of the Banco Nacional de México,
the central bank in the days of Limantour. The law required
each new bank to possess a minimum capital of no less than
500,000 pesos, half in cash assets. In actuality, the patrons of the
banks invested little of their own money. Generally, the Banco
Nacional granted a concession to friends of the regime who then
founded a state bank with the collaboration of local groups. To
finance their operation, the investors sold shares of stock in the
banks, paying the lucrative interest rate of 25 percent, and then
purchased the shares themselves. Later, using the money of their
depositors, from which they collected their interest payments,
they made low-interest loans to themselves and their friends.[45]

Such were the shaky credit transactions that from the start jeopardized the financial structure of the banks. Many of the loans were made with little provision for their repayment to *hacendados* who mortgaged lands of questionable value. With the collapse of land prices and other investments during the 1907 crisis, the flimsy banking edifice broke apart. Unable to collect on their loans, many provincial banks had to close their doors, wiping out the savings of depositors and cutting off loans to frantic planters, ranchers, miners, and merchants. The reforms of 1908, deemed essential by *El Imparcial* in order to end once and for all a "vicious system" that limited credit to a circle of friends of the banks, pitted provincial banking interests against the Banco Nacional, the organ of the federal administration.[46] The critics of Limantour claimed that his policies exacerbated the credit crunch and favored the interests of the Banco Nacional over the public welfare.[47]

Anger over the new banking policy had dire consequences in the provinces. As indicated previously, it encouraged a revolt in Yucatán. In San Luis Potosí, the tightening of credit helped drive Toribio Esquivel Obregón, an *hacendado,* and ironically, briefly Limantour's successor in the Treasury, into the arms of Madero.[48] A bank debt of 200,000 pesos and the threat of foreclosure encouraged José María Maytorena, a land-poor *hacendado* in Sonora, to take up arms against Díaz.[49] In Coahuila, the planters of the Laguna filed a public protest against the new banking formulas.[50]

However, despite public anger, the reforms were long overdue. The state banks had been blind to the national interest, but, what is more, had acted with malfeasance. In Chihuahua, for instance, it was suddenly learned in 1908 that a glaring shortage of funds had been discovered in the Banco Minero, the state's leading bank, which was controlled by the Terrazas-Creel clan. Local authorities, the same Terrazas-Creel gang, blamed the loss on three employees of the bank.[51] But Silvestre Terrazas, the crusading editor of the leading newspaper in Chihuahua, placed the responsibility for the shortage with the bank's directors, an accusation substantiated in the course of time.[52] The failure of the Sociedad Cooperativista de Ahorros e Inversiones de Sonora, an institution established to aid small enterprise, wiped out the savings of artisans, workers, and clerks.[53] No part of Mexico escaped the plague of bank failures, which were almost always accompanied by charges of mismanagement or wrongdoing. The Banco de Jalisco failed while the Banco de Michoacán required federal assistance to weather the storm. The Banco de Oaxaca survived only by merging with sister banks in Puebla. Huge losses were suffered by the Banco de Veracruz. In Mexico City it was common knowledge that the Banco de Londres y México was in deep trouble. The Banco Central went bankrupt, as did the Compañía Bancaria de Bienes Raíces. Even the Banco Nacional de México, according to Bulnes, had "water in its wine caskets." [54]

III

Yucatán, home of the henequen planters, probably felt the hammer blows of the financial disaster most acutely. Its population suffered the entire range of ills engendered by the failure of the national economy.

As the spring of 1907 turned into summer Mexicans heard to their surprise that the commercial and financial house of Eusebio Escalante Peón, Yucatán's leading business, had gone bankrupt. Behind the debacle lay the story of henequen, the lifeblood of the province. From 1898 to 1902, the ancient land of the Maya had enjoyed a henequen boom about which not even the boldest of the planters had dared to dream. In 1898, the 418,972 bales of henequen fiber of that year had sold for less than 19 million pesos; in 1902, less than half a decade later, the planters had produced 528,246 bales and sold them for 36.5 million pesos.[55] The future of the henequen lords looked bright indeed.

Unfortunately for them, a slow decline set in during the following year. Despite a growth in the number of bales produced, their value began to drop, and continued to decrease in 1907. In 1910, when rebellion broke out in the town of Valladolid, the planters, although able to produce over 30,000 more bales of henequen than in 1902, sold it for less than half of its value nearly a decade before. Edmundo Bolio, a historian of

Yucatán, labeled 1910 the year of "despair." When Díaz fled Mexico City, 170,000 unsold bales of henequen lay rotting in the warehouses of the port of Progreso. No catastrophe of such magnitude had ever occurred before.[56]

PRODUCTION AND VALUES OF HENEQUEN [57]

Year	Bales	Total Value
1902	528,246	36,432,791 pesos
1903	590,430	33,331,154
1904	606,006	32,022,581
1905	587,289	29,625,430
1906	599,566	27,247,222
1907	611,485	24,874,317
1908	652,498	20,777,016
1909	567,427	20,214,627
1910	558,996	17,886,474

Its antecedents dated from the late nineteenth century, when the *hacendados* of Yucatán discovered a heavy demand for henequen fiber on the world market. To meet the calls for fiber, the *hacendados,* following in the footsteps of the sugar planters in Morelos, began to modernize and to expand their operations. They imported the latest machinery for their mills and installed giant steam plants for power. To connect the mills with the henequen fields and with the port of Progreso, from which cargo ships carried the fiber to foreign markets, the planters built a network of narrow-gauge railroads. Hungry mills required more land upon which to plant the slow-maturing henequen. To satisfy the demand and to maximize their profits, the rapacious planters fell upon the adjoining lands of the Maya people, eventually driving them into open rebellion. They put the insurrection down with the aid of federal troops. To finance the modernization and growth of their empires, the planters borrowed heavily from the banks of Yucatán. By the early years of the twentieth century, only the burgeoning markets for Henequen fiber kept the planters abreast of their mortgage payments.

Yucatán built a lopsided economy in the course of this transformation. Its welfare, as was the case of the northern provinces, was dependent upon foreign buyers. Sales of chicle, cattle hides, handicrafts made from tortoise shells, and tropical fruits complimented but hardly helped to diversify the economy. In the meantime, Yucatán annually imported from abroad up to 12 million pesos of machinery, railroad equipment, hardware, ironmongery, lumber, huge quantities of construction materials, clothing, luxury items, carriages, wagons, and automobiles, while purchasing in Mexico goods costing from 13 to 19 million pesos a year.[58] Worse still, Yucatán purchased food, even corn, to feed itself. Despite booming sales of henequen, the fragile economy teetered on a razor's edge.

In the years of henequen's glory, all but the poor lived a splendid prosperity. Relying on their income from the sale of the yellow fiber, and with unlimited credit in Mexico and the United States, the planters squandered millions on luxuries. Ostentatious *hacendados*, rumor had it, had even taken their carriages and their horses on their travels abroad.[59] Houses in Mérida, the capital of Yucatán, and the social Mecca of the *hacendados* when they were not in Mexico City or visiting Europe, sold for many times their original cost. It was in the countryside, nonetheless, where the inflation of property values ran rampant; land once worth 10,000 pesos sold for eight or ten times more.[60] With wealthy customers at their doors, the merchants of Mérida amassed large profits selling at stiff prices goods from well-stocked storerooms.

But the prosperity rested on credit. The buying and selling, the imports of goods, and the bank loans presupposed ever-widening markets for henequen. It was an era of frenzied speculation on the stock exchange, and in *haciendas* and urban real estate at inflated prices. To increase the profits bank directors gambled their reserves on spurious investments and rode the crest of the wave of speculation.[61] By 1907, the landed barons of Yucatán, as well as the merchants and bankers who depended on them for their well-being, spent more than they earned. When the henequen market collapsed as a result of the crisis of 1907 and from the competition of Philippine manila hemp the speculative prosperity disintegrated. With money no longer available to fill their empty coffers, the banks began to foreclose on their loans to merchants and planters.[62] For a while debtors, with the consent of the banks, managed to forestall their creditors by postponing payments on their obligations or by borrowing at ruinous rates from private lenders. Eventually, however, the banks that survived the storm had to take over bankrupt properties.

At the same time, the incapacity of *hacendados,* the principal beneficiaries of bank loans, to meet payments on their mortgages, touched off widespread banking failures. The banking debacle, which had severe consequences for the province, shook the banking structure of the entire Republic as well. The banks of Yucatán, with assets of 25 million pesos, ranked second in importance only to institutions in Mexico City.[63] Again, their collapse revealed not just the faulty judgment of their directors but wrongdoing. An investigation of a theft of 740,000 pesos from the Banco Yucateco, the leading institution in the state, inculpated its former director who had absconded with the federal funds recently granted the bank to weather the crisis.[64] El Mercantil, another major bank, went bankrupt.[65] When the banks tottered, the financial house of Mexico erected on sand fell apart.

By May 1907, the list of business failures included the light and power company of Yucatán, its transport system, and the theater patronized by the social élite of Mérida. The debacle of the railroad trust, with shares worth millions of pesos, raised bitter outcries from investors. Homes with mortgages of 80,000 pesos sold for less than half of that amount—when an occasional buyer appeared—with huge losses to the creditors. One young *hacendado,* reported *El Imparcial,* whose fabulous climb to riches had permitted him to hobnob with financial tycoons and ostentatiously to claim the title of "marquis," became as "poor as the proverbial Job." [66] In Mérida, the building boom disappeared; blocks of new houses—nearly 1,000 of them—in the suburbs of Santa Ana and Santiago, built by workers brought in from other parts of the Republic and even from Spain, stood empty.[67] With home construction at a standstill and the program of public works cancelled, workers by the droves abandoned the city. Those who remained swelled the ranks of the unemployed. Their customers gone, and having previously sold untold quantities of merchandise on credit, stores in Mérida closed. On the plantations, meanwhile, *hacendados* cut wages which at fifty centavos a day—or twice the national average for rural labor—had earlier attracted workers from central Mexico to Yucatán.[68] The railroads, in dire financial straits, but still a major employer, slashed wages by 25 percent which was received without a whimper of protest from their labor force.[69]

To cope with the alarming situation, the planters took steps to curtail production and to limit sales in order to control prices, first through their Cámara Agrícola and then by forming a Sociedad Cooperativa de Henequén. The effort at united action stumbled almost immediately when *hacendados* with heavy mortgage payments to meet broke ranks and sold their fiber to the highest bidder.[70] Seeking to find paying customers, merchants asked authorities in Mexico City to renew the modernization of the port of Progreso, both to restore public confidence in the stability of Yucatán and to provide jobs for potential consumers.[71] Quite understandably, planters in search of a scapegoat began to blame the Díaz administration for the fall of henequen prices. According to them, a small clique led by Olegario Molina and his successor, Enrique Muñoz Arístegui, had manipulated prices for its own benefit with the blessings of Díaz and the henequen "trust." [72]

To hardly anyone's surprise, the campaign to re-elect Díaz encountered a frigid reception in Yucatán. Newspapers in Mexico City even carried accounts of heated activity opposing his re-election on the peninsula. One native of Yucatán briefly considered the idea of running against Díaz' choice for governor. Sesto, an avid admirer of the strongman in the capital, acknowledged what he called "momentary political disturbances" in his travels in Yucatán in 1909.[73] But *El Imparcial* probably came closer to the truth when it complained that "the violence of political agitators knew no limits." Young men from the best families, it went on, spent their time throwing stones at the headquarters of the Unión Democrática, the official political organization.[74] Enemies with a more practical bent, during the interval, attempted to entice the military to rebel.[75] In June 1909, Francisco I. Madero made Yucatán one of his stops in his campaign for the presidency. Nearly 600 admirers braved the ire of local officials to welcome Madero upon his arrival in Mérida. It was also of key significance that one of the first labor unions emerged in Yucatán: the Unión Obrera de los Ferrocarriles de Yucatán.[76]

Events came to a head in June, 1910, when a band of armed

men under the leadership of an army colonel, a former public official, and the *mayordomo* of an hacienda attacked the garrison at Valladolid. Before fleeing, the rebels killed the mayor and sacked the stores.[77] Unfortunately for the cause of reform, the uprising represented narrow political goals. The henequen *hacendados* and their allies advocated political change and not social reform. Once Díaz had fallen and the price of henequen taken an upturn, the ruling *hacendados* gave no further encouragement to revolutionaries. And later in the Revolution with Madero dead, the man Madero had appointed governor of Yucatán—an intimate ally of the *hacendados*—quickly telegraphed his allegiance to Victoriano Huerta, the foe of all rebels.[78]

IV

When Madero and his supporters began to clamor for an end to the Old Regime, the crisis of 1907, with its attendant widespread banking failures, the precipitous drop in the value of mining exports, and the inability of a decrepit agricultural system to take up the slack, in short, an economic depression, had brought the recent progress of Mexico to a standstill. As one bankrupt landlord of Coahuila summed up the picture, a man who had formerly owned stocks in both the local electrical and regional telephone companies, the banking crisis and the foreclosure of his mortgage had cost him everything.[79] Of such disasters rebels are made.

PART II THE CAST OF CHIEFTAINS

NINE

Francisco I. Madero:

Apostle of a Gentlemen's

Rebellion

"The caudillo of the bourgeois revolution whom the bour-geoisie refused to understand."

José Fuentes Mares

I

IN HIS Plan de San Luis Potosí, Francisco I. Madero, dubbed the Apostle by his admirers, set November 20, 1910 as the date to storm the barricades of the Old Regime. Few Mexicans took Madero seriously for only a handful of foolhardy souls answered his call to arms. One reason, perhaps, is that the credentials of the candidate lacked authenticity, especially if Revolution were indeed the goal. A son of the élite of Coahuila, as he acknowledged in his book, *La Sucesión Presidencial en 1910,* Madero was born with a silver spoon in his mouth. "I belong by birth," he confessed, "to the privileged class; my family is one of the largest and most powerful in Coahuila." He added revealingly, "neither I nor any member of my family has the slightest complaint against General Díaz, nor against his ministers, nor against the governor of this state, nor even against the local authorities." [1] Yet history picked this quixotic figure, a spiritualist who spent countless hours contemplating the mysteries of the unknown, to head a rebellion that overthrew the most entrenched regime in Mexican history. Not only did he ignite the tinderbox but his ideals survived his death, and despite modifications, set the tone for much of what occurred in the years ahead. In Madero, therefore, lies a clue to the nature of the Great Rebellion.

The son of the master of the Hacienda del Rosario, Madero was just thirty-seven-years old when he confronted the omnipotent Porfirio Díaz. His wealthy family had a stake in the cotton plantations of the Laguna, banks, textile mills, coal and silver mines, smelters, the wine and grape industry, and guayule. No significant economic enterprise in Coahuila escaped its diverse interests and talents. When twelve-years old, his parents sent him to study at the Jesuit Colegio de San Juan in Saltillo, the capital of Coahuila, where his teachers so impressed him that he toyed briefly with the idea of joining their order.[2] Eventually, Madero spent five years in schools in France and eight months at the University of California in Berkeley. At no time during his educational travels did Madero display an abiding interest in study.

His family, to whom he was devoted, made no attempt to hide its conservative proclivities. Not one of its members applauded his defiance of don Porfirio. "I give you my word of honor," wrote his grandfather Evaristo, the patriarch of the clan, to an old friend José I. Limantour, "that we have not contributed a single penny . . . and that far from sympathizing with the movement, we repudiate it energetically." To men of business, said Evaristo, it could only bring horrendous harm. He scoffed at the effort to "redeem our sins" because of "spiritual revelations," a reference to Madero's absorption with spiritualists.[3] Rafael Hernández, his uncle, roundly castigated the "lunacy" of his nephew.[4] In letters to Limantour, Evaristo and Hernández assured him that they spoke for a family "alien to the idea of insurrection" and totally at variance with the "behavior of Francisco."[5]

For the moment, Madero stubbornly ignored the wishes of his family and plunged on with his plot. Unfortunately, once in office, he sought the advice of his family. When as president he thought to name Luis Cabrera, then spokesman for the "radicals" in Congress, minister of *fomento,* his family put its foot down. His father, Francisco, Sr., and his uncles Ernesto and Rafael L. Hernández, with the concurrence of Pedro Lascuráin, a trusted family ally, argued that Cabrera would antagonize Mexican businessman as well as those foreigners with investments in Mexico.[6] Nor was the Madero clan free of the prejudice of the Mexican upper class. Gustavo, Madero's brother, opposed designating Francisco Vásquez Gómez vice-president for, among other drawbacks, being an "Indian." [7]

Madero, the gentleman rebel, emerged from this mold. He cherished his "friendship" with Díaz. You "honor me," he told don Porfirio, "when you think of me as a friend." [8] Alberto Madero, another uncle, and Daniel, a brother, were related by marriage to Enrique C. Creel, one of the kingpins of the Terrazas' empire in Chihuahua.[9] Limantour, the financial wizard of the Old Regime, was "a close friend" of Madero's father and of his uncles Ernesto and Rafael.[10] Before becoming minister of the treasury, Limantour had been the attorney for the Maderos when the grandfather, Evaristo, ran the family's affairs.[11] In his memoirs, Limantour remembered how Evaristo, as head of the commercial, mining, and industrial enterprises of the Maderos, had sought his advice.[12] At the urging of the family, Limantour had given Lorenzo González Treviño, a rich *hacendado* of Coahuila related to the Maderos, a loan of 3 million pesos to improve his lands.[13] In New York City, with the uprising underway, Madero's father met frequently with Limantour, then returning to Mexico from a European visit, to discuss family problems as well as the rebellion.[14] Earlier, when the question of Díaz' running mate was being debated, Madero had thought of Limantour as the logical candidate. He vowed to work on Limantour's behalf within the Partido Democrático, a group opposing Díaz' re-election "when opportune." [15] After Díaz' flight, according to Hernández, Madero asked Limantour to remain at his old job in the cabinet.[16] When he refused, Madero appointed his uncle Ernesto, who swore never to modify either the system or to change the personnel in the Treasury because, as he informed Limantour, "I am an admirer of yours." The Treasury was like "a fine watch that merely required that you wind it every twenty-four hours." [17] For his part, Limantour helped Madero escape jail when taken prisoner in San Luis Potosí.[18] Both Evaristo and Gustavo served on the board of directors of the exclusive Casino de Monterrey, home of the patriarchs of Nuevo León.

Plainly, Madero had strong links with the Old Regime. Indeed, his political gambit gathered momentum only when the effort to install General Bernardo Reyes as Díaz' running mate in the elections of 1910 failed. Had Díaz substituted Reyes for Ramón Corral, it is highly unlikely that Madero would have disturbed the status quo. Antonio Manero saw "Reyismo," the campaign to place Reyes on the ticket with Díaz, as the baptism of the Partido Democrático, the political vehicle of Madero.[19] When Reyes backed out of the race, his disjointed followers flocked to Madero. As Ramón Prida pointed out, Madero utilized the masonic lodges courted and won by Reyes as well as his political clubs to build his own support.[20] Later Madero invited Reyes to become minister of war.[21] To Francisco Bulnes, a seasoned veteran of Mexican politics, the abortive effort of Reyes and the Madero rebellion were cut from the same cloth.[22] Upon meeting General Victoriano Huerta, then in pursuit of Zapata in Morelos, Madero departed with a fine impression of him, convinced that he "was on very good terms" with Huerta.[23] The general's unconcealed disdain for Zapata had bothered Madero not a bit.

Madero arrived on the national stage for the first time with the publication of his book in 1908. Interestingly, its appearance coincided with the bitter clash between the Compañía Tlahualilo and the planters down stream, where the Maderos had large *haciendas*. Madero had written his book in San Pedro de las Colonias, a town in the Laguna hurt by the monopoly of the Tlahualilo company. Cynical contemporaries traced Madero's anti-Díaz stance to his troubles with the company, the recipient of official benevolence.

Whatever the truth, Madero had already built for himself a reputation as a moderate reformer. As a candidate for the city council of San Pedro, he had spurred neighboring *hacendados* to establish schools for the children of their workers. By 1905, according to one of his biographers, he had become a fervent supporter of public education, a defender of individual liberties, and an enemy of one-man rule.[24] In his "Deberes del Creyente para con la Patria y la Humanidad," he urged Mexicans to work

for "the progress of humanity" which, aside from public schooling, called for "strengthening individual morality by combating
vices and developing virtue." [25] Any endeavor to solve Mexico's
problems by reliance on guns, he explained in *La Sucesión
Presidencial,* would exacerbate domestic discord, prolong the
agony of a military regime, and invite dire international repercussions. In Madero's opinion the ubiquitous revolutions of the
nineteenth century, which continually spawned military dicta-
torships, had given shape to the absolutism of the Porfiriato.[26]

To Madero, therefore, the evil was not just Díaz but the
pernicious formula that brought him to power: reliance on
armed force to achieve political ends. Instead, he wanted Mexicans to accomplish their goals step by step as responsible and
mature citizens. His Partido Democrático, he said, was "re-
formist" in character. As one of his admirers reflected on the an-
niversary of his death, Madero was "an evolutionist who relied
on guns only when everything else failed." [27] The people of this
world in their evolutionary development, Madero told his
cabinet, "must march forward"; but he cautioned, "we cannot in
the short time that I am president expect to transform the Republic; we can only lay the foundations of future greatness." [28]
As his friends explained, Madero wanted to do away with the
obstacles blocking Mexico's progress. Francisco Vásquez Gómez,
a physician to Díaz and briefly an ally of Madero, put the matter succinctly: Madero, rather than carry the banner of rebellion,
counseled a prudent, evolutionary approach that, although slow
to work, "gave better and more lasting results." [29]

Followers of Madero shared like views. Emilio Vásquez
Gómez, lawyer and brother of Francisco, helped establish the
Centro Antireeleccionista for "an evolutionary and not revolutionary movement." He did this, he admitted, "to avoid the pitfalls of revolution." [30] Felix F. Palavicini, who accompanied
Madero on his swing through Yucatán, thought Madero's goals
"merely political." Madero, he alleged, "first and foremost" abhorred autocratic rule by the president and state governors, the
servility of Congress, and the corruption of justice. Above all, he
wanted to rid Mexico of the *carro completo,* the nefarious
practice of distributing public jobs to those in the inner circle.
"The poverty of the people, their plight in cities and villages,"

commented Palavicini, "did not appear to be a weighty concern of dissident politicians in 1910." [31] To the disputatious Roberto Blanco Moheno, writing with the hindsight of half a century, Madero represented "the Porfirista wing that rebelled not to defend popular rights but to gain public office with a change in the presidency." [32]

Madero plainly distrusted revolutionaries. Particularly, he feared the Magonistas, radicals who did not play by the rules. He was willing to believe that the tyranny of *caciques* had invited the attempt of the Magonistas to capture Viesca, a small town in Coahuila, in 1908; but, "whatever the reason," he went on, "I believe that these [abortive] military schemes demonstrate that the people no longer welcome revolutions." [33] Even after openly defying Díaz, Madero flirted only briefly with the Magonistas. But the moment their leaders questioned his intentions, Madero had them disarmed—although on his way to lay siege to Ciudad Juárez. With victory in hand, Madero's forces, under the command of Pascual Orozco, fell upon their erstwhile allies at Galeana and Ahumada.[34] To Madero, the Magonistas symbolized the violence he detested and the destruction of his cherished private property.

He dealt with Zapata in similar fashion. According to José Fuentes Mares, Madero "never stopped thinking as an *hacendado*," and judged Zapata's banner of agrarian reform from that perspective. Madero, Fuentes Mares concluded, "loathed revolution," especially the peasant uprisings in Morelos.[35] His speech to Congress in April, 1912, for example, harped on the "impatience" and the "amorphous agrarian socialism" of the people of Morelos, attitudes "peculiar to the vulgar minds" of peasants. He branded their actions a "perverse vandalism." [36] While he merely jailed Félix Díaz and Bernardo Reyes for their ill-fated *cuartelazos,* and granted them sundry privileges in prison, he left Huerta and his army in Morelos to hunt down Zapata.

Abjuring violence, Madero conceived reform in terms of moral imperatives. "I embraced the struggle," he wrote his father, "to conquer liberty for my country, for it alone can save us from the moral decadence that overwhelms us." [37] The people, he said in *La Sucesión Presidencial,* "ask for liberty because it is the gift they most covet," extolling "liberty of thought" above all others.[38] The workers would not be satisfied, he wrote when commenting on the labor legislation promulgated by Reyes in Nuevo León, "until they enjoy a meaningful liberty." Strikes in the textile industry, he admitted, were brought on by the injustices of long hours of toil and poor pay. The "nation sympathized with the workers," but nonetheless, they must not forget that management could not pay higher wages. Instead, management must be encouraged to deal fairly with labor, to provide decent housing, equitable *tiendas de raya,* and most importantly, schools for the children of the workers. Were this done, he promised, the workers would be satisfied.[39] He had not traveled to Orizaba, he told incredulous textile workers, to "incite passions" or to tell them that government had a moral duty "to raise wages or to reduce the hours of toil." We "who embody your aspirations, are not here to make such a pledge because that is not what you want; you want liberty . . . for liberty will give you bread."[40] Bulnes, with his usual acerbic wit, discovered in Madero's fondness for moral homilies a "national rival of the Virgin of Guadalupe."[41]

Madero's banner, as he acknowledged, juxtaposed "liberty of suffrage" with "no re-election."[42] No one could question the people's right to vote. However, Antonio Manero observed, the ban on boss rule had not been raised before.[43] The cry was "death to bad government." As Manuel Calero told Madero, "we had one objective: that democratic institutions take root in Mexico."[44] At the start, the obstacle had been Corral's claim on the vice-presidency; if honored, little could be done to reshape the future.[45] Only when Díaz refused to accept Madero as his running mate did Corral become an enemy. As Madero explained, he wanted the people to elect their vice-president, their Congress, and their governors.[46] How ironic, mused Manero, that Madero, with his plea for an effective vote and elimination of autocracy, should adopt as his own the discarded shibboleths of Díaz' struggle against Juárez. In his Plan de la Noria, Díaz had bewailed Juárez' long reign in the National Palace, the manipulation of Congress, the loss of state sovereignty, and the absence of justice. "What does Madero say today?" asked Manero. "Exactly the same thing." Despite an interval of nearly forty years, little distinguished the Plan de San Luis Potosí from the

Plan de la Noria.[47] Both pointed an accusing finger at the same evils and proposed comparable remedies.

Neither did Madero condemn the entire political baggage of Díaz' regime. When still thinking that Díaz might replace Corral, Madero had lauded the benevolent use of "absolute power." Exercized by wise rulers such as Díaz, "absolute power" tempered political evils; conversely, "in the hands of intemperate men," it represented a "calamity for mankind." [48] The people, Madero insisted, "did not demand new legislation but merely its implementation." [49] In the opinion of Francisco Vásquez Gómez, Madero had rebelled in search of new men, not new ideals. The Constitution of 1857 contained the hallowed principles; it was time for men of good will to put them into practice.[50] The name of Madero's Partido Constitucional Progresista testified that his movement stood in strict accord with the Charter of 1857. Change would flow legally, eventually conferring individual liberties and guarantees on every segment of society, but with absolute respect for their legitimate interests.[51]

Yet Madero was not blind to the ills of Mexican society, as his *Sucesión Presidencial* bears witness, although only a small part of it discusses social issues. From Madero's perspective, the neglect of education topped the list of social crimes; he lamented that a mere 16 percent of the population could read and write.[52] He saw education as the cardinal remedy for the ills of society. Nor was he callous to social injustice. He applauded Heriberto Frías for castigating the butchery at Tomóchic although he glossed over the theft of lands by Limantour which had precipitated the tragedy. Madero decried the enslavement of the Yaquis and the theft of their lands, and advised Díaz to recognize their right to lands they had tilled for centuries. With patience, he thought, the Yaquis could be civilized and "made useful citizens." He inveighed against the attacks on the Maya of Yucatán.[53]

The Plan de San Luis Potosí, Madero's platform for rebellion, differs little from his book. Only article 3, which condemns the loss of village lands under the Leyes de Terrenos Baldíos and urges their return when "legally possible," is nonpolitical.[54] No matter what its merits, the Plan de San Luis Potosí scarcely ranks with the celebrated designs for land reform in Mexican history. Additionally, its silence on the land question, indicated its facit acceptance of the sacredness of private property. With this attitude, land reform would be difficult, if not impossible.

Madero deviated only with difficulty from this ideological posture. As his timid gesture of September, 1911 documents, he cared little for land reform. Meeting with his adherents in the Partido Constitucional Progresista, Madero promised to encourage the growth of small property; but, to the consternation of many who heard him, he also urged safeguards for the *hacienda,* holding inviolable "the principle of private property." Cabrera's efforts to convince Madero of the contradictions in this attitude got nowhere.[55] When the legislature of Chihuahua asked Orozco to become acting governor, an offer he accepted on condition that he be allowed to begin to subdivide the large estates, Madero pointedly ignored the request and instead replied that 3 million acres of public lands could be sold.[53] Soon afterwards, Orozco severed his ties with Madero, calling in his Plan de la Empacadora for the expropriation of unproductive *haciendas.*

With his letter to the editor of *El Imparcial,* June, 1912, Madero removed all doubt as to where he stood on the land issue. Angered by charges that he had betrayed his commitments, Madero, in this document, set out to clarify the record once and for all. He stated categorically that he had never promised to distribute land to the poor or to subdivide the *latifundios,* whether in the Plan de San Luis Potosí, or in speeches delivered both before and after his uprising, or in his blueprints for government. While he believed in creating small property, he did not intend to do it by "stripping any landlord of his properties." It was "one thing to create small property by dint of hard work and another to redistribute large landholdings, something I have never thought of doing or offered in any of my speeches or programs." He reminded the editor that article 3 of the Plan de San Luis Potosí had merely pledged to restore, whenever legally permissible, lands arbitrarily seized from their rightful owners.[57]

The negotiations paving the way for the Treaty of Ciudad Juárez, began with the discussions in the New York City hotel suite of Francisco León de la Barra, Díaz' ambassador to Washington. The discussions were between Limantour and De la

Barra on the one hand, and Madero's father, brother, and Francisco Vásquez Gómez, on the other. This treaty outlined eloquently the hesitant vision of the rebel leadership. According to Limantour, the Maderos and Vásquez Gómez asked for limited concessions. These included the resignation of Corral, ten new governors (for Sonora, Chihuahua, Coahuila, and Yucatán among them, but interestingly, not for Morelos) for additional appointments to the cabinet, voting reforms, and for the end of one-man rule by the president, the governors, and municipal officials. Don Porfirio, meanwhile, would be allowed to finish his term although, as Vásquez Gómez recognized, since the insurgents distrusted him, peace appeared unlikely until he gave up the National Palace. The new governors would be chosen from men "whose standing in society offered guarantees to all of its segments." [58]

Similarly at Ciudad Juárez, Madero and the rebels equivocated. However, unlike the negotiations in New York City, where gentlemen of the old school alone conferred, Madero met his rivals at the dusty border town under the watchful vigilance of Pascual Orozco and his troops. Men of Orozco's stripe had not risked life and limb just to see Madero sit down with don Porfirio in the National Palace. Not unexpectedly, therefore, Madero initially told the government negotiators, Oscar Braniff and Toribio Esquivel Obregón, that Díaz must resign; De la Barra would temporarily replace him. However, even De la Barra, a smooth-talking, lawyer-diplomat with aristocratic airs, hardly pleased Orozco and his allies. Despite this, Madero, apparently fearful of domestic consequences, and worried about what impact the resignation might have on Washington, withdrew his demand that Díaz leave office. According to Braniff, Esquivel Obregón, and Hernández, Madero merely wanted a letter from Díaz offering to resign that would not be made public. [59]

At this juncture, Orozco and his troops, over Madero's objections attacked Juárez and, to the astonishment of the world, captured it. Furthermore, Vásquez Gómez had already informed Madero that he thought poorly of permitting Díaz to remain in office, and in a telegram to De la Barra, had suggested that negotiations be concluded "far from the Maderos." [60] Surprisingly, the capture of the border town brought the government to its knees. With its surrender, bemoaned Jorge Vera Estañol, "public opinion turned hostile to the government, its friends panicked while the enthusiasm of its enemies, drunk with victory, knew no bounds." [61] Writing to Limantour, Hernández warned that with the fall of Juárez, Madero's allies, "more intransigent and radical than he," had become "proud and haughty." Yet Madero, to the anger of his companions, handled the defeated enemy as an equal, asking that the "reasonable and wise be consulted" in the selection of the new governors and cabinet ministers. To get that advice, he would turn to the "best moral and intellectual segments" of society.[62] His cohorts, however, partly thwarted Madero's designs. The peace terms, as a result, were a compromise between what he wanted and the desire of his ambitious companions for total victory.

Yet the peace of Juárez scarcely spelled revolution. Of course, it went beyond what the Maderos wanted in New York City, but only peripherally. Díaz and Corral were told to pack their bags; the victors were to name fourteen interim governors and four cabinet ministers, Gobernación, War, Justice, and Education; and federal troops must evacuate Chihuahua, Coahuila, and Sonora. As for "liberal principles, or political, social, and administrative reforms," recalled Limantour, the peace said "nothing, absolutely nothing." At Juárez, the rebels simply wanted the government turned over to them.[63] As Palavicini remarked, this preserved intact the entire financial and administrative structure of the Old Regime.[64]

A malignancy that sooner or later would plague the visitors survived the Treaty of Ciudad Juárez. To his later sorrow, Madero permitted the old army to keep its weapons, with the idea that the plethora of aging generals who had fought for Díaz would defend Madero. The army brass hats, meanwhile, adamantly refused to recognize as equals any of the rebel chieftains. They were willing only to give them an equivalent rank in the corps of *rurales* in Sonora and Chihuahua.[65] With the signing of the Juárez accord moreover, Madero disbanded the rebel forces. When Emilio Vásquez Gómez, then interim-minister of *gobernación,* attempted to keep them together, De la Barra, with the concurrence of Madero, dismissed him.[66] By a strange quirk in history, the Old Regime had collapsed but its conquerors had made their peace with its military. Without his trusted allies, Madero became a captive of his guardians. Worse still, prospects for reform dimmed, for the army, a confederate of Porfirista society, could hardly be expected to sit idly while the rebels dismantled it.

By deciding he must be legally elected before crossing the threshold of the National Palace, Madero gave the vanquished enemy a further opportunity to recover from the shock of Ciudad Juárez. In order to stump the country, Madero turned the reins of government over to De la Barra, recently elevated to minister of foreign affairs by Díaz.[67] No one had ever the slightest grain of suspicion of De la Barra's impeccable conservative credentials. According to Mexican law, he was next in line for the presidency once Díaz and Corral had resigned. Ironically, by designating De la Barra interim-president, Madero, the rebel chieftain, had assured the constitutional transition of authority. But, in that transition, the old guard weathered the storm. Madero had, furthermore, paradoxically accepted the choice of Díaz for the presidency. Madero picked De la Barra, according to Fuentes Mares, because of his "legalistic spirit, so accentuated that it made him feel a deep repugnance for the role of the victorious revolutionary." [68] By endorsing De la Barra, the constitutional successor to Díaz, Madero could wipe the despised stigma of illegality from his record.

As one wag remarked, "The King had died, long live the King." Díaz had gone off to Europe to nurse his wounds but his regime lingered on. De la Barra, said the trusting Madero, "is fully committed to us." To "avoid further revolts and difficulties," Madero asked Congress and the state legislatures to stay on the job, asking only that their members "fully accept the new regime." [69] Madero's victory, in the interim, had set off a wave of jubilation that, from the perspective of Manero, "reminded one of the dances of savages around their idols." [70]

Madero had merely deceived himself when he claimed De la Barra for the rebel camp. An aristocrat who bore the family crest with honor, De la Barra would later serve Victoriano Huerta, the general who betrayed Madero. His cabinet, chosen in consultation with Madero, excluded radicals. Two wealthy uncles of Madero controlled key ministeries, Ernesto in the

Treasury and Hernández in Fomento. One portfolio went to Manuel Calero, a young lawyer who had sat at the feet of don Porfirio. The Vásquez Gómez brothers, Emilio in Gobernación and Francisco in Public Instruction, perhaps the least conservative, ran immediately into trouble; both ultimately resigned. To the delight of crusty die-hards, only the trappings of the new government were different. De la Barra, a seasoned veteran, gave orders in the National Palace; Díaz had picked the Congress and the state legislatures; nearly half of the governors owed their jobs to the departed strong man; and the army, with officers loyal to the past, guaranteed the peace.[71] To complicate matters for reformers, the national economy took a turn for the better, checking the spread of political discontent.[72]

Madero's presidential ambitions somehow outlasted De la Barra. He carried all of the states in the elections of November, 1911. Nonetheless, the results should have alerted him to the trouble brewing. His running mate, José María Pino Suárez, whom Madero picked over Francisco Vásquez Gómez, lost in Jalisco to De la Barra, that state's choice for the vice-presidency. The old establishment, as Fuentes Mares states, had recuperated sufficiently from the defeat at Ciudad Juárez to dare suggest a national ticket of Madero and De la Barra.[73] As the idea implied, the flower of the Old Regime was alive and well.

Of Madero's cabinet, only three represented the men who defied Díaz. Both Ernesto Madero and Hernández remained, as did Manuel Bonilla, a well-meaning but timid friend of reform. Abraham González in Gobernación, the most notable of the rebel figures, was also governor of Chihuahua. Nothing better described the nature of the incoming government than the choice of Calero for Foreign Relations. To cite Bulnes, Díaz, who judged Calero "an intimate friend," had once offered him the vice-presidency.[74] A congressman, Calero, by his own admission, had been with Díaz just hours before police shot and killed Aquiles Serdán in Puebla.[75] Married to one of Justo Sierra's daughters, Calero, according to Prida, had sympathized with the *científicos*.[76] Rebels and conservatives alike agreed that with Calero, Madero had picked for his cabinet one of the "most opportunistic politicians in the history of the country." [77] Moreover, with the exception of González, Bonilla, and Miguel Díaz

Lombardo, the other ministers were either out of touch with popular sentiment or "irreconcilable enemies" of revolution.[78]

Madero's appointments received few plaudits from reformers. Meanwhile, by breaking with the Vásquez Gómez, Madero antagonized one element of support. With it, he abandoned the Partido Nacional Antireeleccionista, the rebel bandwagon, to form the Partido Constitucional Progresista, a vehicle for legal reform. To those opposing re-election, their old leader seemed bent upon "conciliating and establishing ties with the *científicos*," thus endangering "the hopes of the rebellion of 1910;" they ultimately became Madero's foes.[79] On the other hand, wrote Bulnes, the former *científicos* "were always grateful" to Madero "and never conspired against him." [80]

II

Madero governed approximately thirteen months. In February, 1913, a *cuartelazo* led by Huerta, whom Madero had asked to defend his regime, cost the Apostle his life. While in office, Madero had run his government as he had promised in San Luis Potosí. His beneficiaries and admirers, in the opinion of one scholar, were the discontented members of the élite who, with the middle classes, decried the clinquish control of politics and the privileges of the few. His policy was to embrace capitalism, to attempt to update it, and to rescue the economy from the depression it had suffered under Díaz.[81] During his short stay in Mexico City, Madero merely tinkered with the machinery of government. His accomplishments, declared an editorial in *El Microbio,* scarcely disturbed the plight in which Díaz had left the Mexican people.[82] Continuity, said one worker, superseded reform. Madero died abandoned by tens of thousands of his early supporters. Only two of his governors, José María Maytorena in Sonora and Venustiano Carranza in Coahuila, rejected Huerta's tutelage. Maytorena, however, had so little faith in armed opposition to Huerta that he gave up his job and took up residence across the border.

TEN *Venustiano Carranza:*

The Patrician as a Rebel

"And above all, he is white, very white. His Spanish ancestors were natives of Alava, Guipúscoa, and Biscay. . . ."

Vincente Blasco Ibáñez

I

AT THE DINNER TABLE in Nogales, Martín Luis Guzmán recalled in *El Aguila y la Serpiente,* don Venustiano rode herd on the conversation with a firm hand. His guests, invariably lawyers, physicians, engineers, journalists and other men of learning, city dandies impeccably dressed in coat and tie, listened attentively while the First Chief, Francisco I. Madero's successor as head of the Revolution, spiced his remarks with "historical allusions" to the Reforma, his cherished topic.[1] His history, like that of many amateur historians, was often faulty. But whatever the weaknesses in his interpretations, it was clear that Carranza looked for guidance and inspiration to the Reforma, the soul of nineteenth-century Mexican thought. To the astonishment and anger of partisans of reform, his views never went much beyond the ideals of Benito Juárez, over half-a-century old when the Constitutionalists began their crusade.

Don Venustiano, who ultimately challenged General Victoriano Huerta, was a native of Coahuila and patriarch of a distinguished family. Born in 1859 on an *hacienda* near the Villa of Cuatro Ciénegas, he was nearly sixty years of age when he took up the rebel cause. His father, an army officer who had fought in the Indian wars of Coahuila and Chihuahua, had loyally served Juárez against both the Conservatives and the French invaders sent by Napoleon III. As a boy, Carranza attended school in Saltillo, the capital of Coahuila, and graduated from the Escuela Nacional Preparatoria in Mexico City. Upon his return home, he became a successful *hacendado,* and in time, the patrician of Cuatro Ciénegas.

Like Madero, Carranza could not claim that he was an outsider in the days of Porfirio Díaz. His father, a prosperous *hacendado,* enjoyed the esteem of the rulers of Mexico. Carranza himself, shortly after his return from school, had been appointed *presidente municipal* of Cuatro Ciénegas, a post he held again from 1894 to 1898. He served in the state legislature, and then as deputy and senator from Coahuila to the national Congress for seventeen years. In 1908, he became interim-governor of Coahuila and appeared likely of being confirmed in that office by the coming elections. Unfortunately, his espousal of the political ambitions of Bernardo Reyes incurred the wrath of don Porfirio who, in retaliation, opposed Carranza's confirmation.[2] Critics say that he was an enthusiastic ally of the Old Regime so long as Díaz supported his efforts for political office. To please Díaz, wrote Alfonso Junco, a Catholic journalist and scholar, Carranza sided with the Compañía Tlahualilo in its disputes with the Maderos.[3] Carranza, Francisco Bulnes pointed out, was an "inflexible, unconditional adherent of the dictator."[4] When Díaz put an end to his candidacy Carranza turned against him. Díaz was eventually to say that the "danger was not Madero but don Venustiano Carranza."[5]

Carranza's triumphs in the world of politics stemmed partly from his friendship with Reyes, the *caudillo* of Nuevo León. Reyes, who wielded enormous political clout in the northeast, had opened the path for Carranza's election to the senate and later designation as interim-governor.[6] Carranza never lost his faith in Reyes; even after the debacle at the National Palace, where Reyes needlessly had himself killed, Carranza glowingly remembered his memory. From his perspective, "only Reyes could have saved Mexico from the revolution and carried out truly transcendental reforms."[7] Díaz, who wanted no rivals, put an end to Reyes' dreams of the vice-presidency and to Carranza's hopes for the governorship of Coahuila. When Madero's revolt broke out in 1911, Carranza fled to Texas.

However, even at this juncture, Carranza had not forsaken Reyes. He still debated whether to support him should Reyes leave Europe to confront Díaz and Madero. To learn if Reyes would indeed return, Carranza went to New York City to talk with José I. Limantour, then on his way home from a trip to Paris, where he had spoken to Reyes.[8] Carranza returned to Texas apparently convinced that he could not count on Reyes. However, according to Alfonso Madero, a brother of Francisco, Carranza refused to commit himself to any rebel faction. To join Madero, he wanted either 200,000 pesos, the money needed to recruit a small army, or an army of 1,000 men.[9] Not until Madero, whose fortunes were improving, threatened to name someone else governor, did Carranza join the rebellion and invade Coahuila. Even then, he waited for Madero to capture Ciudad Juárez.[10] Still, according to General Juan Gualberto Amaya, Madero received only an "ambiguous promise" of support from Carranza.[11] As other potential rebels, Carranza, doubting Madero's ability to lead a successful revolt against Díaz, hesitated before committing himself.

Meanwhile, as Madero's governor of Coahuila from May, 1911 to March, 1913, Carranza, while eager to tinker with the political structure, revealed no zest for drastic change. As expected of any rebel, he wielded a vigorous broom, sweeping out of office judges and other public officials and replacing them with men of his choosing. He took steps to revise the state's antiquated law codes, to modernize the tax system, and to rid the municipalities of the hated *jefes políticos*. A paternalistic moralist, Carranza made a great effort to stamp out vice, particularly gambling, drunkeness, and prostitution, and like his Protestant neighbors in Texas, to pass "blue laws" to keep the Sabbath free for worship. He spent nearly 400,000 pesos on schools, renovating old ones and building new ones. But, he denied the miners' request for higher wages, siding with the coal barons, and running out of Coahuila "outside labor agitators," among them Lázaro Gutiérrez de Lara. Carranza harbored no love for outspoken union leaders.[12]

Carranza learned of Huerta's betrayal on February 9, 1913.

From the available evidence, it is thought that he had yet to decide if he would recognize Huerta sixteen days later. His ambiguous telegram to Alberto García Granados, Huerta's minister of *gobernación*, could be read both ways. [13] His defenders argue that he was playing for time. That may be true. All the same, it is doubtful that Carranza would have broken with Huerta without news of the rebellion in Sonora and of the uprising in neighboring Chihuahua. The rebellion, in the meantime, had also gained ground rapidly in Durango and Zacatecas, and in the *sierra* where San Luis Potosí, Querétaro, Hidalgo, and Veracruz meet.[14] Having denounced Huerta, Carranza took flight to Sonora, which the rebels controlled. As the sole governor to sever his ties with Huerta, he could rightly claim to bear the seal of constitutional legitimacy; he alone represented the government elected to office by popular acclaim in 1911. Because of this, and because the rebel chieftains in Sonora distrusted each other, the men who gathered in Nogales picked Carranza to lead them.[15] Almost by historical accident, therefore, Carranza became the First Chief and symbol of unity but, certainly, as José Vasconcelos said, hardly the spokesman for reform.[16]

II

Regardless of why he became a companion of rebels, Carranza was the logical choice to captain the war against Huerta. Who else, asked the Mexican consul in El Paso, "can inspire the confidence and respect . . . of the austere and virtuous Carranza?" [17] The consul phrased it well. The First Chief, a mature and seasoned politician, outshone all of his rivals, who were nearly all political neophytes. In the opinion of one conservative partisan—Robert Lansing, the American secretary of state—don Venustiano, "dignified" and of "gentlemanly bearing," pulled the insurgents together.[18] First and foremost, he was a man of principle, devoted to what he believed, refusing to compromise for the sake of expediency or personal profit. When hostile factions captured his brother, General Jesús Carranza, and notified Carranza that they would kill him if their demands went unmet, Carranza stoically stood fast. In anger, the captors shot his brother. Unlike a legion of mercenary rebels, who acquired fortunes during their adventures, Carranza, a rich man when he began the challenge to Huerta, died an *hacendado* of modest means.[19] State authorities in Coahuila had placed a tax value of only 35,000 pesos on his lands, approximately a third of their true worth.[20]

Urbane but provincial, he prized learning and held Western culture in high esteem. He wanted to send to Europe for travel and study fellow rebels whom he thought would profit from the experience.[21] He read widely if not thoroughly, especially in history. Luis Cabrera, an admirer and aide, boasted that Carranza had an "encyclopedic knowledge" of Mexican and South American history.[22] He considered himself an historian and kept a copy of Plutarch by his bedside. He was a moralist but flexible. All the same, despite cries of alarm from doomsayers who predicted the ruin of the family, he sponsored a divorce bill. When citizens of Matamoros complained of gambling in town, Carranza asked Andrés Osuna, the governor of Tamaulipas, to put a stop to it.[23]

Above all, Carranza was a politician. He knew intimately the twists and turns of Mexican politics, their weaknesses and strengths. He accepted as inevitable the crass opportunism characteristic of many of his revolutionary colleagues. His letter to Alvaro Obregón, his erstwhile military cohort, written just days before each went his separate way, which thanked him for his expression of concern for his wife's health, reveals no trace of bitterness.[24] Loyalty he viewed as a fleeting hope. Unlike Madero, he knew that it would take more than a change of guard to transform Mexico.[25] Still, he was stubborn, suspicious of others, and unable to tolerate criticism. He loathed rivals. According to José Fuentes Mares, Carranza hated Pancho Villa not so much because of his cruelty, but because he was a strong, exuberant opponent, a winner.[26] Like many Mexican politicians, he wore tinted glasses, not because of poor eyesight, commented Villa, but "to better conceal his thoughts."[27] Visitors discovered that he sat with the sun at his back, so that in speaking to him they were always at a disadvantage. His slogan was "walk carefully and do not slip."[28]

Carranza's public speeches, like Madero's, occasionally hailed the virtues of Western democracy. Unlike Madero, however, he knew that only a strong man could govern Mexico. Given the nature of their societies, Mexico and similar countries required firm and vigorous leadership, of the type Díaz had provided. Along with Emilio Rabasa, the political soothsayer of the Old Regime, he believed that only a robust and powerful government could enforce the laws. "In Mexico," he told José Santos Chocano, a distinguished poet from Peru, "those who oppose the dictator are against him because he is not with them." Santos Chocano eventually mistakenly concluded that Carranza merely hungered for power for its own sake.[29] As Díaz before him, Carranza manipulated politics, twisting Congress, the state legislature, and the governors to suit his own ends. Of the nineteen governors "elected" in 1917 when Carranza became president of the Republic, just three belonged to different political camps.[30] Theoretically, he headed a revolutionary regime; in practice, as one American resident of Mexico said, he wanted "law and order." [31] He emphasized his "legitimacy," baptizing his political machine the Partido Liberal Constitucionalista. Convinced that only a civilian should govern Mexico, he died a tragic death at Tlaxcalantongo, the victim of military treachery and the unbridled presidential ambitions of General Obregón—which Carranza had intended to foil as Díaz had those of Reyes a decade earlier.

A conservative and a traditionalist, Carranza wanted men of his own ilk around him. Extremists of the left never gained his confidence. True, he appointed Plutarco Elías Calles, a radical by hearsay, minister of war, because he wisely saw the reputation as a myth and because he wanted to placate the Obregón wing in Sonora. Given his choice, however, he picked moderates and conservatives to work with him. Cabrera, a lawyer with an abiding faith in private property and a gradualist view of reform, best represents the men of Carranza. When Díaz and Madero were at loggerheads in 1911, he had urged a compromise that left the honor of Díaz untarnished, but satisfied "just demands" and restored peace before the rebellion "got out of hand.'" Had he been asked to draw up its terms, he would have allowed Díaz to stay in office, told Corral to pack his bags, and held an election to choose his successor.[32] Others in Carranza's braintrust were the lawyers Luis Manuel Rojas and Alfonso Cravioto,

both lukewarm rebels, and José Natividad Macías, once an enthusiastic Porfirista.[33] Felix F. Palavicini, a civil engineer named
head of Public Instruction by the First Chief, at one time urged
"sincere democrats" to shun Madero and support Díaz.[34] Heriberto Barrón, a special confidante and muckraking journalist,
pandered to Díaz and then to Carranza with equal fervor. Carranza's headquarters at Veracruz, grumbled the excitable Dr. Atl,
seethed with the intrigues of the die-hards the First Chief had
gathered about him.[35] Both Palavicini and Barrón incurred the
wrath of Obregón who, in a fit of pique, called on Carranza to
discharge them, a demand that almost split the Constitutionalists
into warring camps.[36]

Carranza's political principles were basically those of the nineteenth century. As Madero, he was essentially a classical liberal,
a disciple of Juárez and José María Luis Mora, but shaped to
fit the mold of the northern *hacendado*.[37] His suggested modifications of the constitutional articles 3 and 130, leaving local
control of education undisturbed and keeping intact the anticlerical provisions of the Charter of 1857, exemplify his philosophical ties to the past. His revolution, he proudly proclaimed
in his *Manifiesto a la Nación* in 1915, had met with success because it promised not just to purge Mexico of the putrified
bureaucracy but to substitute "liberty" for "oppression." [38] Issued after Carranza had become master of Mexico, however, it
said nothing specifically about major social or economic reforms.

That should not have surprised anyone. Since the Plan de
Guadalupe, a bland recipe for rebellion, Carranza had skipped
lightly over social issues. His famous speech of September, 1913,
before an audience in Hermosillo, although lamenting the absence of economic and social justice, rated the loss of "liberty"
the worst of Díaz' crimes. He was setting out, he claimed, to end
a "tyranny of thirty years," the "pervasive immorality" of the
army, and to avenge the murders of Madero and his vice-
president.[39] True, the regime of don Porfirio had aggravated
social inequalities dating from the colonial period, injustices his
crusade would abolish, bringing with it a peace resting on the
well-being of the majority and on equality before the law. But,
as he lectured Congress in 1917, without order the state did not
exist; and without laws or where the laws were "impudently

violated," there could be no order. And without respect for life, liberty, and property, he added, morality and individual rights, the substance of order, withered and died.[40] As he had said in 1913, he battled "for the return of constitutional order." [41]

A liberal in the familiar mold, he upheld the basic tenets of capitalist doctrine. He believed that a healthy society thrived on competition and bewailed the "immoral monopolies of business-men who for centuries had sucked dry the public coffers of the Republic." [42] He condemned the acquisition of wealth by the few, deplored the poverty of the "masses," but insisted that these evils had no links with the ideal of private property; but, to the contrary, they stemmed from monopolies in business and un-checked speculation for profit that, in turn, fostered an an-tagonism between classes." [43] Carranza, moreover, had matured amidst the language of free trade and eulogies to Herbert Spen-cer's survival of the fittest. He wanted an export tax on raw materials, particularly henequen and petroleum, as he explained to Congress in 1917, because "the protected industry, rather than an asset, is a burden." [44] Assured of an easy profit, it would grow fat and flabby. Competition, on the contrary, hardened muscles and strengthened industry. Some Mexican industries might well falter and fall by the wayside competing with foreign companies; but, he went on, the unsuccessful would have been of negligible benefit anyway. The efficient and vigorous, meanwhile, would survive and thrive, to the benefit of the Mexican people. Legis-lative trickery could and should not decide the fate of business.

Nationalistic considerations, nonetheless, tempered admira-tion of classical ideals. Competition might be the cutting edge of success, but practice had to accommodate to Mexican reality. A fervent nationalist, Carranza anxiously awaited the day when Mexicans would own and manage their own industries. Only in this manner, he stressed, would Mexico ever become even partly self-sufficient. He had learned this lesson during World War I, when despite profitable sales of raw materials abroad, Mexicans could not buy needed manufactured articles.[45] Out of necessity, as well as conviction, Carranza ultimately had to embrace the tariffs advocated by protectionists. Carranza also had to modify his classical principles in the interest of settling domestic conflicts.

In 1915, when the textile industry could not buy Mexican cotton at reasonable prices, Carranza bluntly told the planters of the Laguna to cut prices or risk the seizure of their harvest. From his perspective, the sale of Mexican cotton at war-inflated prices on the international market jeopardized the national welfare. Unless the textile industry could count on a supply of cheap cotton, that Mexican planters alone could provide, it would have to shut its doors, leaving an army of mill workers jobless.[46]

Carranza's goal was equality, said Cabrera, "in everything that touched on civil, economic, political, family, moral, and religious life." [47] Its quest ruled out all special privileges. Translated into fiscal policy, it meant that all Mexicans, rich and poor alike, must share the national burden and pay their taxes.[48] A just tax, however, did not endanger property, a sacred right to Carranza. In his *Manifiesto,* he had sworn to respect legitimately acquired property, so long as it was neither a monopoly nor a special privilege.[49] Once the military had restored peace, he would return all property to its rightful owners, except for that of individuals who had, directly or indirectly, helped to sabotage the Madero regime. He understood, he said, why the rebels, in retaliation for years of exploitation by the rich, had occupied private property. It was the case of "an eye for an eye, and a tooth for a tooth." [50] But abuse could not justify abuse; that attitude, obviously, would not redistribute wealth or income. On matters of property rights, it was abundantly evident, Carranza had little stomach for revolutionary remedies.

Carranza's version of agrarian reform rang a similar bell. At no time did he fully sympathize with the plea to redistribute the land. While he was not above using the rhetoric of land reform, he sat on his haunches when it came to implementing the slogans. To Santos Chocano, he said that he did not think the "agrarian problem important." [51] José Vasconcelos remembered Carranza saying frequently that he "could not understand the constant harping on the agrarian problem because it was not the main issue in Mexico." [52] When Lucio Blanco, one of his charismatic generals, boldly dared to divide the lands of an *hacienda* among its peasants in 1913, Carranza punished him. Blanco, he explained to Bernardino Mena Brito, by anticipating history had gone beyond the Plan de Guadalupe; in 1913, "we were unauthorized to dictate a social or political formula. Our mission was solely to destroy the dictatorship and to establish a government of the Revolution." It was up to the people, and not the rebels, to choose the blueprint they wanted. Common sense, furthermore, made mandatory a policy that would "not alarm the landlords, industrialists, and capitalists." A frontal attack on property, he added, would have antagonized the power brokers in Washington who, to avoid having a socialist neighbor, would have sealed their peace with Huerta.[53]

Yet, whatever the merits of Carranza's argument, it is likely that he exploited fears of frightening the rich and the powerful to justify his own views.[54] Despite his stated readiness to live with Article 27 of the 1917 Constitution, the gospel on land reform, Carranza never truly empathized with the suffering peasantry.[55] No wonder, therefore, that he left its implementation "to the future."

III

The Plan de Guadalupe of March, 1913, the justification for rebellion, marked Carranza's initial venture into the world of ideology. Yet all seven of its articles dealt with political questions. They called for elections, named Carranza interim head of the Republic, and repudiated Huerta.[56] No mention was made of economic or social ills. In defense of the Plan, Carranza at Hermosillo had argued that he did not want to deceive the people of Mexico, adding immediately that they required no "false promises" in order to bear arms to defend their rights. His platform, he said, enshrined no "bastardly pledges that would go unfulfilled." Only after victory, he cautioned, could the battle for social justice begin.[57] Not until events beyond his control compelled him to update his principles did Carranza depart from his narrow platform. Until then, admitted Cabrera, the defeat of Huerta had sole priority.[58] At best, however, such a commitment drew a lukewarm popular response. To Emiliano Zapata, fighting to regain the lands robbed from the people of Morelos, the revered Plan de Guadalupe counted for less than the paper it was written on: nowhere did it hold out a modicum of hope to the humble and poor. To install Carranza in the National Palace —this was its sole objective.[59] Even to Manuel Calero, a city dandy politically opposite Zapata, the empty rhetoric of Guadalupe was a cover for the hoary political game of "get out so that I can come in." [60] Or, as Jorge Vera Estañol commented, it was "exclusively a political denial" of Huerta's legitimacy, an attempt, added another critic, to restore the Constitution of 1857.[61]

Of course, in the Adiciones al Plan de Guadalupe, his subsequent definition of goals, Carranza reluctantly experienced second thoughts. To achieve social justice, he pledged to pass laws to encourage the growth of small property, the subdivision of the giant estates, and the return of lands stolen to their legitimate owners, as well as new labor legislation. Shortly after, he published his celebrated Decree of January 6, 1915, the brainchild of Cabrera and the basis of Article 27 of the 1917 Constitution. But his metamorphosis occurred only after Villa had abandoned the Constitutionalists and gone off to plot with Zapata. With Villa out of the way, he forgot his promises.

More truly indicative of Carranza's thinking was his speech to a gathering of army brass in Mexico City in the fall of 1914, soon to adjourn to Aguascalientes, where Villa went his errant way. In Mexico City, Carranza devoted less than a fifth of his message to labor and agrarian questions. According to Santos Chocano, who heard the speech, Carranza, in his haste to review the political crisis with Villa, mentioned social reform merely in passing. He "discussed briefly the independence of the municipalities, spoke four words on labor legislation," and touched lightly on taxes, banking difficulties, and civil marriage. Santos Chocano left the meeting convinced that Carranza "instead of imitating Juárez had copied Díaz." [62]

When he spoke to the delegates at the Constitutional Convention in 1916, Carranza had a third major opportunity to express his sympathy for meaningful reform. Yet again, he simply dusted off shopworn panaceas. Had his suggestions been approved the delegates at Querétaro would have endorsed the Charter of 1857. In a eulogy to it, Carranza had claimed for the Charter the highest principles known to mankind, forged, he contended, in reference to the French Revolution, on the anvil of the greatest upheaval of the eighteenth century. These principles, pontificated the First Chief, had withstood the test of time, "sanctioned by their use in England and the United States, two of the largest and most powerful nations on earth." [63] Although incorporating the Adiciones, Carranza's remedies basically left unchanged the character of the old Constitution. As he said, his draft "preserved its liberal spirit and its form of government." His recommendations "merely sought to purge it of the no longer applicable, to correct its deficiencies, to clarify its precepts, and to cleanse it of aberrations inspired by the selfish desire to perpetuate dictatorship." [64] The first goal at Querétaro was "unquestionably to spell out carefully the defense of human liberty." [65] At the core of Carranza's suggestions was the ideal of freedom. To Carranza, the Reforma had marked a milestone in the history of Mexican progress; unfortunately, Díaz had corrupted its accomplishments. [66]

The reforms he urged, in some instances only corrections in the language of the old Charter, glossed over key popular demands, including the agrarian issues, labor legislation, and public education. He never believed that government had a right to control "individual initiative and social activity" for that, in his opinion, converted the individual and society into "slaves of government's omnipotent will." He felt more at home when advocating municipal autonomy, universal suffrage, a ban on the re-election of public officials, and divorce. Questions relating to property rights frightened him. He wanted placed in Article 27 merely the authority of government to acquire property when public utility demanded it. With that authority, government could do whatever was necessary to acquire lands and redistribute them, and in that manner, stimulate the growth of small property. [67] As Calero observed, Carranza obviously did not speak for the peasants of Mexico, most of whom probably sympathized with Villa and Zapata. [68] Amaya, a Carrancista general, calculated that up to 50,000 armed men still held out against the Constitutionalists, especially in Chihuahua and southern Mexico. [69] In the opinion of Salvador Alvarado, a Constitutionalist general from Sonora, "Carranza was never a revolutionary or a reformer." [70]

IV

When don Venustiano, the second of the revolutionary *caudillos* took the oath of office in 1917, the time appeared ripe for change. As Alvarado wrote, "everyone voiced hope and confidence in the task of rebuilding Mexico." With the defeat of Villa, factional strife had ended; only Zapata, more a nuisance than a military problem, disputed Carranza's authority. Across the northern border, the United States, the old nemesis, had marched off to war in Europe. All the same, Alvarado spoke with exaggerated optimism. To begin with, he had not taken Carranza into account.

Carranza, of course, had sworn to defend the Constitution of 1917 but enforcing its reform legislation was another matter. To implement its key articles, Congress had to pass *leyes reglamentarias*. By not asking for them, Carranza let the legislation lapse when it suited his purpose.[71] With Zapata, the First Chief proved an implacable enemy. When the Constitutionalists captured Mexico City from Huerta, Carranza kept the federal troops fighting Zapata in their trenches until his own soldiers could replace them. In 1919, when General Pablo González had Zapata ambushed and killed, Carranza sent his crony a telegram of congratulations, and promoted the killer, a mangy colonel by the name of Jesús Guajardo, giving him 50,000 pesos.

On his commitment to defend Mexican sovereignty, on the other hand, Carranza seldom wavered. He was a typical son of the north, and northerners, to quote Fuentes Mares, himself a native of Chihuahua, "are *pochos,* Mexicans infatuated with the ways of the Yankee or carry deep in their soul the ecumenical ideal of the Hispanic," and Carranza scorned *pochos.*[72] Above all, he was a patriot, a tireless enemy of "yankee greed." [73] Large and powerful nations, he emphasized time and time again, had no license to exploit the small and weak. He wanted to rid Mexico of the special rights enjoyed by foreigners at the expense of its own citizens. Everyone residing in Mexico must obey its laws, without recourse to protection from foreign governments. "No more bayonets, no more cannon, no more battleships to be used to protect a man who sets out to build a fortune and to exploit the wealth of another country"—this was Carranza's motto.[74] But, whatever his virtues, and they were legion, Carranza neither worshipped reform nor carried it out in practice. For revolutionaries, he had only suspicion.

ELEVEN

Alvaro Obregón: The Self-Made Man

"Mexico must be saved from its redeemers."

Alvaro Obregón

I

TEACHING SCHOOL, whatever its merits, never bestowed fame or wealth on anyone in Mexico, and Alvaro Obregón, the mastermind of Venustiano Carranza's army, early coveted both. So, after a short stint as a schoolmaster in the town of Moroncarit, Sonora, he abandoned the classroom for more fertile pastures. With the triumph of Francisco I. Madero, and the aid of his brother José, one of the resident *caciques,* he became *presidente municipal* of Huatabampo. According to José María Maytorena, governor of Sonora under Madero, José, without consulting public opinion, arbitrarily appointed his brother.[1] But he did so with the compliance of the state legislature where Adolfo de la Huerta, a future rebel leader and intimate of Obregón, served.[2] Ironically, when named to his first public office, Obregón had not lifted a finger against the Old Regime.

Not until Madero was safely in the National Palace did Obregón reveal his "revolutionary" sentiments. In 1912, when Pascual Orozco, angry with Madero, invaded Sonora, Obregón, spurred on by his nephew and crony Benjamín Hill, went off to the wars. Obregón, whom Hill called a *caciquillo,* became a lieutenant colonel and commander of 250 men, a majority recruited and armed by state authorities.[3] Obviously, if Obregón

had not already won his spurs in the community, Governor Maytorena would not have named him the chief of the military forces
sent to stop the invading Orozquistas. With his victory, Obregón
began his ascent up the ladder of political success. In December,
1920, the former *presidente municipal* and foe of Orozco, with
time out for military campaigns against Victoriano Huerta and
Francisco Villa, became president of Mexico, having, in the
course of events, ousted Carranza and acquired a reputation as a
liberal reformer. At the Constitutional Convention of 1916–17,
delegates claiming to speak for him, substantially modified Carranza's blueprints for reform. When Obregón took office in 1920,
many predicted a sharp break with the politics of Madero and
Carranza. Yet, to the anger and dismay of a host of his followers,
Obregón's rupture with the past proved more rhetorical than real.

II

Obregón, however, draped himself in the mantle of the self-made
man admired by his contemporaries in the Western world.[4] He
was, despite his reputation as a reformer, a politician with whom
bankers and businessmen could sympathize. His ideals were in
tune with the rhetoric of the self-proclaimed practical men. On
one occasion, in defending himself against the vitriolic attacks of
Antonio Díaz Soto y Gama, who accused him of temporizing on
the agrarian question, Obregón replied that he missed the advice from "practical men, for very often practice teaches us better than theory." What might sound "good in theory," he warned
in "practice . . . may result in failure." [5] Obregón, moreover, had
another much admired side. He loved to tinker with mechanical
gadgets. With some justification, he could claim the title of inventor. In 1909, he had designed a machine to plant garbanzo
beans that planters along the Río Mayo adopted for use on their
lands. He built the first machine out of wood, strengthening it
with bits of scrap iron. Its success inspired him to design a better
machine, with iron parts built by the foundry in Mazatlán. On a
limited scale, Obregón "mass-produced" his planter for sale to
farmers in Sonora and Sinaloa.[6] By 1910, the future municipal

president of Huatabampo had become, if not a rival to Cyrus McCormick, a successful inventor and salesman for his machine.

As Madero and Carranza before him, Obregón was light of skin, so "white," recalled Vicente Blasco Ibáñez, the Spanish intellectual who visited Mexico, "that it is impossible to tell whether he has a drop of Indian blood." Obregón, mused Blasco Ibáñez, could easily pass for a Spaniard on the streets of Madrid.[7] Born in Siquisiva, Sonora, in 1880, Obregón was the youngest of eighteen children by Francisco Obregón and Cenobia Salido.[8] While always boasting of his humble origins, Obregón actually was born, recalled Juan de Dios Bojórquez, in "a large house." [9] Cenobia, his mother, was the sister of Jesús, Martín, and José María Salido, owners of *haciendas* (Rosales, Tres Hermanos, and Santa Barbara) in the Mayo River valley. The brothers were on good terms with Ramón Corral, Luis Torres, and Rafael Izábal, the *caciques* of Sonora.[10] While Obregón's father never attained the social rank of the Salido family, still, in the opinion of Emilio Portes Gil, a distinguished *politico* in his own right, don Alvaro was at least of "middle class" background.[11]

María, Rosa, and Cenobia, the older sisters who raised him, were school-teachers. The three were avid readers and one an aspiring poet. The family moved to Huatabampo in 1889 where José, an older brother, became the *cacique*. For awhile, Obregón farmed rented lands. In 1907, with the profits from his harvests of garbanzos, he purchased 150 hectares of land near Huatabampo, soon after buying another fifty hectares.[12] He called his farm, considered a *"rancho"* by Dios Bojórquez, the "Quinta Chilla," the impoverished country manor.[13] By 1911, the Quinta Chilla had become the center of a profitable operation in garbanzos. When Hill, already deeply committed, urged him to join the Madero bloc in Sonora, Obregón refused.[14]

Essentially a self-taught man, Obregón had little formal education, but he had completed primary school and learned much from the tutelage of his sisters. Friends claim that he read widely and voraciously, at least when not at the cock fights, playing cards with his *amigos*, or looking for ways to make money as an inventor or farmer. Admirers report that he read the labor journals of his time: *El Radical*, *El Socialista*, and *El Tipógrafo*. He had seen the *Manifiesto* published by Ricardo Flores Magón in 1906. According to Portes Gil, who reached the presidency on the shoulders of the Sonora clan, Obregón had read the writings of Vargas Vila, Vicente Blasco Ibáñez, Peter Kropotkin, Anatole France, Henri Barbuse, and Francisco Ferrer Guardia.[15] In particular, Obregón admired Vargas Vila, whom he thought of as "a great *liróforo*" (lyric poet).[16] One of his uncritical admirers, General Juan Gualberto Amaya, understood Obregón to be a faithful reader of *Regeneración,* the revolutionary journal of the Flores Magón, and an ardent sympathizer of the miners in their strike against the moguls of Cananea.[17] Obregón even tried his hands at writing poetry, as the following stanza testifies:

> "I have chased after victory,
> And I have won it;
> But upon grasping it,
> I despaired.
> The rays that outlined it,
> Revealed in all their light,
> The ashes of the dead;
> The suffering of the living."

His *Ocho Mil Kilómetros en Campaña,* or as one wit quipped, "eight thousand kilometers of politics," made Obregón an author as well as a poet. Of the rebel chieftains, Obregón was the first to welcome intellectuals and artists. If he seldom asked their advice, at least he tolerated them. Some, the celebrated painter, Dr. Atl, for example, in trying to convert Obregón into a radical reformer, ended up doing the general's bidding.

Few manipulated Obregón, for he generally knew what he wanted. One of his goals was power. Plutarco Elías Calles, ally and friend of don Alvaro, blamed Obregón's betrayal of principles on his "unchecked hunger for power."[18] That thirst for power, for high public office, had an early beginning. From the start, friends and foes of Obregón frequently mentioned his poorly concealed political ambitions. "General," so goes an apocryphal story, "you have excellent eyesight. It is so good," replied Obregón, "that I could see the presidency from Huatabampo." Supposedly, Obregón told the story on himself, and he very well may have because, as one who knew him explained, "he was cocky." [19] His ambition and his "cockiness" on more than one occasion cost Obregón dearly. His unwillingness to tolerate potential rivals drove scores of early allies from Sonora to join the enemy camp, including De la Huerta and Salvador Alvarado. He punished disloyalty swiftly and harshly, especially that of friends and allies, as Martín Luis Guzmán graphically depicted in *La Sombra del Caudillo*. When he felt it necessary, Obregón did not hesitate to order the death of men who had served with him since the days of the rebellion in Sonora. On the evidence available, he was at least morally responsible for the murder of Venustiano Carranza. He viewed Mexican politics with cynicism, once remarking that no Mexican general could "withstand a cannon ball of fifty thousand pesos." Whenever possible, he manipulated those around him with a pat on the back, a word of praise, or by opening the door to the public trough; when opposed, however, his fury knew no bounds. He was a wonderful story-teller, an encyclopedia of anecdotes and jokes, a speaker able to hold his audience for hours at length. People who met him usually found him an intelligent, charming, and witty conversationalist. But his gregarious nature also included a tough and frequently vindictive element. He never forgave De la Huerta, despite a friendship antedating the days of Madero in Sonora. To Obregón, "bastardly ambitions" had impelled De la Huerta to break with him.[20] Nor, as he told the Chamber of Commerce of Monterrey, then preaching national forgiveness and unity, would he forget that it had lodged no protest against the murders of Felipe Carrillo Puerto and his brothers in Yucatán.[21] Yet, in truth, the brutal killings had shocked De la Huerta as much as Obregón.

After forsaking school-teaching, Obregón had worked briefly as a traveling shoe-salesman in Sonora and Sinaloa. History does not record the success or failure of this aspect of his career. That job, however, undoubtedly marked the low point of his life. By 1920, when he occupied the National Palace, Obregón had built a paltry income into a fortune that, as Maytorena remarked, made pale by comparison the "wealth of the most hated *científicos*." [22] While his old foe may have exaggerated, no one disputed that Obregón was a man who loved money. Writing to Luis

Cabrera in 1919, he joyously explained how he had agreed to supply railroad ties to the Ferrocarril Sud-Pacífico. The ties, he boasted, "had turned out plentiful and cheap, something that, while pleasing the company, enriches my pocketbook and helps my credit rating, and that has put me in such a good mood that I am happy in whatever I do." [23] By 1912, one Sonora banker testified, Obregón had "enough money to live well." [24] That proclivity for wealth did not confine itself to the most famous offspring of the Obregón family. José, "the general's dull-witted brother," had become "excessively zealous in appropriating to himself both cash and property." [25] Obregón took pride, as he said once, in having taken up arms against Orozco even though materially successful. As he stated, he had not turned rebel to "satisfy mundane wants." The men who joined him, he proudly exclaimed, were of the same group, "men of work, well known, and respected in their communities." [26] One adulator, Luis L. León, then a fixture in the Chamber of Deputies, recalled Obregón as a "businessman who had never tarnished his revolutionary creed." [27]

More than anything else, Obregón was a man of the soil. Despite his talents with machines, his later military exploits, and his political victories, he never lost touch with the lands of his native Sonora. Unlike a legion of other politicians, the bright lights of Mexico City failed to seduce him. Until his death, he remained a loyal son of the countryside, with the mentality of a successful farmer, or as the case may be, a twentieth-century *hacendado*. His Quinta Chilla eventually became an estate of 3500 hectares, while later in the Yaqui valley he acquired additional lands for his sons to cultivate.[28] To till his lands, on which he planted garbanzos for export, Obregón employed a work force of 1,500 men.[29] As a prosperous planter, as well as the nephew of *hacendados*, he easily acquired the mentality of the northern planter class. Modern in his outlook upon the land and its cultivation, he combined the knowledge of the farmer with the sagacity of the businessman. Unafraid to exploit his political prestige for personal profit, he built a garbanzo empire in Sonora.[30] The Quinta Chilla, the "impoverished country estate," as he described it, was the first step in his upward climb. It was from the land that he became *presidente municipal* of Huatabampo, head of the army in Sonora, and ultimately Carranza's military brain. When he resigned as minister of war in 1917, he went home to farm his estate, where he set about planting garbanzos in larger and larger quantities, raising cattle for export as hides and beef, and purchasing stock in mines.[31] He numbered among his friends the old planters, as well as the "revolutionaries" who acquired new lands for themselves or the estates of the Díaz élite now in exile. As president of Mexico, he not infrequently spent vacations with his family on the *haciendas* of friends. One such favorite retreat was the Hacienda Atequiza in Jalisco, the property of Agustín R. Esparza, an *hacendado* with old ties to the region.[32] Despite his reputation as an ally of the working-man, he felt at home with *hacendados,* the bane of the Mexico of Díaz. Obregón symbolized the modern-day *hacendado,* the landowner who cultivated his lands wisely and efficiently, harvested crops for export, and grew rich from the profits of his enterprise. When he left the presidency in 1924, Obregón returned to the lands he knew so well.

But Obregón, the "self-made man," had amassed his wealth not merely by tilling the land, but by dabbling in sundry other business enterprises. The less reverent dubbed him the "garbanzo merchant." His correspondence from the National Palace included countless observations on the state of the garbanzo industry. Yet garbanzos, while a principal preoccupation, did not monopolize his time. Upon his return from Mexico City in 1917, he had established his business headquarters in Nogales, a border town. Named the Oficina Comercial de Alvaro Obregón, it soon was known by its shortened title, Casa Obregón. In a letter written in 1917, where he advertised its opening, Obregón told how it would handle exports and imports by both Americans and Mexicans, with particular emphasis on the sales of garbanzos and cattle, as well as the purchase of all types of machinery. For a commission, added Obregón, his office would also buy and sell lands and mines, as well as engage in other kinds of business ventures.[33] That same year, Obregón helped organize the Unión de Agricultores de Sonora y Sinaloa, an association of garbanzo planters, and became its first president.[34] Named a member of the exclusive Casino Unión de Navolato, Obregón, as president of the Republic, accepted with alacrity, commenting that its membership included "many of my old and good friends and companions" in business and agriculture.[35] When he abandoned the National Palace, he purchased a costly Lincoln automobile.[36]

Obregón was an entrepreneur, whether in business, agriculture, or real estate. At no time in his life, not even as president, did he forsake these activities. That he should carry the attitudes and values that made him a business success into the world of politics and reform hardly seems incongruous. What does appear illogical is that reformers should have expected revolutionary magic from the entrepreneur who built the Quinta Chilla into a profitable business.

III

Obregón was a political animal, concluded Narcisco Bassols Batalla, "perhaps the most representative of his epoch." [37] His political acumen rallied together all the diverse factions of 1920. To scores of his followers, according to León, Obregón was "the key figure in our social revolution." [38] Or, as another disciple phrased it, "the mighty figure of Obregón expressed the legitimacy of our legal institutions." [39] To José Angel Ceniceros, who later became minister of education, Obregón had spoken for the main currents of reform: the Constitutionalist emphasis of Madero and Carranza; the proletarian upheaval of Francisco Villa; and the agrarian crusade of Emiliano Zapata.[40]

Whatever the merits of these opinions, they fail to come to grips with the crux of Obregón's convictions. If in actuality he embodied these diverse modes of thought, it was not because he could be all things to all men, but because he placed politics and personal relations above principle. Given a certain leeway, he could live with a wide range of opinion. Within reason, Obregón was flexible, if his allies and rivals accepted his pragmatic middle road. He had nothing in common with messiahs of either the right or the left.

Until 1919, when his enemies attempted to thwart his ambitions, the Man from Huatabampo had lived in peace, if not always in accord, with Carranza, to whom he owed his political career. As a loyal adherent of the First Chief, Obregón had won the plaudits of the Casa del Obrero Mundial, helped recruit Red Battalions for Carranza's war against Villa and Zapata, and probably backed the liberal reforms of the Constitution of 1917, which Carranza opposed. When he departed from Carranza's cabinet in 1917, he left with his liberal reputation untarnished. All the same, his backers ran nearly the entire gamut of politics, from firebrands such as Antonio Díaz Soto y Gama to Francisco Serrano and Aarón Sáenz, men of ambition. History will surely not remember these staunch disciples of Obregón, Rafael Zubarán Capmany, Jesús Urueta, and Alberto J. Pani as stalwarts of social change. In Michoacán, a province that played a salient role in the rebellion of 1920, Pascual Ortiz Rubio, its governor and a conservative with the backbone of a jellyfish, deserted Carranza to join Obregón.[41] Meanwhile, Francisco Múgica, the conscience of Michoacán, also sided with Obregón. With victory in hand, however, Obregón embraced Ortiz Rubio, driving Múgica to sympathize, if not join, the rebellion of 1923. Yet Obregón kept the allegiance of General Lázaro Cárdenas, an intimate of Múgica, a reformer, and *cacique* of Michoacán. To survive in politics, Obregón learned, it was important to keep one's finger on the public pulse. The successful politician, as Obregón's record demonstrates, had to march with the wind at his back, to neither lag behind or get too far ahead of his army. How do you judge Porfirio Díaz, an aide once asked Obregón. "As a man of his times," Obregón replied. His tragedy, said the Man from Huatabampo, "was to have grown old." [42] By outliving his usefulness, Díaz had fallen behind the thinking of his age. Had Díaz left office at the appropriate juncture, in the opinion of Obregón, he would have assured himself a revered niche in history. Obregón was a perceptive historian.

Obregón proved a cautious political leader. He looked upon patience as a virtue, a trait that served him admirably at the battle of Celaya where he outwaited Villa. Theoretically, he believed in a large measure of authority for the president while wary of claims to local autonomy.[43] Still, to settle problems at the local level, he encouraged subordinates to make the decisions. Confronted with a dilemma, he was apt to turn the matter over to the governor or the military boss. Before acting, Obregón waited for the right opportunity. He seldom seized the initiative, and rarely went out of his way to oppose groups with political clout.

Obregón had tested this formula of "wait and see" long before he had scaled the political ladder. While he boasted in his book that enemies of the dictatorship had recognized Madero as "our man," the facts tell a different story.[44] To repeat, he stayed out of the battle between Madero and Díaz. If he sympathized with Madero, or with the writings of the Flores Magón, as he later claimed, mindful of the fate of General Bernardo Reyes, whom Díaz had exiled to Europe, Obregón kept his opinions to himself. He said nothing when Zapata issued his Plan de Ayala and remained silent during the strike at Cananea. Not until Madero had triumphed and Orozco invaded Sonora did Obregón jump on the rebel bandwagon.[45] General Amaya, whose admiration for Obregón knew no bounds, had to confess that his hero "was no more than a platonic sympathizer of Madero's candidacy." [46] Still, in *Ocho Mil Kilómetros*, its author says nothing about Madero's ideas or indicates how he felt about them. Upon hearing of Madero's death, he wrote, he decided to battle Huerta.[47] Maytorena, his archenemy, claimed the opposite to be true. In *Verdades Sobre el General Alvaro Obregón*, he states Obregón, had even contemplated recognizing Huerta. Maytorena, whatever the distortions in his account, knew Obregón intimately; he believed that Obregón had not participated in the Madero uprising because he doubted its chances for success, and by the same token, owed a debt of gratitude to politicians of the Old Regime in Sonora.[48]

Obregón met Carranza—a man he followed until his appetite for the presidency overcame his loyalty—in September, 1913, after the First Chief arrived in Sonora. In April, the Constitutionalists had affixed their signatures to the Plan de Guadalupe, which uttered not a word on the subject of social reform. In his book, Obregón swore that he gave this plan his unequivocal endorsement.[49] For their part, in their war on Huerta, Obregón and his companions spoke of their duty to defend the sovereignty of Sonora but were mute on matters of reform and ideology.[50] If the testimony of his friends can be trusted, at Querétaro Obregón broke with Carranza's model for the future. Over the objections of the First Chief, the "radicals" at the Convention, with the blessings of Obregón, put meaningful reform planks into the magna carta. But, as Félix F. Palavicini reminded his readers, Obregón and his closest cohorts were barely involved with the Convention. Only their sympathizers attended, for fundamentally the Obregón clan shared little enthusiasm for the document. They would make up their minds once public opinion had expressed itself.[51]

Not wishing to be identified with the Carranza regime, Obregón retired to his Quinta Chilla. Yet, strangely enough, the Plan de Agua Prieta, Obregón's later call to rebellion, scarcely differed from the Plan de Guadalupe. It was, said Francisco Vásquez Gómez, essentially a political declaration, without social commitments.[52] Of the seven justifications for his candidacy in *Ocho Mil Kilómetros,* just one censured the "absence of social reforms." The others focused on liberty, honest elections, the endangered peace, and the fear of dictatorship.[53] Antenor Sala, the man with the troubled conscience, meanwhile, admonished Obregón that while "the leaders discussed elections, the vote, constitutions, and legal niceties, the humble and poor" thought only of "liberty and land." [54] On the other hand, perhaps the view from Sonora had blurred Obregón's vision of national priorities. In 1917, he had returned to one of the provinces least afflicted by economic maladies, where mining, agriculture, and the livestock industry, well on their way to recovery, offered jobs at good pay to their workers.[55]

Almost the entire military machine, from generals with chests heavy with medals to lowly lieutenants and privates, supported Obregón's *cuartelazo* in 1920. At that time, he applauded the turnabout of the army brass who, just three years before, had sworn to uphold Carranza. But he felt differently in 1923, when over half of the soldiers and their commanders, including generals who had sided with him against Carranza, embraced De la Huerta's abortive coup. He called the campaign to squelch his old comrades-in-arms one of the decisive struggles in the history of social reform.[56] Yet, until the army chieftains challenged his right to pick his successor, Obregón had only cautiously tinkered with the ancient labor and agrarian structure of the Republic.

As Díaz earlier, and unlike Madero and Carranza, Obregón put little faith in political parties.[57] Like don Porfirio, Obregón was an expert chess player, a manipulator of men. He did not want a political party to tie his hands. He welcomed the Partido Laborista, knit together by Luis Morones to help Obregón's bid for the presidency, only until he ruled the political roost. He usually ignored the Partido Nacional Agrarista, to the despair of Díaz Soto y Gama, although he had encouraged its birth to checkmate Morones and his labor bloc. His trusted allies whom he picked carefully, were generally moderates and occasionally conservatives. None of his intimate collaborators advocated radical measures. To the contrary, the men who survived the Obregón years were, in the mold of their leader, cautious politicans. Some, Sáenz and Abelardo Rodríguez, to cite the example of two, became millionaires. Others, such as Arnulfo R. Gómez, the cruel and blood-thirsty general from Sonora appointed minister of war in 1922, squandered fortunes on women and the profligate life. "Tell me who your friends are and I will tell you who you are," runs an old Mexican proverb. Judged by its wisdom, Obregón fares only moderately well. Certainly, if the character of friends defines a man, Obregón was no social revolutionary.

As a self-made man, Obregón had always worshipped the pragmatic, that which produced results. His political philosophy rested on that assumption. He was not an idealogue but rather a man of his era.[58] Writing in 1917, he professed to have smiled benevolently upon all of the foes of Díaz, the Flores Magón as well as Bernardo Reyes.[59] The ideology and method of the two camps, nonetheless, were miles apart. Reyes timidly begged for a spot on the national ticket while Ricardo Flores Magón ultimately preached a revolutionary socialist doctrine. As late as 1915, Dr. Atl recalled, Obregón had merely a vague notion of reform, essentially that of a businessman and soldier. In Atl's version, neither socialist doctrines nor radical panaceas had darkened Obregón's thoughts; not until 1915 did Obregón begin to piece together a philosophy of reform.[60]

Little in his political career, however, demonstrates that Obregón adopted more than a moderate version of social change. True, he helped Atl and his Syndicalist colleagues sway labor over to Carranza and, at the Constitutional Convention may have encouraged the reform mavericks. Still, these were the highlights of his "revolutionary" career. As president, he trod cautiously. Despite his relative youth, like Madero and Carranza earlier, Obregón had matured with the ideas of the nineteenth century. As an editorial in *Excelsior* in 1919 pointed out, he was a "classical liberal." [61] He was cast in the mold of men such as Woodrow Wilson. While he expressed sympathy for the underdog, consciously or not, he accepted as gospel Spencer's notion of the survival of the fittest. In a world where inequality prevailed, the vigorous and strong, the more intelligent and industrious, triumphed over the weak and lazy. [62] The sons of Arizona and Texas, he told a Dallas audience in 1920, "are strong and vigorous . . . because they have gained strength in the struggle to survive; because what they possess they owe to their own personal efforts." [63] The cause of social justice and equality was not advanced, he admonished his listeners on another occasion in Mazatlán, by "robbing the rich of their shoes and hats in order to give them to those who wore *huaraches* and straw *sombreros*." [64] The liberal dogmas of the nineteenth century, the worship of individual rights, the spirit of private enterprise, and free competition—these were the theoretical cornerstones of the Man from Huatabampo. [65] To update and streamline Mexican capitalism was his cardinal goal. In its pursuit, he tolerated the survival of the ancient ruling class: industrialists, bankers, merchants, and even *hacendados,* while urging them to become authentic men of enterprise. [66] He believed in a society where classes lived in harmony, the workers alongside of the capitalists, the poor with the rich. [67] All would profit in such a world. Political extremes, doctrines incompatible with the liberal faith, found no sanction in his mind. As he rejected a decoration offered him by Benito Mussolini in 1924, so he turned a deaf ear to the siren calls of the Soviet Union. [68]

On capital-labor relations, Obregón shared views in common with Wilsonian Progressives in the United States, enlightened perhaps but certainly not radical. Apostles of capitalism had little to fear from them. The "problems of the working class will be solved," he volunteered, when capitalists enjoyed security for their investments in Mexico. [69] His prescription for economic growth called for "saving capital while guaranteeing the rights of labor." [70] To Obregón that meant establishing an equilibrium

between capital and labor, giving business and industry the opportunity to earn a just profit, and in the process, to provide labor with adequate wages and a decent standard of living. He
blamed the conflict between capital and labor on the poorly designed legislation of professional politicians, written so "am-
biguously," that it encouraged labor to strike but in the end favored management.[71] For Mexico, Obregón wanted a system
that protected the worker without attacking capital; to deny
capital sensible guarantees would block the development of "our
natural resources." [72] The purpose of labor legislation was to
"mark where the rights of the worker ended and the rights of the
employer began." Such a demarcation would abolish labor strife,
establish a "perfect harmony between the two classes and encourage the aggrandizement of Mexico." [73] He asked the worker
to understand that the most menial job offered pleasure as well
as opportunity for self improvement. Honorable work was the
best teacher: the "school of hard knocks was the noblest of all
schools." [74] While he regretted the lack of harmony between
capital and labor, he warned that he had not become president
to deepen the chasm, "because a good ruler, rather than take
sides, encourages harmony and equilibrium between the two
classes." [75]

Yet, although a champion of the "happy family," Obregón
foresaw the role of his government as merely that of a neutral
arbitrator. On their own, labor and capital must hammer out a
just relationship. Justice would be meted out to labor, he told
the workers of a cigar factory, without the necessity of government interference. We must acknowledge that "duty is our sole
judge," he warned his listeners, that "justice will be granted by
those above to those below, without resort to laws or authorities." [76] His government would simply see to it that both capital and labor, on a plane of equality, worked to mutual advantage. A spirit of laissez faire, anachronistic in light of the
rhetoric of Revolution, motivated Obregón.[77] He looked upon
"neutrality" as the best of possible worlds for the state. The government would merely arbitrate as a neutral referee. Still, despite
these traditional attitudes, Obregón conferred upon labor rights
and benefits denied it by both Madero and Carranza.

No one can deny, nonetheless, that Obregón, in his Plan de

Agua Prieta, walked with the ghosts of Madero and Carranza. His campaign for the presidency raised aloft the tattered banner of administrative morality.[78] Perchance it was with tongue in cheek that he declared universal suffrage a remedy for national ills—as had Madero a decade earlier. To Obregón, Sonora and its sister provinces in the north had revolted in quest of liberty. Once in office, he made public education a prime goal of his administration—as any moderate reformer might who saw evolution as a cure for his country's ills.[79] But, then, as early as January 1915, Obregón, while acknowledging the urgency of social reforms, had concluded that the "most important were moral in character." [80]

IV

On questions of rural reform Obregón adopted a gradualist approach, as he had when dealing with capital and labor. During his campaign of 1919, he walked gingerly over the agrarian issue. He was silent on the *haciendas,* refusing to commit himself to their subdivision. Earlier, at the time of the Aguascalientes Convention, when asked whether he favored the Plan de Ayala, Obregón had replied that he was not opposed to it, but in reference to a strident declaration on its behalf by Díaz Soto y Gama, he was against long-winded and demagogic speeches.[81] He maintained that he sympathized with the plight of the peasants. Nevertheless, as Bassols Batalla underlines, Obregón had never distinguished himself for his kinship with the apostles of the peasants. Commenting on Article 27, the land reform plank of the Constitution of 1917, Obregón informed a group of congressman that "its architects were . . . overfilled with the noblest of enthusiasm but totally destitute of a practical sense and agricultural knowledge." [82] When asked to clarify his stance, he hastened to explain that he indeed foresaw the subdivision of the great estates. But, when queried as to how long it would take, he replied that he did not know. Small property, however, was the wave of the future.[83] Obregón's commitment, nonetheless, lacks the ring of truth; at best it appears illogical. Had Obregón, an *hacendado* himself, truly believed in the partition of the mammoth estates, he would have hung the sword of Damocles over his own head. In the light of that stubborn reality, two other accounts probably strike closer to the truth. "Thank God, in Sonora we have no apostles of agrarian reform," Alfredo Breceda recalled that Obregón jubilantly told Carranza upon meeting him for the first time in 1913. "We are in arms," said Obregón, "out of patriotism and to avenge the murder of Madero." [84] On another occasion, on a journey by train to Fortín de las Flores, Obregón had invited along ten congressmen. According to Israel del Castillo, one of the guests, Obregón, in discussing a bill he had asked Congress to endorse, pointed out that it made possible the subdivision of the *latifundios* but left the executive to carry it out. The lands would be given to those qualified to farm them. But, he went on, there was a joker in the deck: because most peasants were unprepared to till the lands, they would be ineligible to ask for them. This, he chuckled, was the perfect solution because now nobody could say that his government had not attempted to redistribute the land.[85]

Obregón's heralded affinity with the worker excluded the peasant. Little in his record, either in speeches or deeds, indicates that he fully understood or sympathized with their plight. To the contrary, his attitude casts doubts on his intentions. Possibly, this may explain why military chieftains with dreams of agrarian reform broke with him. One of them was General Lucio Blanco, who supervised the initial subdivision of an *hacienda* in Mexico. In 1914, at a meeting in the home of Blanco, after the defeat of Huerta by Villa at Torreón, reported Colonel Eduardo C. González, Obregón, sensing a final victory in the immediate offing, had declared that it was time to begin to think about the future. We, he exclaimed, "shall be the *científicos* of tomorrow." Obviously irritated, Blanco answered that he had not risked his life merely to turn back the clock. At this point, said González, Obregón launched into a tirade against the *calzonudos*, peasants, claiming among other things, that he was worth more than five peasants.[86] Some of his closest allies, admitted Obregón, referred to Huerta as an "Indian," a racial slur that did not disturb him.[87] He ridiculed Zapata's army, predicting that when Zapata and Villa met in the National Palace, "a convulsion of repugnance would sweep over Mexico." [88] On the other hand, if Bassols Batalla is correct, Obregón while he thought Zapata misdirected still respected him, but Obregon had no use for Villa.[89] On his lands in Sonora, said a visitor, Obregón, while not overly friendly with his workers, dealt with them openly.[90] But his relations with the Yaquis, often the workers in his fields, were ambiguous. He labeled them "savages," and they retaliated by trying to kill him.[91] At other times, complained an American farmer in Sonora, he kept the military from chasing the Yaquis.[92] No one can deny, furthermore, that many of his finest soldiers were Yaquis. He occasionally boasted of their merits as farmers.[93] Still, whatever contemporaries may have thought of Obregón, his record hardly indicates he was a friend of peasants and land reform. While he outshone Madero and Carranza, he distributed fewer lands in four years than his successor in half that time.

V

A striking feature of the rebellion against Díaz was nationalism. The slogan was "Mexico for the Mexicans." Carranza, unquestionably, spoke its language. He made his forte the defense of Mexican interests. Obregón's position, by the same token, defies analysis. As in related matters, ambivalence best describes his attitude, although he was a nationalist, a Mexican who awaited the day when his countrymen would control their own affairs. When Wilson sent the marines to invade Veracruz, he urged Carranza to declare war on the United States. Still, he bent his nationalism to fit the occasion. Deep in his heart, he probably admired the United States. He looked upon Mexico and its neighbor across the border, as he stated in El Paso in 1920, as "sister nations." [94] He wanted "fraternity and harmony between the two countries." At Springfield, Illinois, during a visit to the United States, he expressed admiration for Abraham Lincoln who had "made of his country, with its democracy, one of the nations of the civilized world truly worthy of praise and love." [95] Obregón's basic ideals, after all, were compatible in large measure with the philosophy of the American people. Both believed in the Horatio Alger myth, in the rugged individual, in private enterprise, and in the virtues of free competition. He attributed the success of the United States to its principles, and looked upon them as the salvation for Mexico.

Obregón, furthermore, linked both his business and political success to foreigners. He exported his garbanzos to Spain and endeavored to enlarge the garbanzo market in the United States. He established a business house in Nogales to exploit the trade between Sonora and the American Southwest, counting on his good connections with American merchants. As president, he encouraged the growth of chambers of commerce and industry and their ties with sister organizations abroad. He sent agents to Europe and the United States to lure investment capital to Mexico, offering inducements and guarantees.[96] He equated foreign investments with the development of Mexico's resources.[97] When Obregón entered Mexico City after the fall of Carranza, one general in his entourage was Manuel Peláez, a man for years in the pay of the foreign oil companies. When confronted with a military uprising in 1923, he made his peace with Washington, exchanging, critics charge, Mexican sovereignty and the ideals of the Constitution of 1917 for American recognition of his regime. Maytorena, his ancient enemy, never tired of castigating Obregón for his defense of foreigners and their properties in Mexico. It was partly because of Obregón's lukewarm defense of Mexican interests that Carranza refused to back his presidential ambitions, contended Miguel Alessio Robles.[98]

VI

Judged by what he said, as well as by his record, Obregón may have earned his spurs as a reformer but was hardly a radical or social revolutionary. The self-made man proved a cautious spokesman for change. A figure of his age, he worshipped the capitalist and middle class values of his contemporaries. He looked askance at exotic doctrines. Only on the issue of the Catholic Church did he share the adversion of his intemperate contemporaries.[99] But, it must be kept in mind, so had the classical liberals of mid-nineteenth century Mexico.

TWELVE *Francisco Villa:*

The Mexican Robin Hood

"He behaves as a committed radical, confiscating the goods of the enemy and purging the corrupt."

Silvestre Terrazas

I

THE UNPREDICTABLE LIFE of Francisco Villa best exemplifies the pitfalls of attempting to judge evenhandedly the ambiguities of the rebel leadership. Hero of Torreón and Zacatecas and a man of humble birth eulogized as the Robin Hood of Mexico, Villa became a powerful and much feared *hacendado*. He died planning to join a *cuartelazo* hatched by opportunistic military officers in 1923. Shortly after, Alvaro Obregón, then president of Mexico and an enemy of Villa, received a letter signed by scores of villagers in Chihuahua who applauded the demise of the "master of the *Hacienda* of Canutillo." [1] Yet, as the opinion of Silvestre Terrazas, an irascible foe of the Old Regime, testifies, Villa had his legions of devoted admirers. His career, however, only marginally verifies his credentials as a reformer. To the contrary: the story of Villa, anathema to Mexicans who cherished middle-class values, fits into the ideological picture set by Francisco I. Madero and embellished by Venustiano Carranza and Obregón.

II

Villa was born on July 7, 1878 as Doroteo Arango in La Coyotada, a small hamlet in Durango, to a family of sharecroppers. By 1892, he had earned his spurs as a petty thief, eventually joining a gang of bandits led by Francisco Villa, from whom he took his new eponym. A decade later he moved to Parral, a mining town in Chihuahua, and added cattle rustling to his list of clandestine escapades, practicing his trade in southern Chihuahua and northern Durango. By 1908, he captained his own band of cattle rustlers and thieves. Juan Gualberto Amaya, a native of Durango whose family knew Villa, writes that Villa included murder among his crimes.[2] In 1910, Villa the cattle thief wanted for murder, joined Pascual Orozco and Madero for their assault on Ciudad Juárez.

No one knows precisely why he did. In *El Hombre y Sus Armas* Martín Luis Guzmán, who had the ear of Villa, attributed the metamorphosis to Abraham González, an early disciple of Madero and a cattle buyer. According to Guzmán, González convinced Villa to identify his battle against legal authorities with the plight of the poor and exploited. By espousing their cause, Villa no longer would be simply a *bandolero,* a highwayman, and a purloiner of cattle.[3]

What Villa's change of heart really signified, nonetheless, remains shrouded in controversy. Only with difficulty does the evidence demonstrate that Villa truly embraced the crusade for social justice. For example: in 1914, Villa and Obregón, in a joint declaration of principles, urged the holding of elections, a purge of the judicial system, and a political house-cleaning. Of the nine points in their declaration, only one, the last on the list, discussed social ills, requesting that state governors designate committees to study the agrarian question and suggest remedies for it.[4] From this statement derives Carranza's reply for a "convention" of military leaders in Mexico City to consolidate the Constitutionalist movement. When Villa refused to journey south, the convention met in Aguascalientes. If Guzmán's version can be trusted, Villa believed in an "organized revolution, captained by a leader who behaved prudently, with men who loved order, respected property, and upheld the rights of others."[5] In his answer to Villa's appeal to arms, Carranza taunted his erstwhile subordinate with defending the status quo because of his "desire to install a constitutional system of government before the Revolution had time to enact the social reforms demanded by the Nation." Villa, reported Carranza, wanted the adoption of "radical and social reforms" postponed until a constitutional government could study, discuss, and resolve them. To Carranza, who conveniently forgot that he, too, defended the identical formula, "only enemies of the Revolution" could endorse such a plan.[6] By 1915, Obregón and Lucio Blanco, a reformer of impeccable standing, had jointly published a manifesto calling Villa "the conservative of today."[7]

Nor did Villa, like his rival Obregón, disregard the benefits of pecuniary gain. He displayed a sharp eye for profit; while a rebel, he was also an entrepreneur. From the start, these elements existed side by side within Villa. For helping his brother take Juárez, Gustavo Madero gave Villa 10 thousand pesos, which Villa employed to buy a butcher shop in Ciudad Chihuahua, and eventually a house.[8] He bought a meatpacking plant for 50 thousand pesos in Juárez, a business venture he kept out of the public eye by registering it in the name of one of his sundry wives. When his enemies blew the plant up, Villa asked Obregón for 40 thousand pesos to cover his losses. Obregón sent the money.[9] Villa numbered the Hotel Hidalgo in Parral among his properties.[10] Luis Aguirre Benavides, his former personal secretary, recalled that Villa reserved for himself the most lucrative enterprises. In Juárez, he ran the gambling casinos where, said Aguirre Benavides, Villa collected over 20 thousand pesos a month for nearly a year-and-a-half from money spent by visitors from across the border. On El Fresno, an *hacienda* he owned on the outskirts of Ciudad Chihuahua, Villa enjoyed the life of the country squire.[11] After his death, tenant farmers on his Hacienda de Canutillo accused Villa of pocketing over 20 thousand pesos given him to pay his bodyguard. According to his accursers, Villa had even profited from their labors, buying their wheat for less than he sold it for. When they complained, Villa threatened to shoot their spokesmen.[12]

To his followers, Villa was a Robin Hood, rewarding loyalty

with gifts. During his bountiful moods, he showered his trusted lieutenants with *haciendas,* mines, and businesses. He gave El Nuevo Mundo, a store in Ciudad Chihuahua, to Juan B. Baca, a relative of one of his lieutenants, and a flour mill to Vidal de la Garza, a companion. A textile mill in Santa Rosalía went to José Martínez.[13] He persuaded Obregón to grant rights to explore for oil along the Gulf of Mexico to a group of his relatives and friends.[14] General Rodolfo Fierro, ran the copper mines in Casas Grandes.[15] Hipólito, Villa's oafish brother, after making a fortune on gun-running in the United States, inherited a sheet metal shop in Jiménez, a small town not far from Parral.[16] When Villa died, Hipólito attempted to make himself master of the Hacienda de Canutillo.[17] Obregón rejected the request and Hipólito went off to fight with the coup leaders of 1923.

III

At the battle of Celaya in 1915, Obregón put an end to Villa's dreams of glory. Conflicting ambitions and not ideological rivalries, however, underlie the clash between the Constitutionalists and Villa's army of the North. Both cloaked themselves with mantles of similar color. As L. Rivas Iruz, an intimate of Carranza, admitted, the Villistas included "many who sympathized with the Constitutionalists but who, in a moment of error and because of special circumstances, took a false step." Given the similarity of goals, he continued, these elements would either return to the Constitutionalists's fold or abandon the struggle. By the same token, Villa's allies, the Zapatistas, he added perceptively, were different in ideology and in class structure.[18] Obregón, himself, wondered why Villa had marched off alone, thinking the break with Carranza a misunderstanding on Villa's part that frank discussion between the two chieftains could have resolved.[19] Plainly, Obregón, an extremely able politician, saw no major ideological barriers standing between Villa and the Constitutionalists.

The opinions of Obregón and Rivas Iruz stand up under scrutiny. Unquestionably, scores of leading civilians in Villa's tent, as well as key military chieftains, could have served with distinction in the ranks of the Carrancistas. Indeed, many had, and scores of others did so again. Both generals Felipe Angeles and Maclovio Herrera, Villista stalwarts, spent time among the Constitutionalists. Angeles, once director of the Military Academy in the days of don Porfirio, had taken orders from Madero and been named minister of war by the First Chief in 1913—until Obregón's jealousy and envy undercut the appointment. Unwilling to play second fiddle to Obregón, a neophyte in the art of war, Angeles decided to teach Villa how to handle his artillery. Herrera, on the other hand, embraced Carranza after fighting alongside Villa, as did General Manuel Chao, who had at one point been military governor of Chihuahua. The Aguirre brothers, Eugenio and Luis, sons of one of the cultivated families supporting Madero, had their feet in both army camps. To capture Durango, Villa relied for advice on an officer who up to that point had been in the Porfirista army.[20] General Juan N. Medina, a career military man, was Villa's chief of staff.[21] In Ciudad Chihuahua, Villa appointed an old bureaucrat to head the telegraph office, a key post in 1914.[22] Eulalio Gutiérrez, a president of Mexico in the days of the Convention of Aguascalientes, took Villa to task for soliciting former federal officers for his armies.[23]

The coat-and-tie brigade in Villa's camp, moreover, bore a striking resemblance to their rivals under the First Chief. Among them were the Maderos who had bolted Carranza to follow Villa. The brothers and uncles of the fallen Apostle in Villa's camp spoke the language of Carranza but because of old animosities and inflated ambitions had broken with him. Raul and Emilio, the two Madero brothers, shared Carranza's views. Heriberto Barrón, the controversial ally of the First Chief, blamed Ernesto Madero, an uncle, for the break between Villa and Carranza. According to Barrón, Ernesto, with Villa's help, hoped to replace Carranza as First Chief.[24] Villa, said another aide of Carranza, had promised large tracts of land to Alberto and Evaristo Madero in return for their support.[25] Whatever the dubious merits of these opinions, not one placed the responsibility for the political somersaults of the Maderos on ideological differences. Moreover, when Carranza seized his properties, Ernesto loudly protested that he had never sympathized with Villa.[26]

The similarity of ideological views included a host of other distinguished Villistas. José María Maytorena, an *hacendado* and colleague of Villa in Sonora, had obeyed both Madero and Carranza—until the First Chief sided with Obregón. Nothing in the records of Roque and Federico González Garza, both Villistas at one time, indicates that an irreparable gap separated them from the men around Carranza. Roque, the more famous of the two, was a native of Coahuila, a Maderista, twice a congressman—once as a Constitutionalist. Miguel Díaz Lombardo, a former law professor, minister of public instruction under Madero, and Villa's minister of foreign relations let a wounded ego sever his ties with his old companions. Another of Villa's key subordinates, Enrique C. Llorente, a diplomat under Díaz and Mexican consul in El Paso during the Madero era, abandoned the Carrancistas at the Convention of Aguascalientes; until then, he had been chief of Carranza's consular corps. Manuel Bonilla, a lukewarm reformer in Madero's cabinet, more than likely joined Villa because Carranza failed to include him in his inner circle. Under Madero, Francisco Lagos Cházaro had been governor of Veracruz, and then military magistrate for the Constitutionalists. When Carranza appointed Cándido Aguilar, his son-in-law, governor of Veracruz, a job coveted by Lagos Cházaro, the Villistas had a new adherent.[27] Villa's commercial agent in Juárez, Luis Gaxiola, had once rubbed shoulders with the socially élite of Mexico City and was hardly a political radical.[28] Villa, reported General Pablo González, could count on the support of the rich in Coahuila and Nuevo León.[29] For intellectuals, however, regardless of their politics, Villa had scant esteem, on one occasion saying that the degree of their "servility grew in proportion to their learning." [30]

On the issue of the Catholic Church, a question that supposedly divided reformers from stand-patters, furthermore, Villa was ambivalent. The early Villa hated priests and seldom lost the opportunity to attack them. As one scholar says, Villa was a "deep-dyed clerophobe." [31] Nonetheless, after his rupture with Carranza, Villa reversed his attitude, discarding his anticlericalism to become a defender of the Church. He even indicted Carranza, a politician with no stomach for senseless forays against the clergy, for sanctioning attacks on religion. By closing his eyes to the violation of constitutional rights, particularly liberty of thought, and by permitting governors of states to ban religious services that, Villa reminded his rival, "the law of the country allows," Carranza had deeply offended "the religious sentiments of the people." [32] Carranza, meanwhile, rightly charged Villa with hypocrisy and with courting the clerical party.[33] For their part, Obregón and Blanco, who had known Villa for many years, ridiculed his sudden conversion and scoffed at his allegations of Carranza's crimes against "civilization." [34]

More important, Carranza's nationalistic badge easily outshone Villa's. From the beginning, on the question of Mexican sovereignty, Villa equivocated, especially when his political ambitions got in the way. His catering to Washington's designs dulled his sense of integrity. When Woodrow Wilson dispatched troops to Veracruz, Villa, then feuding with Carranza, told the press that he saw the Americans as "friends," adding that he had no wish "to go to war with them." [35] Chao, Herrera, and Orestes Pereyra, his chief lieutenants, sharply censored Villa for this statement. According to a Mexican historian, Villa told George C. Carrothers, Wilson's agent in Mexico, that, so far as he was concerned, the American troops could cut off "every drop of water" from Huerta's army in Veracruz.[36] Obregón, who momentarily lost his usual calm and urged a declaration of war against the United States, accused Villa of currying favor with Wilson. Obregón reported that another Washington agent had tried to persuade him to circumvent Carranza, as Villa had, in his dealings with the United States. Two representatives of Villa, Díaz Lombardo and Miguel Silva, reported Obregón, had brought the American agent to him.[37] In August, shortly before he ended his courtship of Washington, Villa made into law in the territory he still controlled health regulations for the wholesale meat industry identical to those of the United States Department of Agriculture. With this decree, according to some, he was making sure that Americans would continue to buy meat from the packing plant that he and John Payton, his American partner, owned in Juárez.[38] At about the same time, if Obregón and Blanco can be believed, Villa promised to safeguard the properties of foreigners in Mexico. Earlier, it was said, Villa had sold an American a store he had taken from Mexicans in Juárez, as well as another, to two other American merchants—at a time when foreign ownership of properties in Mexico was being strongly questioned.[39]

Villa never shook himself free of his rumored links with Americans. One such report in April, 1915 called attention to the backing Villa enjoyed "of certain American capitalists with interests in Mexico," and another to the fact that "all of the Americans" living in the capital of Guanajuato supported him.[40] Again, in the same year, Barrón told Carranza that he had heard on good authority that General Hugh L. Scott of the American army thought highly of Villa, while another Mexican living in New York City reported to Carranza that General Leonard Wood was of the same opinion, and that wealthy Americans in New York City were sending money to Villa.[41] An official of the State Department, in a letter to Welford Smith, which he turned over to Ignacio C. Enríquez, a Constitutionalist politician, stated that William Randolph Hearst was "back of the Villa faction." [42] Obviously, these accounts may have exaggerated or distorted the facts, or been patently false; still, the frequency of their appearance does cast doubts on Villa's nationalistic credentials—a badge of the reformer.

Washington's *de facto* recognition of Carranza in October, 1915 ended Villa's courtship. Hoping to embroil the Constitutionalists and the Wilson administration in war, Villa recklessly crossed the border to raid Columbus, a town in New Mexico. To the distress of Mexican nationalists, he almost succeeded. With domestic politics in mind, Wilson sent General John J. Pershing and his troops in pursuit of Villa, jeopardizing the survival of the Carranza regime. For the sake of a personal vendetta, with this madcap adventure, Villa had endangered the sovereignty of his country and the future of reform. On this score alone, Villa scarcely merits the label of revolutionary, if that signified a concern for nationalistic aspirations.

The behavior of Villa's cronies further blackens his reputation as a social reformer. Scores of his leading generals not only lacked a social conscience but glorified brutality. Tomás Urbina, a *compadre* and an early companion, already wanted for murder by 1902, enhanced his nefarious fame riding with Villa. He died according to an eyewitness, at the hands of Rodolfo Fierro on the instruction of Villa, who wanted him punished for deserting, and in the presence of Villa, and his wife and children.[43] Fierro, a former railroad man, a drunkard and degenerate known as *el carnicero*, the butcher, for his wanton killing of prisoners, met his end in quicksand because he would not free his horse of the loot he carried. Yet Fierro, often labeled Villa's right arm, had the affection of his chief. Villa, himself, bloodied his hands and soiled his fame by killing his rivals and on occasion bystanders. Nothing can expunge from the record his legendary cruelty to Spaniards and the defenseless Chinese.

All the same, no rival *caudillo* won the hearts of a larger army of believers. Although the better part of the *gente decente* judged Villa a "criminal," the poor idealized him as their "avenging angel," and as Juan Barragán, Carranza's chief of staff conceded, looked to him for social justice.[44] According to Arnaldo Córdova, "a mass of workers, sharecroppers, muleteers, and peddlers, none of whom had ever owned a piece of land, filled the ranks of Villa's armies." [45] Most of them were natives of the northern provinces, particularly Chihuahua and Durango; yet others came from as far away as Chiapas to gamble their lives with him.[46] In 1915, Villa had a hard core of supporters in Veracruz, among them the elders of tiny Tlalcotlalpan, a fishing village on the edge of society.[47] The combined armies of Villa and José María Maytorena, General Benjamín Hill wrote Carranza, outnumbered Obregón's in Sonora, Obregón's own habitat.[48] Pehaps the better part of the Mexican population sympathized with the government of the Aguascalientes Convention that Villa manipulated. At Aguascalientes, furthermore, Villa had extended the hand of friendship to Zapata, thus theoretically endorsing the Plan de Ayala, the banner of the agrarian rebels. In his book, Obregón acknowledged that Villa, with his political maneuvers at Aguascalientes, had covered himself with the aura of legitimacy.[49] Nor did every stalwart of the middle classes turn his back on Villa. Silvestre Terrazas, one of a host of the reverent, exalted Villa because he thought him a social reformer. Carranza, to the contrary, said Terrazas, encircled himself with men antipathetic to change.[50]

IV

Terrazas, a bundle of contradictions himself, nonetheless, voiced a debatable opinion. On the cardinal question of agrarian reform, Villa's stance was at best ambiguous. Many of his companions-in-arms doubted his commitment. Villa, according to Francisco Vásquez Gómez, a politician out of favor with the Constitutionalists, never intended to subdivide the great estates.[51] Marte R. Gómez, an advocate of land reform from Tamaulipas and one of the few to study carefully Villa's social blueprints, points out that no lands changed hands in Chihuahua between 1912 and 1915, years of Villa's ascendancy.[52] For that time, at least, the Villistas had shelved land reform. To cast further doubt on Villa's commitment, after the split with the Constitutionalists in 1915, his northern bloc promised to uphold the property guarantees in the Charter of 1857.[53] Later, the defeated Villa condemned Article 27 of the Constitution of 1917, claiming that it invited intervention by the United States and kept alive the conflict in Mexico.[54]

To further confuse the picture, Villa apparently endorsed two agrarian reform measures, a law for Chihuahua in 1914 and the platform of the Aguascalientes Convention shortly after. Unfortunately, there is no evidence to reveal the extent of Villa's own participation, if any, in the drafting of these measures, or the degree to which they reflect his own convictions. The Chihuahua legislation appeared during the months of September and November when Villa had left the state government in the care of General Field Jurado and Silvestre Terrazas.[55] Whether Villa initiated the legislation, cosponsored it, or simply went along is not known. Villa sanctioned the blueprints of Aguascalientes; but whether he did so enthusiastically, however, remains a mystery.

The architect of the Chihuahua decree was Manuel Bonilla, a civil engineer from Sinaloa and kingpin of the local club opposing Díaz' reelection. For siding with Madero, authorities in Sinaloa had put him in jail. When released, he joined Madero during the capture of Juárez. Interim-President Francisco León de la Barra, surely at Madero's behest, picked Bonilla for minister of communications. When Madero became president, he named Bonilla as minister of *fomento*.[56] Quite likely, Bonilla and Madero shared comparable philosophical views. After Madero fell, Bonilla, who in the interval had become a senator, remained at his post until Victoriano Huerta shut down the Senate. At this point, Bonilla joined Carranza, traveling with him to Chihuahua where Bonilla, believing himself unappreciated by the First Chief, switched allegiances to Villa. In September, 1914, Bonilla was chairman of the Comisión Agraria of Chihuahua organized by Governor Jurado and his legislature to devise a land reform program.

The Chihuahua legislation, therefore, mirrors Bonilla's ideas, and those of Henry George who, writes Marte R. Gómez, influenced Villista thought.[57] If judged by his legislation, Bonilla proved a timid disciple of agrarian reform. Never implemented, the Proyecto de Ley Agraria asked for the prompt payment of lands seized. For reasons of public utility, *haciendas* could be subdivided into small plots and sold for cash. Not all of them would be broken up, however. Bonilla, writes Gómez, believed that *hacendados*, seeing the handwriting on the wall, would sell off their surplus lands. The goal, he concluded, was not the destruction of the *hacienda* but to improve the yields of lands best cultivated in small parcels. Meanwhile, the state budget, although setting aside money for health and education, including schooling for young women, earmarked none for the local agrarian commissions, entrusted with overseeing the legislation.[58]

The decree of May 24, 1915, promulgated by Villa as commander of the army of the Aguascalientes Convention, bore a marked resemblance to Bonilla's proposal. Probably the brainchild of Francisco Escudero, director of the Departamento de Hacienda y Fomento of Chihuahua, the decree authorized the subdivision of *haciendas* in order to create small private property. The new owners, nonetheless, had to buy their parcels, either with their own funds or with loans granted at low interest rates by the government. Designed to support itself, the program would not cost the government a penny. The *hacendado* was to be paid for his lands before they were either subdivided or occupied by their new owners. Except for sanctioning expropriation, the decree copied most of what Madero had suggested in

December, 1911. The individual plots of land would be large enough to support a family but not beyond the capacity of one man to cultivate alone. Also included in the decree were gifts of plots of twenty-five hectares to heads of families of Indian communities. Conversely, these villages would retain in communal ownership only the pasture lands and wooded lots. Despite their embrace of Zapata, Villa and the Aguascalientes leadership exhibited little faith in communal land systems. Still, by including the ownership of water in their decree, Escudero and his allies anticipated a key feature of Article 27.[59] But the insistence on prior compensation hardly signaled the start of a radical drive to eradicate the *latifundia*. By the same token, by asking for immediate indemnification and the subdivision of *hacienda* lands into small private plots, Villa and the northern bosses at Aguascalientes revealed their high regard for property rights and their intent to build a society modeled along lines suggested by Benito Juárez half a century earlier.

Not too surprisingly, Villa, in keeping with a custom of the day, did not always live by what he said. As his army advanced southward, he permitted, as noted earlier, if not the expropriation of private property, its seizure and use by his lieutenants.[60] To cite Luis Aguirre Benavides, Villa freely distributed *haciendas* among his favorites, allowing them, said Carranza, to exploit their lands for private profit.[61] By 1915, Gómez added, the Villistas, who had taken over *haciendas* of the Terrazas, Creel, Falomir, and Luján families in Chihuahua, wanted no part of any plan to break them up. Instead, they ran them as if they were theirs: Hormigas, Torreón, El Carmen, San Lorenzo, Encinilla, Gallego, Los Sauces, Agua Nueva, and El Sauz.[62] Where the *haciendas* escaped the sticky fingers of Villa's generals, they were left in the hands of their owners. This pattern prevailed wherever Villa's armies conquered. In the Laguna, the military commander of Villa, appointed a *comisión agraria* not to subdivide the *haciendas* but to help get them back on their feet.[63] Its secretary, Jesús R. Ríos, told Carranza that just the lands of Spaniards and of vocal Huerta supporters were seized. Although sharecroppers had been allowed to cultivate the lands of some of the "intervened" *haciendas,* most of them, for all intents and purposes, were run by Villa's generals. The Hacienda Avila y

Anexas, previously the property of Feliciano Cobián, a Spaniard, had been entrusted to General Máximo García and his brother Benito.[64] The García brothers, formerly wealthy *hacendados,* "owners of immense tracts of land," according to John Reed, had come out for Madero just a few years before. When neighboring farmers tried to buy some of the lands of the Cobián *hacienda,* then controlled by the Garcías, the Villistas turned a deaf ear.[65] Ramiro Reyes Sáenz Pardo, a *compadre* of Villa, helped himself to the Hacienda Amador. Lázaro de la Garza watched over the Hacienda La Concha y Anexas. On his travels through northern Durango, Reed spent a night on the Hacienda El Canutillo, the property, he learned, of General Tomás Urbina. For one day "and all next day we drove through its wide lands," he recalled. All of the *haciendas* in this region had been confiscated by Urbina, "who ruled them with his own agents, and, it was said, divided fifty-fifty with the Revolution." Not long ago, one humble follower said in awe, Urbina "was just a peon like us; and now he is a general and a rich man." [66]

At the close of his military adventures, Villa, too, retired to an *hacienda.* In return for laying down his arms, Interim-President Adolfo de la Huerta gave Villa the Hacienda Canutillo, once the delight of his *compadre* Urbina. Villa swore that he would spend the rest of his life tilling its fields.[67] To placate him, the government had purchased Canutillo from its owners.[68] Valued at 800,000 pesos, Canutillo encompassed over 87,000 hectares, approximately 2,000 of them irrigated. Before fighting laid waste its lands, the plantation had fed 24,000 cattle, 4,000 goats, 6,000 sheep, and 4,000 horses.[69]

From the sanctuary of Canutillo, Villa reigned like a monarch over the surrounding countryside. Only his opinion counted, De la Huerta informed President Obregón, to say nothing of Villa's adamant resistance to land reform.[70] When the Ministry of Agriculture tried to give the people of Villa Coronado lands controlled by his cronies lying along the borders of his *hacienda,* Villa employed guns to stop it.[71] The angry citizens of Coronado appealed to Ignacio C. Enríquez, the governor of Chihuahua, who, upon learning from the local military commander that nothing could be done, asked Obregón to intercede.[72] Villa, however, although castigated for his dog-in-the-manger attitude, stood his ground.[73] Not until Villa's death did Obregón order that the lands be distributed to the people of Coronado.[74] When authorities attempted to subdivide the Hacienda El Pueblito occupied by General Albino Aranda, an old companion, Villa blocked their path with guns. Ironically, the people asking for land were his former soldiers. El Pueblito had been originally acquired by the federal government for subdivision among Villa's soldiers, but was instead, turned over to Aranda, who permitted Villa's old comrades-in-arms to till just a fraction of its fields.[75] Again, justice had to await the death of Villa.[76] In the meantime, Villa, in handling the pleas for aid from the *buenos campesinos* of the Laguna, had limited his help to giving them work building irrigation canals and paying them one peso a day in place of the customary 75 centavos so that they would not "pillage" and "steal food." Villa, the *hacendado,* wanted order in society and security for property.[77]

V

In Obregón's opinion, Villa and Carranza merely had incurred a lover's quarrel.[78] Yet irony of ironies, Villa's angry exit from the Constitutionalist tent, and his subsequent embrace of Zapata, the perennial priest of land reform, drove the conservative Carranza to seek the plaudits of men of broader vision. To survive as First Chief, he had to add reform planks to his skimpy Plan de Guadalupe. Villa, because of his alliance with Zapata and his wish to rule the roost at Aguascalientes, partly deserved credit for don Venustiano's abbreviated metamorphosis. All the same, Francisco Villa's commitment to social change, particularly if agrarian ideals help to define it, is ambiguous if not shaky.

THIRTEEN   *Emiliano Zapata:*
The Unorthodox Rebel

"Today the North and the South are not fighting for the same ideals, as the former contemplates a government, such as they have lived under for years, but slightly modified, with a bit of justice and humanity injected, while the latter are entirely anarchistic in their ideas, confiscatory in their methods, and extremely arbitrary in their dealings. . . ."

A. Bell, January 26, 1915

I

TAKE HEED, L. Rivas Iruz, the blunt-talking medical doctor, warned Venustiano Carranza, the uprising in Morelos "has a distinct hue." [1] As the anonymous A. Bell succinctly noted, the dirt farmers from the south were "as different as chalk from cheese, as unalike as Macedon and Monmouth" from their northern rivals.[2] Only infrequently, the world heard tell, did these men of the soil march in accord with the "legal revolutionaries" of the border provinces. By culture and ethnic background, Rivas Iruz intuitively sensed, the two camps were worlds apart. Nor, he might have added, did the *calzonudos,* as Alvaro Obregón once mockingly tabbed them, peasants almost to a man but for a tiny band of highbrows with city learning, come from the same classes or fight for similar goals.

To the anger of Carranza and the bewilderment of Francisco I. Madero, Emiliano Zapata, the *caudillo* of Morelos, cherished alien ideals. Judged by the standards of the northern bosses, Zapata, from the start, proved an unorthodox rebel, a man who marched in step with the martial airs of social revolution, timidly perhaps but dramatically and violently nonetheless. For the legal revolutionaries from the north, Zapata was nearly "un-Mexican," a noncomformist who did not play by their rules. A complex man of simple revolutionary faith, Zapata never captured the imagination or loyalty of the man on the street. He was always a provincial figure.[3]

Yet, paradoxically, the holy scriptures of Zapata, because of their identification with the hallowed propaganda of the decade of turmoil, weathered the abuse heaped upon them by hostile contemporaries to emerge as one of the hallmarks of what Mexicans refer to as the "Revolution." Unfortunately, linking Zapata's quest for social justice, and that of kindred souls, with the gospel of their foes from the north, distorts the record of the battle against the Old Regime. Without making a sharp distinction between the war in Morelos and events outside, the student of Mexico's history runs the danger of confusing reform with revolution. Still, of the five major insurgent *caudillos,* only Zapata truly made the plight of the rural poor his special passion. Because he lived by the golden rule, practicing what he preached, contemporaries from Madero to Carranza ostracized him. He became an untouchable, judged guilty of crimes against middle-class mankind. Zapata, his enemies shouted to the four winds, did not speak for them. By the same token, those who would chronicle the events of the past cannot write the history of the rebellion begun in 1910 just by telling what Zapata fought and died for. To the contrary, his story runs counter to the currents in the mainstream.

II

Emiliano Zapata, slight but sinewy, with a face the color of the brown earth of his native land, was a country man from Anenecuilco, a village of four hundred people just a stone's throw from Cuautla, the hub of Morelos.[4] He was thirty-one when he stood up to the rulers of Morelos. Orphaned at fifteen and on his own for all of his adult life, Zapata matured early. Unlike his neighbors who spent their lives within the confines of their villages, Zapata had seen something of the outside world. While caring for the horses of a Morelos sugar planter he had lived in Puebla and experienced the hectic life of Mexico City. Poor in comparison with the wealthy Madero or the patrician Carranza, but in contrast to his neighbors, Zapata was a man of substance, the proud owner of a solid house built of adobe and stone. No *hacendado* had ever paid him to work as a day laborer. Instead, he had tilled his small piece of land and raised livestock, adding to his income by running a pack train of mules through the villages in the vicinity and sharecropping the lands of an adjoining *hacienda.* A veteran horseman, he brought home extra income by training the spirited stallions of the *hacendados.* He admired fine horses and good clothes, and nothing pleased him more than to ride through town in his Sunday best. But Zapata was no drugstore *charro.* His brother Eufemio, whose reputation would become questionable in the days ahead, had gone off to Veracruz as a traveling salesman rather than plow the soils of neighboring *haciendas.* When he married in 1911, Zapata chose as his wife Josefa Espejo, the daughter of a well-to-do livestock dealer from Ayala who, upon his death, had left her a modest dowry. In 1909, the elders on the town council of Anenecuilco picked Zapata to speak for the entire village, a singular honor and token of the high esteem he enjoyed. By then, Zapata was "both a sharecropping dirt farmer whom villagers could trust and a mule-driving horsedealer whom cowboys, peons, and bandits could look up to; both a responsible citizen and a determined warrior." [5]

To Madero, the first of the northern nabobs to confront him, Zapata was a trouble-maker, a stubborn country bumpkin with inflexible and impractical attitudes. However, from the perspective of his worshippers today, Zapata could do no wrong; he was all things to all men. He was a simple man, they say, determined to purge Morelos of tyrants who robbed the people of their lands and who took the bread from their lips. The truth, as always, is more complicated. No man, and Zapata least of all, is born a revolutionary. Zapata became one almost against his will, a victim of fate, the hostilities of his enemies, and a conscience that would not let him quit until the wrongs he saw had been eliminated. In June, 1911, while waiting in a railroad station in Mexico City for a train to take him back to Morelos, Zapata had told a reporter that he had only joined "the revolution . . . to defeat the dictatorial regime." Once that was done, he was going home to farm. "It can't be said that I went off to battle because of poverty. I've got some land and horses . . . which I earned through long years of honest work . . . and which give me and my family enough to live comfortably." [6] These were hardly the words of a Trotsky. Until the first days of 1913, Zapata seemed willing to go along with the slow pace of political reform, determined to sign a truce and to lay down his arms; but something always occurred to keep him from doing so.[7] From this background and experience evolved the dogmatic revolutionary, the conscience of the militant reformer.

By 1919, the year of his death, nothing short of total victory could have convinced Zapata to give up his weapons. Carranza, in contrast, in his keynote speech in Hermosillo wanted to postpone reform until after the conquest of the enemy. Zapata, noted Jenaro Amezcua, a devoted companion, believed in putting first things first. Honor and integrity, if worth a farthing, required that gut issues be studied before others, and that the people be told what the goals were. From Zapata's viewpoint, it was morally wrong to await the ultimate triumph before converting promises into reform.[8] As the Plan de Ayala, the gospel as seen by Zapata, stated, Mexico had endured its fill of "men who lied and of traitors who pose as liberators offering countless solemn oaths but who upon taking office forget them and become tyrants." [9] Like José I. Limantour and Francisco Bulnes, city dandies who abhorred the country men from Morelos, Zapata eventually concluded that false saviors had grasped the sword not to combat injustice but to "satisfy vulgar political ambitions." [10] The "Acta de Ratificación" of the Plan de Ayala, signed by Zapata and his generals in July, 1914, bluntly condemned the idea that a mere change of the guard would abolish tyranny and guarantee social justice.[11] Zapata had not jumped into the fray in search of public office. The peace of Juárez devised by Madero, Zapata told Pascual Orozco, was a "shameful" farce that "brought a blood-letting" but solved nothing.[12] The men of Ayala declared that Madero had not successfully concluded the revolution he had initiated, having left in office some of the original scoundrels and having continued the iron heel of tyranny.[13] Yet, although aware of the errors of Ciudad Juárez and with General Victoriano Huerta's army killing and pillaging in Morelos, Zapata was still ready to make his peace with Madero—if the *hacendado* from Coahuila had only met him halfway.[14]

Nevertheless, Zapata had scant faith in Carranza, viewing him with "disgust, distrust, and disappointment." [15] Huerta had fled, but the nation had rid itself of one Porfirista only to have another, in the person of the bearded tyrant from Cuatro Ciénegas, take his place. Zapata had ample grounds for his low opinion of the First Chief who, in the days after Huerta's flight, had told envoys of General Genovevo de la O, a lieutenant of Zapata, that the "business of dividing up the land is ridiculous." [16] For Carranza shared little of Zapata's enthusiasm for a Mexico shorn of the *hacienda*. A man who boasted of his prudence in speech and behavior, Carranza wanted to mend what was wrong with the system. On the life or death issue of agrarian reform, charged Zapata, Carranza had sat on his hands. Victory for Carranza, said Zapata, boiled down to his own triumph, although no lands changed hands, guarantees were given to the people, or benefits conferred on peasant and worker; the revolution had ended with his conquest of power. To Zapata, the false prophet from Coahuila had made himself a virtual dictator, eliminating in that process, even the pretense of the elections of yesterday.[17]

For his part, Zapata had an explicit, unambiguous target. While his Plan de Ayala ended with the words "liberty, justice, and law," its message, given expression in articles 6, 7, 8, and 9, were in the language of the dirt farmer.[18] Signed on November 25, 1911, the Plan declared land reform synonymous with social justice. As Zapata verbalized his battle: "we fight so that the people will have lands, forests, and water." [19] To return the land to its rightful owners was the end in view. Of course, others, too, had unfurled the agrarian banner, but only Zapata persisted.[20] Nor did he await the election of Madero to restore justice to the people of Morelos. With the peace of Juárez, which coincided with his capture of Cuautla, Zapata began to encourage the villagers to take back the lands stolen from them. To Madero's ire, he justified his actions with article 3 of the Plan de San Luis Potosí, calling for the return of lands illegally seized from Indian communities. After all, to a dirt farmer from Morelos, dark of skin and unsophisticated in the ways of city anthropologists, Indian and *campesino* were one and the same. Surely Madero, ignorant of the reality of the southern country-side, had simply confused the two terms.

From the perspective of Carranza, Zapata stood at the vortex of the radical crusade. Beyond him, only a tiny band of Socialists and Anarchists marched in discord, isolated from the flow of popular opinion. Between Zapata and the "legal revolution-aries," there was a large gap; by any test of political ideas, Zapata walked far to their left—which is why they wanted no truck with him. But Zapata bore the stamp of the radical only when compared with his enemies. In truth, he advocated a moderate recipe for revolution. In contrast to V. I. Lenin, already plotting the downfall of Czarist Russia, Zapata hoisted a timid banner.

The Plan de Ayala, while dwelling at length on the land question and justifying expropriation as a remedy for past wrongs, side-stepped the bread-and-butter issues of income distribution and ownership of wealth. Stolen lands, stipulated article 6, would be restored to their former owners. Article 7, the key point, sanctioned the distribution to the landless, by way of expropria-tion, of one-third of the lands of each *hacienda*. Recalcitrant *hacendados* who refused to cooperate, according to article 8, would lose their entire lands. No lands, furthermore, not even the paltry one-third, swore the patrons of Ayala, would be seized from the *hacendados* without prior indemnification.[21] Farmers might occupy the land and till "it on an *ad hoc* basis," but Zapata "never for a moment contemplated permanent occupation without payment." [22] *Haciendas* and land-owning villages would live side by side in the society envisaged by Zapata. Moreover, not until the irreparable break with Carranza did Zapata en-force article 8, sanctioning the confiscation of property, both rural and urban, of intransigent landlords. Until then, Zapata had enforced just article 6: the return of lands illegally taken from their owners. The contradictions in the thinking of the Zapatistas caught the attention of General José Siurob, one of their companions at the Aguascalientes Convention, who wanted to know why they safeguarded a part of the properties of the *hacendados.*[23] By the same token, by leaving two-thirds of the real estate in the hands of the land barons, and by asking for payment for lands taken, the Plan hardly disturbed the wealth and income of the rich. Despite its narrow scope, the farmers of Morelos gave the Plan de Ayala overwhelming endorsement, some dying with a copy of the document in their hands.[24]

However, Zapata, to his credit, learned as he went along, maturing intellectually and gaining a wider grasp of Mexico's social ills. When he died, he was no longer just a dirt farmer and *charro* with only the "land, forests, and water" of Morelos on his mind. His growing sophistication ultimately led him to see more of the problems confronting the lower classes, urban as well as rural.[25] Specifically, this meant paying attention to the hopes of the urban worker, a regard conspicuously absent from the blueprints of the Plan de Ayala. Unhappily, industrial labor viewed the Zapatistas with suspicion and distrust, going so far in 1915 as to form, under the prodding of the Casa del Obrero Mundial, Red Battalions to fight the soldiers of Zapata and Villa. One battalion of railroad workers, the third, fought off the Zapatista attack on the penitentiary of the city of Puebla. Yet the *caudillo* from Morelos eventually linked, at least in his own mind, his struggle with that of labor, as he wrote in a bitter letter to Carranza in 1919, accusing him of playing off the workers against each other, of suborning their leaders, and of destroying the dream of the independent labor union.[26]

Yet on the question of the Church, Zapata budged not an inch from his original beliefs. In contrast to the rabid anti-clericals who saw a priest behind every social evil, Zapata held on to his Catholic faith. Like Manuel Hidalgo and José María Morelos, the patriot priests of the Independence Wars, he wanted no quarrel with religion or the Church. On matters of the faith, he was a conservative and a traditionalist. Yet, unlike fanatical Catholics, who gave their Church a monopoly of virtue and truth, Zapata urged tolerance and respect for all creeds, among them "Protestants, free-thinkers, Muslims and Buddhists." [27] Misunderstanding the reasons for his religious commitment, conservative exiles tried to exploit it, always unsuccessfully, to advance their own schemes.[28]

Nor was Zapata totally in step with the militant nationalism of his times. From a small, isolated village, he failed in the beginning to grasp fully nationalism's revolutionary implications. That he loved Morelos requires no documentation; but, at the same time, he had a cloudy view of Mexico. By contrast with Carranza, a nationalist among nationalists, Zapata judged the defense of the *patria* a peripheral issue, and not the crux of his revolution. When American troops trampled the sovereignty of Mexico at Veracruz, it did make his "blood boil," [29] but he left Huerta to uphold the national honor; if need be, he would defend it on his own, although not in company with others. While the First Chief doggedly insisted on Mexico's right to settle its own affairs, fulminating against Woodrow Wilson's meddling, Zapata jumped at the offer of the Pan American Conference, to whom Wilson had turned for help, to help Mexicans put their house in order. [30]

With Zapata's death, resistance to Carranza's bland palliatives, for all intents and purposes, evaporated. To the extent that the rebel *caciques* of Morelos had stood together against don Venustiano, Zapata had been responsible. Even in his lifetime, nevertheless, the revolutionary fervor of his companions had wavered; and on occasion, it had been just skin deep. With the demise of Madero in 1913, a number of Zapatista stalwarts had shamelessly rushed off to join Huerta, including Otilio Montaño, a patron of the Plan de Ayala, who eventually repented. Jesús Morales, another bellwether, on the other hand, left the fold forever. [31] After the costly struggle against both Madero and Huerta, scores of Zapata's supposed enthusiasts clamored for peace with Carranza. General Guillermo García Aragón, a "sunshine" rebel from Guerrero, warned that if Zapata did not make his peace with the Constitutionalists, he would lose untold numbers of his followers to the enemy. [32] With their beloved leader dead, Zapata's lieutenants abandoned the fight and went their separate ways, occasionally, as a letter from Cuautla says, with pitched battles between their dwindling columns. [33] Most of his old standard bearers switched their support to Obregón. Both Antonio Díaz Soto y Gama and Gildardo Magaña fell in step with the Man from Huatabampo who, from notice given by Soto y Gama, had "voiced a total commitment to our ideals." Now that Obregón had severed his ties with Carranza, said Soto y Gama, "it is our duty to join" him.[34] Evidently, General Genovevo de la O, one more Zapatista leader, had not gotten the message, for he had announced to his flock that the new messiah was Francisco Vásquez Gómez. Zapata, he stated, had named Vásquez Gómez his successor shortly before his death; by 1922, notwithstanding, De la O was safely in the nest of Obregón.[35] For his part, Jenaro Amezcua, also a former pacemaker, was preaching the sanctity of the charter of 1857, still unwilling to have anything to do with legislation concocted by Carrancistas.[36] Reinaldo Lecona, meanwhile, who had gone off to join the enemies of Obregón in 1923, was urging De la O to emulate his example.[37] De la O kept his own council but General José Rodríguez, a *compadre* of Zapata, followed Lecona into the camp of Adolfo de la Huerta and his dissident brass hats.[38] Ironically, in the uprising of 1923, partisans of De la Huerta brutally murdered Felipe Carrillo Puerto, the reform governor of Yucatán who, as an engineering student, had gone off to Morelos to help Zapata begin to distribute land.[39]

III

On one point the historical record requires no additional proof. For almost a decade, from 1910 to 1919, the ringleaders of Mexico vented their ire on Zapata. In the story of this drive to cleanse Mexico of Zapata, one implacable enemy of the *caudillo* of Morelos, General Huerta, obeyed three masters: don Porfirio, Francisco León de la Barra, and Madero. Just before taking passage on the *Ypiranga,* Díaz had dispatched Huerta and his troops to Morelos; his successors lost little time in aping the precedent.[40] Yet Díaz, but for the blandishments of Madero, nearly made his peace with Zapata, or at least Limantour thought so.[41] De la Barra, the diplomat in tails and top hat, upon taking office, sent Huerta to Morelos to hunt down Zapata. For a while, Emilio Vásquez Gómez, minister of *gobernación* under De la Barra, clandestinely supplied Zapata with guns; but when De la Barra and Madero learned of this, they fired him. His successor Alberto García Granados, an *hacendado* from Puebla with rancor in his heart for Zapata, wanted no truck with rebels. He would take their arms away even if he had to call on the army assembled by Díaz to do it. Zapata was a bandit, to be hunted down by Huerta and his soldiers.[42] While Madero watched from the sidelines, García Granados gave Zapata just one alternative: to surrender unconditionally and to stand trial for his crimes.[43] Huerta, meanwhile, as if to confirm García Granados' prejudices, wired De la Barra that the Zapatistas were indeed a bunch of "bandits." [44]

Madero shared the distorted perspective on Zapata of García Granados. He, too, wanted Zapata to disarm his men and to stop harrassing the sugar plantations. Madero judged "a hostile act against . . . the *haciendas*" as tantamount to "an act of war." [45] When Madero reneged on his promise to return the stolen lands, De la Barra, with Madero's blessings, dispatched General Arnaldo Casso López and his men to help Huerta quiet the furor in Morelos. Again with the approval of Madero, De la Barra named Ambrosio Figueroa military governor of Morelos. Figueroa, a prosperous farmer and manager of a rice mill owned by the powerful Ruiz de Velasco family, and an officer in the army reserves as well as Inspector General of Rurales, was an old foe of the dirt farmers of Morelos.[46] To Zapata, Figueroa, a native of Guerrero, was a carpetbagger, a traitor who had sold out to the sugar mafia.

The appointment of Figueroa amply revealed the degree of Madero's antipathy for Zapata. He was no innocent bystander in this affair. From the start, he knew that Zapata would not look kindly upon the choice of Figueroa. But, as Madero said to De la Barra, "it was time to stop pussyfooting and to act decisively." [47] When Figueroa voiced doubts about the wisdom of accepting the governorship, Madero personally begged him to agree and "to put Zapata in his place for us, for we can no longer put up with him." [48] As governor, Figueroa did what he could "to end the vandalism wrought by enemies of the public order" and to defend the "honorable men of property." [49] To help Figueroa pursue Zapata, Madero imported rebel soldiers from as far away as Coahuila.[50] When Figueroa faltered, Madero replaced him with Francisco Naranjo, a native of Nuevo León, and lent him General Juvencio Robles, who had earned his spurs killing Yaquis in Sonora. Robles, like Huerta, took delight in burning the villages of Morelos. Cruel and despotic, he introduced into Morelos the infamous resettlement camps popularized by the Spaniards in Cuba and the Americans in Philippines.[51]

Madero's military lieutenants failed to bring Zapata to his knees. Robles, in his haste to lay waste to Morelos, offended prominent *hacendados*. That, as well his inability to kill Zapata, led to his recall. To replace him, Madero sent General Felipe Angeles, reputedly an exponent of "civilized" warfare, to chase Zapata. At first, Angeles fought "fairly"; but, stymied by Zapata, he, too, began to burn villages.[52] Yet, to his credit, he permitted men sympathetic to Zapata to control a town council here and there.[53] From Mexico City, in the meantime, Madero, with the concurrence of his minister of *gobernación*, Jesús Flores Magón, brother of Ricardo, dispatched fresh contingents of troops to Morelas to protect the sugar *haciendas* against depredations by the Zapatistas.[54]

This sorry chronicle occurred with Madero fully aware of Zapata's immense popularity among the dirt farmers of Morelos. He could not plead ignorance for the facts were not withheld from him. As early as November, 1911, Gabriel Robles Domínguez, fresh from a peace mission to Morelos, had asked Madero to meet Zapata half way, else, he warned, Madero would have a problem because "Morelos has as many [Zapatistas] as inhabitants, and so do the neighboring districts of Guerrero and, it must be added, many of Puebla and all of the southern rim of the Federal District." [55] His soldiers, Governor Figueroa had informed Madero, faced insurmountable obstacles "because of the hostility of the lower classes, almost always obstinately Zapatista." The people helped Zapata and his men in a "thousand ways, now providing them with food, now with horses and rifles, and now telling them the hiding place of the enemy." [56] Even with the irregulars at his command, and those of General Aureliano Blanquet, complained Figueroa, Zapata's soldiers outnumbered his. Despite his efforts to pacify Morelos, the Zapatistas "had grown stronger." [57] Huerta, in a speech at the Jockey Club, had acknowledged that the dirt farmers of Morelos were "all Zapatistas." [58] Said Rivas Iruz to Governor Figueroa: "Zapatismo is the protest, the gesture of desperation of a people no longer willing to endure more outrages, more abuse, more infamous deeds." [59] But the Apostle, in mortal dread of the *calzonudos,* and frightened by revolution, refused to listen to the truth. By December, 1911, Zapata had tagged Madero "the most fickle, most vacillating man I've ever known." Nothing, he confessed, would give him greater pleasure than to pull Madero out of Chapultepec castle and hang "him from one of the highest trees in the park." [60]

By killing Madero, Huerta rescued Zapata from his ordeal with the Apostle. But, unhappily, the First Chief, Madero's successor, followed essentially the same policies. It was the old stage, the same drama, but with a slightly different cast of actors, although the leading man was also an *hacendado* from Coahuila. Carranza looked askance at land reform, seeing Zapata and his "country renegades, [as] upstart field hands who know nothing of government." If they refused to lay down their weapons, he would punish them as "bandits." [61] Carranza, so the story goes, made one effort to come to terms with Zapata. In August, 1914, prodded by Lucio Blanco and others sympathetic to Zapata in Constitutionalist ranks, Carranza let Luis Cabrera, Antonio I. Villarreal, and Juan Sarabia meet with Zapata in Morelos. The *caudillo* gave them a cold reception. His demands were unambiguous: acceptance of the Plan de Ayala and of land reform. He would settle for nothing short of it. His inflexibility, lamented his enemies, barred any agreement. [62]

Yet, to believe in the likelihood of an accord, required a flight of fantasy. All things considered, as Juan Gualberto Amaya knew, it was madness to visualize an understanding because, "speaking candidly, the two stood miles apart." [63] As Zapata told General Pablo González, a buddy of Carranza, "nothing bound the Plan de Guadalupe to the Plan de Ayala." [64] Even Carranza's delegates to the meeting in Morelos had at best questionable ties with dirt farmers. Cabrera, a lawyer politician, worshipped moderates, private property, and Carranza; Villarreal, an oracle of land reform from the north, had a different vision in mind; while Sarabia, once a blind admirer of Ricardo Flores Magón, had cleansed his soul of radical doctrines. Carranza although ready to embrace his famous Adiciones al Plan de Guadalupe, with his defeat of Villa, immediately shelved his metamorphosis.

Obregón, who had lost an arm saving the National Palace for Carranza, also had little in common with Zapata. An entrepreneur with a hankering for the life of an *hacendado,* and a master of pragmatic politics, Obregón, at the Convention of Aguascalientes, had forsaken Zapata and Villa. In his *Ocho Mil Kilómetros en Campaña,* published in 1917, he glossed over Zapata, and later in his Plan de Agua Prieta, ignored the land issue. Of course, when dealing with human beings, everything is possible in this world. Perhaps, the gains that Obregón as the occupant of Chapultepec castle granted the people of Morelos might have satisfied Zapata—although, in the interval, the one-armed general had made his peace with landlords and business-men. However, that appears unlikely because by 1919, the year of his death, Zapata, in marked contrast with other rebel standard bearers, had gone beyond thinking of patchwork remedies for the country's ills. Obregón's timid version of change would hardly have placated the militant and embittered Zapata. Nor, must it be forgotten, the military bosses who cut their apron strings to Carranza, only rhetorically sympathized with revolution. As General Gertrudis G. Sánchez said to Joaquín Amaro, a kingpin in Obregón's army, until Huerta fell everyone must stick together. But, "sooner or later we will take care of Zapata." [65]

Thanks to General González, a brass hat without a military victory to his name, the prophecy came true during Carranza's regime. "Lower-class country hicks, illiterate and uneducated," González had lamented earlier to a reporter, "continue, in large numbers, to sympathize, in a blind and irrational manner, with Zapata." Opposed to them were the people of "some learning . . . who want to work." [66] Fate placed in his hands the opportunity to rid Mexico of the foe he had pursued unsuccessfully. In command of troops Carranza had dispatched to Morelos to end the insurrection, González, with the timely help of Jesús M. Guajardo, a colonel in his army, had Zapata betrayed and murdered.[67] "It is my honor," crowed González in a message sent to the state governors, to announce "that the celebrated southern *caudillo* has been killed in combat." [68] For this deed, González promoted Guajardo to general while Carranza conferred a medal on the colonel. So died the revolutionary from Anenecuilco, by the lights of González, a dirt farmer who had wasted his "miserable and vulgar life," and because of his "stupidity, [had lost] the chance to be an apostle, a savior, a hero"; instead, he died "a bandit, a criminal, an accursed calamity for his native land." [69]

IV

The tragic end was inevitable. Seen from the balcony of the victors, the men in the forefront of the battle against don Porfirio, Zapata's crusade was too radical. It was out of step. As one admirer of Madero bewailed to Carranza, "to our sorrow," the antics of Zapata had been mistakenly "confused with the revolution." But, he hastened to explain, "we who have known them for what they were, prefer to die than to besmirch our name with such a disreputable identification." [70] Revolutionaries, in this gentleman's view, were of a different stripe, for Zapatismo was solely the voice of "bandits." It "could be no other way for its ringleaders, including its supreme chief, belong to the lowest classes." [71] That, in the mind of the middle-class reformers, was probably Zapata's major crime, not simply to have been born a country hick, but to have endangered the private property upon which their world rested.

Until his death, Zapata had kept alive his ideals. Whatever else he came to believe, he wanted land for those who tilled it. He lost his life seeking to convert the ideal into reality, as did, prophetically for the future, Otilio Montaño, found guilty of treason by a court martial formed by, among others, Díaz Soto y Gama, a coat-and-tie lawyer and future ally of Obregón. On the date of Zapata's tragic death, little had been done to solve the agrarian question, the country's ulcer.[72] As for Zapata the faithful revolutionary, his death left his family impoverished, so much so that some of his old companions, then safely lodged in Congress, upon hearing of the plight of Zapata's son, ill and suffering in Morelos, asked their comrades to open their hearts and to give charity.[73]

FOURTEEN

A Profile of Rebels

"Those bastards! The moment they sense an opportunity, they want to get their fingers in the pie, and off they go to where the sun shines brightest. . . . Quickly they change their political stripes, now going off with Carranza or with whomever appears the likely victor."

Emiliano Zapata

I

OBSTINATE MINORITIES plot rebellions, but those whom Fate blesses draw hordes of jubilant latecomers eager to climb on the bandwagon. In May, 1913, shortly after the murders of Francisco I. Madero and his vice-president, the rebels in arms, estimated Jorge Vera Estañol, then minister of education, added up to no more than eight thousand men.[1] Even in Coahuila, home of the slain Apostle, Governor Venustiano Carranza, the future First Chief of the Revolution, unceremoniously had to flee for his life, while in Yucatán, the land of José María Pino Suárez, just a hardy band of insurgents defied Victoriano Huerta.[2] However, less than a year later, Carranza learned from his friend, L. Rivas Iruz, that the victorious rebels had attracted a huge array of court retainers with dubious credentials.[3] Many of them became the architects of public policy as well as the political bosses, the cabinet ministers, advisers, and lesser kingpins of Carranza and Alvaro Obregón.

II

Don Porfirio, addressing Congress for the last time in 1910, had spoken of an uprising of peasants, humble dirt farmers, in the western mountains of Chihuahua.[4] History proved him only partially correct. Not peasants but small-time entrepreneurs and others eager to improve their station in life, mature heads of families, *rancheros,* the owners of lands often left behind in the care of their sons, swelled the ranks of the Maderistas.[5] They were men "with the good fortune of knowing, although perhaps poorly, how to read and write, able to think for themselves." [6] All the same, their chieftains and political bosses were almost always a notch or two above them in social class and learning. With few exceptions, moreover, the Great Rebellion turned into a young man's crusade. An astonished Vicente Blasco Ibáñez, the Spanish writer, described don Venustiano, then sixty years of age, as the "principal of a school" who surrounded himself with "generals of 26 years of age and cabinet ministers who took on airs of importance at the ages of 29 and 30." [7] When dealing with General Francisco Múgica, a distinguished architect of the Constitution of 1917 and a man he esteemed, Carranza called him "son." [8]

Despite the anarchy of the early years, the thinking of rebel leaders, whether young or not, early or latecomers, began to reflect certain basic tenets, particularly moderate social and economic goals. A pattern of continuity with the past slowly emerged, notwithstanding the rhetoric of revolution. To cite an interpretation popular among the rebel bourgeoisie of the day, the Constitutionalist's crusade, like an oak born of an acorn, had risen as an offshoot of the nineteenth-century Revolution of Ayutla, the door to political power for Benito Juárez and his Liberals.[9] The goal, said one partisan, who baptized Madero the "hero of democracy," was to transform into reality the Charter of 1857 and the laws of the Reforma.[10] To the president of the Club Liberal of Acula, a small hamlet in Veracruz, Carranza had picked up the baton dropped by Madero.[11] For disciples of this view of political virtue, which prevailed from 1911 to 1924, the rights of private property, no less so than in the United States and Western Europe, were worshipped, along with the other sacred symbols of capitalism.[12] As one loyal colonel confided to Carranza, the solution for the country's ills was to "boldly protect private enterprise while offering guarantees to commerce and banking." [13] With that sagacious opinion, particularly during the days of Madero, went a fear, at times bordering on panic, of widening the conflict to include the peasantry. To recall the observation of one gentleman from Jalisco to Madero, if the guerrillas operating in the vicinity of Cocula were to receive help from the Indians, it would be difficult to put down the rebellion.[14]

From the start, these views testify that moderates, the timid prophets of reform, discovered a home in the rebel camp. Equally to the point, the opportunistic Luis Cervantes in Mariano Azuela's *Los de Abajo,* a stinging indictment of the corrupted rebellion, had countless counterparts among the rebels. "It is public knowledge," Rivas Iruz told Carranza, "that many persons . . . although claiming to be revolutionaries and sympathizers . . . have never fully supported the Great Redemptionist Movement . . . but, instead, exploit it for personal profit." [15] In the opinion of another friend of the First Chief: the men who have taken up arms in Chiapas "do so solely for selfish gain." [16] Or, according to Salvador Alvarado, a successful general from Sonora turned enemy of Carranza, the First Chief had about him a flock of "servile sycophants hoping to line their pockets with money." [17]

Alvarado exaggerated, but he did not entirely distort the truth, for the upheaval set off by Madero unlocked channels for opportunistic men. Not a few equated the new order with the possibility of making a "fast buck." Emiliano P. Navarrete, one of an army of Constitutionalist's generals, in asking his First Chief for a special concession to build a railroad between Matamoros and Tampico, put the matter well: "revolutionaries stuffed with energy and with blueprints for new enterprises" felt "a moral duty to help develop the country." [18] That he would undoubtedly profit from his venture he left unsaid. In a Sonora mining company with 10,000 shares of stock, one alert colonel had cornered all but one share.[19] "If you want to increase the number of your followers," a sympathizer candidly advised Carranza, "you must stop the outrageous chicanery of your underlings," for even their subordinates, he explained, "censured them, men who took for themselves the homes and automobiles of friends and foes alike and, on occasion, even the furniture." [20]

The grab for the almighty peso, so went the national lament, too often coexisted with the willingness to shed old loyalties and convictions. With startling dexterity, as Zapata remarked, erstwhile stalwarts of dignity and honor climbed on and off political bandwagons to emerge eventually with a distinct set of principles or, at least, of allegiances. A mere minority in the higher echelons of the rebel phalanx probably kept their political honor unblemished. More typical were the ideological adventures of General Francisco Coss, a native of Ramos Arizpe, who began his rebel career with Ricardo Flores Magón, switched to Madero, served the Constitutionalists, and ended up siding with the abortive *cuartelazo* of 1923, discarding, in the course of a decade and a half, one set of commitments for others at the opposite extreme.

III

Of the rebels who climbed the ladder of high public office nearly all were at least of middle class status. Not illogically, in a tug-of-war pitting Mexico City, the seat of power of the Old Regime, against the malcontents, the left-outs, most of the new *politicos* and bureaucrats had come from the small towns of the provinces. Yet of the rebel luminaries, the bosses of ministries and their coterie of subordinates, only a handful had come from rural villages. Peasant leaders were conspicuously missing from the cabinet posts captured by the victors.

Instead, lawyers were the most dominant among the high public officials. Typical of the early dissidents was Emilio Vásquez Gómez, whose brother, Francisco, hunted game with don Porfirio. A liberal reformer, he helped smuggle arms to the Zapatistas while serving briefly in the cabinet of Francisco León de la Barra. However, judged by the convictions of radical agrarian reformers, he was at best a tepid rebel. José María Pino Suárez, Madero's vice-president and also a lawyer, had rallied together malcontents in Yucatán. The son of a wealthy family from Tabasco, Pino Suárez, nonetheless, had worked for Simón Bastar, the owner of rubber and cacao plantations in Tabasco.[21] The cautious Madero placed him on the national ticket because he felt comfortable with his ideas. Pedro Lascuráin, who replaced Manuel Calero as minister of foreign affairs in Madero's cabinet, was a noted jurist, a rich urban landlord, and an active Catholic layman.[22] A few months later, wittingly or not, he delivered Madero into the hands of Victoriano Huerta. Antonio Díaz Soto y Gama, a rebel of a different stripe from Vásquez Gómez and Pino Suárez and offspring of a middle-class family in San Luis Potosí, had fared poorly under Díaz, having to work as a law clerk for an American firm. He catapulted to fame as part of Emiliano Zapata's kitchen cabinet after a short sojourn in the Casa del Obrero Mundial, becoming a congressman, head of the National Agrarian party and oracle for Obregón. In 1911, however, he labeled the old military the "guardians of democracy" and increasingly became disenchanted with reform.[23] Another politician from the bar was Rafael Zubarán Capmany, an astute wheeler-dealer who, during his life, championed Díaz, Bernardo Reyes, Madero, Carranza, the government of the Aguascalientes Convention, Carranza again, Obregón and then De la Huerta in 1923.[24] Along the way, he held choice appointments as minister of *gobernación,* head of the Department of Industry, Commerce, and Labor, and mayor of the Federal District. Often in the shadows of political intrigue, he helped widen the rift between Pancho Villa and Carranza. A partisan of the De la Huerta uprising, he later offered to sell its records and papers to Obregón who had earlier dismissed him from the cabinet, accused, along with his brother, Juan, a Campeche congressman, of peddling their influence.[25]

One flamboyant lawyer, José Vasconcelos, appointed minister of education by both Eulalio Gutiérrez, chief of the government of the Convention of Aguascalientes, and Obregón—itself a feat not to belittle—had been a member of the Ateneo de la Juventud, a small circle of young intellectuals who took it upon themselves to bring down the philosophical edifice built by the positivists. By conviction and temperament miles apart from radicals, and a worshipper at the altar of classical beliefs, he looked across the seas for his inspiration, to the ancient history of the Mediterranean world. He thought himself the Ulises Criollo of Mexico, a facsimile of the legendary hero of Greek mythology he knew and loved so well. To educate Mexico, including its dirt farmers, he had printed and distributed the writings of Dante, Homer, Cervantes, Pérez Galdós, Rolland, and Tolstoy, although those masters had not written for illiterate Mexican peasants. A disciple of José Ortega y Gasset, he believed in the superiority of an educated aristocracy. His idol was Faustino Domingo Sarmiento, the headstrong, conservative Argentine thinker and politician of the nineteenth century. He believed Argentina's success was due to Sarmiento's racist attack on the rustic *gaucho*. For Vasconcelos education was a moral crusade, upholding platonic ideas, stressing the three R's, and scorning the thrust of modern pedagogy, finding his inspiration in the ancient Greeks and the Spanish friars of the conquest. Education was primarily a defense of culture, rather than a mattter of economics. He envisaged a school to develop Mexico's peculiar brand of culture, primarily along Hispanic lines, Spanish and Latin-European. His values excluded the Indian contribution. Mexico was Hispanic; where not, its civilization must be made so.[26]

Andrés Molina Enríquez, lawyer and polemicist of the middle road, trusted advisor of Luis Cabrera, distinguished scholar and bumbling *politico,* served Reyes, Huerta, the Constitutionalists, and Obregón. His *Grandes Problemas Nacionales,* published with funds provided by Reyes and written with a positivist slant, hardly concealed his racist views of Indian Mexico. With his Plan de Texoco, he was among the first to raise the standard of revolt against Madero. Huerta's chief of the Department of Labor, Molina Enríquez survived this mistake to become a key advisor to the committee that drew up Article 27 of the Constitution of 1917.[27] Afterwards, as a member of the National Agrarian Commission, he labored mightily on behalf of small, private property and to halt the spread of the collectivist *ejido.*

No one, however, better exemplifies the cautious lawyer turned politician and reformer than Luis Cabrera, a brilliant thinker, journalist, and confidant to Carranza. Son of the owner of a small bakery in Zacatlán de las Manzanas, Cabrera, after a short stint as a school-teacher, obtained a law degree in 1901. He practiced law first with Rodolfo Reyes, son of the *caudillo* of Nuevo León, and from 1909 to 1912 with the law firm of William A. McLaren and Rafael L. Hernández, the latter being the wealthy and conservative uncle of Madero. He joined Madero because Reyes, whom he supported, refused to take on Díaz.

Cabrera, baptized "the voice of the ideological Revolution" by
Antonio Manero, fell out with Obregón during the days of the
Aguascalientes Convention and lobbied against his presidential
designs in 1919.[28] For his part, Obregón distrusted Cabrera, once
telling him in a letter that "no one believes what you say because you never say what you think." Carranza, however, relied
on Cabrera for advice on financial affairs, naming him minister
of the treasury in 1914, a post he filled for two years, and again
in April, 1919. Cabrera had long thought highly of Carranza,
having suggested him for the vice presidency in 1911.[29]

As his defense of Carranza and the Compañía Tlahualilo,
at the time under British control, demonstrates, Cabrera shared
little in common with militant revolutionaries. According to one
Mexican opinion, "in no way can Cabrera be considered a revolutionary. All of his life he was the most intelligent, satirical, aggressive, and brilliant mouthpiece for the bourgeoisie, the *gente
decente* driven by the restrictive practices of the *científicos* to seek
revenge with Madero." [30] He voiced the aspirations, not of
the poor, but of the middle classes, denied a seat on the *carro
completo* of the Porfiristas. He viewed social upheavals with
horror. In a letter of April 27, 1911, he warned Madero that the
"movement initiated by you in Chihuahua verges on becoming
a national conflagration." The entire Republic, he went on, "confronted an upheaval more powerful and more vast than what you
had in mind." Because it threatened to turn into a runaway
revolution, all Mexicans had "begun to work to stamp it out." [31]

Yet Cabrera had scant faith in standpatters. His own ideas,
furthermore, matured with the passage of time. In April, 1911,
for example, he had believed that the land question could be
solved simply by equalizing taxes on small and large property.
By late that year, however, he had modified his opinion, accepting the need for legislation to spur the growth of small property.[32] As a member of the Bloque Renovador in Congress, he
urged Madero to push ahead with social legislation lest the old
guard climb back into power. In a speech to Congress in 1912, he
laid the foundations for the famous Decree of January 6, 1915,
Carranza's response to the Plan de Ayala. Combining land reform
with guarantees for private property, Cabrera visualized a system
with a place for both *ejidos* and *haciendas*. The peasants would

have lands to cultivate, but not enough to support themselves and their families. To make ends meet, they would require an additional source of income. The neighboring *hacienda*, in need of a seasonal supply of labor, would provide it, while the peasants would offer the *hacendado* a reliable pool of labor for the planting and harvest periods. Cabrera's ingenious formula, as he saw it, satisfied the demand for land but kept alive the traditional *hacienda*. As Cabrera spelled it out in 1916, the goal was "to spur economic development through free competition." [33]

IV

School-teachers, too, supplied a large share of the political nabobs and rebel officials. One Mexican historian has noted the similarity in the role of the insurgent schoolmaster with that of the lower clergy during the wars for independence a century before.[34] Yet, while the list of school-teachers turned rebels was long and impressive, only a handful were actual radicals. The straight and narrow, moderate reform, appealed to most of them.

Teachers entered the fray early. Esteban Baca Calderón, one of their precursors, helped instigate the strike at Cananea in 1906; before that, he had taught school in Tepic.[35] According to rumor, Braulio Hernández, teacher and personal secretary to Abraham González, inspired his cautious boss to rebel in Chihuahua.[36] The son of a wealthy family from Guanajuato, Praxedis Guerrero, the first to unfurl the flag of rebellion in Chihuahua, was also a school-teacher. David G. Berlanga, a rebel dignitary, had been superintendent of public education in San Luis Potosí. Luis G. Monzón, unlike his companions a radical and a delegate to the Constitutionalist Convention at Querétaro, was a native of Sonora and the former director of the Escuela de Varones in Moctezuma. Born in San Luis Potosí in 1872, Monzón had come to Sonora during Ramón Corral's efforts to expand and upgrade public schooling. One of the handful of left-wing ideologues, he had collaborated with Ricardo Flores Magón on *Regeneración*.[37] For siding with Flores Magón, he was exiled from Mexico and jailed in Douglas, Arizona, as a syndicalist agitator. In 1923, he joined the Communist party, and eventually died honest but poor.[38] Manual Chao, governor of Chihuahua in the time of Villa, less radical and more successful than Monzón, had spent his youth in Tuxpan, a port of Veracruz. A graduate of the teachers college in Jalapa, Chao answered Madero's call as a teacher in Chihuahua, served Villa and Carranza, and lost his life for supporting De la Huerta in 1923. Chao, whose thinking ran with the mainstream of rebel thought, had taken the field against Huerta to defend "democracy" and "the rights of man." [39] Born and educated in Saltillo, capital of Coahuila, Gertrudis G. Sánchez, a teacher in Agua Nueva, became a commandant of *rurales* in return for his support of Madero. Sent to Guerrero, he initially sympathized with Zapata. But when Madero faltered, he fell in step with Huerta, and then with the Constitutionalists because, as he said, Carranza "upheld his principles." [40] He stayed out of the quarrel between Carranza and Villa; when he regained his loyalty to the Constitutionalists, the Villistas killed him. Meanwhile, during the course of his vacillations, he had abandoned Zapata. In like manner, Antonio I. Villarreal, another schoolmaster from the north, became a stalwart of the Constitutionalists after finding the climate of the Partido Liberal Mexicano, an allegiance of his early political days, overly invigorating. Once a backer of land reform, he ultimately shed this conviction, rejecting even Obregón's cautious stance.

Of the schoolmasters of moderate bent, Plutarco Elías Calles undoubtedly stood at the head of his class. Unlike most of his companions, however, Calles had forsaken the schoolroom even before don Porfirio went into exile. A man of ups and downs during his early life, Calles was the illegitimate son of Plutarco Elías Lucero, an influential *hacendado* in Sonora, and doña Jesús Campuzano. His step-father, from whom he took his last name, was Juan B. Calles, while his half brother, Arturo M. Elías, as a diplomat served Díaz and Huerta and later the Constitutionalists. Calles launched his teaching career in the Colegio de Sonora, one of the many schools built by Corral, and then moved to Guaymas as its school superintendent. When he lost his job in Guaymas, because of his heavy drinking, he moved to Fronteras where he unsuccessfully tried farming. Fortunately for him, at the urging of Governor Rafael Izábal, the city council of Fronteras appointed him its secretary, while his natural father made

him the *mayordomo* of one of his *haciendas*. To add to his income, Calles also managed the local flour mill. By 1909, given
his multiple activities, he was earning 300 pesos a month, a
goodly sum for that time. Yet again, circumstances, probably of
his own making, compelled Calles to leave Fronteras for a job
as manager of the Hotel California in Guaymas.[41]

Calles' political life dated from 1911, when he ran unsuccessfully for Congress. Like Obregón, with whom he was closely
linked, Calles did not support Madero, preferring to watch events
from the sidelines. But, he and José María Maytorena, appointed
governor of Sonora by Madero, shared mutual friends, who prevailed upon Maytorena to appoint Calles chief of the police of
Agua Prieta and Cananea. Maytorena wanted someone he could
count on to curb the activities of disciples of the Flores Magón,
for whom he had no sympathy. True to his orders, Calles kept
Agua Prieta from falling into the hands of the Magonistas.[42]
With the death of Madero, Calles pledged his allegiance to the
Constitutionalists, siding with Carranza in his quarrel with Villa
and Maytorena. Between 1915 and 1918, he was Carranza's
minister of industry, commerce, and labor, governor of Sonora,
and its military boss. In 1919, he abandoned Carranza for Obregón, served briefly as minister of war under De la Huerta, later
as Obregón's minister of *gobernación*, and then as president of
Mexico.

Until 1927, the year of his conversion to conservative principles (some say with the encouragement of Dwight Morrow, the
Yankee ambassador), Calles had occasionally toyed with unorthodox doctrines. To his enemies, he symbolized the radical fringe
of the Sonora dynasty. W. A. Julian, the American consul in
Nogales, described with horror Calles' ideas during his term as
governor. Calles, he said, had started a "back to the farm" movement, while harboring "hatred" for the Cananea Consolidated
Copper Company and the Cananea Cattle Company.[43] Still, whatever the validity of this opinion, Calles had another side. As
military boss of Sonora, alleged Villarreal, Calles had not only
become the scourge of urban and rural workers but had two
precursors of Mexican socialism, Lázaro Gutiérrez de Lara and
Manuel H. Hughes, shot.[44] He ruled with a brutal hand, as one
Mexican physician who clashed with Calles, then military chief of

Nogales, testified. Only the timely intervention of Obregón had saved the doctor from death by a firing squad for having, against the wishes of Calles, gone to the United States in search of medical help for a stomach ailment.[45]

The former schoolmaster quickly left behind the austerity of the classroom. He built not only a "political clan," but a "financial dynasty reminiscent of the *científicos*."[46] The "radical" who had sent shivers of fear down the spine of the American consul in Nogales became the proud owner of the Hacienda Santa Barbara on the outskirts of Mexico City—lands originally designated for subdivision into small farms.[47] By 1921 he could speculate, at a loss of 50,000 pesos, on the purchase of El Tramado, a lead and silver mine.[48] He owned the controlling stocks of the Compañía Mercantil y Agrícola de Sonora, and shared the others with members of the Elías family.[49] In 1925, Rodolfo, one of his sons, on the advice of Obregón, purchased 390 hectares of land in the Río Yaqui Valley by writing a check for 50,000 pesos on his father's account.[50] In the meantime, another son, Plutarco Elías, Jr., had acquired the Hacienda Soledad de la Mota in General Terán, Nuevo León, where he cultivated cotton, alfalfa, corn, and citrus fruits.[51]

V

Engineers furnished an additional contingent of the public officials and planners. Like the men they obeyed, they wanted reform and not revolution, and easily mastered the art of adaptability, the need to adjust to political realities. Adalberto Tejeda, for one, the son of a distinguished family from Veracruz, chief of staff of General Cándido Aguilar, Carranza's son-in-law, and Constitutionalist senator from 1916 to 1920, became governor of his native state under Obregón. To his credit, he worked hard for reform. Pastor Rouaix, an engineer from Durango, helped write articles 27 and 123 of the national charter. Wealthy and successful, he had been governor of Durango, which under his leadership was the first state to adopt a land reform program. While loyal to Carranza and no kin of radicals, Rouaix nevertheless boldly broke with his chief's timid recommendations at Querétaro in order to sponsor meaningful labor and agrarian measures. At the time, Rouaix was Carranza's minister of agriculture and *fomento.* Yet, for all his contributions, Rouaix, a believer in private property, merely hoped to update Mexican capitalism and to add a measure of social justice.

Another Carranza favorite, Félix F. Palavicini, weathered the unpredictable political winds until 1917. Son of a rich family from Tabasco, the owner of cacao and rubber plantations, Palavicini had been sent to Europe for travel and study by Justo Sierra. Not illogically, he thought well of Díaz. At best a man of moderate political views, Palavicini accompanied Madero on his campaign swing through Yucatán. Yet, upon learning that Díaz had jailed Madero, Palavicini did an about face, vowing, in a letter he sent to Rafael Reyes Spindola, editor of *El Imparcial,* to fight for Díaz if a revolt broke out against him. "I condemn mutiny," he said, adding that he preferred "the stagnation of democracy to civil war." [52] Evidently, Madero forgave him, for with his victory Palavicini entered the hallowed halls of Congress—despite strong objections to him. He stayed in Congress until Huerta decided to jail its occupants, and then left to join up with Carranza in Veracruz, where he encountered the bitter enmity of the reform element among the Constitutionalists. To the dismay of many of his followers, Carranza stood by Palavicini, naming him minister of public instruction and director of propaganda. Then, over the heated objections of scores of delegates, Palavicini, at the behest of Carranza, attended the Constitutional Convention at Querétaro. Yet, as he wrote in *El Universal,* he believed that you could not "better the lot of a people by taking from the rich in order to give to the poor; that could only be done by increasing both national wealth and productivity." [53] Hardly a revolutionary doctrine, that hypothesis could only please conservatives. As publisher of *El Universal,* he adamantly opposed efforts to organize his employees into a union, refusing to recognize their right to strike. Instead, he founded a company union that, ironically, Obregón called "independent." [54] Despite these views, Palavicini, who died in the arms of the Old Guard, served Madero, Carranza, and De la Huerta, and helped write the Constitution, the magna carta of the "Revolution."

Pascual Ortiz Rubio, appointed president of the Republic by Calles in 1930 was cast from a similar mold. Less dogmatic and with a keen sense for the politically expedient, Ortiz Rubio, nevertheless, worshipped idols revered by Palavicini. He was the holder of an engineering degree from Mexico City, and the son of a wealthy and powerful family of Michoacán, beneficiaries of high public office in the days of Díaz. A late arrival on the Madero bandwagon, Ortiz Rubio, at the time a lieutenant colonel in the militia of Michoacán, later served Huerta for an embarrassingly long interval.[55] Ultimately, he saw the error of his ways, deserting Huerta for General Pablo González. In 1916, Carranza appointed him director of Bienes Intervenidos, an office established to handle properties occupied by the Constitutionalists. With Carranza's blessings, he became governor of Michoacán; but, nonetheless, defected to Obregón in 1920. As a reward, Obregón made him minister of communications, where he promptly embroiled himself in an attempt to oust the reform governor of Michoacán, Francisco Múgica, and also became involved in a battle with De la Huerta, minister of finance, over the role of labor on the railroads. Yet this "man without a backbone," as Emilio Portes Gil described him, who claimed "as his own the ideas of the last person to speak to him," enjoyed cabinet jobs, political prestige, and the presidency.[56] Not once in the two decades of his glory, however, did he advocate social revolution.

Alberto J. Pani, also an engineer and technocrat, obeyed the dictates of Madero, Carranza, and Obregón. Born to wealth and a worldly man with a taste for old paintings and women, Pani held a series of public jobs in Díaz' regime that, he acknowledged, had given him "economic independence." [57] He earned his political spurs with Madero, serving as his under-secretary of education. Carranza appointed him head of the ministry of commerce and industry, and then sent him abroad as Mexico's ambassador to France, a post that Pani, with his fondness for the elegant life, surely enjoyed. Under Obregón, he ran the Ministry of Foreign Affairs, and helped bring about Washington's recognition of the Mexican government. When De la Huerta resigned as head of the Treasury, Obregón picked Pani to replace him. In these diverse jobs, Pani never failed to urge orthodox fiscal policies, good relations with the United States, and aid to business. His one social goal was to create "an autonomous middle class." [58] One band of senators accused Pani of bringing to the Treasury "every enemy of the Revolution": men loyal to Díaz, Limantour, and Huerta—as well as the Knights of Columbus.[59]

VI

Barring scattered exceptions, neither did the physicians who jumped into the political fray fit the picture of the social revolutionary. From middle-class background, and not uncommonly from wealthy families, the physician who heeded the siren call of politics cherished moderation and distrusted unorthodox schemes. Occasionally, one of them, Jenaro Amezcua, for instance, a physician with the Zapatistas, battled vigorously for social change. Still, Amezcua never sided with the die-hards in Zapata's camp, advocating from the start ties with the Constitutionalists. He ended his political career as the agent of Obregón's Ministry of Agriculture in Morelos, scarcely a place to shape national policy.

More typical was Francisco Vásquez Gómez, brother of Emilio and a physician who entered politics by linking his fate to Bernardo Reyes. A man who went hunting with don Porfirio, Vásquez Gómez, while to the left of Madero, bid farewell to his orthodox views when he lost his political prestige. When Reyes left his admirers high and dry, Vásquez Gómez, like others in the identical plight, turned to Madero. Although he belatedly tried, with the help of his brother to keep the rebel militias alive, Vásquez Gómez never felt at home with radicals. Yet, to his credit, after Madero cut him off, he ultimately accepted the necessity for some kind of land reform. José Manuel Puig Casauranc, another physician and officeholder in the 1920's, rode to fame on the shoulders of Calles. Before that, he had cared for the sick of El Aguila, a foreign oil company. According to Jorge Prieto Laurens, Calles had once judged Puig a "reactionary" and a *burgués*.[60] But Puig had the good sense to side with Calles in his battle with De la Huerta, and as a reward, became minister of education

where, happily for public education, a coterie of dedicated pedagogues did his work for him. Puig died a millionaire with a
palatial home in the Lomas de Chapultepec in Mexico City.

VII

Middle-class journalists were also among the *políticos* of the
coming order. A muckraking newspaperman, Silvestre Terrazas,
publisher of *El Correo de Chihuahua* and a stubborn critic of
the local bosses, supported Madero and served briefly as governor of Chihuahua. By choosing Villa over Carranza, Terrazas
cut short his political career. Yet despite his angry denunciations
of the ruling clan in Chihuahua, he hardly fitted the picture of
the wild-eyed radical; instead, he displayed a sharp eye for
profitable investments, having acquired a small fortune of 200,000
pesos by 1912. Besides his newspaper, he owned real estate in the
city of Chihuahua and rural property.[61] With the approval of
Villa, who also was savy in business matters, Terrazas, in 1915,
had signed an agreement with Generals Manuel S. Avila, the
military commander of Chihuahua, and Fidel Avila, giving him
one-fourth of the profits from two coal mines on public lands.
At the time, Terrazas was the *secretario de gobierno* of Chihuahua.[62]

Juan Sánchez Azcona, who wrote for *El Presente* and *El
Diario,* rivals of *El Imparcial,* tasted a larger measure of political
success, perhaps because of his amorphic views. Born and raised
in Tabasco, and the child of a respected family, Sánchez Azcona,
nevertheless, as a Porfirista congressman between 1904 and 1908,
represented Chihuahua.[63] He was an ally of Reyes and, as editor
of *México Nuevo,* a backer of Patricio Leyva in Morelos. When
Díaz sent Reyes off to Europe, Sánchez Azcona fell in step with
Madero, publishing *Nueva Era* for him. He was the private secretary, a prestigious job, of both Madero and Carranza. However,
upon hearing of Madero's death, he had wired Governor José
María Maytorena to urge him to "collaborate patriotically for
the success of the government headed by President Huerta." [64]
Meanwhile, he kept his ears alert for news of good investments,

as evidenced by a letter to him from Luis Casarrubias, his *compadre,* advising Sánchez Azcona not to put money into the *"baños de Axocopan* but in Chignahuacan." [65]

A newspaperman of unsavory reputation, Heriberto Barrón enjoyed Carranza's confidence. Formerly a congressman and once militantly pro-Díaz, he had helped undermine the second liberal Congress held in San Luis Potosí in 1902.[66] As *El Imparcial* acknowledged, Barrón had a knack for "political schemes." [67] While editor of *La República* near the close of the Díaz era, he had supported Reyes; but, in an effort to cover all of his political bets, privately worked for an alliance between Reyes and Corral, the person Reyes would replace on the ticket with Díaz.[68] His newspaper, in the interval, printed eulogies to Corral. In 1909, Barrón, in company with Diodoro Batalla, "the two biggest demagogues in the country," recalled Francisco Bulnes, lent his talents to Pablo Escandón, a wealthy *hacendado* and rival of Leyva for governor of Morelos.[69] Notwithstanding, Barrón carved a niche for himself in the revolutionary family, first as a commercial agent in New York for Madero and Carranza and then as a governor of Yucatán in 1915. The man Ramón Prida said "no one took seriously" met his Waterloo at Querétaro in 1916 when the credentials committee rejected Carranza's recommendation that Barrón be seated as a delegate. The "only thing Barrón had going for him," declared one delegate, "was his friendship with Carranza; aside from that, he was a 'reactionary'." Cándido Aguilar, son-in-law of Carranza, labeled Barrón "the most immoral figure in the Constitutionalist camp." [70]

VIII

Even bankers scaled the heights of exalted public offices. One of them, Adolfo de la Huerta, son of "one of the most beloved and most powerful merchants of Guaymas," and a graduate of the Preparatoria in Mexico City, had majored in the unlikely combination of accounting and voice.[71] When not performing on the stage, he kept the records for the Banco de México. From that job he went on to be manager of the Negociación Industrial, and by 1909 ran one of the largest companies in Guaymas, the tannery-

hacienda of San Germán. In the waning of Díaz' regime, De la Huerta flirted briefly with the Partido Liberal Mexicano, but its intoxicating idealism proved too strong for don Adolfo who, while a reformer of sorts, stopped short of embracing militants.[72] Occasionally a friend of labor, kind and generous, De la Huerta, perhaps one of the most liberal in the Sonora dynasty, also advocated streamlining Mexican capitalism, not its elimination. When governor of Sonora, he sanctioned the small, private farm over the *ejido*.[73] To the delight of the American consul in Nogales, he displayed a "conservatism that has proven a surprise to most persons"; an American mining mogul, according to the consul, after a conversation with De la Huerta, had returned "agreeably surprised by the governor's reasonable attitude." [74] He was a diplomat for Carranza in Europe and Obregón's minister of the treasury. Had Obregón picked him as his successor, the two would have lived happily ever after. When he marched off in a huff over the political rebuff, quixotically along with a large body of workers, he also drew the applause of the rich, greedy generals and die-hards.

Abraham González, banker, cattle buyer, and governor of Chihuahua for Madero, like De la Huerta, toyed momentarily with the Flores Magón but quickly discovered that he had no heart for their socialist doctrines. Well meaning, he envisaged reform within a political framework, giving his attention to municipal autonomy and state's rights, both, he believed, trampled by the old oligarchy in Mexico City. As governor of Chihuahua, and as a cabinet minister for Madero, he never swore to destroy the huge *latifundia*. Had he outlived Madero, in all likelihood he would have loyally served Carranza as well as Obregón.

Antonio Manero, a banker not adverse to trafficking in shady deals, hung on until 1923. Intelligent, erudite, the author of a perceptive study of the Banco de México, and knowledgeable in economics, Manero pulled his chestnuts out of the fire more than once. Under Díaz, Huerta, and Madero, he was an employee of the Banco de México. But, to his misfortune, he and his brother, Enríque, also with the Banco, were convicted of forgery and the theft of bank funds just days before Huerta fled the capital.[75] With the occupation of Mexico City by Obregón,

Manero became a Constitutionalist, leaving with them for Vera-cruz when Villa and Zapata drove his new allies to the port city. There, Palavicini, minister of education, used Manero as an editorial writer for *El Pueblo* and *El Demócrata,* and named Enríque a paymaster for the military.[76] When Luis Cabrera and his assistant Rafael Nieto, appointed Manero to a banking post, his critics revealed his sordid record.[77] Manero, nonetheless, weathered the storm, becoming, according to one report, the "factotum" in the Treasury.[78] From there Manero went to Congress and by 1920 headed the Committee on the Treasury and Public Credit. Under Obregón, he presided over congressional sessions dealing with agrarian legislation.[79] By 1923, evidently having circumvented his tarnished reputation, he belonged to the Committee on Statutes of the Banco de México. Always ambitious for higher glory, Manero bolted Obregón to join De la Huerta's retinue. When the *cuartelazo* failed, Manero, with Rafael Zubarán Capmany, offered to sell documents of the plot to Obregón.[80] Not once in this controversial career had Manero, an ally and colleague of rebels, uttered a sincere revolutionary thought. Yet, he enjoyed choice public jobs for over a decade.

IX

"Unquestionably, men of business and property sympathize with your administration," a merchant told Madero. We want to help you, he added, "not just with our hearts but with guns in our hands." [81] Shopkeepers and merchants, almost always from towns in the provinces, from the start participated in the rebellion; eventually, large numbers of them filled government jobs, and some in key positions.

The list of salesmen, clerks, and merchants on the make who swore allegiance to the Constitutionalists is particularly long. General Celedonio de Villarreal, for example, a native of Nuevo León and the son of wealthy parents, had run a produce and dairy business in Monterrey.[82] Another Constitutionalist general, Ildefonso V. Vásquez, had been a student in a commercial college in Fort Worth, Texas.[83] Captain Ernesto Martínez had sold Singer sewing machines in the coal towns of Coahuila.[84] Former store clerks, Crispín Treviño and David R. Neave became respectively a colonel and a general for Obregón.[85] Everardo G. Arenas, a traveling salesman, distributed Maderista propaganda, including *La Sucesíon Presidencial*, in the state of Puebla. In 1909, he founded in the city of Puebla, where he made his home, the Club Central Anti-Reeleccionista and worked closely with Aquiles Serdán, the young newspaperman who fired the opening shot of the Madero rebellion. Made a general by Madero, Arenas helped organize Puebla for him, and subsequently became its attorney general, a political bellwether, and an inspector for the army. With Madero's death, he went over to the Constitutionalists.[86] Ramón F. Iturbe, governor of Sinaloa and a man who knew how to benefit monetarily from the influence of public office, owned a small grocery in 'Alcoyonque. Another storekeeper, Eulalio Gutiérrez, went from mayor of Concepción de Oro, his home in Zacatecas, to general and eventually became president of Mexico. Gutiérrez, who surmounted the misfortunes of his aborted rule, acquired a mine in San Pedro, where he paid his miners poorly, and a *tienda de raya* that sold goods at inflated prices.[87]

Gregorio Osuna, another Constitutionalist bigwig, friend of Pablo González and a store clerk during the old regime in Puerto del Carmen in Coahuila, began his upward climb by working in Carranza's campaign for the governorship of Coahuila. In 1911, Osuna took up arms on behalf of Madero and later, in company with González, went off to fight the Magonistas and Pascual Orozco. Soon after, he was in the south combating Zapatistas alongside of General Aureliano Blanquet, one of Madero's assassins. He remained in Mexico City after the "Tragic Ten Days," compelled, he claimed, to serve Huerta. Sent to Lower California as military boss of its southern district, he deserted Huerta for Obregón. Carranza named him governor of Aguascalientes in 1916, governor of Tamaulipas the following year, and then mayor of Mexico City. Osuna, like his friend Pablo González, walked in step with Carranza's less than radical views.[88]

Other partisans held minor bureaucratic posts or jobs on the fringes of business, or in lesser professional occupations, such as General Francisco Murguía, a photographer in Monclova before joining Carranza's circle of trusted lieutenants. At the time of his death by a firing squad in 1922, Murguía owned the Hacienda Santa Isabel in Tamaulipas, six homes in the best *colonias* of Mexico City, as well as gambling dens in the capital and Tampico.[89] General Luis Herrera Cano, brother of the famous Maclovio, was the agent in charge of the railroad station at Mesa Sandía, between Parral and Durango.[90] One of the clique of Sonora bosses, Ramón P. DeNegri was a telegraph operator, the job also of Rodolfo Fierro, the blood-thirsty ally of Villa.[91] General Francisco Serrano, a devotee of night clubs, beautiful women, and one of Obregón's cabinet officers, had been a bookkeeper in Sonora. A crony of Obregón's since their days together in Huatabampo, Serrano entered politics as the private secretary of the *hacendado* Maytorena.[92] No one took him seriously, certainly not anyone with a social conscience.

A beneficiary of Carranza's trust, General Pablo González, a native of Nuevo León, had been a traveling salesman in Coahuila and Chihuahua for American companies and boasted of his friendship with Americans. He was on the town council of Nadadores in 1907 and at one time a candidate for the job of mayor.[93] He rode the coattails of Carranza to the pinnacles of power: commander of the Army of the Northeast, governor of Coahuila, and military boss of Morelos. While in Morelos, González, reported Gildardo Magaña, pocketed the profits from the sales of harvests of five *haciendas*.[94] To no one's surprise, he built a considerable fortune, acquired rural and urban real estate, as well as a bank and the Hotel Bender in Laredo, Texas.[95] Notwithstanding his debt to Carranza, he turned on his mentor in 1920 and ran for the office himself. Among those who contributed to his campaign for the presidency, according to Magaña, were the *hacendados* of Yucatán, "contractors who bought and sold human beings, the worst slave merchants in the Republic." [96]

Of somewhat different fabric were two other former entrepreneurs. One was Pascual Orozco, the son of a shopkeeper in San Isidro, a village in Chihuahua, who hauled goods between the mining camps on mule-drawn wagons, and with two companions, ran a lumber and feed store.[97] Until quite late in the movement, Orozco paid scant heed to politics.[98] But, when a business competitor received special privileges from the Terrazas clan during the aftermath of the crises of 1907, Orozco joined the foes of re-election and took to the hills with Madero.[99] Denied a post he coveted, the governorship of Chihuahua, Orozco rebelled against Madero, advocating in the Plan de la Empacadora, a concoction of liberal reforms, including land distribution, and conservative panaceas. However, behind his revolt stood the Terrazas and the old oligarchy in Chihuahua. Defeated, he ended up in Huerta's camp. Salvador Alvarado, once a leading Constitutionalist and afterwards one of its critics, had owned a profitable drugstore in Potam, Sonora. Born in Sinaloa, he had come north with his parents, proprietors of a small business.[100] A rival of Obregón, he became military boss of the southeast and eventually governor of Yucatán, where he ran a well-oiled political machine. Sympathetic to labor, he helped found the Socialist party of Yucatán. Yet, despite his scores of worthwhile social measures and his socialist rhetoric, his most acclaimed accomplishment was a committee to regulate the price and sale of henequen to foreign buyers.[101] The henequen planters, nonetheless, outlived his term in office. Not so the priests, most of whom he drove out of Yucatán. Always unhappy with Obregón, he joined De la Huerta's coup in 1923 and paid with his life for his treason.

Not every petty job holder or entrepreneur, however, proved timid or cautious in his politics or ideology of reform. Two, in particular, left their imprint on the history of revolution. One was Lucio Blanco, who came from Nadadores, the town in Coahuila that gave Pablo González his start in politics. The first rebel to subdivide an *hacienda,* Blanco was the offspring of a prominent family and had gone to school in Saltillo and Texas. One of his ancestors was Miguel Blanco, minister of war for Juárez. Blanco's godfather, Atilano Barrera, a backer of Madero, presided over the state legislature.[102] Until he took up arms, Blanco had managed his father's properties. Unfortunately, Carranza punished Blanco for daring to subdivide an *hacienda,* and sent him to serve under Obregón in Sonora. A partisan of the government of the Aguascalientes Convention, and one of the few northerners to want to patch up the rift with Zapata, Blanco died at the hands of former companions in arms. As the lives of

Blanco and Zapata illustrate, social revolutionaries often paid dearly for their convictions. A similar fate befell Felipe Carrillo Puerto, an engineering student and later a train conductor in Yucatán. A supporter of Zapata and a Socialist, Carrillo Puerto became governor of Yucatán in 1922, and spent his short span in office attempting to help the peasants, eradicating illiteracy and combating the clergy. Of impeccable reform credentials, Carrillo Puerto committed the mistake of organizing the peasants against the henequen lords, and lost his life for his efforts. During the De la Huerta uprising, his enemies captured and shot Carrillo Puerto and his brothers.

X

Hacendados, too, strangely enough, attended the banquet of the victorious rebels, either as sympathizers or as "revolutionaries" who had, in the course of their adventures, made themselves masters of *haciendas.* No one knows how many successful rebels acquired estates, but no one disputes that many did. Not surprisingly, a handful of *hacendados,* whether of Porfirista vintage or of the newly inaugurated, championed reform, but rarely land redistribution. Antenor Sala, *hacendado* and proponent of land reform, walked a lonely path. Madero and Carranza, vintage *hacendados,* died, so to speak, with their boots on; neither lost his lands during his stay in office. Nor did Obregón, a "revolutionary" *hacendado.*

From the start, Madero, Carranza, and Obregón counted *hacendados* among their friends and backers. Carlos Morton, an *hacendado* in Hidalgo, even borrowed money from the Banco de Monterrey to help equip his brother-in-law who had taken up arms on behalf of Madero.[103] Genaro Dávila, a landlord in Coahuila, lent the rebels nearly 10,000 pesos and gave lands for Carranza to distribute among the landless of Zaragoza to insure, as he said, the "pacification" of the country.[104] Manuel Cuesta Gallardo, an *hacendado* and former Díaz *político,* from his haven in New York was telling Carranza in 1915 that he was a "devoted follower of the Constitutionalists, whose victory he awaited so that Mexico might savor an era of peace, prosperity, and progress."[105] Unquestionably, some of the enthusiasm of *hacendados* for Carranza, particularly during the period of factional fighting, reflected a fear of the more radical rebels. Manuel Ruíz Lavín, an *hacendado* in the Laguna, to cite one instance, pledged his allegiance to Carranza while offering to dispatch his own soldiers to combat the "Villista yoke." [106] At that time, Villa had taken to rewarding his *compadres* with lands of *hacendados* he disliked. Roberto Castro, master of the Hacienda San Miguel in Puebla, probably turned Constitutionalist in order to protect his properties.[107]

Still, landlords did go to battle to challenge the rule of Díaz and his puppets. Such a landlord was José María Maytorena who governed Sonora for Madero and was the son of an *hacendado*. His father, the offspring of a distinguished family, had long waged political warfare against Lorenzo Torres and Corral, the state's *caciques*. The Maytorenas were allies of the Pesqueira family, another landowning clan that broke with Díaz. A moderate politically, Maytorena had studied at Santa Clara College in California and had backed Reyes. He owned eight *haciendas*, mines of silver and copper, and urban real estate in Guaymas.[108] He employed large numbers of Yaquis on his *haciendas*, and at times, before casting his lot with Reyes, had received special permission from Governor Alberto Cubillas, a Corral henchman, to recruit additional Yaquis to harvest his garbanzos.[109] Yet, Maytorena became one of Madero's earliest disciples in Sonora, as he claimed, "to defend its sovereignty." [110] When Obregón asked him to break with Huerta, Maytorena replied that he could not: "It is useless to ask me to do it," he replied. "I have family ties with the elements you label *científicos*, and anyway, my stomach is not up to eating raw meat in the mountains." Huerta's soldiers, he abjectly confessed, "would destroy my properties and burn my *haciendas*, and frankly, I am simply not cut out for it." [111]

Benjamín Hill, like Maytorena a native of Sonora, general and buddy of Obregón until his sudden death in 1920, was another "revolutionary" with lands. One of the first to endorse Madero in Sonora, *El Imparcial* noted that Hill, as a member of the reception committee for Madero, arrived with his *"peones."* [112] Hill was a descendant of a Confederate Army physician who had settled in Mexico. On his mother's side, the Salido family ranked with the leading families and was related by blood to Obregón. Hill embodied the typical characteristics of the Sonora rebel. He was young, just 36 years of age in 1910; a budding entrepreneur, he owned a flour mill, and was the master of a small *hacienda* and of 2,494 hectares of land acquired under the Leyes de Terrenos Baldíos; he exhibited a good sense for business from the beginning.[113] He had visited Italy and married one of Obregón's sisters. By 1916, he told Carranza, he had 4,526 hectares of land lying fallow in Huatabampo; but, he added, if the government were willing to help develop the land, he was ready to invest money of his own.[114] Eventually, he purchased the Hacienda Encarnación, an estate in Hidalgo originally taken from its owner by General Juan Barragán.[115] Hill called his own the Hacienda Coapan just outside of Xochimilco. At no time did Hill, a cabinet minister of Obregón, display a fondness for social reform. As mayor of Agua Prieta in 1911, he had urged that federal soldiers replace the rebels who occupied the border town. While political boss of Cananea, he jailed the leaders of a labor strike for disturbing the public order, judging their demands, essentially shorter hours of work, unjust. Hill, writes Hector Aguilar Camín, had a "phobia about disorder." [116] At his death, according to a letter sent by his widow to Obregón, Hill left behind a small fortune: the Hacienda de Coapan; rights to 40 percent of the gate receipts from the bullfights in Mexico City; one-fourth of the profits from three *haciendas* in the state of Mexico; two petroleum concessions, one in Tamaulipas and the other in Puebla, valued at 1 million pesos; lands acquired as *tierras baldías* on the Río Mayo; rural property; and a healthy bank account.[117]

Hill and Maytorena were not the only landed gentlemen unhappy with the status quo in Sonora. The Pesqueira clan also furnished its quota of rebel paricipants. Roberto V. Pesqueira, politican and diplomat, was the owner of the Hacienda de Chuchuta and the titular head of a family that, as Luis Terrazas in Chihuahua, had bitterly opposed Díaz' coup of Tuxtepec but in time made its peace with him.[118] Ignacio Pesqueira, an intimate of Obregón, had been on the governing council of Cananea in the days of Corral. When Maytorena refused to disown Huerta, Pesqueira became governor of Sonora. Another ally of Obregón,

Ramón Ross, destined to represent Mexico in the discussions that led to the Treaty of Bucareli in 1923, cultivated garbanzos on his lands in Sonora. Like Obregón's older brothers, Francisco and José, Ross had signed a formal pledge of loyalty to Díaz in 1911.[119]

Elsewhere, Tomás Garrido Canabal, a partisan of Obregón and Calles in thought and politics, and as governor of Tabasco, notorious for his persecution of priests and his Red Shirt goons, was the son of a wealthy *hacendado*. Julián Malo Juvera, governor of Querétaro between 1923 and 1925 and an *hacendado*, joined Madero, worked closely with Huerta's governor in Querétaro, and then supported Carranza. When Villa's army chased the Constitutionalists out of Mexico City, Malo Juvera, by then a general, stayed behind. Although the author of a special study on land reform for the government of the Aguascalientes Convention, Malo Juvera kept his lands.[120] Madero's choice for governor of Jalisco, José López Portillo y Rojas, was a rich *hacendado* as well as a novelist. His family's wealth dated from colonial days. A lawyer by training, he had been a Díaz' favorite and senator. As vice-president of the Círculo Nacional Porfirista in 1909, he had signed its *Manifiesto a la Nación,* calling Díaz the "indispensable man" and urging his re-election.[121] When Madero fell, López Portillo y Rojas accepted Huerta's tutelage, becoming his minister of foreign affairs. Juan Barragán, Carranza's chief of staff at age 27, was the heir of a former Díaz governor of San Luis Potosí and of one of its "largest landowning families." Until 1911, young Barragán worshipped Díaz, but then went over to Madero. A playboy who loved glittering uniforms, Barragán became governor of San Luis Potosí in 1917.[122] During the course of his "revolutionary" life, he acquired the Hacienda Encarnación, which he lost to Hill, additional properties in San Luis Potosí, and if Obregón can be believed, fled Mexico after the debacle of his mentor Carranza with large sums of money pilfered from the national Treasury.[123]

XI

Additionally, students, similar to others in the *carnaval,* as José Clemente Orozco called events from 1910 to 1920, had their quota

of politicians, public officials, and generals. Aarón Sáenz, intimate of Calles, abandoned law school on behalf of rebellion and
ended up a cabinet minister, presidential hopeful, and a millionaire. Emilio Portes Gil, president of Mexico between 1928
and 1930 and also a millionaire, rose from the ranks of the law
students, along the way serving as a clerk in the law courts of the
Huerta regime, and if Prieto Laurens' version is authentic, as an
"enthusiastic Huertista." [124] He wrote articles in defense of
Huerta, but finally made his peace with Carranza and Obregón,
becoming senator and political boss of Tamaulipas.[125] To his
credit, as president of the Republic, he pushed ahead with land
reform. General and politician Juan Andréu Almazán, with
an "impressive talent for hoax and skulduggery," had been a
medical student in Puebla and then, as he proclaimed, a loyal adherent of Madero. However, with the triumph of Huerta, he
changed colors, parroting Huerta's condemnation of Zapatismo
as "the banner of bandits who kill, rob, and pillage." It was a
"flag to be destroyed completely . . . because it was a shameful
blot . . . on the motherland." Yet Almazán, an opportunist hostile
to social reform, held high public office, won national honors and
died a rich man.[126]

FIFTEEN

Soldiers as

Revolutionaries

In a clash between you and Villa, three alternatives are
possible:
  *I. That a large majority of military chiefs sides with
     Villa. You are the loser.*
  II. That a large majority sides with you. Villa is the loser.
  *III. That the military chiefs divide their loyalties between
      you and Villa. The Nation is the loser.*

      Anonymous letter to Venustiano Carranza, 1914

I

THE EXPLOSION touched off by Francisco I. Madero gave birth
to an arrogant military caste. Almost immediately, the
brass hats captured huge slices of the national wealth as
well as large measures of the Republic's political power. Ironically, despite populist roots, the military became not just a ladder to the top, but one of the biggest "obstacles" in the path of
reform, and a shabby agent for the perpetuation of the ancient
"agrarian structure." [1] The army chiefs, more often than not,
equated reform with the enjoyment of opportunities previously
denied. Beyond the fulfillment of vulgar avarice, many lacked
goals.

    Nor, as Luis Cabrera recognized, was the military truly a na-
tional unit. Until 1924, despite its formal reorganization in 1917,
the rebel army kept its earlier disparate character. For cohesion
and discipline, it relied on the personal loyalty of its leading

chiefs to the president; of its generals to their chiefs; of its officers to the generals; and of the soldiers to their officers. If the president kept a tight control, the army was a military oligarchy; if he did not, the system was controlled by military *caciques*.[2]

In the nascent stages of the battle against Victoriano Huerta, the rebel chieftains had recruited soldiers and officers where they found them. Most of the soldiers, the privates, corporals and sergeants, were of humble background, workers or peasants. The officers, by contrast, tended to come from a higher social class. Before taking up arms wrote Jorge Vera Estañol, they had been sharecroppers or tenant farmers, clerks in drugstores, labor bosses in mines, trainmen, police, craftsmen, carpenters, trolley conductors, "without taking into account the many rustics and ne'er-do-wells." [3] Alvaro Obregón, in Sonora, for example, recruited Yaquis as privates for his army; but he chose his officers from among the men of the north, "white, creole . . . and partly educated and politically aware." [4] Of the thirty-four generals chosen to be cabinet ministers, vice-ministers, or *oficiales mayores* between 1920 and 1935, only four had earned professional degrees before joining the military.[5]

Not surprisingly, many in the military displayed a dubious loyalty to reform. Antonio Manero, an eyewitness to the surrender of the Porfiristas at Ciudad Juárez in 1911, and a perceptive observer, returned with a poor impression of Madero's army, the *Ejército Libertador,* more or less controlled by Pascual Orozco with the help of Francisco Villa. After speaking to officers and soldiers, Manero concluded that they suffered from "bad habits and a total ignorance, not only of their rights but of how to earn a livelihood." [6] Not much different was a majority of the soldiers wounded in the battle for Monterrey in 1913 who, according to their commander, General Pablo González, "were drunk when the fighting began and, because of that, were captured and shot by the enemy" while withdrawing.[7]

Obviously, not all of the officers and their men fell into this camp. Peasant soldiers with an abiding faith in land reform died by the thousands while countless workers fought for their rights. Not everyone joined the rebel hordes simply for adventure or the opportunity for personal gain. Equally true, many rebel officers held strong reform convictions. The greedy, the opportunistic and the adventurous were also accompanied by those who aspired to build a just Mexico, some of radical bent and others of moderate views. While General Genovevo de la O, a former stalwart of Emiliano Zapata, jeopardized his principles serving Obregón in Morelos, his old colleague, General Francisco Mendoza, the military commander in the district of Jonacatepec, kept faith with past commitments.[8] Although ordered again and again to attack Zapata, Lucio Blanco, a Constitutionalist general and prophet of land reform, refused. "I will not fight . . . against Zapata," he said.[9]

II

"If they are going to kill me tomorrow, let them kill me now," runs one stanza of *La Valentina*, a popular ballad of the Constitutionalist armies. To Vicente Blasco Ibáñez, this phrase captured "the psychology of the Mexican people, their fatalism, their disregard for death." [10] Still, in spite of a certain degree of validity in the observation, Mexicans neither volunteered freely to fight nor eagerly risked death. To the contrary, with few exceptions, the military chieftains constantly faced a recruiting problem. Everyone had to lure peasants and workers with more than the rhetoric of liberty or the promise of land. To gain adherents, the rebel leaders had to offer concrete rewards, not just nebulous promises of a better future. In most instances, this meant money to compensate for the risks taken. To convert peasants and workers into privates required paying them more than they earned by staying home. Clearly, the ravages of war, the destruction of jobs in mines, industry, and agriculture depriving thousands of their wages, drove the jobless to join the rebel armies. But the idealistic and selfless probably constituted a minority.

Grievances against the Old Regime notwithstanding, a minority, particularly as casualties mounted during the factional struggle, gambled their lives for the promise of a better life. Even Madero, who had expected throngs of volunteers to greet him upon his return to Mexico in 1910, had to flee back to Texas when a mere handful awaited him. Only after he and his fellow plotters had provided money and guns did they manage to organize the semblance of an army. However, as Manero pointed out, scores of officers and men under Orozco and Villa had no clear perception of why they were fighting. In *Los de Abajo,* Mariano Azuela, a physician in Villa's army, made this attitude the crux of his novel. Even so Madero did not have as great a recruiting problem as his successors. The Old Regime succumbed to a minuscule force. But after years of fighting, even Zapata, who personified a popular crusade, no longer could count on large numbers of volunteers for his military adventures. Before peace returned, northern chieftains had dispatched agents to recruit soldiers as far south as Chiapas. But, as they learned, soldiers recruited in one province were unwilling to fight in another. As Colonel Vicente Segura complained to General González, one company of his soldiers had refused to follow their captain because they had no wish to abandon their native state.[11] General Guadalupe Sánchez, military boss of Veracruz in 1921, reported that even the threat to pay only in Jalapa, the capital of the state, had failed to convince the "mountain Indians" who formed the 46th Battalion to leave their *patria chica.*[12]

Large-scale recruiting dated from the effort to unseat Huerta. The north, without question, suffered the brunt of the conflict. With the exception of Morelos and adjoining regions where Zapatistas operated, the southern states either put up token resistance or fought internal squabbles just faintly linked to Huerta. The north, meanwhile, had to build immediately a military capable of taking on the federal army. Despite his victory at Ciudad Juárez, Madero had not vanquished it. By the same token, Madero, confronted with the uprising of Orozco, had ironically revitalized the army.[13] To defeat it, Carranza, Obregón, and Villa, the principal antagonists, had to find thousands of men for their armies.

From the start, to recruit privates, the *soldado razo* or *Juan* as he was known in the old army, meant paying men to take up arms. At first, along with those who coveted military command and usually recruited their own men, local political groups helped recruit "volunteers." For instance in Agujita, a town in Coahuila, the Centro Constitucionalista asked Carranza for authority "to recruit men, to give military training" and "to reward the families of soldiers in the field or those that had lost loved ones in battle." As of May 12, 1913, the Centro reported that 108 families had been given meat.[14] The soldiers, through their families, in short, had been compensated with either food or money for their services.

The split between Villa and the Constitutionalists exacerbated recruiting difficulties. As a result, nearly all of the burden fell upon the shoulders of the military leaders. It was up to them to replenish their ranks, a problem made worse by almost two years of fighting. By then, not even the promise of good "wages" enticed men in the northern states to volunteer. With this turn of events, the southern states became important hunting grounds for recruits. On a regular basis, the leading chieftains sent out emissaries, usually captains or majors but also colonels at times. By November, 1914, the commander of Puerto México, a port in Veracruz, was sending his colonels, their pockets filled with money, to find men as far south as Chiapas.[15] When guerrillas sympathetic to Zapata invaded Oaxaca in 1914, Francisco Canseco, its governor, had to ask Carranza for funds to hire additional defenders and to pay his forces.[16] The governor of Puebla used women to help recruit.[17] When Captain Rafael Nieto went off to look for men in the towns of Oaxaca, he wired Carranza for the money required to entice men to join.[18]

Not unexpectedly, as the fighting showed no signs of decreasing, fewer men volunteered. As an aide explained to Carranza in March, 1915, to find soldiers he had to print propaganda leaflets advertising opportunities in the military and had to open a recruiting office in Saltillo. In fifteen days, he boasted, he had recruited one hundred men, "more or less." He could have found additional volunteers, he added, had he not run out of money to pay them.[19] But, it was commonly acknowledged, many of the recruits eventually deserted and returned to their old jobs. Even Zapata, as early as 1912, had learned to burn the cane fields if he wanted soldiers.[20] With nothing to do, their former workers, jobless and hungry and with families to support, readily took up arms. As one foe of Zapata complained to an official in Madero's cabinet in 1912, when the cane fields burn there were "thousands of men without work in the countryside who, undoubtedly, will become a threat to the public order by joining the ranks of the Zapatistas." [21]

In Sonora, moreover, the rebel leadership had, from the beginning, relied on a paid military. The men recruited by Obregón to halt Orozco's invasion of Sonora in 1911—the backbone of the military that eventually confronted Huerta, says Hector Aguilar Camín—enlisted for money. "For this type of man," he went on, "the career of arms offered security of employment . . . as did any other job." If they were not paid, they did not work—bear arms. Money (income), he emphasized, more than partisan politics, ideological convictions, or loyalty to a military chieftain "was the key to the first revolutionary militias in Sonora." The majority of the soldiers, the alcalde of Oputo bluntly admitted, "are men who need a daily wage in order to support themselves and their families." Lamenting the failure to recruit large numbers of soldiers in Cananea in 1911, Benjamín Hill, the prefect of Arizpe, placed the blame on "the low pay offered" recruits, particuarly since in Cananea "the minimum daily wage in the mines is from 2.50 to 3.00 pesos." [22] I. Thord-Gray, a soldier of fortune, reported that Obregón's officers paid their men 1.50 pesos each morning after review. This was more money than they earned as workers on the *haciendas*. [23]

To the rebel leadership in Sonora, victory depended more on the acquisition of military supplies, food, and money to pay troops than on any effort to win popular backing with a meaningful program of social reform. Obregón and his allies managed their revolt as they would have a war with a foreign power. Sonora and its needs dictated policy, not any necessity to respond to the political demands of the fighting element. As Aguilar Camín pointed out, "the quest for wealth, a daily wage, and the adventure of soldiering, as well as regional enthusiasm and loyalty to a military chief, kept the army together." Obregón and his cohorts wanted a professional army. Their soldiers, added Aguilar Camín, shared with their leaders an "absolute lack of a revolutionary conscience defined as a vindication of the social needs of the soldiers themselves." The rank and file never asked for more than Obregón, Salvador Alvardo, and the other generals offered: money, help to their families, clothes, and "martial music." With their material needs satisfied, fear vanished that the soldiers themselves would take advantage of the fighting and political chaos to ask for land, higher wages, and housing. In this disappointing picture, the Yaquis may be a possible exception. Although willing to risk their lives for money, they had often volunteered because Obregón and his companions had promised to return their lands. These Yaquis, nonetheless, were a minority in Sonora.[24]

Villa, whose troops ran matters as they saw fit between Chihuahua and Zacatecas, adopted a similar system. He "always paid his men well." The key to the loyalty of his soldiers, Villa knew, "was a full pocketbook."[25] He had begun to pay his men during the Orozco revolt when he had served under Huerta. At that time, he told Madero, he paid all of his enlisted men, regardless of rank, 1.50 pesos for a day's soldiering. Later, he decided to pay by rank. Each morning at five he paid both the enlisted men and their officers.[26] When he rebelled against Madero, Orozco promised new recruits 2 pesos a day for their services.[27] The Constitutionalists, to cite Luis Cabrera, never lacked soldiers because they made compensation the first priority.[28] Further, L. Rivas Iruz believed, the wages of soldiers had to stay ahead of inflation. In 1910, this meant paying soldiers between 3 and 5 pesos a day, a sum sufficient to encourage them to fight well and to insure their loyalty. At that time, soldiers in the federal army were earning 45 centavos for one day's work.[29] With the modification of the Plan de Ayala in May, 1913, Zapata promised to pay his men regular wages; his officers were to raise the money with forced loans levied on merchants and landlords.[30] Paid soldiers, moreover, did not pillage as one letter informed Madero. "You should know," he went on, "that Colonel Costodio Rodríguez, a native of Carrizal de Arteaga, with his own funds paid the revolutionary forces in the vicinity so that the landlords and foreigners . . . would not be hurt." All told, the colonel had spent 20,000 pesos—which he wanted repaid.[31] To insure the loyalty of his troops, Governor Juan José Ríos had paid them by collecting a tax on foodstuffs. Despite complaints from consumers, he kept the tax, and by implication the higher price on food, until Obregón sent money to pay his men.[32]

Nor were soldiers and officers reticent about asking for monetary rewards. "I have just received a letter from the Ministry of War," Colonel J. Aguirre León reproached Carranza, "telling me that I must chose between my salary in Communications and what I earn as a Colonel; I am told that I cannot have the two salaries." From his perspective, he needed both, what with the high cost of living and a household of ten that included his "children and his servants." [33] Alfredo Ricaut, a literate and intelligent Constitutionalist general, brazenly asked Carranza for a "Cadillac automobile, vintage 1916, one of those you gave General Luis Caballero." [34] To keep his minister of war happy, Obregón, in the middle of a financial crisis in 1921, approved the expenditure of 9,000 pesos for the purchase of a Packard automobile. [35]

Privates, corporals, and sergeants, too, had their eyes on the pot-of-gold. Six months before asking for his Cadillac, Ricaut had complained to Carranza that he had lost over 600 men since leaving Matamoros. The majority had deserted to other brigades "where . . . unscrupulous officers, despite orders to the contrary, admit into their ranks soldiers from other units who enlist without prior permission." To attract them, the officers offered "higher ranks or better pay; in fact, there are brigade leaders who pay soldiers 2 pesos a day and food." Such behavior hurt discipline and weakened the unity of the army, argued Ricaut, "at times making it impossible to rely on men supposedly under your command." Given this situation, he concluded, it was difficult to find men because of the competition "among the countless recruiters operating in the territories we control." The common man, he confessed, had learned to "play the game, to deceive one and all, enlisting in various brigades without ever serving in any." [36] Behavior of this sort hardly built a revolutionary conscience.

In the meantime, the triumphant military of the Constitutionalists, numbering 150,000 by 1917, had blossomed into an enormously costly branch of government. The national budget for 1917, the year for reform to begin, set aside over 656.8 million pesos for soldiers and guns; Communications, ranking next, had only 43.9 million pesos, and education half of that. [37] Out of a budget of 348 million pesos in 1923, the military received 113 million pesos, compared to 42 million for Communications and Public Works, basic tools of reconstruction.[38]

From the start, the growth of the military blocked peace and hurt the economy. The problem began with Madero. To build an army to stop Orozco, Madero had paid volunteers up to 1.50 pesos a day, and in the process, taken them away from jobs in industry that paid less. But since Orozco offered comparable benefits, both he and Madero recruited with equal facility. The clash with Huerta, and later the factional fighting, exacerbated the competition for soldiers. At this rate, testified a physician, Mexico would never enjoy peace, since both friends and foes of the men in office would pay whatever was necessary to hire soldiers. Their inflated pay guaranteed a surplus of warriors but few farmers, miners, laborers, and artisans.[39] The defeat of Villa and Zapata only slightly altered the picture. Despite an order to stop recruiting, according to a confidential report to Carranza, it went on unabated. By paying 1.75 pesos a day for soldiering, with little risk of battle, the military attracted more men to its ranks, while industry and business complained about the scarcity of labor. Even government shops had to advertise for workers.[40]

When volunteering, moreover, soldiers as well as candidates for commissions as officers kept their eyes on rank and opportunities for promotion. It was a scramble for the stripes of a corporal or sergeant or the gold insignia of a field officer. To win a promotion to a higher rank, men changed commanders and even went over to the enemy. "Since I have been given a commission at a higher grade," read the laconic message of a Constitutionalist officer in 1913, "I am joining General Emiliano Zapata." [41] In Michoacán, General Gertrudis G. Sánchez fretted and fumed when Zapatistas, promising promotions, raided the ranks of his officers. Meanwhile, officers with detachments of men loyal to them sold themselves and their units to the highest bidder. These flip-flops, reported Sánchez, raised eyebrows in the villages and towns.[42] When Villa severed his ties to the Constitutionalists, his commanders began to woo their former companions. "Join us," wrote General Raul G. Ruíz, Villa's military governor of Veracruz, to a Constitutionalist colonel, and "you will never again have to worry about rank." [43]

III

To the unhappiness of Mexicans who looked to the rebel militias for salvation, their officers and men too often appeared primarily motivated in filling their pockets with loot. At Ciudad Juárez, contrary to orders by Madero, the motley band of fighters under Orozco and Villa had celebrated their victory by pillaging the border town. The inhabitants of Juárez were the first to suffer as a result of their liberators' hunger for spoils. Until the very end, despite sundry orders to keep the military in check, officers and men fell upon the land like birds of prey. Some commanders even made the right to pillage a reward for victory. All the same, other military chiefs, perhaps a minority, struggled to enforce the rules of war on soldiers engaged in the bloody civil strife where passions and ancient animosities dictated behavior. "We do not want thieves," General González warned his troops in 1913, "we want selfless men who fight to emancipate the motherland and not to stuff their pockets." He had ordered Colonel Antonio Treviño shot, he reminded his followers, for looting during the capture of Monterrey and for stealing money from a defenseless old man.[44] A few months later, González called attention to roving bands of armed thugs who pillaged and robbed, telling Carranza that he had told them to join his army immediately or else be labeled bandits and shot upon capture.[45] From Oaxaca, General Fortunato Maycotte promised Obregón that he would see to it that his officers did not enrich themselves at public expense in the belief that he would not punish them.[46] One of Obregón's sundry letters on the subject, written to General Eugenio Martínez in 1924, pointed a finger at the corruption among army units in the state of Veracruz. He referred specifically to a general who demanded payment of a *mordida,* bribe, before he would supply banana planters with railroad cars. "As I told you in our last conversation," Obregón explained, "if the chicanery of certain commanders is not stopped promptly, it will predictably undermine discipline in the army and damage the prestige of the national government."[47] For his part, Martínez, apparently unable or unwilling to act, urged Obregón to take "energetic steps to stop the knavery that, unfortunately, is the way of life for large numbers of our generals and commanders." [48] Even Zapata had to publish an injunction against any "revolutionary . . . who committed crimes in the towns and villages and broke into homes without their owners consent." He promised swift punishment for such crimes.[49]

Obregón and González had ample justification for their alarm for, as an article in *El Regenerador,* a newspaper in Tuxtla Gutiérrez argued, "a mule driver who loses his animals to soldier thieves will see no difference between the Constitutionalists and the Old Regime." [50] Victory would go to the group that kept the public confidence. Yet, unquestionably, the tumult of the times, *la bola* in popular slang, drew uncommitted men to the life of the warrior. Opportunists plagued all rebel factions. As the unhappy wife of a colonel said to General González, her husband, "a man shorn of noble sentiments . . . had embraced soldiering for money and personal gain." [51] According to another informant, Colonel Ramón Corona, an individual of "the worst antecedents," had once been sentenced to death for murder but won his release from jail by enlisting in the army of the Constitutionalists. Sent to the 24th Battalion, he had fled when he and other soldiers, dispatched to guard a shipment of money, had killed its captain and absconded with 17,000 pesos. Promoted to colonel, he looted at will.[52] A native of Temascaltepec, a village in the state of Mexico, described how General Jesús H. Salgado, eventually governor of Guerrero, allowed his soldiers to rob and pillage, "leaving the people to beg for charity." [53] Governor M. Triana of Aguascalientes had to ask Carranza for help in dealing with the 4,000 troops of General Pánfilo Natera, a Villista who had just surrendered, because to set them free, without food or jobs would jeopardize the peace of his state. The vast majority of them, "accustomed to the life of a soldier . . . and without jobs would surely split up into bands of thieves." [54] The attorney general of Chiapas, writing in 1924, told of officers and men who pillaged estates, raped women, and, with the knowledge and permission of their commanders, stole what they wanted from merchants.[55] General Cándido Aguilar spoke of rebel factions that controlled entire regions, who were "at least as hated" by the inhabitants as the *"jefes politicos* of the recent dictatorship." [56] An angry General Conrado Cevero, in a public declaration from Jonacatepec, Morelos in 1918, castigated generals who robbed "by the darkness of night or the bright light of day, raping and committing countless crimes," while their officers and men could not even feed their families.[57] In Coatepec, Veracruz, to cite a complaint from the Casa del Obrero Mundial, a Constitutionalist colonel had sold the 200 shoes sent the 20th Red Battalion, a workers unit, to local merchants. The worker volunteers had to go without shoes.[58] The generals attending the Convention of Aguascalientes spent over 18,000 pesos on wine, cognac, champagne, cigars, music, and servants.[59] To conclude military campaigns against Huerta and Villa, Carranza had to give his field commanders (Obregón, González, Alvarado, Jacinto B. Treviño, Manuel M. Diéguez, and Plutarco Elías Calles) millions of pesos without demanding an accounting either to himself or to Congress. Obregón, for example, was given the lump sum of 2.8 million pesos at one point in 1915.[60] Demands for accountability, recalled Cabrera, had led to 90 percent of the military coups in the history of Mexico. Well versed in the lessons of the Mexican past, Carranza, mused Cabrera, had to approve all of the expenditures "(or, in other words . . . sanction the thefts) in order not to commit the historic error of other epochs." [61]

But it was Zapata who put the matter succinctly. A few days before his death, he sent a bitter letter to Carranza, outlining graphically the character of the Constitutionalist's blight. Agrarian reform, he wrote, was in effect a countryside with *haciendas* in the hands of generals, either as owners or renters; of old *hacendados* replaced by modern landlords wearing epaulets, stiff hats with high crowns, and pistols in their belts. Popular hopes had been mocked. The soldiers labelled Constitutionalists had turned into the scourge of the people and of the land, robbing seeds, cattle and draft animals at will, burning and sacking the homes of the poor, killing by the light of day, and converting thievery into a major industry.[62]

In this situation, loyalty to cause and commander was not present. "At times," bewailed General Juan José Ríos, "I have concluded that loyalty among the military "is a sad virtue." [63]

The willingness to change horses in midstream had old antecedents. Subsequent claims to the contrary, friends of Madero had not immediately or unanimously turned on his assailant. Of the governors, only don Venustiano had defied Huerta; in Sonora, the other state to rebel, Governor José María Maytorena had fled to Arizona rather than confront the usurper. Nor did all of the rebel forces remaining in the field unite to battle Huerta. When General Martín Espinosa challenged Huerta, only one other officer in Tepic joined him.[64] The mayor of San Juan de Sabinas, in Madero's native Coahuila, had to take refuge in Texas because the local troops went over to Huerta.[65] With equal ease, however, many who had soiled their reputations in the Huerta coup had, by the fall of 1914, just as easily joined his enemies.

The era of turbulence produced impressive lists of military men with flexible loyalties. A few were holdovers from the Porfirista army, generals such as Benjamín Argumedo who marched with equal enthusiasm with soldiers loyal to Madero, Orozco, Huerta, and the Aguascalientes Convention. At the time of the Convention, even the Constitutionalists were courting him, although as Ramón P. DeNegri, the Mexican consul in San Francisco, acknowledged, "it casts a shadow on our honor." [66] In Oaxaca, General Alfonso Santibáñez, a follower of Félix Díaz and a Huerta conspirator, embraced the Constitutionalists, and then murdered General Jesús Carranza when his brother, don Venustiano, refused to pay a ransom. With victory assured in 1915, a host of converts rushed to the Constitutionalists' camp. In 1920, General Epigmenio Jiménez pledged to betray Carranza if Obregón met his four conditions: to keep his rank and that of his men; be given an *hacienda* or *rancho* in a region of his choice and a gift of 20,000 gold pesos; and that his army be left under his command in his home state.[67] Even González, a general who owed everything to Carranza, turned on his mentor in 1920. Half of the army deserted Obregón to follow De la Huerta three years later. Obregón in an angry reply to treasonous army officers in jail in Guanajuato, who claimed that they had been compelled to join the De la Huerta coup against their will, told them bluntly to thank their captors for not standing them up before a firing squad.[68]

IV

At Teoloyucan, on the outskirts of Mexico City, Obregón accepted the surrender of the remnants of the federal army. As of August 13, 1914, it ceased to exist. Yet, while the hated army had disintegrated, its officers did not necessarily fade away. The rebel armies provided countless Porfirista officers and soldiers with fresh military careers. General Felipe Angeles, the director of the Colegio Militar in the days of Díaz, and a salient figure under Madero and Villa, was merely the most prominent. One delegate to the Constitutional Convention charged that former federal officers had found a second home in Carranza's armies.[69] One report told how González, the commander of the Army of the Northeast, had built a particularly notorious reputation for accepting Díaz' officers in his ranks.[70] Félix F. Palavicini, a close ally of the First Chief, urged their use in the struggle against Villa and Zapata, frequently vouching for their loyalty.[71] Young lieutenants of the old federal army fought in the Brigada Jesús Carranza.[72] Both Higinio Aguilar and Rafael Erguía, Porfirista generals, went over to Zapata after the fall of Huerta, although many of Zapata's officers did not take kindly to serving under their former enemies.[73] One lieutenant colonel, representative of the willingness of "revolutionaries" to employ remnants of the old army, had been a cadet in the Colegio Militar, won his commission under Huerta, served Villa, and subsequently Lucio Blanco, Obregín, Villa again, and finally the Constitutionalists. General Treviño, for years a Constitutionalist kingpin in the northeast and a graduate of the Colegio Militar, started his military adventures under Díaz, backed Madero, signed the Plan de Guadalupe, and then in an about face, the Plan de Agua Prieta, which pitted the military against Carranza, his friend and mentor. As late as 1923, a group of congressmen warned that former Porfirista officers were teaching military tactics to regiments of the army.[74]

From Madero to Obregón, the use of military men as cabinet ministers, subministers and *oficiales mayores,* the pinnacle of the political ladder, grew by leaps and bounds. Soldiers, almost always generals, held 15 percent of these jobs under Madero;

28 percent under Carranza; 48 percent in the interim-government of Adolfo de la Huerta; and, after the "election" of Obregón, 59 percent.[75] Outside of Mexico City, military bosses, charged with keeping the public order, enjoyed a political role rivaling and often dwarfing the authority of governors, usually generals themselves.

Clashes between military and civilian authorities erupted from the start. The attack on Ciudad Juárez in 1911, urged by both "General" Orozco and "Colonel" Villa, occurred over the objections of Madero, the civilian head of the rebellion. To generals in pursuit of Zapata in Morelos, the wishes of President Madero hardly mattered. The conflict, however, developed symptoms of an acute disease in Carranza's time. He was First Chief of the Constitutionalists, but his generals claimed immunity from civilian supervision. His troubles with Villa were legendary, ultimately leading to an irreparable rift between them. As Luis Mesa Gutiérrez informed Zubarán Capmany, Carranza's minister of *gobernación,* the military in Chihuahua paid scant heed to civilians, and only when it suited them. General Eugenio Aguirre Benavides, the military boss he served, flaunted his disdain for civil authorities.[76] In Durango, Governor Mariano Arrieta gave warning that he would resign if held accountable to General Francisco Murguía.[77] According to Pascual Ortiz Rubio, governor of Michoacán in 1918, General Enrique Estrada did as he wished, going on his merry way while shunting public officials aside. His troops disarmed the police, violated private property, and robbed.[78] Earlier, in 1916, Ortiz Rubio had complained to Carranza that generals had driven his Departamento de Bienes Intervenidos out of its headquarters in the Jockey Club and barred the use of Limantour's home, formerly occupied by them.[79] When Ramón P. DeNegri, subsecretary of agriculture in 1922, asked Obregón to have the military provide students of the National School of Agriculture with uniforms because they had nothing "to wear," Obregón after consulting the brass hats, could merely reply that the military would not do it.[80] Sánchez, a general turned ally of *hacendados* and conservatives, openly defied Governor Adalberto Tejeda in Veracruz.[81] During the elections of 1916 in Tlaxcala, said Governor H. M. Machorro, General Máximo Gómez and his staff had—to guarantee the selection of their choices—put pressure on every municipal president. When municipalities balked, pistol-wielding officers had run election officials out of the voting booths.[82] Generals and their underlings, to cite Luis Cabrera, selected the members of Congress during Carranza's last two years in office.[83]

In 1923, the military, in league with politicians backing General Calles for the presidency, turned Congress into a circus. In October, General Arnulfo Gómez, a crony of Calles and chief of the army stationed in Mexico City, sent army officers dressed as civilians to harass and kill congressmen friendly to De la Huerta, the rival of Calles. Jorge Prieto Laurens, head of the De la Huerta band in the Senate, was earmarked for death. The plot failed, but not before fifty to sixty of the army officers, accompanied by Luis Morones, head of the Confederación Regional Obrera Mexicana, had boldly disrupted Congress, and in passing, fired pistol shots into the nearby headquarters of the De la Huerta election committee. More than 130 congressmen, some scared half out of their wits, addressed a letter of protest to Obregón who, in a curiously worded reply, denied their right to solicit his assistance.[84] If one were to believe them, said Obregón, a majority of the officers in the army had set out to cast shame on the government they served; but, to the contrary, the army, with only scattered exceptions, had remained faithful to its duties and obligations.[85] Obregó did not budge from this stance —even after two army captains, in a public confession, testified that they had participated in the affair.[86]

Events in Mexico City had their sequels in the provinces. In November, 1923, with the connivance of the military, assassins murdered eight members of the Partido Socialista del Sureste, including Felipe Carrillo Puerto, the governor of Yucatán. Soldiers killed the two stalwart revolutionaries, Blanco and Zapata. By his own admission, General Higinio Aguilar in 1915 had apparently bribed Miguel Sánchez Bravo to kill Carranza for 20,000 pesos.[87] In 1927, when news leaked of the appointment of General Eulogio Ortiz as military chief, businessmen in Chihuahua threatened to flee to Texas because, in the days when he fought alongside Villa, Ortiz had wantonly looted and killed.[88] Quarrels between General Heriberto Jara, the liberal governor, and General Agustín Millán, the military chief, kept the political pot boiling in Veracruz in 1916.[89] A similar rivalry disrupted the peace of Guerrero until well into Carranza's administration. At one point, generals Rómulo Figueroa, Julián Blanco, Jesús H. Salgado, and Silvestre Mariscal fought each other. All but Figueroa, of nefarious fame in Morelos, had at some time supported Zapata. Salgado remained loyal to him until the end, while Mariscal ambushed and killed Blanco, who had signed the updated Plan de Ayala in 1913. Mariscal, who had obeyed both Madero and Huerta, murdered Blanco even though both now served Carranza. Meanwhile, Mariscal had built a reputation for rape, pillage, and murder, as well as political double-dealing.[90] In 1918 with victory in his grasp however, Mariscal, then governor of Guerrero, found himself in jail when the minister of war, in his quarrel with General Maycotte, the commander in Acapulco, turned against him.[91]

The antics of the military brass peaked in 1920 when the generals, with Obregón at their head, rebelled against Carranza, and again in 1923 when a majority of them, ironically, broke with Obregón. Cabrera, who witnessed the murder of Carranza by a renegade colonel in Tlaxcalantongo, tagged Obregón's *cuartelazo* "a military strike." During the nineteenth century, he recalled, the army had picked presidents and set itself up as the bulwark of national institutions. It was foolhardy to expect it to relinquish what it considered one of its "prerogatives." Carranza had never controlled the military; he survived because the rivalries and ambitions of the generals kept them disunited. Carranza's choice of Ignacio Bonilla, a civilian for president was a pretext. Regardless of what civilian Carranza chose, the brass hats would have rebelled. Had Bonilla or any other civilian won the presidency in an election, the results would have been the same. Obregón, Benjamín Hill, Alvarado, and Calles, the generals who captained the *cuartelazo,* would have broken with Carranza unless he had picked one of them.[92]

By 1920, as Cabrera noted, the army had become "the arbiter" of the country's destiny. Soldiers, approximately 50,000, led by moderate if not conservative officers, held the balance of power in "revolutionary" Mexico.[93] Obregón had to worry about the defeated brass hats who, as one Mexican summed it up, expected him in recognition of their past service, to set aside "political differences" and bring them back into the revolutionary family and to satisfy the ambitions of the victorious generals.[94] One of them, General Estrada, the lord of Jalisco, began to feud with his civilian companions who, in his opinion, falsely accused him of harboring designs on the National Palace.[95] To the chagrin of Obregón, the suspicions proved prophetic when, Estrada, Guadalupe Sánchez, and Maycotte encouraged De la Huerta to captain a barrack's revolt against him. By December 1923, Obregón's allies against Carranza just three years before, the military *caciques* of Jalisco, Veracruz, Oaxaca, Guerrero, Aguascalientes, and Zacatecas, had betrayed Obregón. "The military," Obregón wrote to Samuel Gompers, the American labor czar, "had utilized De la Huerta to mask their treason." [96] Ironically, the perfidy of his generals spurred Obregón to quicken the pace of land reform. With half of the army in revolt, he needed all the help he could get, even from land-hungry peasants.

VI

But, whether allied with or antagonistic to Obregón, the medal encrusted military turned out to be a fickle comrade of the poor. One historian writes that the army of the "revolution," when asked to police the countryside, went beyond the brutality of the military of don Porfirio. Only occasionally, had the soldiers of Díaz handled the peasantry with the inhumanity of the new army.[97] Yet its behavior was consistent with its origins. The army shaped by Obregón, the master of Villa and Huerta, quixotically, rose out of the *hacendado*'s fear of the Yaquis. After the flight of Díaz, Governor Maytorena had persuaded Madero to allow Sonora to maintain an armed force to combat marauding Yaquis; to oppose Huerta, Obregón and his companions had enlarged it into an army.[98] Theoretically a voice for reform, this military apparatus, converted into a national army in 1917, had, as when a skeleton force to check the Yaquis, made an about-face to become the enemy of peasants and workers.

Significantly, the shift occurred because the years of turmoil upset the equilibrium between social classes, particularly in the countryside where, to entice recruits to their ranks, the rebels, first in the battle against Huerta and, later, as they split into factions, had promised a rich bounty to the peasantry. A cardinal pledge was land, enshrined in Article 27 of the Constitution. Not illogically, the peasants, the privates in the army in countless instances, came to believe in the promise. When the fighting ended, these hordes of have-nots wanted that pledge honored, despite the hostility of both the old and the new *hacendados,* their allies, and the reluctance of Carranza and Obregón. Given this picture, the army, particularly in the provinces, inherited the task of upholding law and order, in other words, the status quo.[99]

Unfortunately, the rebel officer class, usually from a provincial petit bourgeoisie, proved especially susceptible to the flattery and bribes of the rich and powerful. Additionally, in a country still essentially rural, where ownership of land signified success, the climb up the social ladder for the ambitious rebel required that he, too, join the landed gentry. Before long, countless new landlords, often the masters of *haciendas* and almost always from the military, made their debut in the countryside. Under their command, or under old comrades-in-arms, the military became a tool used against unruly peasants. Moreover, most of the enlisted men who stayed on, or who were eventually recruited, had left destitute villages; nearly all were illiterate, were usually of Indian ancestry, and lacked any sense of class conscience or solidarity. Themselves the victims of poverty and exploitation, they quickly learned to wield their weapons against peasants at the behest of their officers—just as the peasant soldiers of Díaz had done so in the past.

By 1923, it was commonplace to hear of "revolutionary" officers converted into rural tyrants. Both governors with military rank and Jefes de Operaciones Militares, the provincial brass, won a nefarious fame for their antagonism to agrarian reform. The offenders among Obregón's henchmen were legendary, particularly governors Amado Azuara in Hidalgo, Ignacio Enríquez in Chihuahua, César López de Lara in Tamaulipas, and Angel Flores in Sinaloa, as well as Guadalupe Sánchez and Enrique Estrada, commanders of key military zones. Whatever his beliefs, Obregón found it convenient not to trifle with these subordinates.

Accept "no gift or favor from *hacendados* or businessmen,"

General Juan de Anaya, the military chief of Puebla, told his officers. He issued this order, he explained, because of efforts of *hacendados* and businessmen with labor problems "too woo influential officials and especially army commanders in order to impose their views." Meanwhile, he went on, the humble "who struggle for social benefits duly theirs" lost faith in military men "perhaps because of their lamentable experiences with them." [100] As a group of dirt farmers in Durango told Obregón, the army officers in their village took advantage of the poor but groveled before the wealthy. [101] In Acapulco, General Silvestre Castro, according to a complaint, hobnobbed with the rich who showered him with gifts of money and cattle. Unfriendly to reform, Castro had disarmed peasants demanding land in Tecpan de Galeana and the Sierra de Atoyac and sold their weapons to their enemies. He threatened to "punish any who dared utter one word about land reform." [102] On his own authority, General Rómulo Figueroa in Guerrero had stopped the granting of *ejidos* becáuse, he explained, the plots were too large. Fearful of "an anarchy worse than Russia's," he had squelched demands for land with his troops, telling a delegation of peasants, as one of them reported to Obregón, that "if we want lands, we should buy them." [103] One colonel turned *hacendado*, upon hearing that his lands had been subdivided, warned that he would "greet with bullets" those who dared farm them. [104] In Morelos, General De la O, lamented old companions, had cast his lot with a "gang of opportunists" in league with *hacendados* "who exploited . . . the revolution for personal profit." In the meantime, old Zapatista soldiers, either landless or without tools or draft animals to till their tiny parcels, looked ahead to a bleak future. [105] As a congressman and head of the Partido Nacional Agrarista, Antonio Díaz Soto y Gama repeatedly begged Obregón to defend land-hungry peasants from the military. [106] General Félix Barajas, for example, the military lord in Antlán, Jalisco, labeled as "bandits" peasants who solicited lands, and had allowed his name to appear as the buyer of lands of the *hacienda* in Tepantla so as to keep them out of the hands of the villagers. All the same, the Liga de Comunidades de Jalisco had failed to get Barajas transferred; not only had the Ministry of War turned a deaf ear, but had named an *hacendado* to command the soldiers stationed in the nearby municipality.[107] In Puebla, added Díaz Soto y Gama, the generals helped shield *hacendados* from laws distributing idle lands to peasants.[108] In Michoacán, the state agrarian commission accused General Estrada of using his troops to prevent dirt farmers from taking over lands awarded them.[109] Obregón, nonetheless, thought Estrada a splendid *agrarista,* until compelled to withdraw his appointment as minister of agriculture upon reading in the newspapers that Estrada had condemned even mild agrarian reform.[110]

For diverse reasons, these clashes between soldiers and peasants multiplied and became more acute during the Obregón administration. While Article 27 dated from 1917, Carranza's obvious dislike for agrarian reform had discouraged demands for land. Similarly, the Decree of January 6, 1915, a war measure, had enjoyed limited success in the countryside. Despite these measures, the landless had not immediately organized themselves to take lands away from the *hacendados.* It took time for them to realize that legislation existed that, if properly utilized, might yield a harvest of lands. This is not to deny that conflict over lands did not begin early. By January, 1914, reports of *hacendados* in Yucatán using soldiers and *guardias blancas,* armed bands in the pay of the landlords, to protect their properties had caught the attention of Carranza. Some of the *hacendados* had hired former soldiers of Díaz' army.[111] The election of Obregón, however, seemed to offer a golden opportunity to invoke the legislation; after all, Obregón had entered the National Palace with the halo of the reformer. Besides, to gather popular support for his battle with De la Huerta, Obregón had publicly proclaimed his sympathy with the landless.

Not all of the Republic, nevertheless, underwent these violent conflicts over land. Generally, they occurred when peasants developed an awareness of their rights, organizations to enforce them, and where men friendly to their pleas became governors. This took place in the central states, the Bajío, and Yucatán, all regions of landless peasants and *haciendas.* By the same token, the *hacendados* in these states increasingly relied on the military or *guardias blancas,* to safeguard their properties. As the emboldened peasants multiplied their demands, the *hacendados,* more and more, called on the military for help, turning the army into a stalwart defender of their economic interests. Few clashes occurred in the border states where, from the start, the rebel rulers opposed the breakup of the large estates—unless it meant land for themselves, as in Chihuahua where Villa's officers occupied the *haciendas* of the Terrazas clan. In Sonora, a traveling salesman notified Carranza that the military had openly allied itself with the *hacendados* by 1914.[112]

The generals, colonels, and their underlings did not just side with *hacendados* or fight land-hungry peasants. Many acquired *haciendas*. Asked if Obregón and his allies had sponsored Article 27, Carranza had replied "no, because Obregón as well as the majority of the generals and civilians who grew rich" during the fighting "want to become landlords." [113] Obregón himself acknowledged that most military chiefs thought the agrarian problem solved once they "owned the best *haciendas*." [114] To Obregón, this marred the record of the Carranza regime. Among the military landlords who turned their backs on Carranza in 1920 were Aguilar, Diéguez, Juan Barragán, and Rafael de la Torre. Cesareo Castro, another Constitutionalist general, enjoyed the life of the cotton planter in the Laguna.[115] The governor of Querétaro, previously in the days of don Porfirio a public employee in Coahuila convicted of theft, now owned a "magnificent *hacienda*." [116] General Joaquín Amaro, of humble Indian stock, was a rich *hacendado* in the state of Mexico, while General José V. García, dead by 1918, owned an *hacienda* in Chiapas.[117] General Maycotte had gone into the *pulque* business on an *hacienda* on the boundary of Puebla and Tlaxcala. Both generals Eulalio Gutiérrez and Agustín Millán acquired *haciendas* without paying a cent for them.[118] In short, the list of generals turned *hacendados* would take up space for countless columns.

Both don Venustiano and don Alvaro watched the antics of their generals with the pragmatism of the seasoned veteran of Mexican politics. Carranza probably with regret: an *hacendado* himself, he had never fully advocated the subdivision of the great estates, or a change in their ownership because their masters had backed Díaz. In contrast, Obregón added dramatically to his properties during his career in the military. He could hardly deny his cohorts equal opportunity; yet the shameless grab for land shocked even Obregón. Further, Obregón, like Carranza before him, although not to the same degree, could not control his military. To condemn the deeds of his commanders, or of their subordinates, would have alienated Obregón from his principal allies, something the pragmatist from Sonora was careful not to do. Compelled to choose between peasants and his generals, Obregón wisely picked the camp with the heaviest firepower.

Obregón, as the following episode reveals, had a healthy regard for the rights of generals. When generals and politicians formed alliances, the interests of peasants fared badly. On April 4, 1922, Obregón had received a telegram marked urgent from the Comité Agrarista of Ajacuba, asking him to stop General Enrique Espejel and his soldiers from harvesting the maguey plants on lands given the villages of Tlamaco and Atitalaquía six years earlier.[119] With the consent of Governor Amado Azuara of Hidalgo, Espejel had taken up the *pulque* business, evidently in cahoots with an *hacendado*, Ignacio Villamil, who had lost part of the lands of his *hacienda* to the neighboring villagers. To prohibit the villagers from taking the land, Espejel had become a partner of Villamil. If Obregón did not stop Espejel's activities, another telegram warned, the villagers would solve the matter themselves.[120] Obregón's reply, offering to look into the problem, promised swift punishment for those who took the law into their hands.[121] However, when Obregón investigated, consulting General Francisco Serrano, the minister of war, he learned that Espejel had the "law on his side," and that the troops he employed to "protect himself against the plaintiffs" had been furnished by Governor Azuara.[122] Shortly thereafter, Obregón received another plea for help from the villagers because Espejel, Azuara, and their henchmen had not only seized their lands but had driven them from their homes.[123] At this juncture, finally, Obregón asked General Serrano to order Espejel to report to Mexico City where, to the surprise of no one, he went unpunished. By April 1923, a few months later, he was back with his *pulque* trade in Hidalgo, new complaints against him had been filed, and Obregón was again asking him to justify his behavior.[124] Meanwhile, in Hidalgo the executive and administrative committees of the villagers had been jailed, while a judge had ordered the arrest of their spokesman. Sadly, lamented one of them to Obregón, while "honest men" are put in jail the "word of criminals is honored." [125]

The clash between the general and the dirt farmers of Tlamaco and Atitalaquía, with Obregón in the middle, ended on a victory note for Espejel and his *hacendado* partner. Rendered impotent by choice or circumstance, Obregón could merely castigate Espejel's behavior. "You have allowed the *hacendado* to use you against the people," he scolded the general; by hiding behind Espejel's epaulets, the *hacendado* had "salvaged his own interests." Espejel, said Obregón, had "soiled the honor of the National Army." [126] To Espejel, however, he had "done nothing more than to collect the sap from the maguey," adding that Tlamaco had more land than it needed.[127]

Governor Azuara, meanwhile, who emerged unscathed from this episode, had earlier employed troops, on this occasion against the wishes of General Juan C. Zertuche, to help the owner of the Hacienda Hueyapan in his battle with the people of Ahuazotepec, who had been recently awarded a slice of his lands, including a forest. Upon learning of the decision by the National Agrarian Commission, the *hacendado*, Joaquín Eguía Irizarri, had cut down many of the trees in hopes of selling them for lumber. When the villagers occupied their lands, the timber was lying on the ground. Eguía Irizarri, adamantly insisting on his right to the timber, obtained the backing of Azuara, who dispatched state troops to honor his claims. According to Zertuche, Azuara's troops immediately began a reign of terror against the people of Ahuazotepec. In response, the National Agrarian Commission persuaded Zertuche to use his soldiers to defend the village. For his part, Azuara accused Zertuche of invading the Hacienda Hueyapan.[128]

To complicate the picture, while the Hacienda Hueyapan was in Hidalgo, Ahuazotepec was in Puebla. Zertuche, the military chief of Puebla, had sent his troops to the aid of a village under his jurisdiction, while Azuara's soldiers defended an *hacendado* in Hidalgo. Further, José María Sánchez, the governor of Puebla, supported Zertuche. But Obregón, to the chagrin of Ahuazotepec, sided with Azuara, ruling that the National Agrarian Commission lacked authority to circumvent the governor of Hidalgo, and asked the Commission to suspend the granting of land to Ahuazotepec. It was up to Azuara to decide.[129] In a reply on behalf of the commission, Julio Mitchell reminded Obregón that both the former governor of Puebla, Alfonso Cabrera, and interim-president De la Huerta, by a decree of November 11, 1920, had given the lands to Ahuazotepec.[130] Moreover, in a previous message, Governor Sánchez had carefully explained this to Obregón, saying that Ahuazotepec had received final confirmation of ownership by May, 1921.[131] Despite this, troops from Hidalgo, from the start, had harassed the people of Ahuazotepec. During the interval also, Zertuche had informed Obregón that a relative of Azuara, General Francisco P. de Mariel, controlled the soldiers tormenting Ahuazotepec.[132] Obregón, instead of applauding Zertuche, reprimanded him.[133] Faced with Obregón's ire, Zertuche recalled his soldiers, leaving Ahuazotepec at the mercy of Azuara and Eguía Irizarri.[134] Obregón's one concession was to tell the *hacendado* that he could remove only the trees already cut.[135] All the same, two years later, to the sorrow of the local dirt farmers, the governor of Hidalgo, relying on his troops, had stopped them even from farming the lands granted them in 1920.[136]

The conflict between the military and the peasants, exemplified by events in Hidalgo and Puebla, were daily occurrences in Veracruz. Urged on by peasant and labor groups, Governor Tejeda, a general himself, had sought to carry out reform; his protagonist, General Guadalupe Sánchez, the military *cacique* and spokesman for the *hacendados,* fought it. When the pace of land distribution quickened, the conflict turned into a bitter war as *hacendados* and their military allies resisted. During the height of the imbroglio, the legislature of Veracruz labeled the military "a social plague." As one critic said, "the National Army is the dirt farmers' principal enemy . . . the persecutor of the poor." [137]

The interpretation fitted the facts. Until he sided with De la Huerta, General Sánchez had employed his troops, according to the Union of Workers and Peasants of Jalapa, to make life miserable for the poor. Soldiers had destroyed crops by riding their horses over cultivated fields; robbed, pillaged, raped, and driven dirt farmers from their homes; they had collaborated with the *guardias blancas,* hunting down and killing agrarian leaders. General Sánchez, in the view of the union, had embraced the attempt of the *hacendados* to rid Veracruz of the "land reform movement" and workers' groups.[138] With his blessings, the *"guardias blancas* had declared agrarian legislation null and void." [139] One reason for his attitude, emphasized the state treasurer of Veracruz, was that Sánchez, as well as his lieutenants, had lands of their own. How, he asked, could you expect them to go against their interests? [140] Yet Sánchez, a general always on the alert for an "abandoned" *hacienda,* as one of his letters to Obregón reveals, had launched his career as a tobacco worker and enemy of the rich.[141] To the despair of reformers in Veracruz, Obregón, nevertheless, had supported Sánchez until the latter's defection to De la Huerta; even then, Obregón continued to believe that the military had acted to suppress illegal acts by the peasants.[142] It was Sánchez' treason, not his antipathy to land-hungry peasants, that troubled Obregón.

VII

Labor, too, felt the wrath of the military. The rift flared with Madero, when the federal army, in spite of having a new national commander, insisted on thinking in the time-honored Mexican tradition. For instance, discussing the causes of a textile strike in Nogales, a factory town in Veracruz, the minister of war, instead of looking at both sides of the issue, blamed labor agitators; most of the strikers, he asserted, wanted to work. This reliable information, he confided, had been provided by Isidro Torres, the captain in charge of the soldiers stationed in Nogales, who wished to teach the agitators a lesson. His opinion, Torres had assured his superior officer, had been corroborated by the manager of the textile mill shut down by the strike.[143] In Atlixco, a mill town outside of the city of Puebla, the owners of the textile plants hard hit by the strikes had federal troops keep their workers in line.[144] At their behest, soldiers captured and jailed Jesús Montes, a spokesman for the Comité Central de Obreros, Madero's labor body.[145]

Land-reform rhetoric to the contrary, the military of the

Constitutionalists handled labor with similar methods. When the workers of a textile mill near Monterrey, the capital of Nuevo León, defended it against the assault of Constitutionalist soldiers, the invaders sacked their homes.[146] The mayor of Guadalajara, with the approval of the governor of Jalisco, Manuel Aguirre Berlanga, used troops to protect a trolley company employing scabs to break a strike by its workers.[147] With the support of generals Obregón and Hill, Carranza put down the general strike in Mexico City in 1916 with bayonets. That same year, to silence labor militancy in Tampico, General E. P. Navarrete, the military *cacique*, banned the Casa del Obrero Mundial from the city, giving labor leaders just thirty-six hours to justify their complaints against industry. Under no circumstance, he warned, would he tolerate crimes against the public order and "individual rights." He pledged swift punishment for any worker attending "a meeting of more than nineteen of them." [148] Soldiers in Mexico tortured and killed José Barragán Hernández, a delegate of the Partido Socialista Obrero to the national labor conference in Tampico in 1917. A founder of the Sindicato de Artes Gráficas, and a key figure in the Casa del Obrero Mundial, Barragán died in agony in an army barracks. An outraged Federación de Sindicatos Obreros del Distrito Federal blamed the murder "on an insolent and arbitrary caste." In Tampico, in the interval, soldiers disrupted a parade of workers protesting the murder of their companion.[149]

Nor did Carranza's departure from the National Palace brighten the picture. Pleas from labor leaders asking Obregón to keep the military from busting strikes were commonplace; angry letters from Veracruz, Coahuila, and Tamaulipas make that abundantly clear.[150] In Ciudad del Carmen, soldiers crushed efforts to organize the dock workers.[151] At Amozac, Puebla, said Eduardo Moneda, a leader of the Confederación Regional Obrera Mexicana, with a wanton display of cruelty soldiers prevented unemployed workers from building homes on the unoccupied lands of an *hacendado*.[152] The military boss of Puebla, General Gómez, did not hesitate to send troops to crush strikes in the textile mills, or to tell workers that he wanted an end to labor protests.[153] In Ciudad Campeche, General Alejandro Mange openly sided with employers who hired scabs to disrupt a trolley lines strike protesting poor pay and long hours of toil. Mange went so far as to have soldiers man the trolleys.[154] But the governor of Campeche wrote Obregón that not only would the city be better off without a single soldier but that its labor strife would come to an end.[155] Of like opinion was Carrillo Puerto, who reminded Obregón that the Constitution guaranteed labor the right to strike, saying that he thought the strikers were justified in asking for an eight-hour day and a daily wage of three pesos, as against the current schedule of a sixteen-hour day during the week and eighteen hours on Sunday for a daily income of one to two pesos.[156] However, despite Obregón's assurances to Carrillo Puerto that he had directed Mange to stay out of the strike, Mange continued to harass labor. To the north, in Coahuila, the military in Saltillo allowed the mine operators in Sabinas, Agujita, Cloete, and Palau to use scabs in their war with the Unión Minera Mexicana.[157] When a clash occurred between the Unión and scabs in Cloete, soldiers, called in to disperse the melee, fired into the crowd, killing and wounding members of the Unión and jailing two of its leaders. One of them Jacobo Flores, an official of the Unión, was beaten to death in the barracks, in a manner, "to make even Torquemada," the genius of Spain's hated Inquisition, "blush with shame." [158]

PART III A CHRONICLE OF WHAT WAS DONE

SIXTEEN

Labor's Ambiguous Springboards

"In that manner was born in Mexico the struggle for liberty; thus were organized the first phalanxes that fought for the socialization of the instruments and machines of production."

Rosendo Salazar

I

THE "ROMANTIC HONEYMOON of the proletariat," so were the years of 1911–1912 baptized by Rosendo Salazar, harbinger of the labor crusade, printer, and author of the monumental *Las Pugnas de la Gleba*.[1] With the flight of don Porfirio, bold men set out to build a just labor structure. It was a golden age for the fledgling leaders, when a Mexico suddenly rid of old rulers began to relax and allow reformers to plot a healthier future for the workers. With their efforts, Salazar reminisced, they awakened the "sleeping lion." [2]

A host of individuals and groups laid the basis for labor organizations, and added color and excitement to this period. There were the radicals Juan Sarabia, Paulino Martínez, and Antonio I. Villarreal; parliamentary Socialists such as Fredesvindo Elvira Alonzo and Antonio de P. Araujo; the Syndicalists Luis Méndez and Pedro Junco, a native of Spain and the founder of the Cámara Independiente del Trabajo in Veracruz; and the Anarchists, Juan Francisco Moncaleano, a primary-school teacher from Spain and later head of the stonecutters union in Mexico

City, and Ricardo Flores Magón and his brothers Enrique and Jesús, fathers of the Partido Liberal Mexicano. Anarchists were led by Amadeo Ferrés, a Spaniard who arrived in Mexico near the close of the Díaz regime and established the Confederación Tipográfica de México, quickly in the forefront of union activity. From Mexico City, the *tipógrafos,* or printers, carried their efforts to the provinces and, as they branched out, changed their name to the Confederación Nacional de Artes Gráficas. Among its collaborators were José López Dónez, Ezequiel Salcedo, Rafael Quintero, Alfredo Pérez Medina, Jacinto Huitrón, and Enrique Arce, all to become successful labor leaders in the years ahead.[3]

The success of the Confederación inspired the cobblers, tailors, bakers, carpenters, and musicians to organize. Funds contributed by the Confederación helped spur their strikes. Later, the Confederación joined up with the stonemasons, the Unión de Canteros y Albañiles Mexicanos—the brainchild of Moncaleano. The Confederación survived until 1915. Its journal, in the meantime, *El Tipógrafo Mexicano,* circulated in such distant provinces as Sonora, Tamaulipas, Sinaloa, Yucatán, and Guanajuato. From the Confederación emerged the Sindicato de Tipógrafos, a labor union, the genius of Antonio Díaz Soto y Gama, Rafael Pérez Taylor, and Luis Méndez. By 1912, the Unión Miner Mexicana, a militant northern band, claimed sixteen miners' affiliates. Miners in La Rosita, a small town in Coahuila, banded together in a Sociedad de Obreros Mineros, and their companions in Sonora formed the Mineros de Cananea. Casa affiliates surfaced in other parts of the Republic: the Confederación del Trabajo in Torreón, a cotton and transportation hub; a Gremio de Alijadores in Tampico; and the Confederación de Sindicatos de la República Mexicana in Veracruz.[4] Before his untimely death in 1915, the saintly Lázaro Gutiérrez de Lara labored unstintedly with notable success to unite workers and peasants in Zacatecas. A Partido Obrero Socialista de la Revolución Mexicana flourished briefly in 1911. The groups in Mexico City jointly celebrated May 1st as labor day in 1912, a first in the history of Mexico.

Mexico City, in the interval, became a haven for the ideologues of the labor movement. One of their meeting houses was the tailor shop of Luis Méndez where generally in the evenings, and on Sundays, labor supporters of radical persuasion under the tutelage of Moncaleano congregated to discuss the downfall of capitalism. Moncaleano and his colleagues read the works of Peter Kropotkin, Max Simon Nordau, and Jacques Elisee Réclus, among others, meanwhile publishing a journal called *Luz*. From these meetings was born the Casa del Obrero, eventually the headquarters for the labor leadership that blossomed in the summer of 1912. As a result of a massive labor parade sponsored by the Casa on May 1, 1913, during which 25,000 workers marched, the Casa, in keeping with the ideal of international solidarity, added the word Mundial to its title. From that point on it became known as the Casa del Obrero Mundial or COM.[5]

At the start, the Casa relied for its support on workers and artisans in the immediate vicinity of Mexico City. It represented a small segment of the total labor bloc, essentially tradesmen (stonemasons, bricklayers, printers, bakers, tailors, and carpenters), workers in transportation (trolleys), employees in the service industries, and students and intellectuals. Its links with industrial labor were weak at best. Not until 1914 did the Casa begin to build ties with labor groups outside of the Federal District—in Veracruz, Jalisco, Nuevo León, and San Luis Potosí.[6]

The patrons of the Casa had two goals in mind. Their first was to make it a center for the study and promulgation of modern labor and economic doctrines. An attempt would be made to teach advanced ideas to the workers, to make them politically active, and in the process, to instill a sense of class consciousness. The Casa's other goal was to put theory into practice, to make the worker see the fallacy of relying on mutualist societies developed in the nineteenth century. It was time to convince the worker that only by building labor unions and using strikes and boycotts could he improve his life and transform the character of bourgeois society. But this second objective evolved slowly because, as the spokesmen for the Casa understood, little could be accomplished politically with a largely illiterate and naïve working class. It was first necessary to carry out the educational and political goals before the task of organizing labor could begin. This gradualist blueprint undoubtedly reflected the influence of the printers, among the best read of the skilled tradesmen.[7] When the Casa did turn to its second goal, the organization of labor, it excited the hostility of government, then, as in the days of Díaz, unfriendly to the idea of independent labor unions.

On Sunday, when more workers were free, the Casa came alive. Usually, it sponsored lectures and discussions open to anyone who wished to attend. At these meetings, Salazar, Pérez Taylor, Méndez and their companions, and frequently a visitor, held forth on the latest social doctrines. Of eclectic bent, the speakers, among whom were refugee Spaniards, discussed ideas as diverse as Christian socialism, utopianism, positivism, anarchism, and particularly the Escuela Racional, the ideal advanced by Francisco Ferrer Guardia, a Spanish professor martyred in 1909.[8] Until winter, 1914, the messiahs of the Casa cautioned workers to stay out of national politics; from their point of view, nothing could be gained by backing any of the factions battling for supremacy in Mexico. To help itself, to build a spirit of class solidarity, and to achieve its goals, labor had to stay clear of the murky political arena lest as befell the workers' movements of the 1870's, it be victimized by opportunistic politicians.[9] It was during the Casa's educational stage that Francisco I. Madero governed Mexico, as did his successor, General Victoriano Huerta. The nuts-and-bolts stage, the organizational effort, had to await the downfall of Huerta and the end of the factional struggle between Venustiano Carranza and his leading enemies, Francisco Villa, and Emiliano Zapata. By mid-1912, therefore, the Casa as well as other labor groups, especially in the mining and industrial centers and in the port cities, had planted the seeds of an independent, if fragmented, labor movement.

II

The deteriorating economic picture, dating from the 1913 battle to unseat Huerta, added fresh impetus to the drive to organize labor. Violence plagued the era between the murder of Madero and the defeat of Villa in 1915. For over two years, war and its pestilence ravaged the land. This turbulence, which brought normal activity to a standstill, had widespread political repercussions.

With Carranza, Villa, and Zapata in pursuit of Huerta, and then at each other's throats, the economy tottered and collapsed. The Treasury, inherited by Madero with a surplus of 70 million pesos, had not a penny when Huerta fled the country.[10] To complicate life for the workers the factional squabbles exacerbated economic conditions. By 1916, Mexico confronted a crisis of major dimensions, with many of the states on the verge of bankruptcy. Without federal aid, as the governor of Tlaxcala wrote Carranza, a catastrophe loomed ahead.[11] Most of the municipalities, for their part, had long since exhausted their tiny resources. In Coahuila, the home state of the First Chief, the municipalities were destitute as in Durango, perhaps the province hardest hit in early 1915.[12] Few had funds to pay teachers and other employees, while essential public services simply ceased.

Confronted with this agonizing picture, the Constitutionalists, the ultimate victors, cast reform aside on behalf of recovery. To the cautious Carranza, this was no time for drastic change lest Mexico's society and economy disintegrate. Recovery meant putting together again the pieces of the economy, permitting business and industry to revive, and agricultural production to return to normal. The goal of recovery tempered enthusiasm for tinkering with reform and acted as a brake on the spread of revolution. Increasingly the middle sectors of society felt that, if reform were to come, it would have to await better times.

Conversely, however, the civil strife pushed the rebel leadership in the direction of reform. To wage war against Huerta required popular backing, which would not be available unless his enemies committed themselves to labor and agrarian reform. When the factional battle broke out in the fall of 1914 both Villa and the Constitutionalists stepped up their propaganda campaign: Carranza with his Adiciones al Plan de Guadalupe, and Villa by accepting the reform planks of the Aguascalientes Convention. In the interval, Zapata, an ally of Villa, had broadened his platform to include the needs of labor. At the same time, the military strife and the competing promises had begun to encourage peasants to invade the lands of *haciendas* and labor to assume a militant stance. The Constitutionalists, perhaps the larger faction, had either to placate the destitute, each day rendered more desperate and less willing to wait for future reform, or watch them swell the ranks of their adversaries. The disruption of the economy in summary, became a double-edge sword, acting both as a brake and as a spur to reform.

No one, least of all Madero, would have predicted the social and economic repercussions arising from the challenge to the Old Regime. The value of the Mexican peso fell, from an exchange rate of two pesos for a dollar to five pesos by 1916.[13] As the peso depreciated, essentially because of the flight of foreign investment, the rebel leaders resorted to the printing of paper money. To finance his military machine, Carranza, on April 26, 1913 began to issue paper money, in subsequent months distributing some 5 million pesos. With his permission, Alvaro Obregón, Francisco Villa (then still loyal to the First Chief), Pablo González, Manuel Diéguez, Francisco Murguía, Luis Caballero, and other commanders did the same. Six states controlled by the Constitutionalists had bills of their own. By his own account, Carranza alone put into circulation an estimated 30 million pesos by 1917. From the beginning, nonetheless, the public placed scant faith in the value of the paper currency. Even Carranza's *papel infalsificable,* supposedly safe from counterfeiters, quickly dropped in value.[14] Early in 1915, Carranza prohibited the circulation of currency issued by the states further complicating economic transactions in the northern provinces.[15]

The cost of toppling Huerta and defeating Villa was placed on the shoulders of the public.[16] The reliance on paper money exacerbated the rise in the cost of living, including prices for corn, wheat, and beans. To the anger of labor, countless merchants refused to accept the paper money, or added huge markups to the price of their goods. In Veracruz, for instance, the peso fell to a low of two cents.[17] By the summer of 1915, one report had it, the public could no longer carry the burden of the paper currency or help pay the domestic debt.[18] Jobless workers in industry, mines, and agriculture were in no mood to respect the rights of property when the paper currency did not cover the cost of basic necessities.

To compound the financial plight, agricultural production remained abnormally poor, as it had in the final days of Díaz. For most of the second decade of the twentieth century Mexico suffered a series of poor harvests. Corn and wheat, staples of the urban diet, were especially hard hit. The corn harvest of 1913 was less than a fifth of the amount normally consumed, and the harvests of the next two years continued the dismal record. In the years between 1909 and 1915, only the corn harvest of 1910 met national demands.[19]

CORN PRODUCTION [20]

Year	Harvest (millions of kilogrames)
1909	1,839
1910	4,705
1911	2,307
1912	2,296
1913	448
1914	Under 500 (estimate)
1915	" "

Further while the surplus of 1910 carried the country through the poor harvest of the following year, ultimately those reserves were exhausted, as well as funds for buying corn abroad. The devastation of war, plus years of low rainfall, had disrupted the production of corn and wheat. The wanton cutting of ears of corn for food by the rebel armies, approximately 250,000 men under arms in 1915, kept scarce kernels from being planted for the following year and aggravated the problem.[21] With corn in scarcity, its price shot up from twenty to fifty *centavos* a *cuartillo*, a fourth of one peck, to between 2.25 and 2.50 pesos. The rise in the price of corn, along with its scarcity, hit particularly hard the worker in the cities and mining camps.

Even more severe was the shortage of wheat, the flour for the bread rolls never absent from the dinner table of the urban Mexican. In 1914, Mexican farmers harvested only slightly more than a tenth of the 1910 crop of 326 million kilograms of wheat; yet 1910 was merely an average year for wheat. The drastic decline in the size of the wheat harvests, which began in 1913, continued through 1915. As one observer said, the hunger of the urban middle classes, essentially wheat-eaters, which dated from 1914, now equalled the hunger of the poor. By 1914, the harvest of wheat had dropped by 70 percent, and that of corn by 80 percent. As of that year, the people of Mexico had to survive on one-fifth of the corn and wheat usually eaten. The result was hunger, and with that demands that rebel leaders take steps to change a system that could not be counted upon to feed Mexicans.[22]

The destruction of the railroads, a responsibility shared by all rebel factions further exacerbated the shortage of corn and wheat supplies, and concurrently contributed to the rise in the cost of living. As the warring armies monopolized the railroads, it became increasingly difficult to move food from a region of partial abundance to one of scarcity. In some cases, corn was not always unavailable but simply out of reach. During the horrendous food shortage of 1915, for example, four bushels of corn, selling for 30 pesos in the Bajío, cost 280 pesos in the capital.[23] Mexicans in one region of the Republic starved while in the next province were supplies of corn and wheat. By 1915, the eternal military wars had destroyed 76 percent of the boxcars of standard gauge, 40 percent of those built for narrow-gauge roads, and nearly 33 percent of the locomotives.[24] All told, over half of the railroad rolling stock, with a replacement cost of $10 million dollars, had been wrecked.[25]

The shortage of boxcars and locomotives quickly attracted the attention of unscrupulous Mexicans eager to exploit anything, even hunger. Military chieftains, with the complicity of bureaucrats and railroad workers, learned how to extort bribes, rebates, and duties from shippers of grains and other foods. According to a report prepared for General Pablo González, the military in cooperation with trainmen grew wealthy from these bribes. Railroad stock needed for the transportation of food went to the highest bidder, not infrequently a speculator who purchased the rights to boxcars and locomotives and then sold them to desperate grain merchants. According to Eduardo Fuentes, the author of the report, even a superficial investigation would reveal the culprits; but, he cautioned, to punish them was impossible because back of them was a powerful *político*. Because of this, nothing had been done to punish the guilty.[26] Not surprisingly, therefore, workers on the railroads often collaborated with all warring bands since the opportunity for profit had no political allegiance.

For all of these reasons and because thousands of small

farmers left their lands unplowed, want and hunger increasingly cast their shadow over the Republic. Food shortages, John R. Silliman, the special agent of the State Department, noted, afflicted much of Mexico, and particularly the capital.[27] Hunger stalked the northern states—in the presence of clandestine shipments of corn, beans, and garbanzos to the United States; [28] meanwhile food prices skyrocketed. Soldiers stationed along the Texas border, reported General Luis Caballero, could not buy food with what the army paid them.[29] To purchase food, he sent agents to Veracruz where it was rumored to be abundant. But, shortages of food in Veracruz had led local authorities to prohibit the export of corn and beans to neighboring states.[30] Like Caballero in Tamaulipas, the military commanders of Veracruz reported growing scarcities of cereal crops. People were dying of hunger in Chinameca by 1915, a situation described as "desperate" by the military.[31] Inhabitants of Jalapa each day found it more difficult to buy corn, beans, flour lard, and barley, or if they did, to find the means to pay the exorbitant prices.[32] The high cost of food, clothing, and medicines in the port city of Veracruz led authorities to take steps to punish profiteering merchants.[33] Unable to buy grains and other foods, the workers in the textile mills in Orizaba sent a committee to purchase food in Puebla, only to be told by authorities there that "not one grain of corn" would be permitted to leave Puebla because of local food shortages.[34] To halt the fantastic rise in the price of foodstuffs in Puebla, Carranza ordered its governor to sell corn and beans to the workers at a loss.[35] Corn, wheat, flour, and lard were in critically short supply in Campeche, Tabasco, and Yucatán, while the entire Isthmus of Tehuantepec, said workers on the railroads, confronted an "acute situation." [36] Attempts to recruit soldiers for the Constitutionalists failed because the people blamed Carranza and his allies for their plight.[37] Merchants in Oaxaca were attempting to buy food in Chiapas. In Guerrero, where the entire corn harvest of 1915 was lost, people died from hunger.[38] One Constitutionalists' brigade survived by eating green fruit and another on brown sugar.[39] In Mexico, in the opinion of one physician, 1,000 persons died of hunger each month by 1915.[40] Yet, despite this lamentable picture, in the fall of that year, Carranza had to officially ban the export of rice, sugar, beans, garbanzos, lima beans, flour, lentils, corn, and chicken-vetch.

Bad as the picture was in the provinces, Mexico City suffered more. With over 700,000 people, it felt the food crisis acutely. So many people died of starvation that physicians began to list other maladies as the cause of death. In August, 1915 alone, over 200 individuals died of malnutrition.[41] According to another opinion, 100 persons died daily of starvation.[42] Between February and April of 1915, the capital had been a beseiged city, as the Constitutionalists and Villa fought for control of it. During this interval, the workers and the other poor had been driven to scavenge for food in garbage dumps and on occasion to eat dead animals.[43] To their growing anger, the middle classes, mainly bureaucrats and employees of commerce and business on a fixed income, had been forced to share the fate of the less fortunate.[44] A cup of coffee in the restaurants of the capital reached the astronomical price of seventy centavos.[45] Scenes depicted by the photographer Gustavo Casasola record long lines of housewives before shops, stores, and bakeries, the looting of stores, and the public shooting of counterfeiters. The city became a jungle as the workers and the middle classes struggled to survive the holocaust that had engulfed them. By 1916, elements of the middle classes had come to accept the idea of peace at any price, even at the cost of substantial concessions to workers and peasants.

Labor, in the meantime, grew increasingly restive. "Only one path is open to us," declared an angry spokesman for the workers in a shoe factory in Tacubaya: "to take up arms" in defense of our lives and families.[46] The root of the problem, concluded David Pastrana Jaimes, a delegate to the Constitutional Convention in 1916, was the worker's inability to live on what he earned.[47] The rise in the cost of living had far outdistanced meager wage gains. As the military turmoil disrupted production, the worker found himself squeezed between the skyrocketing cost of basic necessities, increasingly in short supply, and wages that failed to keep pace. No wonder that some workers joined the rebel armies.

The plight of the worker was especially hard in the port cities of Veracruz and Tampico, both of which imported their food. In Tampico, a single egg cost 25 centavos and a liter of milk more than twice as much, while even water had to be purchased. Despite that, longshoremen earned approximately 30 pesos a month; after paying a third of their income on housing, they had 20 pesos to spend on food, clothing, and medical care. For a time, the expanding petroleum industry served as a safety valve, absorbing many poorly paid longshoremen and dock workers, but concommitantly, luring thousands of refugees to Tampico with promises of better jobs. Upon entering a city unprepared to employ them, or to provide adequate housing and food, the immigrants crowded into slums and shanty towns rampant with disease. By 1915, economic difficulties had transformed Tampico into a center of revolutionary unrest. The worker endured similar hardships in Veracruz. There, however, a vintage surplus of unemployed workers compounded the misery. Circumstances, therefore, determined that both Tampico and Veracruz turn into centers of radical agitation. In the two cities, a large population of workers, ill-paid, poorly housed, and often hungry and jobless, offered fertile soil for rebel propaganda.[48]

Elsewhere in the Republic, labor confronted nearly identical problems and voiced similar complaints. Inflation, the scarcity of food, and the violence of the times hit equally with sledgehammer blows, northern miners, textile hands in Nuevo León, Querétaro, and Puebla, stevedores in the port of Mazatlán, and workers on the national railways. Unemployment ran high everywhere. Not more than 3 percent of the mines stayed open. The others were flooded or caved in; the plants damaged or destroyed; machinery and equipment wrecked; supplies exhausted; management and workers scattered or demoralized; and transportation either wholly lacking, or obtainable with the greatest difficulty and in insufficient capacity. In the opinion of one American mine operator, the restoration of the mining industry would not come for many years.[49] In the mining camps, as reported to Carranza, "the misery was frightful." [50] Unless something were done to cope with this "alarming situation," which daily brought with it larger food shortages, additional rises in the cost of living, and a multiplication of the jobless, warned the governor of Guerrero, the hungry and destitute might take matters into their own hands.[51]

As industries shut down, jobless workers swelled the ranks of the rebel armies, fueling the chaos and violence of the era. One such band of recruits came from the Fábrica de la Estrella in Parras, a town in Coahuila, the property of the Maderos, which closed its doors early in 1913.[52] The gap between income and the cost of living drove scores of textile workers in Orizaba to join the Constitutionalists. According to the Unión Minera Mexicana, over 5,000 of its members lost their lives fighting under rebel chieftains.[53] This pattern repeated the length and breath of the Republic. One reason for granting concessions to labor, acknowledged Pastor Rouaix at the Constitutional Convention of 1916, was that if this were not done the restless workers would constitute "an imminent danger to the public order." [54]

III

Inflation, and the economic dislocation which cost countless workers their jobs, exacerbated the conflict between Mexicans and foreigners. Complaints against foreigners grew in frequency and intensity under Madero, and exploded into a chorus of hatred under Carranza. Charges of discrimination, whether justified or not, were rampant. Mexican workers accused foreigners of attempting to keep alive their old prerogatives on the national railways; foreign managers, it was said, acted arbitrarily by cutting wages on the Ferrocarril Nacional de Tehuantepec.[55] Accusations of racial prejudice and favoritism on the part of Americans multiplied in the coal towns of Coahuila where, bemoaned Mexican miners, the axiom of "equal pay for equal work" was a myth.[56] Demands by Mexican miners to work under native bosses grew by leaps and bounds. While Mexicans looked for jobs, mine owners in Mexico State employed *"gachupines,* Italians, Yankees, and even Chinese,"* so claimed the president of the Confederación Cívica Independiente of Tlalpujahua.[57] Officials of the Constitutionalist regime in 1916 accused El Aguila, the petroleum corporation, of openly discriminating against Mexican workers and employees at its plant at Minatitlán, Veracruz. Mexicans, they declared, were the last hired, the first fired, and the worst paid.[58]

The experience of Sonora, always a seedbed of rebel sentiment, documents both the impact of the revolution on labor and the intensity of the conflict between natives and foreigners—

Americans usually. By 1919, observed the American consul in Nogales, all industry languished because of the turmoil. The state treasury was empty. The plight of Caborca, a small town in the midst of the rich farming and mining district of Altar was "but an illustration of the general conditions throughout Sonora." Business, mining, agriculture, and manufacturing in Caborca had come to a standstill. Of the 241 stores and homes, half were unoccupied.[59] With industry and agriculture in the doldrums, the jobless abandoned their homes to seek work in the cotton and beet fields or the railroads of the American Southwest. Several thousand, reported the consul, had passed through the port of Nogales in the fall of 1919 alone. It was a vicious circle because, as Mexicans fled their homes, mining companies in Sonora began to speak of shortages of labor which impeded their operations. At Cananea, for instance, 400 miners had left their jobs to go to the United States, presumably to pick cotton.[60]

Meanwhile, in response to workers' demands for protection against the abuses of foreign management, authorities in Sonora had passed labor legislation in 1916. One of its stipulations demanded the payment of adequate compensation—the amount to be determined by local courts—to victims of industrial accidents; in one decision judged unfair by the Americans, the amount was 5,000 pesos. In Cananea, mining company officials, the American consul lamented, were "hauled before labor union courts and browbeaten before a crowd of admiring witnesses." Foremen he went on, were "afraid to reprimand a lazy workman for fear that he will be jailed for using offensive language." [61] The governor, as the consul described it, had even compelled El Tigre Mining Company to give merchandise from its company store to striking miners.[62]

IV

With this scene as background, first Madero, and increasingly Carranza turned to confront the demands of a labor force slowly awakening to the currents of the twentieth century. Unfortunately, despite the revolutionary rhetoric, the politicians and labor were on a collision course.

SEVENTEEN *Labor Confronts*

the New Rulers

---

*"If the Revolution had as one of its cardinal goals the
destruction of capitalist tyranny, all the same it must not
allow another to arise as pernicious for the welfare of the
Republic as would be the tyranny of the workers."*

Venustiano Carranza

I

THE MEN WHO OUSTED Porfirio Díaz, disciples of an age
worshipping Herbert Spencer's interpretation of the "fittest," had no stomach for the more radical messiahs of labor.
The fear of revolution, along with the defense of traditional interests, led them to take a position often at odds with the hopes
of workers. By 1923, with the Revolution more than a decade
old, various spokesmen for labor had sadly concluded that the
past had been only rhetorically repudiated. In the tradition of
Venustiano Carranza, an *hacendado* deeply distrustful of labor
militants, both Francisco I. Madero and Alvaro Obregón shared
an abiding faith in the traditional doctrines of private property
and laws of supply and demand. Nor did the new rulers, like the
previous élite, openly welcome independent labor unions. Yet
changes did occur; when Obregón handed over his office to
Plutarco Elías Calles, many workers, on paper at least, had said
good-bye to the nineteenth century; the problem was that practice lagged behind rhetoric.

Labor jubilantly greeted the disappearance of the ancient

potentates. Its spokesmen accepted at face value the promise of the Madero administration to open politics to all parties. For labor, furthermore, there was the pledge of Madero and his disciples to "improve the material, intellectual, and moral lot of the worker." [1] The rash of strikes that erupted in 1911 immediately tested the stated intentions of the *politicos*. As their political stability was endangered, like it or not, they had to respond to the demands of labor. To labor's disappointment, it readily became apparent that, despite Madero's vows, his administration had neither abandoned sacrosanct principles nor committed itself to new ones. But deal with labor it must, for the waves of strikes in industry ruled out a hands-off policy. Compelled to act, the administration embarked on a tortuous road that in the decade ahead would lead to a system of government-controlled labor unions.

The retreat from the previously inflexible attitudes, which equated labor unions with the sabotage of property rights, began in December, 1911, when the administration discarded as unwise and impractical a policy of government neutrality in times of industrial disputes endangering the public order. According to the oracles in the Ministry of Fomento, modern states must safeguard the interests of every class that helped produce the wealth of a society. While progressive rulers, who stayed within the bounds of their authority and responsibilities, had no right to meddle with natural laws controlling wages, they nonetheless, had a moral duty to enact legislation bettering relations between capital and labor. And when necessary, government could help settle industrial disputes.[2]

The rejection of "neutrality" augered no startling philosophical metamorphosis. Díaz had never kept his distance in industrial disputes, and no one in government urged the adoption of remedies giving preference to labor over business. After all, Madero, an *hacendado* and businessman, had dealt with labor in the custom of the day, no better and no worse than others. Business, it became clear, could still count on benevolent treatment; nothing would be done to regulate it or to control its size. And to the contrary, private enterprise and bigness, the offspring of free competition, called for government protection. Strikes would be handled quickly and firmly. Included in this guarantee were foreign businessmen, for all industrialists enjoyed similar rights and privileges. Whether native or not, businessmen contributed to the national well-being. Property rights claimed no nationality.[3]

But Madero had gone on record during his political campaign: no longer would Mexican rulers close their eyes to the dreams of the workers who, the victims of exploitation and neglect, hungered for justice. Madero, despite his orthodox economics, was a humanitarian, and a kindred soul of the progressives of his era. At Orizaba, he had expressed shock at the plight of textile workers, condemned the long hours of toil, and acknowledged the right of labor to form unions.[4] To many of his subordinates, the charter of 1857 guaranteed that right—so long as the behavior of labor left undisturbed the country's peace and stability. A hands-off policy, in truth, invited disaster. The ferment in labor circles could not be ignored.

Ambiguity and hesitancy colored the administration's approach to the labor problem. Policy vacillated between reliance on the carrot and the use of the stick. Thinking in Fomento, which dealt with labor, followed the teachings of Adam Smith. Madero's ascension to power hardly dampened the earlier faith in laissez faire economics. Friends of labor's rights, cautioned Rafael Hernández, chief of Fomento, a cousin of the president and a *científico* of the old school, "must not forget that the laws of supply and demand set wages." The "larger the profits the higher the wages." [5] Ernesto Madero, the president's brother and head of the Treasury, held identical views. With their allies in the cabinet, these two ministers, representatives of the Madero family fortune, charted policy in the National Palace. Until the downfall of Madero, this policy held labor leaders largely responsible for the country's industrial problems, and admonished strikers to return to their jobs and to practice "prudence and discretion." They were to emulate the wisdom and moderation of businessmen and to "abandon the stupid and pernicious custom of relying on strikes to settle labor questions." Strikes, instead of offering a solution, exposed to the glare of day the bankruptcy of labor's leadership.

Labor, in the interim, had denied the administration a political honeymoon. Instead, strikes became endemic in the key industries of the Republic, as remedies devised by Díaz failed. Strikes paralyzed the textile mills of Veracruz, Puebla, and Mexico State, approximately forty of them between January and September, 1912. As dwellers of Mexico City sat down to celebrate the feast of the Virgin de Guadalupe in December, dockworkers walked off their jobs in the port of Veracruz, while miners and railroad men shut down operations in Guanajuato and Aguascalientes. As the administration tottered on the brink of disaster, strikes flared in Hidalgo and Jalisco.[6] Clearly, unless repressive measures were once again embraced, fresh formulas must be worked out to deal with labor unrest.

The administration, with the passage of time, hit upon a solution composed of the carrot and the stick. The latter element obviously had roots in the past. When miners at Matehuala, La Paz, and Catorce stubbornly refused to return to work, the authorities of San Luis Potosí, with the blessings of Mexico City, ordered soldiers to break the strike. In Coahuila, the home of the Apostle, the political bosses of Ciudad del Oro also employed guns to silence miners.[7] The pattern repeated itself again and again. To silence the political propaganda of the group *Luz,* the government exiled its foreign-born leaders from Mexico, among them Francisco Moncaleano, suppressed its journal, and jailed its Mexican spokesmen. In this instance, the attack went awry; while languishing in Belem Prison, the jailed leaders decided to found the Casa del Obrero, a militant labor center.[8]

Reliance on the stick, to the credit of the administration, was merely a first step. Less inflexible than the Old Regime and more in tune with current political thought, the Maderistas recognized that repression alone provided only a temporary remedy. The changing industrial picture required more imaginative measures. Labor must be courted, if necessary some of its demands met, and more significantly, its leadership controlled by government. To give voice to the policy, the administration established the Departamento del Trabajo, an office in the Ministry of Fomento. Its main task was to prevent work stoppages, solve them when they occurred, and keep the budding labor movement under control. Its birth marked official acknowledgement of the growing importance of the labor movement, and additionally, represented a concession to worker's demands for a bureau in government responsive to their needs. With no authority of its own, the Departamento could mediate, solely on a voluntary basis, disputes between labor and management. Its goal was to "encourage harmonious relations between capital and labor," but on a budget hardly sufficient for its mission.[9] To head it, Hernández picked Antonio Ramos Pedrueza, a lawyer and former Díaz' congressman, who believed in the responsibilities of citizenship and in respect for authority, viewing both as the cornerstones of peace. Although hostile to strikes, he sympathized with the hopes of the workers, yet rarely ignored the interests of businessmen, upon whom he lavished praise for their patience and prudence, attitudes he asked workers to adopt. As he interpreted his duties, he was to endeavor to prevent strikes, and by taking measures to improve the lot of workingmen, to win their backing for the Madero administration.[10] But according to *El Ahuizote,* a labor journal known for its biting criticism, the "ballyhooed Departamento del Trabajo was worthless." [11]

The spadework began in the textile industry, where the Departamento organized a Comité Central de Obreros to collaborate closely with it. Under the guidance of Ramos Pedrueza, the Comité acted as an intermediary between labor and management in the mills. When troubles flared, Ramos Pedrueza despatched the Comité to the scene of the conflict where, invariably, its members exhorted their companions to return to work. "The Departamento," to cite Ramos Pedrueza, counted "on the Comité to stop agitation." [12] Also, in a further effort to control labor and to checkmate the plans of the Casa del Obrero, the administration attempted to organize a Confederación Mexicana del Trabajo. A portent of the government-controlled union of the future, the Confederación failed to capture the support of the workers.[13] Enactment of labor legislation was another item in the official formula. It symbolized an attempt to court the worker and a recognition that industrial peace required a response to the pleas for higher wages and better working conditions. A contrary course would encourage crippling strikes. The administration had picked the strife-ridden textile industry for its pioneer effort at social engineering.

To develop the legislation, the administration met twice with the mill owners and managers, in January and July 1912 in

Mexico City, and urged them to draw up measures that Congress could enact into laws. Hernández, nonetheless, left no doubt that he anticipated no legislation harmful to industry. Still, bringing peace to the troubled mills required going beyond the recommendation of Díaz at Río Blanco. At the meetings, businessmen made the decisions; the Comité Central de Obreros, invited to observe, could consult with Fomento but not vote.[14]

In the opinion of Hernández, the workers wanted higher wages, a shorter workday, an end to the exploitation of women and children in the mills, and the right to have their representatives speak for them. He suggested three specific concessions; a workday of ten hours with a minimum wage of 1.25 pesos, and a general wage boost of 10 percent. Also, he explained, workers complained that employers ran them off their jobs for joining a labor union, but he did not push the issue further. When owners objected to the cost of wage increases Hernández implied that they could be passed on to consumers.[15] Labor, however, wanted a uniform wage system for the entire textile industry, eliminating inequalities at all levels, and especially a government edict compelling management to bargain with its representatives.

The accord left labor unhappy; the delegates had adopted a timid blueprint of labor reform. The revised regulations for the textile industry included a ten-hour day; limited management's right to dismiss workers to grounds of "insubordination, disobedience, ineptitude or obstreperous behavior"; abolished fines for damage done to company property; and established a six-day week. Instead of a uniform wage scale, the textile barons adopted a minimum wage of 1.25 pesos for the "average" worker and, to stimulate him to work harder, offered him the incentive of doing more piecework to add to his income. The harder he worked the more he earned.[16] But management bluntly refused to accept labor unions. To encourage the mills to adopt the revised regulations, Congress later increased the tax on textile goods from 5 to 8 percent, while offering to refund half of the tax to mills adhering to the regulations. The textile industry would pay a smaller tax and pass on the savings to the worker who, as a consumer, would pay higher prices for cotton goods. As a result what the textile barons had given with one hand, they had taken back with the other. Ramos Pedrueza called the regulations a victory for labor, although conceding that some labor spokesmen might disagree and warning the workers not to listen to these "malcontents and agitators." [17] Events proved Ramos Pedrueza mistaken. Not all mill owners adopted the revised regulations and some continued to pay their workers as little as thirty centavos a day.[18]

These cautious steps taken by the Madero administration failed to improve the lot of labor. For its part, labor remained skeptical of the good intentions of both government and industry. Genuine labor reform had yet to appear. However, with its attempts to watch over labor and to control its leadership, the Madero administration had set a precedent for the future.

III

Not until 1915 did Madero's disciples again claim the National Palace. Labor's problems, during the interim, had grown more acute. The struggle to unseat Huerta and the ensuing factional wars between the Constitutionalists and their rivals dealt harshly with the economy. Inflation, hunger, and unemployment left misery in their wake. As the economy deteriorated, so did the well-being of labor, and with it the militancy of its leadership increased. Before the turmoil ended, workingmen had put together the framework of scores of unions and labor confederations. Yet those dominant among the victorious Constitutionalists viewed with suspicion and hostility embryonic efforts to build an independent labor movement. No sooner were the Constitutionalists back in the National Palace when the battle to control labor, for which the Madero regime had laid the beginning, burst forth again.

To win the fray, the Constitutionalists had to turn back the clock. The regime of the hated usurper Huerta, to start with, had courted labor. Labeled neo-Porfirista by its enemies, it nonetheless had fallen in step with the reforms of its predecessor, championed labor legislation, and learned to coexist with the nascent labor movement. Before being driven from office, it had drawn up blueprints for a Ministry of Industry, Commerce, and Labor—a tribute to the growing importance of industrial labor.

The recommendation to upgrade labor affairs reflected practical reality. Heavy fighting in the northern provinces, Huerta's major antagonists, made imperative the search for allies. The Huertistas had a stake in maintaining political stability and industrial output lest national revenues decline and unemployment and the scarcity of goods drive the worker into the arms of the insurgents.

Huerta, obviously, had not seized power to befriend labor. Like Madero's government, his administration had the welfare of the worker only marginally in mind. It too, employed the policy of the carrot and the stick. To suppress labor ferment, it shut down the Casa del Obrero Mundial—but not until May 27, 1914, just weeks before Huerta fled Mexico City.[19] As had Madero, Huerta jailed radicals. Yet his administration allowed the giant labor parade of May 1, 1913.[20] It wooed successfully a number of labor groups, including the Unión de Conductores, Maquinistas, Garroteros y Fogoneros.[21] To manipulate labor it upgraded the Departamento del Trabajo, placing it in the hands of Andrés Molina Enríquez and Rafael Sierra, two friends of the worker. For the first time in Mexico, admitted a Constitutionalist, its rulers had given the Departamento its due importance. Its budget, twice that granted by Madero, exceeded the funds later provided by the Constitutionalists.[22] The Departamento lent a helping hand to labor groups seeking recognition from management, among them the Gremio de Alijadores de Tampico, recommended the enactment of legislation to cover industrial accidents, while endorsing the regulations for the textile industry laid out by the Madero administration. The Constitutionalists could not easily ignore this record.

The Constitutionalists, also, had pledged aid to labor. With Villa's armies in Mexico City, it became imperative to attract neutral political blocs to the Constitutionalist camp, or at least to keep them from linking up with Villa and Zapata. At this juncture, Constitutionalists willing to cooperate with labor convinced Carranza to share his fate with the Casa del Obrero Mundial. Practical politics, therefore, made bedmates of Carranza and the Casa. The alliance, signed in February, 1915, occurred none too soon for already Antonio Díaz Soto y Gama and Luis Méndez, two regulars of the Casa, had embraced Zapata. Carranza and his principal allies, however, never meant to include an independent labor bloc in their vision. As General Pablo González, a crony of the First Chief, told striking miners at El Oro, the Revolution was not just for the benefit of labor, but "also for industries seeking government safeguards for their interests." The workers were sorely mistaken if they thought in terms of a "proletarian revolution." [23]

Still, the Constitutionalists had embraced the Casa. But the agreement brought into the Constitutionalist camp a political bloc not entirely in step with Carranza and a majority of his partisans. Carranza if presently willing to cooperate, would eventually want control; an open break was just a matter of time. The merger, furthermore, shattered the neutrality of labor which, until 1915, had wanted nothing to do with any of the military factions. By embracing the Constitutionalists, the Casa assured government meddling in labor's affairs. Worse yet, the marriage shattered hopes for a solidarity among workers, pitting industrial labor against peasants in Zapata's army and the poor allied with Villa. By backing the Constitutionalists' assault on the messiah of the peasants, one bloc of workers had befriended politicians unsympathetic to their blood brothers. That decision aided the conservative Carranza and his partisans to consolidate their lealership, thus placing another obstacle in the path of social reform. In the future, the more politically sophisticated industrial worker would pursue his goals independently, and if need be at the expense of the peasant.

The ink had hardly dried on the quid pro quo when the Constitutionalists and the Casa began to suspect each other's motives. By the pact of 1915, the Casa had sworn to provide soldiers, and in return, the Constitutionalists promised to permit it to establish branches in the provinces, as well as to better the lot of the workingman. The Red Battalions, composed almost entirely of workers from Mexico City and the textile industry of Veracruz, result from this agreement. A marriage of convenience, it embodied distinct goals for each partner. Leaders of the Casa undoubtedly looked upon it as a means to help solidify their leadership of labor; to Carranza and his friends, it meant additional and much needed soldiers, but also an ally who would require watching in the future. If Carranza welcomed the Red Battalions, he had no intention of allowing the Casa to use them to build a base from which to challenge his authority. The First Chief wanted no rivals, especially left wingers or labor revolutionaries.

That the Carranza wing of the Constitutionalists meant to keep in check its labor partisans soon became apparent. The recruitment of soldiers immediately dissolved into a tug of war between the Casa and the Departamento del Trabajo, an office loyal to Carranza. Both the Casa and the Departamento were playing a double game. The Casa, which sent emissaries to the textile mills of Orizaba to recruit for the Red Battalions, had not done so out of loyalty to the Constitutionalists. To the contrary: in their meetings with the workers, its emissaries blatantly began to undermine the prestige of Carranza. To cite Dr. Atl, one of the emissaries, conservative politicans and businessmen understood only guns and bullets.[24] The Departamento, on the other hand, set about subverting its rivals by exhorting the workers to enlist in military units led by orthodox Constitutionalists' commanders and even to stay on their jobs. It endeavored to get the workers' loyalty and to circumvent the Casa which, to Carranza and his wing, spoke for a rival labor bloc, or equally pernicious, acted on behalf of the ambitious General Alvaro Obregón and his crowd.

The rivalry exacerbated the split in the ranks of labor. At Orizaba, to give one example, it divided the workers into three camps. Of the workers voting to bear arms, one group elected to join a Red Battalion, but the other decided to follow the commands of an officer loyal to Carranza. A third group chose to stay on its job. The two groups remaining in Orizaba, either as soldiers or workers, pledged their loyalty to the Departamento del Trabajo. Similar splits occurred in other parts of Veracruz and Puebla; at Atlixco, a textile center in Puebla, a majority of the workers elected to collaborate with local military units and not to join the Red Battalions.[25]

Significantly, the contest was not just over who would control the workers but over the character of their organizations. The initial skirmishes occurred in the textile industry where the Carrancistas confronted two major problems, both of which the ambitions of the Casa complicated. They must keep the workers out of the Casa's grasp, and conversely, to assure their loyalty, get management to deal with their representatives who, at the same time, would be beholden to the Departamento del Trabajo. The task was to build labor organizations satisfying the demands of the workers but which would not get out of hand. To complicate the task, the organizations had to be acceptable to management. The Constitutionalists, in short, expected to mold the shape of labor organizations and to control them.

It fell to Marcos López Jiménez, the director of the Departamento, to carry out the complex task. It was he who began to organize *agrupaciones de resistencia* among the textile workers of Orizaba. To compel management to deal with their spokesmen, the Departamento conferred legal status, *personalidad jurídica,* on them. But there was a joker: the government retained for itself the right to regulate the *agrupaciones* and to punish their infractions. To cite a memorandum of the Departamento, the formula would permit government to "curtail effectively strikes and other disorders by workers and agitators . . . put an end to the power of independent labor groups . . . and to their conspiracies against the constituted authorities." No independent particular, body would receive either "direct or indirect legal status." The memorandum left no doubt as to the identity of the agitators: the committees of the Casa, "impudent and fraudulent groups . . . concerned solely with parochial interests and hostile to all authority." [26]

Still, Carranza and his partisans were not yet out of the woods; independent labor had been merely blunted. No sooner was Carranza back in Mexico City than strikes began again. The Casa, meanwhile, was busily engaged in building a labor network in the Republic. Labor unions, either affiliated with the Casa or independent of it, had blossomed in nearly every industry, spurred on by hard times and the revolutionary euphoria.

The inevitable showdown occurred in the summer of 1916, when the Federación de Sindicatos Obreros of Mexico City called a general strike that immediately paralyzed the public utilities. The strike, which infuriated government leaders, led Carranza to brand as traitors spokesmen of the Casa. To put it down, Carranza, with the concurrence of Obregón, invoked a law dating from 1862 sanctioning the death penalty for treason, jailed the leaders of the Casa, and had troops close its offices.[27] Then the administration went after the branches and affiliates of the Casa in the provinces, using soldiers to destroy their headquarters and to jail their leaders. Governors and military commanders were ordered to confiscate radical propaganda and to punish its authors. In Mérida, Yucatan, according to Felipe Carrillo Puerto, the army burned down the headquarters of the Partido Socialista, pillaged and sacked its cooperatives in the villages, and murdered Socialists.[28] By late 1916 the rulers of Mexico had given a death blow to the Casa and to the independent labor movement.

The Carrancistas, whatever their inclinations may have been, however, could not just do nothing. The days of the stark repression of don Porfirio at Cananea and Río Blanco were over. Even among the Constitutionalists who looked to don Venustiano for guidance, a large majority favored a measure of labor reform. With the activities of the Casa—anathema to all wings of the Constitutionalists—effectively blocked, and the independent labor movement in disarray, it was time to start afresh. Besides, the downfall of the Casa had not dampened the proclivity of the workers for strikes.

Between 1916 and 1918, the Constitutionalists, revolutionaries of practical bent, slowly evolved a new formula for dealing with labor. At Querétaro, they incorporated Article 123 into the national charter, establishing a modern labor code. This gave workers a legal right to join labor unions and to bargain collectively with management. But the Constitutionalists apparently did not intend to include an independent labor movement in their formula. Ironically, because of Article 123, itself partly an offshoot of the pressure of labor on the Constitutionalists, the drive to organize unions had gained ground. Meanwhile, strikes, sanctioned by Article 123, disrupted the recovery of the economy. Caught between the need for industrial peace, the necessity of courting labor, and fear of an independent labor bloc, the administration decided to build a captive national labor organization, and in the process, deter efforts by workers to organize their own.

That labor would try to build one was a foregone conclusion. A conference in the port city of Veracruz in 1916 had already produced the short-lived Confederación del Trabajo de la Región Mexicana (CTRM); its radical platform called for a class struggle and the socialization of the means of production. Its failure prompted two other abortive attempts, both in 1917. Anarchists, Syndicalists and Socialists had founded a Partido Socialista Obrero. At Tampico, remnants of the CTRM and the Casa, at the invitation of the Gremio de Alijadores, had convoked a meeting attended by delegates from the Federación de Sindicatos Obreros del Distrito Federal, and by spokesmen for miners and the electricians' unions; they had urged the communization of the means of production.[29] To insure the failure of the undertaking, government had deployed troops to harass the delegates. Obviously, if it was to forestall additional efforts, the government had to take the initiative.

At the behest of Carranza, or according to others, at the urging of Obregón, Governor Gustavo Espinosa Mireles, an intimate of the president, invited all labor groups to send delegates to a meeting in Saltillo, the capital of Coahuila, in the summer of 1918. The puprose was to develop a national labor body. For the meeting, the government paid the expenses of delegates from eighteen states representing 116 groups.[30] Three major elements were present: Anarcho-syndicalists, with the largest following in organized labor; Socialists, backed by supporters of the USSR; and the Unionists, with the benediction of the administration and the American Federation of Labor. Luis Morones, a leader active in earlier attempts to build a national body, arrived at Saltillo as the spokesman of the unionists. Morones had dealt with the AFL since 1916 when, as head of the Mexican Telephone Company, he had opposed the general strike in Mexico City.[31]

From Saltillo emerged the Confederación Regional Obrera Mexicana (CROM), which promptly set out to "unite" labor and to "emancipate it from political manipulations." By 1920 it claimed 350,000 members.[32] Its birth, however, ended "the romantic, idealistic period in the Mexican labor movement."[33] Despite its platform rhetoric, the CROM dedicated itself to seeking an "equilibrium between capital and labor." Opportunistic and pragmatic, its leaders easily learned to accommodate themselves to capitalism and to live with employers and government.[34] Their success set the stage for the successful manipulation of labor and for its subservience to government. Morones, the crown prince of the CROM, lost no time in gaining notoriety for "the extravagant revelry at [his] . . . weekend parties and his ostentatious display of automobiles and diamonds." [35] The initials of the CROM, as one wit said, came to stand for "Como Robó Oro Morones" (how Morones stole money). Still, its birth and triumphs marked a milestone in the history of Mexican labor. Unlike the Old Regime and Madero's administration, Carranza and his disciples had come to terms with the labor union, going so far as to sponsor a national labor network. With the birth of the CROM, however, government began to have the control.

IV

It had taken a decade to draw up a workable blueprint for the handling of labor. Although some of its features clung to past practices, its general tone had the color of modern legislation. It was up to the administration of Alvaro Obregón to make it run smoothly.

Obregón's administration probably best exemplifies the ambivalence of the upheaval of 1910. Contrasted with its predecessors, it seemed more progressive, espousing twentieth-century rhetoric, but paradoxically, Obregón's administration walked in step with nineteenth-century economic doctrines. It advocated reform, not drastic change. To cite Obregón, his administration "watched over the interests of all classes." [36] Industry and investors who cooperated had nothing to fear. Quite the contrary: government conferred a plethora of safeguards on businessmen, natives and foreigners alike.

Obregón and his supporters captured office not at a propitious time. The military coup of Agua Prieta had revived fears of political instability, especially among conservatives and Americans who distrusted Obregón's liberal image. Efforts to revive business and restore confidence drew top priority. Unfortunately, a bloated military that elevated Obregón to the presidency but nearly toppled him from office three years later, had to be placated and fed. Generals and politicians grew fat off the national budget while graft and corruption became commonplace. It was the decade of the revolutionary rich who built palatial estates in the hills of Chapultepec and spent weekends on their *haciendas*. In the meantime, the aftermath of World War I brought a world depression, undercutting the prices of silver and copper, key Mexican exports. Landlords, during the interval, with a worried eye on Article 27, hesitated to till their lands, setting back the recovery of agriculture. Confronted with a paper-thin budget, the administration cut the salaries of public employees. To exacerbate matters, Washington withheld recognition of Obregón's regime until 1923. Officials had to rebuild Mexico without the markets of its chief customer, while confronting the hostility of American mining and petroleum corporations. Given this situation, to implement radical labor measures spelled doom to the administration.

The lot of labor, during the interlude, had hardly improved. Still prevailing were low wages, long hours of toil in squalid, dangerous conditions, industrial accidents without adequate compensation, and arbitrary decisions by management.[37] As late as 1923, nothing had been done to enforce Article 123; *leyes reglamentarias*, enabling legislation had not been passed.[38] Yet labor had backed Obregón's bid for the presidency. The Partido Laborista Mexicano, an offspring of the CROM, had sent delegates to all of the provinces to work for his candidacy, while Morones had accompanied Obregón on his campaign tour. As a reward, the Obregonistas permitted the Partido Laborista to win half of the seats on the city council of the capital in the municipal elections of 1920, and named Celestino Gasca, a luminary of the CROM, its mayor. Both Morones and Eduardo Moneda, another CROM chieftain, received lucrative posts in government.[39]

The CROM, likewise, enjoyed a monopoly of official benevolence. The decade from 1918 to 1928 was the *esplendor* of the CROM when, in return for financial and political support, its leaders manipulated labor for the benefit of government and business. In the opinion of Jorge Basurto, Obregón and Calles took advantage of the era of the industrial peace resulting from the CROM's manipulation of labor to strengthen capitalist development; "that is, to encourage and protect native and foreign capital." [40] The triumph of Morones and his henchmen, which destroyed local autonomy in labor circles, encouraged the growth of the captive or *charro* union, impeding the awakening conscience of labor. A tiny coterie of twelve, with Morones at its head, ruled the roost. Critics labeled the twelve the *Apostolado de la Vaqueta,* the apostleship of the thick-skinned, because of their insensitivity to public criticism and censure.[41]

With the aid of the CROM, government brought labor under control. One result was a marked decline in the number of strikes. Independent labor groups, by the same token, fared badly. Nevertheless, dissident groups challenged the CROM, mainly the textile and streetcar workers who established the Confederación General de Trabajadores (CGT) in 1921. An industrial union, it held aloft the unity of peasants and workers and the communization of the means of production. The CGT, which enjoyed Communist support, had only marginal success. A few labor groups, additionally, weathered the monopoly of the CROM, essentially railroad brotherhoods and the Sindicato Mexicano de Electricistas.[42]

Meanwhile, in 1920 the Church also founded a short-lived rival to the CROM, the Confederación Nacional Católica del Trabajo which, through its activities in the textile zone, clashed head on with the CROM and CGT. From its headquarters in Guadalajara, the archbishop of Jalisco watched over it. While endorsing Article 123, the Catholic union opposed agrarian reform, calling expropriation a theft of land. The Catholics enjoyed limited success; in the textile industry, for example, they failed to gain control of a single mill.[43] However, the Catholic challenge in textiles helped weaken the influence of the CGT, particularly in Atlixco.[44]

In its dealing with the CROM, government had a lion by the tail. Whatever the motives of Morones and company, they had not joined with Obregón's politicians just to permit the Republic to savor industrial peace. The merger had to yield benefits to both groups, an axiom which kept the CROM leadership constantly in the battle for higher wages and bargaining rights. The vast majority of industrial disputes, almost 200 in 1922 alone, occurred because management turned deaf ears to the representatives of the workers. To insure industrial peace—the key to reconstruction and reform—government had to revamp the previous formula for dealing with labor questions.

To do so, it had to bear in mind that it was necessary to satisfy a heterogeneous constituency. Contrary to popular myth, Obregón never deviated far from his base of power. To insure his position, he had to placate powerful groups in society: businessmen, landlords, mining and petroleum interests, politicians of diverse stripe, military unfriently to labor, as well as the CROM. Political success, a lesson Obregón mastered in Sonora, required a healthy regard for individual ambitions and provincial autonomy. Unless strikes jeopardized the national welfare, or threatened the political status quo, it was best to leave their solution to the CROM and to local officials. The Obregón formula contained a large dose of deliberate inaction. The better part of wisdom was to plead legal inability to intervene in industrial disputes. When politically necessary, Obregón took no liberties with the Constitution. "The President of the Republic," he told striking miners in San Luis Potosí, "lacks the authority to intervene in disputes between management and labor in the states." [45] A belief in the efficacy of the free play of forces underscored this attitude. However, as events time and again showed, this reluctance played into the hands of groups hostile to labor's pleas. Most local politicians, it must not be forgotten, shared a stake in the status quo.

Still, pragmatism rather than principle shaped policy. When politics required a populist response, government could become a champion of labor; in some situations, labor could rely for sympathy and help on the "revolutionary" family. Unfortunately, the economic difficulties of the early twenties hardly encouraged government to side with labor. Recovery, economic development, and the need to increase production dictated this response. Given the gloomy picture, the administration usually relied on the law of supply and demand to settle its dilemmas; more so because it had decided to hold the line on prices, regardless of the consequences to labor. The consumer, it was said, had top priority. Nor did government hesitate to lecture workers on the importance of self reliance and respect for law. Under no circumstances were workers to take the law into their hands, an approach that merely hurt their cause.[46] Circumstance, therefore, colored government's interpretation of law and morality.

Notwithstanding legal principles and morality, officials

meant to make labor toe the line. Rebellious and angry workers jeopardized economic recovery, disrupted political stability, and frightened off foreign investors, key ingredients of the official blueprint for the welfare of Mexico. In the decade just concluded, Madero's regime had organized a Departamento del Trabajo to steer labor's development; Carranza and his followers had persecuted independent labor groups, utilized the Departamento as a tool for their own ends, and eventually sponsored the formation of a "manageable" national labor confederation. Under Obregón, the Departamento, one division of the Ministry of Industry, Commerce, and Labor, ceded many of its functions to the CROM, which was called upon to keep the worker orderly and to end the rash of strikes.

"LEGAL" STRIKES, 1920–1928 [47]

Years	Number of Strikes	Workers Involved
1920	173	88,536
1921	310	100,380
1922	197	71,322
1923	146	61,403
1924	125	23,988
1925	51	9,861
1926	23	2,977
1927	15	1,005
1928	7	498

As these figures show, while Obregón fought the battle, Calles harvested the fruits of victory. The year 1924 began a dramatic decline in the number of workers on strike. These statistics, however, reported merely "legal" strikes sanctioned by law; that is, by unions recognized by the government, almost always under the control of the CROM or allied with it. Wildcat strikes, the illegal kind, usually led by the CGT, and with the odds against success, went unreported in the official statistics.

The decline of strikes demonstrates not just the success of the official policy, to keep labor in its place, but the consolidation of the CROM's political monopoly. In the early years, the CROM, although blessed by the National Palace, had continued to face challenges from recalcitrant labor groups, usually unions friendly to the CGT. With its triumph, signaling the demise of the CGT and the Catholics, the number of strikes decreased until only a handful occurred in 1928. Thus success, with its goal of industrial peace, came with the rise of the CROM and the destruction of independent labor. But Obregón and Calles never intended to allow the CROM to challenge their authority. At best, the merger of big labor and government was an uneasy alliance. When Morones and his henchmen stepped out of line, the political bosses of Mexico withdrew their support. This occurred in 1927 when Morones and Celestino Gasca who, having coveted the National Palace, looked coldly on Obregón's designs for a second term in office.

The regime, however, did not rely on the CROM to bring labor to heel; it also took a direct hand. The opening shot against rebellious labor groups was fired from the National Palace. The initial victim was the Confederación de Sociedades Ferrocarrileras de la Repúblic Mexicana, the largest and most powerful of the railroad brotherhoods. At its birth in 1920, it spoke for sixteen unions, including the Unión de Conductores, Maquinistas, Garroteros y Fogoneros, and the Orden de Maquinistas y Fogoneros, two groups with leaders on friendly terms with the CROM. Designed to end their constant quarrels, the merger of the rival unions collapsed a year later when Federico Rendón, the chief of the conductors and their allies, abandoned the Confederación. With the split, Francisco Pérez, the director of the National Railways of Mexico, broke his promise to bestow official standing to the Confederación, arguing that the departure of Rendón and his unionists invalidated its claim to speak for the railroad workers. Even without Rendón, nevertheless, the Confederación represented most of the railroad unions, nearly all of the railroad workers, as well as a majority of the conductors and engineers. Its members charged that Pérez had sided with Rendón, an ally of Morones and the CROM, in order to destroy their independence. Pérez and the CROM, with the backing of the Obregón administration, had decided to put an end to the one brotherhood with a valid claim to speak for the Republic's railroad workers.

To compel Pérez to honor his pledge, the Confederación called a strike; approximately 80 percent of the railroad workers honored it. From the beginning, the strike won wide backing from diverse labor groups throughout the Republic, among them the textile workers, the Alijadores de Tampico, and the trolley and electricians unions of Mexico City, allies of the CGT. The strikers demanded the recognition of the Confederación and the dismissal of Pérez. Instead of heeding their demands, Obregón boasted "that the strike would triumph only if he were driven from office." He dispatched troops to quell the strikers, and during the interval ran the trains with scabs and soldiers and Mexicans who worked on railroads in the United States, by offering financial rewards to get them to come home. Additional help came from Rendón's union which, naturally, stayed at work. Obregón's hostility broke the strike. By his tactics, he had taught the railroad men a lesson in Mexican revolutionary politics: they could have their unions only if they marched in step with the administration. Ultimately, the railroad workers lost their independence.[48]

The Unión Minera Mexicana, another segment of labor in sympathy with the CGT, fared even worse. The Unión, embodying the aspirations of the coal miners of Coahuila, had engaged in bitter disputes with management since the days of Carranza. Local authorities, according to the Unión, had refused to compel management to bargain with its representatives, going so far in their hostility as to use *rurales* against it. In March, 1923, after the owners had refused to rehire fourteen miners fired for union activity, their companions had gone on strike. When they staged a public protest against the coal company, troops fired on the workers, killing three and wounding others. A public uproar followed, with even the CROM protesting the shootings. Yet Obregón, rather than punish the guilty, placed the blame for the tragedy on the victims who, in his opinion, had acted imprudently. The shootings, and Obregón's refusal to intervene on its behalf, badly hurt the Unión, many of whose members were pleading with the government to help them find jobs by 1926.[49]

Nor did the government go to battle to protect the rights of workers in the textile industry. At Atlixco, a mill town outside of the city of Puebla and scene of intense labor strife, the complaints of workers included all of the old grievances: long hours of toil, low wages, poor conditions of work, and the adamant refusal of management to talk to their representatives. To exacerbate the situation, foreigners owned and managed the mills, while innumerable textile workers sympathized with the CGT. The CROM, meanwhile, was competing to enlarge its foothold. For the Obregón regime, the trouble dated from March 1922, when the workers at the Carolina mill shut it down after management had dismissed five members of the executive board of their union. Management bluntly refused to negotiate the dispute, choosing to employ scabs and to open the doors of the mill to Catholic workers. The tactics backfired and the strike spread to the neighboring mills. To protect them, Obregón eventually permitted the stationing of troops in Atlixco, meanwhile alleging that he lacked authority to settle the conflict. To no one's surprise, the soldiers fired on the strikers, killing scores of them. According to the workers, *obreros libres,* scabs, with arms furnished by the employers had joined the attack. When company police killed a worker and wounded others at Metepec, the entire labor force at Orizaba staged a massive protest demanding that Obregón punish the guilty and protect the workers.[50]

However, even when the governor of Puebla urged the expulsion of the *obreros libres* from the mills, the Ministry of Industry, Commerce, and Labor replied that it would be unfair to deprive the members of the Confederación de Obreros Católicos of their jobs.[51] To the administration, the right to work superseded the right to organize labor, and certainly took precedence over the closed shop. As Marjorie R. Clark noted, the Obregón administration left the textile industry in a state of "complete chaos in wages and working conditions." She might have added that the authority of the independent union was undercut.[52] At Atlixco, the CROM eventually emerged the victor.[53]

With its marriage to the CROM, the Obregón regime passed on to its successor a tested system for the manipulation of labor. Initiated by the government of Madero, the plan had finally become effective. Whether the administration, as critics charge, had converted the leaders of the CROM into its puppets, however, may be debatable. At times, Morones, Gasca, Moneda and their companions displayed a surprising degree of independence. They were not beyond playing their own game. Although at the beck and call of politicians in Mexico City, and similarly willing to align with management, the stalwarts of the CROM also coveted power for themselves, and obviously, for their organization. Adherents, therefore, often stood to gain. The affiliates of the CROM, for example, won a majority of their disputes with management in the years between 1920 and 1924.[54]

Graft and corruption, in the meantime, accompanied the rise of the CROM; its leaders unashamedly flaunted their wealth. Morones and his friends became millionaires. The rise of the CROM meant the disappearance of the independent labor movement, so dear to the hearts of pioneer labor leaders. In the world of the CROM, there was no room for rivals. Nor had workers much to show for over a decade of struggle. Wages still lagged behind prices while working conditions had barely changed since the days of Díaz. Despite a supposedly redeeming revolution, lamented the Comité Estudiantil Pro-Paz in 1924, "greedy and powerful capitalists still victimized the weak"; the ills of the colonial era continued consuming the "workers and their children, and to exacerbate their plight, the ills grew worse." [55] Or to cite the Federación Obrera de Hilados y Tejidos, the gulf between the rich and the poor widened; while the "rich feasted . . . the workers and their families lived in stark misery." [56] In 1923 an army of workers flocked to the banners of De la Huerta, especially followers of the CGT and the railway brotherhoods.[57] The uprising even split the CROM, with state affiliates threatening to bolt to the rebels.[58]

EIGHTEEN

The Faltering Pledge

"At this moment, the political situation renders unwise any attempt to alter dramatically economic ills centuries old. Because of the obvious peril, we rely on your intelligence, wisdom and patriotism to silence demands for agrarian reform."

> Antonio Ramos Pedrueza to Governor of
> Guanajuato, 1912

I

To the dismay of the penniless dirt farmers and their vindicators, the ageless *hacienda* weathered the galewinds of insurgency. Claims to the contrary notwithstanding, its survival was neither ironic nor unpredictable because the victors in the bloody civil strife had, from the start, hardly masked their dislike of radical change. Ridding Mexico of the *hacienda,* the growing plea of the landless, tempted only the boldest.

Still, like it or not, dirt farmers—peasants in the opinion of city folk, their aspirations given voice by the rebels—eventually began to clamor for land to call their own. "The poor in . . . Veracruz want nothing more than to own a plot of land to work freely . . . without the weight of the *hacendados* upon them," a friend wrote Francisco I. Madero in 1912.[1] Before he died, Madero was to hear this plea of the dirt farmer time and time again. Yet his Plan de San Luis Potosí hardly took it into account, while his ship of state, navigating in turbulent political waters, at best sponsored half-hearted measures. In December, 1911, the Maderistas adopted a blueprint for the purchase of *hacienda* lands for resale as small plots, but the powerless measure failed to induce *hacendados* to sell their lands at prices the poor could pay.[2] Two months later, the architects of policy took another cautious step, sponsoring legislation to subdivide into parcels the public lands, the heralded *terrenos baldíos*.[3] To survey them the Dirección Agraria, a bureau in the Ministry of Fomento, began to establish branches in the provinces. Believing that these offices were meant to handle their pleas for land, humble dirt farmers began to flock to them. "They think that we have come to settle the agrarian problem," the agronomist in Guerrero told Madero; "they think that you have sent us to bring justice to them, the poor who cannot afford lawyers, whose lack of schooling cost them their rights." One complaint overshadowed the others: "the theft of lands by the rich and powerful." They did not "understand," said the agronomist, "that this was not our job." [4]

To the contrary: if the experience of Villa de Reyes, a village in San Luis Potosí, is symbolic of the actual situation, leaders in Mexico City exhibited greater concern for the wishes of *hacendados*. Since the days of don Porfirio, Villa de Reyes had been fending off the invasion of its lands by the neighboring *hacienda*. All efforts had failed and the *hacienda* now stood at the very door of the village. In July, 1912, to the consternation of Villa de Reyes, the Dirección Agraria authenticated the claims of the *hacendado,* nullifying the land titles of the villagers.[5] Reform fared no better at the hands of the Comisión Nacional Agraria, designated by Rafael Hernández, minister of *fomento,* to study and resolve the tangled land issue. He filled the Comisión with "progressives from the conservative classes," and thus to no one's surprise, little came of its labors.[6]

State governors adopted a similar stance. Abraham González, Governor of Chihuahua and an intimate of Madero, for example, had even told his lieutenants, during the struggle to unseat Porfirio Díaz, to respect private property. As governor, he confined his legislation to a tax on large holdings while pledging to subdivide and sell in small plots the public lands on easy credit terms.[7] In Guanajuato, timid efforts by its governor to alleviate the lot of rural workers backfired, frightening *hacendados* there and in adjoining Querétaro. Almost immediately, the Cámara Agrícola of the city of León, a voice for the *hacen-*

dados in Guanajuato, asked Hernández to squelch attempts of "agitators" to stir up the "peons on the *haciendas*." [8] So Antonio Ramos Pedrueza, head of the labor office in Fomento, ordered the governor to halt his "dangerous propaganda inciting agricultural workers to want higher wages." Such a policy, he added "merely stirred up unrest in the state and perhaps in others." [9] All the same, in a letter to the Cámara Agrícola, Fomento still found time to ask how it might serve the distinguished body since its views marched in step with "sound principles of economics." [10] All of this occurred because the governor of Guanajuato had urged the *hacendados* to meet with their *jefes políticos* in order to find ways to end the discord with peasants and to improve rural wages.

Fomento, however, had scant reason to warn the governor of Querétaro, Carlos M. Loyola, to act with caution. His handling of the complaints of two sharecroppers against the Hacienda Jofre y Montenegro made that abundantly clear. The *hacendado*, Fomento had informed Loyola, while having the legal right "to do as he wished with his property," nevertheless, had to recognize that there were "questions that should be handled with a broader criteria because today more than ever before public officials are duty bound to help the unfortunate." [11] Loyola, needless to say, paid little attention to the advice. "My administration," he replied, "is naturally motivated by the best of intentions to aid and protect the destitute"; he piously insisted that he had, "within the limits of justice and equity, always endeavored to resolve conflicts in favor of the workers." Be that as it may, he continued, his government had to maintain law and order and, because of this obilgation, at times had employed "harsh measures which that class of people by its ignorance . . . invites." [12] The coup by Victoriano Huerta ended for the time being attempts to cajole moral behavior from public authorities and *hacendados* by appealing to their sense of *noblesse oblige*.

II

To judge them solely by their legislative accomplishments, the Constitutionalists, the rulers of Mexico between 1915 and 1920, departed sharply from the vacillation of Madero. Had Article 27—the bill of rights of land reform in the Constitution of 1917 —been fully honored, it would have dealt sternly with the *hacendados*. But, unfortunately for the landless, practice did not match rhetoric. No one even modestly in the know about Mexican affairs, Manuel Calero commented in 1920, could examine recent history and judge the Constitutionalists to be crusaders against agrarian ills.[13] From the start, documented the Plan de Guadalupe, Venustiano Carranza and company worshipped mundane goals. To make matters worse, years of warfare, by hampering the cultivation of the land, had cut deeply into the food supply of the Republic. Feeding Mexicans took precedence over schemes to subdivide *haciendas*; the latter plan, in the minds of Carranza and his successor, would further reduce dwindling supplies of corn and wheat. Additionally, added Marte R. Gómez, popular pressure of the kind to compel politicians to champion land reform lay in the future.[14]

Recognition by the Constitutionalists—rebels who worshipped legal niceties, as their title testifies—of the growing importance of land reform matured slowly. By and large, it developed in response to the rising popular clamor, particularly after the promulgation of Article 27 in 1917, a pledge that awakened the hopes of the landless. But from March, 1913, the date of the Plan de Guadalupe, to nearly the end of 1914, the Carrancistas twiddled their thumbs. Field commanders were ordered to safeguard private property, not to split up estates. The Agrarian legislation of October 3, 1913, adopted by Governor Pastor Rouaix in Durango, survived largely on the statute books.[15] When General Lucio Blanco, in defiance of his First Chief, subdivided the Hacienda Los Borregos, Carranza stripped him of his troops. The First Chief and his advisers openly flaunted their dislike for that champion of land reform Emiliano Zapata, once using federal soldiers to keep the Zapatistas out of Mexico City after the surrender to Huerta. They dismantled Huerta's Ministry of Agriculture, reducing it to an office under Fomento, along with mining, colonization, industrial, and commercial properties, and weights and measures.[16]

Only after Francisco Villa and Zapata had driven them to seek refuge in Veracruz did don Venustiano and his comrades add social and economic planks to the Plan de Guadalupe, the famous "Adiciones" of December, 1914. The Decree of January 6, 1915, essentially dealing with *ejidos,* confirmed a fundamental shift in tactics. By hoisting the banner of agrarian reform, admitted Luis Cabrera, the First Chief strengthened his "military and political position." [17] It was scarcely a metamorphosis in his thinking; he kept his faith in private property, both large and small, limiting the *ejido* to the Indian, hoping that it would encourage him to buy additional land. At no time did he think of the *ejido* as a communal system of land ownership; quite the opposite: each Indian farmer would receive title to his plot of land but with the stipulation that he could not sell it. [18] As late as 1915, the legal-minded rebels contemplated no "confiscation of property." [19]

The Carrancistas harbored not merely an antipathy for enemies of private property, but in the judgement of Saturnino Cedillo, *cacique* of San Luis Potosí, they preferred the company of *hacendados* to peons or radicals. [20] His allegations had the ring of truth. For in reality, the majority of the leading Constitutionalists defended the *hacienda* from attacks by land-hungry dirt farmers, particularly those *hacendados* willing to aid their cause. By May, 1913, Colonel Jacinto Treviño, Carranza's chief of staff, had begun issuing orders protecting the property of friendly *hacendados* from the ire of Constitutionalist commanders and their soldiers. [21] On behalf of José Landero, owner of the Hacienda San Juan Hueyapan in Atotonilco, Carranza himself asked the governor of Hidalgo to protect his properties. Yet Landero, the governor told Carranza, had stolen village lands and behaved with wanton cruelty. [22] In Puebla, an *hacendado* had his lands restored despite evidence that he had taken them from nearby villages and had browbeaten their inhabitants. In 1915, Carranza ordered the military in Chiapas to return all properties to their "legitimate owners," and did the same for San Luis Potosí, apparently at the behest of the Barragán family, *hacendados* and friends of his, and for the Laguna. [23] Once safely in command, the Constitutionalists, in the spring of 1916, turned back all properties seized from their owners. By 1919, all but one planter in the Laguna were "tranquilly tilling their lands"; Carranza, meanwhile, had encouraged him to believe that he, too, would soon again have his lands.[24]

The decision, however, led to tragic and awkward situations and stirred vocal protests. The Hacienda de Tochac, the governor of Tlaxcala reported, had previously been subdivided among the inhabitants of Xalostoc; to exacerbate the difficulty, the military garrison there refused to intervene.[25] In Hidalgo, on the other hand, the order restored the Hacienda de Tepenemé to its owner, although dirt farmers in nearby Actopan had cultivated and planted its lands.[26] One family in Hidalgo received back two *haciendas*.[27] From Sonora, Governor Adolfo de la Huerta objected to turning back the properties of Arturo Morales, a Porfirista faithful and archenemy of the Constitutionalists.[28] In Michoacán, the American Land Company got back the *haciendas* Tamándaro and Cojumatlán—in the face of plans to subdivide them immediately.[29] Not surprisingly, telegrams from grateful *hacendados* flooded offices in Mexico.

The course of national legislation reflected this resurrection of the status quo. With its Circular 14 (January 19, 1917), the National Agrarian Commission, established to implement the distribution of land, had begun to put into effect the Decree of January 6, 1915, dealing essentially with the restitution and dotation of lands to *ejidos*. But, two years later, with Circular 34, the Commission, in a reversal of form, solemnly announced that in the future villages seeking to acquire lands by dotation, of far more importance than restitution to most of them, would have to buy their lands. From then on, if one had not lost lands, or could not prove title to them, one would have to buy them. If this were not done, the Circular proclaimed, the government would be unable to pay the *hacendados* for their lands.[30] At this juncture, the future of land reform looked bleak, for few villages had the money to buy land.[31]

Land reform would be on a "pay as you go basis." To comply with this view, Congress, on January 10, 1920, enacted legislation establishing an agrarian public debt. By it, the government promised to idemnify owners for lands taken for both restitution and dotation. It authorized the sale of 50 million pesos of public bonds bearing 5 percent interest annually over a period of twenty years. Appropriately, the decision to sell the land originally promised by the Decree of January 6, 1915 embodied the intention of the Carrancistas to subdivide *ejidal* lands into private plots. Not until January 26, 1922, however, did the Obregón regime put the law into effect.[32]

Concomitantly, Carranza suspended taxes on rural, urban, and industrial properties in Morelos. Even to General Pablo González, military governor of Morelos and chum of the First Chief, the action seemed foolish. It favored the *hacendados*, but not dirt farmers desperately in need of assistance. Additionally, he pointed out, sharecroppers still had to pay a special fee to the *hacendados*, while state authorities required tax revenues to establish schools and to push ahead with the task of rebuilding Morelos, almost totally devasted by a decade of war.[33]

Such policies hardly brought about the subdivision of the huge *latifundios*. Predictably, they had the opposite effect, safeguarding *hacendados* from land-hungry peasants. During the debates at Querétaro, Manuel Cepeda Medrano, a delegate, reported that in Carranza's home state, the birthplace of the Constitutionalists, a handful of *hacendados* continued to monopolize the land; the dirt farmer was conspicuous by his absence.[34] By 1920, only the villages of Castaños in Coahuila had been blessed with land: 3,511 hectares.[35] Next door in Chihuahua, the story had a similar ending. In 1917, after six years of violence and untold deaths, little had been accomplished to break the monopoly of the *hacendados*. Not until August of that year did the National Agrarian Commission send a representative to Chihuahua. As late as May, 1920, authorities had on only four occasions granted ownership of lands to villages, and at that just "provisionally." These decisions, none ultimately sanctioned, applied to a mere 6,282 hectares.[36] The fate of the enormous *latifundios* of the Terrazas still hung in the balance.[37] The picture in Tamaulipas, Sonora, and Sinaloa was similar.

If government were to provide the villages of Mexico with *ejidos*, calculated Fernando González Roa, an ambitious politician from Sonora, it must expropriate 2,735,000 hectares of land.[38] Yet, to cite figures by Manuel López Gallo, an economic historian, the Carrancistas, since the Decree of January 6, 1915, had distributed a paltry 224,393 hectares of benefit to only 50,000

ejidatarios.[39] Only a tiny fraction of the lands given out had water for irrigation.[40] By 1919, furthermore, just 111,065 hectares
had been dispersed by dotation.[41] Obviously, a small fraction
of the population had received a tiny slice of Mexico's farmland;
the land that changed hands was about one-half of one percent.[42]

A healthy slice of the lands expropriated, moreover, often
belonged to political enemies of the regime, as Carranza himself
acknowledged.[43] The disciples of the Plan de Guadalupe made
no blanket condemnation of *hacendados,* but instead, divided
them into two categories: good and bad, depending, more likely
than not, on their past behavior. The "good" ones, General
Vicente Dávila, governor of San Luis Potosí, explained, had sided
with the Constitutionalists, or at least not with the enemy. "Bad"
hacendados had either smiled on enemies of the Constitutionalists, Francisco Villa for instance,[44] or were notorious scoundrels
of the Porfirista era. One such villain was Iñigo Noriega, a
Spaniard in Tamaulipas with a reputation for having committed every crime in the statute books. Only these offenders,
said Francisco León de la Barra, were denied the return of their
properties.[45] The Carrancistas, apparently, regarded private property as sacred, unless in the hands of landlords of opposing
political views. But, it must not be forgotten, reminds Manual
Calero, that the Constitutionalists, despite their allegiance to the
law, not infrequently tarnished their principles by converting
confiscated property into private wealth.[46]

From his hideout in the sierras of Morelos, an unhappy
Zapata, with just a handful of men at his disposal, watched the
drama unfold. The crimes of the Constitutionalists, which
Zapata laid at the doorstep of Carranza, added up to the betrayal
of the solemn agrarian promise. The labors of rebel chieftains
who had given land to the villages had been sabotaged by
Carranza's decision to restore *haciendas* to their former owners.
An *hacendado* and a "disciple of Porfirio Díaz," don Venustiano
had sided with the landlords against the poor. The peasants were
worse off than before. The promised lands had been denied them,
and to exacerbate their plight, they now had to pay "exorbitant
taxes, suffer the consequences of the breakdown of law and order,
and endure the depradations of the military"; all of this, he
went on, was in addition to the "deplorable administrative and

financial chaos, recurrent economic and financial crises, scandalous ups and downs in the value of paper money, . . . and the alarming rise in the cost of living." At the same time, the National Agrarian Commission did nothing, refusing to handle legal petitions for the restitution of lands. Of over 5,000 requests, complained Zapata, at best the Commission had acted on 300. He scoffed at the idea of satisfying land hunger by subdividing and selling the public lands. Nearly all of them were unfit for farming. To populate them would require the wholesale transfer of Indian villages to distant localities, and the separation of their inhabitants from "the home of their birth, where they had spent their lives, and where they venerated their dead." [47]

Zapata was not alone in his anger. To Salvador Alvarado, one of the Sonora dynasty, the pledges heralded at Veracruz lay discarded. The people still awaited their parcel of land.[48] Or, to cite Antenor Sala, the monopoly of the land by the few continued to keep alive the slavery of the majority.[49] By failing to enforce the postulates of Querétaro, bemoaned Gildardo Magaña, Carranza had mocked the faith of peasants who had fought for him because of their belief in his promises.[50] All the same, as the fiery Antonio Díaz Soto y Gama prophesized, no one could lightly brush aside the rising clamor for land. Along the Pacific slope, from Chiapas to Sinaloa, in Michoacán, Colima, Nayarit, as well as in Morelos, Puebla, and Guerrero, dirt farmers with rifles in their hands had taken to the sierra in open rebellion, flying proudly the banner of agrarian reform.[51]

III

The Plan de Agua Prieta, a call to rebellion remarkable for its silence on the land issue, swung open the political gates to a clan from Sonora destined to rule Mexico until 1935. Politically active since 1911, it had never revealed an inclination to change the world. Since the days of Governor José María Maytorena, an *hacendado* and kindred soul of Madero, this clan from the northwest had exhibited a deep regard for the sanctity of private property. Both Maytorena and his successor, Ignacio Pesqueira, who spoke for a group of rebels that included Alvaro Obregón, took care not to trifle with property rights. They headed a revolt against Victoriano Huerta, not against the social order. After coming home from exile in Arizona, Maytorena had invited *hacendados* who, like himself had fled the state, to return and resume the cultivation of their lands, merely asking that they support the war against Huerta. By the same token, a bill introduced in the state legislature, demanding the restitution to former owners of lands acquired fraudently by the *hacendados*, met a quiet death.[52] In the meantime, with Obregón in the lead, enterprising rebels began to carve out landed empires for the cultivation of garbanzos to export.

None better than Obregón epitomized the world of the Sonora dynasty. Yet only in degree did he differ with Carranza, the recently deposed *caudillo;* after all, not until 1919, when don Venustiano mistakenly cast his ballot against him, had the man from Huatabampo clashed with his mentor. The garbanzo lord dealt gently with his kin. In a speech to the *hacendados* of Jalisco, Obregón had underlined the impossibility of solving the agarian problem with unrealistic solutions. This was interpreted by the *hacendados* to mean a pledge by the Sonora *caudillo* to respect private property. Laws could not bring about the desired result if they were out of harmony with logic. The reform of the rural structure could not be brought about by passing laws limiting the size of private property. Such efforts would merely hurt national income, undermine agriculture, and damage the entire country. The future of Mexico required a healthy agriculture.[53]

The solution, said Obregón, lay in the modernization of agriculture, bringing to it the benefits of science. It was imperative to introduce up-to-date technology, to mechanize farming, and to diversify what was planted, but always with an eye on heavy yield crops and on large markets. It required the conquest of desert lands, tropical marshes, and the cultivation of regions hitherto thought unfit for agriculture. To build irrigation canals —to dam the flow of rivers, and to water the fields with engine-driven pumps—is what must be done. As an incentive to modernize, Obregón dangled before the *hacendados* a pledge to safeguard their properties; he would take lands only from the unproductive *haciendas*. This policy would provide, he said, a truce for *ha-*

cendados willing to employ new methods as well as stimulus to improve the condition of agriculture.[54]

The goal, nevertheless, was to stimulate the growth of small, private farms. But the process, as spelled out by Obregón, was neither simple nor quickly achievable. The path ahead was long and labyrinthian. "I am an advocate of the small farm," he explained, "because I believe in helping those who want to help themselves rise above their penurious situation." The vow, strangely, had a quixotic ring: to enact agrarian reform by protecting private property. "In no way," stated the Man from Huatabampo, "do I believe that the *hacienda* should be broken up before the development of small-scale agriculture has occurred." Nor would he look kindly upon the use of violence and plunder to achieve that goal. It bespoke foolishness to divide up the productive units of an *hacienda* among different individuals: its manor house, wells, and lands. That would simply destroy its productive capacity without benefiting anyone. The first step was to build a system of efficient small farms that, ultimately, would out-produce the *haciendas*.[55] Lamentably, Obregón never fully explained how he would create small farms without taking fertile lands away from the *hacendados*.

Obregón, in actuality, had no ready answer, partly because he lacked confidence in the humble dirt farmer. The "great majority of our poor," he assured the *hacendados* in Guadalajara, "have no inkling of what thrift is; they can gather a harvest but not save for another." [56] If the *haciendas* were broken up, much of their lands would go to waste because of the technical ineptitude or the negligence of their owners. The drop in farm productivity would be fatal for Mexico.[57] Give land, "but do it gradually"—was his recommendation.[58] In this manner, eventually the villages would get back their *ejidos*. To allay the fears of the *hacendados,* who viewed with alarm any such suggestion, Obregón hastened to add that he had limited goals: just certain types of communities would have the right to solicit lands, and everything would be done according to the letter of the law. For awhile, Obregón contemplated giving a small plot of land, taken from the unproductive *haciendas,* to those willing to till it, but discarded the idea by 1922. Ultimately, his regime, says Narcisco Bassols Batalla, became identified with Mexicans who objected to the disappearance of the *hacienda* and to the formation of a different system of property. Land reform for the Obregonistas, as it was for the Carrancistas, became a pacification gimmick.[59] "Future revolutions," as Plutarco Elías Calles, a high priest of the Sonora dynasty, learned, "would be averted by converting the rural wage worker, the *campesino,* into a small property holder."

The ideals of the Obregonistas, needless to say, hardly assuaged the apostles of reform. To Díaz Soto y Gama, the juxtaposition of small property with the defense of the *hacienda* staggered belief; the two stood at loggerheads. Socratic logic had been turned upside down. "The objective" was "to destroy the big estates, but the big estates cannot be destroyed before small property is a fact; but since small property cannot yet be created, the big estates cannot be destroyed." [60] Further, added Bassols Batalla, to believe that social injustices could be rectified merely by restoring rights trampled afoot since colonial days, without taking steps to reorganize the life of the peasant and of agriculture, was foolhardy.[61] By the same token, how would modern technology and machinery transform the *haciendas* of owners accustomed to using cheap labor, tilling the land with primitive methods, and lacking individual initiative—especially in times of violence and disorder? To Bassols Batalla, the longer land reform was postponed, the tougher it would be to carry out.[62]

Not illogically, men with the ambivalent attitudes of the Sonora clan left behind a mixed legislative record. By and large, it went beyond the conservative laws of the Carranza era; it often had a progressive if ambiguous stamp. Objectives were not always clearly spelled out nor, evidently, always the same. Legislative changes began in June, 1920, with a law declaring of public benefit the cultivation of all arable land; it empowered the government to seize and temporarily cultivate lands left idle by their owners. Unhappily, its enforcement proved impossible.[63] On December 20 of that year, Congress enacted a Ley de Ejidos, codifying earlier *circulares,* including stipulations exempting from expropriation up to fifty hectares of irrigated land. But the legislation, as well as adopting cumbersome and lengthy procedures, banned the provisional restitution and dotation of land.

From then on, villages would receive land only after authorities had arrived at a final verdict. This measure further postponed the acquisition of land by the landless. A public outcry against it compelled Congress to abrogate it (November, 1921) and to write a law that, among other stipulations, established Procuradurías de Pueblos, legal offices designed to help peasants, especially illiterate Indians, to acquire land. Meanwhile, on March 5, 1921, Circular 44 of the National Agrarian Commission nullified Circular 34 requiring that peasants buy their lands.[64]

In the Reglamento Agrario (April, 1922), the Obregonistas outlined their views on the *ejido,* its beneficiaries, and its role in society. The legislation fixed the size of the plots of land to be given through dotation to heads of families or individuals eighteen years or older. These were lands over which village had no prior claim: for irrigated lands, three to five hectares; for seasonal (with abundant and regular rainfall), four to six hectares; and for other types (dry), six to eight hectares. Inhabitants of villages within eight kilometers of a city or town, a railroad, or in the proximity of communities with equal rights to land would receive the minimal number of hectares stipulated in the three categories. The Reglamento Agrario, like the Decree of January 6, 1915, did not envisage an *ejidal* plot large enough to support its occupant without need of an outside job for at least a part of the year, more often than not on a neighboring *hacienda.* The *ejido* would simply provide a minimum income for the *ejidatario* and his family. Likewise, the *ejidatario* near a railroad or a city could do with less land.

In the interval, article 14 of the Reglamento Agrario calmed the anxieties of *hacendados.* It exempted from expropriation irrigated lands of 150 hectares or less, but also seasonal lands (with abundant and regular rainfall) of less than 250 hectares and lands of other types (dry) under 500 hectares. More important, it placed in an untouchable category "all properties, which by their character, are working agro-industrial units." Planters in this category could decide what lands to cede when faced with demands for land from their neighbors.[65] This law, Obregón explained, protected the owners of sugar mills in Morelos, and he might have added, planters in the Laguna and Yucatán—as well as in Sonora.[66] Still, from the perspective of Felipe Carrillo Puerto, the Socialist governor of Yucatán, the Reglamento Agrario, besides safeguarding the lands of *hacendados,* stood at odds with Article 27 of the Constitution.[67]

The family rift within the Sonora clan, with Adolfo de la Huerta in rebellion against his erstwhile *compadres,* set the stage for one final legislative statute. Significantly, the Decree of August 2, 1923, a political ploy designed to insure the loyalty of dirt farmers in the face of rebellion, unabashedly acknowledged the failure to implement the earlier agrarian promises. Merely with the restitution and dotation of *ejidos,* it stated, had there been progress. But the small, private farm, the cherished goal of the Obregonistas, languished. In the meantime, countless dirt farmers, unable to till their own lands or to find work, left Mexico for the United States. A small clique still enjoyed a monopoly of the land, and with it, control over the lives of the rural worker. To stop the flight from Mexico and redeem past pledges, the legislation authorized the immediate occupation and colonization of the Republic's *tierras baldías.* Every Mexican eighteen years of age or older could occupy and claim 25 hectares of irrigated land, up to 100 hectares of prime seasonal land, and up to 500 hectares of dry land. To obtain title to them, he had to cultivate them for two years and prove that they were not private property or ejidal lands. For all that, the legislation yielded meager results. A majority of the landless never heard of the decree; others lacked funds to cultivate the lands; and, more to the point, nearly all of the public lands were unfit for agriculture.[68]

Appropriately, no Obregonista lifted a finger to rectify the glaring omission in Article 27 denying *peones acasillados,* workers living on the *haciendas,* the right to petition for the lands they tilled. Yet, until this was done, most of the *haciendas* would survive, a fact not overlooked by Obregón. If the rights of *peones acasillados* were incorporated into the Reglamento Agrario, Obregón predicted dire results for agriculture. No *hacendado* would invest a single penny if he knew beforehand that "after digging irrigation canals, clearing the land for planting, and building his home, the workers he had hired to do the job had the right to ask the government to grant them the land as an *ejido.*" That, he said, was why the Constitution had denied this right—an argument that in no way explained why its reform was unnecessary.[69]

IV

Politics make strange bedfellows. Nonetheless, those who lie between the same sheets do not for long remain unaware of their odd companions. So it was with the apostles of agrarian reform who mistook the Obregonistas for kinfolk. Such was the experience of Miguel Mendoza López Schwertfeger, secretary of the National Agrarian Commission, whose sympathies for Zapata's ideals cost him his job with the Obregonistas.

Wanting to hasten the pace of land distribution, Mendoza López, with the backing of his companions on the National Agrarian Commission, had, in a Circular dated November 16, 1922, cut the time required for the allotment of *ejidal* lands. As he pointed out, only 546 allotments had been approved since the promulgation of the Decree of January 6, 1915. To end the bottleneck, the Circular, designed specifically for Durango, but with obvious implications for the entire Republic, asked agrarian officials to draw up, in the space of one month, a list of the inhabitants in Durango eligible to own land; to locate the lands earmarked for expropriation; and to subdivide them immediately, parceling them out with titles of temporary ownership. The Circular exempted small property from its provisions.[70]

He had written the Circular, Mendoza López told Obregón, because of the dire plight of the dirt farmer who, having petitioned for land, was denied work by the *hacendados*. Unless changes were made, the farmer would continue to suffer the ire of the powerful. Moreover, at the current rate of land distribution, it would take at least 200 years to settle the *ejidal* problem alone. In the interval, the *hacendados,* fearful of losing their lands, left them untilled, while peasants lucky enough to get land but uncertain of the future of their ownership, did the same. As a result, large tracts of land lay fallow. To settle the problem once and for ever, it was imperative to subdivide and distribute the land and to get on with the work of growing food.[71]

But, the Circular lacked Obregón's endorsement. In addition, *hacendados,* politicians, and other enemies of land reform in the Laguna, where the Circular was read, quickly made their unhappiness public. Andrés Molina Enríquez, the touted architect of Article 27, even accused Mendoza López of harboring communist sympathies.[72] As bands of dirt farmers began to invade the cotton plantations of the Laguna, their owners appealed to politicians and the military for aid. When Governor Jesús Agustín Castro wired Obregón for instructions, the reply left no doubt that Obregón neither approved of the Circular nor sympathized with it.[73] At the same time, Obregón ordered General Pablo Rodríguez, the local army boss, to take whatever measures were required to stop violations of private property.[74] The distribution of land must proceed according to "the precepts of law and reason." [75] With Obregón adamantly opposed to it, the Circular met a quick death; villages that had acquired land had to return it; and Mendoza López, its author, fell from grace.[76] Ironically, during the interval, the peasant leagues of Durango had wired their thanks to Obregón for the Circular; and from Guerrero news arrived notifying him of the popular glee that greeted the Circular and the anguish over its demise.[77] All the same, in the Laguna, with the return of the lands to the planters, Governor Castro laconically informed Obregón, "life . . . had gotten back to normal." [78]

Similarly, as the story of the ill-dated Circular documents, the Sonora dynasty worshipped law and order. Land reform must proceed legally.[79] Despite their revolutionary veneer, the men from the northwest wanted the lords of the lands to prevail. Yet law and order, hailed as the golden rule for every Mexican, in practice suffered from blind spots. The law was not always all things to all men. At the bar of justice, the scales tipped in favor of the rich and powerful. Confronted with an "illegal" occupation of his lands, an *hacendado* could invariably count on help from Obregón. Such was his response to a plea from *hacendados* confronted with the attempts of jobless workers to occupy lands in the Laguna. The workers, fortified with the Decree of August 2, 1923, sanctioning the colonization of *tierras baldías,* had taken over lands on the banks of the Nazas and Aguanaval rivers.[80] But, the lords of the Laguna insisted that the entire region belonged to them. Agitators had incited the "worst elements" of the towns and cities of the Laguna to mock the law. The cotton industry of the Laguna, they reminded Obregón, contributed 40 percent of the state revenues of both Durango and Coahuila. With a straight face, they assured Obregón that there were no *hacendados* in the Laguna for the land was owned by large numbers of persons.[81] Regardless of the self-serving testimony of the planters, nonetheless, not only did *haciendas* exist but the "invasions" had occurred following the stipulations of the law, with the blessings of the ministry of Agriculture and the labor office—as Obregón himself acknowledged in his blistering reprimand to the labor inspector in the Laguna. The law did not sanction "anarchy" of this sort, he said.[82] A few days later, soldiers of General Alejandro Mange were busily ridding the land of its invaders.[83] A grateful band of planters applauded "unreservedly" these "just and patriotic measures." [84]

On the other hand, pleas from villages for the enforcement of the law fared less well. A response from Obregón to the *presidente municipal* of Aljojuca, Puebla, spoke eloquently about this official ambiguity. "The *hacendado* threatens to destroy our crops on *ejidal* lands given us," stated the telegram from Aljojuca. "We ask that the law be upheld." [85] But Obregón, in a brief rejoinder, merely stated that he had forwarded the complaint to the governor of Puebla, whose duty it was to enforce the law. When a group of dirt farmers, in mortal terror of an *hacendado* who had hired armed thugs to thrash them for daring to petition for his lands, traveled to Mexico City at tremendous personal sacrifice to beg for help, Obregón refused to talk to them.[86] "Most of your complaints and fears," he lectured another band of villagers in a similar predicament, "take as the truth the immorality of public officials, their complicity with *hacendados,* and allegations that the law favors the rich"; but, he reflected philosophically, this was not the fault of the law. To the contrary, "these were essentially the vices of human nature because, unfortunately, only a tiny minority of men can resist the temptation to profit personally." [87]

Human nature notwithstanding, the danger to peasants from *hacendados* reluctant to relinquish their lands was real. Obregón's gratuitous sermon hardly made more unpalatable the harsh reality of rural life. Since the days of Victoriano Huerta (and

Díaz), *hacendados* had increasingly hired rifle-toting thugs to shield their properties from the landless. These private armies, in the eyes of the poor dirt farmer, bore the sign of the devil himself. To Díaz Soto y Gama, they were the bane of rural Mexico, particularly in Michoacán, the state of Mexico, and sadly in Coahuila, site of the Plan de Guadalupe. Dirt farmers in Guanajuato lived in terror of these brigands. The Revolution, Soto y Gama mourned, instead of putting a stop to their atrocities, had condoned them. Recently, he told Obregón, the leader of one of these gangs of ruffians had murdered five dirt farmers and hung their bodies in the public squares of a village in Michoacán—as a warning to peasants not to ask for land.[88] All the same, countless *agraristas,* dirt farmers who asked for land, forgotten by the law, awaited their fate in provincial jails.[89]

Without the law to defend their legal rights to land, dirt farmers, to the chagrin of the *hacendados,* armed themselves. But Obregón and his friends did not look kindly upon armed peasants who took the law into their own hands. The De la Huerta rebellion, however, postponed efforts to disarm them, and it was not until May, 1924, that Obregón asked the military to do so.[90] The law, curiously, left a loophole, permitting the keeping of arms for the defense of the home, although banning their collective use. A person could keep a rifle in his home, but not use it in company with his neighbors to protect his lands.[91] Not surprisingly, a confused governor of Oaxaca wanted Obregón to clarify what he meant.[92] Both *hacendados* and dirt farmers, nonetheless, took the order to mean the disarming of peasant groups. And that is how it ended, with *hacendados* thanking Obregón for his ruling while the peasants lost their weapons.[93] For the decision, as Calles and others recognized, left dirt farmers at the mercy of the bullies of the *hacendados.*[94] The rulers of Mexico in 1924 bespoke politics markedly at odds with an editorial in *La Voz de Zacatecas,* warning that to "disarm peasants would bring the defeat of the Revolution." [95]

The government of Obregón, like its predecessor, also returned *haciendas* to their owners. For Obregón, this was not an entirely novel procedure. After all, as military chief of the Constitutionalists he had restored to their owners *haciendas* confiscated by Villa. This defense of property rights, nevertheless, excluded the Yaquis in Sonora who, to regain their lands, had gambled their lives with the rebels. But, when they insisted on the return of their lands, Obregón had sent General Manuel Diéguez in pursuit of them. To accede to their demands, pontificated Obregón, would be to "sanction . . . the survival of barbarism and to give them control" of lands now exposed to "civilization." [96] Calles, the sidekick of Obregón and military boss of Sonora, even briefly revived the deportation policy of the Old Regime. [97]

NINETEEN

The Meager Harvest

---

*"Let's give up those fields to the peasants. After all, it is
land that can only be dry-farmed. You will lose very little.
We give it up, so that the Indians will go on raising merely
patch-crops. And you will see that when they are obligated
to us, they'll leave their patches to be hoed by their women,
and return to working our irrigated fields for wages. Look:
you pass for a hero of agrarian reform, and it costs you
nothing."*

Carlos Fuentes, La Muerte de Artemio Cruz

I

AT THE CLOSE of years of revolutionary rhetoric, whatever
the gains, of laws and constitutional statutes pledging
to revamp the pattern of land ownership, the landless
only marginally savored victory. When Alvaro Obregón abandoned Mexico City to look after his garbanzos in Sonora, for the
rural poor, the harvest, at best, was meager. Statistics, notoriously
unreliable and contradictory, nevertheless clearly reveal little
official enthusiasm for drastic measures. From 1920 to 1921, they
show a gentle upswing in land redistribution. During this interlude, government distributed 142,182 hectares of land by restitution and 435,757 by dotation to 229 villages with a population
of approximately 250,000 inhabitants. This was almost twice the
amount of land distributed under the Carranza administration
since the promulgation of the Decree of January 6, 1915. In 1922
however, a decline set in with only 92 definitive grants of land,
and 77 the following year, with another 50 still pending. The
De la Huerta rebellion, which erupted at this juncture, jarred

the Obregonistas out of their complacency. Obregón's report to Congress in 1924, the last of his four messages, revealed a sharp statistical increase. According to his figures, the government had approved 233 resolutions, granting title to 311,939 hectares of land and provisional ownership to 751,125 hectares. All told, his administration, in its four years in office, had stamped its approval on 650 resolutions totaling approximately 1,170,000 hectares of land. If the 3,250,000 hectares given out under provisional ownership were included, boasted Obregón, 400,000 Mexicans had shared in the bonanza.[1]

Statistics notwithstanding, none dwelt on the number of *latifundios* broken up. Did Mexico have fewer *haciendas* in 1924? Or, equally significant, how much and what kinds of lands had the *haciendas* actually lost? Were the villages endowed with fertile, irrigated lands? In reality, no attempt had been made to confiscate the *haciendas,* to strike, to recall the phrase of one observer, while the revolutionary iron was hot.[2] Because of that failure, in large measure, the lands of Mexico still remained in the hands of a small minority. Statistics, meanwhile, followed a curious trajectory, almost always in response to political pressures. Of the 650 final grants of land, 229 were in the first year of Obregón's administration, undoubtedly in answer to the need to court dirt farmers in order to achieve peace in the countryside. Once achieved, the curve dipped sharply, to only 92 final grants in 1922 and to 77 in 1923. With half of the army rebelling, the curve rose dramatically in 1924, with 233 final *resoluciones.* Caught between the demands for land from the villages, on the one hand, and the resistance of the *hacendados,* on the other, the Obregón regime had vacillated, marching off in contradictory directions depending upon the political situation. The pattern of land distribution confirmed that there was no firm commitment to the principle of land reform.

Moreover, laws enacted to speed land reform, as Obregón himself acknowledged, had had legal obstacles placed in their path.[3] One such statute was the *amparo,* the injunction. At Querétaro, delegates who had voted enthusiastically for land reform, with like determination had adopted guarantees for private property. According to Article 14 of the Constitution, no law could be employed retroactively at the expense of an individual.

Nobody could be deprived of life, liberty, or property without due recourse to law. Out of this came the controversial right of *amparo*. A legal precept dating from the Decree of January 6, 1915, the *amparo* gave the landlord the right to appeal to the courts any decision by agrarian authorities affecting his property.[4] It was used, José G. Parres, a recent governor of Morelos said, regularly by *hacendados* to undercut agrarian legislation. It became common practice for landlords to demand from the courts, under the guise of individual rights, protection for their property. Unhappily, Parres charged, the *amparo* left the decision to local judges who, either mistakenly or maliciously, frequently sabotaged the intent of agrarian legislation to the detriment of the poor. In the state of Mexico alone, according to Parres, *hacendados* had asked the courts for 115 *amparos*.[5]

At best, the legal requirements for the granting of land were cumbersome and time consuming. First, the local agrarian commission must approve the petition of the village; if the governor of the state endorsed the recommendation to grant land, the village enjoyed provisional ownership. At this point, the National Agrarian Commission had to review the decision, and if in accord, forward it to the president of the Republic for his signature. He could, of course, reject it. At any time during the course of this lengthy process, the landlord had the right to appeal the decision to the courts. Only after he had either neglected to appeal, or the courts had denied his petition for an *amparo*, did the village receive "firm and irrevocable" title to the land. But, with his right of *amparo*, the *hacendado* had recourse to the entire lineup of federal courts, from the local Juez de Distrito to the Supreme Court. To make matters worse, the Juez de Distrito was not uncommonly a friend of the *hacendado*, and his judgment often reflected it. Yet even Gustavo A. Vicencio, the Chief Justice of the Supreme Court, was far from impartial, urging Obregón in 1922 to halt the granting of land on a provisional basis.[6] Had Obregón listened to him, villages would have to wait for their lands until the entire legal and administrative rigmarole was completed.[7]

Revolutions, by their nature, are set in motion by apostles of drastic change, not by disciples of law and order. The two stand in opposite corners; a law-abiding revolution is a fantasy.

Nonetheless, that is what the Mexicans set out to have. Giving the enemies of social change recourse to the law, nevertheless, quickly put a brake on land reform, thereby making a revolution impossible. As Carlos M. Peralta, the agent in charge of subdividing the Terrazas's estates in Chihuahua, noted, the law (the *amparo*) had torpedoed his attempts at agrarian reform. His efforts to subdivide the *haciendas* San Diego and Tapiecitas near Casa Grandes, he complained, had vanished when their owners, the Corralitos Land Company, obtained an *amparo* from the local court.[8]

The trials and tribulations of Aldama, a village in Chihuahua, is a dramatic example of the use of the *amparo* as a barrier to land reform. The drama eventually had a large cast of characters: the inhabitants of Aldama, *hacendados,* agrarian officials, and the governor of Chihuahua. Additionally, the struggle between Aldama and neighboring *hacendados* involved both clashes over land and water rights to the Rió Chuviscar, a conflict exacerbated by a drought.

The conflict began when Aldama asked for additional lands to supplement its meager holdings. According to the state agrarian commission, the lands it owned were both insufficient to meet its needs, and because they were arid, useless for farming. The village could use them only for pasture. To aggravate the picture, 627 heads of families lacked land. Agrarian officials, in their report to the governor, recommended that lands be given Aldama from the nearby *haciendas:* Dolores, with 90,000 hectares; Hormigas, with 175,000; Encinillas, with 702,000; and Tabalaopa, with 33,000.[9] The recommendation ignited the powder keg. During the course of the litigation that grew voluminously, three *amparos* were granted, two to Martín Falomir and Benjamín Elías, the owners of the *haciendas* Dolores and Tabalaopa, and one to Armando Gameros, the *presidente municipal* of Aldama, who sided with the *hacendados*. Gameros' stance, illogical at first glance, in reality mirrored the decision of his boss, the governor of Chihuahua, General Ignacio C. Enríquez, a politician unsympathetic to land reform, to back the *hacendados*. No less important, Gameros belonged to a family of *hacendados* in the state, a not uncommon relationship for *presidentes municipales* at that time.

A friend of Obregón, Enríquez, had dispatched *rurales* to teach Aldama a lesson. On August 20, 1922, a band of forty of them invaded the village; one of their leaders, Captain Manuel M. Arzate, a landlord himself, had previously staked out claims to its lands. The *rurales,* the inhabitants of Aldama complained to Obregón, "on horseback and with rifles in hand ran our animals off, filled our wells with dirt, and destroyed our farming equipment." All of this, said Ramón P. DeNegri, the subsecretary of the ministry of agriculture, had indeed occurred.[10] Meanwhile, the villagers, evidently distrustful of Obregón, had also appealed to Francisco Villa, the ancient enemy of the Man from Huatabampo and now master of the nearby *hacienda* of Canutillo, for help. Villa, with his customary bluntness, accused Enríquez of deliberately endangering the peace of Chihuahua and angrily demanded that Obregón protect Aldama's rights. Arzate and his troublemakers, to cite Villa, had gone on a rampage, despite "the pleas and tears of the terrified women and children." [11] Villa's message elicited a promise from Obregón to look into the matter.[12]

A few days later, Julio S. Prieto, the agronomist sent to study the problem, endorsed the recommendation of the state agrarian commission that Aldama be given land. Martín Falomir who, with his brother José stood to lose 14,760 hectares, asked Obregón to cancel the award, declaring that Aldama did not need extra lands.[13] However, on November 23, 1922, an *acuerdo* of the National Agrarian Commission signed by Obregón, granted 29,490 hectares of the land to Aldama, leaving the *hacendados* with only the right to demand just payment for the lands lost.[14]

One month later, nevertheless, the Juez Segundo de lo Civil in the District of Morelos issued an *amparo* to Martín Falomir and another to Elías, one of the owners of the Hacienda Tabalaopa. Both *hacendados* argued that the ruling by the agrarian authorities violated Article 14 of the Constitution, specifying that "no one can be deprived of life, liberty, or property" without due recourse to the law. At this juncture, Aldama and the agrarian officials had to go back to the courts in order to get the Juez de Distrito de Chihuahua to revoke the *amparo*.[15] Yet, despite the legal victory, the *rurales* did not let up on their harassment of Aldama, compelling its inhabitants to arm themselves for their own defense since Obregón, in the interval, had denied them the protection of the military. As Obregón was leaving office in 1924, an armed band of fifty men had just attacked Aldama again, while the new governor of Chihuahua, J. A. Almeida, who, like Enríquez, wept for the *hacendados,* was thinking of asking the courts for an *amparo* against Aldama.[16]

But the *amparo* was merely one of a number of tactics called into service by the *hacendados* to sabotage land reform. Another, as the experience of Aldama documents, was the use of terror to discourage villagers from asking for land. The *hacendados* paid armed thugs to drive those daring to petition for land from their homes and even to kill their leaders. Moreover, the *hacendados* refused to hire peasants who had asked for land, leaving them without the means to feed their families. Thus, because of the length of time required to obtain legal title to land, many refused to ask for it for fear of bringing the wrath of the *hacendados* down upon their heads. These tactics, of course, worked well only during the interim when the villagers merely had provisional ownership, one reason why the *hacendados* badgered Obregón to end the provisional allocation of land. For once title to the land had been confirmed, there was little the *hacendados* could do. Still, as in the case of Aldama, even legal title did not always put an end to the chicanery of the *hacendados* and their allies.

To further circumvent the law, the *hacendados* devised other schemes. A common one was to claim that they had voluntarily subdivided their lands among their workers. But, as Andrés Molina Enríquez pointed out, it was a subterfuge for the theoretical owners were the employees and workers on the *hacienda* who, in return for a monetary bribe, had agreed to lend their names to the hoax, and later, when the "heat was off," to give back their plots to the *hacendado.*[17] Others "split up" their *haciendas* among the family and relatives: sons, daughters, sisters, uncles, and aunts and all manner of kin thus appeared as the legal owners of small parcels of land.[18] Given these tactics, and the vacillation of the administration, it was no wonder that a large majority of *hacendados* kept their lands. In the fertile

Laguna, for instance, DeNegri informed Obregón, the owners of over a million hectares were the ones who were leading the fight to deny access to the landless to lands on the banks of the Río Nazas.[19]

Additionally, the *hacendados* waged a heavy propaganda campaign designed to appeal to the conservative proclivities of Mexico's rulers, as well as to frighten them from pushing ahead with the dissolution of the *haciendas.* Supposedly the battle against agrarian reform was not just on behalf of the sanctity of private property, but of like significance, for the public welfare. As the powerful Cámara de Comercio, Industria y Minería de Nuevo León, with headquarters in Monterrey pontificated, the rulings of the National Agrarian Commission were "killing agriculture." With the threat of expropriation hanging over their heads, farmers had no incentive to till their lands. The moment public officials denied the "sacredness of property," faith in government collapsed, and all work came to a halt.[20] To restore confidence in government, Guillermo Pous, president of the Sindicato Nacional de Agricultores, mouthpiece for the *hacendados,* told Obregón that it was absolutely essential to recognize the sanctity of private property and to expropriate only in cases of "true public utility, and then with prior idemnification, to be determined by the courts on the basis of expert testimony." Pous urged the return of all property taken without due process of law and the repeal of Section VII of Article 27, giving state and local governments the right to acquire land for public use.[21] Of course, none of this meant, according to Ramón Sánchez Albarrán, a successor of Pous, that *hacendados,* "public minded men of order, had ever been or were enemies of government." [22]

To aggravate the plight of the landless dirt farmer, their advocates split into two warring camps over whether to stress the distribution of land in the form of *ejidos* or as small parcels of private property. This was an old question, dating back at least a decade. At the time of the Plan de Agua Prieta, friends of the *ejido,* under the dynamic leadership of Antonio Díaz Soto y Gama, had organized the Partido Nacional Agrarista. In 1922, small property advocates, including Molina Enríquez, and ironically, the former Zapatista Gildardo Magaña, formed La

Confederación Nacional Agraria; its goal was the growth of small private property, the size to depend on the nature of the land and the availability of water for irrigation. In some cases, it urged the subdivision of the *hacienda* into *ranchos,* plots of land beyond the ability of the owner to cultivate and plant alone. It asked that federal authorities be entrusted with the care and health of the *ejido,* but wanted small property under the jurisdiction of the states. At its founding, it had applauded Pastor Rouaix, then minister of agriculture under Carranza, for asking that villages pay the *hacendados* for lands received as *ejidos.* While endorsing the subdivision of *haciendas,* on the one hand, it denied, on the other, as it affirmed to the Sindicato Nacional de Agricultores in 1924, any intention of "bringing ruin to the *hacendados* with the subdivision." [23]

Leaders of the Confederación, generally unsympathetic to the use of expropriation, threw their weight on behalf of the adoption of tax policies designed to encourage *hacendados* to sell lands left uncultivated.[24] By this manner, a class of small farmers could be formed without the necessity of government having to bear an onerous public debt. *Ejidos,* by the same token, would be allotted only to villages that in the past had held their lands in common, a small segment of the population and almost entirely Indian.[25] The Carrancistas, particularly Luis Cabrera, had shared a similar vision. The more militant Partido Nacional Agrarista pressed for the distribution of land to *ejidos* by expropriating the large estates, asked the government to bear the brunt of the cost, placed less emphasis on small property, and lobbied incessantly for the cause of the *campesino.* Its members flatly rejected attempts to subdivide the *ejidos* into small private property that, as José Obregón, an older brother of the president, had acknowledged, put their owners at a tremendous disadvantage when competing with *hacendados.* The plantations with large tracts of land to farm, with modern equipment, and with access to ample credit, could easily out produce and out sell them. Only by working their lands in common could *ejidatarios* hope to compete.[26]

Ultimately, Obregón's regime adopted the pay-as-you-go policy of the Carranza years, the position upheld by the Confederación Nacional Agraria. With its activities in Chihuahua, the Caja de Préstamos, the forerunner of the Banco de Crédito Agrícola, a bank organized to encourage the growth of small private farms, began to sell parcels of land to eligible buyers. But the lands sold, formerly parts of the Terrazas' *latifundio,* had already been allotted by agrarian authorities to the villages as *ejidos.* Under this policy, the buyers purchased their plots from the *hacendado,* with the Caja serving as the intermediary.[27] From the beginning, unfortunately, charges of graft and chicanery plagued the history of the Caja. Its officials, according to General Abelardo Rodríguez, president of Mexico a decade later, took advantage of the subdivision of the Terrazas estates to personally cash in on the transaction, selling the plots at a profit.[28] According to information given by the inhabitants of Nueva Delicias, a farming community carved out of lands formerly owned by the Terrazas, agents of the Caja had gone so far as to demand a percentage of the profits from the harvests, while cutting the lumber they wanted to sell from its forests.[29] Governor Enríquez accused the officials of the Caja of holding on to the Hacienda Santa Gertrudis and of refusing to subdivide it.[30] In Nayarit, in a parallel case, the Caja had taken over the Hacienda de San Lorenzo, once the property of Barron Forbes, and reported its administrator, asked natives of El Venado and Puerto de Platanares, neighboring communities, to pay rent on the land they farmed. But, the *hacienda's* administrator said, even the Díaz regime had recognized their titles to these lands. From his perspective, the neighbors had been better off under Díaz.[31]

II

The success of land reform nearly always required the cooperation of state officials who, in the opinion of Parres, played key roles. But Obregón, like Carranza, often had cautious and conservative men in the statehouses: Pascual Ortiz Rubio in Michoacán; Arellano Valle in Aguascalientes; Basilio Vadillo in Jalisco, where *hacendados* still paid fifty centavos for a day of toil stretching from sunrise to sunset; the governor of Puebla, who lobbied with members of his state agrarian commission on behalf of *hacendados* and employed his authority to staff it with men willing to do his bidding; Jesús Agustín Castro of Durango, a state boss who took pride in his ability to keep both the landless and *hacendados* "happy"; the governor of Chiapas who, said his detractors, headed an administration with "only personal gain" for a goal; F. C. Manjárrez in Puebla, noted for his willingness to overrule his agrarian commission; and the head of the territory of Tepic, who permitted the *hacendados* to pay *guardias blancas* to defend their lands.[32] In 1922, according to Gilberto Fabela, a congressman, a group of governors had pooled their talents to stop the further distribution of land. It included Enríquez in Chihuahua, César López de Lara in Tamaulipas, Amado Azuara in Hidalgo, and Antonio Madrazo in Michoacán.[33] Politicians cool or hostile to agrarian reform served under them, and held important posts in the national government. Only the vocal opposition of agrarian and labor militants stopped the appointment of Fortunato Dozal, subsecretary of the ministry of agriculture and a friend of *hacendados,* to oversee the subdivision of the Terrazas estates in 1923.[34]

Petitions for land languished for years in the hands of these officials. Because of their indifference or hostility, a condition aggravated by red tape and bureaucratic inefficiency, countless demands for dotation and restitution never reached the desks of the National Agrarian Commission. This brought widespread dismay and discontent, reported DeNegri, acting head of the Ministry of Agriculture in 1923.[35] Local *políticos,* in the opinion of Parres, openly sided with *hacendados,* helping them to undercut the intent of legislation. In the state of Mexico, an example used by Parres, authorities, instead of giving land in common as the *ejidal* law stipulated, sold it in private plots. The hostility of the governor to agrarian reform filtered down to the municipal officials. Few of them, Parres claimed, had not been suborned by the *hacendados.* To exacerbate matters for the poor, a plague of hungry *caciques* had fallen on the *ejidatarios* like birds of prey. Given the outlines of the picture, not surprisingly state agrarian officials had left unresolved 349 of the 445 petitions for land, some dating back to 1915.[36]

Also alarming, only 13 titles of final ownership had been approved in ten years; the other 83 resolutions had merely granted provisional ownership. In an "absolute state of limbo," that is, neglected and ignored, were 233 petitions. This lamentable situation, Parres concluded, authenticated how little interest state authorities had taken in the performance of their agrarian officials.[37]

LAND DISTRIBUTION, MEXICO STATE [38]

Year	Petitions
1915	43
1916	61
1917	66
1918	31
1919	13
1920	26
1921	95
1922	25
1923	52
1924	33
Total	445

The problems of Mexico State were not unique. Other provinces of the Republic had similar ones. Guanajuato was one of them. There, as the people of Uriangato patiently explained to Obregón, "if he [Obregón] did not compel local authorities to obey the law, the agrarian problem of Guanajuato would outlive all of them."[39] Obregón "must" intervene, declared a congressman from the state, because, he went on, some 100 petitions for land lay gathering dust in official archives. Yet, despite this backlog of cases, the National Agrarian Commission had eliminated half of its agronomists assigned to handle the problems of Guanajuato, while its delegate, along with the *procurador de pueblos*, blocked the petitions for land.[40] Some of the villages of Guanajuato had been asking for land since 1915.[41] Statistics on land distribution corroborated the criticism. According to figures of the state agrarian commission, just 33 provisional titles of ownership had been awarded since 1915, ten of them during the months of June to September, 1924, undoubtedly in response to the De la Huerta uprising.

LAND DISTRIBUTION, GUANAJUATO [42]

Year	Resolutions
1915	0
1916	6
1917	1
1918	7
1919	1
1920	0
1921	2
1922	0
1923	6
1924	10
Total	33

In the north, supposedly the heartland of rebellion, by the same token, only 98 villages, between 1920 and 1924, had received provisional title to lands, 53 of them in Chihuahua. Not one grant was made in Sinaloa, a rich farming state.

PROVISIONAL LAND GRANTS, 1920–1924 [43]

State	Number
Chihuahua	53
Coahuila	11
Nuevo León	3
Sinaloa	0
Sonora	9
Tamaulipas	12
Total	98

Only six states in the entire Republic gave provisional ownership of land to more than a hundred villages: Guerrero, Morelos, Puebla, San Luis Potosí, Veracruz, and Yucatán. Of these, merely San Luis Potosí could be classified a northern province.

PROVISIONAL LAND GRANTS: MOST ACTIVE STATES 1920–1924 [44]

State	Number
Guerrero	107
Morelos	108
Puebla	138
San Luis Potosí	108
Veracruz	129
Yucatán	139

Meanwhile, if the testimony of General Antonio I. Villarreal, briefly minister of agriculture in 1921, merits credence, the Obregonistas had kept ninety *haciendas* for themselves.[45]

The fortunes of the poor, moreover, did not necessarily take a turn for the better in the six exemplar states. Morelos, may have been the exception where under Governor Parres by 1923, 115 of the state's 150 villages, had received provisional title to land.[46] Quite different was the fate of the natives of Yucatán where, despite a substantial number of land allotments, the henequen barons kept the largest and best lands. In 1914, Governor Eleuterio Avila had cancelled the debts of the *peones acasillados,* theoretically ending debt peonage, and given them the choice of leaving the *haciendas* or remaining as day laborers.[47] But, due to the chicanery of the *hacendados* and the inability of the workers to find jobs, little actually had changed. Rural workers, Antonio Ancona Albertos, one of the two senators from Yucatán, told Obregón, were "worse off now than before the Revolution." [48] Further, not until the 1920's had land allotments been made; Salvador Alvarado, governor of Yucatán from 1915 to 1920, had condemned any attempt to limit the size of private property.[49] Under his regime, he had boasted, no worker dared lift a finger against an *hacendado.*[50] He had limited land reform to the estates of his political enemies, *hacendados* who had supported Abel Ortiz Argumedo in 1915.[51] Yet, as the testimony of Senator Ancona Albertos documented, even the rule of Felipe Carrillo Puerto, a Socialist sympathetic to land reform, had scarcely altered the life of the rural poor; furthermore Carrillo Puerto lost his life espousing the land reform cause. In Veracruz, a major farming state, according to one of its legislators, the poor in the countryside had enjoyed the barest of gains, certainly not in keeping with their immense sacrifices.[52] As students in Mexico City lamented, "the peasant who aspired to own land in order to be free . . . today, when he sees the heroic efforts of the liberators and the work of reformers undercut by treachery and deceit, has lost his faith in the future." [53]

III

The willingness to compromise and equivocate, out of conviction or need, dulled even the cutting edge of nationalism, the doctrine so avidly pursued by the rebels since the days of the Apostle. The results, particularly noticeable in the nonenforcement of the statutes of Article 27, brought additional harmful repercussions to the agrarian sector. The attempt to sell the old Terrazas domain to an American speculator, which embroiled Obregón in a national scandal, was one of them.

In April 1920, with Venustiano Carranza still in office, Alberto Terrazas, the son of don Luis and spokesman for the family in the negotiations, had signed an agreement giving Arthur J. McQuatters, the head of an American syndicate, an option to buy the Terrazas lands in Chihuahua.[54] To facilitate the transaction, the government of Carranza had returned the lands in question to the Terrazas. With the consent of his father, then ninety years of age and living in exile in California, Terrazas was to sell at $2.50 dollars an acre. For each acre sold, both Terrazas and McQuatters were to receive one-tenth of the sale price as a commission. McQuatters was to organize the Compañía Agrarista Mexicana, a grandiose real estate firm, to subdivide and sell the 2,322,270 hectares of the Terrazas in individual plots, ranging from 40 to 4,000 hectares, to private buyers, both Mexicans and foreigners.[55] With the downfall of Carranza, the agreement was renegotiated, this time fixing the price of an acre of land at $1.50 dollars. Soon after, McQuatters and his associates had traveled to Mexico City to confer with Obregón who, in their opinion, gave his consent to the venture. The goal, according to Governor Enríquez of Chihuahua who also gave the deal his blessings, was to develop small private property. The state legislature too approved the agreement. All of this was done before any attempt had been made to distribute the lands among the landless and needy. Believing everything settled, McQuatters paid $150,000 dollars to the Terrazas, another $125,000 dollars to cover the cost of the option, and $113,000 dollars to pay for the cost of surveying the land.[56] By 1922, McQuatters and his friends had invested $388,000 dollars in the business deal. Had matters proceeded on schedule, Americans (and Mexicans with money to purchase real estate) would have occupied the lands of the Terrazas' family.

To the chagrin of McQuatters, the enterprise raised a storm of protest once news of it leaked to the public. McQuatters, it was learned, was a mining speculator; his venture had the backing of the Guaranty Trust Company of New York, one of the hated financial lords of Wall Street. In the popular mind, Enríquez, the young governor, had betrayed Mexico. It was brought out that he was related to the Terrazas family, and that he had graduated from the University of Illinois, an American institution. At the insistence of the New York bankers and undoubtedly prompted by Enríquez, the state legislature of Chihuahua had passed legislation exempting the Terrazas' lands from the agrarian reform laws of the Republic. Unless this were done, the bankers wanted no part of the deal.[57] Mexican nationalists, recalling the debacle of Texas in 1836, rightly saw the McQuatters affair as planting the seeds of future troubles with Washington. General Plutarco Elías Calles, the Minister of Gobernación, told Obregón that Enríquez had quoted Terrazas as saying that he was selling the family lands to Americans because it suited his interests and because no laws prohibited it.[58] The Confederación de Obreros y Campesinos of Chihuahua pleaded with Obregón to cancel the agreement as it circumvented Artículo 27. The state legislature lacked authority to sell the lands, and certainly not to Americans. If the Terranzas were permitted to mock national laws, eventually foreigners would own the best lands of Mexico. The duty of the state legislature was to pass land legislation benefiting the people of Chihuahua.[59] In Parral, labor groups pressured Obregón to stop the legislature from giving its consent, and even asked don Luis, the patriarch of the Terrazas family, to give his Mexican compatriots the opportunity to buy his lands.[60] However, Enríquez urged Obregón to approve the contract, advising the president that it "was untrue that there was popular discontent" with the sale.[61]

But, as Obregón acknowledged in a letter to the governor ordering him to stop the transaction, Enríquez was mistaken. News of the sale had gone beyond the boundaries of Chihuahua to alarm the entire Republic.[62] Among the alarmed was Francisco Villa who, from his *hacienda* in Canutillo, firmly warned Obregón that to sell the Terrazas estates to McQuatters, "the faithful servant of the financial lords of the United States, could well be the first step in the downfall of his regime." The venture was not worth the risk. Only the governor and the state

legislature, Villa charged, favored it. "I believe," Villa emphasized, "that given the unanimous protest of the people of Chihuahua, in less than three months bullets will fly unless the deal
is cancelled." Obregón was told to give his immediate reply to
the general who carried Villa's angry letter to Mexico City.[63]

Obregón's prompt response left no doubt that he had undergone a change of heart on the McQuatters affair. The contract,
he conceded, circumvented laws "we are obligated to defend." [64]
Yet nothing in the correspondence between Obregón, on the
one hand, and Enríquez and lawyers for McQuatters on the
other, indicated that until the message from Villa arrived that
don Alvaro had recognized the magnitude of the popular anger.
A few days later, in keeping with the second thoughts in the
National Palace, the Ministry of Gobernación, while paying lip
service to the good intentions of officials in Chihuahua, cancelled the McQuatters concession. It based its decision on the
omissions in the contract—all patently obvious from the start.
The noble goal of creating small private property had been re-
linquished to foreigners; nothing in the contract compelled
McQuatters to subdivide the lands he purchased; McQuatters
and his associates could simply occupy them; the state of Chihuahua had no control over the decisions of the company once
the contract was signed; the company had the right to settle
foreigners on Mexican lands, a right Chihuahua lacked authority to grant; and the concession went against public opinion,
with dire consequences for the nation.[65] The omissions, it might
be added, also sabotaged the nationalistic aspirations of the past
rebellion: to make Mexico a haven for Mexicans.

Still the evidence documents that Obregón had, indeed,
given his approval to the McQuatters venture. To quote a letter
to Obregón from McQuatters, Obregón had "discussed . . . at
length the possibility of our undertaking a great agricultural
development in the northern part of Chihuahua." It "would en-
brace the purchase, development, and sale in their totality of the
rural properties owned by General Luis Terrazas." Because "of
. . . the encouragement we received from our conversation with
you, my friends and myself . . . definitely decided to proceed
with the undertaking." [66] Furthermore, Obregón had given his
written endorsement to McQuatters, Franklin Remington and

James G. McNary in a letter dated December 10, 1921.[67] Obregón's reversal left McQuatters and his colleagues with nothing to show for their already considerable investments. "The above is naturally a great surprise to us," concluded McQuatters in his final letter to Obregón, "and places us in a very embarrassing position on account of payments made, financial commitments, and otherwise. . . ." Meanwhile, Governor Enríquez had reminded Obregón of his letter offering "guarantees" to McQuatters.[68] Lastly, in a memorandum to McQuatters, Obregón himself admitted that he had given his blessings to the sale of Terrazas' lands.[69]

The McQuatters episode ended on a happy, if decidedly unrevolutionary note. According to Obregón, the government expropriated the properties to prevent the Terrazas from selling to foreigners.[70] But it was an expropriation with prompt payment to the Terrazas. In return for their lands, the Terrazas were to be paid 13,600,000 pesos; a down payment of 10 percent, was made immediately; the balance would be paid over ten years with 5 percent interest. Even this large cash settlement was less than what Adolfo de la Huerta, the minister of the treasury, had originally wanted to pay. Had he had his way, he would have given the Terrazas a down payment of 3,600,000 pesos, a sum, according to the head of the Caja de Préstamos, which had to supply the money, that would have left it bereft of funds to lend Mexican farmers.[71] At that, Obregón, who unquestionably intervened to reduce the amount of the cash settlement, felt obligated to tell the Terrazas of his desire to increase it should the national budget take a turn for the better.[72]

With the McQuatters affair out of the way and the Terrazas paid off, Governor Enríquez and the state legislature finally saw fit to pass laws to implement the promises of Article 27.[73] Ironically, the McQuatters episode had helped bring land reform to Chihuahua. During the interval, nationalism, had been rescued from the edge of the precipice to which the leaders of Mexico had brought it, by the common people of Chihuahua and by Villa, an old warhorse waiting for the chance to avenge his defeat at Celaya.

TWENTY

Between Adam Smith and Marx

_____

"I have never said I was a socialist, a communist, a bolshevik or an enemy of private property."

Andrés Molina Enríquez

_____

I

ALONG WITH THE FITS and spurts in land redistribution, the rebel victors additionally had given life to a Constitution. In the Constitution of 1917, drafted and voted upon at Querétaro, the triumphant middle classes spelled out their recipe for the future, vividly displaying both the strengths and weaknesses of the crusade undertaken by Francisco I. Madero. Following an ageless Mexican political habit, Venustiano Carranza and the victorious Constitutionalists kept their enemies, the disciples of Francisco Villa and Emiliano Zapata, at arms length, making a mockery of the election of delegates to the Constitutional Convention. The delegates hypothetically represented the states but were actually hand picked, called to serve from Mexico City.[1] When they convened, only the moderate wing of the rebel factions answered the roll call. The majority at Querétaro, says Moisés González Navarro, an urban middle class, stamped its ideological seal on the Mexico of the future: lawyers, engineers, school-teachers, generals, newspapermen, poets, writers, physicians, store clerks, and salesmen. Even men from the world of business helped chart the course of constitutional reform: Ignacio L. Pesqueira, a politician and general from Sonora with a sharp eye for profits, was the principal stockholder of La Fama Montañesa, a textile mill in the Federal District.[2] Workers and peasants were notable by their absence. The Constitution of 1917, notes Arnaldo Córdova, signaled the victory of the middle classes.[3] After weeks of debate, the delegates hammered out a blueprint often at odds with the dreams of their First Chief, who merely wanted to update the old charter; but they gave their blessings to legislation more in keeping with the principles of Adam Smith than with Karl Marx. Despite the revolutionary rhetoric and the revisions adopted, some drastic in scope, the ideals of Benito Juárez, in essence nineteenth-century liberalism, survived. The statutes on land, labor, and public education starkly illuminate the amorphous and contradictory nature of the legislation adopted.

To a majority at Querétaro, the historic city of the bells, turbulence and unrest would disappear only when a solution had been found for the agrarian question. According to Juan de Dios Bojórquez, a native of Sonora but a delegate from Jalisco, Mexico would not have peace until the land issue had been laid to rest. It was the "cardinal problem" of the Revolution.[4] Indeed, long before Querétaro, even conservatives, as the belated efforts by the Díaz regime testified, had come to accept the inevitability of some kind of land reform.[5] Speaking to Congress in 1911, Francisco León de la Barra had labeled agrarian discontent a salient reason for the rebellion. He joyously anticipated the day when every man would own his plot of ground and the defense of private property had become a universal cause. To get the job underway, De la Barra had appointed a National Agrarian Commission.[6] His successor, Francisco I. Madero, a landlord with the attitudes typical of his class, while vacillating on the agrarian issue in his Plan de San Luis Potosí, had sworn to rectify the theft of village lands.

Victoriano Huerta, whose evil deeds upset the rebel apple cart, partly justified his betrayal of Madero by promising a Ministry of Agriculture to supervise land reform and actually carrying it out.[7] One of his emissaries vowed to Zapata that don Victoriano meant to enforce the Plan de Ayala, a pledge repeated to him by Pascual Orozco's father, by then another of Huerta's agents.[8] Just months after taking office, Huerta's minister of the treasury, Toribio Esquivel Obregón, asked Congress for funds to spend on lands to distribute among the peasants.[9] In a pamphlet titled *El Problema Agrario en México*, Esquivel Obregón, once an ally of Madero and an *hacendado* himself, had urged the government to buy and subdivide *haciendas* and sell the small plots to individuals qualified to farm them.[10] Bonds to pay for the lands taken would be sold. Huerta's administration also began to explore ways to restore the lands of the communal villages, the *ejidos*.[11]

The fall of the Usurper Huerta, an event that split his enemies into quarreling factions, led to additional plans for agrarian reform. Unhappy with Carranza's leadership, a majority of the military and their staff met at the famous Convención de Aguascalientes where, after a brief flirtation, Alvaro Obregón and a host of lesser chieftains walked out, leaving the gathering in the control of Villa, supposedly an ally of Zapata. Land reform was one of the planks voted by the Convention regime, the government set up by the dissidents to replace Carranza. Yet, even with the participation of the Zapatistas, the generals and their disciples approached the issue cautiously. Manuel Palafox, named minister of agriculture, for example, while urging the breakup of the large estates, wanted expropriation with prior indemnification.[12] The Ley Agraria of October 26, 1915, extolled by both Villa and Zapata, sanctioned the right of every Mexican to own land, but all the same, pledged to pay the barons of the countryside for their losses and left its implementaticn to the states.[13] Writing in *La Convención*, the official organ of the dissidents, José María Luján, a former minister under Huerta and an *hacendado*, cautioned that only qualified farmers should receive land.[14] Not until the Convention government moved to Cuernavaca, where Zapata took control, did it take a militant stance on the land issue. When General Rafael Buelna, one of its chieftains and governor of the territory of Tepic, suggested that the sugar *haciendas* under his control be returned to their owners, the Zapatistas unhesitatingly said no.[15]

For their part, Carranza and his band of lukewarm reformers confronted a debacle in the making. Villa had driven them out of Mexico City, compelling them to seek refuge in the port of Veracruz. Villa's *dorados*, with the help of Zapata's motley army in the south, ruled the key regions of the Republic. To win, Carranza explained to Ignacio C. Enríquez, one of his generals and later governor of Chihuahua, it was necessary to woo Zapata away from Villa, or at least to neutralize Zapata's peasant following. Only by embracing agrarian reform could this be done.[16] With this in mind, Carranza, on December 12, 1914 published his Adiciones al Plan de Guadalupe, pledging upon his victory to pass laws to satisfy the social, economic, and political hopes of the Mexican people. He spoke of agrarian legislation, the dissolution of the *haciendas,* and the restoration to the villages of lands unjustly taken from them by rapacious landlords. However, the Adiciones dwelt on the formation of a class of small farmers, relegating the *ejido,* the crux of Zapata's Plan de Ayala, to the Indian communities, a minority of the rural villages. Like Madero, Carranza meant to rectify an ancient wrong, the theft of village lands, conveniently overlooking the fact that most of the villages had lost their lands not by the illegal manipulations of unscrupulous *hacendados,* but by the enforcement of the Ley Lerdo, eventually an integral plank of the Charter of 1857.[17] To give lands to dirt farmers required not merely a remedy for old wrongs, but more importantly, laws to replace the outmoded property concepts. Nevertheless, despite their limited scope, with the Adiciones don Venustiano had abandoned his standpat attitude and taken a view in keeping with the opinions of a large segment of his supporters.

One month later, on January 6, 1915, Carranza converted his pledge into a decree, ultimately the gist of Article 27 of the Constitution of 1917. The decree, the brainchild of Luis Cabrera, represented the thinking of Andrés Molina Enríquez, author of *Los Grandes Problemas Nacionales.*[18] Cabrera had divulged its basic outlines in a speech to Congress on December 3, 1912. To Dios Bojórquez, the Decree of January 6, 1915, which attracted a large contingent of new disciples, spelled the difference between victory and defeat for Carranza.[19]

The decree, according to Molina Enríquez, encapsulated five key aims: to right old wrongs; return stolen lands to their rightful owners; stem the flight of rural workers to the United States; keep peasants from taking up arms; and reward loyalty to the Constitutionalists. Specifically, it nullified the theft of lands, water, and forests of *pueblos, rancherías, congregaciones,* or *comunidades* sanctioned by *jefes políticos,* governors and other local officials contrary to the law of June 25, 1856; it ruled invalid the concessions or sales of lands, water, and forests made by national officials since December 1, 1876 that had led to the illegal occupation of *ejidos* or other lands of the above communities. Finally, it ruled null and void land surveys or demarcations of property boundaries carried out after 1876 by judges or other national or local authorities that illegally alienated the lands, water, and forests of these communities.[20]

To retore lands to the villages, the decree adopted two methods: restitution and, a new concept, dotation. Villages that could prove title to property lost were empowered to petition for their return or restitution; eligible villages without proof of prior ownership must rely on dotation. Governors were given the authority to grant or deny petitions; where war or problems of terrain made action by governors unlikely, military commanders could exercise a similar right. The decree asked federal and state agrarian commissions to judge the validity of the requests, decide the amount of land to be granted, and advise the governors and the Republic's president. A favorable decision gave the village provisional title and the right to farm the land. The final decision, confirming ownership, was up to the National Agrarian Commission and the president of the Republic, who must sign it. No confiscation of property was intended as all lands taken must be paid for.[21]

Unfortunately for land-hungry dirt farmers, the decree only partially met their hopes. Expropriation applied merely to *haciendas* on the edges of villages asking for land. Nothing defined the amount or character of the lands subject to expropriation. Initial possession was provisional, leaving both village and *hacendado* to await impatiently the final decision. Given the limited number of categories, a host of rural communities and individuals were denied the right to ask for land, including agricultural workers not living in villages adjacent to *haciendas,* sharecroppers, and tenant farmers. Worse yet, the decree put *peones acasillados,* the workers on the *haciendas,* in this group, condemning them to a life of toil on the landed estates. Additionally, since in most cases the *peones acasillados* were the only groups with a valid claim to the lands they worked, the decree, for all intents and purposes, protected the *haciendas* from expropriation. The decree, in summary, benefited a small slice of rural inhabitants, nearly always Indians. Additionally, although the grant went to the village, the intent was to make the individual farmer the owner of his plot of land.[22] Cabrera and Molina Enríquez, the architects of the decree, harbored scant sympathy for any form of communal or collective ownership of property. Moreover, a decree of September 19, 1916 expressly forbid the further granting of provisional titles to land.[23] With it, land distribution, in reality, had come to a dead end on the eve of Querétaro.

With this ambivalent record behind them, the creators of the Constitution gathered at Querétaro. Strangely, despite the ambiguity of earlier efforts, and the wide range of opinions among the Constitutionalists over what should be done, the delegates quickly reached an accord. They spent just one evening in general debate on Article 27, as against the heated and angry polemics on articles 123 and 3 dealing with labor and education. The debates on Article 27 occurred late on the agenda at Querétaro, after the discussions on labor and schools, with most of the delegates eager to return home. By this juncture, it had been decided to postpone the difficult job of formulating the *leyes reglamentarias* required to enforce the legislation. When the delegates took up the agrarian question, Pastor Rouaix, chairman of the committee studying it, had met privately with his colleagues in order to iron out differences of opinion.[24] The same committee had previously drafted Article 123, with the exception of Molina Enríquez, who had been invited to serve as a consultant by Rouaix.[25]

A native of Puebla but a political boss of Durango, Rouaix belonged to the loyalists of the First Chief. As governor of Durango, he had backed agrarian legislation (October 3, 1912) designed to encourage the growth of a class of small farmers. Although permitting the expropriation of *hacienda* lands on behalf of the public welfare, the law made the peasants pay for the lands they received and shielded from expropriation *haciendas* under 5,000 hectares.[26] During the days of Querétaro, Rouaix was Carranza's minister of agriculture, a post he held until 1920.

Along with Molina Enríquez, an adviser to the National Agrarian Commission, Rouaix helped shape Article 27. Ironically, in late 1916, almost nothing had been done to solve the agrarian problem [27]—with the exception of Morelos, where Zapata had taken it upon himself to redistribute land.

The quick adoption of Article 27, however, did not signify that a consensus existed on what constituted agrarian reform. From the start, the conservative Constitutionalists, with Carranza leading the way, displayed their distrust of radical measures. By June 1915, the First Chief had made abundantly clear his opposition to any attempt to confiscate property. He wanted to solve the agrarian problem by dividing up public lands into small parcels and selling them for a fair price on easy terms. If need be, he conceded, private lands could be bought for distribution to the rural poor. He meant to end all special privilege and to tax property according to its true value.[28] In his version of Article 27, Carranza suggested only small changes. As written into the Charter of 1857, he explained, Article 27 allowed the government to expropriate, with prior indemnification of course, privately owned lands deemed necessary for the public good. With this authority the government could buy lands to distribute among the landless who wanted to farm and, in that manner, build a class of small farmers, which was the goal as Carranza saw it. He asked only that Article 27 be revised so that the government have authority to decide what was public utility, leaving to the courts merely the right to determine the value of property. Foreigners, in Carranza's draft, while keeping their rights to own land and the subsoil, must obey Mexican laws in matters relating to their holdings. No civil or religious corporation, as specified in the Charter of 1857, could own real estate. *Ejido* lands, the First Chief went on, whether acquired before the adoption of the Charter of 1857 or by restitution or dotation, would be split into individually owned parcels.[29] A majority of the delegates, awaiting a substantial revision of existing legislation, listened in stunned disbelief to Carranza.[30]

Yet, paradoxically, even the radical Francisco Múgica, who presided over the sessions dealing with Article 27, along with others in his political bailiwick, shared with the First Chief a belief in the system of private property. Both, although perhaps not to the same extent, looked upon it as the pillar of society. All were apostles of free enterprise. The elimination of special privilege, the cancer of yesteryear, signaled no demise of free enterprise; on the contrary, the end of monopoly heralded a new day for it.[31] For Carranza and the majority at Querétaro, the objective, Molina Enríquez pointed out, was to "defend, develop, and multiply small property" which would form the nucleus of "a large and strong middle class." Its growth would "prevent the extravagances of the rich, the violence of the poor, and lay the cornerstones for healthy voting practices." A majority of the delegates, moreover, consigned the *ejido,* the one exception to the private ownership of property, to a secondary role, viewing it as a legacy of the past. Only a radical fringe demanded the expropriation at one stroke of the entire class of *hacendados* and foreign landlords in order to distribute their holdings among the hungry. In the opinion of most delegates, this would be folly. Even Múgica and his cohorts saw the abolition of private property as "utopian." [32] Still, to both Múgica and Carranza, the rights of private property should not take precedence over the public need. Individual rights could not be exercised at the expense of the prerogatives of society.[33] They were secondary, for both the land and the subsoil, in theory, belonged to the state. This was the Spanish colonial concept, a principle, said Molina Enríquez, jettisoned by the Charter of 1857.[34]

Nearly all of the delegates agreed on the necessity to pay for property taken on behalf of the public good.[35] Some wanted *hacendados,* to cite the opinion of a delegate from Puebla, paid in hard currency, a practice that would have severely curtailed the pace of land reform in a country on the verge of bankruptcy.[36] Still, a key distinction divided the architects of the constitutions of 1857 and 1917: the early fathers had sanctioned expropriation with prior indemnification, while the men at Querétaro spoke of it "by means of," *mediante,* indemnification, pledging merely to eventually compensate the landlord.[37] Obviously, each delegate interpreted the law in terms of his own political convictions. Múgica and Rouaix might agree but Félix A. Palavicini, a mirror of Carranza's thought, would interpret the legislation differently. Also, the delegates had to bear in mind, any tinkering with the structure of private property would further jeopardize agricultural production, already sorely hurt by years of war and turmoil. Regardless of the political proclivities, the men at Querétaro had to keep an eye not just on the shape of the national economy but also on the necessity to prevent Mexicans from starving to death. The delegates were men of practical bent.

Article 27 reflected this hodgepodge of ambiguities and striking contradictions. To safeguard the public interest, the state had the power to regulate private property, the use of natural resources, and the responsibility to guarantee the equitable distribution of the national wealth and its conservation. To foment the growth of small, private property, Article 27 called for the subdivision, but not the total disappearance, of large property. Since the land barons would be paid for lands lost, the cost would be borne by the buyers. The state simply guaranteed payment. The need to redistribute wealth and income was glossed over, although both would supposedly come with the new legislation. The states were to determine the maximum limits of private property according to their needs. *Hacendados* had to divest themselves of lands beyond those limits. Buyers were given a period of no less than twenty years to pay off their mortgages, plus an interest rate of no more than 5 percent annually. However, the exact length of time and the interest rates were left to the states to decide. The buyer, for his part, could not sell his land for twenty years. Certain types of communities without lands, or with insufficient lands to meet their needs, had the right to ask for lands, to be taken from the adjoining *haciendas*. The legislation exempted small property from expropriation. Additionally, it confirmed titles of lands granted to villages by dotation under the Decree of January 6, 1915. Should the *hacendado* refuse to sell his excess lands, state authorities would expropriate it. The seller had to accept government bonds as payment. Within their respective jurisdictions, federal and state laws would determine when public utility required the occupation of private property. The value of lands seized would be based on the tax assessments accepted by their owners (notoriously low under Díaz). Once a government based on the Constitution of 1917 was established, Congress and the state legislatures were to enact laws, *leyes reglamentarias,* setting up guide-lines for the subdivision of large property.[38] But by leaving to the states the enactment of these laws, essentially the imple-mentation of Article 27, the delegates relegated to limbo the intended agrarian reform. As Fernando González Roa noted, "it would be difficult to imagine the states taking steps harmful to the interests of the *hacendados."* [39] So it should come as no surprise that the first of the *leyes reglamentarias* was not passed until 1923.

Section VI, fundamentally the Decree of January 6, 1915, authorized *pueblos, condueñazos, rancherías, congregaciones,* tribes and other corporate communities, by right or fact living in a communal state, to hold and till their lands, forests, and water in common. It nullified acquisitions of lands at the expense of villages by the Law of June 25, 1856, and in accordance with the 1915 decree, to be restored to them by restitution, or by dotation if need be. Lands of less than fifty hectares held by their owners for at least ten years, whether seized illegally or not, were exempted from expropriation; lands in excess of that figure were to be returned to the community, but with indemnifica-tion.[40] Unfortunately, nothing was done to give *peones acasil-lados* the right to ask for land. Still, the *ejido,* no longer transi-tory as in the decree of 1915, had become a legal fixture, for the time being at least, in rural Mexico.

Mexico for the Mexicans had been a rallying slogan of rebels since Madero, and Article 27 marched in tune with this nationalist cry. Foreigners must accept the supremacy of Mexi-can laws and officials. The government had the authority to review all contacts and concessions made since 1876 that had given individuals or corporations monopolies of land, water, or natural resources, and to nullify them when in conflict with the public interest. Only Mexicans by birth or citizenship, and only national corporations enjoyed the right to acquire mines or wa-ter, or to obtain concessions to exploit the subsoil. However, the state could grant concessions to foreigners who agreed to abide by Mexican legislation and not call upon their governments for special protection. Under no circumstances were aliens to own either land or water resources within 100 kilometers of the bor-ders of Mexico or 50 kilometers of the coasts.[41] (Foreigners owned 22 million hectares in these regions, or 11 percent of the national territory).[42]

Article 27 enshrined diverse schools of thought, the opinions of men as different in political philosophy as the conservative Carranza and the radical Múgica. However, most observers agree, it mirrored the views of Molina Enríquez, ally and adviser to Rouaix, chairman of the drafting committee.[43] His interpretation of Article 27, therefore, merits careful scrutiny.

An inconoclast, with views ranging from the conventional to the unorthodox, Molina Enríquez, by his own admission, was hardly a revolutionary. He understood that change would not come with the consent of those who stood to lose by it. Yet he abhorred violence, whatever its intent. He spent his life defending small, private property, and he later conceded, did not advocate a solution to the agrarian muddle at the expense of the landlords. On the National Agrarian Commission, he urged not merely prompt payment for lands seized but a hike in the interest rate paid the dispossessed *hacendados* from 5 to 8 percent.[44] His book, *Los Grandes Problemas Nacionales,* paid tribute to Díaz, labeling his political leadership "inspired, felicitous, and fortunate." [45] If he wanted to subdivide the *haciendas,* it was because he believed that a healthy society rested on a large and powerful class of small property owners. But, until the departure of don Porfirio, he had worked merely for an evolutionary remedy to rural ills. He wanted to modify the laws of inheritance in order to force the children of *hacendados* to subdivide their fathers' property. By this manner, the *mestizos,* the backbone of Mexico, could buy up parts of the *haciendas.*[46] He belittled the Indian, although he endorsed the right of Indian villages to own and farm their lands in common. He admitted, however, that the idea was not his, but that of Antenor Sala, a progressively minded *hacendado.*[47] A friend of both Cabrera and Wistano Luis Orozco, a pioneer student of rural maladies, Molina Enríquez shared their cautious views. His thoughts, he said, had been voiced by Cabrera in the speech of 1912. Only belatedly did he urge federal intervention to break up the *haciendas,* an opinion Orozco decried because he judged property rights sacred. Still, Molina Enríquez never fully endorsed the subdivision of *haciendas* by expropriation; as late as 1924, he was telling Plutarco Elías Calles to use a progressive tax on property in order to encourage the *hacendados* to subdivide their lands.[48]

To determine the character and size of property, Molina Enríquez divided Mexico into three regions. Each had its own peculiar population: *criollos* (the offsprings of Spaniards); *mestizos* (a blend of Indian and Spaniard); or Indians. *Criollos* predominated in the north, the first of the three regions; *mestizos* in the central zone; and Indians in the south. Property rights, as well as the size of landholdings, he argued, must take into account population and topographical considerations. Each racial group, because of its special relationship to the land, had "instinctively" developed its own form of property. In the north, it was the capitalist *hacienda;* the *rancho* or small property, in the central zone; and the communal village with its *ejido* in the south. Such being the realty, the objective was to divide the arid north into *haciendas;* central Mexico, a region of usually regular rainfall, into *ranchos;* and the south, when tillable lands were available, into *ejidos.*

Mestizos held the key to a prosperous Mexico. They made up 60 percent of the population, the bulk of the middle classes, the majorities in Congress, and represented the true nationality. Small property, he believed, was not just the "basis of domestic and international stability," but the lifeblood of the *mestizo.*[49] To subdivide the *haciendas* was to increase the number of *mestizo* small farmers, and by this policy, enlarge the yield from agriculture. Regional conditions would set the maximum limits of small property. As a general rule, the smallest parcel of land was what the individual farmer could till alone; the maximum would be what a farmer working alongside of wage workers could plant and harvest. On the National Agrarian Commission, Molina Enríquez had attempted to define what he meant by small property in the state of Mexico. With the help of Emilio Vásquez Gómez, the state representative, Molina Enríquez had fixed the limits of the *rancho* (small property) at 700 hectares, a considerable amount of land. The buyers were to pay the fiscal value of the land in cash, and to assume a mortgage at 2 percent interest to compensate the *hacendado* for the difference between the fiscal and true value of the lands he lost. Only the strident opposition of the Partido Nacional Agrarista stopped

Molina Enríquez from testing this scheme, although it would have rendered the term small property virtually meaningless and limited land sales to not unprosperous farmers.[50]

Section VI, according to this apostle of the capitalistic *mestizo*, while ratifying the *ejido* as a permanent fixture, assigned it a secondary role to play in rural Mexico. The delegates at Querétaro had not envisaged the communal system as equal in importance to small property.[51] The *ejido*, essentially, was a stopgap measure to satisfy the demands of communal villages. The legislation barred all other villages from "legally having lands in common."[52] Molina Enríquez saw the *ejido* as a "regressive survival of the communal stage of primitive epochs."[53] Its restoration, either by restitution or dotation, was not meant to be the tool by which to subdivide the *haciendas;* that was the function of small property. Nor were the *ejidos* restored to better the condition of agriculture nor to improve its yield. To the contrary; with the *ejido* the policy makers at Querétaro had simply wanted to liberate the Indian from his total dependence on the *hacendado* and to permit him to sell his labor on the free market. The inhabitants of communal villages would supplement their incomes by working for wages on neighboring farms. Additionally, they had their own lands to fall back on when jobs were scarce, as well as the option of not working for low wages. This made for higher wages in the countryside and gave a measure of independence to rural wage workers. To Molina Enríquez, this was the purpose of the *ejido* in Article 27.[54] The framers of the Constitution had never thought of replacing private property with a communal system of land ownership.

At Querétaro, the delegates, in short, had dealt separately with the questions of the *ejido* and the subdivision of the *haciendas*. With the *ejidos*, they meant to improve the lives of a population bloc, in the majority Indian, "that because of its historical backwardness had failed to develop beyond a communal stage dating from pre-Columbian times." Historical circumstance had prevented the communal village from moving to the more advanced stage of private property.[55] To Molina Enríquez, communal landholdings, and by implication collectively owned property, represented an economic system inferior to that of private property. The hallowed principles of the nineteenth century, not the Marxist ideals adopted by socialist Russia, held the answer to Mexico's future.

II

Like the agrarian formula, Article 123, the labor code, emerged out of a concrete Mexican situation. Its nationalistic patrons unquestionably welcomed the opportunity to utilize the demands of industrial labor to curb the influence of foreigners. This and other extraneous doctrines may account for some of the rhetoric. But, Article 123 responded basically to labor's demands. The modernization of Mexico, the lifetime goal of Díaz, had brought the trappings of an industrial complex: thousands of miles of railroads, a network of textile mills, a conglomerate of mines, smelters, factories, steel mills, ports, and a web of petroleum derricks between Tampico and Veracruz. Industries and mines employed thousands of Mexicans in almost every corner of the Republic. Weighted against the total population in 1910, the industrial labor force appears small. But, judged by its productivity and share of national income, the underpinnings of the progress and welfare of modern Mexico, no other population segment matched its importance.

The industrial worker formed a distinct and increasingly powerful political bloc. Unlike the dirt farmer, isolated in forgotten hamlets, the worker in industry, not infrequently literate, lived in a city or town, within reach of newspapers, pamphlets, and books. He was not a political neophyte.[56] By 1916, he had built unions, marched in the picket lines of strikes, and occasionally stood up successfully to his bosses. In a country slowly emerging from a simple agricultural economy, he enjoyed a monopoly of scarce skills. Yet, the evidence documents, he had just cause for complaint: low wages, long hours of toil, unsatisfactory work conditions in factories and mines, skimpy housing, and the adamant refusal of management to sit down at the bargaining table with his representatives. The workers' battle to survive years of chaos that shut down plants and mines and cost them their jobs put additional political pressure on the rebel leadership. Thus, the framers of the Constitution, had to listen to the demands of industrial labor, a key element of Mexico's economy by 1916.

Even before Querétaro, rebel governors had endeavored to respond to labor's exigent pleas. In Aguascalientes, Governor Alberto Fuentes had limited the workday to nine hours. Eulalio Gutiérrez, governor of San Luis Potosí, had affixed his signature to a labor code stipulating a minimum wage, a nine-hour day, the end of company stores, and the setting up of a department of labor.[57] In Yucatán, Salvador Alvarado had given his blessings to a Ley de Trabajo, pledging an eight-hour day, Sundays off, indemnification for industrial accidents, limits to the work of women and children, but significantly, withholding the right to strike.[58] In December 1915, Governor Luis G. Cervantes of Puebla had boldly conferred "legal status" to labor unions and established boards of arbitration to handle industrial disputes. By 1916, Sonora and Veracruz had labor codes of their own. That of Sonora guaranteed workers a three-peso minimum daily wage, an eight-hour day, Sundays off, banned night shifts for women and children, and organized a Cámara de Trabajo; Governor Cándido Aguilar in Veracruz had conceded to workers the right to organize unions and negotiate with their employers through their representatives. Indeed, even General Pablo González of Puebla had put his name on a labor bill by 1915.[59]

During the interval, Carranza had grudgingly fallen in step with his followers. His Adiciones, a response to harsh political necessity, gave hope of "legislation to improve the condition . . . of the worker." Also, in a decree dealing with the textile mills of Veracruz, he had endorsed the concept of a minimum wage, reduced the hours of toil, declared Sundays a time of rest, stipulated compensation for industrial accidents, and accepted the right of workers to elect their representatives. However, the decree skirted the subject of labor unions, said nothing of government's role in industrial disputes, glossed over health conditions in the factories, and avoided comment on the work of women and children. To José Santos Chocano, the Peruvian poet watching events unfold in Mexico, Carranza's formula, supposedly a plan for revolution, lagged behind the labor laws of Argentina, Uruguay, and the United States, all capitalist countries.[60]

Indeed, don Venustiano and his band of cautious rebels contemplated no granting of major reforms. Carranza's opening remarks to his audience at Querétaro merely discussed the need to shorten the hours of work, to compensate for industrial accidents, to provide sickness and old-age insurance, to adopt a minimum wage, and ban work without pay—debt peonage. He was silent on labor unions, leaving the worker at the mercy of Article 9 of the Charter of 1857, containing a vague reference to the right to associate and unite with others for legitimate goals. Articles 4 and 5 of the Charter, on the other hand, spelled out "right to work" legislation that undercut the principle of labor unions. To the further despair of champions of the worker, Carranza left the enforcement of labor's rights to the states, thus turning over the welfare of the worker to local politicians notoriously friendly to business.[61]

Happily, the majority at Querétaro voted to write a new labor code. Yet, in its drafting, labor had no direct voice, for the Constitutionalists permitted the election of just two workers as delegates. A small circle of *políticos,* generally moderate in outlook, sat down to discuss legislative alternatives. Neither of the two worker-delegates had traveled to Querétaro to speak for the nascent labor movement. Both Nicolás Cano and Carlos I. Gracida, while partisans of labor's rights, attended in another capacity. The worker did not speak for himself. To pour salt on the wound, in the elections of the Twenty-seventh Congress, the first to operate under the new Constitution, every candidate of the labor movement lost his bid for office. Clearly, the Carrancistas disliked sharing political power with labor. The worker had patrons but no generals of his own.

Instead, Rouaix, an engineer, and José I. Lugo, head of the Department of Labor, guided the work of the special committee on labor legislation. Cano, Gracida, Múgica, and representatives from states with progressive labor records gave advice and enthusiastic support. Héctor Victoria, one of their number, for example, had earlier authored a bill in Yucatán to establish boards of arbitration and other labor guarantees. Prodded by delegates of this stripe, the convention at Querétaro eventually wrote a meaningful labor code, one Carranza and other recalcitrants had to accept.

Adopted in late January 1917, Article 123 sanctioned thirty specific measures. It included an eight-hour day, limited the type of labor to be done by women and children, set aside Sundays for rest, called for a minimum wage based on local living costs, stipulated health and accident insurance, and required special company schools for the children of their work force. To settle industrial disputes, it set up boards of arbitration and conciliation. More significantly, Article 123 pledged to labor the right to organize and to join unions. Section 28 explicitly recognized labor's right to strike. The legislation defined the government's obligation to place Mexican and foreign workers, as well as men and women, on an equal footing. Section 7 bluntly stated: "for equal work, equal pay, regardless of sex or nationality." [62]

But the middle-class delegates, while willing to acknowledge a responsibility to protect the worker, had not assembled at Querétaro to dismantle Mexican capitalism. Nothing in Article 123 discussed a socialist paradise for workers. Rather, it sought to establish an equilibrium between the bargaining power of labor and capital. The state, the new leviathan, had the authority to supervise and control relations between the two parties and to decide what was in the public interest. Article 123 did not do away with classes, or the poor, but simply made the state the protector of the worker, who presumably would be better off, although still a worker in a capitalist universe.[63] Theoretically, moreover, laissez faire no longer held sway. Mexico, however, would continue to need capitalists and workers, for both were unquestionably the foundations of national well-being. In Section 19, its authors underscored management's right to shut down plants when overproduction cut into reasonable profits. Like Article 27, the labor code left the formulation of *leyes reglamentarias* to the states. When formulated, some states adopted less liberal measures. Confronted with restrictive legislation in one state, business moved to another less restrictive. The states held on to their right to legislate labor questions until 1929.[64]

III

Public education, too, ranked high on the list of priorities in 1917. At Querétaro no issue kindled a brighter flame of controversy than the character of schooling. Yet the delegates, who hotly debated the issue, gave birth to a misshapen and truncated measure.

The national interest, it was obvious to everyone, called for mass education. If Mexico were to march forward, the poor and their children must be given the skills of learning. Dirt farmers, nearly universally illiterate, particularly needed to learn to read and write if they were to play an active role in the future. Mexico had a long way to go before becoming a nation; when Díaz fled, a minority of the population fully identified with national concerns. Rural Mexico, isolated from the modern world by geography, with rampant illiteracy and with economic inequalities, possessed merely a sense of family and village. National unity was nonexistent. Of the total population, to cite one estimate, at least three out of five Mexicans could neither read nor write.[65] Calculations of illiterates ranged from a low of 8 million to a high of 12 million. At best, in the words of Recios Zertuche, a Constitutionalist chieftain, just 20 percent of the population could be labeled "passably educated" and perhaps 5 percent "well educated."[66] The population of the Republic included over 4 million Indians (30 percent), most of whom could not speak Spanish.[67]

Like other reforms, the crusade to educate the rural poor got off the ground in the waning days of Díaz' administration. Two months before his flight, Jorge Vera Estañol, head of both Gobernación and Public Instruction, had publicized a plan of rural "rudimentary schools" designed to teach peasants to read and write Spanish. Many of these schools were earmarked for Indian communities. Díaz took residence in Paris before the plan could be implemented. However, the interim-De la Barra government, following in the footsteps of Vera Estañol, promulgated a Law of Rudimentary Education, establishing preprimary schools to teach Indian-speaking groups, without distinction to age or sex, to speak, read, and write Spanish and to handle the fundamentals of arithmetic. Tacitly accepted was the concept of federal responsibility for rural education; all the same, the legislation did not intend to substitute local schools with national ones but simply to establish them where none existed. To get the effort underway, Congress appropriated a paltry 300,000 pesos, a sum eventually reduced by half.[68] Ironically, while Madero conferred his approval, the law raised an acrimonious public debate, especially between Gregorio Torres Quintero, famous pedagogue and chief of the Office of Rudimentary Instruction, and Alberto Pani, under-secretary of education, who voiced the fears of the critics.

To Torres Quintero, a disciple of the traditional wisdom on language learning, the plan symbolized progress. Given the circumstance, it was the only measure possible. Later, the program could be enlarged to cover the entire rural population. By establishing 1,000 schools annually, the figures set out by the plan, the goal could be reached in thirteen years.[69] Pani, with ample justification, called the idea poorly defined, narrow in scope, and ill-suited to the needs of the Indian.[70] Additionally, Pani may have voiced the hostility of the provinces, particularly Coahuila, where Governor Carranza saw the legislation infringing upon the sovereignty of his state, although less than a third of Coahuila's natives could read or write. Huerta, free of Pani and his critics, and insisting he was "Indian and not caucasian," also endorsed the rudimentary school plan. To carry it out, he appointed its architect, Vera Estañol, minister of public instruction. From Huerta's perspective, Mexico must educate the Indian "regardless of the cost." [71] According to his report to Congress, Mexico had 200 rudimentary schools with 10,000 pupils by September, 1913.[72] Thus, on the morrow of Carranza's victory, administrations from Díaz to Huerta had agreed to a national school program and implicitly accepted federal responsibility for public education.

The number of school-teachers, 20,000 by 1917, moreover, had grown impressively during the last decade of the Díaz regime.[73] Unfortunately, salaries had failed to stay abreast of numerical growth. In Mexico City, teachers earned less money than janitors.[74] In Las Tres Huastecas, one of his generals told Carranza, teachers earned 15 pesos a month, "a fact that astonished me and caused my soldiers to laugh in disbelief." Yet in the district of Hueyutla, a part of the Tres Huastecas, just 5,000 out of the 110,000 inhabitants could read and write.[75] So, to no one's surprise, scores of ill-paid school teachers became rebel dignitaries. Huerta, paradoxically, had given teachers a 25 percent pay boost—nullified by Carranza because it had occurred during the usurpation of constitutional authority.[76]

To put an end to the illiteracy blight and to pay inequalities, teachers and citizens in diverse walks of life had begun to advocate a federally controlled network of public schools. Justo Sierra's Ministry of Public Instruction, giving the national government responsibility for schools in the Federal District and Territories, had been a step in this direction. Also, the Partido Democrático, one of the first to urge Díaz to leave the choice of his vice-president to the public, had recommended the adoption of a federal system of public education.[77] Teachers in the provinces had given Madero identical advice.[78] The rudimentary-school idea, endorsed by Díaz, De la Barra, Madero, and Huerta, emerged out of this mold.

Yet an older view still enjoyed staunch support. This was the version incorporated into the Charter of 1857, barring the federal government from meddling in the school programs of the states.[79] Public education was the responsibility of the states. Carranza adhered to this opinion. Upon replacing Huerta, he ordered Félix F. Palavicini, whom he appointed minister of public instruction, to end federal intervention in the provinces, and concurrently turn over the rudimentary schools to the states. For his part, Palavicini, indubitably speaking for his chief, publicly declared that the Ministry of Public Instruction, as presently constituted, should be abolished. During the interval, Carranza had made evident his opposition to any attempt to federalize education because, he emphasized, it curtailed state sovereignty.[80]

Still, at Querétaro, many delegates called for federal school legislation. For men of this stripe, the sessions on Article 3, which dealt with education, were crucial. Carranza, to show the importance he attached to the school issue, attended the preliminary debates. At stake was primary education, especially for peasants, as the states and municipalities, when they had built schools, had placed them in urban centers. Federal school legislation, therefore, pertained principally to rural education, one of the avenues to a better life for a majority of Mexicans.

In the face of the significance attached to learning, what emerged out of Querétaro represented a setback for reform and the first of sundry mistakes in school policy. As finally approved, Article 3 merely provided that "primary instruction in public institutions shall be gratuitous." Nothing guaranteed a national network of public primary schools. Incredibly, Article 3 did not make school attendance obligatory.[81] To have done so, critics cogently argued, would have compelled the states, and eventually the federal government, to provide schools. A majority of the delegates were unwilling to assume this responsibility. Worse yet, Sierra's justly famous Ministry of Public Instruction was disbanded. Supporting an unusual concoction of centralized authority and regional autonomy, Carranza left the implementation of Article 3 to the states and municipalities.[82] In the meantime, Article 73 empowered Congress "to establish professional schools of science and fine arts" as well as "agricultural and trade schools . . . and other institutions of higher learning" but carefully omitted primary schools.[83]

To complicate matters, the question of Church schools, which monopolized debate, hampered rational planning. Most of the heated discussions over Article 3 focused on the right of the Church to have schools, with Carranza, under the guise of liberty of learning and thought, advocating their legality, and with radicals opposed to them. However, everyone agreed that public primary education must be secular and free. Ultimately, a compromise was reached: the Church could have secondary but not primary schools. Still the issue of Church schools was a red herring. Had public institutions met the demand for schooling the question of school control might have been a valid issue; but in 1917 Mexico had approximately 9,600 public schools and only 586 Church schools.[84] The combined total hardly satisfied the educational needs of the country's children. The priest-baiting speeches of Múgica and his allies, in reality, had obscured the real issue. Unwilling to admit defeat, Carranza, for his part, in the fall of 1917, asked for a revision of Article 3 to permit the establishment of independent private schools—essentially Church schools for the wealthy.[85]

Leaving primary education to the states and municipalities made no sense whatsoever, for the local bosses and their clients were usually its worst enemy. From exile, Vera Estañol put the matter succinctly: aside from the "obstinate opposition" of Carranza, no plausible reason existed to justify the absence of a national system of primary schools in Article 3.[86] By delivering primary education, essentially the rural school, into local hands, the men of Querétaro had engaged in double talk. Mexico had no genuinely autonomous political units. Everything flowed from Mexico City, including funds required to organize schools in the villages. Clearly, given the nature of the legislation, and of political and economic realities, Carranza and the patrons of the national charter had turned their backs on the heralded obligation to provide the poor with schools.

Ironically, the inability or unwillingness of the states and municipalities to establish schools, fully documented by 1917, prompted Carranza's successors to rectify his error. Less conservative than their former First Chief, they wisely recognized that the reforms demanded by the people who had fought alongside of them could not be postponed indefinitely. Caught between pleas for land and schools, they chose to grant more of the latter. But the schools they built appeared at a time when the ruling classes of Mexico were busily repudiating radical panaceas.

In 1920, at the behest of José Vasconcelos, rector of the national university during the interim-rule of Adolfo de la Huerta, Congress, then the spokesman of the Obregonistas, revised Article 73, giving the federal government authority to build and manage a national system of primary schools. It also restored Sierra's proud design, calling it the Ministry of Public Education. The states and municipalities, nonetheless, retained their right to run separate systems of public instruction. The result was often either local neglect of rural education or duplication and waste, a wide range of standards and goals, and quarrels between local and federal officials over control of schools. Years later, Vasconcelos, appointed chief of the Ministry of Education by Obregón, remembered that its idea had occurred to him while reading "what Lunascharsky was doing in Russia." [87] Be that as it may, with the exception of that one inspiration, everything else in the house that Vasconcelos built had orthodox underpinnings.

Still, by 1924, government had set aside 45 million *pesos* for public education, four times that of any previous administration. Between 1921 and 1931, national expenditures on schools rose from 4 percent to nearly 13 percent of the total national budget; almost a third of it was spent on rural schools. From a mere handful of rural schools in 1921 the situation improved so that ten years later there were 6,796 federal rural schools with 593,183 students, children and adults, and 8,442 teachers.[88] Under the prodding of Moisés Sáenz and Rafael Ramírez, two able officials, the Ministry of Public Education had erected schools for Indian communities, rural normal schools, and sent out teams of cultural missions to countless isolated villages. But, as the pedagogues learned, without basic economic change, particularly land reform, schools alone proved no match for age-old ills.[89]

PART IV THE
UBIQUITOUS
BARRIERS

TWENTY-ONE *Jobs, Politics, and Graft*

"*We have no ulterior motive at stake: because of our not unprosperous situation, we seek no public job, sinecure or political favor.*"

Angel Colina to Governor Cándido Aguilar, 1915

I

UNDERDEVELOPMENT, a term employed by economists to describe the absence of industrial growth, breeds a frantic hunt for public office. With a skeletal economic infrastructure, where industry and business limit opportunities to a handful of white-collar hopefuls, federal and state bureaucracies must take up the slack. Such was the condition of Mexico under don Porfirio; for sundry reasons, the Great Rebellion left this picture undisturbed. Only the success of reform would transform Mexico but, as history verifies, the eradication of social and economic maladies, under the best of intentions, requires years if not decades. Given this axiom, it was logical that the quest for public jobs and the ready acceptance of graft should outlive the Old Regime. To make matters worse, the chaos and general uncertainty of the times, as well as new possibilities for public office, exacerbated ageless ills as ambitious Mexicans struggled to find a niche in society. Alone, the hunt for sinecures merely highlighted the persistence of the underdevelopment of Mexico despite decades of progress under Díaz. But, with time, it also helped sabotage the spirit of reform, as even the middle-class ideals and goals of the rebellion sank deeper into the quicksand of the Mexican past.

No wonder, therefore, that every Mexican leader, from Francisco I. Madero to Alvaro Obregón, from governors to the lowliest public official empowered to employ others, confronted countless applicants for government jobs, special concessions or sinecures of one kind or another, from relatives, friends, political supporters, and strangers convinced that they merited individual consideration. From the moment of their triumph, Mexicans in power had to cope with the craving for public office of their constituents. To write the national *caudillo*, and to claim to speak honestly and forthrightly because "I covet no post or harbor political ambition," as in one letter to Venustiano Carranza, was a mark of singular distinction.[1]

For the quest for the *hueso*, the political plum, quickly became a landmark of post-Díaz Mexico. Be on guard, General Cándido Aguilar warned his colleague-in-arms, Agustín Millán, recently named military commander of Veracruz, against "friends" who betray the Revolution in their search for personal success and wealth. He urged Millán to sever his ties with them, to punish them, "for they are neither friends nor revolutionaries."[2] Aguilar spoke from experience for it was soon common practice to support a candidate for public office, regardless of his credentials, in return for a promise of a job. But Mexico had only a finite number of public posts; filling them with fresh faces meant turning out bureaucrats, not because of incompetence or political differences, but because someone else coveted the office. "My father," wrote a distraught son to Madero, "has been asked to resign his job because I campaigned" for the losing candidate for mayor of Monterrey. The victor "had promised the municipal jobs to those who voted and worked for him."[3]

But the leading office holders also sat on the horns of a dilemma: to continue in the rat race of politics, everyday more enmeshed in rivalries and intrigues, or to accept defeat and go off into exile. Unfortunately, the second alternative, Luis Cabrera learned, proved more illusory than real. "I discovered that . . . a man cannot easily leave politics when he wants to because his decision clashes with the wishes of those who, to some extent, depend upon him for political survival." There were always, he continued, "persons who require that you remain at your job for otherwise they find themselves abandoned, exposed not just to injustices but to abuse because they are seen as your supporters." To Cabrera, public life was a highly partisan activity; the leader who forsook his post, left his subordinates and backers at the not-so-tender mercy of his successors.[4] "For all of us," wrote a newspaperman, "the holy treasury is a deity that we must venerate with fervor." [5]

The hunt for public office and political power, by the same token, rendered ideology and political convictions virtually meaningless. The hungry applicant, like the chameleon, could adjust to any set of principles or to any leader. To cite a native of Ixhuatlán, a small town in Veracruz, its *caciques*, depending on the political winds, "have been Porfiristas and recalcitrant Magonistas; cautious Maderistas; exalted Vasquistas; dedicated Orozquistas; enthusiastic Felicistas, Huertistas, and Carrancistas" and "now are Villistas and Zapatistas." Why?: "In order to continue exploiting the wealth of the miserable Indian communities . . . and to assure their survival as *caciques*." [6]

Still, by 1910, even old party-liners advocated the rejuvenation of the bureaucracy and of public office. Government, conceded José I. Limantour, needed new blood. The days of government jobs at the beck and call of an oligarchy had passed into history; the presidency, governorships, seats in Congress, as well as municipal posts, could no longer be hoarded by the few. Unhappily, lamented Limantour, he had failed to sell Díaz on the need to clean house, while financial limitations had curtailed efforts to expand the number of public jobs.[7] Not illogically, he discovered in 1911, the cement that bound the critics together was their appetite for public office. Upon his return to Mexico, he explained, an army of men had met him, each eager to discuss the political crisis and to offer a solution for it. "I am ashamed to say it," he added, "but if one common thread could be discerned from the jumble of ideas of my visitors, it was the need for a total change of politics and personnel . . . everyone spoke of removing public officials, but when the discussion of substitutes began, the discord erupted." [8] Nobody could agree because all aspired to a public office.

Even Madero, whose panaceas scratched merely the surface

of political ills, had been compelled, although only halfheartedly, to bow before the hoary dictum of politics as public jobs. At the urging of his companions at Ciudad Juárez, he had rightly demanded seventeen of the twenty-seven governorships for his adherents. All the same, he had voiced his determination, recalled Francisco Bulnes, "to keep in office honest and capable employees," and cautioned ambitious bureaucratic underlings "to obey and respect their superiors in office or face dismissal." [9] Since this policy kept at work nearly the entire coterie of public officeholders, it restricted opportunities to the chosen few: men who had participated directly in the rebellion. Because of this, remembered Félix F. Palavicini, "a horde of liberators" had suddenly appeared, men who had "not abandoned their public jobs for one single day" or "their business for a moment." [10] Madero's loyalty to honest and hard-working public servants undercut his popularity and encouraged the shilly-shallyer to cloak selfish ambition with the mantle of revolutionary virtue.

Yet, to the disinherited, Madero's views had the stench of treason. As Cabrera had stated in Congress, "the revolution was the revolution." The army of public employees dating from Díaz, according to this dictum, "would be turned out." [11] As one self-styled warrior complained to Madero, "we who took up arms for you, who voted for you, are saddened when we see you give the best jobs to persons who fired not a single shot." [12] Judging by the number of letters of this type, countless Mexicans had gone to the barricades with Madero. For in truth, Madero had to fend off an army of office seekers. So many pleas for jobs arrived on his desk that he eventually decided to "recommend no one." [13]

Under Carranza, the rush turned into an avalanche of office hopefuls. Not only were jobs of old bureaucrats jeopardized, but so were those of Madero appointees who stayed at their posts during the Huerta interlude, as well as the jobs of disciples of Villa, Zapata, and the Convention government. While Carranza easily embraced holdovers from the days of Díaz, his followers worshiped a different opinion. They intended to wipe the slate clean, and expected Carranza to obey their wishes. "Sir, it is scandalous," warned one of them, "how endless numbers of *cientificos,* Huertistas, and Felicistas occupy public posts . . . so much so that it is said that people are beginning to grumble, to suspect, and to believe that you are not upholding the ideals of Madero, but instead, are driven by ambition," otherwise "you would not permit the enemies of the nation to wield power." [14] With the defeat of Huerta, in reality, the ancient administrative structure lay in shambles, inviting a wholesale assault on it by hordes of office seekers. Employees of a government printshop put the matter succinctly to Carranza: "we ask . . . that you protect our jobs and give jobs to those of us who do not have them or, at least, keep us in mind so that we may be given jobs later." [15]

A man of principle but also a realistic politician, Carranza had no choice but to heed the cry of his hungry followers. When he gave them carte blanche to do as they wished, the purge was on. Asked by Palavicini, newly appointed minister of public instruction, to tell him who was on his staff, Carranza replied that he had not kept anyone of the "old team." Recalled Palavicini: "I ordered the heads of the divisions to meet with me and told them that their services were no longer needed. All of the employees and workers were dismissed." [16] When Cabrera became minister of the treasury, he staffed it with his own loyalists, while Gobernación purged "employees who had, in whatever capacity, served Díaz, Huerta, or the Convention chieftains." [17] A similar house cleaning was carried out by the Ministry of Communications and Public Works.[18] Upon being named head of customs in Veracruz, General Francisco Múgica "threw the rascals" out and replaced them with his own men.[19] But, then so had Villa. By 1916, to weed out "untrustworthy" employees, tests of past political loyalties had been adopted by all branches of administration.[20] Countless bureaucrats, having served enemies of the Constitutionalists "because of necessity or want," lost their jobs.[21] The influential, meanwhile, one member of his family reminded Alvaro Obregón, reserved the best posts for themselves.[22]

The successful coup against Carranza set in motion the process once again. The purges, however, may not have been as widespread as before. After all, Obregón's die-hards had earlier flown the banners of the Carrancistas. Prominent partisans of the First Chief, nonetheless, immediately felt the political axe, among them Cabrera. To satisfy the appetites of his legion of yes-men, Obregón, in the style of his predecessor, looked the other way when his subordinates inflated public payrolls. As Antonio Manero ascertained, the thousands of superfluous employees, with little to do but to claim their paychecks, sank all hopes of balancing the budget.[23] At the same time, the army of officeholders had begun to build a wall between the people and their leaders, while eventually even senators were to complain of government ministries staffed with "cynics." [24]

II

The transfer of power from Díaz to Madero, hailed as the birth of a new era, moreover, also left undisturbed deeply rooted political practices to the bitter anguish of those who believed in panaceas. The pledges of free and honest elections, of voting rights for everyone, and of democratic horizons, proved more apparent than real. Like Mexican rulers before him, Madero, who in his heart worshipped the ideals of Western democracies, succumbed to the traditional vices. Whether with his consent or at his behest, or because of harsh political reality limiting his ability to guarantee the wishes of people he had sworn to consult, Madero fell into step with the Mexican habit of controlling the political process. To the disillusioned, to quote the Plan de Ayala, Madero had made a cruel hoax of his promise of free elections, "imposing against" the popular will "José María Pino Suárez . . . and state governors such as General Ambrosio Figueroa, the executioner and tyrant of the people of Morelos." [25] Or, in the words of one cynical observer, "we had changed collars but the dogs were the same ones." [26]

The free and honest elections theoretically endorsed by Carranza and Obregón, in reality, were impossible to carry out. Alien to Mexican history, the pledges, at best, symbolized goals. The political past had outlived the change in leadership and the rhetoric of revolution. "Whenever possible, I try to encourage honest elections," confessed Juan Sánchez Azcona. "Unfortunately, there is a limit to what one can do because . . . of political intrigues and the range of views among even disciples of our own school of thought." [27] More than likely, Azcona voiced the frustrations of Madero, a political neophyte in the jungle of Mexican politics. Tht triumphant "Revolution" had disowned the past, but its disciples had seen the light of day and grown to maturity in a society with political ills as old as the sixteenth century. They were as Mexican as don Porfirio, whom they accused of having corrupted and subverted a nonexistent, idealized political heritage. Once in power, the new masters of Mexico discarded unrealistic pledges in order to govern in the way they knew best: with the attitudes and tools that had kept the Republic afloat for a century. Nor was the society of 1910 ready to live by the ideals and customs shaped by the experiences of alien societies.

Madero and his successors, whatever their convictions may have been, shut their eyes to political skullduggery out of necessity, but also, their critics knew, because they accepted it for reality in Mexico. Madero could live with the fraudulent elections of 1912, leaving high public offices in the hands of scores of Porfiristas, because he had no fundamental ideological differences with them. Yet, when he permitted Governor Nicolás Méndez, a spokesman for vested interests, to manipulate elections in Puebla, to give one example, he risked the victory of conservative senators and deputies to Congress.[28] Not to intervene, as Madero insisted he could not, left politics to the rich and influential, the groups favored by Díaz. Actually, Madero had two choices: to intervene and betray his vow to uphold democracy; or to remain neutral and betray supporters who wanted men with new ideas in politics. Quixotically, he jumped back and forth between the two alternatives.

The banners of Madero's Partido Constitucional Progresista notwithstanding, the irregularities of the past became the trademark of the future. To begin with, fraud marred elections from the start. While Madero triumphed in what was called the most honest election until then, the political tug-of-war in the states in 1912 bore a distinct stamp. With the approval of his brother, Gustavo, Madero hand-picked the governors of San Luis Potosí and Aguascalientes, both unpopular candidates. Against the wishes of the majority, Delio Moreno Cantón, brother-in-law of Pino Suárez, became governor of Yucatán.[29] Votes were altered in Chiapas, Sinaloa, Oaxaca, Jalisco, and Tlaxcala. In Tamaulipas the people voted for Grácia Medrano but saw their opinion ig-

nored by the state legislature.[30] To control elections in Veracruz, the political bosses elevated a man of their own to the
statehouse.[31] A small band chose the deputies to the national
Congress in Tabasco. "At first," wrote a native of the state to
Madero, "we who had lived through the devious ways of Díaz
paid little attention to what went on; but such were the outrages
committed that we eventually had to vent our anger." [32] In one
key district of Tlaxcala the departing governor, at the behest of
the Liga de Agricultores, the lords of the land, had the mayor
appoint *hacendados* the election judges.[33] In Jalisco, Wistano
Luis Orozco, the distinguished scholar and lawyer, a congressional candidate and avowed Maderista, watched officials
"steal votes" away from him and confer victory on his rival.[34]

Carranza, a veteran of Porfirista politics, made no serious attempt to transform the political behavior of his countrymen.
New faces grasped the reins of government but the methods remained unchanged. While extolling democratic ideals, Carranza,
nevertheless, reserved their implementation for the future. The
fall of 1915, he declared, was no time to sanction diversity of
political opinion. By the same token, so long as they shared the
fruits of the banquet table, Carranza's partisans did not ask for the
impossible. To the contrary, Obregón and others applauded efforts to discourage the formation of political parties until peace
was assured.[35] Political differences, they believed, endangered it.
Still, a few states began to cautiously implement reforms, reor-
ganizing, as Governor Plutarco Elías Calles did in Sonora, municipal governments.[36] But these were hesitant efforts, less successful
in practice than in theory. The hated *jefe político* disappeared but his successor was not very different. Further, everywhere time-honored ways of doing things weathered the rebellion. General Ramón F. Iturbe, the military *cacique* of Sinaloa,
for example, named his father-in-law its governor.[37] Carranza,
meanwhile, had to listen to complaints of the abuse of power in
Sinaloa, making injustice "the order of the day" and "political
murders as common as in the Porfirian epoch." [38] With the
new official bandwagon, the Partido Liberal Constitucionalista,
behind him, Carranza became the choice of Congress for the
presidency, but there were no seats set aside for its opponents.
Earlier, its bosses had controlled the choice of delegates to the

Constitutional Convention, where noted champions of agrarian reform sat on the sidelines but not Gerzayn Ugarte, Carranza's conservative private secretary, who was "elected a delegate." A key plank of the Partido Liberal Constitucionalista demanded that all of its members elected or chosen for public office fill secondary jobs under them with *peleceanos,* party loyalists.[39]

Nor did the First Chief discourage *personalismo,* the cult of the leader. Regardless of protestations to their party, the *peleceanos* paid homage to Carranza. "We bring our complaint to you," to quote a striking passage in a letter to Carranza, "as a son to his father." [40] A partisan of the First Chief wrote angrily of a general in San Luis Potosí who had sworn loyalty to a cause and a set of principles instead of to the First Chief.[41] With equal disbelief another stalwart reported the convictions of a general who had made himself neutral in the coniflict between Carranza and Villa because he believed it anchored in ambition and "personalism." [42] In another version: "What this country needs are men, for without men of noble intent . . . the most perfect legislation is superfluous." [43] With this attitude to rely on, Carranza became, said a Zapatista, "a vulgar tyrant, interested solely in the conquest of personal power and in surrounding himself with adulators, a man totally alien to the revolutionary cause." [44]

The rigging of elections and the use of terror to achieve political ends went on unabated despite the coming of peace. Formal opposition was taboo. However, with Carranza's consolidation of political authority, sanctioned by edict of Congress in 1917, the quest for public office, formerly characterized by flagrant abuses, took on a more sophisticated tone. After all, the *peleceanos* themselves were the sole candidates. Nonetheless, practices of questionable repute endured. As one embittered native of Chiapas described the picture there, the acting governor, an unpopular general lacking qualifications for office, but with ambitions to succeed himself, enjoyed the backing of the bureaucracy and the political bosses; his rival, another general, was equally unqualified. Carranza, he suggested, could help the people of Chiapas by sending both "away on a mission." [45] With the aid of Luis Cabrera, charged General Luis Gutiérrez, Gustavo Espinosa Mireles, the "conservative" state boss and intimate of

Carranza, had deprived him of the governorship of Coahuila in 1917.[46] Had there been no fraud, Gutiérrez would have won, asserted General Conrado Cevera, a Zapatista. In Tabasco, in the meantime, said Salvador Alvarado, governor of neighboring Yucatán, "political leeches" were trying to take over the state-house.[47] By encouraging and manipulating factional strife in Oaxaca for selfish gain, the national political bosses, implied *El Universal,* had alienated progressive elements in the state.[48]

The situation in Puebla in late 1916 encapsulated the larger political picture. In September, the people of its capital city had cast ballots to select a mayor. The municipal council, which counted the votes, declared Ramón I. Guzmán to be the victor over Leopoldo R. Galván, the popular candidate. Galván, in the opinion of his followers, had won overwhelmingly. The two groups in the election stood at opposite poles of the political spectrum. The Partido Político Popular, Galván's group, repre-sented the textile workers, the railroad brotherhoods unionized astisans and mechanics, and the students. Its rival, the Gran Par-tido Liberal del Estado, spearheaded a different constituency: political bosses and bureaucrats in league with the rich and pow-erful of Puebla. Among them was General Marciano González, the governor. It included men who as high state officials had served Victoriano Huerta, been private secretaries to Liman-tour, leaders of the conservative Catholic party of Puebla, and admirers of Díaz. Guzmán, their candidate, had just recently ar-rived in Puebla and was ineligible to hold public office. Yet the city council, ignoring state law, had made him mayor.[49] Car-ranza's decision to pick his successor, a reflection on a national scale of the ills in Puebla, however, cost him his life. His murder at Tlaxcalantongo, commented Francisco León de la Barra, bore a striking resemblance to the death of Madero.[50]

"To be an Obregonista today," stated José Vasconcelos in 1920, "is to have been a Maderista yesterday." [51] On the surface, at least, Vasconcelos judged correctly, since Obregón, like the martyred Apostle, had tossed his hat into the presidential ring supposedly to defend political morality and the sanctity of the vote, both, he believed, trampled afoot by Carranza.[52] He had taken up arms, he told General Enrique Estrada, against a gov-ernment that had "attempted to impede the right to vote in complicity with a gang of governors." [53] Be that as it may, Obregón's methods hardly differed from those of his predecessors. Recognizing this, Vasconcelos, the former enthusiast, resigned his post as minister of education in 1923.

With the collapse of the Carrancistas, the political arena belonged to Obregón and his followers. They organized themselves into the Partido Cooperativista Nacional, and counted upon the support of the Partido Laborista Mexicano, formed essentially to back Obregón's candidacy by Luis Morones and his companions, and the Partido Nacional Agrarista, the genius of Antonio Díaz Soto y Gama. A number of splinter groups, the Partido Socialista del Sureste, for instance, lent additional support. By January, 1923, the Obregonistas controlled Congress, the state legislatures, and every one of the governorships.

A consumate and worldly politician, Obregón, theoretically, allowed a degree of political freedom—so long as it posed no danger. With this approach, he could kill two birds with one stone. The opposition, usually politicians hungry for public jobs, could be silenced by letting some of them feed at the public trough; and, by permitting them seats in Congress, Obregón's regime displayed the façade of a democracy. But to make certain that their rivals did not get out of hand, the Obregonistas kept a tight rein on them. "The sanctity of the ballot, a cardinal postulate of the Revolution since 1910," bewailed Rafael Martínez Escobar, president of the Partido Liberal Constitucionalista in 1922, "has never been so defiled before." To the "dishonor" of Mexico, the Ministry of Gobernación, entrusted with the management of politics, had flagrantly attacked candidates unwilling to toe the party line. Armed thugs had threatened the lives of members of the Partido Liberal Constitucionalista in the Chamber of Deputies. He had been jailed, Martínez Escobar reminded Obregón, for standing up to Carranza's attempt to impose his successor. It appears, he went on, that "you have forgotten your pledge to allow the people to freely pick the man who will succeed you." In order to turn over the presidency to Calles, Obregón and his cadre of servile loyalists had employed soldiers to ride roughshod over the sovereignty of the states, specificially Jalisco and Nuevo León. In a majority of the states, bemoaned Martínez Escobar, members of his party had been denied the vote. Their opposition in the Federal District was not just a party but the Ministry of Gobernación, the army, public officials, the police, and the power of a national regime bent on manipulating the elections. During the process, he concluded, democratic ideals, the dream of those who waged war against the Old Regime, had been prostituted.[54] But, in contrast, on the military chiefs, among them men guilty of murder and theft, said Toribio Esquivel Obregón, who watched events in Mexico from New York, the nation had bestowed rank, money, and *haciendas*.[55]

Neither did Obregón change the picture in the provinces. More likely than not, as in the days of Madero and Carranza, fraud determined election results. An open letter sent by citizens of Puebla to Obregón in 1921 charged that governors had been "imposed" on Veracruz, San Luis Potosí, Campeche, Michoacán, Coahuila, Morelos, Tlaxacala, Nayarit, as well as Puebla. The popular will had been flouted in all of them. In Puebla, José María Sánchez, an incompetent and unpopular governor, had, in the company of his cronies, fallen upon the towns and villages "like ravenous vultures." [56] A few months later the legislature of Puebla granted Sánchez a leave of absence until he cleared himself of charges of the "premeditated murder" of one of its members.[57] Reform governor Francisco Múgica of Michoacán, one of the fathers of the Constitution of 1917, after one year in the statehouse was driven from office by enemies hostile to his policies.[58] Senators and deputies, hypothetically the spokesmen for individual states, often were either not natives of the states they represented or had spent little time in them. Given this state of affairs, Obregón acknowledged, they were unfamiliar with local needs and apt to make mistakes.[59]

The municipalities had their own brand of political maladies. One strange case in Zacatecas involved the efforts of two national congressmen to depose the popularly elected town council of Jerez. Obregón reported that the petty czars cut telegraph lines connecting southern Zacatecas, the site of Jerez, with the rest of the state, and then with the aid of the army attacked the town. The result was two dead and a number of wounded.[60] The tables were reversed in Ciudad del Carmen in Campeche where, according to Congressman J. Certucha, unpopular municipal authorities, with an eye to controlling the results of a forthcoming election, on any pretext whatsoever, had jailed law-abiding citizens or had given them stiff fines.[61] The governor of Veracruz wrote Obregón that one public official, a member of the Monetary Commission with close ties to the *hacendados,* had taken it upon himself to compel peasants to literally sign away their rights.[62]

At the national level, during the interval, the political ambitions that had led Pascual Orozco to defy Madero, and Villa to clash with Carranza, and Obregón to disown Carranza, persuaded Adolfo de la Huerta to confront Obregón in 1923. De la Huerta had been dropped in favor of Calles. Obregón's decision upset the delicate balance in the revolutionary family. Suddenly discontented generals and opportunistic politicians charged Obregón, just as he had Carranza earlier, with attempting to subvert the popular will. The rebel flag of General Estrada, one of the malcontents, immediately chastized Obregón for having betrayed the principle of honest ballots in free elections "sacred since the days of Madero." [63] Before long, all of Obregón's rivals, from De la Huerta to the municipal bigwig, had voiced that accusation. Obregón, the leader sufficiently bold to rescue Mexico from Carranza's claws, lamentably had performed a similar dastardly deed. However, unlike Carranza, Obregón triumphed over his enemies. The defeat of De la Huerta encouraged General Angel Flores, governor of Sinaloa and a man with unrealistic presidential dreams, to mistakenly, if briefly, run against Calles. But the well-oiled political machine refused to permit Flores, a quixotic candidate given the inevitable victory of Calles, to campaign freely. A *Manifiesto* published by him, listing political crimes committed against him, included the usual election irregularities and the jailing, shooting, and killing of his partisans.[64]

III

"How sad," lamented Obregón during his campaign for the presidency, "to see the most distinguished men, civilians, and soldiers, turn the revolutionary movement into a butt for ridicule and devote heart and soul to the pursuit of the almighty peso." [65] Obregón, no stranger to the sport played with public funds, had put his finger on a cancer that outlived the flight of don Porfirio and his coterie of docile millionaires. To the contrary, the appetite of the new rulers, so long denied entrance to the world of the rich, exacerbated the ills of the ancient game of politics for private gain. It was not a time to observe the rules of honesty but an opportunity to make up for what had been lost. So, "revolutionaries" by the scores feasted on the spoils of public office, or acquired fortunes overnight in shady business ventures. Among the rebel figures who basked in the public limelight, those who saved their honor and integrity were singular. Men of principle had to stand by helplessly and watch (and to accept as inevitable) less squeamish companions enrich themselves. "After my disillusionment with so many I thought honest, I fear even my own shadow," confessed De la Huerta. [66] "The entire world anxiously awaits an honest government in Mexico," said Francisco Vásquez Gómez, one "truly patriotic, that will devote itself to the salvation of the country and not to enriching its members." [67] For his part, Manuel Gamio, who months earlier had vowed to move heaven and earth for Mexico, resigned his job as subsecretary of public education and went off to exile in protest against the graft he discovered in the house Vasconcelos had built. [68]

Commonplace in the days of Díaz, the evils of corruption had quickly contaminated the Madero regime. The illness even found receptive organs in the ruling family, for Madero's uncles, owners of a textile mill in Monterrey, negotiated themselves a fat contract to provide the army with uniforms. During his four months in office, testified one Madero official, funds for welfare and education had largely passed into private hands. [69] The legislature of Hidalgo accused Ramón Rosales, Madero's choice for governor, of stealing 79,000 pesos from the state's treasury. [70] In Sonora, complained Governor José Maytorena, the legislature permitted the Banco de Sonora, a private corporation, to control the Río Sonora. [71] Police officials in Mexico City, charged a nephew of Madero, continued to mete out justice only to the rich. [72]

In the aftermath of Huerta's demise, the ancient ills became

an epidemic. Accounts of graft and corruption, of "revolutionaries" who publicly talked of *ejidos* for dirt farmers but went
home to their *haciendas,* amassed fortunes out of public works,
or took money under the table from businessmen and *hacendados,* were prosaic topics of gossip. Jesús Urueta and Rafael
Zubarán Capmany, two of the lawyers and stalwarts among the
Carrancistas, went so far as to agree to handle the case of an
imprisoned *hacendado* eager to win his release from jail and the
return of his property on condition that, if successful, he pay
them 5,000 pesos and 20 percent of the profits from the sale of
his harvest. To keep the scheme from public view, they arranged
for the *hacendado* to sign an agreement with an intermediary.[73]
When a new governor of Chiapas assumed his post, he found
the state treasury "without a single cent to pay for the most urgent services." [74] His predecessor, a nominee of Carranza, had
exempted his cronies from paying taxes, levied onerous dues
on others, reserved public jobs for his friends, and saved money
by reducing the salaries of lowly bureaucrats. He told newspapers what to print, controlled the courts, spent public funds
on himself, tolerated monopolies in business so long as he
received a slice of their profits and, as in former years,
appointed the *jefes políticos,* supposedly banned by the Constitution of 1917. By the same token, the *jefes políticos,* euphemisti-
cally referred to as "Representatives of the Executive,"
mercilessly exploited the Indian communities.[75] One of the first
acts of the governor of Oaxaca, a Carranza loyalist, was to
declare null and void the changes and additions to the Charter
of 1857 approved at Querétaro.[76] Lorenzo Rosado, a confidant
of Governor Ignacio Pesqueira in Sonora, became a millionaire
in less than half a year in public office.[77] Governor Alejandro
Bay, also of Sonora, under the pretext of rebuilding the customs
house in Nogales, imported cement, lumber, and hardware from
the United States for his own use, and sent the bills to the state
treasury.[78] According to testimony given Carranza, "immorality"
on the railroads was widespread in 1915 and involved leading
figures in government.[79] No exile returned home by way of
Laredo without paying a *mordida,* bribe, where, reported an
agent of Carranza, a corrupt immigration official decided their
fate.[80] Under Governor Martín Triana of Aguascalientes, most

rural and urban properties had been returned to their former owners.[81] Meanwhile, to the anger of local merchants, Triana, in cahoots with friends in business, enjoyed a virtual monopoly over the sale of certain goods.[82] To his cronies, Triana granted favors but arbitrarily denied to ordinary citizens their rights. In San Luis Potosí, *hacendados* had given *mordidas* to Rafael Nieto, subsecretary of the national treasury and candidate for governor of the state, for the return of their properties.[83]

Elsewhere, there were similar stories. Iturbe, governor of Sinaloa, in return for a share of the profits, allowed merchants and *hacendados* to traffic with food prices, linked arms with the Redo family, the major *hacendados* in the state, and dabbled in commerce—while the Constitutionalists, the faction to which he belonged, waged a war to the death with Villa.[84] Food prices soared in Culiacán, the capital of Sinaloa, because state and federal officials profited from its sale.[85] The governor of Puebla, Luis G. Cervantes, his enemies charged, had left undisturbed the legal and judicial rigmarole of the Díaz era, and winked at prostitution and vice. In league with the Compañía Pulquera, authorities in the city of Puebla permitted *pulque* bars to flourish; formerly open for business from nine in the morning to three in the afternoon, they now sold *pulque* from seven in the morning to eight at night. Some *barrios* had as many as three *pulquerías* every thirty paces.[86] Antonio G. Azuara, the private secretary of Luis Cabrera, then in Carranza's cabinet, had a record of graft dating from the Díaz epoch, according to an accusation signed by the *presidente municipal* of Tuxpan, a town in Veracruz. Yet Azuara also held an important post in the Treasury.[87] The governor of Yucatán, Salvador Alvarado, had placed the railroads under state control, organizing a Consejo Administrativo to run them. By 1920, under his successor, charged an official of the railroads, the members of the Consejo, in the process of enriching themselves had bankrupted the railroads. While the workers had not been paid in two weeks, the high salaries of the Consejo were paid promptly. On the Consejo, admitted one of its members, for chairman we have "a drunken ex-Argumentista [Benjamín Argumedo, a Porfirista general]; for *official mayor,* a perverse enemy of the worker." [88]

The decade of the twenties, the years of Obregón and Calles

capped this picture. The past, a history of nearly four centuries of moral turpitude in politics and public life, had engulfed the rebellion. By 1921, for instance, in the home state of the ruling dynasty, garbanzo farmers were complaining of being cheated by officials "high in government" working with foreign interests.[89] Two stories, perhaps, add a final footnote on the condition of public morality in Mexico. Writing Obregón, Alejandro Iñigo, then recently dismissed as director of the penitentiary in the Federal District, explained why he lost his job. To his sorrow, he had learned of the sale of marijuana to inmates of the prison; the culprit was the uncle of the mayor of the Federal District. When Iñigo alerted him to what was going on, the mayor, rather than punish his uncle, fired Iñigo.[90] "When I returned to Mexico from exile," recalled Jorge Prieto Laurens in the second of the two stories, "to my surprise I found many of my former companions, such as Emilio Portes Gil, Ezequiel Padilla, Luis L. León, José Manuel Puig Casauranc . . . and others too numerous to list, to be the owners of palatial homes in the Lomas de Chapultepec, on the Paseo de la Reforma, and the Colonia Hipódromo." Prieto Laurens had known them "when they lived in modest apartments in the most humble *colonias*" of Mexico City.[91]

TWENTY-TWO

The Unwilling

Neighbor

"Poor Mexico, so far from God and so near the United States."

Porfirio Díaz

I

T HE YANKEE NEXT DOOR, Mexicans learned immediately, would not easily relinquish his stake in Mexico. To the contrary, investors and their government in Washington watched warily the course of the rebellion, and from the start, worked feverishly to keep it within the bounds of what they believed permissible. They distrusted social revolution and only belatedly tolerated halfway reform. With the Treaty of Bucareli of 1923, say many Mexicans, policy makers in Washington dealt a hammer blow to the hopes of reformers in Mexico. Whatever the truth, history amply documents sundry American efforts to impede and stifle change in Mexico. The claim of American innocence hardly stands scrutiny.

The American attitude, from the perspective of some Mexicans, helps explain why their country stopped short of having a revolution. Given this view, at least three interpretations, all logically defensible, merit careful consideration. Mexicans failed to carry out a revolution because the United States would not permit it. Secondly, in another Mexican version, Yankee attitudes, as understood by Mexicans, frightened sincere reformers into believing that any attempt to implement social change in-

THE UNWILLING NEIGHBOR 383

vited American intervention. Confronted with this harsh reality, Mexicans abandoned thoughts of drastic change. Finally, in a third view, the cautious and conservative Mexican chieftains exploited the bugaboo of Yankee intervention to hide their unwillingness to alter significantly the status quo; in their opinion, Mexico needed American investments and know-how for the prosperity of its capitalist system, and obviously, for their own well-being. To some extent, all three versions have merit.

From the start, it scarcely requires saying, Mexican rebels, as Porfirio Díaz before them, had to come to terms with their gargantuan neighbor. To deny it is to distort the history of Mexico's relations with the United States. To begin with, the wealth, power, and sheer physical size of the United States dwarfed Mexico. The country inherited by Francisco I. Madero had one-fifth of the territory, a fraction of the population, and a tiny slice of the agricultural and industrial capacity of its huge neighbor. By the same token, the Mexican army, small, ill-equipped and poorly led, hardly served as a barrier to Washington's designs. As Francisco R. Serrano, a *político* from Sonora, put it, an ill fate had willed that Mexico lie adjacent to the United States.[1] To Jorge Vera Estañol, American influence had been "decisive" in shaping the destiny of Mexico, so much so that its "political and social structure" shook with every change in Washington's attitude. Any repudiation by a Mexican government of contracts earlier agreed to with American interests, giving them rights and property, brought "onerous . . . consequences."[2] Our foreign problem, added Luis Cabrera, boils down to how Mexico safeguards the investments of foreigners.[3] Intelligent Mexicans know, to quote Félix F. Palavicini, that "it is impossible to long maintain a hostile attitude towards the colossus, to close our doors to its commerce, or worse still, to enter into alliances with Europeans or Asians who, surely, will turn against us."[4] Mexico must put its house in order, lest the United States intervene, if not militraily, with diplomatic measures that, warned Antonio Manero, "could well cost us a loss of territory."[5]

But all the same, after years of pandering to foreigners, Mexicans wanted a "Mexico for the Mexicans." To Venustiano Carranza, perhaps its loudest voice in government circles, love of country meant respect for Mexican sovereignty, nonintervention by outsiders, and the right to deal with domestic questions in light of the national interest.[6] Love of country was equated with antiforeign. Carranza, his disciples reminded him, stood for a unity of Latin Americans and for their right to live independently of the Yankee, the enemy of the Hispanic people.[7] When the governor of Texas invited three counterparts from northern Mexican states to meet with him in Laredo, Gustavo Espinosa Mireles, chief of Coahuila, speaking for his companions, refused, saying that it would look bad for them to come running at the behest of an American politician.[8]

The cardinal question for Mexico to resolve, explained Aarón Sáenz, subsecretary of foreign affairs under Alvaro Obregón, was how to have equitable relations with the United States. The attempt to liquidate economic and political inequities of the Old Regime had disturbed powerful foreign interests that, to defend their holdings, had suborned Mexicans, employed diplomatic blackmail to stop reform, and rode roughshod over Mexican sovereignty.[9] Yet, to bring the Revolution to a successful conclusion, Mexico had to make private interests, both native and foreign, obey its laws. The concept of property rights outlined by Article 27, the crux of the national charter, intended to rescue for the nation title to property and natural resources, particularly mines and petroleum, exploited by foreigners.[10]

However, every try at reform almost always brought Mexico face to face with its neighbor across the border. Prudence, the soul of practical politics, therefore, called for caution lest Mexico unduly antagonize the Yankee. One reason for not pushing ahead with drastic social change, Carranza explained, was because "common sense dictated a policy that would not alarm landlords, business people, and capitalists who would immediately unite to defend their interests, while the United States, to avoid having a socialist country next door, would have embraced Victoriano Huerta."[11] In an effort to justify the slow pace of agrarian reform, Obregón, speaking in 1923, dwelt on the "formidable resistance of both national and foreign" groups.[12] Because of it, Sáenz added, one element in the Ministry of Foreign Affairs had urged Obregón to scale down plans for land redistribution, particularly since foreigners wanted ready payment for lands taken from them.[13] To satisfy the hunger for land, in brief, exacerbated Mexico's international situation due to the hostility of foreign powers.

An added concern that every administration had to live with was the likely possibility that dissident Mexicans would inevitably court Washington's benevolence. Many Mexicans, apparently, saw nothing incongruous in their demand that Carranza and Obregón behave with nationalistic aplomb while, at the same time, asking outsiders to meddle in Mexican affairs on their behalf. Even Obregón, complained Carranza, to hurt him politically at home had stooped to exploiting Washington's paranoia of Japanese activity in Lower California.[14] Carranza, moreover, angrily castigated the schemes of Mexican exiles who, to feather their own nest, plotted the downfall of his regime with foreigners. He saw a sharp similarity between Mexico's situation in 1919 and that of Benito Juárez who, in 1860, had to deal with the disloyalty of Mexican exiles begging Britain, France, and Spain to invade their country.[15]

II

Ironically, however, the men who led Mexico down the path of rebellion had no quarrel with the principle of foreign investment. Like the Porfiristas, the new masters believed that outside capital could help cure the ills of underdevelopment. Without the aid of industrialized nations, little could be done to rebuild and develop Mexico. "Our country," Mexico's consul in Detroit cautioned Adolfo de la Huerta in 1923, "needs foreigners to develop its natural resources." [16] Obregón, particularly, believed inevitable, and perhaps even beneficial, Mexico's dependence on the United States. Leaders of Obregón's stripe merely wanted to end the blatant special privileges of foreigners. While welcomed, foreign investors must abide by national legislation, so that Mexicans might govern as they saw fit. At no time did the rulers of post-Díaz Mexico ask Americans to leave or to stop investing their money in Mexico. If Americans and other aliens did not challenge the supremacy of the state, the new rulers were satisfied. It was not their wealth that preoccupied Mexico's rulers, but the power of the United States, so ubiquitously at their beck and call.[17]

On this point, Article 27 openly displayed its nationalistic bent. Only Mexicans could own land in Mexico or exploit its subsoil. But, added Fernando González Roa, an ally of Obregón, the state could grant a comparable right to foreigners willing to renounce the right to special protection from their governments. However, this was no radical innovation, for no attempt had been made to revive colonial legislation barring foreigners from the Spanish empire. Mexico lived in a twentieth-century world of interdependent countries, where artificial walls were obsolete. Isolation was both impractical and impossible, concluded González Roa, due to the heavy outside investment in Mexico, the large number of foreigners in the country, past international treaties, and Mexico's proximity to the United States. Any scheme to isolate Mexico would surely invite gunboats to beat down "our doors." [18]

This attitude dated from Madero but had roots in the Porfiriato. Madero had only belatedly bowed to popular sentiment, increasingly hostile to foreigners and exemplified by the demands of the strikers at Cananea in 1906. Yet article 3 of his Plan de San Luis Potosí pledged to honor "the obligations with foreign governments of the Porfiristas," while article 8 spoke of respect for the rights of foreigners and their properties. Ernesto Madero, Francisco Bulnes emphasized, had "rightly judged that it was impossible to govern without the full support of national and foreign capitalists, especially in a country that needed funds to develop." [19] Still, Madero was not unaware of the danger to Mexico from the United States. Mexico must build an inner strength based on a sense of national dignity and democracy to withstand the turbulent winds from the north. Madero welcomed foreign capital but only if it contained no strings.[20]

Carranza voiced a similar opinion. One of his first decrees, dated May 10, 1913, had recognized the right of foreigners to collect for damages suffered by their properties since 1910. He promised to abide by the decision of a mixed commission of Mexicans and foreigners that would evaluate the legitimacy of claims and the amount of reparations. Another of his decrees ordered Constitutionalist army chieftains not to permit their underlings to take property or goods away from foreigners. In June, 1915, in another decree, Carranza promised foreigners residing in Mexico "the guarantees to which they are entitled by our laws and to fully protect their lives, liberty, and the enjoyment of their legitimate property rights." He spoke of a solution to the agarian problem without resort to "confiscation." Property legitimately acquired, and not a monopoly or a special privilege, would be respected.[21] During a visit to Piedras Negras, a small border town in Coahuila, Carranza invited American investors to come to Mexico, "but without the promise of special privileges." [22] To the editor of *The Los Angeles Examiner,* he pledged "all of the security and guarantees granted by Mexico's laws" to American capital invested in Mexico.[23] Rafael Nieto, Carranza's minister of the treasury in 1919, told a group of New York bankers that the Mexican government would soon begin to pay the interest on its foreign debt, adding that he believed it highly likely that the bankers and Mexico could reach an agreement of mutual benefit. Mexico, he stressed, welcomed legitimate foreign investors willing to collaborate in its development.[24] When American mining magnates objected to a progressive tax on their properties, Carranza revoked it, although Luis Cabrera had thought it necessary in order to prevent foreigners from holding on to large tracts of undeveloped land.[25]

The clan from Sonora, with Obregón at its head, maintained an even more pragmatic nationalism. With their defiance of Huerta in 1913, the rebels had despatched a note to Washington vowing to protect American interests in Sonora.[26] Obregón believed that Mexico must open its doors to outside capital, especially American, for its own good. Foreign capital could be either beneficial or harmful, depending on its motives.[27] During his campaign for the presidency, he cabled the *Chicago Commerical Herald and Examiner*: Mexico "is eager to embrace, with true hospitality, men who seek a fair return on their work and money, and offers guarantees to those who . . . will cooperate with us to develop our motherland." With the help of American capital, he prophesized, Mexico, with its inexhaustible store of natural resources, could supply the markets of the world to the mutual benefit of both parties.[28] Lest Americans fail to get the message,

Obregón incorporated guarantees to foreign capital in his campaign platform: full recognition of rights legitimately acquired in Mexico; opportunities to Americans who wanted to invest to develop Mexico; and the enjoyment of rights granted by Mexican law.[29] Mexico, said Obregón, knew how "to appreciate" the contributions of foreign investors.[30] "My government," he told a potential American investor, "offers the necessary guarantees." [31] Writing to the widow of General Benjamín Hill, Obregón told her that he approved of her sale of petroleum lands to an American buyer, adding, in a revealing insight into his thinking, that he believed that the property should be passed on to individuals able to exploit it but, at the same time, to "obtain from its sale the highest possible profit." [32] To Pat M. Neff, governor of Texas, Obregón dwelt on efforts by his administration to convince the lower classes, evidently in his mind the most hostile to foreigners, to see workers and other groups of moral integrity in the United States as "friends." [33]

III

But as Mexicans interpreted events, moderation and courtship of American capital, to their disappointment and anger, merely fueled the intransigence of their neighbors. From their vantage point, the dog-in-the-manger attitude of the Yankees was an old and intractable characteristic. To his sorrow, Díaz and his generation had learned that unlocking Mexico's doors to foreign investors failed to make them loyal or grateful. Foreigners, especially Americans, isolated themselves, put self-interest above Mexico's welfare, and wanted their governments to protect their pot of gold. If he catered to their whims, Díaz could count on the sympathy of Washington, which was also the spokesman for European investors; yet Díaz, in his note of resignation, listed fear of American intervention in Mexico as one reason for leaving office. Whether correctly or not, leading Porfiristas had concluded that Washington's less-than-enthusiastic backing of Díaz rendered improbable a successful military campaign against the rebels.

"The danger to Mexico's sovereignty and independence was

no figment of the imagination," José I. Limantour stated emphatically.[34] By 1911, in his opinion, President William H. Taft and his cabinet, for a variety of reasons, no longer supported the Díaz regime.[35] Taft, he declared, had wanted to buy Lower California and, if unsuccessful, was ready to employ other means to acquire it.[36] This issue, in addition to Díaz' rumored plan to permit the Japanese to use Magdalena Bay, his refusal to permit the American navy access to it, and his rejection of Washington's request to stop Japanese immigration to Mexico, partly underlay the change in attitude. Further, his belated efforts to put a brake on the rising influence of American capital in Mexico had led Díaz to back policies labeled hostile by Washington. These policies included plans favoring European investors over their American rivals, demands that Washington pay Mexico for the Chamizal territory, banking reforms to control American commerce in Mexico, the refusal to allow American companies to build the Tehuantepec railroad, the consolidation of the national railways under Mexican control, and the asylum granted President José Santos Celaya of Nicaragua, a recent enemy of Washington.[37]

At first, according to the Porfiristas, the government of the United States had behaved properly, even cracking down on rebel activity north of the border.[38] But then, its policy changed, with Díaz more and more unable to get Washington to help him rid the border of rebels. Washington, for instance, refused to allow Díaz to move his troops over American territory and only half-heartedly attempted to stop the flow of guns and ammunition from Texas to Mexico. When rebels damaged American property in Mexico, Washington wanted immediate reparations from Díaz.[39] In the meantime, the American ambassador, Henry Lane Wilson, had urged Díaz to make concessions to the rebels, as he said, in order to undercut rebel propaganda. All the same, Wilson had persuaded Taft to station soldiers along the border. To Limantour, the order to mobilize troops meant that Taft planned to intervene in Mexico if necessary to protect American lives and property. "No one took seriously," Limantour recalled, "Taft's claims that he called up the soldiers to prevent rebel incursions from the United States into Mexico and to halt the traffic in arms." [40] During his stay in New York City, on his way back to Mexico from a trip to Europe, remembered

Limantour, spokesmen for the American government, especially Hungtington Wilson, under-secretary of state, and bankers, businessmen, and others with a stake in Mexico had openly displayed their impatience with the Díaz regime. Díaz' advanced age, said Limantour, particularly troubled Americans who, fearful that nothing had been done to assure a peaceful transfer of power, believed their interests in Mexico jeopardized. This attitude, and Mexican fear of intervention by the United States, concluded Limantour, helps explain why the Díaz regime decided to negotiate with Madero at Ciudad Juárez.[41] Limantour may have mistakenly interpreted American attitudes and policies, or deliberately distorted them to justify the sudden collapse of a government he served so long. But, nonetheless, his version probably mirrors much of the opinion of Mexicans of his time, even that of the rebels.

Modero, so goes the Mexican view of history, inherited this situation. Almost immediately, according to Manuel Calero, the minister of foreign affairs at the time, Taft warned Madero, whom he considered weak, not to tamper with the property of foreigners in Mexico.[42] Not to be outdone, Wilson, the Yankee ambassador, assumed that it was his duty not just to speak for American investors but for the entire foreign community. He wanted prompt remuneration for damages suffered by foreigners during the recent rebellion. Speaking in defense of the Compañía Tlahualilo, a role he abrogated to himself, declared Bulnes, Wilson "went so far as to make the absurd statement that when there was even a single American stockholder in a . . . company, even if his share were only one cent, it gave the United States . . . the right to make a claim against the Mexican government under the right of aliens." [43] When, in his opinion, Madero responded inappropriately to a note dealing with the payment of damages to foreign investors, Wilson called it proof of the anarchy in Mexico and of antiforeign sentiment.[44]

Wilson's dislike of Madero, Mexicans state, went to pathological extremes. Regardless of the cost, he wanted Madero out of the way. In the opinion of Cabrera, so distorted was Wilson's fear of the Mexican leader that he eventually became the "intellectual author" of the barrack's coup that toppled Madero. Further, Cabrera, along with every Mexican of his time, accused Wilson of helping Felix Díaz, nephew of don Porfirio, during the Tragic Ten Days of February 1913, and of engineering the Pact of the Embassy, where General Victoriano Huerta, entrusted with the defense of the government, embraced Felix Díaz and betrayed Madero.[45] The plot, said Jorge Vera Estañol, had been hatched, "discussed, written, and signed by both military chiefs" in the American embassy.[46] Able to protect the lives of Madero and José María Pino Suárez had he wanted to, Wilson arrogantly dismissed the pleas of the president's wife for his intervention and simply stood by while Huerta had them killed in cold blood.

Madero's death left a lasting imprint on Mexican attitudes. With disastrous consequences, the intervention feared by don Porfirio and his advisers had come to pass. The American ambassador had publicly unmasked the ability of the colossus to unmake Mexican presidents and to manipulate disloyal and opportunistic Mexicans. Washington's big stick did not go unnoticed in the Mexican Congress. "I accuse Mr. Henry Lane Wilson, the ambassador of the United States in Mexico," said Congressman Luis Manuel Rojas in his famous *yo acuso*, "of the moral responsibility for the death of Francisco I. Madero and José María Pino Suárez." [47] Huerta, Governor Carranza of Coahuila told his companions, had carried out the foul deed "with the help of a band of pampered foreigners who surrounded Wilson." [48] It was perfectly clear to Carranza and his allies, states Arnaldo Córdova, that in the future nothing could be done without taking into account the unruly neighbor across the border.[49]

For the Constitutionalists, a huge problem loomed ahead: how to defeat Huerta while courting American diplomatic recognition, but at the same time, keep Washington from meddling in Mexican domestic business. Fittingly, Huerta, eager for Washington's benediction, had instead to listen to President Woodrow Wilson condemn his regime and to watch American marines and sailors invade Mexican soil. To Huerta's allies, and perhaps also to Carranza, Woodrow Wilson appeared to be trying to turn Mexico into a protectorate of the United States.[50] During the interval of Huerta's presidency, and later after Wilson saw fit to recognize the Constitutionalists, Carranza, his sympathizers say, had to put up with almost daily American interference and harassment. In one period, Cabrera recalled, the State Department and its representative in Mexico sent endless notes and telegrams demanding guarantees for foreigners in Mexico. They included complaints against the Carranza regime for its use of the railroads; against efforts to hold prices in check; against the censure of telegrams and mail; against sanitary measures; against everything, in short, that prevented foreigners from enjoying a life of security . . . in a civilized nation." In Cabrera's opinion, J. R. Silliman, vice-consul and special representative of Wilson, was as likely to protest the death of a man in Chihuahua, who turned up very much alive a day or two later, as he was to ask for the return of a mule stolen in Tabasco, on behalf of Americans, Englishmen, Frenchmen, Germans and even Mexicans who flew the Stars and Stripes over their property.[51]

To Mexicans, their country was seldom free of American intervention. Wilson compelled Carranza to lift the siege of the port of Progreso when it cut into the profits of American corporations in Yucatán.[52] In June 1916, the director of Mexican customs reported that officials in Laredo and Eagle Pass, two key border towns in Texas, had arbitrarily banned the export of corn and other basic foodstuffs to Mexico.[53] According to Mexican sources, two years later the United States closed its doors to imports of Mexican vanilla.[54] Washington, said Ignacio Bonilla, Carranza's minister to the United States, had viewed as unfriendly plans by officials in Sonora in 1911 to cancel a concession for water given the Richardson Construction Company ten years earlier.[55] In the fall of 1915, reported Cabrera, authorities in El Paso, Texas were opening Mexican mail to the United States.[56] A month earlier, Ramón P. DeNegri, Mexican consul in San Francisco, had alerted Carranza to a flotilla of naval ships being readied in case armed intervention came about.[57] Efforts by both the Republican and Progressive parties to discredit President Wilson's Mexican policy, reviewed in detail for Carranza by the Mexican consul in Philadelphia, cast a pall over the National Palace in Mexico.[58] If Wilson's political enemies wanted a tougher stance taken against Mexico, what could Carranza expect of them should they capture the White House? No wonder that Mexican agents in the United States gleefully reported Wilson's growing involvement in the war in Europe.

IV

To survive or perish at the whims of Washington—this, said Mexicans, was their fate. Struggle a they might to control their own destinies, Washington pulled the strings. The lament, voiced by Díaz, was subsequently echoed in the halls of the National Palace by his successors. Mexicans especially resented the arms policy of the United States, the handling of Mexican news by the American press, and for both Huerta and Carranza, the invasion of Mexican soil by Yankee soldiers and marines.

The need to rely on the sale of American arms, the key to military victories at home, particularly galled Mexicans, both rebels and government officials. To complicate life for them, Washington frowned on the purchase of arms in Europe or Japan. Yet, by withholding or not withholding permission to buy arms, Washington, for all intents and purposes, decided the outcome of domestic quarrels in Mexico. Díaz had confronted this harsh reality first when, despite Washington's supposed benevolence toward him, his enemies had easily acquired arms across the border. One witness told Manero that he had seen smugglers swim across the Río Grande with weapons in their hands while American soldiers, dispatched to guard the border, deliberately fired over their heads.[59] Huerta watched Washington deny entry to his agents while allowing his enemies to buy guns and ammunition from American suppliers. To Vera Estañol, Huerta's angry cabinet officer, this policy invited civil war in Mexico.[60] Still, when Wilson decided to destroy Huerta, he included all Mexican factions in his arms embargo, making it difficult, Obregón acknowledged, to buy guns "on the other side." [61] Cabrera, Roberto Pesqueira, and an army of other Constitutionalists had to travel to Washington to beg its leaders to lift the embargo against them. The war in Europe, a glorious opportunity for American arms merchants to prosper, complicated the Mexican hunt for weapons.

The Constitutionalists joyfully greeted Washington's order canceling its embargo on the sale of guns to Huerta's enemies. Had Washington dealt with Carranza and Villa as rebels and not as "belligerents," it would have denied them the right to buy arms and condemned them to defeat by Huerta. For Villa, it meant that while he competed with Carranza for Wilson's favors he could buy guns across the border, talk to George C. Carothers, a special American emissary in his camp, and drive a Packard automobile Carothers had given him.[62] Wilson's decision to back Carranza, on the other hand, cost Villa his chance at victory. Without sufficient arms and ammunition, Villa was defeated at Celaya.[63] For Carranza, the lesson was dramatically clear: so long as his government had to depend on the good will of the United States for arms, it was at the mercy of its northern neighbor. By the same token, to obtain permission to buy weapons, Cabrera bitterly exclaimed, Carranza had not only to swear "not to reconquer Texas" but to "behave." [64] Without Washington's benediction, Obregón concluded in 1923, he could not purchase arms across the border and without them he could not put down De la Huerta's revolt.

The courtship of Washington's good will, moreover, required wooing the American press. As Mexicans saw it, to make Washington smile also required a favorable press. Villa was known to have paid as much as $200 dollars to American reporters for a friendly story in their newspapers.[65] But Americans, who knew little of Mexico, had no stomach for revolutions, particularly as described in their journals. William R. Hearst, the Chihuahua landlord who controlled a chain of newspapers in the United States, in the view of Mexicans, displayed singular delight in casting aspersions on the integrity of the Mexican government. "I am saddened to tell you," Alfredo Breceda wrote Carranza from New York, that the American press, "while it gives us no aid, goes out of its way to hurt us." [66] In a letter to the editor of *The New York Herald,* Heriberto Barrón, a special agent of Carranza, accused the American press of deliberately distorting the character of the Mexican Revolution and of calling for an armed invasion of Mexico.[67] American newspapers and magazines, believed Carranza, had misinterpreted the Constitutionalist cause to the American people, to their government, and to the leaders of the entire world.[68] Invariably, said Mexicans, attempts to implement reform in Mexico, while always upsetting to foreigners, brought the wrath of the American press down upon them. Mistakenly or not, a majority of Mexican officials equated the views of newspapers, magazines, and journals with opinion in Washington.

To aggravate matters, Mexicans, as they interpreted events, had to watch helplessly while the American military, at the behest of Wilson, trampled the sovereignty and dignity of their country. The occupation of Veracruz and the invasion of Chihuahua by an army under General John J. Pershing, to which Carranza had to acquiesce, significantly added to the distrust and fear of the Yankee. Ostensibly designed to destroy Huerta, the capture of Veracruz actually nearly united Mexicans behind him. As General Juan Barragán pointed out, Mexicans, believing their independence endangered, rushed to enlist in Huerta's army.[69] In Sonora, the home of Huerta's major enemies, state authorities recruited men, collected arms and munitions, and raised funds for what they thought was the coming Armageddon. Carranza vehemently objected to the invasion of Pershing, wrote Cabrera, "in every manner and tone once and a hundred times." [70] To justify armed intervention, Wilson had used as an excuse his determination to punish Villa for his raid on New Mexico. But to Cabrera, this was just a pretext; Wilson, he thought, actually wanted to compel the Mexican government to endorse his version of Mexico's obligation to foreigners and their properties in Mexico.[71]

Months earlier, Carranza had to ward off Wilson's attempt to meddle in Mexico by using Argentina, Brazil, and Chile to help pick Mexico's ruler. For his refusal to send delegates to the ABC peace conference, Carranza earned the plaudits of Mexicans. Even Mexican businessmen, who stood to lose by the factional quarrels, applauded. I congratulate you, said one of them, "for your correct, energetic, and above all, patriotic reply to . . . the United States." [72] Carranza won even more support for his opposition to the Pershing expedition. Countless telegrams and letters swearing loyalty to Mexico and Carranza arrived at the National Palace. Many came from labor, a group generally distrustful of Carranza. A message from one group of railroad workers, who offered to contribute one-tenth of their wages to the defense of Mexico, ended with the cry "We are not living in '47," a reference to the defeat of a century before.[73]

However, while Wilson's blatant intervention had rallied Mexicans together, his unilateral acts confirmed, in the eyes of Mexicans, the ability and willingness of the *gringo* to intervene in their private business. Carranza, the haughty champion of national dignity, had to stand by and see a foreign army invade his country. That knowledge was not lost on him, or on his successor, Obregón. Care had to be exercized in handling the arrogant neighbor, even at the cost of discarding internal reforms.

V

Equally ominous to Mexico was the bitter dispute with the petroleum corporation. The conflict flared when Mexico attempted to enforce Article 27, declaring the subsoil the property of the Mexican nation. To shield the foreign oil giants, say Mexicans, Washington employed the diplomacy of the big stick. Not to put teeth in Article 27, however, meant undercutting nationalistic goals, and specifically, land reform, the key plank in the Constitution of 1917. Further, the oil companies often refused to obey Article 123, the labor code.

On petroleum, Mexico found itself in a quandary. It wanted to control the subsoil but also needed the revenue from the sale of petroleum abroad. According to the petroleum magnates, Mexico could not enjoy both. While Mexicans battled each other, petroleum production had shot upward, from 3.6 million barrels in 1910 to 157.1 million barrels by 1920.[74] In 1920–21, the peak year of production, Mexico produced 26 percent of the total world output of petroleum. Revenue from its exports helped it to weather the international depression of 1921 and drops in the price of metals and raw materials.[75] Income from taxes on the production and export of petroleum totaled nearly 86 million pesos in 1922, and despite a sizeable drop, 60.6 million pesos the next year.[76] From duties and taxes on the Standard Oil Company alone, the Mexican Treasury received 32 million pesos in 1923. All told, revenues from petroleum represented nearly one-fifth of the entire national revenue. As one Mexican financial expert summed up the picture, the disappearance or decline of petroleum revenues spelled trouble for Mexico, even bankruptcy. Not surprisingly, the oil bonanza put Mexico at the mercy of the petroleum companies, further complicating the enforcement of Articles 27 and 123. As evidence of this, say Mexican leaders, the companies curtailed operations in 1920 and 1921.[77]

In the meantime, national spending had risen sharply, from 283.8 million pesos in 1922 to 348.4 million pesos in 1923.[78] Without other sources of revenue, Mexico increasingly had to rely on its share of the profits from the sale of petroleum. Still, this was not a new development, for as early as 1915 Carranza had to encourage the growth of petroleum exports in order to use its revenues to support the value of the Mexican peso, which had been steadily dropping in price on the international monetary market since the outbreak of the fighting in 1913. To exacerbate the dependency, American corporations determined the price of Mexican petroleum. Additionally, due to its shaky financial situation, the Mexican government, on occasion, had been driven to beg loans from the oil companies, 10 million pesos from the Huasteca Petroleum Company in 1923 and an advance on tax revenues of 2.5 million pesos from El Aguila in 1924.[79] As a friend told Armando Deschamps, governor of oil-rich Veracruz in 1919, the petroleum question "is perhaps the most difficult and perplexing problem confronting our country today." [80]

The controversy over ownership of the subsoil, conferred on the nation by Article 27, dated from the legislation of the Díaz era. Under Spanish colonial law, the land and its subsoil belonged to the Crown; they could not be alienated. In 1885, however, Díaz had granted subsoil rights of ownership to proprietors of the land above.[81] With this interpretation, petroleum speculators, mainly Americans and Englishmen, acquired lands in the petroleum belt of Mexico. Madero had taken the first step, if not to recover ownership, at least to assert Mexico's control over its subsoil. His administration had imposed a tax, the first in the history of Mexico, of twenty centavos per ton weight on crude petroleum.[82] This measure, argues Narciso Bassols Batalla, thought imperative by Madero because Mexico could not modernize while foreigners controlled its chief source of energy, marked the beginning of his downfall.[83]

The Constitutionalists went beyond Madero, raising the tax

on crude petroleum to seventy centavos a barrel in 1914 and, a few months later (January 7, 1915), stopped new drilling for oil pending forthcoming legislation. They set up a committee to study the petroleum industry and to recommend laws and regulations for its better control.[84] Its report ruled property rights not absolute, and justified both taxes and expropriation as legitimate measures of control on behalf of the public good.[85] Then came Article 27, giving the nation ownership of its subsoil.

Carranza, highly nationalistic but realistic, Cabrera stated, never intended to prevent foreigners from exploiting the petroleum, or by ruling Article 27 retroactive, to deprive them of rights acquired earlier. To Carranza, Article 27 merely returned legal ownership of the subsoil to the nation; in the future, subsoil rights, in the form of special concessions, must be obtained from the Mexican government as in the case of mining.[86] With this interpretation, Carranza tempered the "confiscatory nature" of Article 27. At this juncture, a delighted President Wilson extended Carranza *de jure* recognition. By 1918, the two leaders had worked out a *modus vivendi*. Carranza refused to modify the nationalistic character of Article 27 or to settle accounts with foreign investors; but, all the same, he left undisturbed the titles of Americans to property in Mexico, including the holdings of the petroleum companies.[87] In the landmark Texas Company Case, another major concession, the Mexican Supreme Court, acting on behalf of the administration, confirmed the ownership of oil lands acquired prior to 1917. Ownership merely called for proof of a "positive act" that demonstrated intent to exploit the subsoil.

Obregón inherited a blighted economy and the traditional need to rely on petroleum revenues to float the budget. To his dismay, Washington refused to recognize his government, demanding in return for it that he sign a Treaty of Amity and Commerce "interpreting Article 27 in a nonconfiscatory, nonretroactive manner." [88] To Alberto Pani, the treaty, by undermining the authority of the Constitution, asked that Mexican laws favor Americans over Mexicans. Washington, added Bassols Batalla, in return for blessing Obregón, wanted Mexico to safeguard the properties of the international petroleum monopolies, limit the future of agrarian reform, and dispel the notion that it viewed with distrust the role of foreign capital in its basic industries. Ironically, in the Texas Company Case, Mexico, through its Supreme Court, had more or less already met these conditions. Further, Obregón, in his initial address to Congress, had declared himself fully in accord with the ruling of the court. As Bassols Batalla indicated, the question of retroactivity was a red herring. Of the capital invested in oil, just 23 percent had entered Mexico before 1917. Article 27 antedated the bulk of the capital invested.[89] Actually, said Bassols Batalla, foreign interests, with the backing of conservatives in the Obregón administration, had employed the issue of diplomatic recognition to halt reform.[90]

For whatever reason, either to undercut reform, as Bassols Batalla suggests, or to court Washington, Obregón worked diligently to maintain his vow to uphold the Supreme Court's ruling. He pledged help compatible with Mexican legislation to Henry L. Doheny, the oil tycoon; provided backing for the Pierce Oil Company "as well as all others"; he gave concessions to exploit deposits of natural gas to American investors willing to abide by Mexican laws; and he promised solid "guarantees" to C. N. Haskell, former governor of Oklahoma and spokesman for the Middle States Oil Corporation.[91] To keep happy the folks at home, Obregón also conferred drilling rights to Mexicans eager to tap the petroleum wealth, among them DeNegri.[92]

Despite this record of conciliation, according to Mexicans, the oil barons, with the backing of Washington, gave no peace to Carranza and Obregón. Instead, from 1917 on, they redoubled their efforts to render Mexican laws covering the ownership of land and subsoil worthless. Almost every interventionist scheme hatched in the United States enjoyed the support of the petroleum companies. One independent oil operator had informed Charles E. Hughes, Harding's secretary of state, that "untold sums" had "been expended by the oil interests to nourish discord in Mexico."[93] In the Huasteca, the heartland of the oil industry, its moguls kept an army under General Manuel Peláez supplied with money, guns, and ammunition.[94] Alberto Tejeda, governor of Veracruz, sent note after note to Obregón asking him to disarm the private armies of the petroleum companies that, as he stated, made virtually impossible the enforcement of national legislation.[95] The Huasteca Petroleum Company, a lawyer for an independent oil firm said, paid armed mercenaries to kill at will anyone daring to enter its properties.[96] With the local military in cahoots with the Huasteca Company, state authorities were unwilling to uphold the law. Obregón, furthermore, believed that high officials of El Aguila had lent their support to the rebellion of De la Huerta, an opinion partly based on reports by his agents of arms and munitions for the rebels landed on its property.[97] Given this picture, many Mexicans conclude that it is difficult to visualize how even militants could have carried out a revolution, let alone Carranza and Obregón.

VI

In twentieth-century Mexico, no regime stood a ghost of a chance of surviving without Washington's embrace. Until the pope in the White House conferred his benediction, no Mexican president could look to God for help. But the White House, and its advisers in the State Department, usually responsive to the wishes of their business and financial community, judged with suspicion governments out of step with the American dream. Mexican efforts to modify property rights, particularly those of American investors, were met with the wrath of these defenders of private enterprise. Efforts at radical reform, certainly anything that smelled of socialism, had the taint of treason. With conservatives of their own to please, Carranza and Obregón, hardly militants themselves, quickly learned that the successful wooer of Washington's love must exhibit a healthy respect for Western capitalist traditions. Both men, however, were oracles for Mexican nationalism, the goal of teaching Mexicans to run their own house. This meant eliminating the special privileges of foreigners in Mexico, and establishing Mexican ownership and control of the subsoil as a legal principle. On this issue Mexicans clashed with Washington.

From the Mexican perspective, Washington employed diplomatic recognition as a weapon to compel Mexican regimes to toe the line.[98] To cite Querido Moheno, Huerta's minister of industry and commerce, the issue was not whether a Mexican president could govern, but whether he could get Washington's recog-

nition, for without it he could not stay in office.[99] Carranza knew
by 1915 that to govern effectively by Washington's standards
meant to be willing to guarantee the person and properties of
foreigners in Mexico. Conversely for Mexicans, to rule successfully depended upon the willingness of the White House to grant
recognition, a lesson mastered by Carranza after Wilson accepted
him. Yet, to obtain recognition, Carranza had to publicize his decision to leave undisturbed the interests of foreigners in Mexico.[100]
Not until 1917, when Carranza undermined the "confiscatory
nature" of Article 27, however, did Wilson extend *de jure* recognition. Mexicans supporting social reform judged Carranza's
pledge a betrayal of national goals.

Obregón confronted a similar problem. In return for recognition, Washington wanted Obregón to sign a treaty of friendship
and commerce that, in the judgment of Sáenz in Foreign Affairs,
weakened or destroyed the Constitution. Such a treaty, he said,
struck at the heart of Article 27, not only undercutting land
reform legislation but violating the right of the Supreme Court
to interpret Mexican laws. The treaty stipulated immediate payment for any property expropriated and asked Mexico to recognize the properties of foreigners acquired before May 1, 1917.
These, of course, were the oil lands. To add insult to injury,
the treaty contained a clause condemning Mexico's handling of
the Catholic Church, under the guise of insuring freedom of
religion.[101] Obregón rejected the treaty, although he signed the
Lamont-De la Huerta Agreements, pledging Mexico in 1922 to
begin payment on its foreign obligations.[102]

Fate, to the misfortune of Obregón, forced him to give up
his game of watchful waiting. Mexican politics, in the shape of
De la Huerta's uprising in 1923, made Obregón's courtship of
Washington a matter of life and death. In the absence of recognition, the foreign bankers, upon whom Obregón depended for
loans with which to buy weapons to defeat his rivals, would not
open their purse strings. Either don Alvaro won the battle of
Washington or he lost his job in Mexico.

On August 1923, at a meeting on Bucareli Street in Mexico
City attended by delegates from both countries, Obregón received the endorsement he coveted. Obregón chose no revolutionaries to speak for him. Fernando Gonzáles Roa, a lawyer for

the Pierce Oil Company, had been judged unfit to be a delegate to the Constitutional Convention by its credentials committee.[103] His companion, Ramón Ross, an old friend of Obregón's, was a businessman from Sonora. By the Treaty of Bucareli, Mexico made Article 27 nonretroactive, confirming the decision of the Mexican Supreme Court in the Texas Company Case, and acknowledged the validity of American financial claims dating from 1868. It vowed to respect subsoil rights acquired both before and after 1917. On the debt, it agreed to abide by the rulings of a special claims commission composed of one Mexican, one American, and a representative of a "neutral" country selected by the other two.[104] Americans with claims against Mexico could submit their case to the tribunal where the defendant, Mexico, had only one vote. Further, González Roa and Ross, quoting a memorandum from Obregón, promised that Mexico would indemnify Americans for the loss of their lands, at the same time implying that agrarian reform had about run its course.[105] The propertied classes in Mexico could sleep peacefully from then on.

To worshippers at the temple of nationalism, the Bucareli Treaty was a betrayal of their dreams. To stay in power, Obregón had sacrificed noble goals, one of which was national sovereignty. By appealing for help to the United States, Obregón had admitted that a Mexican regime could not alone police its own house, proclaimed General Cándido Aquilar.[106] By the same token, by pledging to pay Mexico's foreign debt, lamented Marte R. Gómez, Obregón had mortgaged money set aside for social reform.[107] One caustic critic, Salvador Diego Fernández, author of *Los Pactos de Bucareli,* (Mexico, 1937) saw a striking connection between the terms of Bucareli and the earlier treaty of friendship and commerce, rejected as unacceptable by Obregón. By ruling Article 27 nonretroactive, in the view of Isidro Fabela, Obregón had exceeded his authority. Antonio Salas Robledo, in *Los Convenios de Bucareli ante el Derecho Internacional,* (Mexico, 1938) viewed the ruling of the Supreme Court in the Texas Company Case—the basis for Obregón's decision not to make Article 27 retroactive—as a betrayal of national legislation in order "to meet the demands of foreign capital." To Bassols Batalla, Obregón and his cohorts had abandoned the field of battle to the

State Department, foreign oil monopolies, and enemies of social change.

VII

The hindsight of over half a century amply verifies the legitimacy of Mexican interpretations of American attitudes and goals. Mexicans had reason to be afraid. The powerful giant across the border was hostile and misunderstood the objectives of Mexican leaders. Washington displayed no tolerance for drastic social change in Mexico. Woodrow Wilson, at the helm of foreign policy during much of the crucial decade, may have stumbled when he tried to curtail violence in Mexico, says an American historian, but he fared "far better in blocking the consummation of revolutionary reform." [108]

But Wilson neither initiated nor ended this sorry chapter in American relations with its smaller and weaker neighbor. His policies had beginnings in the Taft administration and they outlived his death. As Limantour suspected, Taft had dispatched 20,000 troops to the Mexican border not just to "hold up the hands" of Díaz but to the contrary, as Taft told Philander C. Knox, his secretary of state, "to place troops in sufficient numbers where Congress shall direct that they enter Mexico to save lives and property." The navy, Taft confided to Theodore Roosevelt, "is anxious for a contest, and has to be held in leash." [109] Moreover, Henry Lane Wilson, a diplomat with the mentality of Rudyard Kipling, played a significant role in shaping the opinions of Taft.[110] To the ambassador, Madero was "weak" and unresponsive to complaints on behalf of American investors. He warned Madero to give "more hearty consideration" to American business interests lest Taft convene Congress to ask for guidance on Mexican matters. The labor strikes in the textile mills in the days of Madero turned Ambassador Wilson's hair gray. When the army brass revolted in 1913, Wilson arrogantly prevailed upon the ambassadors of Great Britain, Germany, and Spain to support his demand that Madero resign.[111]

Although he rid himself of the bigoted and ungenerous ambassador, President Wilson added a fatal dose of capitalist morality to Taft's diplomacy. He intended to keep alive Mexican capitalism and to defend the American stake in it. His first press release welcomed as "friends . . . those . . . who protect private property." [112] With Huerta and his rivals at war, Wilson began to ponder military intervention, "including blockading Mexico's ports and sending troops across the border . . . to protect American lives and property." [113] Determined to oust Huerta, Wilson lifted the arms embargo on Huerta's enemies; when that failed, he sent troops to invade Veracruz. But Wilson had more in mind than the demise of Huerta. He "wanted a much larger role in Mexican affairs . . . He desired control over Mexico's destiny," ultimately to mold the Mexican Revolution "according to the American experience." [114] Wilson denied any intent to invade Mexico, but nevertheless, cautioned that if "the lives and properties of Americans and all other foreigners are [not] safeguarded . . . we shall be forced to it." [115] His tardy and reluctant recognition of Carranza on October 1915, simply acknowledged the Constitutionalist's mastery of Mexico.[116]

Wilson's pilgrimage to save democracy in Europe granted Mexico a brief respite. To start with, Wilson had to call Pershing home. Still, while the war kept Wilson busy in Europe, and demands for oil and henequen richly benefited both industries, economically Mexico suffered. To aid the allies win the war, the United States upset established commercial patterns, including trade ties with Mexico. Washington barred the export of corn and pork to Mexico, despite surpluses in the United States and starvation in Mexico. The sale of arms to Mexicans was banned, while Mexican gold reserves in the United States were frozen "as hostages to Mexico's good conduct." [117] Determined to protect American petroleum properties in Mexico, Wilson had decided to occupy them with troops if necessary. During the interval, his government helped preserve the status quo in Mexico by loudly protesting decrees tampering with property and subsoil rights. According to Washington, Mexico could not expropriate foreign properties legally acquired before the promulgation of the Constitution without immediate compensation in accordance with due process of law.[118] Congressional opinion was no less hostile. By 1919, the committee of Senator Albert B. Fall was urging intervention if Mexicans enforced their Constitution against the economic stake of Americans.[119] Intervention, according to Congressman Fiorello H. LaGuardia of New York, could be avoided only "if the loyal citizens of Mexico get together, take affairs into their own hands and put out the present administration." [120] On his own, Wilson had concluded that Carranza was a "pedantic ass." [121]

The election of Warren G. Harding, a Republican party hack, scarcely served to console Mexicans. During the elections of 1920, the Republican party had charged Wilson with being soft on Mexico. Hughes, Harding's secretary of state, bluntly stated Washington's attitude: "The fundamental question which confronts the government of the United States in considering its relations with Mexico is the safeguarding of property rights against confiscation . . ." Washington would recognize Obregón only on condition that he refrain from enforcing the Constitution against American interests. Otherwise, stated Hughes, Obregón must deal with the United States as an "unfriendly power." [122] To quote *The New York Times*: "No American administration" can "afford to neglect the interests of investors in Mexico who are threatened with confiscation of their property by arbitrary decrees and predatory legislation." To secure recognition, Obregón had to "undo the mischief of . . . Article 27" and clear American titles to oil lands of all "clouds" and permit investors to develop their concessions without interference.[123] "In order to be recognized as a responsible nation and government," added the *Washington Times,* "Mexico will have to prove that she recognizes the rights of Americans in and out of Mexico." [124] The proposed treaty of Amity and Commerce, said *The Morning Post* in 1922, rightfully asks Mexico to safeguard the rights of property acquired "before the Constitution of 1917 was promulgated." [125] Washington, concludes an American scholar, restored normal diplomatic relations only when "satisfied that American interests would receive special consideration in Mexico." [126] By the Treaty of Bucareli, the *modus vivendi,* "the Mexican government had yielded more than it had won." [127]

Perhaps, without this record of American hostility, of meddling in Mexico's business, Carranza and Obregón, albeit recalcitrant reformers, might have accepted a larger dose of change? Had they done so, Mexico might possibly have enjoyed a modicum of Revolution.

TWENTY-THREE

Reflections

"Here you may witness the blessings of the revolution caught in a single tear."

Mariano Azuela, Los de Abajo

I

WHY AFTER ALL, did Mexicans rebel in 1910?
"Revolutions are not made; they come," wrote Wendell Phillips, an American radical. "A revolution is as natural a growth as an oak. It comes out of the past. Its foundations are laid far back." Following this axiom of Phillips, it is highly likely that the Mexican upheaval developed in response to the growth of those conditions that have almost always characterized societies on the brink of social explosions. Mexican society prior to the rebellion fits into the pattern of France, England, the Thirteen Colonies, and czarist Russia which Crane Brinton describes in his ground-breaking study of the revolutionary process.[1] "Societies, like individuals," to cite R. H. Tawney, author of the masterful *Religion and the Rise of Capitalism,* "have their moral crises and their spiritual revolutions." [2]

To begin with, to use Brinton's first of five "uniformities," Mexican society, as was true in the earlier cases, was not unprosperous, but was, on the contrary, upward-bound. The dissatisfied elements were more annoyed or restrained than oppressed. The protest voiced by Francisco I. Madero, a rich landlord, was not that of a hungry and miserable class without hope in the future. Instead, the middle classes, the spokesmen for rebellion and the progeny of three decades of progress, had grown in numbers, had tasted the fruits of modern life, and had matured politically and intellectually during the Porfiriato. History teaches us that upheavals of the kind that toppled the Old Regime occur in societies that have enjoyed change but still demand further changes.

Class conflict marred the calm of Mexico's pre-1910 society, but not in simplistic Marxist terms. Discontent centered in the middle classes that, to once again fall back on Brinton's analysis, had "made money, or at least . . . have enough to live on, and who contemplate bitterly the imperfections of . . . [the] socially privileged." As he concluded, "Revolution seems more likely when social classes are close together, than when they are far apart." [3] Although economically the middle classes lagged behind the more affluent, nonetheless, in other respects, particularly in the realm of intellectual achievements and social aspirations, they walked a similar path. Further, not only were the middle classes dissatisfied, but industrial labor, a small but potentially important bloc, gave signs of a political awakening that threatened to undermine the economic relationships laboriously hammered out by the rulers of the nineteenth century. Exploited but better off than the peasantry, its rural counterpart, industrial labor wanter a bigger slice of the pie. By sharply curtailing their chances for upward progress, the economic crisis that descended on Mexico in 1907 exacerbated the restlessness of both the middle classes and industrial labor.

At the same time, the old rulers, the Porfiristas, had slowly lost the vigor that had kept them masters of Mexico for thirty years. The energy and ambition that had led them to rally around Benito Juárez and to launch the Reforma over half a century before had been dissipated. Age and success had made them complacent and, given the new problems that arose with the crisis of 1907, ineffectual. In Brinton's terms, the aging rulers, with don Porfirio leading the way, had lost touch not only with changing reality, but in the process, had lost faith in their ability to govern and had lost the moral strength necessary to control the political apparatus. Many of the old class had become dissolute, placing personal gain above the needs of the society they had built, and consequently had abdicated moral and political respectability. The aging élite, which according to some was a plutocracy, had made the economic well-being of Mexico dependent on the *hacienda,* on foreign investment for development, and on outside markets for the sale of minerals and raw material. The land, essentially unproductive in their hands, sustained them. Only a minority of the old élite had ventured forth into the world of business and industry. By 1910, the needs of the ruling class stood at odds with the hopes of youth and the nationalistic aims of white-collar hopefuls, intellectuals, and industrial worker.

Moreover, the machinery of government, its political institutions, had broken down, partly because of its frailty and partly because it failed to respond adequately to problems generated by the crash of 1907. These deficiencies bred dissatisfaction in much of Mexican society, but particularly among the middle classes and industrial labor, both of which had been battered by the economic hard times. A governmental structure that had developed in response to less complicated political conditions during the early years of the Porfiriato became ineffectual in dealing with the demands of social classes eager to implement political and economic reforms. Institutional adaptability, so necessary in order to keep the government effective, was absent.

Mexico lacked the means of peaceful accommodation to the changing scene. It had no political parties, but merely groups at the beck and call of the *caudillo,* don Porfirio, who sat on top of a rigid pyramid; his will, and that of his underlings, always prevailed. Local government at the state and municipal level was conspicuous by its absence. The *jefe político,* appointed by outsiders and responsive to their wishes, had made a shambles of municipal autonomy. State governors looked to Mexico City for their orders. Honesty in public office was a rare virtue as both the "ins" and the "outs" battled for the opportunity to live well off the public trough. Government in Mexico was inefficient, corrupt, and representative of only a favored minority of native rich and influential foreigners.

By the same token, the new intelligentsia, which was primarily middle class formed a bitter, restless, and alienated segment in society. Denied access to public office, one of the few sinecures in an underdeveloped society, and without a voice in government, men of learning gave vent to an increasingly negative view of Mexican society, much of it centered on Mexico's ties with foreigners. Not surprisingly, intellectuals, beginning with their activities in Liberal Clubs and culminating in their support of Bernardo Reyes and Madero, led the demands for change. Ironically, the late years of the Porfiriato had given birth to an intellectual and cultural renaissance which had been absent from Mexico since the banner years of the Reforma. The turmoil of rebellion postponed for nearly an entire decade the flowering of artistic and intellectual endeavors which had been in the offing in 1910.

In addition to the "uniformities" it shared with prerevolutionary England, France, the Thirteen Colonies, and Russia, Mexican society displayed revolutionary symptoms all its own. Every rebellion, obviously, emerges from particular political and economic conditions. In Mexico's case, a strident nationalism that placed the blame for the country's sundry difficulties on its next-door neighbor—the major customer for Mexico's goods but also the source of its investment capital—provided the banner around which Mexicans of diverse backgrounds could rally. Nationalism offered rebel leaders the means to popular support, endorsement for reforms, and backing for their battle against remnants of the Old Regime. Much of the nationalism was anti-American, particularly among intellectuals and elements of industrial labor who believed that to achieve a better society Mexico must dramatically alter its traditional relationships with the Yankees.

Finally, the crash of 1907, which had such disastrous effects on Mexico's export economy, served to light the political fuse that triggered Madero's rebellion. With the economy in the doldrums and opportunities for public office dashed, the frustrations of the ambitious middle classes grew dramatically and ultimately exploded.

II

Still the rebellion, which at some junctures had seemed an out-of-control nightmare, never exploded into a full-scale revolutionary upheaval. Despite its radical rhetoric, which often verged on socialism, the rebellion stayed within the bounds of a capitalistic framework, the traditional formula of the day. Eventually, its leadership merely updated the nineteenth-century cap-

italist model, bringing Mexican theory, if not practice, into line
with reality in Western Europe and the United States. In this
light the Mexican rebellion must be judged one of the last bourgeois protests of the nineteenth century and not, as is so frequently alleged, the precursor of the socialist explosions of the
twentieth century. It had much more in common with the
French Revolution of 1789, the forerunner of the triumph of
the capitalistic middle classes, than with the socialist victory in
Russia in 1917 or its companion in Cuba in 1959. If this be so,
why its limited nature? How were Madero and his successors able
to keep it from getting out of hand?

   It seems probable that any explanation must begin with an
analysis of Mexican society on the eve of Madero's challenge to
Díaz. One key lies in the character of the class sytem in Mexico.
Whatever its weaknesses, Mexico had a well established class
structure. The ruling élite, the upper class, had deep roots and
strength derived from the land and the *hacienda* system, which
was no simple economic unit, but a way of life dating from
colonial times, and intimately woven into the national fabric.
To destroy it meant striking at a class upon which the welfare
of millions depended, and which possessed strong allies in
Church and government. Indeed, *hacendados* and rulers were
often one and the same. The peasantry, generally illiterate and
politically unsophisticated, only belatedly posed a serious challenge to the *hacendado*. Tragically, ownership of land, often in
the form of *haciendas*, represented one of the obvious goals to
many of the malcontents. The élite had a strongly defined set
of values with which to identify itself. It was as Mexican as any
other class. The *hacendados*, the core of the upper class, together
with their allies in business and industry, formed a formidable
barrier to the spread of revolution. Only a prolonged and frontal assault on the upper class, requiring dynamic leadership with
sophisticated popular backing, would destroy it.

   Clearly, in the Mexico of 1910, only the middle classes could
have provided the incentive and leadership for such an attack.
But the middle classes were woefully unprepared to do so. Small
and of recent vintage, they lacked both a strong sense of class
and an ideology of their own. With the exception of a tiny minority of unorthodox thinkers, of whom Ricardo Flores Magón

was one, the chieftains of the middle classes pursued limited goals. Essentially, they wanted a bigger share of the spoils, and entrance into the higher spheres of the system, rather than its destruction. Few wanted to change dramatically Mexico's economic dependency on American markets and capital, an obvious prerequisite for the social transformation of Mexico. They wanted the status quo altered because it had denied them equal opportunity with the élite, the people they aspired to become. Unlike the élite, the middle classes had little group cohesion, they were still in the process of growth and development, still without a consciousness of class. Rather than form their own unique place in society, the middle classes, both rural and urban, mimicked the values and customs of the rich. They had little that was distinctively their own. And they were as afraid of drastic social change, fearful of the rural and urban poor, as were the rich, with whom they sought to identify. To cite one example, Alvaro Obregón, shared the values and aspirations of the upper class, albeit its more modern wing, while having little in common with poor dirt farmers, who formed the majority of the population. For Obregón, as for the majority in his class, to transform Mexico meant to streamline the system, to modernize it so that Western-minded and educated Mexicans might partake of the rich fruit on the banquet table. Leaders of this type hardly envisaged revolution so that the "underdogs," to use Mariano Azuela's phrase, might govern. If Obregón and his allies were to become social revolutionaries, pressure from beneath must be applied to them and it never was, at least not sufficiently, and certainly not in a sustained manner. Nor was there any overwhelming reason for the middle classes to espouse radical or socialist doctrines. After all, the Russian socialist revolution, which might have served as an alternate model to capitalism, did not occur until after the victorious Mexican rebels had publicly baptized their amorphous Constitution of 1917.

Pressure from the lower end of the social scale, furthermore, also failed to manifest itself in a meaningful way because of the character of the worker. Industrial labor failed to offer it. As a class, it comprised a small fraction of the total population, containing less than 800,000 Mexicans. Like its middle-class counterpart, it was of recent origin. At best, its sense of itself as a class was weak; the solidarity of the industrial working class was merely a mirage on the horizon. Geography, as well as the nature of economic activity, had scattered the tiny army of industrial workers to the four winds. Time and additional economic development were needed to unite workers in mines, railroads, factories, and petroleum fields into a homogeneous class with concrete goals of its own. When Madero raised the standard of revolt, the seeds of worker unity had just been planted. Politically, labor was still only just forming a class consciousness. The opportunistic middle-class chieftains of the rebellion easily thwarted the hopes of labor, and by the same token, stifled pressure from below for change.

Further, the peasantry, labor's rural counterpart, with just a few exceptions, only belatedly served to spur the radicalization of the rebellion. Barring the obvious case of the Zapatistas, an untypical phenomenon, the inhabitants of rural Mexico lacked a sense of class, and even of group. Politically they were not yet even neophytes. Ideological questions were alien to them. And, when finally aroused, their political demands hardly went beyond the quest for a small plot of land to till and schools for their children. They were poorly understood by industrial labor, their urban counterparts. Unschooled in the ways of modern political protest, they were separated by geography, and in the case of the Indian population, by culture. A large bloc of the peasantry, approximately 4 million, did not even speak Spanish, the national language. After centuries of neglect and exploitation, the dirt farmer had learned to keep to himself, to distrust outsiders, and to view with skepticism proposals for change by outsiders. True, countless *calzonudos,* cotton-clad dirt farmers, joined the guerrilla armies that ravaged the land during the years of fighting; but, as Azuela argued in *Los de Abajo,* they often lacked a clear idea of what they were fighting for. Not only did this large population of peasants, perhaps two-thirds of the people of Mexico, frequently fail to push for the radicalization of the rebellion, but they often served as a conservative barrier to change.

Additionally, there were other old institutions to be reckoned with. One was the Catholic Church. Although its enemies grossly exaggerated its wealth and influence, the Church and its clergy had an important role to play. Traditionally Mexicans were Catholics, orthodox in their own ways, especially in the forgotten rural villages. The Catholic faith, regardless of how diluted it may have been, and its clergy, helped to unite both rural and urban Mexicans, and to some extent, bring them together in support of traditional ways of doing things. Thus Catholicism, despite its deviations from the Church in Rome, helped build a wall of suspicion and distrust between new ideas and the people they were intended to serve. The Church stood for a historical entity of negligible benefit to reformers who wanted the past either dramatically transformed or destroyed. As radical messiahs eventually learned, even Zapata, the apostle of agrarian reform, at first glance a natural ally, had no quarrel with the Catholic religion or the clergy. To unite Mexico behind the banner of revolution often proved a herculean task because one element of the old order, the Church, while politically and materially weak still wielded a strong ideological influence over a large bloc of Mexicans of all classes, an influence generally in accord with the customs and values of the past.

Yet the usual interpretation of the role of the Church is of doubtful value. True, the Church backed Díaz, opposed Madero, and supported his successor the usurper Victoriano Huerta, and generally fought reform tooth and nail. If there were to be reform, the rebels had to deal with the Church, a pillar of the old society. However, the issue of the Church, while significant, may be essentially irrelevant to a discussion of whether Mexico had a Revolution or not. In short, the polemics over the clerical "problem" serve to camouflage the failure of the rebel leadership to come to grips with the issue of social reform. All the same, no student of the Revolution fails to include in his book or essay a lengthy analysis of the conflict between Church and state. And if liberal and sympathetic to the aims of reform, as most authors are, an accusing finger will be pointed at the Church for its dog-in-the manger attitude.

The bulk of the rebel leadership, for its part, privately scoffed at religion and publicly flaunted a distrust of priests, bishops, archbishops, and the Pope. As General Augustín Millán, Governor of Puebla in 1915, exclaimed, "the view of the clergy as one of the formidable enemies blocking reform lies in the heart of every honest revolutionary." [4] The anticlerical slant of articles 3 and 130 of the Constitution of 1917 vividly testify to the depth of this belief. While Article 3 deals with education, the debate over it focused on the clerical issue, on the question of Church schools. Article 130, meanwhile, put the Church under the political control of the state.

Unfortunately, the traditional picture of the Church-state conflict more often than not obscures its nonrevolutionary character. Because of the absence of serious and impartial research, only its outlines are clearly drawn. To begin with, the clergy sided with the Re-electionist party in 1910. But, to give the devil his due, so did anti-Church Jacobins and atheists.[5] Strangely enough, Madero and his band overlooked the support given Díaz by the clergy. Francisco Vásquez Gómez, a guiding figure in Madero's campaign, even wrote Aquiles Serdán, an anticlerical newspaperman destined to die for his loyalty to Madero, to urge him to put aside "differences over religion," arguing that nothing should "divide clericals and liberals for we are all Mexicans." [6] In Morelia and Michoacán, the Partido Católico Nacional supported Madero for the presidency in 1911. The following year, José López Portillo y Rojas, ostensibly the liberal candidate, became governor of Jalisco, the most Catholic province in the Republic, with the votes of the Catholic party. Wistano Luis Orozco, author of a landmark book on Mexico's social ills, thought the victory splendid, "for even though the Catholic party won," the citizens of Jalisco had thwarted an attempt to impose a governor not of their choice. He assured Madero, with whom he sympathized, that López Portillo y Rojas would "govern in accord with Madero's ideals." [7]

But the Church, to its later unhappiness, ultimately joined the chorus of attacks on Madero, and then fell into line with Huerta who, as president, attempted to turn back the clock. It was claimed that the Church lent 25 million pesos to Huerta. In reality, the Church gave only 25,000 pesos, and that as a forced loan. The Church, moreover eventually saw its error, and abandoned Huerta. As Ramón Cabrera, brother of the legendary Luis, stated in 1914, the "clergy no longer wanted to dip into its coffers" to keep Huerta in the National Palace. He looked forward to the rapidly approaching day when both clergy and *hacendados* would be convinced that "only the Revolution should run the government." [8] Obviously, by embracing Huerta, the clergy had won no friends among the rebels. Still, the Church, before the advent of Huerta, had come to terms with Madero, and if Cabrera truly spoke for popular sentiment, many in the rebel camp were willing to take the Church back.

Not the least among these was Venustiano Carranza, the First Chief of the Constitutionalists, the ultimate victors; he wanted peace with the Church. Had his opinion triumphed at Querétaro, Article 3 would have permitted Church schools—as in the days of don Porfirio. The anticlerical provisions of 1917 were passed over his objections. Even Alvaro Obregón, a president not noted for his sympathy for the clergy, wrote archbishops José Mora y del Río and Leopoldo Ruíz, then in exile as a protest against what they called his anticlerical policies, to assure them that his regime was "fundamentally Christian." Its objectives, he vowed, "would in no way harm the basic aims of the Catholic Church"; if not entirely in accord, "both programs essentially complemented one another." With good faith on both sides, he promised the prelates, "complete harmony would reign." [9]

Despite the willingness of Madero, Carranza, and apparently Obregón to live with the Church, a conflict erupted. One reason was because the rebels believed the Church to be wealthy. To cite one example, the Partido Liberal Democrático of Puebla requested that Carranza stop the Church from collecting money and take its wealth away, especially its real-estate holdings. [10] The Church, along with the bankers, said others, was the leading owner of mortgages. In the opinion of Luis Cabrera, the Church, while suffering losses during the Reforma, had partly recouped its wealth through subterfuge. [11] Undoubtedly, as Cabrera believed, individual prelates of the Church had acquired lands of their own, despite legal provisions against it. One such property was the Hacienda de Jaltipa on the outskirts of Cuautitlán, a village in the state of Mexico. According to the natives there, its owner was a Church prelate. [12] One Constitutionalist officer claimed that a *rancho,* once owned by his grandfather in Michoacán, had been given by Díaz to Archbishop Leopoldo Ruíz.[13] These and similar examples help confirm the ownership of land by some members of the clergy.

However, no statistics exist on the extent of Church property. Certainly, it was not on the scale confiscated by the Reforma of the 1850's and 60's; and even that proved disappointingly low. Had the rebels uncovered a large hidden cache, it seems almost certain, especially in the light of their anticlerical views, that they would have announced their startling find to the world. No such declaration ever appeared.

True, the Church hierarchy committed the unforgivable blunder of taking an adamant stance against articles 3, 5, 27, and 130 of the Constitution. Still, with the exception of 27, each of the articles dealt specifically with a religious matter. Article 3 banned Church schools; Article 5 prohibited convents and monasteries; and Article 130 placed the Church under the political control of public officials. None of these statutes, although involving important issues, touched directly on socioeconomic questions. These statutes were on the outer edge of reform. The religious issue, as Carranza admitted, was not at the heart of the matter; moreover, he argued, it was time to get beyond discussions of what man could or should not believe.[14]

Of course, in its stance against Article 27, the Church carried its obsession with what it called its religious prerogatives too far. As José G. Parres, a member of the Comisión Nacional Agraria, declared, if the clergy did not openly sabotage the granting of lands to villages, it certainly hindered the process.[15] In Puebla, in their opposition to Article 27, the prelates went so far as to dispatch teams of clergy to warn villagers not to ask for lands or risk the loss of priests to perform the rite of confession, say mass, and confer the marriage sacraments. The Church could condone the acquisition of property only when it was done by purchase.[16] Yet, paradoxically, the bishop of Puebla, since his sponsorship of the first Catholic Congress on rural problems in 1903, had urged that the peasantry be given lands and schools, and this advice was endorsed by every succeeding Catholic Congress.[17] In addition, by 1919, the Church had gone on record in support of reforms suggested by Antenor Sala, one of the few *hacendados* to recommend the subdivision of the

large estates. Still, even in its objections to Article 27, the hierarchy had mainly in mind Church property and that of its individual members.

By dealing harshly with the Church, politicians stoked the
fires of controversy. Determined to stamp out the "clerical cancer," officials banned from Yucatán all but six priests, while in
Sonora, another example of extreme irrationality, none were allowed to remain.[18] Governor Plutarco Elías Calles, a future
president of the Republic, equated the ills of liquor with those
of the clergy and outlawed both.[19] All the same, Sonora and the
northern provinces in general, heartland of the rebellion and
often of anticlerical bigotry, had only a handful of men of the
cloth to begin with. In 1895, Sonora had just fifteen, while as
late as 1908, its bishop, Ignacio Valdespino, was desperately trying to bring priests from Mexico City. Until then, only priests
ordained in Sonora had been willing to work there.[20] Neither
had the Church played an important economic role in the northern provinces. Since colonial times the landed estates there had
been almost exclusively in lay hands, and had probably become
completely so after the Reforma.[21] Along with the north, the
southeastern provinces had the fewest priests; yet Yucatán, like
Sonora, spawned some of the worst baiters of the clergy. In all,
only a small number of priests had ministered to the religious
needs of Mexican Catholics: 3,576 in 1895 and 4,553 in 1910, or
approximately three priests for every 10,000 inhabitants.[22]

Not surprisingly, the Church viewed rebellion with jaundiced eye. As in most other parts of Mexico, Bishop Valdespino of Sonora issued a pastoral letter calling on the devil to
cast a thousands spells on supporters of Madero.[23] But surely the
stance of Valdespino fails to explain the virulence of the attacks
on the clergy, who were numerically insignificant and relatively
poor. Elsewhere, moreover, politicians and the clerical hierarchy
learned to live together. In Puebla, for instance the Church
elders, at the request of the ruling Maderistas, undertook to punish priests who meddled in politics.[24]

The ire of nationalists added a further dimension to the
clash. Not only were many clerics foreigners, but nearly all had
come from Spain, the accursed colonial master. This probably
explains some of the rancor against the clergy, for the Spaniard,

whether as priest or *mayordomo* of an *hacienda,* a job he frequently held, won the venomous hatred of nationalistic reformers. Nor did Archbishop Mora help to cool tempers by fleeing
to the United States in order to fulminate against the Carranza
administration. In so doing, *El Dictamen* announced, Mora had
clasped hands with "imperialistic Americans," a view shared by
El Demócrata, another of the rebel journals.[25] By asking foreign
Catholics for aid and sympathy, and in that manner inviting outside intervention in Mexico, Mora and his cohorts endangered
not merely the masters of Mexico but ran roughshod over the
sensibilities of nationalists. Still, had Mexico's rulers handled the
religious issue with wisdom and tact, the hierarchy might have
stayed home.

None of this denies the conservative nature of the Catholic
hierarchy, and perhaps of much of the rank-and-file clergy. From
the beginning, they made little effort to conceal their sympathies
for the status quo. For nearly three decades the Church had
been a bulwark of the Díaz regime. More than a decade after
that administration's fall, a large bloc of prelates backed the
military coup of Adolfo de la Huerta in 1923—the last major
challenge to the new leadership. But not all of the prelates or
the clergy sided with De la Huerta. The archbishop of Guadalajara, one of the most powerful figures in the Church, remained
in the camp of Alvaro Obregón.[26]

Despite its conservative bent, the Church kept the loyalty
of Emiliano Zapata and his peasant armies, spokesmen for the
rebel agrarian wing. In modern terminology, Zapata voiced the
views of "leftists." Significantly, his crusade thrived in regions
where the Church had kept its moral authority alive. Of the old
elements, only the Church, Francisco Bulnes pointed out, had
retained its moral prestige in central and southern Mexico.[27]
It was precisely there that the Zapatistas drew a large following.
Nor did Zapata and his disciples attempt to hide their Catholic
commitment. The Virgin de Guadalupe, anathema to the *come
santo,* saint-baiting, rebels in the rival camps, adorned their banners. As a mayor of a Zapatista enclave declared, "Zampahuacán
is and always will be Catholic." [28] Even the inhabitants of Villa
Ayala, site of the heralded Zapatista plan which bears its name,
rejected any attempt to convert Catholic temples into schools.

"The Church," to cite a letter from Villa Ayala to Zapata, "must not be confused with the profane!" [29] To their dismay, Carrancista politicians discovered that priests, the hated *curas*, had staunch allies in the villages of Oaxaca, whose inhabitants welcomed no attacks on churches.[30] Yet nearly all rebel factions looked upon the Zapatistas, their Catholic faith notwithstanding, as radicals.

Political heritage, too, played a major role. Obviously, Mexico lacked genuine political parties, and outside of the villages and the early municipalities, lacked any tradition of popular decision making. The Spaniards and their Republican successors had long ago implanted a system of government by manipulation and by an élite. That system resulted in widespread cynicism, which became in itself a major hurdle to overcome. After centuries of fraud and deception, of false promises and political skullduggery, few Mexicans were ready to believe even honest reformers. This *desconfianza,* a distrust that verged on the refusal to have faith in fellow Mexicans, and almost in mankind in general, undercut efforts at revolution. To his bitter disillusionment, Ricardo Flores Magón confronted this reality early on. So, paradoxically, a Mexico with weak political institutions had forged one uniquely its own. While nontraditional, and more of the spirit than of the temporal world, this absence of faith in what was possible, a logical product of centuries of chicanery, helped sabotage efforts to make revolution a reality.

Nor was the time ripe for noncapitalist transformations of society, the essence of revolution in the twentieth century. Unsympathetic and distrustful of socialist rhetoric and deeds, Western capitalist countries led by the United States managed the affairs of the world. Few expected the Soviet Union, a recent arrival on the scene, to survive. At best, the 1910s were an age of reform, of Western middle-class progressives who wanted to wipe clean the tarnish accumulated by capitalism during the age of robber barons, to restore free competition, and to eliminate the sins of monopoly. This was the gist of Woodrow Wilson's ideas. In the Western Hemisphere, the Radical party in Argentina, and José Batlle y Ordóñez in Uruguay—the soothsayers of the day—had taken their cue from like beliefs. To complicate life for the social revolutionary, a decade ruled by conservatives set in with the end of the war in Europe. Men satisfied with things as they were, won control of politics in the United States. They would not tolerate radical experiments next door.

Worse still a severe financial crisis swept the postwar world, hitting Mexico with sledge-hammer blows. Silver, copper, and lead, its chief mineral exports, with a value of 187.5 million pesos in 1920, had dropped to 98.6 million pesos by 1921.[31] One-third of Mexico's copper and silver mines shut down operations because of low market prices.[32] Exports of cattle, *ixtle,* and henequen suffered similar sharp drops in price. For a while, the value of petroleum exports rose, but eventually they too went the way of the others when production declined after 1921. As the value of Mexican exports plummeted downward, the Treasury by 1923, reported Aarón Sáenz, tottered on the brink of bankruptcy.[33] So bad was the state of national revenue, according to Adolfo de la Huerta, the chief of the Treasury, that even paying the army on time became impossible.[34] Passage of the Fordney-McCumber Tariff by the American Congress in 1922, a reversal of the Underwood Tariff on 1913, left Mexico with the onerous task of finding a solution to its economic difficulties while, concomitantly, paying higher duties on its exports to the United States, its principal customer. For ironically, despite a decade of revolutionary rhetoric and nationalistic platforms, trade ties between Mexico and the United States had grown stronger. When Obregón left office in 1924, American business-men were both buying more and selling more to Mexico than ever before. Still, if funds were required for reform, the future looked bleak for social change.

Notes

Archival Abbreviations

AGN, AR: Archivo General de la Nación, Abelardo Rodríguez Papers

AGN, F: Archivo General de la Nación, Secretaría de Fomento Papers

AGN, M: Archivo General de la Nación, Francisco I. Madero Papers

AGN, OC: Archivo General de la Nación, Alvaro Obregón-Plutarco Elías Calles Papers

AGN, Z: Archivo General de la Nación, Emiliano Zapata Papers

Condumex: LDB: Centro de Estudios de Historia de México, Condumex, Francisco León de la Barra Papers

Condumex: JA: Centro de Estudios de Historia de México, Condumex, Jenaro Amezcua Papers

Condumex: RC: Centro de Estudios de Historia de México, Condumex, Ramón Corral Papers

Condumex: MG: Centro de Estudios de Historia de México, Condumex, Manuel W. González Papers

Condumex: AVC: Centro de Estudios de Historia de México, Condumex, Archivo de Venustiano Carranza

CHAPTER I

1. Blas Urrea, *La Herencia de Carranza* (Mexico, 1920), p. 106.

CHAPTER II

1. J. C. Enríquez to Venustiano Carranza, New York, January 3, 1915, Condumex: AVC.

2. *El México de Porfirio Díaz (Hombres y Cosas)* (Valencia, Spain, 1910), p. 265.

3. "El Desarollo Económico de México de 1877 a 1911," *El Trimestre Económico*, XXXIII (1965): 405.

4. Francisco Bulnes, *El Verdadero Díaz y la Revolución* (Mexico, 1967), p. 226.

5. Sesto, *México de Díaz,* p. 174.

6. Jorge Basurto, *El Proletariado Industrial en México (1850–1930)* (Mexico, 1975), p. 20.

7. *El Imparcial,* February 13, 1906.

8. Aurelio Pérez Peña, editor of *El Imparcial,* to Ramón Corral, Guaymas, Sonora, March 7, 1909, Condumex: RC.

9. Alfredo N. Acosta, *La Gestión Hacendaria de la Revolución* (Mexico, 1917), p. 52.

10. José I. Limantour, *Apuntes Sobre Mi Vida Pública* (Mexico, 1965), p. 61.

11. "Más de Cien Millones de Pesos de Ingresos," *El Imparcial,* September 19, 1906.

12, Moisés González Navarro, *Estadísticas Sociales del Porfiriato, 1877–1910* (Mexico, 1956). p. 38.

13. James D. Cockcroft, *Intellectual Precursors of the Mexican Revolution, 1900–1913* (Austin and London, 1968), p. 14.

14. "Nuestra Verdadera Independencia Económica," *El Imparcial,* September 30, 1909.

15. (Mexico, 1964), p. 227.

16. *México de Díaz,* p. 148.

17. *The Mexican Agrarian Revolution* (New York, 1929), p. 144.

18. *México y los Capitales Extranperos* (Mexico, 1918), p. 24.

19. Moisés González Navarro, "Social Aspects of the Mexican Revolution," *Journal of World History,* VIII (1964): 281.

20. Enríque González Flores, *Chihuahua de la Independencia a la Revolución* (Mexico, 1949), p. 192.

21. Barry Carr, "The Peculiarities of the Mexican North: An Essay in Interpretation," Institute of Latin American Studies, *Occasional Papers,* No. 4 (Glasgow, 1971): 5.

22. Antonio G. Rivera, *La Revolución en Sonora* (Mexico, 1969), p. 120.

23. Hector Aguilar Camín, "La Revolución Sonorense, 1910–1914" (Ph.D. diss., Instituto Nacional de Antropología e Historia, Mexico, 1975), p. 115.

24. *Ibid.,* p. 117.

25. *Ibid.,* p. 3.

26. *Ibid.,* pp. 16–18.

27. April 12, 1909.

28. Aguilar Camín, "Revolución Sonorense," pp. 44–48.

29. Francisco P. Molina, Presidente, Club Reeleccionista Obreros

de Magdalena, to Ramón Corral, Magdalena, Sonora, March 13, 1910, Condumex: RC.

30. Letter to General José María Rodríguez, Mexico, December 7, 1915, Condumex: AVC; Rivera, *Sonora,* p. 16.

31. Moisés González Navarro, *El Porfiriato. La Vida Social,* Daniel Cosío Villegas, ed., *Historia Moderna de México,* 9 vols., (Mexico, 1955–1973), IV: 546; Jorge Vera Estañol, *Historia de la Revolución Mexicana; Orígenes y Resultados* (Mexico, 1967), p. 38.

32. González Navarro, *Vida Social,* p. 546.

33. Aguilar Camín, "Revolución Sonorense," pp. 109 and 122.

34. *México de Díaz,* p. 138.

35. *Ibid.,* p. 68.

36. González Navarro, *Estadísticas Sociales,* p. 7.

37. *El Imparcial,* October 30, 1910; Sesto, *México de Díaz,* p. 142.

38. "Chihuahua Desarrolla sus Elementos de Riqueza," November 13, 1909.

39. *Ibid.*

40. Sesto, *México de Díaz,* p. 140.

41. Francisco R. Almada, *La Revolución en el Estado de Chihuahua,* 2 vols. (Chihuahua, 1964), I: 55.

42. *La Sucesión Presidencial en 1910* (Mexico, 1960), p. 269.

43. "Torreón Erigida en Ciudad," *El Imparcial,* July 27, 1907; Sesto, *México de Díaz,* p. 152.

44. Bernabé González to Alvaro Obregón, Torreón, Coahuila, November 17, 1921, AGN, OC, P. 41, L-11, 407-C-25.

45. *El Imparcial,* March 20, 1907.

46. Bulnes, *El Verdadero Díaz,* pp. 135 and 228; Vera Estañol, *Historia de la Revolución,* pp. 14–15.

47. *El Correo de Chihuahua,* August 7, 1907; Bulnes, *El Verdadero Díaz,* p. 135.

48. Sesto, *México de Díaz,* p. 143.

49. *Ibid.,* p. 144.

50. January 10, 1906.

51. "Trabajadores para México," *El Imparcial,* February 13, 1906.

52. "Las Quejas de los Agricultores de Durango," January 23, 1906.

53. p. 251.

54. Ramón Eduardo Ruiz, *Mexico, the Challenge of Poverty and Illiteracy* (San Marino, California, 1963), p. 20.

55. "Lo que se ha hecho en Favor del Indio," *El Imparcial,* September 28, 1909.

56. González Navarro, *Vida Social,* p. 675.

57. *Ibid.,* p. 599.

58. *Ibid.*, p. 575.
59. *Ibid.*, p. 595.
60. Alfonso Craviota, cited in Felix F. Palavicini, *Historia de la Constitución de 1917*, 2 vols. (Mexico, 1917), I: 232.
61. *El Imparcial*, September 5, 1906; Francisco R. Almada, *Resumen de la Historia de Chihuahua* (Mexico, 1955), p. 366.
62. *El Imparcial*, April 27, 1907; Almada, *Resumen*, p. 364.
63. González Navarro, *Estadísticas Sociales*, pp. 18–19.
64. José Clemente Orozco, *An Autobiography*, translated by Robert C. Stephenson (Austin, 1962), pp. 26–28.
65. Salvador Mendoza, "Editorial: El Problema Político de Oaxaca," *El Universal*, January 22, 1919.

CHAPTER III

1. *El Antiguo Régimen y a Revolución* (Mexico, 1911), p. 9.
2. *Historia de la Revolucion Mexicana; Orígenes y Resultados* (Mexico, 1967), p. 90.
3. *El Verdadero Díaz y la Revolucion* (Mexico, 1967), p. 351.
4. *La Sucesión Presidencial en 1910* (Mexico, 1960), p. 139.
5. *El Verdadero Díaz*, pp. 21 and 23.
6. *Un Decenio de Política Mexicana* (New York, 1920), p. 15.
7. Ramón Prida, *De la Dictadura a la Anarquía; Apuntes para la Historia Política de México durante los Ultimos Cuarenta y Tres Años (1871–1913)* (Mexico, 1958), p. 288.
8. Bulnes, *El Verdadero Díaz*, p. 200.
9. Blas Urrea, *La Herencia de Carranza* (Mexico, 1920), p. 26.
10. *El Verdadero Díaz*, pp. 356–57.
11. *El México de Porfirio Díaz (Hombres y Cosas)* (Valencia, Spain, 1910), p. 151.
12. Madero, *Sucesión*, p. 192.
13. Fernando González Roa, *El Aspecto Agrario de la Revolución Mexicana* (Mexico, 1919), p. 88.
14. Manero, *Antiguo Régimen*, p. 159.
15. José I. Limantour, *Apuntes Sobre Mi Vida Pública* (Mexico, 1965), p. 188; Bulnes, *El Verdadero Díaz*, p. 59.
16. Limantour, *Apuntes*, pp. 142–144; Bulnes, *El Verdadero Díaz*. p. 340.
17. Aquiles Elorduy, "Proyecto de Reforma de la Constitución," Mexico, November 20, 1916, Condumex: AVC.
18. *Ibid.*

19. *Apuntes Confidenciales al Presidente Porfirio Díaz* (Mexico, 1967), p. 197.

20. "Programa," El Paso, Texas, August 18, 1916, Condumex: AVC.

21. Urrea, *Herencia de Carranza*, p. 26.

22. Antonio Manero, "Informe Rendido al Señor Licenciado don Luis Cabrera, Secretario de Hacienda y Crédito Público, por orden del Señor Subsecretario del propio ramo, don Rafael Nieto, sobre la cuestión bancaria y los trabajos llevados a cabo por la Comisión Reguladora e Inspectora de Instituciones de Crédito," Mexico, November 16, 1916, Condumex: AVC.

23. Urrea, *Herencia de Carranza*, p. 45.

24. *El Imparcial*, September 24, 1909.

25. pp. 165–166.

26. Cited in *Diario de los Debates del Congreso Constituyente, 1916–1917*, 2 vols. (Mexico, 1960), II: 1117.

27. *El Verdadero Díaz*, pp. 165–166.

28. Manero, "Informe Rendido," p. 8.

29. Francisco R. Almada, *La Revolución en el Estado de Chihuahua*, 2 vols. (Chihuahua, 1964), I: 37.

30. Hector Aguilar Camín, "La Revolución Sonorense, 1910–1914" (Ph.D. diss., Instituto Nacional de Antropolgía e Historia, Mexico, 1975), p. 84.

31. *Ibid.*, p. 88.

32. Manero, *Antiguo Régimen*, pp. 313–314.

33. Aguilar Camín, "Revolución Sonorense," p. 106.

34. Antonio G. Rivera, *La Revolución en Sonora* (Mexico, 1969), p. 16.

35. Aguilar Camín, "Revolución Sonorense," p. 97.

36. *Revolución en Sonora*, p. 16.

37. Aguilar Camín, "Revolución Sonorense," p. 19.

38. *Ibid.*, p. 49.

39. *Ibid.*, pp. 26, 33, 62, 83, 108, and 110.

40. *Resumen de la Historia del Estado de Chihuahua* (Mexico, 1955), p. 381.

41. *Ibid.*, pp. 362–63.

42. *The Whole Truth About Mexico; President Wilson's Responsibility* (New York, 1916), p. 154.

43. José Fuentes Mares, *Y México se Refugió en el Desierto. Luis Terrazas: Historia Destino* (Mexico, 1954), pp. 171–72.

44. William H. Beezley, *Insurgent Governor: Abraham González and the Mexican Revolution in Chihuahua* (Lincoln, Nebraska, 1973), p. 10.

45. *Resumen de la Historia,* pp. 362–63.

46. *El Verdadero Díaz,* p. 287.

47. Almada, *Resumen de la Historia,* p. 363.

48. Almada, *Revolución en Chihuahua,* I: 35.

49. *Ibid.,* pp. 20–21.

50. "Historia de un Proceso," Chihuahua, Chihuahua, 1907, Silvestre Terrazas Papers, Box 83, Bancroft Library.

51. Almada, *Revolución en Chihuahua,* I: 63.

52. *Ibid.,* p. 81.

53. Beezley, *Insurgent Governor,* pp. 5–6.

54. *Ibid.,* pp. 13–17.

55. *Ibid.,* p. 18.

56. Almada, *Resumen de la Historia,* p. 383.

57. Manuel Calero, *Un Decenio de Política Mexicana* (New York, 1920), p. 39.

58. Almada, *Revolución en Chihuahua,* I: 150.

59. Esther Lobato Vda. de Barreiro to General Alvaro Obregón, Mexico, February 5, 1915, Condumex: AVC.

60. *Apuntes,* p. 266.

61. Paul J. Vanderwood, "Genesis of the Rurales: Mexico's Early Struggle for Public Security," *The Hispanic American Historical Review,* L (May, 1970): 343–344.

62. Quoted in *El Imparcial,* September 22, 1909.

63. Limantour, *Apuntes,* p. 266; For a similar view of the military see Paul J. Vanderwood, "Response to Revolt: The Counter-Guerrilla Strategy of Porfirio Díaz," *The Hispanic American Historical Review,* LVI (November, 1976): 555, 557.

64. Limantour, *Apuntes,* p. 252.

65. *Ibid.,* pp. 77–79.

66. *El Verdadero Díaz,* pp. 125–126.

67. *Historia de la Revolución Mexicana,* p. 52.

68. *El Antiguo Régimen,* pp. 343–344.

69. *Un Decenio de Política,* p. 37; *El Ejército Villista,* (Mexico, 1961), p. 20.

70. *El Verdadero Díaz,* p. 299.

71. *Ibid.,* pp. 299 and 302.

72. Letter to Federico Gamboa, Los Angeles, California, April 17, 1916, Condumex: LDB.

73. *El Verdadero Díaz,* p. 302.

74. March 24, 1908.

75. Leonardo Pasquel, "Prólogo," Zayas Enríquez, *Apuntes Confidenciales,* p. XII.

76. Limantour, *Apuntes,* p. 267.

CHAPTER IV

1. "La Democracia y la Clase Media," March 13, 1908.
2. Quoted in "La Gleba Intelectual," *El Imparcial,* October 3, 1906.
3. *Historia de la Revolución Mexicana; Orígenes y Resultados* (Mexico, 1967), p. 92.
4. Quoted in "La Democracia y la Clase Media," *El Imparcial* March 13, 1908.
5. *Historia de la Revolución,* pp. 16–17.
6. "El Gobierno y Sus Empleados," April 27, 1907.
7. *El Antiguo Régimen y la Revolución* (Mexico, 1911), p. 405.
8. *El México de Porfirio Díaz (Hombres y Cosas)* (Valencia, Spain, 1910), p. 267.
9. *Historia de la Revolución,* p. 92.
10. Letter to Alvaro Obregón, Mexico, June 28, 1919, Condumex: AVC.
11. Barry Carr, "The Peculiarities of the Mexican North, 1880–1928: An Essay in Interpretation," Institute of Latin American Studies, *Occasional Papers,* No. 4 (Glasgow, 1971): 3.
12. Letter to Plutarco Elías Calles, Mexico, December 30, 1924, AGN, OC, P. 106, L-6, 818-E-28 (2).
13. Quoted in P. Edward Haley, *Revolution and Intervention: The Diplomacy of Taft and Wilson with Mexico, 1910–1917* (Cambridge and London, 1970), p. 18.
14. Carr, *Peculiarities,* p. 6.
15. Moisés González Navarro, *Estadísticas Sociales del Porfiriato, 1877–1910* (Mexico, 1956), pp. 18–19.
16. Carr, *Peculiarities,* p. 6.
17. Moisés González Navarro, *La Confederación Nacional Campesina; Un Grupo de Presion en la Reforma Agraria Mexicana* (Mexico, 1968), p. 45.
18. *Apuntes Confidenciales al Presidente Porfirio Díaz* (Mexico, 1967), p. 11.
19. Sesto, *México de Díaz,* p. 132; "El Descanso Dominical," *El Imparcial,* March 18, 1907.
20. *El Imparcial,* July 29, 1906 and July 5, 1910.
21. James D. Cockcroft, *Intellectual Precursors of the Mexican Revolution, 1900–1913* (Austin and London, 1968), p. 27.
22. *Mi Vida Revolucionaria* (Mexico, 1937), p. 16.
23. *El Verdadero Díaz y la Revolución* (Mexico, 1967), p. 39.
24. *La Sucesión Presidencial en 1910* (Mexico, 1960), p. 253.

25. *Ibid.*, p. 252.

26. *Apuntes Confidenciales*, p. 12.

27. *Historia de la Revolución*, p. 91.

28. *Memorias Políticas (1909–1913)* (Mexico, 1933), p. 12.

29. *Ibid.*, p. 22.

30. *Apuntes Confidenciales*, pp. 11 and 23.

31. José I. Limantour, *Apuntes Sobre Mi Vida Pública* (Mexico, 1965), p. 226.

32. Quoted in Manero, *Antiguo Régimen*, p. 158.

33. Limantour, *Apuntes Sobre Mi Vida*, pp. 249 and 267.

34. *Antiguo Régimen*, pp. 113, 167–168, 176, and 351–352.

35. Quoted in Moisés González Navarro, *El Porfiriato. La Vida Social*, Daniel Cosío Villegas, ed., *Historia Moderna de México*, 9 vols. (Mexico, 1955–1973), IV: 289.

36. Quoted in *ibid.*, p. 388.

37. Bulnes, *El Verdadero Díaz*, p. 261.

38. Francisco Bulnes, *The Whole Truth About Mexico; President Wilson's Responsibility* (New York, 1916), p. 234; González Navarro, *Vida Social*, p. 388.

39. *El Verdadero Díaz*, p. 42.

40. *Ibid.*, p. 252.

41. Sesto, *México de Díaz*, p. 158.

42. "El Sueldo de los Empleados," *El Imparcial*, November 6, 1906; Bulnes, *El Verdadero Díaz*, p. 263.

43. Jesús Urueta to José Ives Limantour, Paris, France, March 25, 1903, in *El Imparcial*, September 21, 1909.

44. *El Verdadero Díaz*, p. 251.

45. *Ibid.*; A much lower figure for lawyers is found in González Navarro, *Estadísticas Sociales*, pp. 18–19.

46. *El Verdadero Díaz*, p. 253.

47. Francisco R. Almada, *La Revolución en el Estado de Chihuahua*, 2 vols. (Chihuahua, 1964), I: 152; Francisco R. Almada, *Resumen de la Historia del Estado de Chihuahua* (Mexico, 1955), p. 378.

48. González Navarro, *Estadísticas Sociales*, pp. 18–19; González Navarro, *Vida Social*, p. 606.

49. "Los Estados y la Instrucción Primaria," May 25, 1908.

50. *El Verdadero Díaz*, p. 259.

51. *The Whole Truth*, p. 142.

52. *Apuntes Confidenciales*, p. 13.

53. Quoted in "Los Científicos y los Puestos Públicos," *El Imparcial*, November 11, 1909.

54. *The Whole Truth*, p. 142.

55. Vera Estañol, *Historia de la Revolución Mexicana*, p. 90.

56. *Revolución en el Estado,* I: 149.

57. José Fuentes Mares, *La Revolución Mexicana; Memorias de un Espectador* (Mexico, 1971), p. 30.

58. *Un Decenio de Política Mexicana* (New York, 1920), p. 16.

59. Quoted in "Los Movimientos Sediciosos y su Influencia sobre la Juventud," *El Imparcial,* December 12, 1910.

60. Letter of Governor M. Ahumada, Guadalajara, Jalisco, June 14, 1909, Condumex: RC.

61. *Cincuenta Años de Política Mexicana, Memorias Políticas* (Mexico, 1968), p. 17.

62. *Apuntes Confidenciales,* p. 12.

63. *Historia de la Revolución Mexicana en Tabasco* (Mexico, 1972), pp. 13 and 22.

64. *De la Dictadura a la Anarquía; Apuntes para la Historia Política de México Durante los Ultimos Cuarenta y Tres Años (1871–1913)* (Mexico, 1958), p. 234.

CHAPTER V

1. *Historia de la Revolución Mexicana; Orígines y Resultados* (Mexico, 1967), pp. 35 and 91.

2. Centro Industrial Mexicano, "Reglamento Interior, Puebla, December 3, 1906, AGN, F, 6, 28.

3. "La Comisión de Obreros Obtiene una audiencia del Señor General Díaz," *El Imparcial,* December 27, 1906.

4. Jorge Basurto, *El Proletariado Industrial en México (1850–1930)* (Mexico, 1975), p. 46.

5. *Ibid.*

6. "Las Nuevas Tarifas," *El Imparcial,* January 12, 1907.

7. "La Huelga de Cananea," *ibid.,* June 26, 1906.

8. *El Imparcial,* November 14, 1906; Marvin D. Bernstein, *The Mexican Mining Economy* (Albany, 1964), p. 86.

9. *El México de Porfirio Díaz (Hombres y Cosas)* (Valencia, Spain, 1910), pp. 131, 134, and 253.

10. Bernstein, *Mexican Mining,* p. 88.

11. October 2, 1910.

12. Bernstein, *Mexican Mining,* p. 88.

13. *Mexico and Its Heritage* (New York, 1928), p. 345.

14. Basurto, *Proletariado Industrial,* p. 55.

15. *Ibid.,* p. 25; James D. Cockcroft, *Intellectual Precursors of the Mexican Revolution, 1900–1913* (Austin and London, 1968), p. 47.

16. *El Imparcial,* June 29, 1906.

17. "Patriotismo y Emigración," *El Imparcial,* October 22, 1907.

18. E. Arnold to Gobernador Alberto Cubillas, Cananea, Sonora, September 17, 1908, Condumex: RC.

19. *El Imparcial,* March 30, 1908; October 25, 1907; October 22, 1910; May 3, 1908; March 2, 1906; and December 17, 1907.

20. Andrés Molina Enríquez, *Los Grandes Problemas Nacionales* (Mexico, 1964), p. 236.

21. Bernstein, *Mexican Mining,* p. 87.

22. Basurto, *Proletariado Industrial,* p. 52.

23. *México de Díaz,* p. 245.

24. José C. Valadés, *El Porfirismo, Historia de un Régimen: El Crecimiento,* 2 vols. (Mexico, 1948), II: 88.

25. Bernstein, *Mexican Mining,* p. 87.

26. Vincente Lombardo Toledano, *Teoría y Práctica del Movimiento Sindical Mexicano* (Mexico, 1961), p. 34.

27. Basurto, *Proletariado Industrial,* p. 77.

28. Servando A. Alzati, *Historia de la Mexicanización de los Ferrocarriles Nacionales de México* (Mexico, 1946), pp. 66–67 and 71.

29. Bernstein, *Mexican Mining,* p. 91.

30. "Reglamento para las Fábricas de la Comp. Industrial de Orizaba, S. A.," Río Blanco, Veracruz, May 1907, AGN, F, 6, 28.

31. Frank Tannenbaum, *The Mexican Agrarian Revolution* (New York, 1929), pp. 149–150.

32. February 9, 1907.

33. David M. Pletcher, *Rails, Mines, and Progress: Seven American Promoters in Mexico, 1867–1911* (Ithaca, New York, 1958), p. 61.

34. Basurto, *Proletariado Industrial,* p. 48.

35. "México para los Mexicanos," August 19, 1906.

36. "Informe Presidencial," *El Imparcial,* September 17, 1906.

37. "La Cuestión Obrera," July 5, 1906.

38. *Apuntes Confidenciales al Presidente Porfirio Díaz* (Mexico, 1967), p. 11.

39. Basurto, *Proletariado Industrial,* p. 78.

40. *Ibid.,* pp. 81–82.

41. Alfred Tischendorf, *Great Britain and Mexico in the Era of Porfirio Díaz* (Durham, 1961), pp. 191–192.

42. Basurto, *Proletariado Industrial,* p. 195.

43. *El Imparcial,* July 26, 27, and 29, and August 2 and 9, 1906; Basurto, *Proletariado Industrial,* p. 105.

44. Alzati, *Historia,* p. 119.

45. "El Congreso de Obreros," *El Imparcial,* August 8, 1906.

46. Robert E. Quirk, *The Mexican Revolution and the Catholic Church, 1910–1929* (Bloomington and London, 1973), p. 18.

47. Basurto, *Proletariado Industrial*, pp. 198–199.

48. Moisés González Navarro, *El Porfiriato. La Vida Social*, in Daniel Cosío Villegas, ed., *Historia Moderna de México*, 9 vols. (Mexico, 1955–1973), IV: 298; Moisés González Navarro, *Las Huelgas Textiles en el Porfiriato* (Puebla, 1970), pp. 12 and 17.

49. Alzati, *Historia*, p. 71; Antonio G. Rivera, *La Revolución en Sonora* (Mexico, 1969), p. 135; González Navarro, *Vida Social*, p. 316.

50. Francisco Bulnes, *El Verdadero Díaz y la Revolución* (Mexico, 1967), p. 225.

51. Marjorie R. Clark, *Organized Labor in Mexico* (Chapel Hill, 1934), p. 12.

52. González Navarro, *Huelgas Textiles*, pp. 78 and 83.

53. *El Imparcial*, July 29, 1906; Pletcher, *Rails, Mines, and Progress*, p. 228.

54. "Escándalos Huelguistas en Cananea," *El Imparcial*, June 3, 1906; "Informe Completo de los Asuntos de Cananea," *ibid.*, June 29, 1906; González Navarro, *Vida Social*, p. 317; Rivera, *Revolución en Sonora*, pp. 20 and 134; Alzati, *Historia*, p. 68; León Díaz Cárdenas, *Cananea, Primer Brote del Sindicalismo en México* (Mexico, 1936), pp. 22, 23, and 34.

55. Pletcher, *Rails, Mines, and Progress*, p. 249.

56. "El Gran Clamor Nacional," August 20, 1906.

57. *Apuntes Confidenciales*, p. 25.

58. *Grandes Problemas*, pp. 222–223.

59. "Informe Completo de los Asuntos de Cananea," *El Imparcial*, June 29, 1906.

60. *Ibid.*

61. *Ibid.*

62. *Díaz y la Revolución*, p. 160.

63. "Las Nuevas Tarifas," *ibid.*, January 1, 1907.

64. González Navarro, *Huelgas Textiles*, p. 90.

65. Vera Estañol, *Historia de la Revolució Mexicana*, pp. 88 and 103.

66. Juan Sánchez Azcona, *Apuntes para la Historia de la Revolución Mexicana* (Mexico, 1961), p. 101; Benjamín Rodríguez to Francisco I. Madero, Cañada, Morelos, December 12, 1911, AGN, M, 18, 1391; Angel Ruíz to Francisco I. Madero, Oaxaca, Oaxaca, June 12, 1912, AGN, M, 18, 1383.

67. Francisco I. Madero to Porfirio Díaz, Mexico, May 26, 1910, in Azcona, *Apuntes*, p. 45.

68. Vera Estañol, *Historia de la Revolución Mexicana*, p. 103.

69. Azcona, *Apuntes*, p. 94.

70. *Ibid.*

71. Consuelo Peña de Villarreal, *Revolución en el Norte* (Puebla, 1968), p. 60.

CHAPTER VI

1. *Apuntes Sobre Mi Vida Pública* (Mexico, 1965), p. 91.
2. *The Whole Truth About Mexico; President Wilson's Responsibility* (New York, 1916), p. 228.
3. Moisés González Navarro, *El Porfiriato. La Vida Social,* in Daniel Cosío Villegas, ed., *Historia Moderna de Mexico,* 9 vols. (Mexico, 1955–1973), IV: 187.
4. Pastor Rouaix, Subsecretario de Fomento, to Gobernadores de los Estados y a los Jefes Políticos de los Territorios, Mexico, July 1, 1916, AGN, F, 5, 3; Charles C. Cumberland, *Mexican Revolution: The Constitutionalist Years* (Austin, 1972), p. 230.
5. Cumberland, *Mexican Revolution,* p. 230.
6. *Vida Social,* p. 240.
7. James D. Cockcroft, *Intellectual Precursors of the Mexican Revolution, 1900–1913* (Austin and London, 1968), p. 51.
8. "Los Pretendidos Revolucionarios," *El Imparcial,* October 3, 1906.
9. *El Aspecto Agrario de la Revolución* (Mexico, 1919), p. 201.
10. Mrs. Alex Tweedie, *Mexico As I Saw It* (New York, 1901), pp. 339–341.
11. *El Mexico de Porfirio Díaz (Hombres y Cosas)* (Valencia, Spain, 1910), p. 268.
12. *The Whole Truth,* p. 230.
13. González Navarro, *Vida Social,* pp. 219 and 222.
14. *Ibid.,* pp. 223 and 227.
15. Bulnes, *The Whole Truth,* p. 231.
16. González Navarro, *Vida Social,* p. 212; Bulnes, *The Whole Truth,* p. 87.
17. John Womack, *Zapata and the Mexican Revolution* (New York, 1970), p. 43.
18. For example on the Hacienda El Malinal in Tepic, *La Tribuna,* April 14, 1914, AGN, F, 31, 23.
19. Moisés González Navarro, *Estadísticas Sociales del Porfiriato,*
20. *Ibid.,* pp. 40–41.
20. *Ibid.,* pp. 40–41.
21. González Navarro, *Vida Social,* p. 210.
22. González Navarro, *Estadísticas Sociales,* p. 41.

23. Arnaldo Cordova, *La Ideología de la Revolución Mexicana; la Formación del Nuevo Régimen* (Mexico, 1973), p. 122.

24. González Navarro, *Vida Social*, p. 279.

25. *The Whole Truth*, p. 38.

26. Francisco Bulnes, *El Verdadero Díaz y la Revolución* (Mexico, 1967), p. 236.

27. Antonio Manero, *El Antiguo Régimen y la Revolución* (Mexico, 1911), pp. 211–213.

28. "La Cosecha de este Año," *El Imparcial*, June 3, 1906.

29. *El Imparcial*, October 16, 1909.

30. "La Situación Económica y la Producción Agrícola y Minera," *El Imparcial*, December 29, 1908.

31. "Escasez de Maíz," *El Imparcial*, January 12, 1906.

32. "La Cosecha de este Año," *El Imparcial*, June 3, 1906.

33. "Se Perderán en México las Cosechas de Trigo?" *El Imparcial*, May 5, 1908.

34. "Informe Leído por el C. Presidente de la República," *El Imparcial*, April 2, 1909.

35. June 2, 1909.

36. *El Imparcial*, September 2, 1909.

37. *Ibid.*, October 24, 1909.

38. "El Año Agrícola," *El Imparcial*, July 27, 1910.

39. May 29, 1907.

40. April 29, 1909.

41. *El Imparcial*, March 26, 1908.

42. Cockcroft, *Precursors*, p. 43; *El Imparcial*, November 25, 1909.

43. *El Imparcial*, March 13, 1907; May 20, 1908; July 10, 1908.

44. *Historia de la Revolución Mexicana; Orígenes y Resultados* (Mexico, 1967), p. 33.

45. Manero, *Antiguo Régimen*, p. 224.

46. Andrés Molina Enríquez, *Los Grandes Problemas Nacionales* (Mexico, 1909), p. 118.

47. Manero, *Antiguo Régimen*, pp. 211–213.

48. November 20, 1909.

49. Frank Tannenbaum, *The Mexican Agrarian Revolution* (New York, 1968), p. 144.

50. "La Carestía de la Vida y la Eficacia del Trabajo," November 16, 1909.

51. Marjorie R. Clark, *Organized Labor in Mexico* (Chapel Hill, 1934), p. 9.

52. Carlos Felix Díaz, *Génesis de la Revolución Mexicana* (La Paz, Bolivia, 1918), p. 165.

53. González Roa, *El Aspecto Agrario,* pp. 167–168.

54. *Ibid.,* p. 168.

55. *Historia de la Revolución Mexicana,* p. 29.

56. October 1, 1908.

57. *El Imparcial,* October 1, 1908.

58. "¿Faltan Brazos o Faltan Energías?" February 14, 1906.

59. "No Faltan Brazos," *El Imparcial,* March 24, 1907.

60. "Faltan Brazos para el Cultivo del Algodón," *El Imparcial,* February 12, 1906.

61. "Exceso de Braceros en Texas," *El Imparcial,* February 6, 1907.

62. November 5, 1909; González Roa, *El Aspecto Agrario,* p. 197.

63. February 12, 1907.

64. González Roa, *El Aspecto Agrario,* p. 197.

65. "Por que Emigran Nuestros Trabajadores," *El Imparcial,* November 4, 1907.

66. *Grandes Problemas,* p. 116.

67. *Ibid.,* p. 117.

68. *Agrarian Revolution,* pp. 149–150.

69. Andrés Molina Enríquez, "El Verdadero Objeto de los Ejidos," Mexico, October 24, 1924, AGN, OC, P. 106, L-6, 818-E-28 (2); also see González Roa, *El Aspecto Agrario,* pp. 196–197.

70. Barry Carr, *The Peculiarities of the Mexican North, 1880–1928: An Essay in Interpretation,* Institute of Latin American Studies, *Occasional Papers,* No. 4 (Glasgow, 1971), p. 3.

71. Bulnes, *The Whole Truth,* p. 87.

72. González Navarro, *Vida Social,* pp. 210 and 213.

73. Toribio Esquivel Obregón, *Democracia y Personalismo. Relatos y Comentarios Sobre Política Actual* (Mexico, 1911), p. 16.

74. González Roa, *El Aspecto Agrario,* pp. 83–84.

75. José Fuentes Mares, *Y México se Refugió en el Desierto. Luis Terrazas: Historia y Destino* (Mexico, 1954), p. 171.

76. González Roa, *El Aspecto Agrario,* p. 132.

77. González Navarro, *Estadísticas Sociales,* p. 42.

78. González Roa, *El Aspecto Agrario,* p. 132.

79. Francisco R. Almada, *La Revolución en el Estado de Chihuahua,* 2 vols. (Chihuahua, 1964), I: 56.

80. González Navarro, *Vida Social,* p. 215.

81. Marte R. Gómez, *La Reforma Agraria en las Filas Villistas, Años 1913 a 1915 a 1920* (Mexico, 1966), p. 53.

82. *Ibid.,* p. 25.

83. González Navarro, *Vida Social,* p. 188; Almada, *Revolución,* I: p. 60.

84. Gómez, *La Reforma Agraria,* p. 29.

85. *El Imparcial,* August 27, 1907; March 19, 1908; and December 16, 1908.

86. *Ibid.,* September 21, 1909.

87. *Ibid.,* September 12, 1909.

88. *Ibid.,* April 3, 1908.

89. *Ibid.,* August 13, 1906.

90. Cosecheros de Algodón de la Comarca Lagunera to Venustiano Carranza, Torreón, Coahuila, October 28, 1915, Condumex: AVC.

91. González Navarro, *Vida Social,* p. 258.

92. "La Cuestión del Yaqui," *El Imparcial,* February 26, 1906.

93. Cited in González Navarro, *Vida Social,* p. 250.

94. Hector Aguilar Camín, "La Revolución Sonorense, 1910–1914" (Ph.D. diss., Instituto Nacional de Antropolgía e Historia, Mexico, 1975), pp. 50–53.

95. *Ibid.,* p. 54.

96. Alberto Cubillas to Ramón Corral, Hermosillo, Sonora, July 22, 1908; Condumex: RC.

97. July 17, 1908.

98. Cited in Alberto Cubillas to Ramón Corral, Hermosillo, Sonora, March 20, 1908, Condumex: RC.

99. *El Verdadero Díaz,* p. 70.

100. *La Sucesión Presidencial en 1910* (Mexico, 1960), p. 205.

101. Antonio G. Rivera, *La Revolución en Sonora* (Mexico, 1967), p. 201.

102. Alberto Cubillas to Ramón Corral, September 4, 1908, Hermosillo, Sonora, Condumex: RC.

103. Womack, *Zapata,* p. 15.

104. *Ibid.,* pp. 42–43.

105. Cockcroft, *Precursors,* p. 32.

106. "El Nuevo Gobierno del Estado de Morelos," February 15, 1909.

107. "Seis Meses de Comercio," April 15, 1907.

108. "El Comercio Exterior y la Reforma Monetaria," April 25, 1907.

109. "El Nuevo Programa del Gobierno," May 23, 1908.

110. "Terreno a Donde Debemos Llevar Nuestras Actividades," September 24, 1909.

111. "Tierras Viejas Frente a Tierras Viejas," December 4, 1909.

112. "El Aumento del Salario," January 1, 1911.

113. "¿Debe México Sacrificar la Minería?" September 1, 1906.

114. "El Problema del Maíz," *El Imparcial,* December 14, 1907.

115. Félix Palavicini, *Mi Vida Revolucionaria* (Mexico, 1937), p. 13; "Fin del Congreso de Zamora," *El Imparcial,* September 19, 1906.

116. Cited in *El Imparcial*, December 11, 1907.

117. *El Imparcial*, December 14, 1908.

118. "Los Patrones y Jornaleros," *El Imparcial*, April 26, 1909.

119. "Lo Unico Verdadero Bárbaro," September 23, 1909.

120. "En Pro de la Agricultura Nacional," *El Imparcial*, January 13, 1910.

121. González Navarro, *Vida Social*, p. 195.

122. Manero, *Antiguo Régimen*, p. 149.

123. *Ibid.*, p. 160.

124. Moisés González Navarro, *La Confederación Nacional Campesina; Un Grupo de Presión en la Reforma Agraria Mexicana* (Mexico, 1968), p. 47.

125. "Agricultura y Revolución," March 30, 1911.

CHAPTER VII

1. *El Veradero Díaz y la Revolu*cion (Mexico, 1967), p. 230.

2. Francisco Roux-López, "El Surgimiento del Imperialismo Económico y los Estados Unidos. La Penetración Económica en México (1876–1910)" (Thesis for the Licenciatura, Universidad Nacional Autónoma de Mexico, 1963), p. 56.

3. *Apuntes Sobre Mi Vida Pública* (Mexico, 1965), p. 54.

4. Secretaría de Hacienda Pública, *Memorias de la Secretaría de Hacienda Pública (1906–07)* (Mexico, 1907), pp. 336–337.

5. Quoted in Adolfo Carrillo, "El Señor Ramón Corral el Futuro Presidente," Mexico [1909?], Condumex: RC.

6. Moisés González Navarro, *El Porfiriato. La Vida Social*, Daniel Cosío Villegas, ed., *Historia Moderna de México*, 9 vols. (Mexico, 1955–1973), IV: 156.

7. *El México de Porfirio Díaz (Hombres y Cosas)* (Valencia, Spain, 1910), pp. 27 and 248.

8. David M. Pletcher, "The Fall of Silver in Mexico, 1870–1910, and Its Effects on American Investments," *The Journal of Economic History*, XVIII (March, 1958): 33.

9. P. Edward Haley, *Revolution and Intervention: The Diplomacy of Taft and Wilson With Mexico, 1910–1917* (Cambridge and London, 1970), pp. 11–12.

10. Cleona Lewis, *America's Stake in International Investments* (Washington, 1938), p. 443.

11. U.S. Senate, *Investigation of Mexican Affairs. Preliminary Report and Hearings of Committee on Foreign Affairs*, [September 8, 1919], 2 vols. (Washington, 1920), II: 3322.

12. Roux-López, "Surgimiento," p. 80.

13. Haley, *Revolution and Intervention*, p. 87.

14. *El Antiguo Régimen y la Revolución* (Mexico, 1911), p. 20.

15. Alfred Tischendorf, *Great Britain and Mexico in the Era of Porfirio Díaz* (Durham, 1961), pp. 139–141; James F. Rippy, "French Investments in Mexico," *Northamerican Economic Affairs*, II (Winter, 1948): 3–16.

16. Jorge Basurto, *El Proletariado Industrial en México (1850–1930)* (Mexico, 1975), p. 21.

17. *El Aspecto Agrario de la Revolución* (Mexico, 1919), p. 299.

18. Fernando Cuesta Soto, "Los Tratados de Bucareli Contra la Revolución" (Thesis for Licenciatura, Universidad Nacional Autónoma de México, Mexico, 1937), p. 10.

19. *Ibid.*, p. 7.

20. Roux-López, "Surgimiento," pp. 100 and 106.

21. "El Comercio Exterior y la Reforma Monetaria," April 25, 1907.

22. Secretaría de Hacienda, *Memorias, 1906–07,* pp. 336–337.

23. *Antiguo Régimen*, p. 218.

24. Servando A. Alzati, *Historia de la Mexicanización de los Ferrocarriles Nacionales de México* (Mexico, 1946), p. 156.

25. Roux-López, "Surgimiento," p. 105.

26. "Los Extranjeros Incapaces para Adquirir Minas," *El Imparcial*, June 11, 1908.

27. August 1, 1908.

28. *El Imparcial*, October 16, 1908.

29. "No Existe el Movimiento Antiextranjero," *El Imparcial*, July 4, 1908.

30. Quoted in Roux-López, "Surgimiento," pp. 66–67.

31. Mariano Miguel del Val, "Un Reportaje al ex-Presidente de México," *Caras y Caretas*, May, 1912.

32. Robert E. Quirk, *The Mexican Revolution and the Catholic Church, 1910–1929* (Bloomington and London, 1973), p. 23.

33. *The Whole Truth About Mexico; President Wilson's Responsibility* (New York, 1916), p. 103.

34. Blas Urrea, *La Herencia de Carranza* (Mexico, 1920), p. 158.

35. Bulnes, *El Verdadero Díaz*, p. 398.

36. Quoted in González Navarro, *La Vida Social*, p. 159.

37. Quoted in *ibid.*, p. 388.

38. Quoted in James D. Cockroft, *Intellectual Precursors of the Mexican Revolution, 1900–1913* (Austin and London, 1968), p. 98.

39. "La Pretendida Revolución Anti-Extranjera," July 31, 1906.

40. *La Sucesión Presidencial en 1910* (Mexico, 1960), pp. 223 and 342.

41. Quoted in González Navarro, *La Vida Social*, p. 380.
42. Blas Urrea, *Herencia*, p. 58.
43. *Los Grandes Problemas Nacionales* (Mexico, 1909, p. 215.
44. *Ibid.*, p. 312.
45. Quoted in Roberto Blanco Moheno, *Crónica de la Revolución Mexicana*, 2 vols. (Mexico, 1958–1959), II: 156.
46. Quoted in Bulnes, *The Whole Truth*, p. 129.
47. Quoted in *ibid.*
48. Quoted in *ibid.*
49. Victoriano Huerta, *Memorias del General Victoriano Huerta* (Barcelona, Spain, 1915), p. 35.
50. Manuel Doblado, *México Para los Mexicanos; El Presidente Huerta y su Gobierno* (Mexico, 1913), p. 129.
51. José Mancisidor, *Historia de la Revolución Mexicana* (Mexico, 1965), p. 45.
52. *Ibid.*, pp. 45–46.
53. Daniel Cosío Villegas, ed., *El Porfiriato. La Vida Económica. Historia Moderna de México*, 9 vols. (Mexico, 1955–1973), VII, Part 2: 1134.
54. Barry Carr, "The Peculiarities of the Mexican North, 1880–1928: An Essay in Interpretation," Institute of Latin American Studies, *Occasional Papers*. No. 4 (Glasgow, 1971): p. 5.
55. April 30, 1909.
56. *La Revolución en Sonora* (Mexico, 1969), p. 138.
57. Hector Aguilar Camín, "La Revolución Sonorense, 1910–1914" (Ph.D. diss. Instituto Nacional de Antropología e Historia, Mexico, 1975), p. 116.
58. Carr, *Peculiarities*, p. 6.
59. Moisés González Navarro, *Estadísticas Sociales del Porfiriato, 1877–1910* (Mexico, 1956), pp. 34–35.
60. "Los Yaquis en Sonora," January 31, 1906.
61. *The Whole Truth*, p. 123.
62. Edmundo R. Puentes to Enrique Creel, Cananea, Sonora, October 14, 1906, Silvestre Terrazas Papers, M-B, 18, Bancroft Library.
63. *La Sucesión Presidencial*, pp. 220–221.
64. *Resumen de la Historia del Estado de Chihuahua* (Mexico, 1955), p. 378.
65. Enrique González Flores, *Chihuahua de la Independencia a la Revolución* (Mexico, 1949), p. 211.
66. *La Revolución en el Estado de Chihuahua*, 2 vols. (Chihuahua, 1964), I: 54–55.
67. Almada, *Resumen de la Historia*, p. 374.
68. Almada, *Revolución en Chihuahua*, I, 64–70.

69. *Ibid.*, pp. 70–80.

70. Quoted in González Navarro, *Vida Social*, pp. 197–198.

71. Cuesta Soto, *Bucareli*, p. 8.

72. April 16, 1909.

73. "El Ultimo Error Económico," *El Imparcial*, June 22, 1907 and September 21, 1907.

74. Almada, *Resumen de la Historia*, p. 380.

75. "El Mexicano Quemado," *El Imparcial*, November 9, 1910, and November 10, 1910.

76. *Diario de los Debates del Congreso Constituyente, 1916–1917*, 2 vols. (Mexico, 1960), II: 552.

77. Quoted in *El Imparcial*, April 3, 1908.

78. Cuesta Soto, *Bucareli*, p. 8.

79. Bulnes, *El Verdadero Díaz*, pp. 268–269.

80. Luis Cabrera, *Obras Completas*, 5 vols. (Mexico, 1975), I: 491.

81. "El Problema del Algódon Nacional," *El Imparcial*, December 13, 1907.

82. Manero, *Antiguo Régimen*, p. 214.

83. *El Verdadero Díaz*, p. 274.

84. Manero, *Antiguo Régimen*, pp. 215–216.

85. Bulnes, *El Verdadero Díaz*, p. 273; For the history of this case see "Compañía Agrícola, Industrial, Colonizadora, Limitada del Tlahualilo, S.A., Contra el Gobierno Federal de la República Mexicana," Cabrera, *Obras Completas*, I: 329–588.

86. Cockcroft, *Intellectual Precursors*, p. 22.

87. *Ibid.*, pp. 17–19.

88. *Ibid.*, p. 40.

89. Edmundo Bolio, *Yucatán en la Dictadura y la Revolución* (Mexico, 1967), p. 65.

90. Diputado Enrique Recio of Yucatán quoted in *Diario de los Debates*, II: 539.

91. "La Crisis en Yucatán," June 10, 1907; "Una Embriaguez de Riqueza," May 20, 1907.

92. Diputado Enrique Recio of Yucatán quoted in *Diario de los Debates*, II: 540.

CHAPTER VIII

1. Antonio Manero, *El Antiquo Régimen y la Revolución* (Mexico, 1911), p. 220.

2. L. Rivas Iruz to Francisco I. Madero, July 8, 1911, Condumex: AVC.

3. James D. Cockcroft, *Intellectual Precursors of the Mexican Revolution, 1900–1913* (Austin and London, 1968), p. 40.

4. See for example issue of January 14, 1907.

5. *El México de Porfirio Díaz (Hombres y Cosas)* (Valencia, Spain, 1910), pp. 128–129.

6. *El Imparcial,* July 4, 1908.

7. "La Marcha de la Crisis," *El Imparcial,* February 14, 1910.

8. "La Revuelta Contra la Prosperidad Nacional," *El Imparcial,* August 8, 1910.

9. Manero, *Antiquo Régimen,* pp. 218–219.

10. *Ibid.,* p. 218.

11. *El Imparcial,* December 26, 1908.

12. "Informe del Señor Presidente," *El Imparcial,* April 2, 1908.

13. Cockcroft, *Intellectual Precursors,* p. 62.

14. "Cuestión Sumamente Delicada," November 16, 1907.

15. Francisco R. Almada, *Resumen de la Historia del Estado de Chihuahua* (Mexico, 1955), p. 373; *El Imparcial,* March 17, 1908.

16. "Cuestión Sumamente Delicada," November 16, 1907.

17. *El Imparcial,* August 6, 1908.

18. Almada, *Resumen de la Historia,* pp. 370–385; William H. Beezley, *Insurgent Governor: Abraham González and the Mexican Revolution* (Lincoln, 1973), p. 48.

19. "Seis Meses de Comercio," April 15, 1907.

20. David M. Pletcher, "The Fall of Silver in Mexico, 1870–1910, and Its Effects on American Investments," *The Journal of Economic History,* XVIII (March, 1958): p. 42.

21. Alfred Tischendorf, *Great Britain and Mexico in the Era of Porfirio Díaz* (Durham, 1961), p. 29.

22. Pletcher, "The Fall of Silver," p. 38.

23. "Las Fluctuaciones de la Plata," August 19, 1906; "¿Por Qué Falta Dinero?" June 14, 1907; "El Mercado Monetario y las Exportaciones," July 30, 1907, all in *El Imparcial.*

24. "¿Se Destruirá el Equilibrio Financiero en el Presente Año Fiscal?" April 21, 1909.

25. Ramón Eduardo Ruiz, *Labor and the Ambivalent Revolutionaries; Mexico, 1911–1923* (Baltimore and London, 1976), p. 19.

26. *El Imparcial,* April 27, 1908.

27. "La Revuelta en Sonora," *El Imparcial,* May 15, 1911.

28. "Entrevista con el Señor Gobernador del Estado de Durango," *El Imparcial,* November 6, 1908.

29. *México de Díaz,* p. 153.

30. *El Imparcial,* August 31, 1907 and July 15, 1908.

31. *Ibid.,* September 8, 1907.

32. *Ibid.*, August 20, 1909.

33. Manero, *Antiguo Régimen*, p. 220.

34. "Informe Presidencial," *El Imparcial*, September 17, 1907.

35. "Informe del Señor Presidente," *El Imparcial*, April 2, 1908.

36. "Oro e Industrias," June 15, 1907.

37. "Entrevista con el Señor Ministro de Hacienda," *El Imparcial*, March 20, 1908.

38. *Ibid.*

39. Antonio Manero, "Informe Rendido al Señor Licenciado don Luis Cabrera, Secretario de Hacienda y Crédito Público, por Orden del Señor Subsecretario del Propio Ramo, don Rafael Nieto, Sobre la Cuestión Bancaria y los Trabajos Llevados a Cabo por la Comisión Reguladora e Inspectora de Instituciones de Crédito," Mexico, November 16, 1916, p. 11, Condumex: AVC.

40. "Por qué los Bancos no Prestan a Todo el Mundo," *El Imparcial*, February 14, 1908.

41. "Cual Fué el Resultado de las Asambleas de Banqueros," *El Imparcial*, April 12, 1908.

42. Manero, *Antiguo Régimen*, p. 221.

43. *The Whole Truth About Mexico; President Wilson's Responsibility* (New York, 1916), p. 146.

44. Francisco Bulnes, *El Verdadero Díaz y la Revolución* (Mexico, 1967), p. 406.

45. Manero, "Informe Rendido," pp. 1–3.

46. "El Crédito de los Bancos," *El Imparcial*, January 9, 1908.

47. Blas Urrea, *La Herencia de Carranza* (Mexico, 1920), p. 27; Manero, "Informe Rendido," pp. 3–5 and 12.

48. Cockcroft, *Intellectual Precursors*, p. 36.

49. Guy Weddington McCreary, *From Glory to Oblivion, the Real Truth About the Mexican Revolution* (New York, 1974), p. 27.

50. *El Imparcial*, October 6, 1909.

51. Almada, *Resumen de la Historia*, p. 372.

52. Bulnes, *El Verdadero Díaz*, p. 245.

53. "Un Desastre Financiero," *El Imparcial*, March 29, 1907.

54. *El Verdadero Díaz*, p. 244.

55. "La Crisis en Yucatán," *El Imparcial*, June 10, 1907; Edmundo Bolio, *Yucatán en la Dictadura y la Revolución* (Mexico, 1967), p. 69.

56. Bolio, *Yucatán en la Dictadura*, p. 58.

57. *Ibid.*, p. 69.

58. Yucatán No Está Quebrado," May 19, 1907 and "La Crisis en Yucatán," May 7, 1907, in *El Imparcial*.

59. "Yucatán No Está Quebrado," *El Imparcial*, May 19, 1907.

60. "La Crisis en Yucatán," *El Imparcial*, May 7, 1907.

61. Julio Rendón, "La Situación Económica en Yucatán," *El Imparcial,* June 8, 1907.

62. Bolio, *Yucatán en la Dictadura,* pp. 69–70.

63. Bulnes, *El Verdadero Díaz,* p. 122.

64. *El Imparcial,* January 9–10, 1907.

65. Bulnes, *El Verdadero Díaz,* p. 161.

66. "La Usura, Consecuencia de la Crisis," May 27, 1907.

67. "La Crisis en Yucatán," *El Imparcial,* May 17, 1907.

68. Moisés Gonzálaz Navarro, *El Porfiriato. La Vida Social,* Daniel Cosío Villegas, ed., *Historia Moderna de México,* 9 vols. (Mexico, 1955–1973), IV: 218.

69. Héctor Victoria to Director del Departamento del Trabajo, Mexico, January 3, 1915, AGN, F, 31, 15.

70. *El Imparcial,* February 18, 1908 and May 24, 1908.

71. "La Crisis en Yucatán," *El Imparcial,* May 7, 1907.

72. Bolio, *Yucatán en la Dictadura,* pp. 57–58.

73. *Mexico de Díaz,* p. 149.

74. October 6, 1909.

75. *El Imparcial,* November 19, 1909.

76. Victoria to Director del Departamento del Trabajo.

77. "¡He Ahí Vuestra Obra!" *El Imparcial,* June 8–9, 1910; Juan Barragán Rodríguez, *Historia del Ejército y de la Revolución Constitucionalista,* 2 vols. (Mexico, 1946), II: 241–242; Juan Sánchez Azcona, *Apuntes para la Historia de la Revolución Mexicana* (Mexico, 1961), p. 104.

78. Bolio, *Yucatán en la Dictadura,* p. 70.

79. "La Cesión de Bienes del Sr. Marcelini G. Galín," Monclova, Coahuila, May 1, 1919, Condumex: AVC.

CHAPTER IX

1. *La Sucesión Presidencial en 1910* (Mexico, 1960), p. 26.

2. Francisco I. Madero, "Mis Recuerdos," Armando de María y Campos, ed., *Las Memorias y las Mejores Cartas de Francisco I. Madero* (Mexico, 1956), p. 15.

3. Evaristo Madero to José Ives Limantour, Monterrey, Nuevo León, January 11, 1911, José I. Limantour, *Apuntes Sobre Mi Vida Pública* (Mexico, 1965), pp. 208–209.

4. José I. Limantour to Roberto Núñez, Paris, France, January 26, 1911, Limantour, *Apuntes Sobre Mi Vida,* p. 117.

5. Limantour, *Apuntes Sobre Mi Vida,* p. 208.

6. Fernando González Roa, *El Aspecto Agrario de la Revolución* (Mexico, 1919), p. 225.

7. Francisco Vásquez Gómez, *Memorias Políticas (1909–1913)* (Mexico, 1933), p. 287.

8. Francisco I. Madero to General don Porfirio Díaz, María y Campos, *Las Memorias,* p. 84.

9. Francisco R. Almada, *La Revolución en el Estado de Chihuahua,* 2 vols. (Chihuahua, 1964), I: 92.

10. Manuel Calero, *Un Decenio de Política Mexicana* (New York, 1920), p. 47.

11. Francisco Bulnes, *The Whole Truth About Mexico; President Wilson's Responsibility* (New York, 1916), p. 160.

12. Limantour, *Apuntes Sobre Mi Vida,* p. 208.

13. Francisco Bulnes, *El Verdadero Díaz y la Revolución* (Mexico, 1967), p. 124.

14. Limantour, *Apuntes Sobre Mi Vida,* pp. 210–213.

15. Francisco I. Madero to Francisco Madero, Sr., San Pedro, Coahuila, January 20, 1909, Juan Sánchez Azcona, *Apuntes para la Historia de la Revolución Mexicana* (Mexico, 1961), p. 23.

16. Limantour, *Apuntes Sobre Mi Vida,* p. 344.

17. Quoted in Roberto Blanco Moheno, *Crónica de la Revolución Mexicana,* 2 vols. (Mexico, 1958–1959), I: 53.

18. Ramón Prida, *De la Dictadura a la Anarquía; Apuntes para la Historia Política de México Durante los Ultimos Cuaranta y Tres Años (1871–1913)* (Mexico, 1958), p. 227.

19. *El Antiguo Régimen y la Revolución* (Mexico, 1911), p. 311.

20. Prida, *Anarquía,* p. 161.

21. Francisco I. Madero to General Bernardo Reyes, Puebla, Puebla, July 16, 1911, Condumex: DLB.

22. *El Verdadero Díaz,* p. 407.

23. Francisco I. Madero to Francisco León de la Barra, Cuernavaca, Morelos, August 14, 1911, María y Campos, *Las Memorias,* p. 170.

24. "Mis Memorias, por Francisco I. Madero," San Luis Potosí, September 20, 1910, María y Campos, *Las Memorias,* pp. 41 and 53.

25. Cited in María y Campos, *Las Memorias,* p. 66.

26. *La Sucesión Presidencial,* p. 18.

27. "Discurso Pronunciado por el Señor Doctor Manuel Mestre Ghigliazzo, en la Velada Celebrada en el Teatro Arbeu en Honor de los Señores Madero y Pino Suárez, José Vasconcelos, ed., *La Caída de Carranza* (Mexico, 1920), p. 108.

28. Francisco I. Madero, Mexico [1912], AGN, M, 3, 751.

29. *Memorias,* p. 60; Madero, *Sucesión Presidencial.* p. 15.

30. Emilio Vásquez Gómez to Venustiano Carranza, San Antonio, Texas, December 10, 1915, Condumex: AVC.

31. *Historia de la Constitución de 1917,* 2 vols. (Mexico, 1917), I: 11.

32. *Crónica de la Revolución,* I: 9–10.

33. Francisco I. Madero to don Francisco, 1908, María y Campos, *Las Memorias,* pp. 80–81.

34. Francisco R. Almada, *Resumen de la Historia del Estado de Chihuahua* (Mexico, 1955), pp. 386 and 390.

35. "Madero," *Excelsior,* August 2, 1970.

36. Moisés González Navarro, *La Confederación Nacional Campesina; Un Grupo de Presión en la Reforma Agraria Mexicana* (Mexico, 1968), p. 58.

37. Francisco I. Madero to don Francisco, San Pedro, Coahuila, Mexico, 1908, María y Campos, *Las Memorias,* pp. 75–76.

38. p. 279.

39. *Sucesión Presidencial,* pp. 211–216 and 277.

40. Speech of Madero to Obreros de Orizaba, Orizaba, Veracruz, May 22, 1910, María y Campos, *Las Memorias,* p. 110.

41. Quoted in Calero, *Decenio,* p. 70.

42. *Sucesión Presidencial,* p. 320.

43. *Antiguo Régimen,* p. 308.

44. Manuel Calero to Francisco I. Madero, Mexico [1912], AGN, M, 3, 751.

45. Manero, *Antiguo Régimen,* p. 313.

46. *Sucesión Presidencial,* p. 368.

47. *Antiguo Régimen,* p. 330.

48. Francisco I. Madero to don Porfirio Díaz, María y Campos, *Las Memorias,* p. 84.

49. *Sucesión Presidencial,* p. 278.

50. Quoted in Toribio Esquivel Obregón, *Democracia y Personalismo. Relatos y Comentarios Sobre Política Actual* (Mexico, 1911), p. 42.

51. Sánchez Azcona, *Apuntes para la Historia,* p. 316.

52. *Sucesión Presidencial,* pp. 221–222.

53. *Ibid.,* pp. 197–199 and 200–207.

54. "Plan de San Luis Potosí, 5 de Octubre de 1910," Jesús Silva Herzog, *Breve Historia de la Revolución Mexicana,* 2 vols. (Mexico, 1965), I: 137–138.

55. González Navarro, *Confederación Nacional,* p. 52.

56. Ramón Puente, *Pascual Orozco y la Revuelta en Chihuahua* (Mexico, 1912), p. 91.

57. Francisco I. Madero to Fausto Moguel, Director, Mexico, Mexico, June 27, 1912, Condumex: JA.

58. Francisco Vásquez Gómez to José Ives Limantour, New York, New York, March 14, 1911, Limantour, *Apuntes Sobre Mi Vida*, pp. 217–219.

59. Limantour, *Apuntes Sobre Mi Vida*, pp. 276 and 328.

60. *Ibid.*, pp. 274–275 and 284.

61. Jorge Vera Estañol, *Historia de la Revolución Mexicana; Orígenes y Resultados* (Mexico, 1967), p. 173.

62. Rafael L. Hernández to José Ives Limantour, El Paso, Texas, May 12, 1911, Limantour, *Apuntes Sobre Mi Vida*, p. 338; Vera Estañol, *Historia de la Revolución Mexicana*, p. 173.

63. Limantour, *Apuntes Sobre Mi Vida*, p. 287.

64. *Historia de la Constitución*, I: 11.

65. Limantour, *Apuntes Sobre Mi Vida*, pp. 325–326.

66. González Roa, *Aspectos del Problema*, p. 216; Vera Estañol, *Historia de la Revolución Mexicana*, p. 196.

67. Limantour, *Apuntes Sobre Mi Vida*, p. 243.

68. "Madero," *Excelsior*.

69. "Manifiesto a la Nación," Ciudad Juárez, Chihuahua, May 26, 1911; Manero, *Antiguo Régimen*, pp. 375–376.

70. *Antiguo Régimen*, p. 361.

71. Fuentes Mares, "Madero," *Excelsior*.

72. Francisco León de la Barra, "Informe al Congreso," 1911, Condumex: LDB.

73. "Madero," *Excelsior*.

74. *El Verdadero Díaz*, p. 411.

75. *Decenio*, p. 26.

76. Prida, *Anarquía*, p. 202.

77. Blanco Moheno, *Crónica*, I: 45.

78. José Mancisidor, *Historia de la Revolución Mexicana* (Mexico, 1965), pp. 167–168.

79. Partido Nacional Antireeleccionista to Venustiano Carranza, Mexico, August 17, 1914, Condumex: AVC.

80. *The Whole Truth*. pp. 160–161.

81. James D. Cockcroft, *Intellectual Precursors of the Mexican Revolution, 1900–1913* (Austin and London, 1968), pp. 39 and 174.

82. "Renuncia Pancho, Te Conviene," *El Microbio*, Mexico, January 7, 1912.

CHAPTER X

1. (Mexico, 1941), p. 58.

2. Alfredo Breceda, *Don Venustiano Carranza; Rasgos Biográficos Escritos en 1912* (Mexico, 1930), pp. 3–7; *El Imparcial*, August 12, 1909.

3. *Carranza y los Orígenes de su Rebelión* (Mexico, 1935), pp. 12–13.

4. *The Whole Truth About Mexico; President Wilson's Responsibility* (New York, 1916), p. 244.

5. Juan Gualberto Amaya, *Venustiano Carranza, Caudillo Constitucionalista; Segunda Etapa, Febrero de 1913 a Mayo de 1920* (Mexico, 1947), p. 8.

6. Bulnes, *The Whole Truth*, p. 244.

7. Bernardino Mena Brito, *Maquinismo* (Mexico, 1933), pp. 118–119.

8. José I. Limantour, *Apuntes Sobre Mi Vida Pública* (Mexico, 1965), p. 194; David Moreno, *Venustiano Carranza, Alvaro Obregón, Plutarco Elías Calles* (Mexico, 1960), p. 22.

9. Alfonso Madero to Federico González Garza, Mexico, March 16, 1932, quoted in Moreno, *Carranza*, pp. 21–22.

10. Moreno, *Carranza*, p. 24.

11. *Venustiano Carranza*, p. 7.

12. William H. Beezley, "Governor Carranza and the Revolution in Coahuila," *The Americas*, XXXIII (July, 1976): 54–56.

13. Venustiano Carranza to Alberto García Granados, Ministro de Gobernación, Saltillo, Coahuila, February 25, 1913, quoted in Jorge Vera Estañol, *Historia de la Revolución Mexicana; Orígenes y Resultados* (Mexico, 1967), p. 316.

14. Ramón Prida, *De la Dictadura a la Anarquía; Apuntes para la Historia Política de México Durate los Ultimos Cuarenta Años 1871–1913* (Mexico, 1958), p. 583.

15. Roberto Blanco Moheno, *Crónica de la Revolución Mexicana*, 2 vols. (Mexico, 1958–1959), I: 173.

16. *La Caída de Carranza* (Mexico, 1920), p. 68.

17. A. Prieto, Cónsul de México, "Información," El Paso, Texas, December 30, 1914, Condumex: AVC.

18. Quoted in Antonio Bulnes Tavares to Venustiano Carranza, Brooklyn, New York, July 7, 1915, Condumex: AVC.

19. Juan Barragán Rodríguez, *Historia del Ejército y de la Revolución Constitucionalista*, 2 vols. (Mexico, 1946), II: 110.

20. Charles C. Cumberland, *Mexican Revolution: The Constitutionalist Years* (Austin, 1972), p. 383.

21. Mena Brito, *Maquinismo,* p. 100.

22. Blas Urrea, *La Herencia de Carranza* (Mexico, 1920), p. 10.

23. Venustiano Carranza to Andrés Osuna, Querétaro, Querétaro, November 17, 1919, Condumex: AVC; Venustiano Carranza, *Codificación de los Decretos del C. Venustiano Carranza, Primer Jefe del Ejército Constitutionalista* (Mexico, 1915), p. 150.

24. Venustiano Carranza to Alvaro Obregón, Querétaro, Querétaro, October 14, 1919, Condumex: AVC.

25. Urrea, *Herencia,* p. 20.

26. *La Revolución Mexicana; Memorias de un Espectador* (Mexico, 1971), p. 143.

27. Blanco Moheno, *Crónica,* I, 27.

28. Amaya, *Venustiano Carranza,* p. 9.

29. *El Conflicto Personal de la Revolución Mexicana. Examen de Todo lo que ha Dicho el Ciudadano Carranza* (El Paso, Texas and New Orleans, 1914), p. 71.

30. Cumberland, *Mexican Revolution,* p. 363.

31. M. D. Carter to Editor, *The Sun,* Baltimore, Maryland, July 20, 1919, Condumex: AVC.

32. Cited in Antonio Manero, *El Antiguo Régimen y la Revolución* (Mexico, 1911), pp. 269 and 270.

33. Félix F. Palavicini, *Mi Vida Revolucionaria* (Mexico, 1937), p. 246.

34. José Mancisidor, *Historia de la Revolución Mexicana* (Mexico, 1965), p. 106.

35. "Obregón y el Principio de la Renovación Social," Editorial Cultura, ed., *Obregón, Aspectos de Su Vida* (Mexico, 1935), pp. 79–80.

36. Barragán Rodríguez, *Ejército,* II: 207.

37. Robert E. Quirk, *The Mexican Revolution and the Catholic Church, 1910–1929* (Bloomington and London, 1973), p. 43.

38. June 11, 1915, Condumex: AVC.

39. Venustiano Carranza, *La Revolución de Entonces es la Revolución de Ahora* (Mexico, 1937), pp. 5–6.

40. Arnaldo Córdova, *La Ideología de la Revolución Mexicana; la Formación del Nuevo Régimen* (Mexico, 1973), p. 243.

41. Venustiano Carranza to Francisco Suárez, Piedras Negras, Coahuila, May 16, 1913, Condumex: AVC.

42. Carranza, *Revolución de Entonces,* p. 7.

43. Alfredo Acosta, *La Gestión Hacendaria de la Revolución* (Mexico, 1917), p. 45.

44. *Ibid.,* p. 42.

45. Urrea, *Herencia,* p. 41.

46. Carranza, *Decretos,* pp. 268–269.

47. *Herencia,* p. 25.

48. Urrea, *Herencia,* p. 45; *The Evening Star,* November 6, 1915.

49. June 11, 1915, Condumex: AVC.

50. Acosta, *Gestión,* p. 44.

51. Santos Chocano, *Conflicto,* p. 71.

52. Vasconcelos, *Caída,* p. 70.

53. *Maquinismo,* pp. 84–85.

54. Narciso Bassols Batalla, *El Pensamiento Político de Obregón* (Mexico, 1967), p. 71.

55. Moreno, *Venustiano Carranza,* p. 9.

56. Carranza, *Decretos,* p. 8.

57. Carranza, *Revolución de Entonces,* p. 6.

58. *Herencia,* p. 14.

59. Amaya, *Venustiano Carranza,* p. 163.

60. *Un Decenio de Política Mexicana* (New York, 1920), p. 179.

61. *Historia de la Revolución,* p. 319; Aurelio D. Canale, *Carta Abierta Dirigida al Señor General Don Alvaro Obregón* (Madrid, 1920), p. 8.

62. *Conflicto,* p. 5.

63. *Diario de los Debates del Congreso Constituyente, 1916–1917,* 2 vols. (Mexico, 1960), I: 385.

64. Venustiano Carranza, *Report by Venustiano Carranza, In the City of Querétaro, State of Querétaro, Mexico, Friday, December 1st, 1916* (New York, [1916?]), p. 5.

65. *Diario de los Debates,* I, 388.

66. Cordova, *Ideología de la Revolución,* p. 88.

67. Carranza, *Report,* p. 11.

68. Heriberto Barrón, *Some of the Facts and Arguments which led to the Recognition of the First Chief of the Constitutionalist Army in Charge of the Executive Power of the Mexican Republic, Mr. Venustiano Carranza, as the de facto Government in Mexico* ([n. p.], 1915), p. 17.

69. *Venustiano Carranza,* p. 409.

70. Salvador Alvarado, *La Traición de Carranza* (New York, 1920), p. 5.

71. Quirk, *Catholic Church,* p. 102.

72. *La Revolución Mexicana,* p. 127.

73. Miguel Alessio Robles, *La Cena de las Burlas* (Mexico, 1939), p. 51.

74. Carranza, *Revolución de Entonces,* p. 7.

CHAPTER XI

1. *Verdades Sobre el General Alvaro Obregón* (Los Angeles, 1919), p. 19.

2. Justino Bermúdez y Cortés, *Verdades—No Adulación; Callismo y Obregonismo Revolutionarios* (Mexico, 1935), p. 28.

3. Maytorena, *Verdades*, p. 13; Hector Aguilar Camín, "La Revolución Sonorense, 1910–1914" (Ph.D. diss., Instituto Nacional de Antropología e Historia, Mexico, 1975), p. 267.

4. Richard H. Dillon, "The Rise of Alvaro Obregón, 1880–1917" (Master's thesis, University of California, Berkeley, 1949), p. 2.

5. Alvaro Obregón, *The Agrarian Problem* (Mexico, 1924), p. 20.

6. Juan Gualberto Amaya, *Los Gobiernos de Obregón y Regímenes "Peleles" Derivados del Callismo* (Mexico, 1947), p. 383.

7. *El Militarismo Mexicano* (Valencia, Spain, 1920), p. 86.

8. F. Torreblanca to Manuel E. Otálora, Mexico, January 25, 1922, AGN, OC, P-6, L-10, 103-B-1; Amaya, *Gobiernos*, p. 381.

9. Djed Bórquez, *Obregón, Apuntes Biográficos* (Mexico, 1929), p. 11.

10. Aguilar Camín, "Revolución Sonorense," p. 255.

11. *En Memoria de Obregón* (Mexico, 1946), p. 7.

12. Feliciano Gil, *Biografía y Vida Militar del General Alvaro Obregón* (Hermosillo, Mexico, 1914), p. 3; Amaya, *Gobiernos*, p. 382.

13. Bórquez, *Obregón*, p. 12.

14. Aguilar Camín, "Revolución Sonorense," p. 257.

15. *En Memoria*, p. 7.

16. Narciso Bassols Batalla, *El Pensamiento Político de Obregón* (Mexico, 1967), p. 10.

17. *Gobiernos*, p. 383.

18. Amaya, *Gobiernos*, p. 223.

19. Juan Gualberto Amaya, *Venustiano Carranza, Caudillo Constitucionalista; Segunda Etapa, Febrero de 1913 a Mayo de 1920* (Mexico, 1947), p. 164.

20. Alvaro Obregón to Convención Cámaras de Comercio, Mexico, February 27, 1924, AGN, OC, P-5, 101-R2-P.

21. *Ibid.*

22. *Verdades*, p. 31.

23. Alvaro Obregón to Luis Cabrera, Culiacán Sinaloa, April 29, 1919, AGN, OC, P. 6-1, L-1.

24. Cited in Alvaro Obregón, *Discursos*, 2 vols. (Mexico, 1932), II: 393.

25. Charles C. Cumberland, *Mexican Revolution: The Constitutionalist Years* (Austin, 1972), p. 78.

26. Obregón, *Discursos*, II: 393.

27. Cited in Bórquez, *Obregón*, p. 4.

28. Alvaro Obregón to José María Villa, Mexico, July 21, 1923, AGN, OC, P. 6-2, 103-E-6.

29. Bassols Batalla, *Pensamiento Político*, pp. 12–13.

30. Maytorena, *Verdades*, p. 4.

31. Bassols Batalla, *Pensamiento Político*, p. 24.

32. Alvaro Obregón to Agustín R. Esparza, Mexico, March 14, 1923, AGN, OC, P-6, L-9, 103-A-20.

33. Alvaro Obregón to Rafael Martínez, Nogales, Sonora, September 18, 1917, cited in Roberto Quirós, *Alvaro Obregón: Su Vida y Su Obra* (Mexico, 1928), pp. 96–97.

34. Bórquez, *Obregón*, p. 44.

35. Alvaro Obregón to D. Alvear, Mexico, July 26, 1923, AGN, OC, P-7-1, L-5, 103-N-3.

36. Cía. Importadora del Auto Universal to Alvaro Obregón, Mexico, December 3, 1924, AGN, OC, P-6, L-9, 103-A-46.

37. *Pensamiento Político*, p. 10.

38. "Prologo," Bórquez, *Obregón*, p. 3.

39. Juan B. Cervantes, *Obregón Ante la Historia* (Mexico, 1924), p. 7.

40. "Discurso Pronunciado por el Señor José Angel Ceniceros, en Representación del Partido Nacional Revolucionario, en Honor del General Alvaro Obregón con Motivo del Aniversario de su Muerte," Partido Nacional Revolucionario, ed., *En Memoria de Obregón* (Mexico, 1936), pp. 13 and 17.

41. Rodrigo López Pérez, *El Movimiento Obregonista en Michoacán* (Mexico, 1920), p. 5.

42. Quoted in Ceniceros, "Discurso," p. 16.

43. Bassols Batalla, *Pensamiento Político*, p. 84.

44. *Ocho Mil Kilómetros en Campaña* (Mexico, 1917), p. 8.

45. Bassols Batalla, *Pensamiento Político*, pp. 13–14.

46. *Gobiernos*, p. 383.

47. p. 42.

48. *Verdades*, pp. 13 and 18.

49. *Ocho Mil Kilómetros*, p. 69.

50. Aguilar Camín, "Revolución Sonorense," p. 333.

51. *Mi Vida Revolucionaria* (Mexico, 1937), p. 291.

52. Francisco Vásquez Gómez to Jenaro Amezcua, San Antonio, Texas, May 10, 1920, Condumex: JA.

53. p. 550.

54. Antenor Sala to Alvaro Obregón, Mexico, June 25, 1919, Condumex: AVC; Alvaro Obregón to Antenor Sala, Nogales, Sonora, July 10, 1919, Condumex: AVC.

55. Arturo Elías to Francisco León de la Barra, Douglas, Arizona, January 14, 1917, Condumex: LDB.

56. "A los Miembros del Ejército Nacional," Mexico, September 22, 1923, AGN, OC, P. 4-1, 101-R2-E-1.

57. Miguel Alessio Robles, *La Cena de las Burlas* (Mexico, 1939), p. 101.

58. Francisco Vásquez Gómez to Jenaro Amezcua, San Antonio, Texas, May 31, 1920, Condumex: JA.

59. *Ocho Mil Kilómetros*, p. 7.

60. "Obregón y el Principio de la Renovación Social," Editorial Cultura, ed., *Obregón, Aspectos de Su Vida* (Mexico, 1935), p. 75.

61. June 9, 1919.

62. Bassols Batalla, *Pensamiento Político*, p. 72.

63. *Discursos*, I, 63.

64. Bassols Batalla, *Pensamiento Político*, p. 72.

65. *Ibid.*

66. Arnaldo Cordova, *La Ideología de la Revolución Mexicana; la Formación del Nuevo Régimen* (Mexico, 1973), p. 30.

67. Obregón, *Discursos*, I: 182 and 244.

68. Bassols Batalla, *Pensamiento Político*, p. 82.

69. Obregón, *Discursos*, I: 73.

70. Quirós, *Alvaro Obregón,* p. 221.

71. Obregón, *Discursos*, I: 244.

72. *Ibid.*, p. 245.

73. *Ibid.*

74. Quirós, *Alvaro Obregón*, p. 101.

75. Obregón, *Discursos*, I: 244.

76. Quoted in Bassols Batalla, *Pensamiento Político, p.* 75.

77. Bassols Batalla, *Pensamiento Político*, p. 75.

78. Alessio Robles, *Cena*, p. 118.

79. Obregón, *Discursos*, I: 281.

80. Dr. Atl, "Obregón y el Principio de la Renovación Social," Editorial Cultura, *Obregón, Aspectos de su Vida* (Mexico, 1935), p. 71.

81. Bassols Batalla, *Pensamiento Político*, p. 42.

82. Obregón, *Agrarian Problems*, pp. 16–17.

83. *Ibid.*, p. 19.

84. Quoted in Aguilar Camín, "Revolución Sonorense," p. 443.

85. *La Batalla de Algibes; lo que queríamos los Revolucionarios de Entonces* (Mexico, 1961), p. 76.

86. Quoted in Maytorena, *Verdades*, p. 78.

87. Obregón, *Ocho Mil Kilómetros,* p. 24.

88. Quoted in *The New York Times,* November 25, 1914.

89. *Pensamiento Político,* p. 24.

90. Quirós, *Alvaro Obregón,* p. 101.

91. Amaya, *Gobiernos,* p. 107.

92. Z. O. Stocker to José María Maytorena, Hermosillo, Sonora, March 11, 1914, Condumex: AVC.

93. Ignacio P. Gaxiola to Fernando Torreblanca, Nogales, Sonora, May 26, 1922, AGN, OC, P-8, L-8, 103-S-12.

94. Obregón, *Discursos,* I, 294.

95. Quoted in Librería de Quiroga, ed., *¿Quién es Obregón?* (San Antonio, Texas, 1922), p. 61.

96. Quirós, *Alvaro Obregón,* p. 218.

97. Alvaro Obregón, *Campaña Política del C. Alvaro Obregón Candidato a la Presidencia de la República, 1920–1924,* 5 vols. (Mexico, 1923), I: 54.

98. *Cena,* p. 179.

99. Juan Barragán Rodríguez, *Historia del Ejército de la Revolución Constitucionalista,* 2 vols. (Mexico, 1946), II: 237.

CHAPTER XII

1. Juan Sáenz, José Aguirre, and others to Alvaro Obregón, Santa María del Oro, Durango, August 19, 1923, AGN, OC, P-3, L-22, 101-V-8.

2. *Venustiano Carranza, Caudillo Constitucionalista; Segunda Etapa, Febrero de 1913 a Mayo de 1920* (Mexico, 1947), p. 482.

3. *El Hombre y Sus Armas; Memorias de Pancho Villa* (Mexico, 1938), pp. 64–65; Arturo Langle Ramírez, *El Ejército Villista* (Mexico, 1961), p. 12.

4. Alvaro Obregón, *Ocho Mil Kilómetros en Campaña* (Mexico, 1917), pp. 278–280.

5. *Hombre y Sus Armas,* p. 86.

6. Venustiano Carranza, *Reply of don Venustiano Carranza to Chief of the Northern Division* (Mexico, 1914), p. 8.

7. Alvaro Obregón and Lucio Blanco, "A la Nación," Mexico, November 23, 1915.

8. Francisco R. Almada, *La Revolución en el Estado de Chihuahua,* 2 vols. (Chihuahua, 1964), I: 240; Guzmán, *Hombre y Sus Armas,* pp. 23, 46, 64.

9. "Acuerdo del C. Presidente de la República para la Secretaría de Hacienda y Crédito Público," Mexico, October 7, 1921, AGN, OC, P-3, L-22, 101-V-3.

10. Victor Ceja Reyes, *Yo Maté a Villa* (Mexico, 1960), p. 135.

11. Quoted in Juan Barragán Rodríguez, *Historia del Ejército y de la Revolución Constitucionalista*, 2 vols. (Mexico, 1946), II: 109.

12. "Algunos Hombres que Estuvieron con Villa en Canutillo," *El Diario*, July 26, 1923.

13. Barragán Rodríguez, *Ejército*, II: 109.

14. Alvaro Obregón, "Acuerdo," Mexico, February 13, 1923, AGN, OC, P. 15-1, L-6, 104-P1-V-1.

15. Barragán Rodríguez, *Ejército*, II: 108.

16. *Ibid.*

17. Hipólito Villa to Alvaro Obregón, Canutillo, Durango, July 28, 1923, AGN, OC, P-3, L-22, 101-V-8.

18. L. Rivas Iruz to Venustiano Carranza, Mexico, October 20, 1915, Condumex: AVC.

19. Lauro Méndez de la Cuenca, *Alvaro Obregón* ([n.p.], [1918?]), p. 31.

20. *The World*, August 25, 1915.

21. Langle Ramírez, *Ejército Villista*, pp. 151–152.

22. Luis Mesa Gutiérrez to Rafael Zubarán Capmany, Chihuahua, Chihuahua, January 19, 1914, Condumex: AVC.

23. General Eulalio Gutiérrez to Francisco Villa, Mexico, January 5, 1915, Condumex: AVC.

24. Heriberto Barrón to President Woodrow Wilson, Washington, D.C., August 18, 1915, Condumex: AVC; Heriberto Barrón, *Some of the Facts and Arguments which led to the Recognition of the First Chief of the Constitutionalist Army in Charge of the Executive Power of the Mexican Republic, Mr. Venustiano Carranza, as the de facto Government in Mexico* ([n. p.], 1915), p. 15.

25. Juan Neftali Amador to Venustiano Carranza, Santa Monica, California, July 26, 1915, Condumex: AVC.

26. Ernesto Madero to Venustiano Carranza, New York, December 14, 1915, Condumex: AVC.

27. Heriberto Barrón to President Woodrow Wilson, Washington, D.C., August 31, 1915, Condumex: AVC.

28. W. Tovar to A. M. Tovar, El Paso, Texas, April 1, 1915, Condumex: AVC.

29. Pablo González to Venustiano Carranza, San Juan, Nuevo León, February 8, 1915, Condumex: AVC.

30. Quoted in Juan M. Caballero to Roque González Garza, Mexico, December 23, 1915, Condumex: AVC.

31. Robert E. Quirk, *The Mexican Revolution and the Catholic Church, 1910–1929* (Bloomington and London, 1973), p. 42.

32. Quoted in Carranza, Reply of don Venustiano, p. 5.

33. *Ibid.*, p. 8.
34. Obregón and Blanco, "A la Nación."
35. Francisco R. Almada, *Resumen de la Historia del Estado de Chihuahua* (Mexico, 1955), p. 406.
36. Langle Ramírez, *Ejército Villista*, p. 72.
37. *Ocho Mil Kilómetros*, pp. 281–282.
38. Almada, *Resumen*, p. 409.
39. Domingo Trueba to Venustiano Carranza, El Paso, Texas, December 22, 1913, Condumex: AVC.
40. W. Tovar to A. M. Tovar, El Paso, Texas, April 1, 1915; S. Aguirre to Venustiano Carranza, Veracruz, Veracruz, July 17, 1915, Condumex: AVC.
41. Heriberto Barrón to Venustiano Carranza, Washington, D.C., September 22, 1915, Condumex: AVC; I. C. Enríquez to Venustiano Carranza, New York, January 3, 1915, Condumex: AVC.
42. Letter from an Official in the U.S. State Department to Jack, New York or Washington, January 2, 1915, Condumex: AVC.
43. *The Evening Star*, September 16, 1915.
44. Barragán Rodríguez, *Ejército*, I: 230.
45. *La Ideología de la Revolución Mexicana; la Formación del Nuevo Régimen* (Mexico, 1973), p. 144.
46. José Manuel Hidalgo to Venustiano Carranza, Mexico, August 14, 1915, Condumex: AVC.
47. Angel Colina to Governor Cándido Aguilar, Veracruz, Veracruz, July 5, 1915, Condumex: AVC.
48. Benjamín Hill to Venustiano Carranza, Naco, Sonora, December 6, 1914, Condumex: AVC.
49. *Ocho Mil Kilómetros*, p. 332.
50. Silvestre Terrazas to General Luis Caballero, Chihuahua, Chihuahua, July 2, 1914, Terrazas Papers, Box, 84, Bancroft Library.
51. Francisco Vásquez Gómez to General Jenaro Amezcua, San Antonio, Texas, September 2, 1919, Condumex: AVC.
52. Marte R. Gómez, *La Reforma Agraria en las Filas Villistas, Años 1913 a 1915 a 1920* (Mexico, 1966), p. 28.
53. Pedro Guzmán to Venustiano Carranza, Mexico, October 11, 1914, Condumex: AVC.
54. Quoted in Jorge Carpizo, *La Constitución Mexicana de 1917* (Mexico, 1969), pp. 148–149.
55. Almada, *Resumen de la Historia*, p. 410.
56. Fernando González Roa, *El Aspecto Agrario de la Revolución* (Mexico, 1919), pp. 225 and 229.
57. Gómez, *La Reforma Agraria*, pp. 42–44.
58. *Ibid.*, pp. 84, 102–106, and 127.

59. Charles C. Cumberland, *Mexican Revolution: The Constitutionalist Years* (Austin, 1972), pp. 234–235.

60. Gómez, *La Reforma Agraria*, p. 87.

61. Quoted in Barragán Rodríguez, *Ejército*, II: 107; Carranza, *Reply of don Venustiano*, p. 4.

62. Gómez, *La Reforma Agraria*, pp. 82 and 84–85.

63. Eugenio Aguirre Benavides, "Nombramiento de una Comisión Agricola de la Laguna," Torreón, Coahuila, May 31, 1914, Condumex: AVC.

64. *Insurgent Mexico* (New York, 1969), p. 157; Jesús R. Ríos to Venustiano Carranza, Torreón, Coahuila, October 24, 1915, Condumex: AVC.

65. Gregorio Moreno, Antonio Mujares and Faustino Martínez to Venustiano Carranza, Lerdo, Durango, October 22, 1915: Condumex: AVC.

66. *Insurgent Mexico*, p. 53.

67. Gómez, *La Reforma Agraria*, p. 130.

68. Eugenio Pesqueira to Alvaro Obregón, January 21, 1921, AGN, OC, P-3, L-22, 101-V-3.

69. "Hacienda de la Concepción del Canutillo y Anexas," Mexico, November 22, 1920, AGN, OC, P-3, L-22, 101-V-3.

70. "Villa Mandará Encerrados en un Ataúd a los Espías que le Mande el Pte. Obregón," *El Heraldo*, Durango, Durango, May 18, 1922.

71. Ramón P. DeNegri, Secretario de Agricultura y Fomento, to Alvaro Obregón, Mexico, February 12, 1924, AGN, OC, P. 105, L-11, 818-C-77.

72. Ignacio C. Enríquez to General P. E. Calles, Chihuahua, Chihuahua, December 8, 1922, AGN, OC, P. 105, L-11, 818-C-77; Ignacio C. Enríquez to Alvaro Obregón, Chihuahua, Chihuahua, January 15, 1923, AGN, OC, P. 105, L-11, 818-C-77.

73. Abelardo S. Amaya to Presidente República, Chihuahua, Chihuahua, January 15, 1923, AGN, OC, P. 105, L-11, 818-C-77.

74. Alvero Obregón to Ramón P. DeNegri, Secretario de Agricultura, Guadalajara, Jalisco, February 14, 1924, AGN, OC, P. 105, L-11, 818-C-77.

75. Secretario Particular to Secretario de Agricultura y Fomento, Mexico, March 11, 1921, AGN, OC, P-108-1, L-9, 818-P-13; "Acuerdo de la Secretaría de Agricultura y Fomento," Presidente Constitucional de los Estado Unidos Mexicanos, Mexico, September 20, 1923, AGN, OC, P-108-1, L-9, 818-P-13; El General en Jefe E. Martínez to Presidente República, Chihuahua, Chihuahua, March 23, 1923, AGN, OC, P-108-1, L-3, 818-P-13.

76. Alvaro Obregón to Secretario Particular, Mexico, April 4, 1923,

AGN, OC, P-108-1, L-9, 818-P-13; Agustín Moye to Alvaro Obregón, Mexico, October 3, 1923, AGN, OC, P-108-1, L-9, 818-P-13.

77. Francisco Villa to Alvaro Obregón, Canutillo, Durango, November 17, 1921, AGN, OC, P-3, L-22, 101-V-3.

78. For another view see Córdova, *Ideología de la Revolución,* p. 164.

CHAPTER XIII

1. L. Rivas Iruz to Venustiano Carranza, Mexico, October 20, 1915, Condumex: AVC.

2. Letter of A. Bell, Mexico City, January 26, 1915, Condumex: AVC.

3. Arnaldo Córdova, *La Ideología de la Revolución Mexicana; la Formación del Nuevo Régimen* (Mexico, 1973), p. 136.

4. Jesús Sotelo Inclán, *Raíz y Razón de Zapata. Anenecuilco. Investigación Histórica* (Mexico, 1943), p. 169.

5. John Womack, Jr., *Zapata and the Mexican Revolution* (New York, 1970), p. 79.

6. *El País,* June 22, 1911.

7. Womack, *Zapata,* p. 108.

8. Jenaro Amezcua to Vicente Sánchez Gutiérrez, Havana, Cuba, July 4, 1919, Condumex: AVC.

9. "Plan de Ayala, Estado de Morelos, Noviembre 25, de 1911," Jesús Silva Herzog, *Breve Historia de la Revolución Mexicana,* 2 vols., (Mexico, 1965), I, 243.

10. "Acta de Ratificación del Plan de Ayala," San Pablo Oxtotepec, Morelos, July 19, 1914, Condumex: JA.

11. *Ibid.*

12. Emiliano Zapata to Pascual Orozco, Campamento Revolucionario en Morelos, April 7, 1913, Condumex: JA.

13. "Plan de Ayala," Herzog, *Breve,* I: 241.

14. Emiliano Zapata to Francisco I. Madero, Cuautla, Morelos, August 17, 1911, Condumex: JA.

15. Womack, *Zapata,* p. 210.

16. *Ibid.,* p. 199.

17. Emiliano Zapata, "Protesta Ante el Pueblo Mexicano," Tlaltizapan, Morelos, May 19, 1917, Condumex: MG.

18. "Plan de Ayala," Herzog, *Breve,* I: 243–244.

19. Emiliano Zapato to Gregorio Sosa y Doroteo Nájera, Campamento de Rancho Nuevo, Morelos, December 29, 1911, AGN, M, No. L, 862.

20. Marte R. Gómez, *La Reforma Agraria en las Filas Villistas, Años 1913 a 1915 a 1920* (Mexico, 1966), p. 99.

21. "Plan de Ayala," Herzog, *Breve,* I: 243–244.

22. Charles C. Cumberland, *Mexican Revolution: The Constitutionalist Years* (Austin, 1972), p. 240; Womack, *Zapata,* p. 212.

23. Gómez, *La Reforma Agraria,* p. 65.

24. Ambrosio Figueroa, Gobernador de Morelos, to Francisco I. Madero, Cuernavaca, Morelos, January 5, 1912, AGN, M, No. L. 862.

25. For a different opinion see Womack, *Zapata,* p. 194.

26. Emiliano Zapata to Venustiano Carranza, Cuartel General del Ejército Libertador, Morelos, March 17, 1919, Condumex: JA.

27. Emiliano Zapata, "Manifiesto a la Nación," Jojutla, Morelos, April 18, 1916, Condumex: JA.

28. Indalecio Jiménez to Venustiano Carranza, San Antonio, Texas, November 10, 1915, Condumex: AVC.

29. Quoted in Womack, *Zapata,* p. 186.

30. "Zapata and Aids Accept Peace Plan," *The New York Times,* August 30, 1915.

31. Womack, *Zapata,* pp. 161–162.

32. General Guillermo García Aragón to Alfredo Robles Domínguez, Mexico, August 5, 1914, Condumex: AVC.

33. Fortunato Macías, "Memorandum para el C. General Pablo González, Jefe de las Operaciones del Sur, Cuautla, Morelos, May 9, 1919, Condumex: MG.

34. Octavio Paz to Jenaro Amezcua, Los Angeles, California, May 28, 1920, Condumex: JA; Antonio Díaz Soto y Gama to Jenaro Amezcua, Campamento Revolucionario del Estado de Morelos, June 24, 1915, Condumex: JA; Antonio Díaz Soto y Gama to Gral. Francisco Mendoza, Mexico, July 1, 1920, Condumex: JA.

35. Gral. Genovevo de la O and others, "Al Pueblo Mexicano," Campamento Revolucionario en el Estado de Morelos, April 15, 1919, Condumex: JA; Gral. Genovevo de la O to Alvaro Obregón, Cuernavaca, Morelos, August 1, 1922, AGN, OC, P-8, L-8, 103-S-11.

36. Jenaro Amezcua to Vicente Sánchez Gutiérrez and others, Havana, Cuba, July 4, 1919, Condumex: JA.

37. General Reinaldo Lecona to General Genovevo de la O, Tehuacán, Puebla, December 12, 1923, AGN, OC, P-4, L-2, 101-R2-A-2.

38. José G. Parres to Fernando Torreblanca, Mexico, June 1, 1925, AGN, OC, P-5, 101-R2-1.

39. Edmundo Bolio, *Yucatán en la Dictatura y la Revolución* (Mexico, 1967), p. 168.

40. José I. Limantour, *Apuntes Sobre Mi Vida Pública* (Mexico, 1965), pp. 266–267.

41. *Ibid.*, p. 273.

42. Womack, *Zapata*, pp. 106 and 108.

43. Adrián Aguirre Benavides to Francisco I. Madero, Mexico, August 22, 1911, Condumex: JA.

44. Victoriano Huerta to Francisco León de la Barra, Yautepec, Morelos, August 26, 1911, Condumex: LDB.

45. Womack, *Zapata*, pp. 89–90.

46. Jorge Vera Estañol, *Historia de la Revolución Mexicana; Orígenes y Resultados* (Mexico, 1967), p. 245; Ramón Prida, *De la Dictadura a la Anarquía; Apuntes para la Historia Política de México durante los Ultimos Cuarenta y Tres Años (1871–1913)* (Mexico, 1958), p. 357; Womack, *Zapata*, pp. 82–83.

47. Francisco I. Madero to Francisco León de la Barra, Tehuacán, Puebla, July 25, 1911, Condumex: LDB.

48. Francisco I. Madero to Gral. Ambrosio Figueroa, Mexico, August 9, 1911, Condumex: JA.

49. Ambrosio Figueroa to Francisco I. Madero, Cuernavaca, Morelos, January 7, 1912, AGN, M, No. L, 862.

50. For example, see Rosalía Flores Viuda de Barrientos to Francisco I. Madero, Piedras Negras, Coahuila, June 5, 1912, AGN, M, 3, 762-3.

51. Womack, *Zapata*, p. 137.

52. *Ibid.*, p. 148.

53. Hesíquio Bravo to Felix Díaz, Mexico, May 14, 1913, Condumex: MG.

54. Jesús Flores Magón to Rafael Martínez Carrillo, Mexico, November 27, 1912, AGN, M, 2-7, 1173; Francisco I. Madero to Rafael Martínez Carrillo, Mexico, November 28, 1912, AGN, M, 2-7, 1173.

55. Gabriel Robles Domínguez to Francisco I. Madero, Mexico, November 20, 1911, Condumex: JA.

56. Ambrosio Figueroa to Francisco I. Madero, Cuernavaca, Morelos, January 7, 1912, AGN, M, No. L, 862.

57. Ambrosio Figueroa to Francisco I. Madero, Cuernavaca, Morelos, January 13, 1912, AGN, M, No. L, 862.

58. Quoted in Womack, *Zapata*, p. 165.

59. L. Rivas Iruz to Ambrosio Figueroa, Mexico, January 30, 1912, Condumex: AVC.

60. Quoted in Womack, *Zapata*, p. 127.

61. Quoted in *ibid.*, p. 199.

62. Juan Gualberto Amaya, *Venustiano Carranza, Caudillo Constitutionalista; Segunda Etapa, Febrero de 1913 a Mayo de 1920* (Mexico, 1947), pp. 149 and 162.

63. *Ibid.*, p. 163.

64. Quoted in *ibid.*

65. Gertrudis G. Sánchez to General Joaquín Amaro, Zirándero, Guerrero, June 5, 1914, Condumex: AVC.

66. "Interrogatoria Presentada al Señor General don Pablo González Sobre la Situación del Zapatismo en el Sur de México, y Contestaciones Dadas por el Jefe del Ejército de Oriente," Cuernavaca, Morelos, August 30, 1916, Condumex: AVC.

67. Coronel Jesús M. Guajardo to Gral. Pablo González, Cuautla, Morelos, April 14, 1919, Condumex: MG.

68. Gral. Pablo González, "A Todos los Gobernadores de los Estados y Jefes de Operaciones Militares," Cuautla, Morelos, April 10, 1919, Condumex: MG.

69. Gral. Pablo González, "Manifiesto del General Pablo González, Jefe del Ejército de Operaciones del Sur, a los Habitantes de Morelos," Cuautla, Morelos, April 16, 1919, Condumex: MG.

70. L. S. Saavedra to Venustiano Carranza, Mexico, April [n. d.], 1916, Condumex: AVC.

71. *Ibid.*

72. Narciso Bassols Batalla, *El Pensamiento Político de Obregón* (Mexico, 1967), p. 26.

73. Antonio Díaz Soto y Gama, Jenaro Amezcua, Emilio Vásquez Gómez, Eulalio Gutiérrez, Gildardo Magaña y demás Diputados a la H. Cámara de Diputados, Mexico, December 20, 1920, Condumex: JA.

CHAPTER XIV

1. *Historia de la Revolución Mexicana; Orígenes y Resultados* (Mexico, 1967), p. 140.

2. Adonay Hernández Cepeda to Venustiano Carranza, Mérida, Yucatán, February 4, 1915, Condumex: AVC.

3. L. Rivas Iruz to Venustiano Carranza, Mexico, November 14, 1914, Condumex: AVC.

4. Cited in Antonio Manero, *El Antiguo Régimen y la Revolución* (Mexico, 1911), p. 142.

5. Ignacio Herrerías, *En el Campo Revolucionario* (Chihuahua, 1911), p. 12.

6. Atenedoro Gámez, *Monografía Histórica sobre la Génesis de la Revolución en el Estado de Puebla* (Mexico, 1960), p. 7.

7. *El Militarismo Mexicano* (Valencia, Spain, 1920), p. 50.

8. Alberto Bremauntz, *Setenta Años de Mi Vida; Memorias y Anécdotas* (Mexico, 1968), p. 66.

9. Rafael Herrera to Venustiano Carranza, Mexico, August 25, 1914, Condumex: AVC.

10. José C. Domínguez to Venustiano Carranza, San Cristóbal, Chiapas, August 29, 1914, Condumex: AVC.

11. Club Liberal de Acula to Venustiano Carranza, Acula, Veracruz, February 29, 1915, Condumex: AVC.

12. Alfonso Romandía Ferreira, "Obregón, Factor Determinante para la Ejecución de la Reforma Agraria, Principio Básico de la Revolución Mexicana," Editorial Cultura, *Obregón, Aspectos de su Vida* (Mexico, 1935), p. 94.

13. Benjamin Morett to Venustiano Carranza, Saltillo, Coahuila, July 3, 1916, Condumex: AVC.

14. Rafael Romero, Jr. to Francisco I. Madero, Cocula, Jalisco, February 27, 1912, AGN, M, 29, 1359.

15. L. Rivas Iruz to Venustiano Carranza, Mexico, December 23, 1915, Condumex: AVC.

16. Cristóbal Ll. y Castillo to Venustiano Carranza, La Provincia, Chiapas, February 5, 1915, Condumex: AVC.

17. *La Traición de Carranza* (New York, 1920), p. 6.

18. General Emiliano P. Navarrete to Venustiano Carranza, Tampico, Tamaulipas, March 18, 1916, Condumex: AVC.

19. "Sociedad Anónima," Hermosillo, Sonora, December 16, 1917, Archivo General de Notarios del Estado de Sonora, Hermosillo, Condumex: AVC.

20. Un amigo anónimo to Venustiano Carranza, Mexico, October 26, 1914, Condumex: AVC.

21. Simón Bastar to Venustiano Carranza, Veracruz, Veracruz, May 1, 1915, Condumex: AVC.

22. Vera Estañol, *Historia de la Revolución Mexicana*, p. 243.

23. James D. Cockcroft, *Intellectual Precursors of the Mexican Revolution, 1900–1913* (Austin and London, 1968), p. 199.

24. Rafael Zubarán Capmany to Luis Cabrera, Washington, December 4, 1914, Condumex: AVC.

25. John W. F. Dulles, *Yesterday in Mexico, A Chronicle of the Revolution, 1919–1936* (Austin, 1961), p. 211.

26. Ramón Eduardo Ruiz, *Mexico, the Challenge of Poverty and Illiteracy* (San Marino, 1963), pp. 26–28.

27. Silvestre Terrazas to Francisco Villa, Chihuahua, Chihuahua, October 29, 1914, Terrazas Papers, Box 84, Bancroft Library.

28. *Antiguo Régimen*, p. 346.

29. Luis Cabrera, "La Solución del Conflicto," *La Opinión*, April 18–19, 1911.

30. Roberto Blanco Moheno, *Crónica de la Revolución Mexicana*, 2 vols., Mexico, 1958–1959), I: 43.

31. Letter to Francisco I. Madero, April 27, 1911 cited in *ibid.*, p. 34.

32. Arnaldo Córdova, *La Ideología de la Revolución Mexicana; la Formación del Nuevo Régimen* (Mexico, 1973), pp. 137–140.

33. Luis Cabrera, *Tres Intelectuales Hablan Sobre México* (Mexico, 1916), pp. 12–13.

34. Moisés González Navarro, "Social Aspects of the Mexican Revolution," *Journal of World History*, VIII (1964): 281.

35. Hector Aguilar Camín, "La Revolución Sonorense, 1910–1914" (Ph.D. diss., Instituto Nacional de Antropología e Historia, Mexico, 1975), pp. 123–124.

36. Francisco Bulnes, *El Verdadero Díaz y la Revolución* (Mexico, 1967), p. 265.

37. Aguilar Camín, "Revolución Sonorense," p. 133.

38. Robert E. Quirk, *The Mexican Revolution and the Catholic Church, 1910–1929* (Bloomington and London, 1973), p. 88.

39. "Declaración," Parral, Chihuahua, July 23, 1913, Condumex: AVC.

40. Telegrama del Sr. Gobernador de Guerrero al Secretario de Gobernación de Victoriano Huerto," March 25, 1913, Condumex: AVC; Gertrudis G. Sánchez to Venustiano Carranza, Zirándero Michoacán, June 3, 1914, Condumex: AVC.

41. Aguilar Camín, "Revolución Sonorense," pp. 201–204.

42. *Ibid.*, pp. 205–207.

43. W. A. Julian, American Consulate Agent, to E. M. Lawson, Nogales, Sonora, September 19, 1917, Consulate Correspondence, Record Group 84, Records of the Foreign Service Posts of the Department of State, Vol. 248, National Archives, Washington, D.C.

44. Antonio I. Villarreal, "A los Campesinos," Veracruz, Veracruz, January 20, 1924.

45. Ricardo Suárez Gamboa to Gral. Pablo González, Hermosillo, Sonora, February 10, 1914, Condumex: MG.

46. David Moreno, *Venustiano Carranza, Alvaro Obregón, Putarco Elías Calles* (Mexico, 1960), p. 56.

47. Jorge Prieto Laurens, *Cincuenta Años de Política Mexicana, Memorias Políticas* (Mexico, 1968), p. 158.

48. "Asamblea General Extraordinaria de Accionistas. Verificada en Noviembre 19, 1921," Hermosillo, Sonora, AGN, OC, P-6-2, 103-3-8.

49. Rodolfo Elías Calles to Plutarco Elías Calles, Hermosillo, Sonora, February 2, 1924, AGN, OC, P-6-2, 103-E-8; José M. A. Almada to Plutarco Elías Calles, Hermosillo, Sonora, April 6, 1925, AGN, OC, P-7, L-4, 103-H-31.

50. Rodolfo Elías Calles to Plutarco Elías Calles, Hermosillo, Sonora, June 22, 1925, AGN, OC, P. 6-1, L-2, 103-C-52.

51. Plutarco Elías Calles, Jr. to Plutarco Elías Calles, General Terán, Nuevo León, February 14, 1925, AGN OC, P-8, L-8, 103-S-31.

52. Félix F, Palavicini to Rafael Reyes Spindola, *El Imparcial,* Mexico, June 9, 1910.

53. Félix F. Palavincini, *Mi Vida Revolucionaria* (Mexico, 1937), p. 366.

54. Félix F. Palavincini to Alvaro Obregón, Mexico, September 11, 1922, AGN, OC, P-41-1, L-1, 407-E-10.

55. Juan Gualberto Amaya, *Los Gobiernos de Obregón, Calles y Regímenes "Peleles" Derivados del Callismo* (Mexico, 1947), p. 393.

56. Cited in José Fuentes Mares, *La Revolución Mexicana; Memorias de un Espectador* (Mexico, 1971), p. 206.

57. Alberto J. Pani, *Mi Contribución al Nuevo Régimen (1910–1933)* (Mexico, 1936), p. 5.

58. Alberto J. Pani, *On the Road to Democracy* (Mexico, 1918), p. 41.

59. Varios Senadores to Alberto J. Pani, Mexico, September 30, 1933, AGN, AR, P. 10, 139.1/4.

60. *Cincuenta Años,* p. 107.

61. Silvestre Terrazas, "Bienes Pertenecientes al Subscripto, en el Estado de Chihuahua," Chihuahua, Chihuahua, September [n. d.], 1912, Terrazas Papers, Box 83, Bancroft Library.

62. "Timbres por Valor de Cincuenta Centavos, Debidamente Cancelados. Minuta de Contrato," Chihuahua, Chihuahua, May 11, 1915, Terrazas Papers, Box 84, Bancroft Library.

63. Francisco R. Almada, *La Revolución en el Estado de Chihuahua,* 2 vols. (Chihuahua, 1964), I: 41–44.

64. Cited in Juan Gualberto Amaya, *Venustiano Carranza, Caudillo Constitucionalista; Segunda Etapa, February de 1913 a Mayo de 1920* (Mexico, 1947), p. 19.

65. Luis Casarrubias to Juan Sánchez Azcona, Puebla, Puebla, October 12, 1912, AGN, M, 3, 759-2.

66. Cockcroft, *Intellectual Precursors,* p. 103.

67. June 25, 1909.

68. Aurilio Pérez Peña to Ramón Corral, Guaymas, Sonora, May 18, 1909, Condumex: RC.

69. *El Verdadero Díaz,* p. 405.

70. Cited in Jorge Carpizo, *La Constitución Mexicana de 1917* (Mexico, 1969), p. 78.

71. Aguilar Camín, "Revolución Sonorense," pp. 79–80.

72. *Ibid.,* p. 81.

73. Charles C. Cumberland, *Mexican Revolution: The Constitutionalist Years* (Austin, 1972), p. 382.

74. Francis J. Dyer to Secretary of State, Nogales, Sonora, September 26, 1919. Consulate Correspondence, Record Group 84, Records of the Foreign Service Posts of the Department of State, Vol. 248, National Archives, Washington, D.C.

75. Rafael Zubarán Capmany and Jesús Urueta to Venustiano Carranza, Mexico, December 14, 1914, Condumex: AVC.

76. Palavicini, *Vida Revolucionaria,* p. 257.

77. Rafael Nieto to Venustiano Carranza, Mexico, December 17, 1915, Condumex: AVC.

78. J. G. Nava to Venustiano Carranza, Mexico, January 2, 1916, Condumex: AVC.

79. *Diario de los Debates de la Cámara de Diputados* (March 14, 1921) (Mexico), II: 1.

80. Dulles, *Yesterday in Mexico,* p. 229.

81. Juan B. Lizárraga to Francisco I. Madero, Mazatlán, Sinaloa, March 17, 1912, AGN, M, 5, No. E.

82. Consuelo Peña de Villarreal, *La Revolución en el Norte* (Puebla, 1968), p. 186.

83. *Ibid.,* p. 310.

84. *Ibid.,* p. 306.

85. *Ibid.,* p. 234; "Datos Biográficos y Documentación Correspondiente Pertenecientes al Ciudadano General Brigadier David R. Neave," Mexico, July 31, 1922, AGN, OC L-15, 101-N-3, P-2.

86. Everardo G. Arenas, "Memorial de los Servicios que he Prestado desde el Año de 1908 a la Fecha," Mexico, October 1, 1915, Condumex: AVC.

87. Manuel Lozano, Director Escuela Rural Federal, El Jaguey, San Pedro, Zacatecas, to Abelardo Rodríguez, Mexico, November 8, 1933, AGN, P. 135, 562.11/1.

88. Gregorio Osuna, "Biografía Política-Militar del que Suscribe, General Brigadier, Gregorio Osuna," Ciudad Victoria, Tamaulipas, March 29, 1919, Condumex: AVC.

89. Juan Barragán Rodríguez, *Historia del Ejército y de la Revolución Constitucionalista,* 2 vols. (Mexico, 1946), I: 247; Rodrigo López Pérez, *El Movimiento Obregonista en Michoacán* (Mexico, 1920), p. 90.

90. Peña de Villarreal, *La Revolución,* p. 325.

91. *Ibid.,* p. 116; Aguilar Camín, "Revolución Sonorense," p. 111.

92. Aguilar Camín, "Revolución Sonorense," p. 346; Blanco Moheno, *Crónica de la Revolución,* I: 170.

93. Gral. F. L. Urquizo, "Breves Apuntes Biográficos Relativos al General de División Pablo González," Mexico, December 16, 1919, Condumex: AVC.

94. Gildardo Magaña to Jenaro Amezcua, Cuartel General del Ejército Libertador, en el Edo. de Morelos, June 30, 1919. Condumex: JA.

95. Amaya, *Los Gobiernos de Obregón,* p. 11.

96. Gral Gildardo Magaña to Jenaro Amezcua, Campamento Revolucionario en el Edo. de Morelos, June 24, 1919, Condumex: JA.

97. Michael C. Meyer, *Mexican Rebel; Pascual Orozco and the Mexican Revolution, 1910–1915* (Lincoln, 1967), p. 16; Silvestre Terrazas to Francisco Villa, Chihuahua, Chihuahua, January 30, 1915, Terrazas Papers, Box 84, Bancroft Library.

98. Ramón Puente, *Pascual Orozco y la Revuelta en Chihuahua* (Mexico, 1912), p. 26.

99. William H. Beezley, *Insurgent Governor: Abraham González and the Mexican Revolution in Chihuahua* (Lincoln, 1973), p. 36.

100. Aguilar Camín, "Revolución Sonorense," p. 132.

101. Dulles, *Yesterday in Mexico,* p. 81.

102. Armando de María y Campos, *La Vida del General Lucio Blanco* (Mexico, 1963), pp. 18–19.

103. Carlos Morton to Francisco I. Madero, Sabinas Hidalgo, Nuevo León, October 16, 1912, AGN, M, 2-7, 1176.

104. Genaro Dávila to Venustiano Carranza, Zaragoza, Coahuila, February 6, 1915, Condumex: AVC.

105. J. N. Amador, Consulado General de México, to Venustiano Carranza, New York, New York, October 14, 1915, Condumex: AVC.

106. Manuel Ruíz Lavín to Venustiano Carranza, Veracruz, Veracruz, July 25, 1915, Condumex: AVC.

107. Roberto Castro to Venustiano Carranza, Veracruz, Veracruz, March 9, 1915, Condumex: AVC.

108. Aguilar Camín, "Revolución Sonorense," pp. 65, 74, and 76; "Relación de las Propiedades Rústicas Intervenidas a Particulares en la República," Mexico, April 22, 1922, AGN, OC, P-81, L-2, 806, P-5; Francisco S. Vásquez to Felix Díaz, Los Angeles, California, May 21, 1913, Condumex: AVC; Guy Weddington McCreary, *From Glory to Oblivion, the Real Truth About the Mexican Revolution* (New York, 1974), p. 5.

109. Alberto Cubillas to Ramón Corral, Hermosillo, Sonora, September 28, 1908, Condumex: RC.

110. Jóse M. Maytorena, *Algunas Verdades Sobre el General Alvaro Obregón* (Los Angeles, 1919), p. 79.

111. Alvaro Obregón, *Ocho Mil Kilómetros en Campaña* (Mexico, 1917), p. 357.

112. January 19, 1910.

113. Aguilar Camín, "Revolución Sonorense," pp. 5–6.

114. General Benjamín Hill to Venustiano Carranza, Mexico, August 1, 1916, Condumex: AVC.

115. Enrique Estrada to Alvaro Obregón, Mexico, June 21, 1921, AGN, OC, P-7, L-4, 103-H-8.

116. Aguilar Camín, "Revolución Sonorense," pp. 116 and 277.

117. Carmen D. Vda. de Hill to Alvaro Obregón, Mexico, June 7, 1921, AGN, OC, P-7, L-4, 103-H-8.

118. Antonio G. Rivera, *La Revolución en Sonora* (Mexico, 1969), p. 172.

119. Aguilar Camín, "Revolución Sonorense," p. 258.

120. Marte R. Gómez, *La Reforma Agraria en las Filas Villistas, Años 1913 a 1915 a 1920* (Mexico, 1966), pp. 58–60.

121. "Manifiesto a la Nación del Círculo Nacional Porfirista," *El Imparcial*, April 3, 1909.

122. Blasco Ibáñez, *Militarismo Mexicano*, p. 50.

123. "Bienes del General Juan Barragán Rodríguez," Mexico, October 23, 1920, AGN, OC, P-7, L-4, 103-H-8; Alvaro Obregón to Plutarco Elías Calles, Mexico, October 10, 1921, AGN, OC, P-6-1, L-1, 103-C-11.

124. *Cincuenta Años de Política*, p. 20.

125. Amaya, *Los Gobiernos de Obregón*, p. 391.

126. Juan Andréu Almazán, "Manifiesto," Mexico, March 31, 1913, Condumex: MG.

CHAPTER XV

1. Hans-Werner Tobler, "Las Paradojas del Ejército Revolucionario: Su Papel Social en la Reforma Agraria Mexicana, 1920–1930." *Historia Mexicana*, XXI: 39.

2. Blas Urrea, *La Herencia de Carranza* (Mexico, 1920), pp. 92–93.

3. Jorge Vera Estañol, *Historia de la Revolución Mexicana; Orígenes y Resultados* (Mexico, 1967), p. 389.

4. Juan de Dios Robledo, "Obregón Militar," Editorial Cultura, *Obregón, Aspectos de Su Vida* (Mexico, 1935), p. 43.

5. Tobler, "Las Paradojas," p. 46.

6. *El Antiguo Régimen y la Revolución* (Mexico, 1911), p. 400.

7. Pablo, González, "Ejecutiva," Guemes, Tamaulipas, November 14, 1913, Condumex: MG.

8. Tobler, "Las Paradojas," p. 53; Alvaro Obregón to General Genovevo de la O, Mexico, September 22, 1924, AGN, NC, P. 2-1, L. 19, 101-S-1.

9. "Apuntes Intimos de López Sáenz," Veracruz, Veracruz, November 1, 1915, Condumex: AVC.

10. *El Militarismo Mexicano* (Valencia, Spain, 1920), p. 199.

11. Coronel Vicente Segura to General Pablo González, Matamoros, Tamaulipas, December 24, 1913, Condumex: MG.

12. General Guadalupe Sánchez to Adolfo de la Huerta, Veracruz, Veracruz, September 13, 1921, AGN, OC, P 2-1, L-19, 101-S-6.

13. Arturo Langle Ramírez, *El Ejército Villista* (Mexico, 1961), p. 30.

14. Centro Constitucionalista Francisco I. Madero, Agujita, Coahuila, to Venustiano Carranza, Agujita, Coahuila, May 15, 1913, Condumex: AVC.

15. General en Jefe, Cuartel General, Puerto México, Veracruz, November 22, 1914, Condumex: AVC.

16. Francisco Canseco to Venustiano Carranza, Oaxaca, Oaxaca, November 24, 1914, Condumex: AVC.

17. Gobernador de Puebla to Venustiano Carranza, Puebla, Puebla, December 5, 1914, Condumex: AVC.

18. Rafael Nieto to Venustiano Carranza, Oaxaca, Oaxaca, March 25, 1915, Condumex: AVC.

19. Francisco Aguirre León to Venustiano Carranza, Veracruz, Veracruz, March 30, 1915, Condumex: AVC.

20. John Womack, *Zapata and the Mexican Revolution* (New York, 1970), p. 157.

21. Rafael Martínez Carrillo to Jesús Flores Magón, Puebla, Puebla, November 21, 1912, AGN, M, 2-7, 1173.

22. Hector Aguilar Camín, "La Revolución Sonorense, 1910–1914" (Ph.D. diss., Instituto Nacional de Antropología e Historia, Mexico, 1975), p. 276.

23. I. Thord-Gray *Gringo Rebel; Mexico 1913–1914* (Coral Gables, 1960), p. 108.

24. Aguilar Camín, "La Revolución Sonorense," pp. 337, 378, 380, and 385.

25. Roberto Blanco Moheno, *Crónica de la Revolución Mexicana*, 2 vols. (Mexico, 1958–1959), I: 195.

26. Juan Barragán Rodríguez, *Historia del Ejército y de la Revolución Constitucionalista*, 2 vols. (Mexico, 1946), I: 233.

27. William H. Beezley, *Insurgent Governor: Abraham González and the Mexican Revolution in Chihuahua* (Lincoln, 1973), p. 133.

28. Urrea, *Herencia*, p. 39.

29. L. Rivas Iruz to Venustiano Carranza, Mexico, October 20, 1915, Condumex: AVC.

30. Womack, *Zapata*, p. 172.

31. Francisco A. Campos to Francisco I. Madero, Mexico, December 25, 1911, AGN, M, 33, 361–1.

32. Juan José Ríos to Venustiano Carranza, Colima, Colima, September 3, 1915, Condumex: AVC.

33. Coronel J. Aguirre León to Venustiano Carranza, Mexico, November 24, 1915, Condumex: AVC.

34. General Alfredo Ricaut to Venustiano Carranza, Matamoros, Tamaulipas, December 20, 1915, Condumex: AVC.

35. Alvaro Obregón to Secretario de Hacienda y Crédito Público, Mexico, July 2, 1921, AGN, OC, P 19-1, L-7, 121-W-A.

36. General Alfredo Ricaut to Venustiano Carranza, Nuevo Laredo, Tamaulipas, July 8, 1915, Condumex: AVC.

37. Alfredo N. Acosta, *La Gestión Hacendaria de la Revolución* (Mexico, 1917), p. 85.

38. John W. F. Dulles, *Yesterday in Mexico. A Chronicle of the Revolution, 1919–1936* (Austin, 1961), p. 121.

39. Pablo C. de Becerra to Antonio Ramos Pedrueza, Saltillo, Coahuila, April 26, 1912, AGN, F, 7, 6.

40. "Informe Confidencial," Mexico, Mexico, November 12, 1915, Condumex: AVC.

41. José Peña to Venustiano Carranza, San Antonio, Texas, May 9, 1913, Condumex: LDB.

42. Gertrudis G. Sánchez to Venustiano Carranza, [n. p.] June 3, 1914, Condumex: AVC.

43. Raul G. Ruíz to Coronel Facundo Tello, Veracruz, Veracruz, November 5, 1914, Condumex: AVC.

44. Pablo González, "Ejecutiva," Guemes, Tamaulipas, November 14, 1913, Condumex: MG.

45. Pablo González to Venustiano Carranza, Matamoros, Tamaulipas, February 8, 1914, Condumex: MG.

46. Fortunato Maycotte to Alvaro Obregón, Oaxaca, Oaxaca, March 14, 1923, AGN, OC, L-14, 101-M-18, P-Z.

47. Alvaro Obregón to General Eugenio Martínez, Mexico, July 4, 1924, AGN, OC, P-2, 101-M-44.

48. General Eugenio Martínez to Alvaro Obregón, Veracruz, Veracruz, July 10, 1924, AGN, OC, P-2, 101-M-44.

49. General Emiliano Zapata, Jefe de la Revolución en el Sur y Centro de la República, a sus Habitantes, Sabed que: Cuartel General en el Estado de Morelos, February 11, 1914, Condumex: JA.

50. Bernardo L. Ríos, "La Propaganda del Constitucionalismo en Chiapas," *El Regenerador,* Tuxtla Gutiérrez, Chiapas, July 1915, Condumex: AVC.

51. Teresa de Chávez to General Pablo González, Mexico, April 20, 1918, Condumex: MG.

52. Coronel Vicente Segura to General Pablo González, Matamoros, Tamaulipas, December 24, 1913, Condumex: MG.

53. V. Romano to Venustiano Carranza, Temascaltepec, Mexico, August 29, 1914, Condumex: AVC.

54. Martín Triana to Venustiano Carranza, Aguascalientes, Aguascalientes, August 18, 1915, Condumex: AVC.

55. Arcadio López Reyes, Procurador General de Justicia to Gobernador de Chiapas, Comitán, Chiapas, August 20, 1924, AGN, OC, P 17-1, L-5, 121-D3-C.

56. General Cándido Aguilar to General Agustín Millán, Mexico, May 13, 1916, Condumex: AVC.

57. General Conrado Cevera C., "Carta Abierta," Jonacatepec, Morelos, March 17, 1918, Condumex: MG.

58. Felipe Sánchez Martínez, Secretario General Comité Revolucionario de la Casa del Obrero Mundial, to Venustiano Carranza, Veracruz, Veracruz, August 15, 1915, Condumex: AVC.

59. Martín Triana to Venustiano Carranza, Aguascalientes, Aguascalientes, October 27, 1914, Condumex: AVC.

60. Venusiano Carranza to Enrique Melgar, Comisionado de la Jefatura de Hacienda de Veracruz, Torreón, Coahuila, October 28, 1915, Condumex: AVC.

61. Blas Urrea, "Segunda Meditación," *El Universal,* June 6, 1917.

62. Emiliano Zapata to Venustiano Carranza, Cuartel General del Ejército Libertador, Morelos, March 17, 1919, Condumex: JA.

63. Juan José Ríos to Alvaro Obregón, Culiacán, Sinaloa, November 18, 1924, AGN, OC, P-2-1, L-18, 101-12-27.

64. General Martín Espinoza to Venustiano Carranza, Hermosillo, Sonora, December 28, 1913, Condumex: AVC.

65. Juan Martínez, Presidente Municipal de San Juan de Sabinas, Coahuila, to Venustiano Carranza, Eagle Pass, Texas, December 29, 1913, Condumex: AVC.

66. Ramón P. DeNegri, Consul de Mexico, to Venustiano Carranza, San Francisco, California, December 18, 1914, Condumex: AVC.

67. Tobler, "Las Paradojas," p. 71.

68. Alvaro Obregón to Mayor Elías Elizondo, Irapuato, Guanajuato, January 1, 1924, AGN, OC, P-4, L-2, 101-R2-C.

69. *Diario de los Debates del Congreso Constituyente, 1916–1917,* 2 vols. (Mexico, 1960), II: 1084.

70. "Informe Confidencial," Mexico, November 12, 1915, Condumex: AVC.

71. Félix F. Palavicini to Venustiano Carranza, Orizaba, Veracruz, November 22, 1914, Condumex: AVC.

72. Genaro Buen Abad y Gabriel Goyta to Venustiano Carranza, Veracruz, Veracruz, March 25, 1915, Condumex: AVC.

73. Barragán Rodríguez, *Historia del Ejército*, II: 29; Eusebio Arzate to Venustiano Carranza, Puebla, Puebla, May 7, 1915, Condumex: AVC.

74. "Memorandum," Congreso de la Unión, Correspondencia Particular de los Ciudadanos Diputados, Mexico, June 5, 1923, AGN, OC, P 4-1, 101-R2-H.

75. Tobler, "Las Paradojas," p. 44.

76. L. Mesa Gutiérrez to Rafael Zubarán Capmany, Ciudad Juárez, Chihuahua, December 31, 1913, Condumex: AVC.

77. Mariano Arrieta to Venustiano Carranza, Durango, Durango, November, 22, 1915, Condumex: AVC.

78. Pacual Ortiz Rubio to Venustiano Carranza, Morelia, Michoacán, January 16, 1918, Condumex: AVC.

79. Pascual Ortiz Rubio to Venustiano Carranza, Mexico, June 21, 1916, Condumex: AVC.

80. Ramón P. DeNegri to Alvaro Obregón, Mexico, June 10, 1922, AGN, OC, P 16-1, L-12, 121-A-F-1.

81. Jesús María Velásquez to Alvaro Obregón, San Juan Cosomatepec, Veracruz, April 17, 1923, AGN, OC, P 40-1, L-8, 307-V-21.

82. H. M. Machorro to Venustiano Carranza, Tlaxcala, Tlaxcala, September 6, 1916, Condumex: AVC.

83. Urrea, *Herencia*, p. 102.

84. Diputados al Congreso de la Unión to Alvaro Obregón, Mexico, November 5, 1923, AGN, OC, P-4-1, 101-R2-H.

85. Alvaro Obregón to Diputados, El Fuerte, Jalisco, November 7, 1923, AGN, OC, P 4-1, 101-R2-H.

86. El Secretario Particular to C. Secretario de Guerra y Marina, Mexico, November 19, 1923, AGN, OC, P 4-1, 101-R2-H.

87. General Higinio Aguilar to Miguel Bravo Sánchez, Cumbres de Acultzingo, Veracruz, October 25, 1915, Condumex: AVC.

88. Comerciantes de Chihuahua, Chihuahua to Fernando Torreblanca, Srío. del Presidente de la República, Chihuahua, Chihuahua, December 1, 1927, AGN, OC, L-16, 101-0-14, P-2.

89. Cándido Aguilar to Venustiano Carranza, Mexico, September 30, 1916, Condumex: AVC.

90. Coronel A. G. González to Venustiano Carranza, Veracruz, Veracruz, December 6, 1914, Condumex: AVC.

91. Legislatura de Guerrero to Venustiano Carranza, Tecpan de Galeana, Guerrero, April 3, 1918, Condumex: AVC.

92. Urrea, *Herencia*, pp. 92-93, 95-96 and 104.

93. *Ibid.*, p. 124.

94. Urbano Flores to General Arnulfo González, Saltillo, Coahuila, November 23, 1920, AGN, OC, P 41, L-10, 407-C-12.

95. General Enrique Estrada to Alvaro Obregón, Mexico, June 10, 1922, AGN, OC, P-2-1, L-18, 101-R-26.

96. Alvaro Obregón to Samuel Gompers, Irapuato, Guanajuato, February 13, 1924, AGN, OC, P-4, L-2, 101-R2-A-2.

97. Tobler, "Las Paradojas," p. 52.

98. Aguilar Camín, "La Revolución Sonorense," p. 309.

99. Tobler, "Las Paradojas," p. 52.

100. General Juan G. Amaya to Plutarco Elías Calles, Puebla, Puebla, October 15, 1925, AGN, OC, P-5, 101-R2-L, L-5.

101. Sindicato de Campesinos Agraristas del Estado de Durango, Durango, April 2, 1924, AGN, OC, P-5, 101-R2-5.

102. Valente de la Cruz to Alvaro Obregón, Acapulco, Guerrero, April 26, 1924, AGN, OC, P 4-1, 101-R2-D.

103. Tobler, "Las Paradojas," p. 60.

104. *Ibid.*, p. 57.

105. Generales Gabriel Mariaca, Vicente Aranda and others to Adolfo de la Huerta, Cuernavaca, Morelos, January 14, 1921, AGN, OC, L-19, P-2-1, 101-S-1.

106. Antonio Díaz Soto y Gama to Alvaro Obregón, Mexico, October 28, 1921, AGN, OC, P 106, L-6, 818-E-28.

107. Antonio Díaz Soto y Gama and R. Lecona to Alvaro Obregón, Mexico, October 27, 1921, AGN, OC, P 106, L-6, 818-E-28.

108. *Ibid.*, Presidente de la Comisión Local Agraria to Alvaro Obregón, Morelia, Michoacán, November 21, 1921, AGN, OC, P 106, L-6, 818-E-28.

109. Alvaro Obregón to Presidente de la Comisión Local Agraria de Morelia, Morelia, Michoacán, December 5, 1921, AGN, OC, P 106, L-6, 818-E-28.

110. Juan Gualberto Amaya, *Los Gobiernos de Obregón, Calles y Regímenes "Peleles" Derivados del Callismo* (Mexico, 1947), p. 39.

111. Breceda to Venustiano Carranza, Mérida, Yucatán, January 14, 1914, Condumex: AVC.

112. Francisco [Armedia?] to Venustiano Carranza, De Lagos [n. p.], August 24, 1914, Condumex: AVC.

113. Quoted in Bernardino Mena Brito, *Maquinismo* (Mexico, 1933), p. 87.

114. Quoted in Narciso Bassols Batalla, *El Pensamiento Político de Obregón* (Mexico, 1967), p. 137.

115. *Diario de los Debates,* II: 550; Urrea, *Herencia,* p. 97.

116. Jorge Vera Estañol to Francisco León de la Barra, Los Angeles, California, May 29, 1918, Condumex: LDB.

117. Cruz R. Vda. de García to Alvaro Obregón, Mexico, January 27, 1922, AGN, OC, P-81, L-2, 806-S-8.

118. Tobler, "Las Paradojas," pp. 64 and 68–69.

119. Juan Cruz to Alvaro Obregón, Mexico, April 4, 1922, AGN, OC, P 104, L-5, 818-A-21.

120. Tomás Hernández y Juan Hernández to Alvaro Obregón, Mexico, October 6, 1922, AGN, OC, P 104, L-5, 818-A-21.

121. Alvaro Obregón to Tomás y Juan Hernández, Mexico, October 7, 1922, AGN, OC, P 104, L-5, 818-A-21.

122. Francisco R. Serrano to Alvaro Obregón, Mexico, April 8, 1922, AGN, OC, P 104, L-5, 818-A-21.

123. Tomás y Juan Hernández to Alvaro Obregón, Mexico, October 9, 1922, AGN, OC, P 104, L-5, 818-A-21.

124. Alvaro Obregón to F. R. Serrano, Mexico, December 9, 1922, AGN, OC, P 104, L-5, 818-A-21; Alvaro Obregón to Enrique Espejel, Mexico, April 3, 1923, AGN, OC, P 104, L-5, 818-A-21.

125. Tomás Hernández to Alvaro Obregón, Mexico, February 12, 1923, AGN, OC, P 104, LL-5, 818-A-3.

126. Alvaro Obregón to Enrique C. Espejel, Mexico, July 13, 1923, AGN, OC, P 104, L-5, 818-A-21.

127. Enrique Espejel to Alvaro Obregón, Mexico, April 5, 1925, AGN, OC, P 104, L-5, 818-A-21.

128. El General B., J. de las O. M. to Gobernador del Estado, Pachuca, Hidalgo, October 19, 1921, AGN, OC, P 104, L-5, 818-A-22; Crispín Martínez to Alvaro Obregón, Ahuazotepec, Puebla, December 14, 1921, AGN, OC, P 104, L-5, 818-A-22.

129. Alvaro Obregón to J. M. Sánchez, Mexico, December 3, 1921, AGN, OC, P 104, L-5, 818-A-22.

130. Julio Mitchell to Alvaro Obregón, Mexico, December 7, 1921, AGN, OC, P 104, L-5, 818-A-22.

131. J. M. Sánchez to Alvaro Obregón Puebla, Puebla, November 28, 1921, AGN, OC, P 104, L-5, 818-A-22.

132. General J. C. Zertuche to Alvaro Obregón, Pachuca, Hidalgo, December 14, 1921, AGN, OC, P 104, L-5, 818-A-21.

133. Alvaro Obregón to General Juan C. Zertuche, Mexico, December 14, 1921, AGN, OC, P 104, L-5, 818-A-22.

134. *Ibid.*

135. Alvaro Obregón to Crispín Martínez, Mexico, December 5, 1921, AGN, OC, P 104, L-5, 818-A-22.

136. Napoleón Molina Enríquez to Alvaro Obregón, Mexico, May 22, 1924, AGN, OC, P 104, L-5, 818-A-22.

137. Tobler, "Las Paradojas," p. 53.

138. El Comité Ejecutivo de la Federación de Sindicatos de Obreros y Campesinos de la Región Jalapeña to Alvaro Obregón, Jalapa, Veracruz, April 7, 1923, AGN, OC, P 2-1, L-19, 101-S-16.

139. José María Velásquez to Alvaro Obregón, San Juan Coscomatepec, Veracruz, April 17, 1923, AGN, OC, P 40-1, L-8, 307-V-21.

140. Quoted in Tobler, "Las Paradojas," p. 74.

141. Alvaro Obregón to General Guadalupe Sánchez, Mexico, April 26, 1923, AGN, OC, P 2-1, L-19, 101-S-15.

142. Alvaro Obregón to Heriberto Jara, Mexico, October 16, 1924, AGN, OC, P-4, L-2, 101-R2-A-2.

143. Secretario de Gobernación to Secretario de Fomento, Mexico, July 24, 1912, AGN, F, 8, 22.

144. Benito Rueda to Departamento del Trabajo, Atlixco, Puebla, July 7, 1912, AGN, F, 8, 29.

145. N. Meléndez Paiz to Antonio Ramos Pedrueza, Puebla, Puebla, April 19, 1912, AGN, F, 31, 12.

146. Jesús Heredia to Santos Pérez y Juan Olivares, Monterrey, Nuevo León, August 11, 1913, AGN, F, 5, 14.

147. Rosendo Salazar, *Las Pugnas de la Gleba*, 2 vols. (Mexico, 1923), I: 182.

148. Circular del General E. P. Navarrete, Tampico, Tamaulipas, April 3, 1916, Condumex: AVC.

149. Salazar, *Pugnas*, I: 239–240, 249.

150. Alejandro Cruz D. to Alvaro Obregón, Alvarado, Veracruz, August 5, 1923, AGN, OC, P 40-1, L-9, 407-A-10; J. Monrreal to Alvaro Obregón, Rosita, Coahuila, October 29, 1923, AGN, OC, P 41, L-11, 407-C-25; T. R. Burgos to Alvaro Obregón, Tampico, Tamaulipas, August 20, 1924, AGN, OC, P 41-1, L-3, 407-H-3.

151. Eduardo Moneda to Alvaro Obregón, Mexico, September 4, 1923, AGN, OC, P 41, L-11, 407-C-24.

152. Eduardo Moneda to Alvaro Obregón, Mexico, March 3, 1923, AGN, OC, P 104, L-5, 818-A-30.

153. Miguel Candia to Alvaro Obregón, Mexico, October 26, 1922, AGN, OC, P 42, L-6, 407-P-12.

154. R. Castillo F. to Alvaro Obregón, Campeche, Campeche, June 3, 1921, AGN, OC, P 41, L-10, 407-C-6; Miguel Inclán to Alvaro Obregón, Villahermosa, Tabasco, June 4, 1921, AGN, OC, P 41, L-10, 407-C-6.

155. Enrique Gómez B. to Alvaro Obregón, Campeche, Campeche, June 3, 1921, AGN, OC, P 41, L-10, 407-C-6.

156. Felipe Carrillo Puerto to Alvaro Obregón, Mexico, June 4, 1921, AGN, OC, P 41, L-10, 407-C-6.

157. General Anatolio B. Arteaga to Alvaro Obregón, Saltillo, Coahuila, May 5, 1923, AGN, OC, P 41, L-11, 407-C-25; Comité Ejecutivo Local de Unión Minera Mexicana to Alvaro Obregón, Rosita, Coahuila, May 13, 1923, AGN, OC, P 41, L-11, 407-C-25.

158. Evaristo Tenorio to Alvaro Obregón, Cloete, Coahuila, May 19, 1923, AGN, OC, P 41, L-11, 407-C-25.

CHAPTER XVI

1. 2 vols. (Mexico, 1923), I: 40.

2. *Ibid.*

3. Jorge Basurto, *El Proletariado Industrial en México (1850–1930)* (Mexico, 1975), p. 154.

4. José Mancisidor, *Historia de la Revolución Mexicana* (Mexico, 1965), p. 171.

5. Basurto, *Proletariado,* p. 164.

6. Barry Carr, "The Casa del Obrero Mundial, Constitutionalism and the Pact of February, 1915," "paper read at V Reunión de Historiadores Mexicanos y Norteamericanos, Pátzcuaro, Michoacán, October 12–15, 1977, p. 3.

7. *Ibid.,* pp. 5–7.

8. Salazar, *Pugnas,* I, 37.

9. Carr, "The Casa del Obrero Mundial," p. 8.

10. José Ives Limantour, *Apuntes Sobre Mi Vida Pública* (Mexico, 1965), p. 300; N. Zambrano, Tesorero General, to Venustiano Carranza, Mexico, December 31, 1915, Condumex: AVC.

11. M. Machorro, Gobernador, to Venustiano Carranza, Tlaxcala, Tlaxcala, August 12, 1916, Condumex: AVC.

12. Aureliano Esquivel to Venustiano Carranza, February 7, 1915, Condumex: AVC.

13. Federico Garza, Administrador General de Minas, to Venustiano Carranza, Piedras Negras, Coahuila, May 8, 1916, Condumex: AVC.

14. Ramón Eduardo Ruiz, *Labor and the Ambivalent Revolutionaries, 1911–1923* (The John Hopkins University Press, Baltimore and London, 1976), pp. 42–43.

15. General Luis Caballero to Venustiano Carranza, Ciudad Victoria, Tamaulipas, February 9, 1915, Condumex: AVC.

16. Blas Urrea, *La Herencia de Carranza* (Mexico, 1920), p. 49;

Miguel Rebolledo to Venustiano Carranza, Veracruz, July 26, 1915, Condumex: AVC.

17. Director del Departamento del Trabajo to Gobernador de Querétaro, Mexico, June 10, 1916, AGN, F, 1, 27.

18. Roberto Limón to Venustiano Carranza, Orizaba, Veracruz, May 29, 1916, Condumex: AVC.

19. Eduardo Fuentes, "Estudio Sobre el Encarecimiento de la Vida en México," September 27, 1915, Condumex: AVC, p. 33.

20. *Ibid.,* p. 18.

21. *Ibid.,* p. 33.

22. *Ibid.,* pp. 22–23, and 34.

23. *Ibid.,* pp. 17–19.

24. Alberto J. Pani, Director General de los Ferrocarriles, "Informe," *El Mexicano,* September 23, 1915.

25. Fuentes, "Estudios Sobre," p. 32.

26. *Ibid.,* pp. 29–30.

27. Letter to Jesús Urueta, Secretario de Relaciones Exteriores, Veracruz, May 28, 1915, Condumex: AVC.

28. J. A. Luna, "Carta a los Revolucionarios Patriotas," San Antonio, Texas, June 3, 1915, Condumex: AVC.

29. Letter to Venustiano Carranza, Ciudad Victoria, Tamaulipas, March 15, 1915, Condumex: AVC.

30. General Emiliano P. Navarrete to Venustiano Carranza, Tampico, Tamaulipas, March 22, 1916, Condumex: AVC.

31. Margarito Niva to Venustiano Carranza, Chinameca, Veracruz, July 4, 1915, Condumex: AVC.

32. Juan Córdova to Venustiano Carranza, Jalapa, Veracruz, March 27, 1915, Condumex: AVC.

33. J. G. Nava to Gustavo Espinosa Mireles, Secretario Particular del Primer Jefe, Veracruz, April 2, 1915, Condumex: AVC.

34. Representantes de los Obreros de las Fábricas de Hilados y Tejidos del Cantón de Orizaba to Venustiano Carranza, Nogales, Veracruz, May 8, 1915, Condumex: AVC; Macario Reyes and others to Venustiano Carranza, Río Blanco, Veracruz, May 5, 1915, Condumex: AVC.

35. Letter to General Francisco Coss, March 31, 1915, Condumex: AVC.

36. Adolfo N. Magón to Venustiano Carranza, Veracruz, June 18, 1915, Condumex: AVC; General Luis Domínguez to Venustiano Carranza, San Gerónimo, Oaxaca, March 27, 1915, Condumex: AVC.

37. "Informe Sobre Oaxaca," June 3, 1915, Condumex: AVC.

38. Coronel A. G. González to Venustiano Carranza, Veracruz, December 6, 1914, Condumex: AVC; Coronel Simón Díaz, Gobernador,

to Venustiano Carranza, Acapulco, Guerrero, April 11, 1916, Condumex: AVC.

39. E. Neri to Venustiano Carranza, Veracruz, July 5, 1915, Condumex: AVC.

40. Fuentes, "Estudios Sobre," pp. 20–21.

41. *Ibid.,* p. 1.

42. C. Rodríguez to Iñigo Noriega, Mexico, August 31, 1915, Condumex: AVC.

43. *Ibid.*

44. C. López Lara, Gobernador del Distrito Federal, to Venustiano Carranza, Mexico, June 9, 1916, Condumex: AVC.

45. Guillermo López Guerrero to Venustiano Carranza, Mexico, August 14, 1915, Condumex: AVC.

46. Bruno Montes de Oca to Venustiano Carranza, Tacubaya, Mexico, January 20, 1915, Condumex: AVC.

47. Ruiz, *Labor,* p. 41.

48. *Ibid.,* pp. 43–44.

49. Sidney C. Neale to Venustiano Carranza, Washington, D.C., in J. N. A. to Carranza, Mexico, November 12, 1915, Condumex: AVC.

50. Ramón Frausto to Venustiano Carranza, Mexico, August 30, 1916, Condumex: AVC.

51. Simón Díaz, Gobernador, to Venustiano Carranza, Acapulco, Guerrero, April 1, 1916, Condumex: AVC.

52. Manuel R. Díaz, Inspector, to Ramón Rodríguez Peña, Subdirector del Depto. del Trabajo, Torreón, Coahuila, March 21, 1913, AGN, F, 7, 21.

53. Evaristo Tenorio to Alvaro Obregón, Cloete, Coahuila, May 19, 1923, AGN, OC, P. 41, L-11, 407-C-22.

54. Cited in Arnaldo Córdova, *La Ideología de la Revolución Mexicana; la Formación del Nuevo Régimen* (Mexico, 1973), p. 235.

55. J. C. Arellano to Francisco I. Madero, Puebla, Puebla, May 31, 1912, AGN, M, 2-7, 1174-2; Luis Domínguez to Venustiano Carranza, Oaxaca, March 27, 1915, Condumex: AVC.

56. Severiano de Hoyos, Minero Mayor, to Venustiano Carranza, Río Escondido, Coahuila, June 25, 1914, Condumex: AVC.

57. Raul Prieto to Pastor Rouaix, Mexico, September 21, 1914, AGN, F, F. 14, 24.

58. General Heriberto Jara to Gerente de la Refinería, Minatitlán, Veracruz, July 10, 1916, AGN, F, 5, 42; T. Llanas, Inspector del Petróleo, to Director de Minas y Petroleo, Minatitlán, Veracruz, July 17, 1916, AGN, F, 5, 42; Subsecretario de Fomento to Gerente de la Cía. Mexicana de Petroleo El Aguila, Mexico, August 11, 1916, AGN, F, 5, 42.

59. Francis J. Dyer, "Prospective Financial Needs of Mexico," Nogales, Sonora, October 21, 1919, Consulate Correspondence, Record Group 84, Records of the Foreign Service Posts of the Department of State, Vol. 277, National Archives, Washington, D.C.

60. Francis J. Dyer to Secretary of State, *ibid.*

61. E. M. Lawson to Secretary of State, Nogales, Sonora, June 25, 1917, *ibid.*

62. *Ibid.*, June 29, 1917.

CHAPTER XVII

1. Juan Sánchez Azcona, *Apuntes para la Historia de la Revolución* (Mexico, 1961), p. 78.

2. "Decreto del Congreso de la Unión, Secretaría de Estado y del Despacho de Fomento, Colonización e Industria," Mexico, December 15, 1911, AGN, F, 1, 4.

3. Departmento del Trabajo, "Convención de Industriales Reunida en México en el mes de julio de 1912, por invitación de la Secretaría de Fomento," Mexico, July 24, 1912, AGN, F, 31, 9.

4. Armando María y Campos, ed., *Las Memorias y las Mejores Cartas de Francisco I Madero* (Mexico, 1956), p. 110; Charles C. Cumberland, *Mexican Revolution, Genesis Under Madero* (Austin, 1952), p. 222.

5. Ministerio de Fomento, "Junta, 20 de enero, 1912," AGN, F, 4, 23.

6. Ramón Eduardo Ruiz, *Labor and the Ambivalent Revolutionaries* (Baltimore and London, 1976), p. 26.

7. Antonio Manero, *El Antiguo Régimen y la Revolución* (Mexico, 1911), p. 384; James D. Cockcroft, *Intellectual Precursors of the Mexican Revolution, 1900–1913* (Austin and London, 1968), p. 49.

8. Jorge Basurto, *El Proletariado Industrial en México (1850–1930)* (Mexico, 1975), p. 159.

9. "Decreto del Congreso de la Unión, Secretaría de Estado y del Despacho de Fomento, Colonización e Industria," Mexico, December 15, 1911, AGN, F, 1, 4; Antonio Ramos Pedrueza to Señor Propietario o Gerente de la Fábrica, Mexico, January 30, 1912, AGN, F, 7, 1.

10. *El Imparcial*, November 20, 1909; Departamento del Trabajo to Sres. José González Soto y Hno., Mexico, July 17, 1912, AGN, F, 8, 11.

11. Cited in Basurto, *Proletariado Industrial*, p. 157.

12. Antonio Ramos Perdueza to Gerente de la Compañía Industrial de Guadalajara, S. A., Mexico, April 19, 1912, AGN, F, 31, 13.

13. Basurto, *Proletariado Industrial*, p. 162.

14. Ruiz, *Ambivalent Revolutionaries*, p. 33.

15. Rafael Hernández, Ministro de Fomento, "Junta de Industriales, 20 de enero de 1912," Mexico, January 20, 1912, AGN, F, 4, 23.

16. Antonio Ramos Pedrueza, "Circular 14," Mexico, August 4, 1912, AGN, F, 7, 1.

17. *Ibid.*

18. Ruiz, *Ambivalent Revolutionaries*, p. 37.

19. Rosendo Salazar, *Las Pugnas de la Gleba*, 2 vols. (Mexico, 1923), I: 80.

20. José Fuentes Mares, *La Revolución Mexicana; Memorias de un Espectador* (Mexico, 1971), p. 78.

21. Basurto, *Proletariado Industrial*, p. 166.

22. Director del Departamento del Trabajo to Secretario de Fomento, Mexico, June 30, 1915, AGN, F, 1, 4; Departamento del Trabajo, "Proyecto de Presupuesto para el Año Fiscal de 1914–1915," Mexico, March 2, 1914, AGN, F, 6, 6.

23. Cited in Basurto, *Proletariado Industrial*, p. 176.

24. Alejandro Iñigo, "Raro Nacimiento, Vida Fecunda," *Excelsior*, September 13, 1970.

25. Ruiz, *Ambivalent Revolutionaries*, p. 53.

26. Departamento del Trabajo, Memorandum, Veracruz, Veracruz, March [no day], 1915, AGN, F, 7, 16.

27. Salazar, *Pugnas*, I, 134.

28. Cited in letter of Plutarco Elías Calles to Adolfo de la Huerta, Mexico, February 1, 1920, Roberto Blanco Moheno, *Crónica de la Revolución Mexicana*, 2 vols. (Mexico, 1958–59), II: 171–172.

29. Basurto, *Proletariado Industrial*, pp. 185 and 187–188.

30. Ruiz, *Ambivalent Revolutionaries*, p. 60.

31. Basurto, *Proletariado Industrial*, p. 192.

32. Salazar, *Pugnas*, I, 46.

33. Marjorie R. Clark, *Organized Labor in Mexico* (Chapel Hill, 1934), p. 69.

34. *Ibid.*, p. 68.

35. John W. F. Dulles, *Yesterday in Mexico; A Chronicle of the Revolution, 1919–1936* (Austin, 1961), p. 281.

36. Comité Ejecutivo de Sindicatos Obreros de la Región Jalapeña to Alvaro Obregón, Jalapa, Veracruz, May 16, 1921, AGN, OC, P.41-1, L-2, 407-F-1.

37. Charles C. Cumberland, *Mexican Revolution: The Constitutionalist Years* (Austin, 1972), p. 390.

38. Moisés González Navarro, *La Confederación Nacional Campesina; Un Grupo de Presión en la Reforma Agraria Mexicana* (Mexico, 1968), p. 81.

39. Basurto, *Proletariado Industrial,* pp. 219 and 222.

40. *Ibid.,* p. 290.

41. *Ibid.,* p. 285.

42. *Ibid.,* p. 197; Dulles, *Yesterday in Mexico,* p. 277.

43. *Ibid.,* pp. 198–200; Robert E. Quirk, *The Mexican Revolution and the Catholic Church, 1910–1929* (Bloomington and London, 1973), p. 43; Memorandum para el C. Presidente de la República, Mexico, April 11, 1922, AGN, OC, P. 41-1, L-3, 407-G-8.

44. Salazar, *Pugnas,* II, 194.

45. Alvaro Obregón to J. C. Rodríguez, Mexico, November 20, 1924, AGN, OC, P-41, L-11, 407-C-32.

46. Alvaro Obregón to Gral. Luis Gutiérrez, Mexico, August 29, 1924, AGN, OC, P-41-1, L-3, 407-H-3.

47. Basurto, *Proletariado Industrial,* pp. 226 and 251.

48. Ruiz, *Ambivalent Revolutionaries,* pp. 86–88.

49. *Ibid.,* pp. 88–90.

50. V. Silva to Alvaro Obregón, Orizaba, Veracruz, October 3, 1924, AGN, OC, P-40-1, L-9, 407-A-22.

51. J. Vásquez Schiaffino to Alvaro Obregón, Mexico, October 8, 1924, *ibid.*

52. *Organized Labor,* p. 186.

53. Basurto, *Proletariado Industrial,* p. 273.

54. *Ibid.,* p. 226.

55. Comité Estudiantil Pro-Paz to Alvaro Obregón, Mexico, March 6, 1924, AGN, OC, P-5, 101-R2-P.

56. Federación Obrera de Hilados y Tejidos del D. F. to Alvaro Obregón, Mexico, August 28, 1921, AGN, OC, P-41-1, L-3, 407-H-2.

57. Aaron Sáenz, *La Política Internacional de la Revolución; Estudios y Documentos* (Mexico, 1961), p. 202.

58. Felipe Hernández to Alvaro Obregón, Mexico, May 12, 1924, AGN, OC, P-4, L-2, 101-R2-C; Jesús E. Mayagoitia to Alvaro Obregón, Mexico, May 9, 1924, AGN, OC, P-4-1, 101-R2-E.

CHAPTER XVIII

1. Virgilio Chanona to Francisco I. Madero, Medellín, Veracruz, March 6, 1912, AGN, M, 3, 78-2.

2. Charles C. Cumberland, *Mexican Revolution: The Constitutionalist Years* (Austin, 1972), p. 235.

3. Jorge Vera Estañol, *Historia de la Revolución Mexicana; Orígenes y Resultados* (Mexico, 1967), p. 246.

4. R. Ochoa to Francisco I. Madero, Chilpancingo, Guerrero, January 18, 1912, AGN, M, 3, 765–1.

5. J. G. Nava to Venustiano Carranza, San Luis Potosí, San Luis Potosí, December 15, 1915, Condumex: AVC.

6. Fernando González Roa, *El Aspecto Agrario de la Revolución* (Mexico, 1919), p. 213.

7. William H. Beezley, *Insurgent Governor: Abraham González and the Mexican Revolution in Chihuahua* (Lincoln, 1973), pp. 61, 98, and 127.

8. A. Gueda and Francisco Durán to Secretario de Fomento, Colonización e Industria, León, Guanajuato, March 8, 1912, AGN, F, 31, 2.

9. Antonio Ramos Pedrueza to Governor of Guanajuato, Mexico, March 14, 1912, AGN, F, 31, 2.

10. Antonio Ramos Pedrueza to A. Gueda, Presidente de la Cámara Agrícola Nacional de León, Mexico, March 18, 1912, AGN, F, 31, 2.

11. Antonio Ramos Pedrueza to Carlos M. Loyola, Mexico, March 16, 1912, AGN, F, 31, 5.

12. Carlos M. Loyola to Antonio Ramos Pedrueza, Querétaro, Querétaro, April 1, 1912, AGN, F, 31, 5.

13. *Un Decenio de Política Mexicana* (New York, 1920), p. 208.

14. *La Reforma Agraria en las Filas Villistas, Años 1913 a 1915 a 1920* (Mexico, 1966), p. 29.

15. *Ibid.*

16. Ricardo Delgado Román, *Aspecto Agrario del Gobierno del General Victoriano Huerta* (Guadalajara, 1951), p. 48; Venustiano Carranza, *Codificacion de los Decretos del C. Venustiano Carranza, Primer Jefe del Ejército Constitucionalista Encargado del Poder Ejecutivo de la Unión* (Mexico, 1915), pp. 29–33.

17. *Observaciones a la Reforma del Articulo de la Ley 6 de Enero de 1915* (Mexico, 1932), p. 7.

18. Quoted in Bernardino Mena Brito, *Maquinismo* (Mexico, 1933), pp. 89–90 and 151–152.

19. Heriberto Barrón, *Some of the Facts and Arguments which led to the Recognition of the First Chief of the Constitutionalist Army in Charge of the Executive Power of the Mexican Republic, Mr. Venustiano Carranza, as the de facto government in Mexico* ([n. p.], 1915), pp. 18–19.

20. General Pedro Ruíz Molina, General S. Cedillo, General M. Cedillo, "Manifiesto a la Nación," Ciudad del Maíz, San Luis Potosí, August 16, 1916, Condumex: AVC.

21. J. Treviño, Jefe del Estado Mayor, Cuartel General, Piedras Negras, Coahuila, May 19, 1913, Condumex: AVC.

22. General Nicolás Flores to Venustiano Carranza, Pachuca, Hidalgo, September 5, 1914, Condumex: AVC.

23. Colonel Preciliano Ruíz to Mariano D. Urdanivia, Puebla, Puebla, May 3, 1915, Condumex: AVC.

24. Gobernador y Comandante Militar de Chiapas, B. Corral, to Venustiano Carranza, Tuxtla Gutiérrez, Chiapas, June 15, 1915, Condumex: AVC.

25. A. M. Machorro to Venustiano Carranza, Chiantempan, Tlaxcala, May 6, 1916, Condumex: AVC.

26. Gobernador de Hidalgo to Venustiano Carranza, Pachuca, Hidalgo, June 21, 1916, Condumex: AVC.

27. Jefatura de Hacienda de Hidalgo to Venustiano Carranza, Pachuca, Hidalgo, May 25, 1916, Condumex: AVC.

28. Adolfo de la Huerta to Venustiano Carranza, Hermosillo, Sonora, June 5, 1916, Condumex: AVC.

29. Pascual Ortiz Rubio to Venustiano Carranza, Mexico, June 23, 1916, Condumex: AVC.

30. Marte R. Gómez cited in Aarón Saénz, *La Política Internacional de la Revolución; Estudios y Documentos* (Mexico, 1961), p. 115.

31. Robert E. Quirk, *The Mexican Revolution and the Catholic Church, 1900–1929* (Bloomington and London, 1973), p. 103.

32. Jesús Silva Herzog, *El Agrarismo Mexicano y la Reforma Agraria; Exposición y Crítica* (Mexico, 1959), pp. 277–278.

33. General Pablo González to Venustiano Carranza, Cuautla, Morelos, April 8, 1919, Condumex: AVC.

34. *Diario de los Debates del Congreso Constituyente, 1916–1917*, 2 vols. (Mexico, 1960), II: 1113.

35. González Roa, *El Aspecto Agrario*, p. 241.

36. Gómez, *La Reforma Agraria*, p. 129.

37. Venustiano Carranza to Andrés Ortiz, Gobernador de Chihuahua, Querétaro, Querétaro, October 20, 1919, Condumex: AVC.

38. González Roa, *El Aspecto Agrario*, p. 241.

39. *Economía y Política en la Historia de México* (Mexico, 1965), p. 370.

40. Marte R. Gómez cited in Sáenz, *La Political Internacional*, pp. 114–115.

41. González Roa, *El Aspecto Agrario*, p. 241.

42. Cumberland, *Mexican Revolution*, p. 385.

43. Quoted in Mena Brito, *Maquinismo*, p. 92.

44. "El C. General Vicente Dávila, Gobernador y Commandante Militar del Estado Libre y Soberano de San Luis Potosí, a sus habitantes, sabed:" San Luis Potosí, San Luis Potosí, November 19, 1915, Condumex: AVC.

45. Francisco León de la Barra to Rodolfo Reyes, Paris, France, July 6, 1920, Condumex: DLB.

46. Calero, *Un Decenio*, p. 174.

47. Emiliano Zapata to General Jenaro Amezcua, Tlatizapan, Morelos, December 15, 1918, Condumex: JA.

48. *La Traición de Carranza* (New York, 1920), p. 6.

49. Antenor Sala to Alvaro Obregón, Mexico, June 28, 1919, Condumex: AVC.

50. Quoted in Romandía Ferreira, "Obregón, Factor Determinante para la Ejecución de la Reforma Agraria, Principio Básico de la Revolución Mexicana," Editorial Cultura, ed., *Obregón, Aspectos de Su Vida* (Mexico, 1935), p. 103.

51. Antonio Díaz Soto y Gama to Jenaro Amezcua, Campamento Revolucionario en el Estado de Morelos, June 23, 1919, Condumex: JA.

52. Hector Aguilar Camín, "La Revolución Sonorense, 1910–1914" (Ph.D. diss., Instituto Nacional de Antropología e Historia, Mexico, 1975), pp. 348, 424, and 431–433.

53. Quoted in Narciso Bassols Batalla, *El Pensamiento Político de Obregón* (Mexico, 1967), pp. 42–43, 47, and 137.

54. *Ibid.*, pp. 45–46 and 133; Alvaro Obregón to Roque Estrada, December 19, 1919, cited in *ibid.*, p. 138.

55. Alvaro Obregón, *Campaña Política del C. Alvaro Obregón Candidato a la Presidencia de la República, 1920–1924*, 5 vols. (Mexico, 1923), I: 398.

56. *Ibid.*

57. Obregón to Roque Estrada, December 19, 1919, cited in Bassols Batalla, *Pensamiento Político*, p. 138.

58. Alvaro Obregón, *The Agrarian Problem* (Mexico, 1924), p. 6.

59. Bassols Batalla, *Pensamiento Político*, pp. 49–51.

60. Obregón, *Agrarian Problem*, p. 13.

61. Bassols Batalla, *Pensamiento Político*, p. 44.

62. *Ibid.*, p. 48.

63. Silva Herzog, *El Agrarismo*, p. 278.

64. *Ibid.*, p. 281.

65. *Ibid.*, p. 283.

66. Alvaro Obregón to Alberto Terrones B., Urbano Luna y Fortino H. Aragón, Mexico, [n. d.], AGN, OC, P 106, L-6, 818-E-28 (2).

67. Felipe Carrillo Puerto to Alvaro Obregón, Mérida, Yucatan, May 18, 1922, AGN, OC, P 106, L-6, 818-E-28.

68. Silva Herzog, *El Agrarismo*, pp. 285–287.

69. Alvaro Obregón to Alberto Terrones B., Urbano Luna y Fortino H. Aragón, Mexico [n. d.], AGN, OC, P 106, L-6, 818-E28 (2).

70. Miguel Mendoza López Schwertfeger, "Circular," November 16, 1922, AGN, OC, P 104, L-5, 818-A-56.

71. *Ibid.*

72. A. Molina Enríquez, "Cuales Pueblos Tienen Derecho a Ejidos; al Sr. Lic. Don Miguel Mendoza López, en Particular y al Partido Nacional Agrarista en General," AGN, OC, P 106, L-6, 818-E-28 (2).

73. J. A. Castro to Alvaro Obregón, Durango, Durango, December 1, 1922, AGN, OC, P 104, L-5, 818-A-56; Alvaro Obregón to J. A. Castro, Mexico, December 7, 1922, AGN, OC, P 104, L-5, 818-A-56.

74. Alvaro Obregón to General P. Rodríguez, Mexico, December 5, 1922, AGN, OC, P 104, L-5, 818-A-56.

75. Alvaro Obregón to Ramón P. DeNegri, Mexico, December 16, 1922, AGN, OC, P 104, L-5, 818-A-56.

76. Juan Torres S. to Alvaro Obregón, Durango, Durango, December 13, 1922, AGN, OC, P 104, L-5, 818-A-56; Alvaro Obregón to Secretario de Agricultura y Fomento, Mexico, December 29, 1922, AGN, OC, P 104, L-5, 818-A-5.

77. Comité Particular Administrativo de Pedriceña, Durango, to Alvaro Obregón, Pedriceña, Durango, December 8, 1922, AGN, OC, P 104, L-5, 818-A-56; B. O. Villa. Procurador de Pueblos, to Alvaro Obregón, Iguala, Guerrero, December 25, 1922, AGN, OC, P 104, L-5, 818-A-56.

78. J. A. Castro to Alvaro Obregón, Durango, Durango, December 27, 1922, AGN, OC, P 105, L-5, 818-A-56.

79. Alvaro Obregón to Roque Estrada, December 19, 1919, cited in Bassols Batalla, *Pensamiento Político,* p. 45.

80. Cámara Agrícola Nacional de la Comarca Lagunera to Alvaro Obregón, Torreón, Coahuila, December 6, 1923, AGN, OC, P 106, L-7, 818-E-51.

81. Pedro Franco Ugarte y Julio Luján to Alvaro Obregón, Mexico [n.d.], AGN, OC, P 106, L-7, 818-E-51.

82. Alvaro Obregón to R. P. DeNegri, Mexico, April 14 and 29, 1924, AGN, OC, P 106, L-7, 818-E-51; Alvaro Obregón to E. M. Flores, Inspector del Trabajo, Mexico, April 14, 1924, AGN, OC, P 106, L-7, 818-E-51.

83. J. M. Huitrón to Alvaro Obregón, Torreón, Coahuila, April 29, 1924, AGN, OC, P 106, L-7, 818-E-51.

84. Cámara Nacional de Comarca Lagunera to Alvaro Obregón, Torreón, Coahuila, April 23, 1924, AGN, OC, P 106, L-7, 818-E-51.

85. Silviano Sandoval to Alvaro Obregón, Aljojuca, Chalchicomula, Puebla, April 4, 1922, AGN, OC, P 104, L-5, 818-A-1.

86. Bonifacio López, Jesús Zepeda y Luis Peña to Alvaro Obregón, Mexico, April 7, 1922, AGN, OC, P 104, L-5, 818-A-44; Alvaro Obregón

to Bonifacio López, Jesús Zepeda y Luis Peña, Mexico, April 5, 1922, AGN, OC, P 104, L-5, 818-A-44.

87. Alvaro Obregón to Alberto Terrones B., Urbano Luna y Fortino H. Aragón, Mexico, [n.d.], AGN, OC, P 106, L-6, 818-E-28(2).

88. Antonio Díaz Soto y Gama to Alvaro Obregón, Mexico, October 28, 1921, AGN, OC, P 106, L-6, 818-E-28.

89. Fernando Torreblanca to Miguel G. Calderón y O. M. Santibáñez, Mexico, June 14, 1923, AGN, OC, P 104, L-7, 818-A-87.

90. E. Paredes to Alvaro Obregón, Mexico, June 20, 1924, AGN, OC, P 104, L-7. 818-A-114; Alvaro Obregón to E. Paredes, Mexico, June 21, 1924, AGN, OC, P 104, L-7, 818-A-114.

91. Alvaro Obregón to R. Sánchez Albarrán, Mexico, August 8, 1924, AGN, OC, P 104, 818-A-114.

92. Gobernador de Oaxaca to Alvaro Obregón. Oaxaca, Oaxaca, August 9, 1924, AGN, OC, P 104, L-7, 818-A-114.

93. Ramón Sánchez Albarrán to Alvaro Obregón, Mexico, August 14, 1924, AGN, OC, P 104, L-7, 818-A-114.

94. N. Galván to Plutarco Elías Calles, Jalapa, Veracruz, June 3, 1925, AGN, OC, P 104, L-7, 818-A-114.

95. "Bien por el Heroe de Trinidad," *La Voz de Zacatecas*, August 16, 1924.

96. Alvaro Obregón, *Ocho Mil Kilómetros en Campaña* (Mexico, 1917), p. 721.

97. Barry Carr, "The Peculiarities of the Mexican North, 1880–1928: An Essay in Interpretation," Institute of Latin American Studies, University of Glasgow, *Occasional Papers*, IV (Glasgow, 1971): 16–17.

CHAPTER XIX

1. Narciso Bassols Batalla, *El Pensamiento Político de Obregón* (Mexico, 1967), pp. 50–51 and 184.

2. Eyler Simpson, "El Ejido: Unica Salida para México," *Problemas Agrícolas e Industriales de México* (Mexico, 1952), IV: 54.

3. Quoted in Bassols Batalla, *Pensamiento Político*, p. 184.

4. *Diario de los Debates del Congreso Constituyente, 1916–1917*, 2 vols. (Mexico, 1960), II: 1183.

5. José G. Parres, "Informe de la Visita de Inspección Practicada a las Oficinas Dependientes de la Comisión Nacional Agraria en la Ciudad de Toluca, Edo. de México," Mexico, October 15, 1924, AGN, OC, P 106, L-6, 818-E-28(2).

6. Gustavo A. Vicencio, Presidente de la Suprema Corte de Justicia, to Alvaro Obregón, Mexico, June 30, 1922, AGN, OC, P 106, L-6, I-E-28.

7. Alvaro Obregón to Gustavo A. Vicencio, Mexico, July 10, 1922, AGN, OC, P 106, L-6, 818-E-28.

8. Carlos M. Peralta to Alvaro Obregón, Chihuahua, Chihuahua, July 25, 1923, AGN, OC, P-81, L-3, 806-T-1.

9. Presidente de la Comisión Local Agraria to Gobernador del Estado, Chihuahua, Chihuahua, October 8, 1921, AGN, OC, P 104, L-5, 818-A-3.

10. Vecinos del Pueblo El Bosque de Aldama to Alvaro Obregón, Aldama, Chihuahua, August 27, 1922, AGN, OC, P 104, L-5, 818-A-3; Ramón P. DeNegri to Alvaro Obregón, Mexico, September 15, 1922, AGN, OC, P 104, L-5, 818-A-3.

11. Francisco Villa to Alvaro Obregón, Parral, Chihuahua, August 31, 1922, AGN, OC, P 104, L-5, 818-A-3.

12. Alvaro Obregón to Francisco Villa, Mexico, September 11, 1922, AGN, OC, P 104, L-5, 818-A-3.

13. Fernando Torreblanca to Secretario de Agricultura y Fomento, Mexico, September 22, 1921, AGN, OC, P 104, L-5, 818-A-3; Martín Falomir to Francisco Bay, Mexico, September 21, 1921, AGN, OC, P 104, L-5, 818-A-16.

14. Alvaro Obregón, "Acuerdo," Mexico, November 23, 1922, AGN, OC, P 104, L-5, 818-A-3.

15. Eduardo Garduño Soto to Alvaro Obregón, Ciudad Juárez, Chihuahua, May 8, 1923, AGN, OC, P 104, L-5, 818-A-3.

16. Toribio Morales to Alvaro Obregón, Chihuahua, Chihuahua, November 20, 1924, AGN, OC, P 104, L-5, 818-A-3.

17. Andrés Molina Enríquez, "La Creación de Nuevas Poblaciones," Mexico, [n.d.], 1924, AGN, OC, P 106, L-6, 818-E-28(2).

18. L. de Palacios to Francisco León de la Barra, New York, New York, February 8, 1921, Condumex: LDB.

19. Ramón P. DeNegri to Alvaro Obregón, Mexico, February 29, 1924, AGN, OC, P 106, L-7, 818-E-51.

20. Cámara Nacional de Comercio, Industria y Minería del Estado de Nuevo León, Monterrey, Nuevo León, January 7, 1922, AGN, OC, P 106, L-6, 818-E-28.

21. Guillermo Pous to Alvaro Obregón, Mexico, October 6, 1921, AGN, OC, P 106, L-6, 818-E-28.

22. Ramón Sánchez Albarrán to Alvaro Obregón, Mexico, August 14, 1924, AGN, OC, P 104, L-7, 818-A-114.

23. Andrés Molina Enríquez to Plutarco Elías Calles, Mexico, December 30, 1924, AGN, OC, P 106, L-6, 818-E-28(2); Andrés Molina Enríquez, "El Verdadero Objeto de los Ejidos," Mexico, October [n.d.], 1924, AGN, OC, P 106, L-6, 818-E-28(2); Andrés Molina Enríquez to Secretario de Agricultura y Fomento, Mexico, December 4, 1924,

AGN, OC, P 106, L-6, 818-E-28(2); Confederación Nacional Agraria to Alvaro Obregón, Mexico, August [n.d.], 1924, AGN, OC, P 106, L-6, 818-E-28(2); César Córdova to Alvaro Obregón, Mexico, December 27, 1921, AGN, OC, P 106, L-6, 818-E-28; Andrés Molina Enríquez, "La Mejor Forma de los Contratos," Mexico [n.d.], AGN, OC, P 106, L-6, 818-E-28(2); Confederación Nacional Agraria, "A los Sindicatos de Agricultores o sea de Latifundistas," Mexico, [n.d.], 1924, AGN, OC, P 106, L-6, 818-E-28(2).

24. Andrés Molina Enríquez, "La Mejor Forma de las Contratos," Mexico [n.d.], AGN, OC, P 106, L-6, 818-E-28(2).

25. Andrés Molina Enríquez, "El Verdadero Objeto de los Ejidos," Mexico, October [n.d.], 1924, AGN, OC, P 106, L-6, 818-E-28(2).

26. M. Mendoza L. Schwertfeger to Alvaro Obregón, Mexico, May 30, 1923, AGN, OC, P 104, L-5, 818-A-56.

27. Manuel Vargas, Gerente de la Caja de Préstamos Para Obras de Irrigación y Fomento de la Agricultura, S.A., to Alvaro Obregón, Mexico, July 13, 1923, AGN, OC, P-81. L-3, 806-T-1; Caja de Préstamos to Fernando Torreblanca, Mexico, November 18, 1926, AGN, OC, P 81, L-3, 806-T-1.

28. Abelardo Rodríguez, AGN, P 122, 552.14/1280, Extracto, Ramón Vargas Flores, Jefe Depto. Agrario del Comité Estado., Chihuahua, Chiahuahua, June 5, 1934, AGN, OC.

29. Colonos de Nueva Delicias to Plutarco Elías Calles, Chihuahua, Chiahuahua, November 16, 1925, AGN, OC, P-81, L-3, 806-T-1.

30. Ignacio C. Enríquez to Alvaro Obregón, Chihuahua, Chihuahua, January 25, 1923, AGN, OC, P-81, L-3, 806-T-1.

31. Ramón Camacho to Señor Gerente de la Caja de Préstamos, Santiago Ixcuintla, Nayarit, September 27, 1922, AGN, OC, P 106, L-5, 818-E-26.

32. Justino Bermúdez y Cortés, *Verdades—No Adulación; Callismo y Obregonismo Revolucionarios* (Mexico, 1935), p. 197; Manuel Medina to Alvaro Obregón, Aguascalientes, Aguascalientes, October 30, 1921, AGN, OC, P 106, L-6, 818-E-28; Apolonio González y demás to Alvaro Obregón, Guadalajara, Jalisco, November 29, 1921, AGN, OC, P 106, L-6, 818-E-28; Rubén Ortiz, "El Problema Agrario Mexicano," Puebla, Puebla, December 4, 1921, AGN, OC, P 106, L-6, 818-E-28; Jesús Agustín Castro to Ramón P. DeNegri, Mexico, April 29, 1922, AGN, OC, P 16-1, L-12, 104-A-D-1; General Fausto Ruíz to Alvaro Obregón, Tuxtla Gutiérrez, Chiapas, November 8, 1922, AGN, OC, P-2-1, L-18, 101-R-5; F. C. Manjárrez, to Alvaro Obregón, Puebla, Puebla, September 11, 1923, AGN, OC, P 104, L-5, 818-A-30; General Luis F. Mireles to Alvaro Obregón, Tepic Nayarit, AGN, OC, P-2, L-15, 101-N-4.

33. Quoted in "Se ha Formado una Liga entre Gobernadores," *El Sol,* December 17, 1922.

34. Partido Agrarista y Cooperatista Chihuahuense to Alvaro Obregón, Chihuahua, Chihuahua, October 12, 1922, AGN, OC, P-81, L-3, 806-T-1; Casa del Obrero to Alvaro Obregón, Chihuahua, Chihuahua, January 29, 1923, AGN, OC, P-81, L-3, 806-T-1.

35. Ramón P. DeNegri to Alvaro Obregón, Mexico, September 26, 1923, AGN, OC, P 106, L-7, 818-E-48.

36. Parres, "Informe de la Visita de Inspección. . . ," Mexico, October 15, 1924, AGN, OC, P 106, L-6, 818-E-28(2).

37. *Ibid.*

38. *Ibid.*

39. El Pueblo de Uriangato to Alvaro Obregón, Uriangato, Guanajuato, November 21, 1923, AGN, OC, P 106, L-5, 818-E-13.

40. José A. Aguilera to Alvaro Obregón, Mexico, March 27, 1924, AGN, OC, P 106, L-5, 818-E-13.

41. M. Mendoza L. Schwertfeger to Alvaro Obregón, Mexico, November 10, 1924, AGN, OC, P 106, L-5, 818-E-13.

42. "Relación de los Expedientes Tramitados y Aprobados por la Comisión Agraria Local en el Estado de Guanajuato, con Expresión de sus Fechas," Guanajuato, Guanajuato, [September, 1924?], AGN, OC, P 106, L-5, 818-E-13.

43. Departamento Agrario, *Memoria de Labores, 1946* (Mexico, 1946).

44. *Ibid.*

45. General Antonio I. Villarreal, "A los Campesinos," Veracruz, Veracruz, January 20, 1924, AGN, OC.

46. John Womack, *Zapata and the Mexican Revolution* (New York, 1970), p. 373.

47. Eleuterio Avila, "Decreto Número 4," Mérida, Yucatan, September 11, 1914, AGN, F, 11, 3.

48. Senador Antonio Ancona Albertos to Alvaro Obregón, Mexico, September 3, 1924, AGN, OC, P 17-1, L-5, 121-D3-C.

49. Manuel López Gallo, *Economía y Política en la Historia de México* (Mexico, 1965), p. 388.

50. Arnaldo Córdova, *La Ideología de la Revolución Mexicana; La Formación del Nuevo Régimen* (Mexico, 1973), p. 211.

51. Edmundo Bolio, *Yucatán en la Dictadura y la Revolución* (Mexico, 1967), pp. 108–109.

52. N. Galván to Plutarco Elías Calles, Jalapa, Veracruz, June 3, 1925, AGN, OC, P 104, L-7, 818-A-114.

53. Comité Estudiantil Pro-Paz to Alvaro Obregón, Mexico, March 6, 1924, AGN, OC, P 5, 101-R2-P.

54. "Contract of Option of Promise of Sale Executed by Alberto Terrazas, Arthur J. McQuatters, Mexican International Corporation and McQuatters Corporation," New York, New York, April 16, 1920, AGN, OC, P 81, L-3, 806-T-1.

55. Roberto V. Pesqueira, "Memorandum para el C. Presidente de la República. Asunto: Terrazas," Mexico, May 11, 1922, AGN, OC, P 81, L-3, 806-T-1.

56. *Ibid.;* "Contrato Celebrado entre los Señores General Don Ignacio C. Enríquez, Gobernador Constitucional del Estado de Chihuahua y Arthur J. McQuatters, para la Adquisición, Estudio, Clasificación, Mejora, Subdivisión y Venta al Público de Terrenos en el Estado de Chihuahua," Chihuahua, February 4, 1922, AGN, OC, P 81, L-3, 806-T-1.

57. Philip Kinsley, "Mexico—Land of Promise; That's All, Promises," *Chicago Daily Tribune,* April 4, 1922; Domingo Gallegos Medina to Alvaro Obregón, Ciudad Camargo, Chihuahua, May 1, 1922, AGN, OC, P 81, L-3, 806-T-1.

58. General Plutarco Elías Calles to Alvaro Obregón, Mexico, March 14, 1922, AGN, OC, P 81, L-3, 806-T-1.

59. Federación de Obreros y Campesinos del Estado de Chihuahua to Alvaro Obregón, Chihuahua, Chihuahua, March 1, 1922, AGN, OC, P 81, L-3, 806-T-1.

60. Srío. Jesús C. Hinojosa y Presidente Carlos López to Alvaro Obregón, Parral, Chihuahua, March 5, 1922, AGN, OC, P 81, L-3, 806-T-1; Sociedad de Obreros "Miguel Hidalgo" y Unión de Panaderos "Ignacio Zaragoza" to Alvaro Obregón, Parral, Chihuahua, March 23, 1922, AGN, OC, P 81, L-3, 806-T-1.

61. I. C. Enríquez to Alvaro Obregón, Chihuahua, Chihuahua, March 3, 1922, AGN, OC, P 81, L-3, 806-T-1.

62. Alvaro Obregón to General I. C. Enríquez, Mexico, March 6, 1922, AGN, OC, P 81, L-3, 806-T-1.

63. Francisco Villa to Alvaro Obregón, Canutillo, Durango, March 12, 1922, AGN, OC, P 81, L-3, 806-T-1.

64. Alvaro Obregón to General Francisco Villa, Mexico, March 17, 1922, AGN, OC, P 81, L-3, 806-T-1.

65. Secretaría de Gobernación, "Dictamen Sobre el Contrato entre los Señores General Don Ignacio C. Enríquez, Gobernador Constitucional de Chihuahua, y Arthur J. McQuatters, para la Adquisición, Estudio, Clasificación, Mejora, Subdivisión y Venta al Público de Terrenos en el Estado de Chihuahua," Mexico, March 28, 1922, AGN, OC, P 81, L-3, 806-T-1.

66. Arthur J. McQuatters to Alvaro Obregón, El Paso, Texas, February 9, 1922, AGN, OC, P 81, L-3, 806-T-1.

67. A. J. McQuatters and Associates to Alvaro Obregón, New York, New York, March 31, 1922, AGN, OC, P 81, L-3, 806-T-1.

68. I. C. Enríquez to Alvaro Obregón, Chihuahua, Chihuahua, March 3, 1922, AGN, OC, P 81, L-3, 806-T-1.

69. "Obregón Memorandum," Mexico [n.d.], AGN, OC, P 81, L-3, 806-T-1.

70. Alvaro Obregón to Manuel Vargas, Mexico, May 13, 1922, AGN, OC, P 81, L-3, 806-T-1.

71. Manuel Vargas, "Informe para el Señor Presidente de la República Sobre las Negociaciones Llevadas a Cabo con el Señor Don Alberto Terrazas para la Compara de las Propiedades de la Familia Terrazas, en el Estado de Chihuahua," Mexico, May 23, 1922, AGN, OC, P 81, L-3, 806-T-1.

72. Alvaro Obregón to Manuel Vargas, Mexico, May 30, 1922, AGN, OC, P-81, L-3, 806-T-1; Alberto Terrazas to Alvaro Obregón, Chihuahua, Chihuahua, February 26, 1923, AGN, OC, P 81, L-3, 806-T-1.

73. Ignacio C. Enríquez to Alvaro Obregón, Chihuahua, Chihuahua, June 21, 1922, AGN, OC, P 81, L-3, 806-T-1.

CHAPTER XX

1. Francisco de A. Guerrero to Venustiano Carranza, Mexico, October [n. d.], 1916, Condumex: AVC.

2. *La Confederación Nacional Campesina; Un Grupo de Presión en la Reforma Agraria Mexicana* (Mexico, 1968), p. 73; *Diario de los Debates del Congreso Constituyente, 1916–1917*, 2 vols. (Mexico, 1960), II: 1081.

3. *Ideología de la Revolución Mexicana; la Formación del Nuevo Régimen* (Mexico, 1973), p. 262.

4. *Diario de los Debates*, II: 1084.

5. José Ives Limantour, *Apuntes Sobre, Mi Vida Pública* (Mexico, 1965), p. 261.

6. Francisco León de la Barra, "Informe al Congreso," Mexico, September [n. d.] 1911, Condumex: LDB.

7. Secretaría de Fomento, "Proyecto de Exposición de Motivos para Ley Sobre Accidentes en el Trabajo," Mexico, [n. d.], 1913, AGN, F, 14, 18; Librería General, ed., *De Como Vino Huerta y Como se Fúe; Apuntes para la Historia de un Régimen Militar* (Mexico, 1914), p. 30.

8. Simón Beltrán to Emiliano Zapata, Cuervanaca, Morelos, March 24, 1913, Condumex: JA; "Proposiciones del Presidente Usurpador al

General Emiliano Zapata, por conducta del Coronel Pascual Orozco, Sr.," March [n. d.], 1913, Condumex: JA.

9. Francisco Bulnes, *The Whole Truth About Mexico; President Wilson's Responsibility* (New York, 1916), p. 232.

10. González Navarro, *Confederación Nacional Campesina,* p. 63.

11. *Ibid.,* p. 65.

12. Marte R. Gómez, *La Reforma Agraria en las Filas Villistas, Años 1913 a 1915 a 1920* (Mexico, 1966), p. 54.

13. Córdova, *Ideología de la Revolución Mexicana,* p. 167.

14. Gómez, *La Reforma Agraria,* pp. 55–56.

15. *Ibid.,* pp. 94–95.

16. I. C. Enríquez, "El Sistema Ejidal, en Juicio," *Excelsior,* February 9, 1971.

17. Félix F. Palavicini, *Historia de la Constitución de 1917,* 2 vols. (Mexico, 1917), I: 17; Charles C. Cumberland, *Mexican Revolution: The Constitutionalist Years* (Austin, 1972), pp. 232–233.

18. González Navarro, *Confederación Nacional Campesina,* p. 70.

19. Quoted in *Diario de los Debates,* II: 1084.

20. "Ley de 6 de Enero de 1915 que Declara Nulas Todas las Enajenaciones de Tierras, Aguas y Montes Pertenecientes a los Pueblos Otorgadas en Contravención a lo Dispuesto en la Ley de 25 de Junio de 1856," Jesús Silva Herzog, *Breve Historia de la Revolución Mexicana,* 2 vols. (Mexico, 1965), II: 171.

21. *Ibid.,* pp. 172–173.

22. Cumberland, *Mexican Revolution,* pp. 233–234; M. S. Alperovich and B. T. Rudenko, *La Revolución Mexicana de 1910–1917 y la Política de los Estados Unidos* (Mexico, 1960), p. 223; Córdova, *Ideología de la Revolución Mexicana,* p. 203.

23. "Memorandum para el Señor Ministro de España," Mexico, October 10, 1921, AGN, OC, P 106, L-6, 818-E-28.

24. Jorge Carpizo, *La Constitución Mexicana de 1917* (Mexico, 1969), p. 133.

25. *Ibid.,* p. 131.

26. González Navarro, *Confederación Nacional Campesina,* p. 68; Moisés González Navarro, "Social Aspects of the Mexican Revolution," *Journal of World History* VIII (1964): 286.

27. Juan de Dios Bojórquez quoted in *Diario de los Debates,* II: 1085.

28. Venustiano Carranza, "Manifiesto a la Nación," Mexico, June 11, 1915, Condumex: AVC.

29. *Diario de los Debates,* II: 391 and 508.

30. Carpizo, *Constitución Mexicana,* p. 130.

31. Córdoba, *Ideología de la Revolución Mexicana,* pp. 27 and 33.

32. *Ibid.,* p. 24; *Diario de las Debates,* II: 1071.

33. Pastor Rouaix, *Génesis de los Artículos 27 y 123 de la Constitución Política de 1917* (Mexico, 1959), p. 154.

34. Córdova, *Ideología de la Revolución Mexicana,* p. 225.

35. *Diario de los Debates,* II: 1186; Cumberland, *Mexican Revolution,* p. 240.

36. *Diario de los Debates,* II: 1087.

37. *Ibid.,* p. 1186; Córdova, *Ideología de la Revolución Mexicana,* p. 229.

38. *Diario de los Debates,* II: 1072 and 1074–1075.

39. *El Aspecto Agrario de la Revolución* (Mexico, 1919), p. 383.

40. *Diario de los Debates,* II: 1075.

41. *Ibid.,* pp. 1071 and 1073.

42. Silva Herzog, *Breve Historia,* II: 279.

43. Córdova, *Ideología de la Revolución Mexicana,* p. 224; Rosendo Salazar, *Las Pugnas de la Gleba,* 2 vols. (Mexico, 1923), I: 225.

44. Andrés Molina Enríquez to Alvaro Obregón, Mexico, December 27, 1921, AGN, OC, P 106, L-6, 818-E-28.

45. (Mexico, 1909), p. 63.

46. Andrés Molina Enríquez cited in Córdova, *Ideología de la Revolución Mexicana,* pp. 133–134; Andrés Molina Enríquez, *Los Grandes Problemas Nacionales* (Mexico, 1909), p. 107.

47. Gómez, *La Reforma Agraria,* p. 75.

48. Andrés Molina Enríquez to Plutarco Elías Calles, Mexico, December 30, 1924, AGN, OC, P 106, L-6, 818-E-28(2).

49. *Ibid.*

50. Andrés Molina Enríquez to Alvaro Obregón, December 27, 1921, AGN, OC, P 106, L-6, 818-E-28.

51. Andrés Molina Enríquez to Plutarco Elías Calles, Mexico, December 30, 1924, AGN, OC P 106, L-6, 818-E-28(2).

52. Confederación Nacional Agraria to Señor Presidente, Mexico, August [n. d.], 1924, AGN, OC, P 106, L-6, 818-E-28(2).

53. Andrés Molina Enríquez to Plutarco Elías Calles, Mexico, December 30, 1924, AGN, OC, P 106, L-6, 818-E-28(2).

54. Andrés Molina Enríquez, "El Verdadero Objeto de los Ejidos," Mexico, October [n. d.], 1924, AGN, OC, P 106, L-6, 818-E-28(2).

55. *Ibid.*

56. Opinion of Eduardo Hay, *Diario de los Debates,* II: 991.

57. Ramón Eduardo Ruiz, *Labor and the Ambivalent Revolutionaries; Mexico, 1911–1923* (Baltimore and London, 1976), p. 63.

58. Edmundo Bolio, *Yucatán en la Dictadura y la Revolución* (Mexico, 1967), p. 141.

59. Ruiz, *Ambivalent Revolutionaries,* pp. 63–64.

60. José Santos Chocano, *El Conflicto Personal de la Revolución Mexicana. Examen de Todo Lo Que Ha Dicho el Ciudadano Carranza* (El Paso, and New Orleans, 1914), pp. 8–9.

61. Ruiz, *Ambivalent Revolutionaries,* pp. 67–68.

62. *Diario de los Debates,* II: 1213–1216.

63. Córdova, *Ideología de la Revolución Mexicana,* p. 234.

64. Ruiz, *Ambivalent Revolutionaries,* p. 69.

65. Professor Carlos Arias, "Proyecto de Reivindicación de Analfabetos," Aguascalientes, Aguascalientes, January 18, 1916. Condumex: AVC.

66. General Recios Zertuche, "Una Verdadera Administración tiene por Consecuencia Ineludible el Progreso de la República Mexicana," Querétaro, Querétaro, March 24, 1916, Condumex: AVC.

67. "Mexicanicemos al Indio," *La Tribuna,* April 7, 1914, AGN, F, 31, 23.

68. Ramón Eduardo Ruiz, *Mexico, the Challenge of Poverty and Illiteracy* (San Marino, 1963), p. 13.

69. Gregorio Torres Quintero, *La Instrucción Rudimentaria en la República* (Mexico, 1913), pp. 2–3.

70. Alberto J. Pani, *Mi Contribución al Nuevo Regimen* (Mexico, 1936), pp. 64–73.

71. Librería, *De Como Vino Huerta,* p. 232.

72. "Informe Leído por el C. Presidente de la República al Abrirse el Segundo Período de Sesiones del 27⁰ Congreso de la Unión," Mexico, September 16, 1913, Condumex: MG.

73. *Diario de los Debates,* II: 626.

74. Félix F. Palavicini, *Mi Vida Revolucionaria* (Mexico, 1937), p. 164.

75. Letter to Venustiano Carranza, Tampico, Tamaulipas, December 25, 1914, Condumex: AVC.

76. Palavicini, *Mi Vida,* p. 167.

77. Ramón Prida, *De la Dictaduro a la Anarquía; Apuntes para la Historia Política de Mexico Durante los Ultimos Cuarenta y Tres Años (1871–1913)* (Mexico, 1958), p. 208.

78. José Manuel Ramos to Francisco I. Madero, Colima, Colima, June 3, 1912, AGN, M, 18, 1389.

79. Palavicini, *Mi Vida,* p. 330.

80. *Ibid.,* pp. 162 and 215; *Diario de los Debates,* II: 629–634.

81. *Diario de los Debates,* II: 1181–1182.

82. Pani, *Mi Contribución,* p. 112.

83. *Diario de los Debates,* II: 1200.

84. Robert E. Quirk, *The Mexican Revolution and the Catholic Church, 1910–1929* (Bloomington and London, 1973), p. 92.

85. *Ibid.,* p. 103.

86. Jorge Vera Estañol, *Historia de la Revolución Mexicana; Orígenes y Resultados* (Mexico, 1967), p. 528.

87. Ruiz, *Challenge of Poverty,* p. 33.

88. *Ibid.,* p. 40.

89. M. Morfín, Presidente de la Escuela Normal de México, "Manifiesto a la Nación y al Profesorado de la República," Milpa Alta, Distrito Federal, December 22, 1924, AGN, OC, P 18, L-9, 121-E-M.

CHAPTER XXI

1. Un Amigo Anónimo to Venustiano Carranza, Mexico, October 26, 1914, Condumex: AVC.

2. General Cándido Aguilar to General Agustín Millán, Mexico, May 13, 1916, Condumex: AVC.

3. Francisco J. Navarro to Francisco I. Madero, Monterrey, Nuevo León, March 13, 1912, AGN, M, 2-7, 1183.

4. Luis Cabrera to Alvaro Obregón, Mexico, March 14, 1919, AGN, OC, P 6-1, L-1, 103-C-31.

5. Bernardo L. Ríos, "La Empleomanía," *El Regenerador,* July 1915.

6. Ignacio Rosaldo to Venustiano Carranza, Ixhuatlán, Veracruz, January 16, 1915, Condumex: AVC.

7. José Ives Limantour, *Apuntes Sobre Mi Vida Pública* (Mexico, 1965), p. 281.

8. *Ibid.,* p. 231.

9. Francisco Bulnes, *The Whole Truth About Mexico; President Wilson's Responsibility* (New York, 1916), pp. 159–160.

10. Félix F. Palavicini, *Mi Vida Revolucionaria* (Mexico, 1937), p. 71.

11. Bulnes, *The Whole Truth,* p. 235.

12. José García to Francisco I. Madero, Chihuahua, Chihuahua, January 16, 1912, AGN, M, 33, 360.

13. Alfredo Ortega to Francisco I. Madero, Mexico, June 19, 1912, AGN, M, 3, 769-1.

14. Carta Anónima to Venustiano Carranza, Mexico, October 24, 1914, Condumex: AVC.

15. Empleados de Oficina Impresa de Billetes to Venustiano Carranza, Veracruz, Veracruz, July 14, 1915, Condumex: AVC.

16. Palavicini, *Mi Vida,* p. 208.

17. Heriberto Barrón to Venustiano Carranza, Washington, D.C., September 2, 1915, Condumex: AVC; Simón Díaz, Gobernador de

Guerrero, to Venustiano Carranza, Iguala, Guerrero, April 7, 1916, Condumex: AVC.

18. Y. Bonillas, Subsecretario de Comunicaciones y Obras Públicas, to Venustiano Carranza, Mexico, May 22, 1916, Condumex: AVC.

19. "Apuntes Intimos de López Sáenz," Veracruz, Veracruz, November 1, 1915, Condumex: AVC.

20. J. G. Nava to Venustiano Carranza, Mexico, January 2, 1916, Condumex: AVC.

21. Un Amigo Anónimo to Venustiano Carranza, Mexico, October 26, 1914, Condumex: AVC.

22. Esther Lobato Vda. de Barreiro to Alvaro Obregón, Mexico, February 5, 1915, Condumex: AVC.

23. Antonio Manero, *El Banco de México; Sus Orígines y Fundación* (New York, 1926), pp. 258–259.

24. L. Rivera to Venustiano Carranza, Veracruz, Veracruz, July 10, 1915, Condumex: AVC; Varios Senadores to Alberto J. Pani, Mexico, October 14, 1933, AGN, AR, P 10, 139.1/4.

25. "Plan de Ayala," Ayala, Morelos, November 28, 1911, Condumex: JA.

26. Carta Anónima to Gustavo Espinosa Mireles, Mexico, October 25, 1914, Condumex: AVC.

27. Juán Sanchez Azcona to Luis Casarrubias, Mexico, November 5, 1912, AGN, M, 3, 759–2.

28. Manuel Mitre to Francisco I. Madero, Tlatlanqui, Puebla, January 12, 1913, AGN, M, No L, 853–3.

29. Bulnes, *The Whole Truth,* p. 168.

30. David Labransal to Francisco I. Madero, Mexico, April 12, 1912, AGN, M, 5, No E.

31. José Díaz to Francisco I. Madero, Jalapa, Veracruz, December 12, 1911, AGN, M, 33, 371–1.

32. Atenedoro Castillo to Francisco I. Madero, Cunducán, Tabasco, July 11, 1912, AGN, M, 3, 760.

33. Emilio Carvajal to Juan Sánchez Azcona, Huamantla, Tlaxcala, June 27, 1912, AGN, M, 3, 762.

34. Wistano L. Orozco to Francisco I. Madero, Guadalajara, Jalisco, July 4, 1912, AGN, M, 3, 755–1.

35. Alvaro Obregón, Benjamín Hill, J. B. Treviño, Dr. Atl, F. Murguía y demás to Venustiano Carranza, Torreón, Coahuila, October 23, 1915, Condumex: AVC.

36. Plutarco Elías Calles, Gobernador y Comandante Militar del Estado, "Decreto Número Seis," Hermosillo, Sonora, August 31, 1915, Condumex: AVC.

37. Comandante del Resguardo to Carlos Félix Díaz, Mazatlán, Sinaloa, March 22, 1915, Condumex: AVC.

38. Manuel Acuña to Venustiano Carranza, Culiacán, Sinaloa, April 3, 1915, Condumex: AVC.

39. G. A. Velásquez to Venustiano Carranza, Mexico, December 7, 1916, Condumex: AVC.

40. Anselmo Cortés, Anacleto Vargas y Miguel Cano to Venustiano Carranza, Oaxaca, Oaxaca, March 26, 1915, Condumex: AVC.

41. José Vidaurri to Venustiano Carranza, San Luis Potosí, San Luis Potosí, January 18, 1916, Condumex: AVC.

42. Francisco Aguirre to Venustiano Carranza, Veracruz, Veracruz, March 30, 1915, Condumex: AVC.

43. Manuel Zamora to Venustiano Carranza, Veracruz, Veracruz, February 4, 1915, Condumex: AVC.

44. Gral. Conrado Cevera C., "Carta Abierta," Jonacatepec, Morelos, March 17, 1918, Condumex: MG.

45. Carta a Venustiano Carranza, Comitán, Chiapas, December 26, 1919, Condumex: AVC.

46. Gral. Luis Gutiérrez, "Manifiesto al Pueblo de Coahuila," Monclova, Coahuila, December [n. d.], 1917, Condumex: MG.

47. Gral. Conrado Cevera C., "Carta Abierta," Jonacatepec, Morelos, March 17, 1918, Condumex: MG; Salvador Alvarado to Venustiano Carranza, Mexico, January 29, 1919, Condumex: AVC.

48. Salvador Mendoza, "Editorial: El Problema Político de Oaxaca," *El Universal*, January 22, 1919.

49. Obreros de Puebla a Venustiano Carranza, Puebla, Puebla, September 23, 1916, Condumex: AVC; Los Comisionados de Puebla to Venustiano Carranza, Mexico, September 29, 1916, Condumex: AVC; Carlos Aguirre to Venustiano Carranza, Mexico, October 4, 1916, Condumex: AVC.

50. Francisco León de la Barra to Tomás Macmanus, Paris, France, June 14, 1920, Condumex: LDB.

51. José Vasconcelos, "No Permanezcamos Neutrales," José Vasconcelos, ed., *La Caída de Carranza* (Mexico, 1920), p. 63.

52. Miguel Alesio Robles, *La Cena de las Burlas* (Mexico, 1939), p. 46.

53. Alvaro Obregón to General Enrique Estrada, Mexico, December 8, 1923, AGN, OC, P 4–1, 101-R2-H.

54. Rafael Martínez de Escobar to Alvaro Obregón, Mexico, June 17, 1922, AGN, OC, P 40-1, L-8, 307-P-21.

55. Toribio Esquivel Obregón to Francisco León de la Barra, New York, New York, September 3, 1920, Condumex: LDB.

56. Carta Abierta a los Ciudadanos, Presidente de la República,

Diputados al Congreso de la Unión y Senadores, y Magistrados de la Suprema Corte de la Justicia de la Unión, Sierra Norte del Estado de Puebla, Puebla, November [n. d.], 1921, AGN, OC, P 40-1, L-8, 307-P-1.

57. W. Macip e Hilardio Galicia, Diputados Secretaríos de la Legislatura del Estado, to Alvaro Obregón, Puebla, Puebla, March 13, 1922, AGN, OC, P 42, L-6, 407-P-1.

58. Alberto Bremauntz, *Setenta Años de Mi Vida; Memorias y Anécdotas* (Mexico, 1968), p. 62.

59. Alvaro Obregón to General Matías Romero, Jefe de Operaciones, Zacatecas, Zacatecas, Irapuato, Guanajuato, December 27, 1923, AGN, OC, P-5, L-5, 101-R2-I.

60. *Ibid.*

61. J. Certuche to Alvaro Obregón, Mexico, November 20, 1922, AGN, OC, P 41, L-10, 407-C-4.

62. Adalberto Tejeda to Alvaro Obregón, Jalapa, Veracruz, July 21, 1924, AGN, OC, P 4-1, 101-R2-H.

63. Enrique Estrada, "Manifiesto," Puruándiro, Michoacán, January 17, 1924, AGN, OC, P-4, L-2, 101-R2-A-2.

64. Angel Flores, "Manifiesto," Culiacán, Sinaloa, December 1, 1924, AGN, OC, P-4, L-2, 101-R2-A-2.

65. Alvaro Obregón, "Manifiesto del Ciudadano Alvaro Obregón," Alvaro Obregón, *Campaña Política del C. Alvaro Obregón Candidato a la Presidencia de la República, 1920–1924,* 5 vols. (Mexico, 1923), I: 44–45.

66. Aldolfo de la Huerto to Alvaro Obregón, Hermosillo, Sonora, June 9, 1921, AGN, OC, P 2-1, L-19, 101-S-12.

67. Francisco Vásquez Gómez to Jenaro Amezcua, San Antonio, Texas, May 10, 1920, Condumex: JA.

68. Manuel Gamio to Alvaro Obregón, Mexico, September 24, 1923, AGN, OC, P 16-1, L-12, 104-A-D-1.

69. Carta al General José María Rodríguez, Mexico, December 7, 1915, Condumex: AVC.

70. Manuel Martiarena to Ignacio A. de la Peña, Pachuca, Hidalgo, February 27, 1913, Condumex: MG.

71. José M. Maytorena to Francisco I. Madero, Mexico, January 16, 1913, AGN, M, 5, No E.

72. Enrique Navarro to Francisco I. Madero, Mexico, February 7, 1912, AGN, M, 2-7, 1183.

73. Jesús Urueta y Rafael Zubarán Capmany to Teófilo M. Rioja, Veracruz, Veracruz, November 20, 1915, Condumex: AVC.

74. Carta del Gobernador Interino de Chiapas to Venustiano Carranza, Tuxtla Gutiérrez, Chiapas, December 11, 1919, Condumex: AVC.

75. "Síntesis de la Administración Politica del Sr. Villanueva," *El Tribuno,* November 1, 1919.

76. Narciso Bassols Batalla, *El Pensamiento Político de Obregón* (Mexico, 1967), p. 38.

77. Charles C. Cumberland, *Mexican Revolution: The Constitutionalist Years* (Austin, 1972), p. 78.

78. I. P. Gaxiola to Fernando Torreblanca, Nogales, Sonora, July 19, 1921, AGN, OC, P 40-1, L-8, 307-N-1; Procurador General de la República, E. Delhumeau, to Secretario de Hacienda y Crédito Público, Mexico, March 7, 1923, AGN, OC, P 40-1, L-8, 307-N-1.

79. Angel J. Lagarda to Venustiano Carranza, Mexico, November 30, 1915, Condumex: AVC.

80. Jefe del Servicio de Seguridad to Gersayn Ugarte, Nuevo Laredo, Tamaulipas, November 25, 1915, Condumex: AVC.

81. J. G. Nava to Venustiano Carranza, Aguascalientes, Aguascalientes, December 9, 1915, Condumex: AVC.

82. J. G. Nava to Venustiano Carranza, Aguascalientes, Aguascalientes, December 10, 1915, Condumex: AVC.

83. J. G. Nava to Venustiano Carranza, San Luis Potosí, San Luis Potosí, December 1, 1915, Condumex: AVC.

84. Comandante del Resguardo to Carlos Felix Díaz, Mazatlán, Sinaloa, March 22, 1915, Condumex: AVC.

85. Manuel Acuña to Venustiano Carranza, Culiacán, Sinaloa, April 3, 1915, Condumex: AVC.

86. Un Correligionario to Venustiano Carranza, Puebla, Puebla, July 4, 1915, Condumex: AVC.

87. El Coronel, Jefe de Armas y Comandante Militar de la Plaza, to Venustiano Carranza, Túxpan, Veracruz, December 23, 1914, Condumex: AVC.

88. Atolio B. Y. Buenfil to Alvaro Obregón, Mérida, Yucatán, December 2, 1920, AGN, OC, P-41, L-10, 407-C-6.

89. "Anónimo Acompañado de un Programa para Festival, en el Teatro Mayo, en Cuyo Programa se Dedica Sarcásticamente la Función a los Garbanceros del Río Mayo," Mexico, November 19, 1921, AGN, OC, P 40-1, L-8, 307-N-1.

90. Alejandro Iñigo to Alvaro Obregón, Mexico, November 13, 1922, AGN, OC, P 7-1, L-6, 103-0-20.

91. Jorge Prieto Laurens, *Cincuenta Años de Política Mexicana, Memorias Políticas* (Mexico, 1968), p. 158.

CHAPTER XXII

1. Quoted in Arnaldo Córdova, *La Ideología de la Revolución Mexicana; la Formación del Nuevo Régimen* (México, 1973), p. 312.

2. *Historia de la Revolución Mexicana; Orígenes y Resultados* (Mexico, 1967), pp. 288 and 465.

3. Blas Urrea, "Los Partidos Políticos de México ante la Próxima Campaña Electoral," Alvaro Obregón, *Campaña Política del C. Alvaro Obregón Candidato a la Presidencia de la República, 1920–1924,* 5 vols. (Mexico, 1923), I: 93.

4. *Mi Vida Revolucionaria* (Mexico, 1937), p. 347.

5. *El Antiguo Régimen y la Revolución* (Mexico, 1911), p. 407.

6. Cordova, *Ideología de la Revolución,* p. 257.

7. Antonio Hernández to Venustiano Carranza, San Salvador, República de El Salvador, July 2, 1919, Condumex: AVC.

8. Gustavo Espinosa Mireles to Venustiano Carranza, Saltillo, Coahuila, December 17, 1918, Condumex: AVC.

9. Aarón Sáenz, *La Política Internacional de la Revolución; Estudios y Documentos* (Mexico, 1961), p. 19.

10. Córdova, *Ideología de la Revolución,* pp. 257 and 259.

11. Quoted in Bernardino Mena Brito, *Maquinismo* (Mexico, 1933), p. 84.

12. Narciso Bassols Batalla, *El Pensamiento Político de Obregón* (Mexico, 1967), p. 52.

13. Sáenz, *Política Internacional,* p. 115.

14. Blas Urrea, *La Herencia de Carranza* (Mexico, 1920), p. 37.

15. Venustiano Carranza, "Manifiesto del C. Presidente de la República, a la Nación," Obregón, *Campaña Política,* I: 16.

16. Alfredo Serratos to Adolfo de la Huerta, Detroit, Michigan, December 12, 1923, AGN, OC, P-4, L-2, 101-R2-A-2.

17. Córdova, *Ideología de la Revolución,* pp. 31, 260, and 295.

18. *El Aspecto Agraria de la Revolución* (Mexico, 1919), pp. 297–298.

19. Francisco Bulnes, *The Whole Truth About Mexico; President Wilson's Responsibility* (New York, 1916), p. 160.

20. Córdova, *Ideología de la Revolución,* p. 252.

21. Venustiano, Carranza, *Codificación de los Decretos del C. Venustiano Carranza, Primer Jefe del Ejército Constitucionalista Encargado del Poder Ejecutivo de la Unión* (Mexico, 1915), pp. 14–15, 25, and 219.

22. Quoted in *The Evening Star,* November 6, 1915.

23. "Entrevista Concedida por el C. Venustiano Carranza, Primer

Jefe del Ejército Constitucionalista y Encargado del Poder Ejecutivo de la Nación, al Periodista Howard E. Morton, Editor y Representante del Periódico *Los Angeles Examiner*," Mexico, April 18, 1917, Condumex: AVC.

24. "Dice que México Necesita Establecer su Crédito," Mexico, March 13, 1919, Condumex: AVC.

25. Juan Neftalí Amador to Venustiano Carranza, Washington, November 12, 1915, Condumex: AVC; Venustiano Carranza to Juan Neftali Amador, Matamoros, Tamaulipas, November 28, 1915, Condumex: AVC.

26. Hector Aguilar Camín, "La Revolución Sonorense, 1910–1914" (Ph.D. diss., Instituto Nacional de Antropología e Historia, Mexico, 1975), p. 332.

27. Bassols Batalla, Pensamiento *Político*, p. 81.

28. Obregón, *Campaña Política*, V, 235.

29. Alvaro Obregón, *Manifiesto a la Nación* (Mexico, 1919), p. 15.

30. Alvaro Obregón, *Discursos*, 2 vols. (Mexico, 1932), II: 15–16.

31. Alvaro Obregón to Elmer Dover, Mexico, August 25, 1921, AGN, OC, P 15-1, L-6, 104-R1-D.

32. Alvaro Obregón to Carmen D. Vda. de Hill, Mexico, June 12, 1922, AGN, OC, P-7, L-4, 103-H-8.

33. Alvaro Obregón to Pat M. Neff, Governor of Texas, Mexico, April 5, 1923, AGN, OC, P-16, L-8, 104-R1-E-10.

34. *Apuntes Sobre Mi Vida Pública* (Mexico, 1965), p. 204.

35. José I. Limantour to Francisco León de la Barra, Paris, France, November 14, 1915, Condumex: AVC.

36. Limantour, *Apuntes Sobre Mi Vida*, p. 197.

37. *Ibid.*, pp. 197–198.

38. Díaz quoted in Manero, *Antiguo Régimen*, p. 143.

39. Limantour, *Apuntes Sobre Mi Vida*, pp. 203, 205, and 271.

40. *Ibid.*, pp. 199 and 201.

41. *Ibid.*, pp. 136, 201, and 277; Manero, *Antiguo Régimen*, p. 349.

42. *Un Decenio de Política Mexicana* (New York, 1920), p. 102.

43. Bulnes, *The Whole Truth*, p. 124.

44. Manuel González Ramírez, *La Revolución Social de México*, 3 vols. (Mexico, 1960–1966), I: xiii.

45. Urrea, *Herencia*, p. 59.

46. *Historia de la Revolución*, pp. 306–307.

47. Quoted in Librería General, ed., *De Como Vino Huerto y Como Se Fe; Apuntes para la Historia de un Régimen Militar* (Mexico, 1914), p. 212.

48. "Manifiesto a la Nación," Mexico, June 11, 1915, Condumex: AVC.

49. Cordova, *Ideología de la Revolución*, p. 253.

50. Manuel Doblado, *México para los Mexicanos, El Presidente Huerta y su Gobierno* (Mexico, 1913), p. 121.

51. Urrea, *Herencia*, pp. 35 and 70.

52. *Ibid.*, p. 71.

53. L. Mesa Gutiérrez, Director General de Aduanas, to Venustiano Carranza, Mexico, June 24, 1916, Condumex: AVC.

54. J. Vidal Serrano y demás firmantes to Cándido Aguilar, Papantla, Veracruz, June 6, 1918, Condumex: AVC.

55. Ignacio Bonillas to Venustiano Carranza, Washington, D.C., February 24, 1919, Condumex: AVC.

56. Luis Cabrera to Venustiona Carranza, New York, New York, September 26, 1915, Condumex: AVC.

57. Ramón P. DeNegri to Venustiano Carranza, San Francisco, California, August 27, 1915, Condumex: AVC.

58. Consul de México to Venustiano Carranza, Philadelphia, Pennsylvania, January 20, 1916, Condumex: AVC.

59. Manero, *Antiguo Régimen*, p. 232.

60. *Historia de la Revolución*, pp. 318–319.

61. *Ocho Mil Kilómetros en Campaña* (Mexico, 1917), p. 150.

62. Agente Confidencial to Venustiano Carranza, El Paso, Texas, June 23, 1913, Condumex: AVC.

63. Arturo Langle Ramírez, *El Ejército Villista* (Mexico, 1961), p. 154.

64. Urrea, *Herencia*, pp. 36–37.

65. Consul de Mexico to Venustiano Carranza, New York, New York, December 11, 1914, Condumex: AVC.

66. Alfredo Breceda to Venustiano Carranza, New York, New York, July 22, 1915, Condumex: AVC.

67. Heriberto Barrón to Editor of *The New York Times,* Washington, D.C., August 12, 1915, Condumex: AVC.

68. Venustiano Carranza, "Manifiesto a la Nación," Mexico, June 11, 1915, Condumex: AVC.

69. *Historia del Ejército de la Revolución Constitucionalista,* 2 vols. (Mexico, 1946), I: 452.

70. Urrea, *Herencia,* p. 64.

71. P. Edward Haley, *Revolution and Intervention: The Diplomacy of Taft and Wilson With Mexico, 1910–1917* (Cambridge and London, 1970), pp. 238–239.

72. Esteban Bracamontes (Julio Albert y Cia. Sucs., La Gran Sedería) to Venustiano Carranza, Mexico, September 14, 1915, Condumex: AVC.

73. Departmento del Servicio de Locomotoras, Gremio Ferrocar-

rilero, to Venustiano Carranza, Mexico, June [n. d.], 1916, Condumex: AVC.

74. Manuel López Gallo, *Economía y Política en la Historia de México* (Mexico, 1965), p. 438.

75. John W. F. Dulles, *Yesterday in Mexico. A Chronicle of the Revolution, 1919–1936* (Austin, 1961), p. 107.

76. Rafael Curiel, Jefe de la Inspección Fiscal del Petróleo, to Secretario de Hacienda y de Crédito Público, Tampico, Tamaulipas, December 17, 1924, AGN, OC, P-14, L-1, 104-P1-C.

77. Dulles, *Yesterday in Mexico*, p. 107.

78. Antonio Manero, *El Banco de México: Sus Orígines y Fundación* (New York, 1926), p. 257.

79. Alberto Pani, *Mi Contribución al Nuevo Régimen (1910–1933)* (Mexico, 1936), p. 304; Rodolfo Montes to Alvaro Obregón, Mexico, March 4, 1924, AGN, OC, P 41-1, L-1, 407-E-22.

80. Letter to Armando Deschamps, Paris, France, July 30, 1919, Condumex: AVC.

81. Urrea, *Herencia*, p. 74.

82. Secretaría de Hacienda y Crédito Público, "Reglamento," Mexico, June 24, 1912, Condumex: AVC.

83. *Pensamiento Político*, pp. 15–16.

84. Carranza, *Codificación de los Decretos*, pp. 67, 157–158, and 192–193.

85. Charles C. Cumberland, *Mexican Revolution: The Constitutionalist Years* (Austin, 1972), p. 251.

86. Urrea, *Herencia*, p. 75.

87. Ramón Eduardo Ruiz, *Labor and the Ambivalent Revolutionaries: Mexico, 1911–1923* (Baltimore and London, 1976), p. 105.

88. *Ibid.*, p. 106.

89. *Pensamiento Político*, p. 61.

90. Ruiz, *Labor*, p. 106.

91. Alvaro Obregón to H. L. Doheny, Mexico, September 8, 1923, AGN, OC, P-15, L-2, 104-P1-P-5; Alvaro Obregón to Fernando González Roa, Mexico, May 21, 1923, AGN, OC, P-14, L-1, 104-P1-C; Alvaro Obregón "Acuerdo," Mexico, October 31, 1922, AGN, P-14, O-C, L-1, 104-P1-G-1; Alvaro Obregón to C. N. Haskell, Mexico, April 3, 1923, AGN, OC, P-14, L-1, 104-P1-G-1.

92. Alvaro Obregón, "Acuerdo de C. Presidente de la República," Mexico, April 4, 1923, AGN, OC, P-14, L-1, 104-P1-D.

93. A. B. Butler to Charles E. Hughes, Washington, D.C., August 21, 1921, AGN, O-C, P-15, L-2, 104-P1-P-3.

94. Eugenio Méndez, Diputado, to Cándido Aguilar, Mexico, Oc-

tober 3, 1917, Condumex: AVC; Lopez Gallo, *Economía y Política*, p. 442.

95. Adalberto Tejeda to Alvaro Obregón, Jalapa, Veracruz, February 16, 1921, AGN, OC, P-2-1, L-18, 101-R-6; Adalberto Tejeda to Secretario de Estado y del Despacho de Gobernación, Jalapa, Veracruz, March 25, 1922, AGN, OC, P-2-1, L-18, 101-R-6.

96. W. H. Mealy to Alvaro Obregón, Mexico, May 26, 1923, AGN, OC, P-14, L-1, 104-P1-C.

97. Alvaro Obregón to General Amado Aguirre, Irapuato, Guanajuato, January 17, 1924, AGN, OC, P 41-1, L-1, 407-E-32; Amado Aguirre to Alvaro Obregón, Mexico, February 15, 1924, AGN, OC, P 41-1, L-1, 407-E-32.

98. Sáenz, *Política Internacional*, p. 15.

99. Querido Moheno to Francisco León de la Barra, Mexico, March 9, 1914, Condumex: LDB.

100. Fernando Cuesta Soto, "Los Tratados de Bucareli Contra la Revolución" (Tesis de Licenciatura en Derecho, Universidad Nacional Autónoma de México, 1937), p. 23.

101. Sáenz, *Política Internacional*, pp. 3, 24, and 43.

102. *Ibid.*, p. 27.

103. Félix F. Palavicini, *Historia de la Constitución de 1917*, 2 vols. (Mexico, 1917), I: 78.

104. Sáenz, *Política Internacional*, pp. 52, 56–57, and 59.

105. Cuesto Soto, "Los Tratados de Bucareli," p. 36.

106. Cándido Aguilar, "A los Mexicanos," San Antonio, Texas, September 2, 1924, AGN, OC, P-4, L-2, 101-R2-A-2.

107. Quoted in Sáenz, *Política Internacional*, p. 119.

108. Haley, *Revolution and Intervention*, p. 259.

109. *Ibid.*, pp. 26 and 29.

110. *Ibid.*, pp. 15–16.

111. *Ibid.*, pp. 34, 46–47, and 65.

112. Quoted in *ibid.*, p. 84.

113. *Ibid.*, p. 111.

114. *Ibid.*, p. 136.

115. *Ibid.*, p. 114.

116. Cumberland, *Mexican Revolution*, p. 212.

117. Haley, *Revolution and Intervention*, p. 80.

118. *Ibid.*, p. 79.

119. Robert E. Quirk, *The Mexican Revolution and the Catholic Church, 1910–1929* (Bloomington and London, 1973), pp. 101–102.

120. Fiorello H. La Guardia to Francisco León de la Barra, Washington, D.C., December 15, 1919, Condumex: AVC.

121. Quoted in Cumberland, *Mexican Revolution,* p. 397.
122. Quoted in Quirk, *Mexican Revolution and the Catholic Church,* p. 114.
123. "Recognition for Obregón," February 1, 1921.
124. "Fair Dealing with Mexico and What It Means." January 29, 1921.
125. "The Mexican Situation," June 30, 1922.
126. Quirk, *Mexican Revolution and the Catholic Church,* p. 115.
127. Haley, *Revolution and Intervention,* p. 79.

CHAPTER XXIII

1. *The Anatomy of Revolution* (New York, 1965).
2. (New York, 1952), p. 277.
3. *Anatomy of Revolution,* p. 251.
4. Letter to Alvaro Obregón, Puebla, January 16, 1915, Condumex: AVC.
5. Antonio Manero, *El Antiguo Régimen y la Revolución* (Mexico, 1911), p. 305.
6. Mexico, June 13, 1909, Condumex: JA.
7. Wistano L. Orozco to Francisco I. Madero, Guadalajara, Jalisco, October 11, 1912, AGN, M, 3, 755-1.
8. Ramón Cabrera to Rafael Zubarán Capmany, New York, January 30, 1914, Condumex: AVC.
9. Letter to Señores Arzobispos José Mora, Leopoldo Ruíz y demás firmantes, Mexico, January 27, 1923, *Excelsior,* February 2, 1923.
10. Partido Liberal Democrático to Venustiano Carranza, Puebla, Puebla, July 6, 1915, Condumex: AVC.
11. Urrea, *Herencia de Carranza,* p. 29.
12. Vecinos de la Villa de Cuautitlán to Venustiano Carranza, Cuautitlán, Mexico, July 31, 1916, Condumex: AVC.
13. Letter to Venustiano Carranza, Contepéc, Michoacán, September 22, 1916, Condumex: AVC.
14. Quoted in Bernardino Mena Brito, *Maquinismo* (Mexico, 1933), p. 86.
15. José G. Parres, "Informe de la Visita de Inspección Practicada a las Oficinas Dependientes de la Comisión Nacional Agraria en la Ciudad de Toluca, Edo. de México," Mexico, October 15, 1924, AGN, OC, P. 106, L-6, 818-E-28(2).
16. J. J. Lugo, Subsecretario de Gobernación, to Fernando Torreblanca, Mexico, November 25, 1921, AGN, OC, P. 106, L-6, 818-E-28.
17. Moisés González Navarro, *El Porfiriato. La Vida Social,* Daniel

Cosío Villegas, ed., *Historia Moderna de México,* 9 vols. (Mexico, 1955–1973), IV: 265–271.

18. Francisco Orozco y Jiménez, Archbishop of Guadalajara, "Joint Memorial of the Archbishops of Mexico on the Conditions of the Church in Mexico," Chicago, Illinois, January 15, 1919, Condumex: LDB.

19. Mena Brito, *Maquinismo,* pp. 48–49.

20. *El Imparcial,* July 13, 1908.

21. Barry Carr, "The Peculiarities of the Mexican North, 1880–1928: An Essay in Interpretation," Institute of Latin American Studies, *Occasional Papers,* No. 4 (Glasgow, 1971), p. 2.

22. González Navarro, *Vida Social,* p. 485.

23. *El Imparcial,* March 30, 1911.

24. Luis Casarrubias to Juan Sánchez Azcona, Puebla, Puebla, October 31, 1912, AGN, M, 3, 759-2.

25. Both published on April 1, 1915.

26. Francisco Orozco y Jiménez, Arzobispo de Guadalajara, to Alvaro Obregón, February 28, 1924, AGN, OC, P-4, L-2, 101-R2-C.

27. *El Verdadero Díaz,* pp. 260–261.

28. Pablo Dorantes, Presidente Municipal, to Emiliano Zapata, Zumpahuacán, Mexico, March 25, 1915, AGN, Z, NC.

29. Regina Pérez y demás firmantes to Emiliano Zapata, Villa de Ayala, Morelos, June 4, 1915, AGN, Z, NC.

30. Antonio Palacios Rojo, "Memorandum" January 14, 1915, Veracruz, Veracruz, Condumex: AVC.

31. John W. F. Dulles, *Yesterday in Mexico. A Chronicle of the Revolution, 1919–1936* (Austin, 1961), p. 106.

32. *The New York Times,* December 13, 1920.

33. *La Política Internacional de la Revolución; Estudios y Documentos* (Mexico, 1961), p. 206.

34. Cited in *ibid.*

Bibliography

Archival Sources

Archivo General de la Nación, Mexico City, Mexico
Abelardo Rodríguez
Fomento
Francisco I. Madero
Alvaro Obregón–Plutarco Elías Calles Presidential Papers
Emiliano Zapata

Centro de Estudios de Historia de México, Condumex,
Mexico City, México
Francisco León de la Barra
Jenaro Amezcua
Ramón Corral
Manuel González
Venustiano Carranza

Bancroft Library, University of California, Berkeley
Silvestre Terrazas Papers

National Archives, Washington, D.C.
Consulate Correspondence, Records of the Foreign Service Posts of
the Department of State

Newspapers

Mexico
Diario del Hogar, Mexico Cty
El Ahuizote, Mexico City
El Correo de Chihuahua, Chihuahua, Chihuahua
El Diario, Mexico City
El Dictamen, Veracruz, Veracruz

El Demócrata, Mexico City
El Economista, Mexico City
El Heraldo, Durango, Durango
El Imparcial, Mexico City
El Microbio, Mexico City
El País, Mexico City
El Presidente, Mexico City
El Progreso Latino, Chihuahua, Chihuahua
El Pueblo, Veracruz
El Regenerador, Tuxtla Gutiérrez, Chiapas
El Sol, Nogales, Sonora
El Tipógrafo Mexicano, Mexico City
El Tribuno, San Cristóbal de Las Casas, Chiapas
El Universal, Mexico City
Excelsior, Mexico City
La República, Mexico City
La Tribuna, Tepic, Tepic
La Voz de Zacatecas, Zacatecas, Zacatecas
México Nuevo, Mexico City
Nueva Era, Mexico City

United States

Chicago Daily Tribune, Chicago, Illinois
La Democracia, Tucson, Arizona
Los Angeles Examiner, Los Angeles, California
The Evening Star, Washington, D.C.
The Morning Post, Washington, D.C.
The New York Times, New York, New York
The Sun, Baltimore, Maryland
The World, New York, New York
Washington Times, Washington, D.C.

Books and Pamphlets

Primary Sources

Albino, Acereto. *El General Obregón a Través de Sus Discursos.* Mexico, 1920.
Alessio Robles, Miguel. *La Cena de las Burlas.* Mexico, 1939.
Alvarado, Salvador. *La Traición de Carranza,* New York, 1920.
———. *Mi Actuación Revolucionaria en Yucatán.* Mexico, 1918.
Barragán Rodríguez, Juan. *Historia del Ejército y de la Revolución Constitucionalista,* 2 vols., Mexico, 1946.

Barrón, Heriberto. *Some of the Facts and Arguments which led to the Recognition of the First Chief of the Constitutionalist Army in Charge of the Executive Power of the Mexican Republic, Mr. Venustiano Carranza, as the de facto government in Mexico.* (n. p., 1915).

Breceda, Alfredo. *Don Venustiano Carranza; Razgos Biográficos Escritos en 1912.* Mexico, 1930.

Bremauntz, Alberto. *Setenta Años de Mi Vida; Memorias y Anécdotas.* Mexico, 1968.

Bulnes, Francisco. *El Verdadero Díaz y la Revolución.* Mexico, 1967.

———. *The Whole Truth About Mexico; President Wilson's Responsibility.* New York, 1916.

Cabrera, Luis. *Obras Completas,* 5 vols., Mexico, 1975.

———. *Observaciones a la Reforma del Artículo de la Ley de 6 de Enero de 1915.* Mexico, 1932.

———. *Tres Intelectuales Hablan Sobre México.* Mexico, 1916.

Calero, Manuel. *Un Decenio de Política Mexicana.* New York, 1920.

Canale, Aurelio D. *Carta Abierta Dirigida al Señor General don Alvaro Obregón.* Madrid, 1920.

Cárdenas, Lázaro. *Obras.* Mexico, 1972.

Carranza, Venustiano. *Reply of don Venustiano Carranza to the Chief of the Northern Division.* Mexico, 1914.

———. *Codificación de los Decretos del C. Venustiano Carranza, Primer Jefe del Ejército Constitucionalista Encargado del Poder Ejecutivo de la Unión.* Mexico, 1915. ·

———. *La Revolución de Entonces es la Revolución de Ahora.* Mexico, 1937.

———. *President Venustiano Carranza Corrects Statements Made by Senator Knox of Pennsylvania in the Senate.* Washington, D.C., 1917.

———. *Report by Venustiano Carranza, in the City of Querétaro, State of Querétaro, Mexico, Friday, December 1st.* New York, (1916?).

Casasola, Gustavo. *Historia Gráfica de la Revolución Mexicana,* 5 vols. Mexico, 1967.

Castillo, Israel del. *La Batalla de Algibes; lo que Queríamos los Revolucionarios de Entonces.* Mexico, 1961.

Comisión Nacional para la Celebración del Sesquicentenario de la Proclamación de la Independencia Nacional y del Cincuentenario de la Revolución Mexicana, *Diario de las Debates del Congreso Constituyente, 1916–1917,* 2 vols., Mexico, 1960.

Delgado, Miguel R. *El Testamento Político de Otilio E. Montaño.* Mexico, 1920.

Díaz Dufoo, Carlos. *México y los Capitales Extranjeros.* Mexico, 1918.

Didapp, Juan Pedro. *Los Estados Unidos y Nuestros Conflictos Internos.* Mexico, 1913.

Doblado, Manuel. *México Para los Mexicanos, El Presidente Huerta y su Gobierno.* Mexico, 1913.

Espinosa, Luis. *Rastros de Sangre; Historia de la Revolución en Chiapas.* Mexico, 1912.

Esquivel Obregón, Toribio. *Democracia y Personalismo. Relatos y Comentarios Sobre Política Actual.* Mexico, 1911.

Fabela, Isidro, ed. *Documentos Históricos de la Revolución Mexicana; Emiliano Zapata y el Plan de Ayala y su Política Agraria.* Mexico, 1970.

Gil, Feliciano. *Biografía y Vida Militar del General Alvaro Obregón.* Hermosillo, 1914.

González Navarro, Moisés. *Estadísticas Sociales del Porfiriato, 1877–1910.* Mexico, 1956.

González Roa, Fernando. *El Aspecto Agrario de la Revolución.* Mexico, 1919.

Guzmán, Martín Luis. *El Aguila y la Serpiente.* Mexico, 1928.

———. *El Hombre y Sus Armas; Memorias de Pancho Villa.* Mexico, 1938.

Herrerías, Ignacio. *En El Campo Revolucionario.* Chihuahua, 1911.

Huerta, Victoriano. *Memorias del General Victoriano Huerta.* Barcelona, Spain, 1915.

Kaplan, Samuel. *Combatimos la Tiranía, Conversaciones con Enrique Flores Magón.* Mexico, 1958.

Librería General, ed. *De Como Vino Huerta y Como Se Fue; Apuntes para la Historia de un Régimen Militar.* Mexico, 1914.

Limantour, José Ives. *Apuntes Sobre Mi Vida Pública,* Mexico, 1965.

López Pérez, Rodrigo. *El Movimiento Obregonista en Michoacán.* Mexico, 1920.

Luquín, Eduardo. *El Pensamiento de Luis Cabrera.* Mexico, 1960.

Madero, Francisco I. *La Sucesión Presidencial en 1910.* Mexico, 1960.

Manero, Antonio. *El Antiguo Régimen y la Revolución.* Mexico, 1911.

———. *El Banco de México; Sus Orígenes y Fundación.* New York, 1926.

María y Campos, Armando de, ed. *Las Memorias y las Mejores Cartas de Francisco I. Madero.* Mexico, 1956.

Maytorena, José M. *Algunas Verdades Sobre el General Alvaro Obregón.* Los Angeles, California, 1919.

Mena Brito, Bernardino. *Maquinismo.* Mexico, 1933.

Méndez de Cuenca, Laura. *Alvaro Obregón.* (n.p., 1918?).

Molina Enríquez, Andrés. *Los Grandes Problemas Nacionales.* Mexico, 1909.

Monroy Durán, Luis. *El Ultimo Caudillo.* Mexico, 1924.

Obregón, Alvaro. *Campaña Política del C. Alvaro Obregón Candidato a la Presidencia de la República, 1920–1924,* 5 vols., Mexico, 1923.

——. *Discursos,* 2 vols., Mexico, 1932.

——. *Manifiesto a la Nación.* Mexico, 1919.

——. *Ocho Mil Kilómetros en Campaña.* Mexico, 1917.

——. *Teatro de Aguascalientes.* Aguascalientes, 1927.

——. *The Agrarian Problem.* Mexico, 1924.

Orozco, José Clemente. *An Autobiography;* translated by Robert C. Stephenson. Austin, 1962.

Palavicini, Félix F. *Historia de la Constitución de 1917.* 2 vols. Mexico, 1917.

——. *Mi Vida Revolucionaria.* Mexico, 1937.

Pani, Alberto J. *Las Conferencias de Bucareli.* Mexico, 1953.

——. *Mi Contribución al Nuevo Régimen (1910–1933).* Mexico, 1936.

——. *On the Road to Democracy.* Mexico, 1918.

Peña de Villarreal, Consuelo. *La Revolución en el Norte.* Puebla, Mexico, 1968.

Portes Gil, Emilo. *En Memoria de Obregón.* Mexico, 1946.

Prida, Ramón. *De la Dictadura a la Anarquía; Apuntes para la Historia Política de México Durante los Ultimos Cuarenta y Tres Años (1817–1913).* Mexico, 1958.

Prieto Laurens, Jorge. *Cincuenta Años de Política Mexicana, Memorias Políticas.* Mexico, 1968.

Puente, Ramón. *Pascual Orozco y la Revuelta en Chihuahua.* Mexico, 1912.

Reed, John. *Insurgent Mexico.* New York, 1969.

Rouaix, Pastor. *Génesis de los Artículos 27 y 123 de la Constitución Política de 1917.* Mexico, 1959.

Sáenz, Aarón. *La Political Internacional de la Revolución; Estudios y Documentos.* Mexico, 1961.

Salazar, Rosendo. *Las Pugnas de la Gleba,* 2 vols., Mexico, 1923.

Sánchez Azcona, Juan. *Apuntes para la Historia de la Revolución Mexicana.* Mexico, 1961.

Santos Chocano, José. *El Conflicto Personal de la Revolución Mexicana. Examen de Todo lo Que Ha Dicho el Ciudadano Carranza.* El Paso, Texas and New Orleans, 1914.

Serrano, Petronilo. *Breves Memorias de la Revolución, Desde el Año de 1906 Hasta 1910 en las Zonas Veracruz, Puebla y Tlaxcala.* Tlaxcala, Mexico, 1932.

Sesto, Julio. *El México de Porfirio Díaz (Hombres y Cosas).* Valencia, Spain, 1910.

Thord-Gray, I. *Gringo Rebel; Mexico 1913–1914.* Coral Gables, 1960.

Torres Quintero, Gregorio. *La Instrucción Rudimentaria en la República*. Mexico, 1913.

Tweedie, Mrs. Alex. *Mexico As I Saw It*. New York, 1901.

Urrea, Blas. *La Herencia de Carranza*. Mexico, 1920.

U. S. Senate. *Investigation of Mexican Affairs, Preliminary Report and Hearings of Committee on Foreign Affairs* (September 8, 1919), 2 vols., Washington, D.C., 1920.

Vasconcelos, José, ed. *La Caída de Carranza*. Mexico. 1920.

Vásquez Gómez, Francisco. *Memorias Políticas (1909–1913)*. Mexico, 1933.

Vera Estañol, Jorge. *Historia de la Revolución Mexicana; Orígenes y Resultados*. Mexico, 1967.

Zayas Enríquez, Rafael de. *Apuntes Confidenciales al Presidente Porfirio Díaz*. Mexico, 1967.

Secondary Sources

Acosta, Alfredo. *La Gestión Hacendaria de la Revolución*. Mexico, 1917.

Aguilar Camín, Héctor. "La Revolución Sonorense, 1910–1914," Ph.D. thesis. Instituto Nacional de Antropología e Historia, Mexico, 1975.

Almada, Francisco R. *La Revolución en el Estado de Chihuahua*, 2 vols., Chihuahua, 1964.

———. *Resumen de la Historia del Estado de Chihuahua*. Mexico, 1955.

Alperovich, M. S. and Rudenko, B. T. *La Revolución Mexicana de 1910–1917 y la Política de los Estados Unidos*. Mexico, 1960.

Alzati, Servando A. *Historia de la Mexicanización de los Ferrocarriles Nacionales de México*. Mexico, 1946.

Amaya, Juan Gualberto. *Los Gobiernos de Obregón y Calles y Regímenes "Peleles" Derivados del Callismo*. Mexico, 1947.

———. *Venustiano Carranza, Caudillo Constitucionalista; Segunda Etapa, Febrero de 1913 a Mayo de 1920*. Mexico, 1947.

Azuela, Mariano. *Los de Abajo*. Mexico, 1915.

Bassols Batalla, Narciso. *El Pensamiento de Obregón*. Mexico, 1967.

Basurto, Jorge. *El Proletariado Industrial en México (1850–1930)*. Mexico, 1975.

Beezley, William H. *Insurgent Governor: Abraham González and the Mexican Revolution in Chihuahua*. Lincoln, 1973.

Bermúdez y Cortés, Justino. *Verdades—No Adulación; Callismo y Obregonismo Revolucionarios*. Mexico, 1935.

Bernstein, Marvin D. *The Mexican Mining Industry, 1890–1950*. New York, 1964.

Blanco Moheno, Roberto. *Crónica de la Revolución Mexicana*, 2 vols. Mexico, 1958–1959.

Blasco Ibáñez, Vicente. *El Militarismo Mexicano*. Valencia, Spain, 1920.

————. *Mexico in Revolution*. New York, 1920.

Bolio, Edmundo. *Yucatán en la Dictadura y la Revolución*. Mexico, 1967.

Bórquez, Djed. *Obregón, Apuntes Biográficos*. Mexico, 1929.

Brinton, Clarence Crane. *The Anatomy of Revolution*. New York, 1938.

Carpizo, Jorge. *La Constitución Mexicana de 1917*. Mexico, 1969.

Carr, Barry. *El Movimiento Obrero y la Política en México, 1910–1929*, translated by Roberto Gómez Ciriza, 2 vols. Mexico, 1976.

Castañeda, Daniel. *Caudillo y Gobernante*. Mexico, 1936.

Ceja Reyes, Victor. *Yo Maté a Villa*. Mexico, 1960.

Cervantes, Juan B. *Obregón Ante la Historia*. Mexico, 1924.

Cervantes M., Federico. *Francisco Villa y la Revolución*. Mexico, 1960.

Clark, Marjorie Ruth. *Organized Labor in Mexico*. Chapel Hill, 1934.

Cockcroft, James D. *Intellectual Precursors of the Mexican Revolution, 1900–1913*. Austin and London, 1968.

Córdova, Arnaldo. *La Ideología de la Revolución Mexicana; La Formación del Nuevo Régimen*. Mexico, 1973.

Cosío Villegas, Daniel, ed. *Historia Moderna de México*, 9 vols. Mexico, 1955–1973.

Cuesta Soto, Fernando. "Los Tratados de Bucareli Contra la Revolución," Tesis de Licenciatura en Derecho. Universidad Nacional Autónoma de México, 1937.

Cumberland, Charles C. *Mexican Revolution: The Constitutionalist Years*. Austin, 1972.

————. *Mexican Revolution, Genesis Under Madero*. Austin, 1952.

Delgado Román, Ricardo. *Aspectos Agrarios del Gobierno del General Victoriano Huerta*. Guadalajara, 1951.

Díaz, Carlos Félix. *Génesis de la Revolución Mexicana*. La Paz, Bolivia, 1918.

Díaz Cárdenas, León. *Cananea, Primer Brote del Sindicalismo en México*. Mexico, 1936.

Dillon, E. J. *President Obregón, A World Reformer*. London, 1923.

Dillon, Richard H. "The Rise of Alvaro Obregón, 1880–1917," Master's thesis. University of California, Berkeley, 1949.

Dulles, John W. F. *Yesterday in Mexico, A Chronicle of the Revolution, 1919–1936*. Austin, 1961.

Fernández de Castro y Finck, Jorge. *Madero y la Democracia; Estudio Sobre la Doctrina de la Superación*. Mexico, 1966.

Fuentes, Carlos. *La Muerte le Artemio Cruz*. Mexico, 1962.

Fuentes Mares, José. *La Revolución Mexicana; Memorias de un Espectador*. Mexico, 1971.

————. *Y México se Refugió en el Desierto. Luis Terrazas: Historia y Destino*. Mexico, 1954.

Gámez, Atenedoro. *Monografía Histórica Sobre la Génesis de la Revolución en el Estado de Puebla*. Mexico, 1960.

Gámiz Olives, Everardo. *La Revolución en el Estado de Durango*. Mexico, 1963.

Gómez, Marte R. *La Reforma Agraria en las Filas Villistas, Años 1913 a 1915 a 1920*. Mexico, 1966.

González Calzada, Manuel. *Historia de la Revolución Mexicana en Tabasco*. Mexico, 1972.

González Flores, Enrique. *Chihuahua de la Independencia a la Revolución*. Mexico, 1949.

González Navarro, Moisés. *El Porfiriato, La Vida Social*, Daniel Cosio Villegas. ed. *Historia Moderna de México*, 9 vols. Mexico, 1955–1973.

———. *La Confederación Nacional Campesina; Un Grupo de Presión en la Reforma Agraria Mexicana*. Mexico, 1968.

———. *Las Huelgas Textiles en el Porfiriato*. Puebla, 1970.

González Ramírez, Manuel. *La Revolución Social de México, 3 vols.* Mexico, 1960–1966.

Gruening, Ernest. *Mexico and Its Heritage*. New York, 1928.

Guzmán, Martín Luis. *Febrero de 1913*. Mexico, 1963.

———. *La Sombra del Caudillo*. Madrid, 1930.

Haley, P. Edward. *Revolution and Intervention: The Diplomacy of Taft and Wilson With Mexico, 1910–1917*. Cambridge and London, 1970.

Junco, Alfonso. *Carranza y los Orígenes de Su Rebelión*. Mexico, 1935.

Langle Ramírez, Arturo. *El Ejército Villista*. Mexico, 1961.

Lewis, Cleona. *America's Stake in International Investment*. Washington, D. C., 1938.

Librería de Quiroga, ed. *¿Quién es Obregón?* San Antonio, Texas, 1922.

Lombardo Toledano, Vicente. *Teoria y Práctica del Movimiento Sindical Mexicano*. Mexico, 1961.

López Aparicio, Alfonso. *El Movimiento Obrero en México*. Mexico, 1958.

López Gallo, Manuel. *Economía y Política en la Historia de México*. Mexico, 1965.

López Pérez, Rodrigo. *El Movimiento Obregonista en Michoacán*. Mexico, 1920.

Luquín, Eduardo. *La Política Internacional de la Revolución Constitucionalista*. Mexico, 1957.

María y Campos, Armando. *La Vida del General Lucio Blanco*. Mexico, 1963.

Mascisidor, José. *Historia de la Revolución Mexicana*. Mexico, 1965.

Mena, Mario. *Alvaro Obregón, Historia Militar y Política, 1912–1929.* Mexico, 1960.

Mendieta y Núñez, Lucio. *El Problema Agrario de México.* Mexico, 1946.

Meyer, Michael C. *Mexican Rebel: Pascual Orozco and the Mexican Revolution, 1910–1915.* Lincoln, 1967.

Moreno, David. *Venustiano Carranza, Alvaro Obregón, Plutarco Elías Calles.* Mexico, 1960.

McCreary, Guy Weddington. *From Glory to Oblivion, The Real Truth About the Mexican Revolution.* New York, 1974.

Ochoa Campos, Moisés. *La Revolución Mexicana,* 4 vols. Mexico, 1966–1970.

Partido Radical Tabasqueño. *La Labor Presidencial de Obregón.* Villahermosa, Mexico, 1927.

Pletcher, David M. *Rails, Mines, and Progress: Seven American Promoters in Mexico, 1867–1911.* Ithaca, 1958.

Quirk, Robert E. *The Mexican Revolution, 1914–1915; The Convention of Aguascalientes.* Bloomington, 1960.

———. *The Mexican Revolution and the Catholic Church, 1910–1929.* Bloomington and London, 1973.

Quirós, Roberto. *Alvaro Obregón: Su Vida y Su Obra.* Mexico, 1928.

Rivera, Antonio G. *La Revolución en Sonora.* Mexico, 1969.

Ross, Stanley R. *Francisco I. Madero, Apostle of Mexican Democracy.* Austin, 1955.

Roux-López, Francisco. "El Surgimiento del Imperialismo Económico y los Estados Unidos. La Penetración Económica en México (1876–1910)," Tesis para la licenciatura en Ciencias Diplomáticas. Universidad Nacional Autónoma de México, 1963.

Rudenko, B. T. *México en Vísperas de la Revolución Democrática-Burguesa de 1910–1917.* Mexico, 1960.

Ruiz, Ramón Eduardo. *Labor and the Ambivalent Revolutionaries; Mexico, 1911–1923.* Baltimore and London, 1976.

———. *Mexico, The Challenge of Poverty and Illiteracy.* San Marino, 1963.

Sánchez González, Francisco. *Obra Económica y Social del General de División Abelardo L. Rodríguez.* Mexico, 1958.

Silva Herzog, Jesús. *Breve Historia de la Revolución Mexicana,* 2 vols., Mexico, 1965.

———. *El Agrarismo Mexicano y la Reforma Agraria; Exposición y Crítica.* Mexico, 1959.

Smith, Peter D. *Labyrinths of Power; Political Recruitment in Twentieth-Century Mexico.* Princeton, 1979.

Smith, Robert F. *The United States and Revolutionary Nationalism in Mexico, 1916–1932.* Chicago and London, 1972.

Tannenbaum, Frank. *The Mexican Agrarian Revolution.* New York, 1929.

Tischendorf, Alfred. *Great Britain and Mexico in the Era of Porfirio Díaz.* Durham, 1961.

Valadés, José C. *El Porfirismo, Historia de un Régimen: El Crecimiento.* 2 vols., Mexico, 1948.

Womack, John. *Zapata and the Mexican Revolution.* New York, 1970.

Articles

Anderson, Rodney D. "Mexican Workers and the Politics of Revolution, 1906–1911." *The Hispanic American Historical Review* 54, February, 1974.

Beezley, William H. "Governor Carranza and the Revolution in Coahuila." *The Americas* 33, July 1976.

Calvert, Peter. "The Mexican Revolution, Theory or Fact?" *Journal of Latin American Studies,* 1, pt. 1, May, 1969.

Carr, Barry. "The Peculiarities of the Mexican North, 1880–1928: An Essay in Interpretation." Institute of Latin American Studies, University of Glasgow, *Occasional Papers* 4, 1971.

Ceniceros, José Angel. "Discurso Pronunciado por el Señor José Angel Ceniceros, en Representación del Partido Nacional Revolucionario, en Honor del General Alvaro Obregón con Motivo del Aniversario de su Muerte." PNR, ed. *En Memoria de Obregón.* Mexico, 1936.

García, Belisario. "Relación Histórica de la Revolución Democrática en Sonora a Favor del C. Francisco I. Madero." *La Democracia,* Tucson, (1911?).

González Navarro, Moisés. "Social Aspects of the Mexican Revolution." *Journal of World History* 8, 1968.

Hearst, William R. "Obregón Has Brought Peace to Mexico and Deserves Recognition." *New York American.* November 12, 1921.

Malcolmson, J. W. "The Erection of Silver-Lead Smelting Works." Institution of Civil Engineers (London). *Minutes,* 112 (1893).

Manufacturer's Record. "Let the Obregón Government be Recognized Immediately." September 22, 1921.

Pletcher, David M. "The Fall of Silver in Mexico, 1870–1910, and Its Effects on American Investments." *The Journal of Economic History* 18, March, 1958.

Rippy, James F. "French Investments in Mexico." *Northamerican Economic Affairs* 2, 1948.

Rosenzweig, Fernando. "El Desarrollo Económico de México de 1877 a 1911." *El Trimestre Económico* 32 (1965).

Simpson, Eyler. "El Ejido: Unica Salida para México." *Problemas Agrícolas e Industriales de México* 4 (1952).

Tobler, Hans-Werner. "Las Paradojas del Ejército Revolucionario: Su Papel Social en la Reforma Agraria Mexicana, 1920–1930." Sobretiro de *Historia Mexicana* 21, No. 1, Mexico.

Vanderwood, Paul J. "Genesis of the Rurales: Mexico's Early Struggle for Public Security." *The Hispanic American Historical Review* 50, May, 1970.

————. "Response to Revolt: The Counter-Guerrilla Strategy of Porfirio Díaz." *The Hispanic American Historical Review* 56, November, 1976.

Warren, Charles B. "Mexico's Trade With the United States." *Michigan Manufacturer and Financial Record* 32, September 29, 1923.

Index